INSIDERS' GUIDE® SERIES

INSIDERS' GUIDE® TO THE

MAINE COAST

SECOND EDITION

ANDREW VIETZE

INSIDERS' GUIDE®

GUILFORD, CONNECTICUT
AN IMPRINT OF THE GLOBE PEQUOT PRESS

The prices and rates in this guidebook were confirmed at press time. We recommend, however, that you call establishments before traveling to obtain current information.

INSIDERS' GUIDE®

Text design by Nancy Freeborn
Maps by XNR Productions, Inc. © Morris Book Publishing, LLC

ISSN: 1547-8939
ISBN: 978-0-7627-4406-0

Manufactured in the United States of America
Second Edition/First Printing

CONTENTS

Directory of Maps

Maine Coast

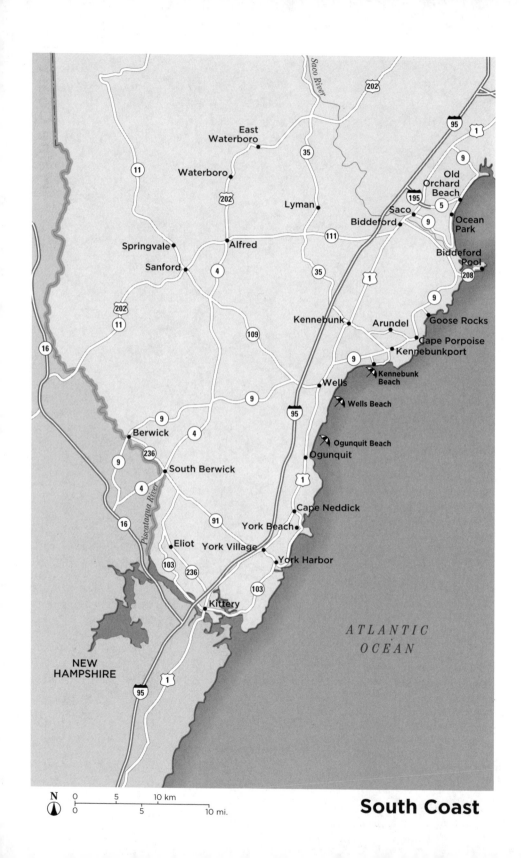

South Coast

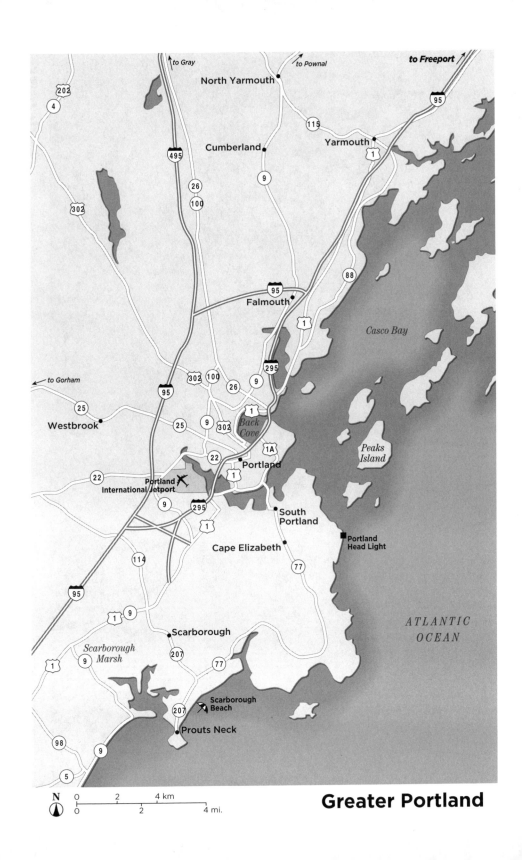

Greater Portland

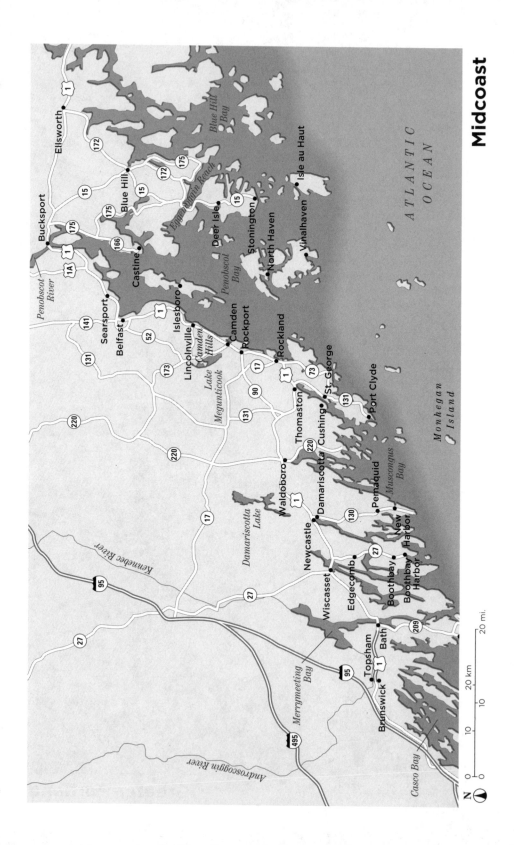

Midcoast

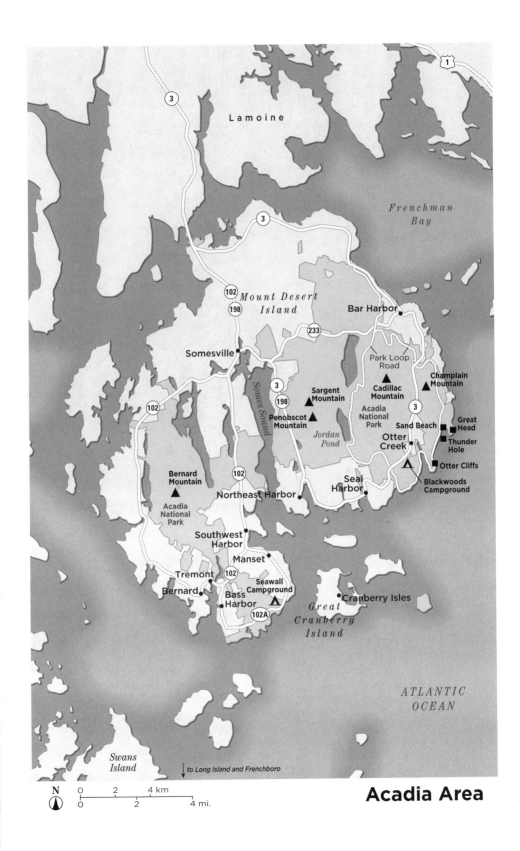

Acadia Area

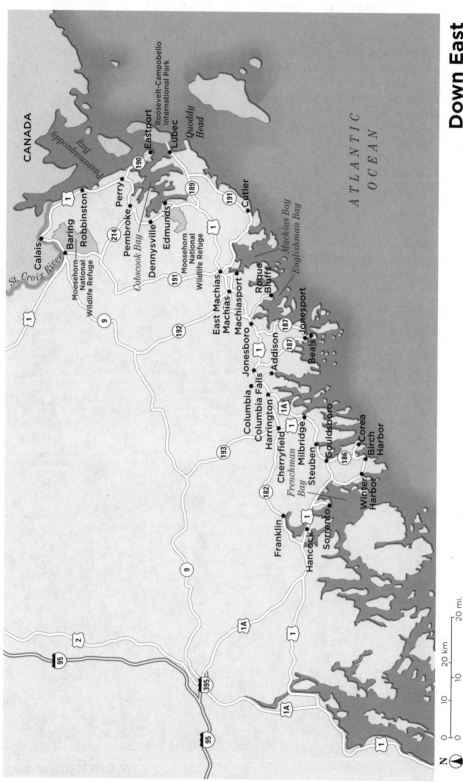

Down East

PREFACE

One of the nicest things about exploring the Maine coast is that it's just the right size. The state's grand waterfront is long enough at 280-some miles to be home to innumerable adventures, sights, and discoveries, but at the same time it's small enough that it's manageable—easy to travel and you can get to know it. If you had to, you could drive from one end to the other in five or six hours. But if you did so, you'd be missing out on so much.

If you started at Kittery and spent weeks meandering your way Down East, finally landing in Calais many days later, you'd happen upon all sorts of great stuff—waterfront restaurants, fine inns, exceptional meals, beautiful beaches, extraordinary trails, and scenery that has few rivals. And the nice thing is, if you were to return at some point and make the trip again (and of course you're going to want to), it would be the same—and entirely different. So many changes occur in the course of even one year here—new eateries, new B&Bs, new outfitters, new outdoor opportunities—that there is always something captivating and unexpected to be found in even those places you think you know. It makes poking about this great state a never-ending pastime.

Whole generations of people have found this to be the case, returning every summer. The first "summercators" began coming here in the late 19th century to escape the heat and noise of the city. They were hooked, and the tides of visitors haven't let up since, making this smallish state in the nation's northeasternmost corner into "Vacationland." Thanks to this annual influx, all the services you could need as a guest are there for you. A whole industry—one of Maine's largest—has been built to cater to your needs.

So get out there and explore.

ACKNOWLEDGMENTS

This book would never have come to your hands without the hard work and gracious assistance and support of Mike Urban and Gillian Belnap at The Globe Pequot Press; Paul Doiron, Dawna Hilton, Jeff Clark, Allister Timms, Clover McCallister, and Josh Moore at Down East: The Magazine of Maine; Losers/Weepers Records, the afflictions, and rural electric ("The Way Life Should Sound") for providing the soundtrack; everyone Down Point; the Maine State Office of Tourism; and all the parties listed inside.

Special thanks go to my Mom, principal archivist and number one fan, for all the afternoons watching the boy, and to my Dad, too. To Karin at Pen Bay Physical and Occupational Therapy, because the book would have read funny without any S, W, or Xs, and I needed the encouragement. And lastly to Lisa and Gus, with whom all my adventures begin and end.

HOW TO USE THIS BOOK

The Maine Coast—everyone has a different idea what those three words mean. To some the phrase conjures up resort communities on big white sandy beaches. To others it means little fishing villages far from the madding crowds. Still others think of it as cities like Portland or remote islands offshore. And they're all correct—beginning with beach and ending in cliffs, the state's coast is a rich and varied place, and it can be a lot of different things to a lot of different people.

But how exactly does one define the coast? How far inland does the term coast apply? (Maine weather forecasters, when they weren't predicting doom and posing in their sweaters, have spent years attempting to answer these questions.) For the purposes of this book, the counties with sea frontage will be considered coastal, and they'll be divided into five regions: South Coast, Greater Portland, Midcoast, Acadia Area, and Down East.

Each chapter will be arranged regionally, following the coast north by east, beginning at Kittery and ending up near Quoddy. So don't be confused when things are listed geographically rather than alphabetically. And also remember that while many people think head-ing to Eastport from Brunswick, say, is going north, it's actually east. Down East, for that matter. The farther you go, the better it gets.

This book will lay out the best in sites to see, things to do, dining, lodging, kidstuff, and more. Watch for the ⓘ—those Insiders' tips that let you in on the (shhh!) local secrets.

One of the nicer aspects about the state of Maine is that it functions like a big small town, and it also is always yielding new treasures to explorers. Doesn't matter how many times you've been to Waldo County, for example; every trip will reveal something unexpected and worthwhile, making travel here endlessly fun.

Over the years, thousands upon thousands of people have decided that they just don't want to leave when their vacation ends. Within these pages you'll also find plenty of resources if that describes you and you're relocating to the state. From private schools to area churches to hospitals to tax information, it's in here.

So whether you're on your first visit or are new Pine Tree State residents—Welcome to Maine.

AREA OVERVIEW

The Maine coast stretches for some 3,000 miles when all its islands and coves are included (some estimates even have it up over 5,000 miles). That's roughly the distance from Portland to Los Angeles, so it's no surprise that Maine is a widely varied place, beginning with miles of sandy beaches and resort communities and ending with rocky cliffs and tiny fishing villages. Along its length are a cosmopolitan city in Portland, vacation hot spots like the Kennebunks, Ogunquit, and Boothbay Harbor, suburbs like Cape Elizabeth and Falmouth, retirement meccas like Damariscotta and Topsham, enchanting islands like Monhegan, cottage communities like Bayside, national parks like Acadia, and hardscrabble Down East fishing villages like Jonesport and Lubec.

Because of this diversity, Maine means different things to different people. Some come for shopping, hitting the outlet towns of Kittery and Freeport, others for sun worshipping, setting up for vacation at a beachside motel in Old Orchard. Still others visit Maine to stay in an island bed-and-breakfast, like the Keepers House on Isle au Haut, to enjoy the old architecture of communities like York and Belfast, to explore the wildlands on the shore at places like Cutler, or to kayak the isles and shoals of Muscongus Bay or Stonington.

Whatever you're looking for—small towns or big, the outdoors, great food, fairs and festivals—you'll surely find it here. In this chapter we'll walk up the coast, from Kittery to Calais, discovering each community on the way.

SOUTH COAST
Kittery Area

Maine's front door can be found in Kittery, a town most people associate with outlet shopping. The vast majority of visitors to the state drive up Interstate 95 from New Hampshire across the big green Piscataqua bridge and into this town of 9,400. Carved up a bit by highways and exits, Kittery is a pretty, old community that most people never discover, pulling off just to go to the 120 outlets that sprawl for a mile along U.S. Route 1 within view of I-95, temptingly flashing sale signs. This outlet row is where you'll find all of the big name brands—Banana Republic, Ralph Lauren, J. Crew, Old Navy, Tommy Hilfiger, Reebok, Gap, Timberland, Eddie Bauer, Brooks Brothers, and on and on—as well as local favorite Kittery Trading Post, an outfitter to rival L. L. Bean. Some amazing deals await in town—if you can remain patient enough to navigate the crowds.

But there's a lot more to Kittery than highways and half-priced shoes. Before the outlets arrived in the late 1970s and early 1980s, Kittery was known for its naval shipyard, which is still active on Seavey Island, spared by 2005 defense cuts. Because of its name—Portsmouth Naval Shipyard—and because of its location in Portsmouth Harbor, the yard has been the source of constant dispute between Maine and New Hampshire. (Taxes, you see. New Hampshire residents who work at the shipyard, repairing naval submarines, don't want to pay them to Maine.) Historic documents, maps, and the state border place the yard squarely in Maine, though, and the U.S. Supreme Court agreed, ruling in the Pine Tree State's favor when the dispute arose again a few years back. Regardless of where it is, visitors are welcome to tour the base's museum.

Kittery is also home to Kittery Point, one of scads of historic neighborhoods in the South Coast but with legitimate claims to being the oldest (York, just up the road, would argue, though). Kittery was settled in 1623 and has the architecture to prove it. Many distinctive colonials sit along the water in Kittery Point, some of which are owned by commuters who work in Boston, about an hour away. There are a couple neat old forts here, which once protected Portsmouth Harbor, as well as a pleasant strand down at Seapoint Beach, and a section of the Rachel Carson National Wildlife Refuge, an estuarine sanctuary for beasts but especially for migrating birds.

Inland from Kittery are the Eliots and the Berwicks, picturesque old communities that have north and south sections and sit on the Piscataqua River. Once shipbuilding and farming towns, they now have a suburban cast to them and send residents to work in Portsmouth, Portland, and Boston.

The Yorks

Many Maine towns are divided into villages—North Everytown, South Everytown, etc.—and are thus referred to in the plural, but the Yorks take the cake. Mark Twain used to spend a lot of time here, and he once quipped that you couldn't throw a brick in any direction without it hitting a postmaster. That's because there's one in York Village, York Harbor, York Beach, and Cape Neddick, all distinctly different villages and all in the town of York.

York is the first real beach community one comes to driving north in Maine, with four stretches of sands reaching out to embrace the cold waters of the Atlantic. About 10,000 people now call the area home, and the population quadruples come June with the arrival of all the summer people and tourists. This population swell is most evident in York Beach, which has the densely packed cottages, the taffy and T-shirt shops, the carousel, the arcades, the amusement park, the zoo, and the other sorts of superficial amusements you find in such places.

York Beach is a world away from York Village, the earliest chartered town in Maine (always challenging Kittery for the title). York Village was founded as Georgeana in 1640,

i For an inside look at a community, there's no better resource than the local paper. Most coastal communities in Maine have a weekly paper that details all the issues concerning residents, and it's usually published on Thursday. Find out more in the "Weekly Newspapers" section of the Arts and Entertainment chapter.

taking its name from Sir Ferdinando Gorges, who governed the area on behalf of the king of England. (It was renamed in 1652.) The architecture here is pure early American, with pretty gables and white clapboards everywhere, and the town has had the good sense to preserve it. About 50 buildings are listed on the National Register of Historic Places (a spooky old cemetery, the Old York Burying Ground, said to be haunted, holds the remains of many of their first residents). There are enough historic sites open to the public—the Old York Gaol (ca. 1653), the Old Schoolhouse (1745), the Emerson-Wilcox House (ca. 1740), and the Perkins House (1730)—to occupy a few afternoons.

York Harbor, likewise, wears its history well, only it was developed in an entirely different era, the late 19th century, when wealthy summercators discovered this shipbuilding center and began to transform it into a resort. Several neighborhoods of tidy Victorian cottages line lanes on the way down to the waterfront, and a lot of new summer places, part of the development boom York County has seen in the past few decades, are tightly squeezed in beside them. Between the two of them, York Harbor and York Village house much of the area's services, shops, and restaurants. Cape Neddick, also home to its share of old houses and cottages, is best known for Cape Neddick Light, affectionately known around town as the Nubble (see the Lighthouses chapter).

In 2002 *Money* magazine called the Yorks one of the best places to vacation in the country, so they must be doing something right.

Ogunquit and Wells

Like many of the other resort communities on the South Coast, Ogunquit was built around its beach, which some claim is Maine's finest. Its broad white sands cover more than 3 miles, and there's rarely a day when someone isn't out on them. Native Americans were the first to recognize the very obvious appeal of the strand, coming to frolic in the surf and giving Ogunquit its name, which means "beautiful place by the sea." Vacationers haven't let up since, regularly flocking here and overwhelming the 930 souls who call the town home.

The community has three principal areas: the beach itself; Perkins Cove, a fishing village on a narrow inlet at the south side of town that's been consumed by restaurants and boutiques; and downtown Ogunquit, a walkable Main Street of still more shops, inns, and eateries. A dozen art galleries can be found in town, testament to the community's rich history as an art colony, and there is an excellent local art museum as well as a summer theater that has welcomed some of Hollywood's biggest names over the years.

But it all started with the beach. Locals have made an effort to preserve the sanctity of these sands, and they've done a good job, keeping development several steps behind the grassy dunes at the edge of the beach. If you stand on the beach, back to town, all you see is glorious sea and surf, a wilderness of water. Lifeguards patrol in summer, when the sands are absolutely thronged with bikinis, umbrellas, beach balls, crying babies, coolers, and several acres of towels and blankets. Access is via Beach Street, right in the village, where there are changing rooms and restrooms; at Footbridge Beach, which is just north of downtown, and at Moody Beach, which is reached via Wells. All tend to be busy on a hot day—come early if you want a spot.

Perkins Cove, a mile down the coast, gets hopping, too, and parking is famously difficult at this little harbor. It's still a working waterfront—with Maine's only footpath drawbridge—but the activities of the local lobstermen based here have been eclipsed by all the boutiques and restaurants that have been retrofitted into old fishing shacks. Some of Maine's better restaurants can be found in Perkins Cove, and getting a table at any one of them—say, Hurricane—is about as hard as finding a parking spot if you don't make a reservation.

Perkins Cove is connected to the rest of Ogunquit by the fantastic 1-mile walking path called the Marginal Way, which traverses rocks and shore, overlooking the open ocean and with benches set up to enjoy the view. Paved and very easy going, the walkway is used by many people to get between town and cove, rather than trying to drive on congested Route 1. Some like to jump down to the tide pools below, others have a seat and survey the sea, and still others power walk while enjoying the views. The going is almost always elbow to elbow in midsummer. Best to show up early or late.

Marginal Way deposits you in downtown Ogunquit, a place of inns, B&Bs, resorts, restaurants, and hustle and bustle all crowded around a three-way intersection at the center of town. The community has become known as a gay-friendly place through the decades, with many businesses run by same-sex couples.

Like several other Maine towns, Ogunquit was "discovered" by artists in the late 19th and early 20th centuries, and once word got around, it became a veritable creative colony with some of the nation's biggest names in residence during the summer. The first to start throwing paint around here was Charles Woodbury, who arrived in Perkins Cove in 1888, calling it an "artist's paradise." Other painters were similarly impressed, and over the course of the next several decades he was joined by Walt Kuhn, Peggy Bacon, Elihu Vedder, Hamilton Easter Field, Yasuo Kuniyoshi, and Henry Strater. Their parties and hijinks were legendary. Strater would go on to found the Ogunquit Museum of American Art, a superb collection of works by these and other American greats, with a fine view of the water.

Ogunquit once was actually a village in the greater municipality of Wells, another beach town a few miles up Route 1 with a population of about 10,000. The pair split in 1980, and it's easy to see why, because they have very different personalities. While Ogunquit is relatively walkable and compact, Wells is a long, several-mile strip with no real town center. Like the one in Ogunquit, though, the town's beach is impressive—some 7 miles long. Also on the waterfront, sort of at odds with the Coppertone zone to its south and the commercial district to its north, are a couple of marshy spots dear to nature lovers and birds—the Wells National Estuarine Research Reserve and the Rachel Carson National Wildlife Refuge (see the Green Space chapter).

Over the years Wells has become famous as a go-to place for antiques and used books, and some of the goods are even affordable. In more recent years, a couple of factory outlets have located here as well.

The Kennebunks

In high summer the Kennebunks—the name given to the villages of Kennebunk, Kennebunkport, Arundel, Cape Porpoise, and Goose Rocks—are as busy as Maine communities come. The population of 13,500 here probably quadruples in July and August as tourists, summer residents, and beach fans arrive to play on the wide sandy beaches, swim in the surf, shop boutiques, dine at some of Maine's best restaurants, stay in fun old inns, head out deep-sea fishing and whale watching, and maybe even catch a glimpse of the Bush family, who have summered here for ages.

The layout of the Kennebunks proves confusing to some as many people are unaware that Kennebunk has a waterfront. Because the town of Kennebunk Beach is closer to Kennebunkport than it is to the brick-lined downtown of Kennebunk, many people assume that it's part of the 'Port. Just remember that the Kennebunk River serves as the border between towns, and you'll know where you are. Better still to think of the place as one community, because that's largely how it functions.

The first European on the scene was likely Bartholomew Gosnold in 1602 or Martin Pring

in 1603. Kennebunkport was settled a couple of decades later in 1629, Kennebunk in 1650, and in 1653 Kennebunkport incorporated as Maine's fifth town. This part of what is now Maine was particularly hard-hit during the French and Indian Wars, enduring many Indian attacks, but the colonists persevered, and in 1730 the community entered a prosperous time of shipbuilding. By the 19th century there were six shipyards along this stretch of coast, which combined to launch some 638 vessels. Trade with the West Indies was particularly important, and the seagoing success of these twin towns fueled a building boom of gracious sea captains' homes. (Kennebunk has some 156 structures on the National Register of Historic Places and there's a fantastic walking tour of the finest streets.) Few Maine towns can rival its colonial revival and late Victorian architecture. During the industrial revolution, small mills were built along the Kennebunk River that turned out shoes and twine (one of these is now home to the renowned Tom's of Maine Natural Living Store).

Tourism has been at the forefront of the economies of Kennebunk and Kennebunkport since at least the turn of the 20th century, when the Kennebunkport Sea Shore Company decided to position the community as a trendy summer resort the likes of Newport or Rhode Island. According to local historian Joyce Butler, the company saw to it that the place was kept neat and tidy, promoted it to the world, and attracted people in droves. Among the newcomers was the Walker family, who purchased the spit of land on Cape Arundel known as Damon's Park and Flying Point in the early years of the 20th century. The Walkers built a summer complex there that became known as Walker Point and was the summer playground for the young George Herbert Walker Bush, who'd go on to become the 41st president of the United States. Though not as popular as a tourist site now as it was during the first Bush presidency, Walker Point is still the subject of a lot of photographs and gawking—it's easily seen from Ocean Avenue—especially when word comes down that

George Walker Bush, the 43rd president, is paying it a visit. Why people bother is a good question, because the whole community is awash with Secret Servicemen, who, while just doing their job, make it difficult for everyday folks to travel from place to place.

The Kennebunks have quite the history of the famous and fortunate. The area became a popular retreat for artists, and several world-renowned authors have lived or summered here. The best known of these is probably Kenneth Roberts, a historical novelist and legendary curmudgeon who was born in Kennebunk and lived at Kennebunk Beach. His books of colonial and Revolutionary America—among them *Rabble in Arms, Arundel, Oliver Wiswell,* and *Northwest Passage*—were huge sellers in their day. Roberts can attribute some of his success to his friend, Pulitzer Prize–winning writer Booth Tarkington, who summered in Kennebunkport and helped the younger writer with his narrative structure.

Today many of the old homes in the Kennebunks have become inns and restaurants, and Dock Square, the small town center, has become a tourist haven with shops and boutiques and businesses hot for the summer dollars.

Biddeford and Saco

The twin cities of Biddeford and Saco stare across the Saco River at one another, and though they are distinctly different communities, their destinies have been entwined since the two were established in the 1630s. The larger of the pair, Biddeford has long been a manufacturing center, with Saco a more residential area. Neither has been a particularly big tourist draw, relative to the resorts to the south and Old Orchard Beach to the north, but each has its own summer enclave in Biddeford Pool and Camp Ellis. If visitors would take the time to explore a bit, they'd find enough to keep them occupied for a few days. Ferry Beach State Park, Saco Museum, the Saco Heath, and Camp Ellis Beach are in Saco, and the University of New England and East Point Sanctuary are in Biddeford.

The English explored the Saco area when Captain John Smith sailed by in 1614 and took a look-see. Two years later, Sir Ferdinando Gorges sent the itinerant Richard Vines across the sea to do some prospecting in the area he had been granted. Homes started going up in 1630 or so, and the river and the village on its northside was originally called Pepperellboro, after Sir William Pepperrell, a large landowner. The name was changed in 1805 to Saco, after what the indigenous people called the Sawacatucke, which meant "burnt pine."

Factories emerged with the onset of the industrial age, and soon an ironworks was forging on the Saco side of the river. This development was followed by textile mills in Biddeford, which drew a large in-migration of French-Canadian workers. The twin cities have been a manufacturing center since, and many of the current 21,000 inhabitants of Biddeford can claim a Franco heritage.

Old Orchard Beach

If your idea of fun is suntanning in a skimpy Speedo, playing arcade games, entering bikini contests, riding Ferris wheels, or shopping for two-dollar shot glasses, Old Orchard Beach is your kind of place—and you're in good company. The honky-tonk atmosphere of the town reels in vacationers in summer, making it into what might be Maine's largest city. Some 100,000 fun seekers have been known to be in town on any given weekend in August, turning the 7-mile beach here into one giant carnival. Fanning out from the old pier in the center of town are scores of hotels, motels, condos, pizza stands, and fried seafood shacks, as well as an arcade and an amusement park. You'll look a long time for parking and will probably never find the stand of apple trees that gave the town its name.

That orchard used to be a landmark to sailors, sitting high up above the beach. One of the first European settlers to see it was an Englishman named Thomas Rogers, who set up residence here in 1657, calling the place Garden by the Sea. He was rather quickly burned out by the Native Americans already living there. The territory here was considered part of the town of Saco until the 1880s, when it was incorporated and named Old Orchard (the Beach was added later). By then it was already a summer mecca. Back in 1837 an entrepreneurial gentleman named Staples had begun taking summer boarders on his farm for $1.50 a week, and his enterprise did well enough that he built the first inn in town. In 1847 trains began running from Boston to Portland right through Old Orchard's backyard, and that led to the development of a restaurant selling shore dinners. Six years later a connecting train was added to the route, bringing large numbers of Canadians down from Montreal. A resort was born.

After the Civil War things really started to boom, with trolley service to Saco and better train access. By the turn of the 20th century, Old Orchard had many of the same amusements that it does today, with roller skating, a merry-go-round and other rides, games of chance, and refreshment stands sprouting along the beach. A disastrous fire set things back a bit in 1907, but by the 1920s everything was rip-roaring again, with Guy Lombardo and Duke Ellington bringing their big-band acts to play for the masses.

And still they come. The 475-foot pier on the site today was built in 1980, and you can often hear French being spoken upon it in midsummer as Canadians continue to pour in for fun in the sun. The town has been attempting to broaden its appeal a bit by getting rid of some of the seedier elements that have crept in over the years and by adding beautifying things like flowers and landscaping in a quest to get families here.

There's certainly plenty to do. Old Orchard boasts Maine's largest waterslide, a gondola Ferris wheel and a roller coaster, championship miniature golf, championship real golf, Jet Ski rentals, parasailing, live music, karaoke, and more. Accommodations number in the hundreds, running the gamut from double-deck motels a la the Alouette Hotel and Cottages to slightly more refined options like the Old Orchard Beach Inn, an 18-room hostelry

that dates to 1730 and is on the National Register of Historic Places. And there are plenty of places to find eats as well. As Maine goes, Old Orchard is one of a kind.

GREATER PORTLAND

Mainers like to joke that the nice thing about Portland is that it's so close to Maine. The state's largest city is so much more cosmopolitan and urban than anywhere else Down East that it seems almost like another place. But there's actually still a lot of Maine left in it. First, the Portland Peninsula is small enough—just 3 miles across—that it's walkable and compact enough that it functions almost like a very big small town. People still know each other here.

Second, fishing remains a staple in the economy in Portland, just as it does in much of Maine. The waterfront is a working one, and the city's 64,000 residents have voted in the past to keep it that way, to keep the hip boots in and the high-rises out. Tourism long ago established a beachhead—vacationers flock to DiMillo's Floating Restaurant, to shops on the city side of Commercial Street, and to whale-watch boats—but it's still a fairly real place. In recent years, there's been talk of replacing the old Bath Iron Works dry docks, the victims of shipbuilding consolidation, with a hotel, but it hasn't happened yet.

The city also shares the architectural appeal of the rest of the state, being a treasure trove of Victoriana. The peninsula burned twice over the centuries, once during a punishing Revolutionary War bombardment and again as the result of a 19th-century warehouse fire. Many blocks were rebuilt immediately after that conflagration, so there are streets and streets lined with pretty old Victorian brick buildings, especially in the 6 blocks of the Old Port.

So with the sea, the fishermen, the small-town vibe, and the historic facade, the city remains rooted in Maine traditions even if people these days walk around with video cell phones and pink hair.

The first settlers in the area arrived in 1623. A gentleman by the name of Christopher Levett built a stone house on nearby Hog Island, but he returned to England to encourage others to come join him in this place he called Quack (from Casco, perhaps?), and whether he ever came back no one knows. After him came the notorious George Cleeve, who arrived in the 1630s, gained a small mandate from the patent holder of the area, and soon had tyrannical control over Casco Bay and its environs. He held onto it tightly until about 1658, when the district of Maine came under the control of Massachusetts and his influence waned.

In the years after Cleeve, the community here grew and prospered until a series of devastating Indian attacks emptied the town. When Samuel Moody was granted permission to set up a garrison here by the Massachusetts government, the site began to develop again, and soon it became an important port for trade with the West Indies and for shipbuilding.

The Revolutionary War years were tough on Portland, then called Falmouth. Locals were none too impressed with the British and their Stamp Act and threw their lot in with the Continental Congress and its militias. One fateful day, when a British sloop appeared in Casco Bay, a group of Mainers captured the vessel's captain, a man named Mowatt, and accused him of espionage. He was eventually released and would return to the city—with a vengeance. Mowatt came back on October 16, 1775, with four warships, and, when the colonists refused to give up their arms, he mercilessly opened fire, raining bombs. Remarkably no one was killed—despite Mowatt's order to "remove all human specie from the town"—but Falmouth was effectively wiped out. Two thousand people were left to face the oncoming winter homeless, and 414 buildings were destroyed.

Though their town was a heap of wreckage, 700 people stayed on to rebuild, and by the 1780s the city—then known by its current name—was back in business, a hive of commercial activity. Portland became one of the largest cities in the young nation and boomed all the way up to the Civil War. During that conflict the staunchly abolitionist city sent 5,000 of its 25,000 residents to join the Union cause.

And then it burned again, this time due to a fire that began in a boat shop before sweeping across the peninsula. In this 1866 fire, little was spared. Most public buildings, many businesses, and scads of homes went up in a blaze worse than the 1775 bombardment. The city vowed to rebuild and did so with help from the rest of the nation. Many of the finest structures in town date back to this late-19th-century period of reconstruction.

This architecture, the surrounding sea, and the pleasant way of life in Portland have attracted all sorts of comers and earned accolades from magazines like *Men's Journal,* which called the city one of the 50 best places to live in America (Portland came in at number 45), and *Outside,* which lauded the small metropolis as being a good home base for adventure. Portland has long been known as the Forest City, and while it's too developed now to have the kind of foliage it once did, it is still surprisingly green and pleasant, especially in its northernmost half. Parks sit on both flanks, overlooking Casco Bay and the harbor—the Eastern Promenade on one side and the Western Promenade on the other—and there are several woodsy areas spread about. The setting is further enhanced by the fact that the city is not even an hour and a half from Boston and less than that to the White Mountains, so getaways are easy.

But there's certainly enough to keep you busy here. In the past decade the city has been transforming Congress Street, the heart of the downtown and once Portland's principal retail corridor, into an arts district, anchored on one end by City Hall, home of Merrill Auditorium and the Portland Symphony Orchestra, and on the other by the I. M. Pei–designed Portland Museum of Art. In between are the Maine College of Art, the Maine Historical Society, the boyhood home of poet Henry Wadsworth Longfellow, several galleries, and a number of clubs, restaurants, and shops.

Retail has moved in large part to the Maine Mall in South Portland and, a few blocks down from Congress Street, to the Old Port, the distinctive shopping district retrofitted into old ship chandleries and Victorian warehouses just up from the waterfront. Six blocks of boutiques, specialty shops, and watering holes are located along the cobblestoned streets of the Old Port, and there are still more local establishments than chain stores among them. Portland is all about food—people like to say there are more restaurants per capita here than anywhere else in the country, save San Francisco—and this district is where a great many of them can be found.

The quaint streets of the Old Port give way to Commercial Street and the waterfront, where boats come and go constantly and where the ferries that provide access to Casco Bay's famed Calendar Islands (so named because there are allegedly more than 365 of them, one for every day). Several of these islands, such as Peaks and Long, have year-round populations, with people commuting across the bay on a daily basis and returning to their quiet seaside homes at night.

South of the city are the towns of Scarborough and Cape Elizabeth, which, while both being largely suburban areas, boast beaches and shopping centers. Scarborough begins to the west at Scarborough Marsh, a fantastic estuarine area that's the site of a popular Audubon sanctuary, and it ends in the congestion and chaos and commercialism of the Maine Mall area near South Portland. Some of the state's best beaches line its eastern front, which is also where Prouts Neck, a very exclusive summer community made famous by Winslow Homer, is located. Cape Elizabeth likewise has its own beaches as well as a pair of exceedingly popular state parks—Two Lights and Fort Williams. The latter is adjacent to Portland Head Light, Maine's best-known lighthouse.

South Portland, usually thought of as little more than a mall explosion, thanks to rampant chain development at the Maine Mall, is actually an interesting city with a personality all its own. With a population of about 23,000, it's Maine's fourth-largest urban area (behind Portland, Lewiston-Auburn, and Bangor) and is a diverse mix of industry, retail, and residential areas. Most of its appealing features are on the opposite side of the city from the scores of stores at the mall, where visitors will find a compact and attractive downtown, a network of greenways, Southern Maine Community College, Willard Beach, and Spring Point Ledge Light.

North of the city are the communities of Falmouth, Cumberland, and Yarmouth, each of which has a waterfront section of expensive homes and a more rural inland half. Housing development has been going great guns since the 1980s in all four, making way for more and more commuters. And to the west is the mill town of Westbrook, where the Sappi paper mill belches smoke from its location above the Presumpscot River. Much of the rest of Westbrook, the state's fifth biggest city, is a mix of quiet suburban streets, big office buildings, and industrial park zones.

Freeport

Usually getting cold feet puts an end to something, but in Freeport a pair of soggy boots was just the beginning. Leon Leonwood Bean went hunting one fateful afternoon and, not happy with his footwear, conjured up a design in his head. The Maine Hunting Shoe, better known as the "Bean boot," was launched in 1911, and the company Bean founded to sell them has never looked back, establishing a presence on Main Street in Freeport in its early years and leaving the door unlocked since. In these days of corporate scandals and cheap Chinese goods, the story of L. L. Bean is quite refreshing. From day one the young entrepreneur unconditionally guaranteed his products, most of which were hand-stitched on the premises, and he made customer service and shopping satisfaction the backbone of the company. It was—and still is—open 24 hours a day, every day, and it's filled with employees who know their stuff. (The company is one of the biggest catalog retailers in the world to boot.) You can still bring those old, hole-ridden Bean boots back with no questions asked.

Since the 1980s this great anchor store has attracted dozens of major retailers to downtown Freeport, creating one of the biggest outlet towns in the country. You want Anne Klein, Polo, North Face, and Banana Republic? You've got them, all in a pleasant downtown where you can walk rather than drive around. It may be a mall, for all intents and purposes, but it's all packaged up like a Maine village and is pleasant to walk around. That is, if you can find a place to park your car.

The 7,000 current residents of Freeport get a little tired of their community being defined by shopping (they should have thought of that when they let the stores flood in to begin with), and there is admittedly a lot more to the town. First, it has an important place in Maine history—the papers that granted Maine statehood, certifying the split between Maine and Massachusetts, were signed in Freeport's Jameson's Tavern, which is now a restaurant (right near L. L. Bean). Second, it's a coastal community, a fact about which 90 percent of its visitors are probably unaware. South Freeport feels about as far from the bargain-bin bonanza as you could imagine, a genuine fishing village with a hardy lobster fleet and lobster in the rough available at Harraseeket Lunch and Lobster Company.

Down on the waterfront is where you'll also find a trio of fine parks. Wolfe's Neck Woods State Park is the largest, a 233-acre forest along the edge of Casco Bay. Then there's Winslow Memorial Park, a 90-acre, town-owned oasis on the bay in South Freeport with a small beach and picnic area. The third park is Mast Landing Sanctuary, a 140-acre site owned by the Nature Conservancy. Once a source of trees for Royal Navy masts, it's now a preserve well known for birding. There's a popular walking trail that clocks in at a little over a mile and a half.

On the north side of town is a real curiosity. People drive by the sign for Desert Road in Freeport all the time without thinking much of it. In fact there is a genuine expanse of sand in town, a tourist attraction known as the Desert of Maine that's just enough of a hoot to make it worthy of your time. A 300-acre farm until 1797, the site was overgrazed and overcleared until the topsoil had eroded completely away, revealing a sandy base. Now it looks like the Middle East, with vast sands and rolling dunes. Where there's an odd landmark, there are sure to be souvenirs, and that's the case here, too. A gift shop and information center on the premises will fill all your needs.

MIDCOAST
Brunswick

Brunswick is the state's largest town and dwarfs many of its cities, with 21,500 residents. (Population doesn't determine whether a community is a city or town in Maine; the type of municipal government does.) It sits at the point where Route 1 and I–95 diverge and has become a commercial and cultural center for the Midcoast. Two great institutions have come to define the town and have made the world at large aware of Brunswick, Maine—Bowdoin College and Brunswick Naval Air Station (BNAS).

Each has influenced the way the town has grown, Bowdoin and its 1,500 students have kept the downtown vibrant, and the navy and all its personnel helped spawn the retail development of Cooks Corner, an outpost of shopping centers on the eastern side of town.

Founded in 1794 as the first institution of higher learning in Maine, Bowdoin College has a long and rich history, filled with personalities of statewide, regional, and national note. Counted among its alumni are many of the most prominent Mainers of the past 300 years—from Henry Wadsworth Longfellow, to Civil War hero Joshua Chamberlain, to Arctic explorer Robert Peary, to Olympian Joan Benoit Samuelson, to distinguished senators and U.S. leaders including William Cohen and George Mitchell. A dozen Maine governors were educated here, as were writer Nathaniel Hawthorne, U.S. President Franklin Pierce, poet Robert Tristram Coffin, and scads of other national figures. The 110-acre campus itself is leafy and pleasant, with all the ivy and brick and granite a top-shelf liberal arts school is supposed to have and with a stand of pines that are among the oldest in the state. Many Brunswick residents have been known to take their lunch at the campus cafe and to use the bookstore as well. There are a pair of very good museums that are also open to the public (see Attractions chapter).

From Bowdoin's campus it's a half-mile walk down Maine Street, past the picture-perfect town green, to the center of Brunswick, several brick-lined blocks. This commercial corridor is the second-widest avenue in any New England town (behind Keene, New Hampshire), and the shops and restaurants here have a vitality to them that many other Maine downtowns have lost, thanks to all the students and the tourists who replace them in the summer. In the neighborhoods behind Maine Street are block after block of classic white-clapboard homes and pretty churches—138 buildings are in the National Register's Federal Street Historic District. At the end of Maine Street opposite Bowdoin, there is old Fort Andross, a mill building on the Androscoggin River.

For the impact it has on the local economy and for the number of pilots and sailors stationed just up the road from the shopping plazas of Cooks Corner, Brunswick Naval Station is a relatively quiet presence. And it's soon to get quieter—in 2005 BNAS was marked for closure by the Department of Defense. The base is the last active-duty airfield in the Northeast and the second-largest employer in Maine, with almost 5,000 people working here, so the community is scrambling to figure out what to do next.

Across the tumbling Androscoggin River from Brunswick is Topsham (pop. 9,000), known for neighborhoods of attractive old homes and rampant development in the 1980s and 1990s. Shopping centers dominate one end of town, and they just seem to keep spawning more stores. Civic leaders have made efforts to keep the historic vibe downtown afforded by the homes on Elm Street and by the big Topsham Mill, now an office complex, by establishing a village center and by putting in a park. Shipbuilding and textiles were the main industries here in centuries past; today it's a bedroom to much bigger Brunswick.

Brunswick is also the jumping-off point to get to the magnificent Harpswells (pop. 6,000), eight distinct villages linked by bridges on an archipelago of 45 islands. The best known are Orr's and Bailey's Islands, popular cottage colonies exquisitely sited on Casco Bay. This is where you'll find a unique granite cribwork that lets the sea pass through, a curious span that's on the National Register of Historic Places. Cundy's Harbor is another Harpswell stunner, a fishing village on the briny New Meadows River.

Bath

Like its southerly neighbor Brunswick, Bath relies heavily on Defense Department dollars. While many Maine towns used to be shipbuilding centers, Bath still is one—and in a very large way. Navy contracts keep massive cranes and some 8,500 shipbuilders busy in the city on the banks of the Kennebec River. (Those shipbuilders change shifts at about 3:30 P.M., and you'd be wise not to be anywhere near here at that point. Bottlenecks are famous.) At any given time, big destroyers will be parked in the river, in full view of Route 1 motorists passing by on the tall and imposing Bath Bridge.

It's said that nearly half of the ships built in the United States in the second half of the 19th century were built in Bath. Today most of the shipbuilding in the city takes part at Bath Iron Works, founded in 1889 and the state's largest single employer. The yard lords over Bath, sprawling in a tangle of industrial buildings and high-rise-size cranes for about a mile along the Kennebec. At the moment BIW, a subsidiary of General Dynamics, is turning out Aegis-class destroyers. Huge crowds turn out for launches in the summer.

You can learn all about the history of ship-building in Bath just up the road at the excellent Maine Maritime Museum (see Attractions chapter). Farther down the road from the museum is the Popham Peninsula, home of exceedingly popular Popham Beach. On a peninsula opposite Popham is another favorite beach at Reid State Park in Georgetown.

But there's more to the City of Ships than huge vessels. The community of 10,000 has a cool, historic downtown, which Mel Gibson fans might recognize from his 1993 movie *The Man Without a Face,* and some of the state's finest architecture in its armada of old sea captains' homes. The city is also something of a cultural center with its museums, excellent library, a handful of good restaurants, and the whimsical Chocolate Church, a gothic-spired former Congregational Church that is indeed painted chocolate brown and hosts a slate of concerts, dances, and arts shows.

Wiscasset

In recent years, Wiscasset has become known for its traffic tie-ups—they can go on for miles and miles on a hot August afternoon—but it would rather be known as the Prettiest Village in Maine. A sign on Route 1 just below the village actually lays this claim, and while some other communities like, say, Castine or Belfast, Monhegan or Stonington, might have a legitimate right to argue, there's no denying Wiscasset (pop. 3,600), stacked up on a hill overlooking the Sheepscot River, is a good-looking place.

The downtown is pleasant, from the church and courthouse on a slight rise above Main Street to the rows of Victorian-era brick buildings that line it. Antiques stores fill many of them. But the really pretty parts of town are the neighborhoods that fan out from the town center. Many fine Federal and Greek Revival homes can be found here, once owned by the sea captains and merchants who flourished in the 19th century when Wiscasset was one of the biggest shipbuilding centers north of Boston. Several small historic homes and history museums are popular draws in summer,

and the town has made a name for itself as an antiques hot spot. An underappreciated gem of a park, Fort Edgecomb sits across the Davey Bridge in Edgecomb with great picnic grounds on a Sheepscot cove.

For decades the eyesore of the Maine Yankee nuclear power plant detracted mightily from the prettiest village, but it has since been removed. The town certainly enjoyed the taxes back when the plant was pumping out electricity, but it's making do thanks to all of the tourist dollars that wind up here, sucked in by the downtown—home of a pair of notable Midcoast eateries, Sarah's and Red's Eats—and to the businesses that line the approach to it on Route 1.

Just inland from Wiscasset are a pair of tiny communities that would hold their own in a prettiest village contest, Sheepscot and Head Tide, the latter in Alna, a fine pastoral town of hills and meadows on the Sheepscot River.

Boothbay Harbor

Boothbay Harbor was among the first places to be settled in Maine, and it's easy to see why people would have chosen to set up on this peninsula between the Damariscotta and Sheepscot Rivers. One of the deeper inlets on the coast, it is a very pretty place—that is, if you're standing on the harbor with your back to the land and looking out toward far away Damariscove Island, where those fishermen laid their claim before being driven off by Native Americans. If you turn around, you'll see the result of decades of barely restrained development, which in high season can turn the town into one big madding crowd.

Boothbay Harbor (pop. 2,347) has long been a resort community, one of the most popular in Maine. Shops, galleries, restaurants, B&Bs, and motels all fight for space downtown, and for anyone interested in shopping, day sailing, minigolf, or seafood, this is the place to be. (There is a wicked cool bowling alley, Romar Bowling Lanes, housed in a log cabin on the water, that's right out of a movie, established in 1946.) Where there isn't a motel in Boothbay Harbor there's a T-shirt shop. The harbor still has a fleet of lobstermen who try to eke out a living among all the pleasure craft and hurly-burly, and it is also home to Cap'n Fish's cruises, which are near legendary for whale watching and deep-sea fishing at this point (see the On the Ocean chapter). Many people enjoy strolling out onto Boothbay's famous 1,000-foot footbridge across the harbor to watch all the comings and goings.

If the throngs get to you, find one of the Boothbay Region Land Trust's excellent preserves. The busy conservationists have acquired 850 acres in the Boothbay region for use by the public and wildlife and turned them into six preserves. Some are woodsy, some are riverine—all are welcome after the bustle of the harbor. Or try visiting East Boothbay or Ocean Point, relaxed enclaves of summer homes.

The area was popular among fishermen from the get-go. They set up on Damariscove Island in the early 1600s, and year-rounders were here by the latter half of that century but were driven out by Indians. By 1729 white folks returned, in the form of 60 Scotch-Irish settlers, who called their neighborhood Townsend. Over the centuries residents here did a lot of fishing, even some whaling, and tried their hands at farming and woodcutting, too, supplying Boston with timber for a time. Shipbuilding was another profit maker, and in the late 1800s ice making and sardine canning were big. And while fishing remained a constant, and continues to this day, tourism has eclipsed just about everything else.

Damariscotta

The name of this community of 2,000, tucked alongside the Damariscotta River just below Route 1, has proven to be a tongue twister for many Maine visitors. The Abnakis named Damariscotta for the number of alewives they found in the river here. (The tiny herring still run in great numbers in springtime—you could walk across their backs, so numerous are they as they swim upstream—and are fun to watch in Damariscotta Mills. Ask around.) If

you want to avoid embarrassment, pronounce it *"Dam-uh-ri-Scott-uh."* The small town of Newcastle is just across the river, and many people don't know where one begins and the other ends, so closely are the villages entwined.

Downtown Damariscotta is a historic village of well-preserved blocks that span the 19th century, and in its redbrick buildings are a mixture of tourist-oriented boutiques; good old Maine staples like Reny's, a discount department store; and a handful of restaurants. (The town is becoming known as an antiques hot spot, too.) Damariscotta is a service center for much of Lincoln County and has some cultural attractions as well, like the Round Top Center for the Arts.

Just inland from the saltwater Damariscotta River is Great Salt Bay, a broad swath of brine, and Damariscotta Lake, a long, skinny freshwater body ringed with cottages. The Damariscotta Shell Heaps are the famous site of ancient Abnaki oyster feasts, and a few years back the exceptional local conservation organization, the Damariscotta River Association, made a park in the area, a fantastic place for long walks in bayside meadows.

Pemaquid Peninsula

Damariscotta is the gateway town to the Pemaquid Peninsula, a long point of land that reaches down to the water like a lobster claw. Two towns, Bristol and South Bristol, occupy the largest part of the peninsula, and they are divided into a half dozen villages. There's Walpole, which is hardly recognizable as its own entity, save for the Old Walpole Meetinghouse, a beautiful municipal gathering place built in 1772, and Bristol proper, a nifty community of older homes at the base of the Pemaquid River. Farther along are Round Pond, a summer colony that wraps around a cove on the east side of the peninsula; Christmas Cove, another enclave of vacation homes, which was "discovered" by Captain John Smith on Christmas Day in 1614; and the fishing village of New Harbor, which has a couple of great lobster wharves where you can grab some crustaceans fresh off the boats. Everyone loves the swinging bridge in South Bristol, which turns 45 degrees to make way for lobster boats passing through what is known as the Gut.

The real treat down in these parts, though, is Pemaquid itself, site of Pemaquid Light, Colonial Pemaquid, Fort William Henry, and Pemaquid Beach. The area practically drips with history, and Fort William Henry, a replica of a 1692 garrison that was originally built to beat back the Indians, the French, and a few pirates, too, is a good place to start looking for it. It has truly great vistas of Johns Bay. Not a quarter mile away is the Colonial Pemaquid Museum and a semipermanent archaeological site (see Attractions chapter).

Around the corner is one of the few sand beaches in the Midcoast, Pemaquid Beach, which arcs for 575 glorious yards on Johns Bay (see Beaches chapter). And no visit to Pemaquid would be complete without a walk on the rocks of Pemaquid Point. With fantastic views of the open Atlantic—next stop France—and of one of Maine's more distinctive lighthouses, it's a great place to picnic or smooch. Watch out during storms, though, because huge waves have been known to carry people off here.

Waldoboro

Waldoboro is one of the most underappreciated of Maine's towns, though its residents are probably happy about this fact. People typically cruise through on a fairly unattractive stretch of Route 1, full of convenience stores, pawnshops, and discount cigarette shops, and then stop at the top of the hill at now legendary Moody's Diner (see Restaurants chapter) for a bite before pushing on. That's a shame, because there's a lot more to this town of 4,800 than great pie and gas pumps.

Waldoboro was settled by a colony of Germans who migrated here before the Revolutionary War at the invitation of General Samuel Waldo, whose name the community bears. The good Saxons—40 families worth—thought that they were going to be settling in a prosperous city and were sorely disappointed to find only a raw pine forest at the head of the Medomak River. They persevered through rough winters and clashes with Indians and built the community they were looking for. The most obvious signs of this history are the Old German Meetinghouse, a fine structure that dates to the 1770s and still has its original box pews, and the nearby Old German Cemetery, where there are graves dating back to those early settlers.

Over the years Waldoboro became known as a shipbuilding center, and an industry was built around the incredible run of alewives, those small anadromous fish from the herring family. Today a lot of people make their living clamming out on the Medomak River, and others commute to larger towns for work. Besides Moody's, the other well-known local business is *Maine Antiques Digest*, a newspaper that got its start covering the growing antiques-dealing scene in Maine and now is a national monthly with subscribers around the globe.

Waldoboro's downtown is a small but fun place, perched on a hill overlooking the saltwater Medomak, where there is a handful of shops, restaurants, and banks. Many, many fine old homes and river vistas can be found if one takes the time to drive the roads that wander from here to places like Dutch Neck and Cove Road.

Travel far enough on one of these byways and you'll land in the gregarious-sounding town of Friendship. A working fishing village with a population of a little over 1,000, Friendship has two claims to fame. First, it's where the Friendship Sloop originated. These old sailing workboats are now valued as cruising vessels. Second, it's where Casper the Friendly Ghost made his home. Of course, when they filmed the 1995 movie about the spritely spirit, Hollywood producers determined that Friendship, as authentic as could be, with its active fleet of lobster boats and unspoiled vibe, didn't look enough like a Maine fishing village, so they chose to shoot much of the movie in the resort town of Camden. Their loss. The beautiful waters of Muscongus Bay spread out before Friendship, and since the late 1980s they've been discovered in a big way by kayakers.

Thomaston

Talk about reinventing your town. For more than 100 years, the stately community of Thomaston was dominated by the Maine State Prison, a dark dungeon of brick and cement and razor wire ominously set at one end of Main Street, right on Route 1 in full view of everyone passing through town. The state's maximum-security facility, full of lots and lots of bad guys, it was the inspiration for the prison in the 1994 film *The Shawshank Redemption* and had a reputation for being overcrowded and antiquated. No one was particularly sad to see it unceremoniously torn down in 2001 (though some area residents thought it might be great as a tourist site, maybe a quaint inn) and its inmates shifted to a new penitentiary on a back road in nearby Warren.

With the prison gone, the focus in Thomaston is squarely where it should be—on its historic brick downtown, filled with book stores, a cafe, and gift shops, and on the miles of fine Federal and Greek Revival homes built for the sea captains who ruled the town in the 18th and 19th centuries. The community was long ago called "the town that went to sea" because of the number of vessels built in shipyards on the St. George River and because of the merchants and sailors who shipped out of Thomaston's tiny waterfront.

Down on the water you'll find a plaque that commemorates the visit to the region paid by British explorer Captain George Waymouth in 1605. Not too long later, the spot became home to a trading post, and it really started to boom in the years after the American Revolution. The town was incorporated in 1777, named for war hero General John Thomas, and it was put on the map when George Washington's secretary of war, Henry Knox, set up in a mansion on a hill at the end of Main Street. Montpelier, a replica of that colonial showplace, was built on the site in the 1930s and is the most impressive structure in town now that the prison is gone.

Lime quarries were a staple of the economy for years, along with shipbuilding, brickmaking, and farming. Now townspeople do a lot of commuting. Some work at the imposing Dragon Cement plant, which sullies the view behind the Knox Mansion, while others head into the neighboring city of Rockland.

St. George River Area

The wide St. George River sweeps in between two communities on its way up to Thomaston, Cushing to the west, and St. George to the east. The latter pair were joined until 1803, when they split into a more manageable duo (they were already composed of almost a dozen distinct villages). This is the country that the Wyeth family of painters have made famous since early last century. A rural area of woods and fields, saltwater farms and fishing villages, the region first seduced N. C. Wyeth, a well-known illustrator, in the 1920s, when he set up household at Port Clyde.

His son Andrew would use an old, creaky Cushing farm—the Olson House—and the hardy couple that lived in it, Christina and Alvaro Olson, in a series of works, including Christina's World, one of the most famous American paintings of all time. Scores of his other paintings depict the area's windswept meadows, rolling hills, and tidal river. Wyeth fans routinely make the pilgrimage downriver to explore the countryside, especially now that the Rockland-based Farnsworth Museum has purchased the Olson House and opened it to tours (see Attractions chapter). Another artistic icon, sculptor Bernard "Blackie" Langlais, lived down in Cushing as well, and many of his old wooden sculptures can still be seen in front of the house he shared with his wife.

The community took its name from a Massachusetts lieutenant governor, Thomas Cushing, back in 1789 when the town was incorporated (remember, Maine originally was part of Massachusetts). It was settled about

150 years prior to that by an English trader in 1634. The trader was chased out of the area by the French, who held this place until 1654 and who harassed English settlers until the French and Indian War drove them out. After the American Revolution there was a slow influx of residents drawn by farmland and fishing potential. Fishermen still work from various points down here, and the population has leveled at about 1,300.

Where Cushing is largely open and meadow strewn, the town of St. George is more woodsy and broken by a handful of villages—Port Clyde, Tenants Harbor, Martinsville, Spruce Head, Long Cove, and Clark Island. Granite quarrying became a huge industry here in the 19th century, and lots of old quarries remain (many, like those on Clark Island, make for great swimming holes).

Port Clyde, across the river from Cushing, is a stunner, a fishing village occupying a headland overlooking the Georges Islands. A cluster of homes and businesses make up the center of town right at the tip of the St. George Peninsula, among them the funky Port Clyde General Store, a 200-year-old gem with groaning floors, newspapers, pizza, and videos. The Dip Net Restaurant is behind the store, offering seafood with a fine view of the harbor.

The waterfront is a busy place in Port Clyde because it's here that vacationers and islanders catch the ferry to Monhegan. The Monhegan-Thomaston Boat Line sends the *Laura B.* and the *Elizabeth Ann* on the hourlong crossing a few times daily (see the next chapter, Getting Here, Getting Around).

Other attractions on this side of the St. George River are Marshall Point, home of Marshall Point Light (see Lighthouses chapter); Tenants Harbor; and the fishing community of Spruce Head. Bicycles might just be the best method of travel in these parts, and a local conservation group, the Georges River Land Trust, has put together a handful of routes and maps.

Monhegan Island

Many people have this idea that Monhegan Island makes for a great day trip, and it does, if that's all the time you have. But this 1-square-mile island 12 miles off the Midcoast is worth more than the six or eight hours you get between ferries. Everything good about the Maine coast can be found packed onto this bit of rock at sea. It has the woodsy heights, the surf crashing on the serrated coast, the blinking lighthouse, the miles of hiking trails, the old capes and cottages of weathered gray shingles, the classic New England inn, the small-town vibe, and the picture-perfect harbor with its lobster boats. (If you can't take a good photograph here, your camera must be malfunctioning.)

The island's history is particularly rich, too. Monhegan is generally regarded as the first place European explorers landed in the Gulf of Maine—they stopped by as early as 1497. Some say they even used the harbor here to repair vessels and wait out storms before Columbus ever made it to the New World. Native Americans were here first, of course, and the name Monhegan is thought to be a variation of a Maliseet or Micmac word for island. They likely traveled out here for the same purpose that early Europeans did—fishing. European fishermen began visiting in the early 17th century, sometimes staying, sometimes moving on, until about 1625, when a trading post was set up on the island. Permanent settlement followed in 1674.

Fishing remains one of the key elements of the local economy, and the Monhegan lobstermen have set up a program that has become a model in Maine, limiting their fishing to seven months of the year, between December 1 and June 25. They have a beautiful tradition of not heading out on day one of the season unless everyone is ready, and they make quite an effort to make sure everybody is, getting together in the weeks beforehand, repairing nets and boats and lending hands. The harbor is very active with fishing vessels through the winter and spring, and in summer several

Painters flock to Monhegan, the famed "Artist's Island." MAINE OFFICE OF TOURISM

entrepreneurial islanders change their focus to the other economic force here—tourism.

The island is home to roughly 90 year-rounders, and a few hundred others move in for the summer months. Thousands more arrive each week on the *Laura B.* and *Elizabeth Ann,* ferries from Port Clyde. Other mainland points send visitors, too. Many are day-trippers, some are arriving for a weekend at one of the excellent hostelries, and still more set up for a week at a rental cottage. Those in the know bring flashlights—electricity is limited out here—and wear good walking shoes, because there are no vehicles, save a few work trucks, on the island's dirt roads. The conveniences of modern life are few—no Internet cafes, no phones or TVs in your room—but that's really the point.

Art draws a lot of vacationers to the island, whether they're making it themselves, perusing the couple dozen galleries and artists' studios in town, or checking out sites made famous by all of the world-famous greats who have lived and worked on the island—from Robert Henri to Rockwell Kent to George Bellows to Edward Hopper to Jamie Wyeth.

Many others, though, come to enjoy the natural world. More than half of the island has been preserved as woods, and the vistas of crashing sea from atop cliffs are some of the best you're ever going to get. In the spring and fall, the island is known for birding—it's a real avian hot spot during these migratory periods. The trail network through these forests is rather extraordinary—that islanders have managed to blaze more than 17 miles of footpaths on little more than a mile and a half of island is something to wonder at.

Idyllic is the word on Monhegan. Those who schedule only a day trip to the island are often regretful when they board the 4:00 P.M. ferry back to the mainland.

Rockland

These are renaissance days for the city of Rockland. Once a down-at-the-heels fishing port known for its bikers and its smell, the burgh has reinvented itself since the early 1990s, thanks in large part to the success of the Farnsworth Art Museum downtown (see Attractions chapter). Long one of Maine's best art collections, the Farnsworth went through a major period of renovation and revival in the late 1990s, debuting the Wyeth Center, expanding display areas, and, perhaps most importantly, establishing a presence on Route 1 in the heart of downtown. Its new entrance on Main Street attracted other galleries to locate here and helped inspire the opening of a bunch of restaurants and shops and the restoration of the old Strand Theater into a showplace of movies and performances.

There's always been a lot to like about Rockland; it's just that the city's reputation got in the way. The location on the west side of Penobscot Bay is very nice, offering beautiful vistas from a variety of points (the best perhaps being the mile-long Rockland Breakwater, a wall of granite stones that protects the harbor). The 19th-century brick downtown, with its Greek, Italianate, and colonial revival blocks, looks like what a Maine downtown should look like, and there are streets of older homes in the neighborhoods beyond Broadway. You might recognize all this from the 2001 movie *In the Bedroom,* which was filmed at various points around town. The city boasts an excellent Carnegie library, too.

Lobsters have been a staple of the economy here as long as anyone can remember, and the city calls itself the Lobster Capital of the World, staking a mean claim to that title by processing millions of pounds of the tasty "bugs" a year. The lobster fleet shares space on the waterfront with a handful of schooners from the Maine Windjammer Association, graceful vessels that pretty up what's largely an industrial harbor. A resident Coast Guard station and an arm of Outward Bound also moor boats down here, and ferries come and go to the populated islands of Penobscot Bay on a regular basis. A relatively new mile-long boardwalk on the side opposite the breakwater is another good place to check out the waterfront.

Before the lobster industry became king in Rockland, the city was a big shipper of lime and granite and, like so many other Maine ports, had its share of shipyards turning out vessels. Many of the city's 8,000 residents today are involved in the seafood business in one way or another, but plenty are also employed in retail and the service industry, at manufactories like Fisher Corporation, which makes snowplows; at PenBay hospital in Rockport; and at many stores and restaurants downtown.

Thanks to the Farnsworth Art Museum, the downtown is still a vital place where it can be difficult to find a parking spot in high summer, despite competition from two shopping plazas and a Wal-Mart on the edge of the city. On Main Street and in the blocks surrounding it are a handful of fine restaurants, many galleries, shops selling everything from high-end furnishings to yupscale women's clothes to used books, and, for some reason, at least a half dozen barber shops. Some in the city wonder if everything happened too fast and whether the population can support all these fancy restaurants—several are now shutting down for winter.

The joke used to be "Camden by the Sea, Rockland by the Smell," referring to the picturesque resort community up the road, and the city of Rockland is certainly turning itself around. It can still stink on a hot August day, thanks to fish processing plants—but that's just keeping it real.

Penobscot Bay Islands

Poet Edna St. Vincent Millay, who grew up in Rockland and Camden, made her first impressions on the literary world with the poem "Renascence," in which she wrote: "All I could see from where I stood / were three long islands and a wood." She's referring to the isles of Penobscot Bay, several of which have year-round communities on them. These are romantic, windswept places, well worthy of poetry, and it's hard to visit without wanting to up and move to a cottage on one. The panoramas are spectacular almost anywhere you go

on them, thanks to the fact that they're surrounded by the Atlantic Ocean and other islands and they overlook the Camden Hills and the mountains of Acadia. But there's something to the deep and rich sense of community that thrives on islands—everyone knows everyone, looks out for everyone, and all that good stuff—in a way that no longer happens in Any Suburb, USA. Plus, no Wal-Mart is going to move in and ruin the neighborhood any time soon.

Vinalhaven

This hardy isle of fishermen and artists is the largest of the 14 year-round islands of Maine, sitting right in the middle of the great inlet next to its sister island, North Haven. Lobstering is the mainstay of the economy, with shrimp, scallops, and urchins also contributing. Of Vinalhaven's 1,200 residents, 200 work on the water. The others do a little bit of everything, whatever it takes to be able to live on this 17-mile isle, an 80-minute ferry ride from Rockland. Many artists and writers have set up on Vinalhaven, the most notable being Robert Indiana—he of the love sign fame—and there are a few amenities for tourists. Libby House, Payne Homestead at the Moses Webster House, and the Tidewater Motel take in guests, and the latter rents bikes and cars (proprietor Phil Crossman is a hoot). Another local character, George Harrison, is a real-estate agent and gives tours. A half dozen eclectic stores serve the islanders and sell T-shirts, film, and take-out food to visitors. And there is a good little museum in the old town hall that's run by the historical society, where you can learn a bit about the island's beginnings.

Archaeological evidence on the island suggests that the Red Paint People, an ancient Native American society known for its red ocher graves, visited Vinalhaven 5,000 years ago. Europeans didn't follow until the 1500s. English explorer Martin Pring sailed by in 1603, and supposedly the hungry captain witnessed gray foxes running about and named Vinalhaven and North Haven the Fox Islands. It wasn't until the 1760s that the island had a permanent resident, and the community began to build, becoming a town in 1789. Townspeople named the new municipality after John Vinal, a Boston lawyer who represented them in their 1785 bid to secede from Massachusetts. Early settlers like Thaddeus Carver of Marshfield, Massachusetts, who lent Carver's Harbor his name, came looking for lumber and shipped plenty out, but what they discovered of real and unique value was granite—and lots of it. This discovery came at a time when the big cities of the northeast were building at a rapid rate, and granite from Vinalhaven quarries was used in such prominent structures as the Brooklyn Bridge, the Cathedral of St. John the Divine, and the U.S. Customs Houses and Post Office in New York; post offices in St. Louis, Kansas City, and Buffalo; the railroad station and the Board of Trade in Chicago; and the Washington Monument.

Vinalhaven has made a significant blip on the radar of tourism since, but it's still not overrun by any means. (Some local teens might feel it is, though, because they've been known to insult visitors.) Day-trippers enjoy walking and biking the miles of roads, swimming in Lawson's and Booth's quarries, kayaking offshore, and playing in the island's several parks and preserves, places like Lane's Island, a breathtaking island of meadows, coves, and wildflowers linked by a bridge to Vinalhaven.

North Haven

You could almost jump across the Fox Island Thorofare from Vinalhaven to North Haven, so close are the two. Because of this proximity the early history of the two islands is very similar—they even claim the same gentleman as their first resident. But not long after granite was being discovered on Vinalhaven, the wealthy elite of Boston began discovering North Haven. The island became something of an exclusive enclave, which it remains to a certain extent. Tourist facilities are very limited—there are few bed-and-breakfasts and inns and only a single sit-down restaurant, the Coal Wharf.

North Haven is 12 miles off Rockland and about an hour by ferry. It's only 24 square miles and has two primary neighborhoods, North Haven Village and Pulpit Harbor (not including the intriguingly named hamlet of Sleepyville). The year-round population of 300 blooms in July and August to about 2,000 with the arrival of the summer people, many of whom are descendants of families that started coming here in the late 19th century.

Day-trippers will find excellent bicycling, a neat old golf course, pleasant walking, local artist Eric Hopkins's fine gallery, another art showplace at the North Haven Gift Shop, and picnic fixings at Brown's Market, a general store that stocks one of everything.

Matinicus

Twenty-two miles out into the drink, Matinicus is the farthest removed of Maine's populated islands. A local cottage rental company describes the isle as "extraordinary, but not for everyone." That is a very apt way of putting it. This rental agent continues, "If you would like to visit an island that is remote, a bit rustic, and that requires a sense of adventure, tolerance, independence and humor from its visitors, read on."

Enticing visitors to this 1.5-square-mile island, which isn't even on most maps, is an uphill battle. First is simply the time and distance. The ferry ride is 2 hours and 15 minutes long, and the ferry comes only three times a month in summer, less often than that in winter (but private boats are available—see www.matinicusexcursions.com or www.wildwoodcharters.com—as is air service). Second is the reputation of the place—it's generally considered the most insular of all of Maine islands, the East Coast's version of the Wild West. Simply put, many islanders don't want to see outsiders.

But if you can deal with stony glances and a bit of rudeness, you'll find a lot to like on Matinicus. The natural world is the most obvious attraction. Walking trails squirrel here and there across the island and, unusual for a piece of rock at sea, there are two fine sand beaches. (The water's still cold, though.) Birding is exceptional—with boats available to take people out to see the puffin colony on Matinicus Rock—and many rare plant species inhabit the island as well. Simply strolling and looking around here is fun, like a walk back to the 1940s, corny as that may sound. This is also one of the few places anywhere where you can call and order a lobster dinner and have it delivered to your door. (Lobstering is the chief industry here.) Artists and photographers have long been drawn to Matinicus, dating back to the great George Bellows. If you make the effort, you'll see why.

Camden-Rockport Area

It would be hard to invent a better setting for a coastal Maine resort town than the one found in Camden. When he visited in 1605, Captain John Smith (yes, him again) was impressed, writing "under the high mountains of Penobscot, against whose feet the sea doth beat." And indeed Penobscot Bay laps picturesquely at the town's protected harbor, with a lighthouse-topped island sitting at the mouth and two round peaks looming imposingly above. A series of small summits—the Camden Hills—trundle inland from there past big Megunticook Lake. From the tops of Mounts Battie and Megunticook you think you can see forever out across the glistening expanse of the bay and over its spiny islands. Soaring cliffs, plenty of wildlife, rivers and streams, a waterfall—the area's got it all.

Which makes it too bad that so many people have discovered it. Camden is now notorious for the congestion that clogs its picturesque downtown, and it seems like every other week some magnate or other is moving into one of the gracious colonial revival homes that line High Street or sit above the harbor. Camden is one of the few places—perhaps the only spot in Maine—where Route 1, the highway up the Maine coast, yields to a local road. Hollywood sets up shop many a summer filming some picture or other—*The Man Without a Face* (1993), *Casper* (1995), *Thinner* (1996), and *In the Bedroom* (2001) in recent years.

The town has a year-round population of about 5,000 relatively affluent souls, and during June, July, and August they are joined by probably three times that number with the arrival of the tourists and summercators. People come for a variety of reasons, and many have similar aims—hiking or camping in Camden Hills State Park; shopping in the innumerable boutiques, specialty shops, and gift stores downtown; or heading out to sea on windjammers. The numerous eateries, offbeat movie theater, kayak tours, grassy parks, and historic homes only add to the appeal. Two excellent auditoriums bring name acts to this wee town—the Camden Opera House and the Strom Auditorium at the impressive high school. Then there is the Camden Snow Bowl, which is everything a ski area should be: small, community run, friendly, and inexpensive. Obviously a bigger draw in winter, it sees its share of hikers and bikers in the summer.

The sea built Camden. Shipyards were a mainstay of the economy for years (and still are, with huge Wayfarer Marine repairing yachts). Lime from area pits and wool from the Knox Woolen Mill employed many workers in subsequent years, and of course fishing fed many families. When East Coast business leaders discovered Camden in the 1950s, the summer trade began. The rich moved in, first for the summers and eventually for the remainder of the year, bringing their yachts with them. Camden Harbor is always awash in boats, from the majestic schooners like the *Mary Day* that anchor there to the raft of ostentatious yachts, colorful kayaks, and dinghies. A few hardy fishermen bravely navigate through the crowded basin on their way out in search of lobster.

Things are a little better in Rockport. Camden's sister town is also a haven for the affluent—many former CIA and Foreign Service workers among them—and has a busy little harbor, but it's not quite as overrun because there simply aren't as many touristy things to do here. The population here is 3,000, and in summer it too triples, with the influx of summer people and with students at the Maine Photographic Workshops, a world-class film

On a sunny summer day, Camden Harbor bustles. JENNIFER SMITH-MAYO

and photography school that draws some of the top names in the field to Rockport.

Downtown are an arc of brick buildings and the pretty old Rockport Opera House, which sits on a hill above the harbor. Around the corner and up the road, the miles of summer homes and "cottages" begin. Some are neat old capes, some shingle-style, others the showy wannabe palaces of the nouveau Mainers.

The town's history is intertwined with Camden's, but it does have its own chapters, one of which is the life of Andre the Seal. Down on the waterfront in Rockport Marine Park is a monument to the beloved harbor seal, who jumped through hoops for audiences all summer long, shooting baskets, counting, singing, from the 1960s until late in his life. He was only a summer resident, swimming back to Boston Aquarium in the fall, and he was killed by a rival on the way in 1986.

Just northeast of Camden and Rockport is the town of Lincolnville, which is technically the southernmost municipality in character-laden Waldo County but behaves more like a suburb of Camden. Lincolnville is best known for its short sandy beach, along which a few restaurants, gift shops, and the always fun Beach Store are located. Bathers in the know travel another mile or so up the road to a tiny rock beach called Ducktrap, where the Duck-trap River empties into Penobscot Bay. There's better, more private swimming here. A skip up the road takes visitors to Tanglewood 4-H camp, which is filled with trails through the woods along the river. And several miles beyond that is Lincolnville Center, a swell village of old homes and vistas in the rolling Camden Hills.

Islesboro

Lincolnville Beach sends a ferry 3 miles across Penobscot Bay to the island of Islesboro several times daily. Like North Haven, Islesboro has an air of exclusivity about it, especially the village of Dark Harbor, which anchors one end of the skinny, 12-mile isle. Here the rich and famous built grand mansions in the Victorian era, many of which still exist. Back then the island's local population were the serving people for the wealthy. Today things are a little more real, though the social calendar of Dark Harbor is busy. John Travolta and Kirstie Alley have been some of the better known of the town's 600-some residents, but they have kept relatively low profiles.

The island was settled in the years before the American Revolution, with an influx of fishermen and farmers. When the War of 1812 gripped the mainland town of Castine, not too far away across East Penobscot Bay, the residents of Islesboro had a rough go of it, forced into cooperating with the British. Later in that century, they had to swallow their pride again after Jeffrey Bracket, a young, rich Boston fellow, visited the island and was smitten, and a few hundred wealthy people from the city moved in and colonization began. An informal caste system went into place that the island took more than a century to be rid of.

As on most of the other populated islands, lobstering is the big breadwinner on Islesboro, but there are also three boatyards turning out vessels, and many islanders commute to jobs on the mainland—or work from their homes, thanks to Internet connections, faxes, and e-mail—since ferries are frequent and the crossing takes only 20 minutes.

Vacationers will find plenty to see and do and a few places to lay their head. Because the island is long and flat, it makes for great biking, and kayakers love all the coves and inlets and smaller satellite isles all around it. One of these islands is home to Warren Island State Park, a great camping area if you have your own boat. There's a nice beach—called, originally enough, Town Beach—at Pendleton Point, and there are also a few shops and even a performing arts center that gets busy in July and August.

Belfast

USA Today in the late 1990s printed a piece recommending Belfast as a "culturally cool"

city, and while a lot of things have changed since then, it still remains a funky and eclectic community. How many other cities of 7,000 have their own vegetarian cafe, classes in African drumming and foil fencing, a professional theater company, another nationally known theater organization, a hip art deco movie cinema, a supermarket-size food co-op, a curling club, several art galleries, an environmentally friendly department store, naturopaths, homeopaths, acupuncturists, and two newspapers? Outside of California, that's a pretty hard place to find. (And maybe even in California.) As the shire town of wacky Waldo County, a collection of cool rural towns with a lot of unique inhabitants, Belfast has become a truly amazing place.

The city underwent a profound and sometimes difficult change during the mid-1990s and today is dominated by Bank of America. The credit card giant MBNA built a massive headquarters here and buildings larger than anything found anywhere else in the Midcoast outside of Bath Iron Works, and then the company staffed them with 6,000 tie-and-dress-wearing telemarketers. This development was a bit difficult for many of the locals to swallow, since up to that point Belfast's populace was a mix of fishermen and back-to-the-land émigrés from the early 1970s, most of whom threw away their ties long ago. People stopped grousing a bit when MBNA started throwing money around to worthy causes, from the schools to the hospitals. And it was hard to argue that Belfast didn't need the jobs. Now that MBNA has been sold to Bank of America, those jobs are in question.

Named for Belfast, Ireland, the city was settled by a Scotch-Irish band of pioneers back in 1770. These tough folks had previously made their home in Londonderry, New Hampshire, and were bothered enough by the British that they upped and left. They liked what they found at this spot above the Passagassawaukeag River (that's Passy for short) and built a thriving little hamlet that grew and grew over the years as shipbuilding and lumbering prosperity moved in. You can walk around and literally see those good times written in wood and shingle—the city is well known in Maine for its distinctive Greek Revival, Federal, and Italianate homes (more than 200 structures in town are on the National Register). When Belfast burned in 1865 and again in 1873, the city rebuilt, and the result is a fine downtown of Victorian Gothic and Greek Revival brick. Some of these old buildings will cause crooks in your neck, you'll stare at them so long—they're that good-looking.

By the mid-20th century the focus of the economy changed from the water to the wings—of chickens. The city became for a while the biggest chicken processor in the world, and while this industry wasn't good for the harbor, which ran with blood, it kept the citizenry at work. Things got a bit down at the heels here when Frank Purdue and others proved they could produce and ship chickens quicker and the broiler industry went bust. So, many people were glad to see the green-and-tan empire of MBNA move in. Many civic leaders recognize the potential of tourism, but Belfast isn't the Maine summer theme park that is Camden down the road. Far fewer people explore Belfast, and it doesn't tart itself up for them.

The city is eminently walkable—at least the good parts are—and there's a stroller's tour all scripted and printed down at the Belfast Chamber of Commerce that will take you through the most attractive neighborhoods. The downtown has a handful of good restaurants—from the hip vegetariana of Chase's Daily to the pricier fare of the Twilight Café to the cheap but good Bay Wrap—and the shopping is nothing if not eclectic. If you see something you like, buy it, because several of these stores won't be here on your next pass through town. These storefronts have quite the history of turnover. The city's park, right on Penobscot Bay, is worth a look, as is the harborfront park established by MBNA.

Plenty of various types of accommodations are available, so you'd best give yourself more than one day. Make sure to travel into Waldo County, too, where you'll find innumerable treasures in towns like Searsmont, Freedom, and Liberty. The further you look into Belfast and Waldo County, the more unexpected delights you'll find.

Searsport

Searsport has two claims to fame: It's an antiques hot spot, and it has a rich maritime history, producing more sea captains per capita than anyplace else in the universe (or something like that) back in the days of tall ships. The former you can see evidence of just by driving around—there are antiques stores every half mile or so. The latter is less evident these days—you don't see mustachioed characters with muttonchops wandering around in gold-buttoned jackets—but you can find out everything you ever wanted to know about Searsport and the sea at the Penobscot Marine Museum (see Attractions chapter).

Turns out 200 or so Searsport residents became ship captains, or 1 in 10 of all American heads of ship in the late 19th century. Shipbuilding was also booming by this period, with six shipyards spread across the city's waterfront on Penobscot Bay. The captains who went to sea returned with all sorts of exotic goods and experiences, and they built themselves impressive homes, like those found in Belfast and Thomaston. One family, the Nichols, had 35 members born at sea.

Searsport has one of the deepest ports in Maine, which it greatly benefited from in those early days and which in more recent years has made it one of a trio of ports—Portland and Eastport are the others—in the state's three-pronged cargo-shipping scheme. The waterfront in town remains a working one, but it is less about fishing and more about moving cargo—and, thanks to some big, ugly Irving and GAC plants—oil and chemicals. Over the years, there has been a lot of talk at the local and state level about using the town's Sears Island, a beautiful, relatively unspoiled, 940-acre isle connected to the mainland by a causeway, in any number of industrial capacities, from nuclear power plant to expanded cargo port. It sits in that deep channel almost exactly halfway up the coast and right near the point where the Penobscot River pours into Penobscot Bay, so its location is truly prime. But it's also the largest undeveloped island left in Maine and has been a favorite, hiking, swimming, fishing, and camping spot for locals, so each time new ideas come up, there is great opposition, and the proposals have been quashed. Now the state, which owns the land, is considering using it as a park, which is probably its best use anyway. There's another great state park south of town off Route 1 at Moose Point.

Aside from the sea captains' homes, which can be truly impressive, like the homes of the Homeport and Brass Lantern inns, the town is rather unassuming. Downtown is a hodgepodge of brick and wood storefronts— a National Register historic district that isn't quite as impressive as the one down the road in Belfast (a search for a good meal here will bring you back to Belfast, so you can compare)—and convenience stores and flea markets are the main features as you head north. However, the past couple of years a real effort has been made to make the town more attractive to the millions of people headed past en route to Acadia—and it's working.

East of Searsport is Stockton Springs, another old shipbuilding port astride Route 1. Named Stockton after a seaside English town, the community added the *Springs* later when it was trying to make a name for itself in the bottled-water industry. The downtown has faded since that enterprise evaporated and others like poultry processing did, too.

Down on its waterfront, though, is Fort Point State Park and its attendant Fort Point Light, and up the road is the handsome hamlet of Sandy Point, where a handful of white clapboard historic homes flank a big white church —the very picture of a New England village.

Bucksport

Witch tale, paper mill, imposing fort, vertiginous suspension bridge, and new marina—

the Bucksport area has a little of everything. The town's situation at the head of Penobscot Bay, exactly the point where the Penobscot River descends to the sea, was ideally suited for the European settlers who made their way here in the 1760s. The Penobscot Indians came here to fish prior to that, seeking the river's famous salmon, but they were pushed out of the way by the English.

Colonel Jonathan Buck of the Massachusetts Bay Colony incorporated "Buckstown" in 1792 and opened a mill on the shore of the river. Quite aside from naming the community for himself and helping launch a shipping and trade industry here, Buck is remembered for an incident that occurred in the late 18th century. Everyone locally is tired of the story now, but it persists because of its creepy nature. Legend has it that while serving as a town magistrate, Buck sentenced a woman to die for witchcraft. She supposedly laid a curse on him, something to the effect that she'd follow him until he died and into the beyond, and now his tombstone bears the uncanny outline of a woman's leg—many consider this stripe a flaw in the granite, but it has reappeared every time it's been ground or buffed away. So the story goes. The grave is clearly visible from Route 1, but it's best to pull into the Hannaford parking lot and cross the street if you want to have a look.

The town would rather be known as an important Maine port and changed its name to Bucksport in 1817, remaining a vital shipping town because its of location on the river and thus on the route to Bangor. Fort Knox, the dramatic, medieval-looking bastion that hangs on a hill on the opposite side of the Penobscot, was built in the 1840s to protect the port and the river when border tensions began to arise with the English. A few decades later, hunters and fishermen begin to discover the North Woods of Maine, and they often traveled to the area via Bangor, through Bucksport.

Today oil flows from Bucksport Harbor to Bangor, fueling homes and the Bangor airport, and the Verso Paper mill employs about 1,000 people. The latter produces glossy papers for catalogs like L. L. Bean and JCPenney and for magazines like *Time* and *Newsweek*. Other businesses that line Main Street, paralleling the river, include a decent bookstore in Bookstacks, software developer Locus Technology, and Ergonomics Plus, an office supply company. Cultural highlights are the Northeast Historic Film Archive, which resides in the Old Alamo Theatre and helps preserve old films—and regularly screens them, too. And Bucksport just opened a new 500-seat theater to bring drama and music to town. Several restaurants, inns, and B&Bs serve the community, including Jefferds Tavern, where Presidents Martin Van Buren, Andrew Jackson, John Tyler, and William Henry Harrison have all signed the guest book.

To reach Bucksport, you have to be prepared to drive over the soaring Waldo-Hancock Bridge, a dramatic, half-mile-long span that's known colloquially as the Bucksport Bridge. Undergoing repairs, the narrow span rises 35 feet above the Penobscot, its steel suspension towers flying 206 feet up, and it feels much higher. First opened to traffic in 1931, it was a toll bridge for 20 years, paying its $846,000 price tag before becoming free to use. Even though today there is no charge, some people who are afraid of heights find the bridge impossible to cross, but there's no other way over the river until the Bangor area.

Blue Hill Peninsula

Though a lot of Mainers say the "real Maine" begins east of Ellsworth, many miles up the road, it's hard to improve on the Maine found on the Blue Hill Peninsula. This is the wide finger of land on which (or near) are located the villages of Blue Hill, Castine, Deer Isle, Stonington, Brooksville, Brooklin, Sedgwick, and Surry. It's an unhurried place where the vistas are drop-dead gorgeous, the roads are punctuated by fantastic old homes, the communities are just that—close-knit, small towns where people still wave at one another and the postal clerks know everyone—and it's still unsullied by chain development. Lobster fishing remains an important part of the economy, as does traditional boatbuilding, and yet there are all sorts of great cultural outlets and interesting populations of artists and writers. Very cool indeed.

With a population of just over 2,000, Blue Hill is the biggest town around, a place of stately old homes, a bustling downtown filled with shops and galleries, and a summer colony that gets things busy on August afternoons. The town had a big fight with the Rite Aid drugstore chain a few years back, not wanting what it considered an eyesore on its main drag, and it's easy to see what Blue Hill residents were keen on preserving. The community is uncommonly attractive, making a U around Blue Hill Harbor and backed up against the peak that gave the town its name. Points and peninsulas and coves are the norm around here, with many homes along them. The architecture is pretty fine, too, with 68 Federal and Greek Revival representatives on the National Register. The area has attracted enough artists, writers, and musicians (like Noel Paul Stookey of Peter Paul and Mary fame) to keep things interesting and berthed the always popular and ever eclectic WERU, a community radio station well known in eastern Maine (89.9 FM).

According to the excellent local history put together by writer and resident Esther Wood, two men from North Andover, Massachusetts, migrated north to settle Blue Hill in 1762 (though they called it North Andover). Several villages sprouted over the ensuing years as people followed the pair—Head-of-the-Bay, the Neck, East Blue Hill, and North Blue Hill—each with its own school, store, and church. The current center of town developed around Head-of-the-Bay, and shipbuilding helped it prosper.

The first ship was built in 1792, and 132 more followed over the course of the next 90 years, resulting in a lot of nice homes in town. One of these houses belonged to Jonathan Fisher, parson of the local church. A true renaissance man, Fisher built his house, taught at the local Blue Hill Academy (now George Stevens Academy), and was also a poet, a scientist, a farmer, a painter, and a businessman. The Parson Fisher house, now a museum, is a fine place to learn about the rich history of the community.

When shipbuilding went to the wayside with the emergence of steel vessels and steamers, another industry arose in Blue Hill, one that conflicts mightily with the genteel, artsy reputation the town has now—mining. The ground beneath Blue Hill seemed to contain a fair bit of copper and some zinc, too, and in the late 19th century, companies and individuals rushed in to extract the valuable minerals. A Canadian company attempted to resume operations in the 1970s to much local opposition.

Residents liked the emergence of crafts as a cottage industry much better. Blue Hill has become known for its pottery—Rowantree is a nationally recognized outfit—and there are a couple other companies making names for themselves as well.

Castine

The flags of four nations have flown over the town of Castine. For 200 years the British, the French, and the Dutch battled over the village, each occupying it for stretches at a time before being beaten on by the next country to move in. The French were the first to set up on the ax-head-shaped peninsula at the edge of Penobscot Bay. Explorer Samuel de Champlain, who sailed and mapped much of the Down East coast, sent a chart back to France for the perusal of King Henry IV in 1612 that showed the prime location of what's now Castine, overlooking Penobscot Bay and the entrance to the Penobscot River. Within a year the site was a French trading post.

Of course, Captain John Smith just so happened to cruise by in 1614 and included the headland on a map he was drawing of English territory. It would go back and forth from there, with the town changing hands numerous times. In 1667 the region was granted to

the French officer Jean Vincent d'Abbadie de Saint Castin by the king of France, and the spot would ultimately take his name. Not 10 years later it would be bombarded by the Dutch, who occupied the peninsula twice, in 1674 and 1676, and then destroyed many buildings and forts in their wake.

The British moved back in and held the site, prompting colonial forces to attack from the bay in 1779 with a fleet of 18 warships and 24 personnel transports carrying 1,400 soldiers. It would go down as one of the worst, if not the worst, naval defeats in United States history as the British snuck up on the armada in the bay and wreaked havoc, and it would ruin the military career of officer Paul Revere. The British would hold Castine through War of 1812 until finally it was liberated by the United States. We still own it today.

What's all this got to do with anything? The town of Castine is one of the finest-looking historic communities in Maine, with neat battlements and buried bastions all over the place, and a squillion 19th-century National Register homes (really, it's only 255). It's particularly comely, with street after street of fine Greek Revival and Federal buildings on the tidy grid on either side of it. More than 100 historic markers chronicle the town's turbulent history and make for a compelling walking tour. You can stop at several small historic-home museums while you're at it, and if you're up for a real walk, stop by Dyce Head Lighthouse on your stroll. If ever there was a town for taking a constitutional, it's Castine.

Today you may see people walking about town in quasi-military-looking dress and wonder who's invading this time. These folks are cadets from Maine Maritime Academy, a college-level institution that prepares students for careers in the merchant marine, as well as in engineering and marine biology. The school's massive training vessel, the *State of Maine*, dominates the waterfront, and tours are available when it's in port.

Maine Maritime's 700 students, along with Castine's 1,300 residents, help keep the restaurants and inns busy during the cold winter months when the town's cottage owners are away.

Deer Isle

Deer Isle is the second-largest island on the Maine coast behind Mount Desert, dangling between Penobscot and Blue Hill bays. To reach the island you pass before or over a couple of state landmarks—Caterpillar Hill, a gradual rise with an astonishing view of Eggemoggin Reach and East Penobscot Bay, and the Deer Isle Bridge, a tall, arcing suspension span that strikes fear in a lot of people. When the state wanted to build a road across Eggemoggin Reach in 1939, connecting the island of Little Deer Isle to the mainland, islanders were not happy, afraid that they were losing their way of life.

Cruise the back roads of Deer Isle, and you can again understand what islanders wanted to protect. Split into three communities—Deer Isle, Little Deer Isle, and Stonington—it's a magnificent place. Because the island is so skinny, you're never far from a cove or a pocket beach or a headland. Jaw-dropping vistas of ocean and island are commonplace.

The bridge deposits you on Little Deer Isle, which is connected to Deer Isle proper by a winding causeway. The smallest of the three Deer Isle hamlets, it's home to a cottage community and Harbor Farm, a gift shop and housewares store, and the local chamber of commerce, which seems to be open only sporadically.

From there you cross the narrow causeway, which is frequently brutalized by storms, and then you hit the village of Deer Isle itself, where historic homes line the main drag and there can be found a thriving gallery and antiques scene, featuring the work of many graduates of the famed Haystack Mountain School of Crafts, which is located on the island. The school has converted so many of its students into island residents it's become a local joke. Eleven B&Bs, inns, and campgrounds cater to visitors needing a place to rest their head.

At the end of the road is the fantastically picturesque fishing village of Stonington, terraced on a hillside that looks out across Deer Island Thorofare and its constellation of small isles. Far from the nearest police station, Stonington had a reputation for lawlessness years ago, thanks to carousing fishermen. These days there are several fine inns, restaurants, and shops, and a couple of guide outfits thanks to Stonington's burgeoning reputation as a kayaking hot spot. Stonington also serves as the jumping-off point for Isle au Haut (*Ile-a-HO*), an idyllic, 4,700-acre gem that features a large and woodsy parcel of Acadia parkland (see Acadia chapter).

The Stone in Stonington comes from the granite on which the island rests. It's long been prized for its pink hue, and quarrying it was the principal industry here for more than a century. Before that and since, the town's been a fishing center. The rugged stone was extracted by an international cast of quarrymen, and it was shipped out to be used in the building of New York bridges, Rockefeller Center, the Boston Museum of Fine Arts, and the Smithsonian. The only active quarrying operation in Maine now is out on Crotch Island, a skip from Stonington across the harbor.

Ellsworth

Acadia's gateway town is Ellsworth, the point where travelers driving north on Route 1 have the option of following the coastal highway on its run Down East or breaking off onto State Route 3 toward Bar Harbor. Many Mainers consider this the exact point where the "real Maine" begins (after Ellsworth, that is). With three million tourists pouring past on an annual basis, you might imagine Ellsworth businesses popping up to lure them in, and you'd be right. The north half of this city of 6,200 is a strip-mall circus, one of the places Maine towns point to when they discuss out-of-control development and its negative effects on a town.

That's too bad, because as a community, Ellsworth otherwise has a lot going for it. The first local landmark one comes to traveling up Route 1 is the legendary Big Chicken Barn, an antiques and used books emporium that's worth half a day in itself. Traveling on you'll come to a steep hill that jogs left before heading down through some fine old homes to the Union River, which put Ellsworth on the map a couple of centuries ago. Then you hit a stoplight, and the city's historic downtown, a crux of brick buildings and attractive storefronts, spreads out before you. There's some nice shopping to be done here—from women's clothes to specialty foods to high-end cookware—and the city is also home to a couple of decent restaurants as well as an art deco theater that regularly shows films and schedules musical acts of regional repute.

The Penobscots and the Passamaquoddies were the first to make camp on the Union River, and they were followed by the French, who claimed most of the territory to the east. The English arrived and began to develop in 1763, when Benjamin Milliken built sawmills on the river powered by its 60-foot drop. The community grew and grew, becoming a center of shipbuilding and lumbering, before incorporating as a town in 1800, named for Oliver Ellsworth, a delegate to the Constitutional Convention of Philadelphia in 1787. Thirty-seven years later, Ellsworth would become the shire town of Hancock County.

An overwhelming fire decimated the downtown in 1855, but residents recovered and rebuilt and kept the wood and ships flowing. In 1868 the town became a city, with a population of about 5,000. Soon, though, the area's old-growth trees were gone and sailing ships out of vogue, and the city turned its attention to manufacturing, churning out shoes and bricks. Another inferno tore through town in 1933, leveling many buildings, but the city once again rose to the challenge and is now a thriving retail center for Hancock County, sucking in those tourists.

ACADIA AREA

Bar Harbor

Bar Harbor was originally named Eden, and the town and the island it resides on are certainly a garden of natural delights. Dozens of mountains rumble across Mount Desert Island, their round pates carved by ice age glaciers, their feet sticking into the chilly Atlantic. The sea relentlessly pounds the shore here, making spectacular displays, and lakes and woods occupy the isle's interior, filled with all manner of beasts and critters. Tempting indeed.

The town of Bar Harbor, on the northeast edge of Mount Desert, has a rich history—literally. Quite aside from its wealth of natural wonders, it became famous for being a summer home for the überaffluent. Curious scions of New York society came up to see the fabulously scenic island in the mid-19th century and found this Eden to be the apple of their eyes. So they told all their friends, and soon Bar Harbor had become the fashionable place to be in July and August, a resort of luxury and privilege where servants catered to the every wish of rusticators ensconced in "cottages" that would be called mansions anywhere else. If your last name was Rockefeller, Astor, Vanderbilt, or Carnegie, this was where you wanted to be.

People have been summering here for ages. The Native Americans were awestruck by this mountainous island and the excellent fishing grounds that encircled it, and they set up camp here during the warm weather months. (The excellent local Abbe Museum is a good place to learn about the island's earliest inhabitants.) French explorer Samuel de Champlain cruised past in 1604 on his way up the coast and labeled the spot I'lle de Monts Deserts, "island of bare mountains," on his charts. The name stuck.

Settled in 1786, Bar Harbor was a simple fishing town until Thomas Cole, a painter of the Hudson River school, showed up one day in the 1840s with his easel. His romanticized renderings of the island, its round peaks and thundering surf, attracted the attention of New York society, which, tired of sweltering in the summer heat of Manhattan, decided to migrate north. A few decades later, fancy magazines were comparing Bar Harbor to Newport, until then the queen of the social scene.

Scores of cottages went up—and alongside them grand hotels—and people were practically tripping over one another to get to croquet tournaments, garden parties, afternoon teas, and sumptuous soirees.

Then a couple of things happened: Acadia National Park opened in 1919, and in 1947 much of the island burned, taking 170 homes, 5 hotels, and 67 summer estates along with it. Acadia attracted a new type of person to the island—the camera-toting tourist. The fire just about killed the hoity-toity summercator scene in one fell swoop. (Although Martha Stewart, the heiress to all things Waspy and societal, bought the old Edsel Ford place in nearby Seal Harbor several years ago before she went to jail.)

These days Bar Harbor's grand age is an interesting historical footnote that middle-class moms and dads learn about at the historical society museum when they're in town to explore the park, play miniature golf, and go kayaking. Tourism is what Bar Harbor is all about now, and unfortunately, a lot of it is of the mainstream variety (T-shirt and sunglass shops, waterslides, go-kart rides, and knick-nacks and gewgaws, that sort of stuff). But there's enough Eden remaining here—the beautiful Shore Path walkway, the blocks and blocks of distinctive old buildings, the cool College of the Atlantic, Bar Island, and, of course, Acadia—that it's most definitely worth your time, especially before June and after September.

Northeast Harbor

Discovered by rich summer people shortly after Bar Harbor, Northeast Harbor has a decidedly tony air when compared to the island's busiest town. First a haven for Philadelphians of means, who still show up in July and August every year, it has diversified a bit in recent years to include affluent summer residents from other cities on the eastern seaboard. There's only one place to stay for those not lucky enough to own a gray shingled manse overlooking Somes Sound, and that is at the fine—and quite pricey—Asticou Inn.

But the small village has enough to entertain anyone for an afternoon, especially if you enjoy gardens, offbeat museums, impressive yachts, and expensive boutiques.

Northeast Harbor (pop. 2,000) boasts one of the island's more accommodating harbors, so it's always had an appeal to visiting yacht owners. And because of the community's cachet, they often arrive in large and luxurious boats, so it can be fun just wandering around the harbor and gawking. Two of Maine's best public gardens—Asticou and Thuya—are located here, the former famous for its azaleas in springtime, the latter for its Oriental overtones, so you'll want to allow time to pay each a visit. The town also is home to a pair of unusual museums. One is Petite Plaisance, former home of famed French writer Marguerite Yourcenar, and the other is the Great Harbor Maritime Museum, filled with boats and models.

Southwest Harbor

On the western or "quiet side" of the island, Southwest Harbor feels less like a playground and more like a real place than Bar Harbor or Northeast, which is because it is. While a lot of people do make it here in the summer to visit Acadia lands and there are plenty of seasonal homes, most here are year-rounders living peacefully in a very appealing, tight-knit community. Southwest (pop. 2,000) is also a working place, with a fishing fleet, a Coast Guard base, and several boatbuilding yards, most notably the headquarters of world-famous Hinckley Yachts. The small downtown is less tourist-oriented than some of its island neighbors, with a school, post office, library, a couple of restaurants, and some shops selling actual necessities.

But you'll find loads to do over here and, thankfully, a lot fewer people to compete with. The Southwest area—we're including Somesville, Manset, Bass Harbor, and the town of Mount Desert—has some of the best of Acadia's hiking trails, several nice inns, a couple of outing companies, freshwater swimming at picturesque lakes, great bicycling, and

Though it gets busy in summer, Southwest Harbor remains an alternative to the overcrowded, tourist-happy haven that is Bar Harbor. JENNIFER SMITH-MAYO

camping, too. Access for the sweet islands of Swans and Frenchboro is from Bass Harbor, and they are great fun to explore.

Many people in the know who prefer a slower, simpler vacation limit their time on the island to this western side and avoid the rush of Bar Harbor.

DOWN EAST

Schoodic Point Area

Traffic and tourism go from a scream to a sigh on Route 1 once you get past Ellsworth and the turnoff for Bar Harbor and Mount Desert. Though they have their own summer colonies and even a section of Acadia National Park, the next few peninsulas Down East couldn't be more different than the merry madness of MDI. Hancock Point is only a few miles down the road from Ellsworth, and it is virtually unknown to day-trippers. Those who do come to stay at the pleasant Crocker House inn find themselves in an exclusive summer enclave of grand cottages and clay tennis courts. A Harvard historian, Frederick Jackson Turner, is said to have been the first to move in for the summer in the 1880s, and he was soon joined by a host of other scholars, giving the point a reputation as an intellectual and cultured retreat. According to a film about the hamlet—*A Century of Summers: The Impact of a Summer Colony on a Maine Coastal Town, 1886–1986*—prominent Bangor residents soon joined these professors, and Vassar and Princeton students had informal summer programs here as well. Famed conductor Pierre Monteux of the Metropolitan Opera and the Boston and London Symphonies set up a school for musicians in 1943, and it's still active. Today's summer residents include Senator Olympia Snowe and former senator and secretary of defense Bill Cohen.

Beyond Hancock Point is Gouldsboro, where author Louise Dickinson Rich spent her summers. She profiled the village of Corea, a part of the town of Gouldsboro (pop. 2,037), in her 1958 book *The Peninsula*. There are few amenities for tourists in Corea, but it rewards visitors with a look at an unspoiled fishing community. South of Gouldsboro is Winter Harbor (pop. 1,240), which is another little-known summer haven for the wealthy. A bunch of families with roots in Philadelphia occupy a spit of land called Grindstone Neck. The other notable resident of Winter Harbor is Acadia National Park, which owns the tip of land at the end of the Schoodic Peninsula (see Acadia chapter). There also used to be a hush-hush U.S. Navy communications post here, but it closed in 2002.

Milbridge

In 1890 Milbridge had a population of 1,963—at the height of the town's shipbuilding boom. Milbridge was one of the centers of boat construction Down East, thanks to loads of available timber and its fine situation on the Narraguagas River. Today there are 1,200 or so residents, dependent upon fishing, worming, gathering Christmas greens and trees, and, especially, blueberrying. (Washington County is the largest producer of wild blueberries in the nation, and one of the bigger processors, Jasper Wyman and Sons, is based in Milbridge.) If people knew better, they'd be descending upon Evergreen Realty and moving in like the wind. The town is amazingly appealing, with its old homes, pleasant Main Street, and truly exquisite scenery. The best time to pay a visit, if you want a dose of Americana, is during the town's popular festival, Milbridge Days, in July.

Just up the coast are the villages of Cherryfield, Harrington, Addison, and Columbia Falls, each of which is a historic, coastal gem.

Machias

It's a wonder, too, more people haven't discovered Machias and fallen in love. The Down East town of about 2,000 has just about everything people come to Maine to find—a magnificent stretch of coastline, pretty old architecture, an inviting downtown, friendly people, woods all around, and a host of natural delights in the surrounding area. The town makes for a great base for a Down East adventure. From here you can easily reach Jonesport, a rugged fishing village; Great Wass Island, famous for its wildflowers; and the Cutler public lands unit, a truly spectacular hiking and camping area.

That is, if you can bring yourself to leave Machias. The town straddles the Machias River and was named Mechises, which meant "bad little falls," by Native Americans. You can see why, driving into town, by stopping at Bad Little Falls Park and watching the churning, tumbling water and imagining a birchbark canoe going over. From here you pass a campus of the University of Maine system, with about 1,000 students, before hitting Court Street and downtown. Machias is the county seat for Washington County and thus has courts and federal buildings; they are joined by shops and a couple of good restaurants in a compact and attractive historic district.

British pirate Samuel "Black" Bellamy was one of the first to put Machias on the map. Famous for stealing the treasures of Spanish ships off the coast of the New World, the charismatic "pirate prince" attempted to set up a "pirates' republic" here in the 17th century, a sort of old folks' home for aging buccaneers. He was hanged in 1717 before it could ever happen.

The town was settled when a group of southern Mainers decided it was growing too crowded down there and decided to venture east in search of grazing lands for their cattle. (It's a wonder more folks from southern Maine aren't migrating here today.) They set up in what would become Machias in 1763, building a sawmill and getting right to work shipping timber, which became a huge industry hereabouts and helped build the town.

By the time of the American War of Independence, there were enough people in Machias to gather at Burnham Tavern, now a landmark and considered the oldest building east of the Penobscot, and discuss how they could help the colonies with the war effort. These early patriots gave the British a bit of what-for in 1775 when they attacked HMS *Margaretta*, which was in town to protect area Loyalists. A small group of men boarded the vessel, fatally wounded its captain, and forced the surrender of the crew, giving the rebels their first naval victory. The British returned to burn neighboring Machiasport two years later, both as punishment for the taking of the Margaretta and because they suspected—rightly so—that the colonists were preparing an assault on English holdings in Nova Scotia.

Nothing quite as exciting as that has happened here since, but it's a nifty town.

Eastport

Welcome to Small Town X. When Fox TV producers were looking for the setting for their reality/mystery show *Murder in Small Town X*, broadcast in the summer of 2001, they chose tiny Eastport, Maine, to be the small town in question for a variety of reasons. First, it's terrifically photogenic, the very picture of what a small New England town should look like, with legions of fine old homes sitting on Moose Island overlooking a distinctive Victorian brick downtown and the fair waters of the bay beyond. Second, most of the town was available to be invaded by cameras and crews, with many storefronts empty downtown and several buildings elsewhere vacant after decades of downturn in the local economy. They named the faux town Sunrise, a reference to the fact that Eastport, being the most easterly city in the United States, sees the rays of the sun before any other city in the nation.

Despite the fact that Eastport is one of Maine's best-looking cities, it's so far off the proverbial beaten path—102 miles from Ellsworth at the farthest reaches of the Maine coast—most people can't imagine moving there. It's simply too remote. Such wasn't always the case. Back when ships were the primary mode of travel, the city was a prosperous place, a center of trade and fishing. Europeans used the deep channel here as a port as early as the 1600s, but settlement didn't come until 1772. The city was originally called Freetown, and its bailiwick included

what's now called Lubec as well. Eastport was renamed when it incorporated in 1798.

In 1807, after the Embargo Act was passed limiting trade with foreign nations, the city of Eastport became a smuggling center, ferrying goods in and out of Canada. The War of 1812 clamped down on this activity, and in July 1814 the British invaded and occupied Eastport for four years. When they left, things began to pick up in the fishing industry, and in 1875 the process of canning was invented here, so that sardines could be packed and made to last. The city had its heyday during the late-19th-century sardine era.

That all crashed eventually, and the city fell on hard times. The 1960s brought the prospect of an oil refinery on the waterfront, an ugly idea that was rejected. A host of positive developments have popped up since the 1980s, though, from the advent of the aquaculture industry—those are salmon farms you see out in the bay—to the newly expanded commercial cargo port, to new crops of more adventuresome tourists, willing to make the drive Down East to see the "real Maine."

What these travelers find is a city that's all their own to explore, uncrowded and friendly. There are a few great places to stay, a few good restaurants, a hiking trail on Shackford Head, a few excursion boats, an excellent local guide service in Tidal Trails. You can witness mustard being made the old-fashioned way, head out on a catered picnic in an old Woodie station wagon, cruise on a whale-watch schooner, or amble along on a self-guided walking tour through the historic districts downtown. If you're anything like other visitors, you'll find yourself keenly eyeing real estate ads, which show absolutely incredible deals—for example, a four-bedroom Victorian in town for $79,900—for old homes with views of the water.

Lubec

If Eastport is the most easterly city in the United States, Lubec is the most easterly town, connected via the Franklin D. Roosevelt Memorial Bridge to New Brunswick, Canada's

Campobello Island. (F.D.R. was a summer resident of the Canadian island, and there's an international park there in his honor.) The town is, in fact, the most easterly point in the nation. Once part of Eastport, Lubec has a similar history, which can be read by simply walking downtown, where many storefronts and buildings are vacant or boarded up. Sardine canning was the big deal here, just as it was in Eastport, and the aquaculture industry swept in about the same time as in Eastport to provide a few jobs. Even with the rough times it's seen, Lubec remains an appealing place; *Men's Journal* gave the town a nod in an August 2006 feature on affordable land in "paradise." The town has a couple of neat B&Bs, a few shops, a new marina, and, of course, West Quoddy Head State Park.

Calais

Another border community, staring across the St. Croix River at St. Stephen, New Brunswick, Calais sits at the point where Route 1 takes a hard left, leaves the coast, and heads up toward the end of its run in Fort Kent. The city of 4,000 takes its name from the French port, a thank-you gesture for the help France gave to the colonists during the American Revolution. But you'll be real embarrassed if you say Calais the way the French would—here it's pronounced "callous." Sometimes called "the international city of Maine," the community enjoys a close relationship with its Canadian

neighbor, offering mutual support for fires and other emergencies, sending a lot of shoppers across the border to take advantage of the exchange rate, and whooping it up together at the International Festival in August.

Driving into Calais on Route 1 along the St. Croix, there are several nice homes and a handful of gingerbread Victorian places that have an almost fairytale vibe. The downtown is a pleasant grid of streets that attest to the city's prosperous past as a thriving shipping port. The brick Main Street is a registered Historic District, and it's a sleepy place as most major industry has left town. The city is largely dependant upon the Georgia Pacific paper mill up the road in Woodland.

First a lumbering center and then a shipbuilding port, Calais was settled in 1779, but a French colony attempted to carve out a home on tiny St. Croix island in 1604. Famed explorer Samuel de Champlain led the party, and they made it through the winter—the first Christmas celebrated in the New World was right here—but had a rough go of it in the snow and ice and left for Nova Scotia in the spring. The National Park Service has set up a nifty interpretive walking trail that tells this story.

Shipbuilding began in earnest with the launch of the *Liberty* in 1801 and continued for much of the century. Farming and fishing were also substantial industries, and fishing remains an economic staple.

GETTING HERE, GETTING AROUND

It would be hard to use the old Maine expression, "you can't get there from here," with a straight face these days. Getting to Maine—and getting around when you're here—has never been easier. The state is served by major airports in Portland and Bangor and by several smaller local airports in communities up and down the coast. High-speed train service between Portland and Boston is enjoying record-breaking ridership, giving the two bus companies that operate in Maine runs for their money. Ferries connect the state to its islands and to Canada. And the two principal automotive arteries—the Maine Turnpike and coastal U.S. Route 1—have undergone modernization in recent years in an effort to make driving simpler and safer. Not only can you get there from here but you can do so quickly and efficiently.

BY CAR

Getting around without a car in Maine is nigh impossible as public transportation is scarce outside the cities. The majority of visitors to Maine consequently arrive by automobile, driving across the big green bridge over the Piscataqua and breathing a sigh of relief once they do. (Maine is, as the sign says, the way life should be.) The bridge connects Maine to New Hampshire via Interstate 95 and connects to the Pine Tree State in Kittery, its southernmost town. From there, the highway proceeds up the coast as far as Portland before it begins to cut up into the interior of Maine toward Augusta. I-95, which is called the Maine Turnpike up to Portland, parallels Route 1 as it heads north, and these are the primary thoroughfares for accessing the Maine coast. To get where you're going quickly, stick to the fast-moving turnpike. For a more leisurely

drive with a lot of local color and frequent stops, take Route 1.

The Maine Turnpike is a fairly straightforward piece of pavement—a modern four- and six-lane highway with a 65 mph speed limit—until it hits Greater Portland, where I-95 all of a sudden becomes I-295 and you have to start paying attention to signs. In the winter of 2003–04, the Maine Department of Transportation decided to make more sense of things here and started changing exit numbers—and even the roadway designations themselves. But what you need to know for now is that most people heading up the coast leave the turnpike at exit 44 in Portland and follow I-295 north for another 20 miles to the Route 1 Coastal Connector in the Brunswick area. Rest areas are uncommon on either I-95 or Route 1, so stop when you see one rather than waiting for the next.

Route 1 used to be called the Atlantic Highway and has a reputation as a scenic, seaside road. Don't be fooled. The two-lane highway does go through many picturesque villages, beginning in Kittery and following the coast to Calais, but ocean vistas are a rarity. Route 1 also has become known for traffic—if you visit in summer and don't want to sit for a bit in your car, avoid driving Route 1 north. If you're heading to the Midcoast, take I-95 to Augusta and cut back over to the coast on State Route 17 or State Route 3. These highways are just as big as Route 1 but don't become nearly as congested. Another option, if you're heading to Acadia or points Down East, is to take I-95 as far north as Bangor and cut over to Bar Harbor on U.S. Route 1A.

U.S. Route 1, Down East

From the point where most of the cars turn off Route 1—onto Route 3 en route to Bar

ℹ Wondering where the bottlenecks are on any given day? Want to avoid the construction delays that pop up like spring flowers on Maine roadways? Visit the Maine Department of Transportation's well-done Web site at www.maine.gov/mdot-stage/. You can find the answers to these questions and more, from road advisories to scenic highways to traffic cams showing the current conditions at several locations.

Harbor—all the way to the end of the coast down near West Quoddy Head, this part of Maine is one epic scenic drive. Mainers like to call it the "real Maine" because it has yet to be overdeveloped or overrun.

BY AIR

Compared to airports in major metropolitan areas, the jetports at Portland and Bangor are real pleasures. Getting in and out is a fairly simple affair at both, but especially in Bangor, and parking is never too much of a problem. Portland has only 11 gates and two luggage carousels, so getting lost or waiting forever is unlikely, and Bangor has only a handful of gates. But just because they're on a smaller scale than most airports doesn't mean they are backwards. Both have all the important amenities found elsewhere.

Portland International Jetport

The Portland International Jetport serves close to 1.4 million passengers annually and is perfectly sited for anyone who wants to visit southern Maine or coastal destinations as far north as Rockland. Flights come in and go out on a daily basis by several major carriers.

Commercial Airline Phone Reservation Numbers

Continental Airlines	(800) 525–0280
Delta Airlines	(800) 221–1212
Jet Blue	(800) 538–2583
Northwest Airlines	(800) 225–2525

United Airlines	(800) 241–6522
US Airways	(800) 428–4322

Car Rentals

Alamo	(207) 775–0855
Avis	(207) 874–7500
Budget	(207) 772–6789
Hertz	(207) 774–4544
National	(207) 773–0036

More information can be found at the airport's handy Web site: www.portlandjetport.org.

Bangor International Airport

Bangor International Airport bills itself as the "intelligent alternative" to other airports serving northern New England (Boston; Manchester, New Hampshire; and Portland), and in many ways it is. Travelers will be hard-pressed to find a simpler, friendlier way to fly the friendly skies than they will in this city-owned airport. It's especially easy and convenient if you're arriving intent on a visit to Acadia, Bar Harbor, the Down East coast, or even south as far as Camden or Rockland. Parking is a cinch, finding the terminal even easier, and just about everyone you encounter is pleasant and helpful. (If your plane is late they might even apologize. Imagine!)

Commercial Airline Phone Reservation Numbers

American Eagle	(800) 433–7300
Continental Airlines	(800) 523–3273
Delta Airlines	(800) 221–1212
Northwest Airlines	(800) 225–2525
US Airways	(800) 428–4322

Car Rentals

Avis	(207) 947–8383
Budget	(207) 945–9429
Hertz	(207) 942–5519
National	(207) 947–0158

The airport's Web site is genuinely helpful: www.flybangor.com.

Avoiding Traffic

On a busy August weekend, Maine's highways can get maddeningly crowded. Traffic here still doesn't amount to what one might expect on the way to Cape Cod, say, but things do get bumper-to-bumper at the tollbooths on the Maine Turnpike (I–95) and in touristy places like Wiscasset and Camden. And the lines can remain backed up for an hour or more on rare occasions. Mainers know better than to even try driving into certain communities in high summer and instead use some alternate routes. These can be handy to know. Here are a few tips and even a few secrets.

- *To avoid traffic on the turnpike:* Plan to arrive sometime other than a Friday afternoon, and try not to depart Sunday afternoon. Avoid driving on holiday weekends if at all possible.
- *To avoid traffic in Greater Portland:* Don't plan on passing through the city at rush hour. Congestion isn't really a problem in Portland except when commuters are traveling to and from work.
- *To avoid traffic in Brunswick and Bath:* Steer clear when the state's largest private employer—Bath Iron Works—lets out. The Bath Bridge, opened in 2000, has helped alleviate the traffic snarls that result when thousands of shipbuilders head home, but it still gets busy in both of these Midcoast communities around 3:30 P.M.
- *To avoid traffic in Wiscasset:* Take a left onto State Route 127 in Woolwich shortly after the Bath Bridge. Follow it 10 miles inland to Dresden Mills and cut back toward the coast on the Bog Road. Stay on this dirt road until it ends at State Route 218 in picturesque Head Tide, and then follow State Route 194 to Newcastle and take State Route 215 back to Route 1. This is a lengthy detour—and it's easy to get lost—but it's also quite pretty and can be quicker in the long run. A map would help, though.
- *To avoid traffic in Rockland/Thomaston:* Take a left off Route 1 onto State Route 90 in Warren and follow it to Rockport, skirting both of these Midcoast communities.
- *To avoid traffic in the Camden/Belfast area:* Grit your teeth and bear Route 1 through downtown Camden. Then take a left onto State Route 52 and follow it all the way to Belfast, bypassing a particularly slow stretch of Route 1.
- *To avoid traffic en route to Bar Harbor:* Route 1 can be a poky road, often backed up with convoys of RVs. Try heading first to Bangor and then taking Route 1A to Bar Harbor. There are fewer headaches that way.

Other Air Options

A pair of smaller airports, both with daily airline service, provide further possibilities to travelers on the Maine coast.

Knox County Regional Airport

Knox County Regional Airport (207–596–0617; www.knoxcounty.midcoast.com/departments/airport) is served by Colgan Air, a Virginia-based US Airways Express carrier, which offers regularly scheduled flights between Rockland and Boston. Call (800) 428–4322 for tickets and reservations. You can also book a flight to the islands of Penobscot Bay through Penobscot Island Air, a charter company based here. It's pricey, though. Call (207) 596–7500 for details.

Hancock–Bar Harbor Airport

Hancock–Bar Harbor Airport (207–667–7329; www.bhbairport.com), on Route 3 between Ellsworth and Bar Harbor, is another airport served by Colgan Air, connecting the Mount Desert Island area with Boston and the world. Car rentals are available through Hertz (207–667–5017). Local taxi service is also available. Local taxi service is available, and you can also connect with the Acadia area's exceptional Island Explorer bus fleet (www.exploreacadia.com).

BY TRAIN

When a new passenger train service between Boston and Portland was first proposed in the late 1980s, naysayers pooh-poohed the idea, saying it would never see any sort of ridership. The train began rolling in December 2001, and within a month or so the Amtrak Downeaster had proved all its critics wrong. It was soon averaging 25,000 riders per month, and by the end of 2002 more than 300,000 passengers had taken to the rails. Revenues in its first year were up by 44 percent over projections, and 2006 ended strong as well. Everyone, it seems, loves the train.

There's a lot to like. It's a simple, efficient, and relatively inexpensive way of getting to Maine. (Parking, for example, is a mere $3.00 a day at the Portland Transportation Center.) The train makes four round-trip journeys between the two cities every day, beginning at 6:20 in the morning and rolling to a stop at 2:00 at night. The trip takes a little over two-and-a-half hours, because the train stops twice in Massachusetts and three times in New Hampshire before it makes its first station visit in Maine at Wells. Then it heads to Saco and Old Orchard Beach (between May and October only) before arriving at the Portland Transportation Center off Congress Street and I–295. Tickets are $22 one-way between Boston and Portland and are $25, $17, and $19, respectively, to Old Orchard, Saco, and Wells.

There are several options for ground transportation once you've arrived at the Portland Transportation Center. The Portland Explorer bus service connects the train station to the airport, the ferry terminal, the Maine Mall, Eastland Park Hotel, Sheratorn Hotel, and the Fairfield Inn. One-way fare is $2.00. Call (207) 772–4457 for details.

The Greater Portland Transit District's METRO buses leave the train hub regularly for downtown Portland, the Maine Mall, and the airport. The fare is $1.25. Call (207) 774–0351 for more info.

Taxi fares from the train station to downtown Portland are about $8.00, and taxis are readily available. Car rentals can be handled at the airport.

For further information, call Amtrak at (800) USA–RAIL, call the local Northern New England Passenger Rail Authority at (207) 780–1000, or visit the Downeaster's well-done Web site at www.thedowneaster.com.

BY BUS

Concord Trailways

The sight of a Concord Trailways bus rolling down Route 1 with its windows all aglow from multiple TVs is a common one these days. The New Hampshire–based company provides daily service from Boston to 12 communities in Maine via its Maine Coastal Route. Express trips go straight from Boston to Portland and Bangor. Fares are $25 one-way, $40 round-trip. The Maine Coastal Route makes the following stops in Maine: Portland, Brunswick, Bath, Wiscasset, Damariscotta, Waldoboro, Rockland, Camden, Lincolnville, Belfast, Searsport, and Bangor. Fares range from $45 round-trip in Brunswick to $60 in Searsport. Call (800) 639–3317 for more information or visit www.concordtrailways.com.

Vermont Transit Lines

Vermont Transit Lines, a Greyhound affiliate, also makes stops in Maine, connecting the coastal communities of Portland, Brunswick, and Bar Harbor to Portsmouth and Boston. Its route arcs through the inland cities of Lewiston and Bangor before heading back down to the coast in Bar Harbor, so it's not the most convenient for coastal travelers. But it's the cheapest way to go between Boston and Portland at $18.75. Find out the complete schedule by calling (800) 552–8737 or by visiting www.vermonttransit.com.

BY BOAT

Casco Bay Lines

Maine was first "discovered" by boat, and a good many people still get around that way. In the Greater Portland area, Casco Bay Lines is the lifeline for six islands with year-round populations: Peaks, Long, Cliff, Chebeague, Little Diamond, and Great Diamond. Founded in the 1920s, the company is the oldest continuously run ferry service in the country, and it's now owned and operated by the very people it serves. More than 800,000 passengers a year drive down to Commercial Street on the Portland waterfront and file aboard the Casco Bay Lines' distinctive black-and-yellow ferries. The vessels run on a daily basis year-round, setting off as early as 5:00 A.M. and continuing operations until almost midnight. Summer, with its fair seas, is the ferry's busiest time. Round-trip fares range from $6.25 to Peaks to $9.50 for

passage to Cliff Island. Cars can be ferried as well, for $30 to $70 depending upon what island they're bound to. For more information call (207) 774–7871 or visit www.cascobay lines.com.

Chebeague Ferry

Great Chebeague Island, a part of the town of Cumberland, has its own ferry service, which leaves from Cousins Island, a small isle linked to the town of Yarmouth by bridge. Vans and buses ferry passengers from the Chebeague Transportation Company parking lot on Route 1 down to the tiny dock on Cousins Island for the 15-minute trip out to the island. The ferry makes a dozen trips daily in summer, fewer in the off-season, and round-trip passage is $12. For more information call (207) 846–3700 or visit Web site www.chebeaguetrans.com.

State Ferry Service

It seems only fitting that the Department of Transportation in a seafaring state like Maine would have its own ferry service. The Maine State Ferry Service (www.state.me.us/mdot/opt/ferry/maine-ferry-service.php) sails to six islands off the Midcoast and the Down East coast, moving both passengers and cargo.

To Islesboro, from Lincolnville

The *Margaret Chase Smith* makes the 3-mile crossing to the long, pretty isle of Islesboro, seven times in summer, beginning at 7:30 A.M. and ending at 4:30 P.M. (It makes only five runs daily in winter.) The boat leaves from a ferry terminal at Lincolnville Beach, right on Route 1. Call (207) 789–5611 for more information. The rate is $6.50 for a round-trip.

To Vinalhaven, North Haven, and Matinicus, from Rockland

State ferries leave the big Maine State Ferry Service Terminal on Route 1 in Rockland on a daily basis bound for Vinalhaven (six trips) and North Haven (three trips) but visit remote Matinicus only every great once in a while, even in summer. Call (207) 596–2202 for more

Close-up

The Speedy Cat

Bar Harbor's *Cat* ferry claims to be the fastest car ferry in all of North America. It's a bold statement, but if the *Cat* isn't the swiftest boat, it must be close. The 300-foot catamaran hits speeds of 50 mph or more and makes its daily run between Mount Desert Island and Yarmouth, Nova Scotia, in less than three hours. (The trip would take you some 600 miles and a day's drive if you were to do it on land.) And, high speeds aside, the ride is fun. On board are more than 120 slot machines, a duty-free shop, a movie lounge, and decks for surveying the passing seas. When the long-running cruise ship the *Scotia Prince* quit making the trip from Portland to Yarmouth, the *Cat* expanded down into the Forest City, adding trips out of Maine's largest port on the weekends. The ferry leaves Bar Harbor every day at 8:00 A.M. between the end of May and October, making two trips during the summer. One-way passage for an adult in summer is $63 from Bar Harbor and $89 from Portland. With car, it's $105. Call (877) 359–3760 or visit www.cat ferry.com for more information.

information. Rates are $13.25 round-trip for Vinalhaven and North Haven and $26.00 for Matinicus.

To Swans Island and Frenchboro, from Bass Harbor

The *Captain Henry Lee* sets off for the 40-minute jaunt to Swans Island five times daily in summer and scales back in winter. It makes two trips to Frenchboro. The ferry leaves from the small town of Bass Harbor on the back side of Mount Desert Island. Call (207) 244–3254 for specifics. Round-trip costs $13.25.

Monhegan Ahoy

The beautiful "artists' isle" of Monhegan, an idyllic outpost 12 miles out to sea, is served by boats that depart from three communities.

From Boothbay Harbor

The *Balmy Days II* visits Monhegan daily in summer, pushing off at 9:30 A.M. and returning at 4:15 P.M. Round-trip fare is $32. Call Balmy

Days Cruises for more information at (207) 633–2284 or (800) 298–2284 or visit Web site www.balmydayscruises.com.

From New Harbor

The 60-foot *Hardy Boat III* makes two daily summer runs out to Monhegan, leaving the dock in New Harbor at 9:00 A.M. and picking up passengers on Monhegan at 3:15 P.M. Round-trip fare is $28. Call (207) 677–2026 or (800) 278–3346 for details or visit Web site www.hardyboat.com.

From Port Clyde

Sailing from the mainland point closest to Monhegan, the *Laura B.* and the *Elizabeth Ann* are among the most popular ways to get to the island. The Monhegan-Thomaston boat line offers the hour-long trip three times daily in summertime—7:00 A.M., 10:30 A.M., and 3:00 P.M.—but less frequently in the off-season. Reservations are necessary. Round-trip fare is $30. Call (207) 372–8848 for details or visit Web site www.monheganboat.com.

To Isle au Haut

Relatively few visitors to Acadia National Park are aware that the island of Isle au Haut is part of the park. The 5,800-acre isle is indeed—and it's well worth seeing. The Isle au Haut mailboat takes passengers and freight across isle-strewn Deer Island Thorofare on a daily basis in summer. The boat leaves the dock in Stonington Harbor five times each day in high summer—at 7:00 A.M., 10:00 A.M. 11:30 A.M., 3:15 P.M., and 4:30 P.M.—and runs a shortened schedule in the winter and shoulder seasons. Round-trip fare for the 45-minute passage is $32. Call the Isle au Haut Boat Company for more information at (207) 367–6516 or visit Web site www.isleauhaut.com.

HISTORY

Many people who know the state of Maine well say it makes the most sense from the water. Driving around on U.S. Route 1, you wonder sometimes why this village grew up there or why that community became a population center while the one over there didn't. Hop into a boat, and it all becomes clear. The region's European settlers first arrived on ships, of course, and they migrated north and east on the water, building their homes not far from the shore and its resources. Everything developed from there, spreading inland. History and the coast are inextricably linked.

EARLIEST INHABITANTS

The first aboriginal people on the coast of Maine—and we're talking prehistory here, thousands of years B.C.—that historians and paleontologists know much about at all were called the Red Paint People because they buried their dead in graves of rich red ocher. (Similar burial traditions have been found in Newfoundland, and some historians think the peoples in Maine and northern Canada may be related.) This unusual culture seemed to arrive out of nowhere, but archaeologists have found points, bone, and stone tools that shed a little light on the lifestyle of these nomadic tribespeople.

In 1892 an archaeologist named C. C. Willoughby began to put the pieces together, but it wasn't until 1912 that another professor, Warren Moorehead, began to study them in detail. (This period of Archaic history is now called the Moorehead Phase.) Burial grounds filled with the signature crushed red hematite have been discovered along East Penobscot Bay, at points Down East, and all the way up to the Saint John River Valley at the top of Maine, which suggested that the Red Paint People

migrated with the seasons and were capable of building seaworthy vessels. All of their dead were interred on or near rivers or the coast, except for two small sites. The tools found at these places were of a finer quality than those that later Indian peoples used, and many were of types of stone of unknown origin.

Despite investigations by Harvard's Peabody Museum and other archaeological outfits, there has never been unearthed traces of a village or habitation of the Red Paint People, only the ocher-filled burial grounds. (Early Maine settlers considered it a bad omen to dig up a red grave.) And, in about 1800 B.C., their highly evolved civilization seems to have disappeared without a trace.

The coast was just as important to the Native Americans who followed them. Mainers today like to joke about who qualifies as a native and who's "from away," but there is nobody more native than a member of the Maliseet, Micmac, Passamaquoddy, or Penobscot tribes, which date back centuries. These four bands were collectively called the Wabanaki, which means "people of the dawnland," a name given to them because they were from the most easterly part of North America, where the sun rises first.

Ethnologically, all of these Maine tribes are of Algonquin stock, a people whose nations are found across North America, and the Maine tribes coexisted relatively peacefully compared to the warring Native American nations elsewhere. They'd pay one another visits, intermarry, make treaties, and trade, and their history is confusing due to the sheer numbers of interwoven bands. Early English settlers referred to them by the name of the river or region where they lived—Saco, Androscoggin, Kennebec, Penobscot, and so on, and though there were some cultural differences, these tribal groups had a largely similar way of life. Woodland peoples, they hunted, fished, farmed, and moved about with the seasons. Spring found them planting crops of vegetables and fishing for salmon, herring, and other anadromous fish. Early summer meant trips to the coast in birchbark canoes for more fishing and lobstering—and, of course, to avoid the bugs. Autumn meant harvest and hunting, winter more search for game, which were easier to track and bag due to snow.

The era of European contact, with its strange illnesses, lies, and displacement, was rough on these peoples, and some estimates show the population gutted by disease, going from 35,000 or more in 1616 to about 5,000 a few years later.

Small populations of these tribal groups survive to the present day at three reservations. The Penobscots live on Indian Island in Old Town. The Passamaquoddies live Down East at Pleasant Point in Perry and at Indian Township in Princeton. Micmacs and Maliseets live up-country in Aroostook County. The Abbe Museum in Bar Harbor, the Hudson Museum in Orono, and other collections in Old Town, Perry, Augusta, Hinckley, and New Portland are great repositories of information on Native American culture in Maine, and there are gatherings like the Native American Festival at the College of the Atlantic in Bar Harbor where you can enjoy dancing, singing, boatbuilding, and basketmaking.

EUROPEAN ARRIVAL

Some people say the first Europeans to land in the New World actually did so in Maine. A Norse coin dating back to A.D. 1000 was found in 1957 in the small coastal village of Brooklin, predating Columbus by almost half a millennium. Whether or not the Vikings actually set foot on the shore of what is now Maine is still a matter of debate; many scholars think that the coin was traded farther away and brought to the site by the Native Americans who lived there. Historians are certain that Leif Ericson

The Maine state government has an excellent online history of the Pine Tree State at www.maine.gov/portal/ facts_history/history.html that includes time lines, narratives, and a host of links.

ventured across the Atlantic and attempted to set up a colony in a piece of land he "discovered" in North America and called Vinland. But there are compelling theories placing Vinland in Labrador, Nova Scotia, and even Massachusetts and Rhode Island. No one is quite sure.

Five hundred years later the picture was a bit less murky, though still not entirely clear. A pair of British brothers, John and Sebastian Cabot, gained the permission of King Henry VII of England to sail to this New World of which they'd heard—it was recently "discovered" by Christopher Columbus—to make claims in the name of the English crown. John Cabot crossed the Atlantic in 1497 with a crew of 18, making it to what is now North America, a point that most scholars agree is Cape Breton. He made the trip again a year later, this time landing somewhere much farther to the south. Was it as far down as what is now called the Maine coast? Historians are still unsure.

The first confirmed reports of European explorers in Maine took place a few decades later. Italian explorer Giovanni da Verrazzano cruised the Maine coast under the auspices of the French government in 1524. The English had claimed the land based on the sightings of the Cabots but didn't appear willing to settle there, and the French thought if they swept in and set up villages, they could grab squatter's rights. The services of Verrazzano were secured, and he sailed up the Gulf of Maine, keeping sight of the coast, and wrote a detailed account of his findings for the king of France before departing for Europe. He was impressed with the rugged landscape but wasn't so taken with its inhabitants.

"The people were entirely different from the others we had seen whom we had found kind and gentle," Verrazzano wrote. "These were so rude and barbarous that we were unable by any signs we could make to hold communication. . . . The country which has been discovered, and which was unknown to the ancients, is another world compared with that before known, being manifestly larger than our Europe. . . . In a short time, I hope, we shall have more certain knowledge of these things by the aid of Your Majesty."

Portuguese explorer Esteban Gomez sailed along the coast of Maine in 1525 searching for a way west to the Orient. He was sent on behalf of the Spanish government by King Charles V after word got back about Verrazzano's trip for the French. Gomez's travels took him up the Penobscot River, to present-day Bangor, and all along the coast, but the Spanish were none too interested in his discoveries and kept their focus on New World points south.

A handful of English explorers were similarly inspired by a Verrazzano, this time by the mention of a city called "Oranbega" made by Giovanni's brother, Girolamo, on the 1529 maps he drew of his brother's voyages. The mythology of a city of riches grew with each expedition to the New World and its name was changed to Norumbega, though no one actually set food on its gold-cobbled streets. English sailor David Ingram crossed the pond in the late 1550s and went looking for Norumbega, and added his own embellishments to the tale.

In 1602 winds blew the British captain Bartholomew Gosnold in to what is now southern Maine, and he ventured from there south as far as Martha's Vineyard, looking for a place to colonize, before heading back to England. He too met Native Americans and described them as being very familiar with European fishing customs—he even saw some sailing a Basque boat. (Fishing boats from England, Portugal, and the Basque and Biscay regions of Europe had been crossing on a regular basis to fill up with fish from the banks of Newfoundland, which is surely the source of the Native Americans' vessel.)

The fishing proved just as good in the Gulf of Maine. Gosnold wrote of the rich stocks of cod in the waters they fished. His crew dropped lines and soon found the fish "so pestered our ship . . . that we threw numbers of them overboard." His expedition was quickly followed by that of Captain Martin Pring, who explored sections of the coast in 1603, and by George Waymouth, who landed at a site on the St. George River near present Thomaston in 1605, capturing five Native Americans. His idea was to take them back to the British Isles, teach them English, and gain intelligence about this new land. His dastardly plan worked—the stories the captives told were inspiring, and soon boatloads of Britons were arriving on the shores of what is now Maine.

Among them was George Popham, who had talked King James into granting his family a charter for a new colony in "Virginia." The scouts they sent to look for land—one of whom was Martin Pring—thought there was a preferable site at the base of either the Kennebec or Sagadahoc rivers. So off went 120 colonists aboard a pair of ships, the *Mary and John* and the *Gift of God*, in 1607. The Popham colony built a village, a bastion they called Fort Saint George, and storehouses, and began to barter with the indigenous peoples, but the winter that befell them was more than many were prepared to take, and 75 of the colonists left by December. The rest made it through to the fall of the following year, but the settlement was eventually disbanded.

The French and English continued their duel over the New World, and at about the same time the Popham Colony was being established, French explorer Samuel de Champlain was touring and mapping the coast of what is now Maine under the blue, white, and red stripes of the French flag. From 1604 to 1606, he sailed between Martha's Vineyard and the Bay of Fundy, charting and naming points and places as he went. Many Maine places got their names at this time. In 1604 Champlain and French Lieutenant General Sieur De Monts made an attempt to settle on the island of St. Croix in the St. Croix River, which is now way Down East. But winter

Close-up

The Center for Maine History

There's great irony to the fact that the home of the venerable Maine Historical Society is a decidedly postmodern building. Most of the state's historical societies—there's one in almost every town—use the oldest structure in town as their museum and headquarters, but not in Portland. In the late 1990s, when these chroniclers of Maine's past were looking for a new home, they decided they wanted to stay next to the other properties they own in town—the Wadsworth-Longfellow House and the society's library building just behind it. So they moved into the old bank at 489 Congress Street right in front of them, opening the Maine History Gallery there. This is where you'll find generally exceptional exhibits about facets of Maine life and politics in the past and resources for research into history Down East. The library, too, is a good place to look into all things venerable, with 125,000 volumes, newspapers, and printed items, and it has a handy genealogy section as well. For more information call (207) 879–0427 or visit www.mainehistory.com.

proved harsh—"there are six months of winter in this country," he wrote—and his band also retreated.

Back and forth went the English and the French. Next up for the Brits was famed adventurer and explorer Captain John Smith, who had made a name for himself fighting wars in the Netherlands and Hungary, by helping to settle Jamestown, and by escaping the wrath of Chief Powhatan thanks to the intervention of the chief's merciful daughter Pocahontas. In 1613 he was sent by the English crown to once again look into colonization of this cold northern region, and he was given the title Admiral of New England, for whatever that was worth. He spent the next several years journeying along the Maine coast, mapping what he saw, and ultimately throwing in his lot with Sir Ferdinando Gorges, who was a mucky-muck among the Pilgrims of the Plymouth Company.

As a firsthand witness to the success of the Plymouth colony on Cape Cod, Gorges was sure that the coast of Maine could and should be settled. In 1622 Pilgrim governors jointly gave Gorges and Captain George Mason, another proponent of settlement, the land between the Merrimac and Sagadahoc Rivers, or the chunk of terrain from northern Massachusetts and New Hampshire all the way up to Bath, and they called the land the Province of Maine, the first official use of the word *Maine*. The origins of the name of the state of Maine are still unknown. Some say it's derived from the word *mainland*. Others think it refers to a province in France.

Small settlements were beginning to multiply all along the coast. Monhegan Island, York, and New Harbor became fishing outposts, and some reports count as many as 84 families living along the Saint George and Sheepscot Rivers by 1630. Grants and deeds were multiplying, and by 1639, it became clear that some form of official governance was needed. That year the region was incorporated as the Province and County of Maine. The king of England turned back to Sir Ferdinando Gorges, dubbed him lord of the area, and the Province and County of Maine grew and grew. The first city was incorporated at York in 1641, and

A Maine Coast Time Line

circa 3000–1800 B.C.: Mysterious society of Red Paint People, early Native Americans that historians don't know much about, live along Maine coast. Red Paint People bury their dead along the coast in graves of rich red ocher.

A.D. 80–350: Oyster Shell People, Native Americans known for their huge shell middens, roam Maine coast.

A.D. 1000: Norse explorers discover "Vinland." Some historians say that the Viking land discovered by Leif Ericson was in Maine.

1524: Italian explorer Giovanni da Verrazzano explores the Maine coast on behalf of the king of France.

1525: Esteban Gomez sails the coast of Maine for Spain, "discovering" the Penobscot River.

1569: An Englishman passes through Maine and tantalizes other explorers with tales of a mythical city of gold, Norumbega, on the Penobscot River.

1602: Captain Bartholemew Gosnold visits Maine for the British government, returning with a load of woods cargo.

1603: The coast between the Piscataqua and the Penobscot is surveyed by Martin Pring.

1604: French Lieutenant General Sieur de Monts establishes a colony near present-day Calais. Samuel de Champlain maps many of the islands and much of the coast of Maine.

1605: Captain George Waymouth lands at Monhegan in the *Archangel* and explores up the St. George River. Five Native Americans are captured by Waymouth and his crew and taken back to England for show-and-tell.

1607: The Popham Colony is established by George Popham at present-day Phippsburg.

1614: Captain John Smith explores Maine and maps the region from Cape Cod to Nova Scotia, calling it New England.

1617: A party led by Captain Richard Vines winters over at Saco to prove the Maine climate is palatable by Europeans.

1620: A permanent settlement is set up on Monhegan Island.

1622: The word *Maine* is officially used for the first time to describe the land between the Merrimac and Sagadahoc Rivers.

1629: Plymouth Colonists able to pay bulk of debts incurred on their *Mayflower* passage by selling furs collected in the Kennebec area.

1632: The English cede the area known as Acadia to the French.

1635: A shipyard—the first in the New World—is established on Richmond Island.

1636: King Charles I of England appoints Sir Fernando Gorges lord of New England. Gorges sends nephew William to govern the colonies and later calls the area New Somersetshire.

1639: Region is incorporated as the Province and County of Maine.

1641: York is chartered as the first English city in the New World.

1673–1745: Dutch, English, and French fight over Maine territory.

1675: Settlements at Casco and Scarborough are destroyed by Indian attacks during King Philip's War.

1677: Maine officially becomes part of Massachusetts, having been purchased by the commonwealth from the Gorges heirs for about $6,000. Three years later Maine gets its first "president," Thomas Danforth.

1713: The Treaty of Utrecht helps define the political boundary lines of the modern state of Maine.

1719: First schoolhouse built in Berwick

1740: Population of Maine is about 12,000.

1770: Rebel fervor grips Mainers as John Adams visits York.

1775: Residents of Maine join the rebel cause. Benedict Arnold leads troops through Maine for a disastrous raid on Quebec. The city of Portland (then known as Falmouth) is burned by the British. The first naval battle of the American Revolution takes place as Mainers capture the British ship *Margaretta* off Machias.

1779: Colonial navy suffers its worst defeat in Castine, getting pummeled by British.

1785: First newspaper founded in Maine, at Falmouth (now Portland).

1787: Maine adopts a constitution and becomes a representative district, with 93 towns and plantations.

1788: Slavery is abolished in Maine.

1791: George Washington orders construction of Portland Head Light in Cape Elizabeth.

1800: Population of Maine is 151,719.

1802: Bowdoin College opens in Brunswick.

1807: Poet Henry Wadsworth Longfellow is born in Portland.

1812: The War of 1812 slows shipping along Maine coast and leads to smuggling, the heyday of "rum-running" Down East.

1814: The British occupy the coast from the Penobscot River to the St. Croix until 1815.

1820: Maine becomes a state, admitted to the Union as part of the Missouri Compromise. William King is elected the state's first governor. A state legislature is set up in Portland.

1832: The state capital moves from Portland to Augusta.

1840: Quarrying for granite begins on Vinalhaven Island.

1849: Author Sarah Orne Jewett is born in South Berwick.

1851: Maine enacts first Prohibition laws in nation.

1860: Mainer Hannibal Hamlin elected vice president of the United States on ticket with Abraham Lincoln.

1861: Civil War breaks out. Maine will send about 73,000 men.

1862: Maine State College of Agriculture and Industrial Arts established at Orono (now the University of Maine).

1865: Famed Maine general Joshua Chamberlain is commander of the Union troops during the surrender of the Confederates at Appomattox.

1866: Portland struck by its second great fire, losing more than 1,800 buildings. Aid is rushed in from all over the country.

1870: Maine begins to blossom as a vacation destination with influx of "summercators."

1879: A freak snowstorm hits Portland on July 4.

1884: Bath Iron Works is established. Winslow Homer moves to Prout's Neck.

1892: Edna St. Vincent Millay is born in Rockland. Archaeologist C. C. Willoughby discovers early evidence of Red Paint People.

1900: Population of Maine is 694,466.

1912: Professor Warren Moorehead begins a detailed study of the prehistoric Red Paint People.

1917: As the nation enters World War I, the first navy-built submarine is launched in Kittery at Portsmouth Naval Shipyard.

1919: Lafayette National Park opens on Mount Desert Island (it will be renamed Acadia).

1920: Maine women are the first to exercise right to vote.

1931: Former Governor Percival Baxter makes his first gift to the state, forever wild Mount Katahdin, the basis of what would become Baxter State Park.

1932: Portland-to-Boston steamer service is curtailed.

1935: The Quoddy Tidal Project, a quixotic New Deal attempt to harness tidal power way Down East, is launched.

1941: Nazi spies are captured on the Maine coast.

1946: Rural electrification begins.

1947: Maine Turnpike is built from Kittery to Portland. Forest fires tear through Mount Desert Island, destroying 1,000 homes and more than 17,000 acres at Acadia.

1950: Hurricanes savage the coast, doing $2 million worth of damage. Passenger rail comes to a slow halt on the Maine coast.

1962: Mainer Rachel Carson's book *Silent Spring*, an ecological wake-up call, is published, becoming an inspiration to the burgeoning environmental movement.

1970: Maine's sesquicentennial population is just shy of one million.

1972: Maine Yankee nuclear power plant opens in Wiscasset.

1975: The last river drive, a logging tradition, occurs in Maine.

1976: Maine's Native American tribes file legal claims to more than 60 percent of the state.

1979: Mainer Edmund Muskie becomes President Jimmy Carter's secretary of state.

1980: Jimmy Carter signs the Indian Land Claims agreement, settling disputes with the Native Americans.

1984: Freeport marathon runner Joan Benoit wins a gold medal at the first women's marathon at the Summer Olympics in Los Angeles.

1994: Angus King, a resident of Brunswick, becomes only the second elected Independent governor in U.S. history.

1997: Maine Yankee nuclear plant closes.

1998: A severe ice storm cripples Maine in January.

2001: Passenger rail service between Portland and Boston resumes.

2003: Governor John Baldacci introduces Dirigo Health, a ground-breaking state-run health care program with the goal of providing all Maine residents with access to health care by 2009.

2005: The cruise ship *Scotia Prince* discontinues its Portland-to-Yarmouth, Nova Scotia run.

villages were being established along the length of the coast.

All sorts of internal squabbles arose over the next several years, and Sir Ferdinando Gorges died in 1647, leaving something of a power vacuum. In 1652 the Commonwealth of Massachusetts essentially annexed the Province of Maine—it became formal in 1677—and the commonwealth would hold onto the territory until 1820, much to the chagrin of Mainers.

FRENCH AND INDIAN WARS

Just as they were warring on continental Europe, the French and English continued to fight over the New World, including the Province of Maine. By the middle of the 1600s, as communities were being settled along the length of the coast, the state of Maine as we now know it was divided roughly in half by the Penobscot River, with the English controlling the west and the French the east. It was a natural split, as the English held most of the rest of the territory to the southeast—offshoots of the Plymouth and Jamestown colonies—and the French occupied the land called Acadia, what is now the Down East coast and Canadian Maritimes. The French had a distinctly better relationship with the Native Americans at this point, having lived among them and gained their trust as traders and trappers, and as war spread from Europe to North America, they enlisted the aid of their Native American friends. This alliance was bad news for the English.

Over the course of about a hundred years, 1675–1760, the two nations had at each other in the Province of Maine, and it was a bloody, restless time for the settlers attempting to carve out a home on the Maine coast. A series of wars broke out beginning in 1675 with King Philip's War (1675–1678), which started in the vicinity of Plymouth, Massachusetts, and spread to Maine after a bunch of English idiots in Saco killed the child of an influential Saco chief. These sailors wanted to test the veracity of the old legend that a Native American baby

could swim at birth, so they placed a Saco baby in a canoe and then overturned the canoe. Of course the baby drowned. The baby's father, Squando, leader of the Sacos, eked out his revenge quickly. War spread from Saco to Scarborough to South Berwick to York and beyond.

The conflict and bloodshed would hardly let up over the next century, with turmoil starting anew only a few years after a peace was brokered. King William's War (1688–1699) picked up not long after King Philip's, and then came Queen Anne's War (1703–1713), Dummer's War (1721–1726), King George's War (1744–1748), and finally the war that defined them all, the French and Indian War (1754–1760). As a consequence of the 1713 Treaty of Utrecht, which settled Queen Anne's War, the French lost control of their Acadia lands, an event that helped define the political boundary lines of the modern state of Maine.

REVOLUTIONARY MAINE

The tranquil years that followed the French and Indian Wars resulted in a boom in settlement along the Maine coast. By 1740 the state's population was about 12,000. The census of 1764 reflected a doubling of that, and it doubled again by the time of the American Revolution. These Mainers were as bothered as anyone else by the arrogance of the British toward the colonies, and they showed solidarity with their Boston neighbors when the port of Boston was closed by act of Parliament, sending relief south.

Troops would soon follow. A company of 60 or more men marched from York to Massachusetts as soon as word came about the Battle of Lexington, and several more from the Portland area followed a day or so later. The war under way, Maine paid the price for rebellion when Portland (then called Falmouth) was bombarded in 1775 and much of its infrastructure destroyed. But Mainers would play important roles in the fight for independence, winning, for example, the first naval battle of the Revolution when Machias patriots captured the British warship *Margaretta*.

One of the most famous Maine incidents during the war occurred in 1775 when Colonel Benedict Arnold made a march through the wilderness of Maine to attack the British in Quebec City. The bold and self-possessed Arnold, who had yet to turn traitor, sailed to the mouth of the Kennebec River south of Bath with 1,100 troops and began an arduous journey upstream. The trip was undertaken in the autumn, and the men were beset with fatigue and sickness, almost starved, and got lost on several occasions. The force that arrived at Quebec was less than half of what started the expedition, and the bedraggled troops were handily routed. Another pummeling by the British occurred in 1779, when the colonial navy suffered its worst defeat of the Revolution at Castine.

Hundreds of Mainers served and died in the contest. Those who made it came home to a place now officially known as the District of Maine in the state of Massachusetts. Things were booming along the coast, with towns and cities incorporating left and right and many soldiers and sailors taking advantage of land deals offered by the Massachusetts government—a dollar an acre, including riverfront properties. A 1786 lottery dispensed with more than a million acres Down East, all the way up to the new border of the District on the St. Croix River. A constitution adopted in 1787 made Maine a representative district, with 93 towns and plantations. Slavery was abolished the following year. By the turn of the 19th century, the population of Maine stood at 151,719.

NEW NATION, NEW STATE

Because of its easternmost location, the District of Maine was put in an interesting position when the United States declared war on Britain in 1812. The years prior had seen a boom in smuggling Down East, especially around Eastport, as Mainers tried to cope with the slowing economy caused by President Jefferson's 1807 Embargo Act. One merchant

estimated he was losing as much as $5,000 a month due to this prohibition on trade with foreign nations. Jefferson was attempting to keep sailors safe from the French and English, who were harassing ships at sea, but it was severely hurting the Maine economy, which was built around shipping.

Tensions between the United States and England led to declaration of war, and Maine was right in the middle of things—literally. It sat between the English cities of Quebec and Halifax and was in the midst of a shipbuilding boom, churning out vessels that could be used as warships. The English knew this, of course, and swept in, occupying the coast from Passamaquoddy Bay all the way down to Belfast. They stayed there until 1815, after the war had ended, and Mainers could again set about settling and developing their district.

It wouldn't be a district for long. Ever since the nation was founded, Mainers were on a quest for statehood. As far as time and distance went, it only made sense to have a separate government north of the Piscataqua. New Hampshire, to use a Maineism, was a "gawmy" wedge right in between the district and the Commonwealth of Massachusetts, and Boston, in those days of limited communication and slow travel, seemed so far away. Mainers had to travel for court cases, for trade disputes, and for all sorts of lesser concerns, and many people in the district felt underrepresented politically, with a lot of places having no voice in the legislature. Plus, some Down East felt that the Bay State had been of little help when Maine was under such duress during the recently concluded War of 1812.

So Mainers rallied for statehood. A group representing almost all of the 236 incorporated towns gathered for a constitutional convention at the First Parish Church in Portland to discuss the many facets of state government. First, there was the name of the new state. What would they call it? Some voted for Columbus, others for the Commonwealth of Maine. Many thought that was too fancy-sounding and advocated plain old Maine. The name stuck. They debated the size of the legislature, whether or not to have a lieutenant governor, as Massachusetts had, what qualifications residents would need to meet to be eligible to vote, whether religion should be acknowledged in the state constitution. Finally these framers had a document, and they sent it out to be voted on by the general population on December 16, 1819—10,000 voted yea and only 797 nay.

Next the state had to win admission to the Union. It received approval—but at a price. Maine would become the 23d state as part of the Missouri Compromise, which used the Pine Tree State as a balance to the slave-trading state of Missouri. It was a bitter victory for many Down East, as Maine had long been staunchly abolitionist. But on March 15, 1820, papers were signed at the Jameson Tavern in Freeport, making the old district official. The man who had pushed hardest for statehood, William King, would be elected the first governor in April, and the seat of government would be Portland (though it would change to more centrally located Augusta in 1832). The population of the new state was 228,705 at about that time (1821), and within 20 years it more than doubled again to over 500,000.

THE CIVIL WAR

The peace and prosperity that pervaded the Down East coast would see some waves with the advent of the Civil War. The author of *Uncle Tom's Cabin,* Harriet Beecher Stowe, was living in the Brunswick area while her husband was working as a professor at his alma mater, Bowdoin College, when she was inspired to write the hugely influential antislavery text. This tale of the south, which would sell upward of three million copies in its day and caused President Lincoln to call her "the little lady who started the big war," was written from her home at 63 Federal Street.

The war resonated loudly in Maine, and Mainers rallied to the call for volunteers put out by President Lincoln. The state sent some 72,945 residents to the conflict—more than any other place in the North, per capita—in 32

i The rich history of Maine goes on display every summer at a variety of historic homes, historical societies, and museums along the length of the coast. You'll find them listed in the Attractions chapter, under History.

infantries, three cavalry regiments, seven companies of sharpshooters, one heavy artillery, seven field artillery batteries, seven coast artillery companies, and six companies to fortify coastal points. Thirty-one Union generals hailed from the Great State of Maine, and Ulysses S. Grant, who would navigate the Union to victory, was made a colonel by one of the famous Washburn brothers of Livermore. The state of Maine also contributed warships and, by some accounts, 5 percent of all the gunpowder used by the Union.

Perhaps no one was more important to the Union cause than Bowdoin professor Joshua L. Chamberlain, however. At least that's how things are remembered these days, after the generously mustachioed brigadier general has been immortalized in several well-known books and a couple of major feature films, *Gettysburg* (1993) and *Gods and Generals* (2003). Chamberlain led the Twentieth Maine Regiment at Gettysburg, where he was assigned to the far left flank of the Union line on the exposed hill of Little Round Top. The Confederates had been making gains in the weeks prior and, if things went their way, could sweep past the federal army and make a bold push north against weakened forces. Gettysburg had to be held, and this small hill was strategically imperative. Despite overwhelming odds, Chamberlain and the men of the Twentieth Maine did just that, at one point charging at a Confederate force of superior numbers with only fixed bayonets and surprise on their side. A third of the Mainers died, but the hill held, and with it the Union. Chamberlain was later awarded the Congressional Medal of Honor and actually received the surrender of Robert E. Lee at the end of the war.

The Southern colonel who faced the

Maine Notables, 12 to Know

Joshua Chamberlain (1828–1914)

Joshua Chamberlain was a lot of things to Mainers—governor, president of Bowdoin College, prominent resident of Brunswick, surveyor of the Port of Portland—but he is most revered for his courageous stand at Gettysburg. As commander of the Twentieth Maine infantry regiment during that fateful battle, Chamberlain held Little Round Top against overwhelming odds. Some say that Little Round Top changed the course of Gettysburg, which in turn changed the course of the war. Chamberlain suffered six wounds and survived 24 engagements in the war, earning the Congressional Medal of Honor for still further heroics at the Battle of Petersburg. When Confederate general Robert E. Lee surrendered at Appomattox Court House, it was Chamberlain, by then a major general, who accepted his surrender. The language professor would return home to be elected governor of the state in 1866 by the largest margin in history. He'd later become president of his alma mater, Bowdoin, in 1871, and write a well-received account of his Civil War service entitled the *Passing of the Armies*. He died at the age of 86 from complications relating to his war wounds.

Margaret Chase Smith (1897–1995)

The first woman to become a U.S. senator, Margaret Chase Smith was elected to office upon the death of her husband, Republican congressman Clyde Smith. The Skowhegan native served four terms in the U.S. House and graduated to the Senate in 1949, where she stayed until 1971. Smith became famous as the first Republican senator to denounce Joseph McCarthy with the "Declaration of Conscience" speech she delivered in June 1950, and she was widely praised and admired for her independent streak. "Maggie" was the first woman nominated for a presidential bid by a major party in 1964, and she was an inspiration to many politicians to follow.

Edmund Muskie (1914–1996)

Rumford-born Edmund Muskie became the first Democratic governor in decades when he was elected in 1954, breaking a Republican cycle of dominance dating back generations. A graduate of Bates College and Cornell Law School, he began his political career in the Maine House of Representatives in 1947. After serving as governor, he would go on to serve in the U.S. Senate, where he was a champion of the environment, among other things. He was the Democratic presidential candidate in 1968 and 1972 and became secretary of state under President Jimmy Carter in 1979.

Percival Proctor Baxter (1876–1969)

Born to one of the wealthiest families in Portland, Percy Baxter fell in love with the outdoors at an early age. When he was elected to the Maine Legislature in the early 20th century, Baxter was an advocate for water conservation and other envi-

ronmental legislation. In 1921 he ascended to the governorship and began pushing for creation of a park or preserve centered on Mount Katahdin, the state's
highest peak. The idea was met with a lot of derision, and the legislature refused
to pass several bills sponsoring creation of such a park. So Baxter decided to do it
himself, ultimately buying more than 200,000 acres and donating them to the
people of Maine with the mandate that they remain "forever wild." Today, Baxter
State Park is one of the premier wildernesses in the East and is revered far and
wide. Baxter died at his Portland home in 1969.

Neal Dow (1804–1897)
Portland resident Neal Dow never met a drink that he liked. The founder of the
Maine Temperance Union in 1838, Dow would become known as the father of
Prohibition. He helped launch Prohibition nationwide as author of the Maine Law,
which outlawed the sale of alcoholic beverages in the Pine Tree State in 1851. The
statute stayed on the books until the repeal of Prohibition in 1933. Dow also
served as mayor of Portland and was the Prohibition Party's candidate for president in 1880.

Guy Gannett (1881–1954)
A newspaperman extraordinaire, Guy Gannett rode the news to an extraordinary
media empire. Born in Augusta, Gannett counted among his print publications
many of the prominent papers in the state—the *Portland Press Herald*, the *Kennebec
Journal* in Augusta, and the *Waterville Sentinel*—and he branched into radio and TV
as well, adding stations in Portland and Bangor to his massive conglomerate.

Hannibal Hamlin (1809–1891)
When he was in his 20s, Paris Hill resident Hannibal Hamlin began his public
service career, serving five terms in the Maine Legislature, three of which
included stints as speaker. He moved on to the U.S. House and Senate and then
became the first Republican governor in Maine history in 1857. Just a few years
later, Abraham Lincoln would ask Hamlin to serve as his vice president. The pair
were elected in 1861.

William King (1768–1852)
Maine's first governor, William King, was born in Scarborough. After making his
fortune in shipbuilding and land development, King became active in the movement for Maine statehood. He served in the Massachusetts General Court as a
representative of Maine and helped draw up the Maine Constitution in 1819. The
following year, he was elected to head the executive branch of the newly created
state of Maine.

Robert Peary (1856–1920)
Born well after the golden age of exploration, Peary nonetheless made a name for
himself in 1909 by becoming the first person to reach the North Pole. Though
born in Pennsylvania, he grew up in South Portland, was educated at Bowdoin

College, and spent summers on Eagle Island on Casco Bay, where today there is a museum dedicated to his life and exploits.

Nelson Rockefeller (1908–1979)
Scion of the Rockefeller clan, Nelson was born in Bar Harbor and would spend much of his life in public service. He was an assistant secretary of state in 1944 and 1945, during the World War II years; was a special assistant to President Eisenhower (1954–1955); and eventually served as vice president of the United States under Gerald Ford (1974–1977).

Louis Sockalexis (1873–1913)
One of the most prominent Native Americans in Maine history, Louis Sockalexis was born in Old Town and become the first American Indian to play major-league baseball. He was a Hall of Famer for the Cleveland Nationals in the 1890s.

John Calvin Stevens (1855–1940)
If anyone can be said to have shaped the way Maine looks, it might be John Calvin Stevens. Brought up in Portland, he helped develop the shingle style of architecture, which is now common along the Maine coast. He was influential to Frank Lloyd Wright and a host of other architects to follow.

young Bowdoin man that day later wrote: "There were never harder fighters than the Twentieth Maine men and their gallant colonel. His skill and persistency and the great bravery of his men saved Little Round Top and the Army of the Potomac from defeat. Great events sometimes turn on comparatively small affairs."

RECONSTRUCTION AND THE TURN OF THE 20TH CENTURY

The years after the Civil War were not the best of times in Maine. Portland lost more than 1,800 buildings in a fire that engulfed the city in 1866. Having seen greener grass elsewhere, many Maine war veterans trended westward, planting roots in places they'd visited during the war that seemed to have soil more amenable to farming than the rocks they were used to Down East. ("You can't keep the boys on the farm after they've seen Paree" was a popular quote at the time.) This migration so alarmed state officials that they went out and started actively recruiting settlers.

The state's traditional industries would go into a gradual decline, too. People weren't traveling in wooden ships as much with the advent of steel boats, nobody seemed to want granite after cement was invented, and mills elsewhere presented stiff competition to those turning out textiles in Maine. But the Bath Iron Works was established in 1884 and became successful. Papermaking was one of the few manufacturing industries that was on the rise at the turn of the 20th century, and by 1909 it would place Maine third in the nation, behind Massachusetts and New York, in production. By 1914 papermaking was bringing in more than $40 million a year and employing almost 100,000 people.

The other industry that was growing steadily in the late 1800s was tourism. Many of Maine's great resorts began to prosper in the 1870s, with grand hotels flourishing in places like York, Old Orchard, Kennebunkport, and Bar Harbor. Wealthy summercators were moving to enclaves in Northeast Harbor, Prouts Neck, and Islesboro for July and August and bringing their wallets with them. And it wasn't just the wealthy who were flocking north by east to escape the heat of the cities—the middle-class travel trade was important to Maine as well, and the beaches in southern Maine were soon awash with vacationers. Trains, steamboats, and soon automobiles were depositing people from all over on the coast for a week or two at a stretch. The establishment of Acadia National Park in 1919 helped draw people farther Down East. By 1929 the state was bringing in some $30 million in annual revenue from tourists.

20TH-CENTURY MAINE

By 1900 the state of Maine had about 700,000 residents, most of them living in rural areas. The state managed to send 35,000-plus troops to Europe to fight World War I, and it launched the first navy-built submarine in Kittery at the Portsmouth Naval Shipyard. Hundreds of boats were constructed for World War II, too, with 75 submarines alone at Kittery and 236 Liberty ships in South Portland. Almost 100,000 troops would participate in the Second World War, and bases along the coast were integral to the war effort—Portland did a spell as the naval operating base of the Atlantic Fleet, and Brunswick Naval Air Station helped patrol the skies in search of German U-boats. A pair of Nazi spies were headline news in 1941, going ashore at Hancock Point after being dropped off by a submarine. They would later be arrested by the FBI in New York City.

Between the wars Mainers made history in 1920 by being the first place women voted in the nation after winning the suffrage battle. Maine also became a hot spot for smuggling during the Prohibition era. Teetotalism had had advocates Down East for ages, dating back to Neal Dow, sometimes called the father of Prohibition. A mayor of Portland, he man-

aged to get a law passed in the Maine legislature banning the sauce in 1851. When the rest of the nation enacted Prohibition laws in 1919, though, Mainers were quick to defy them, beginning the rum-running trade Down East. Some say that today's lobster boat races can be traced back to those days when lobstermen would speed over into Canada to procure some hooch and transport it back to Maine under the cover of darkness. The throttle on these vessels was often open as they tried to avoid and evade the authorities.

After the Civil War tourism continued to explode as city slickers from Boston, New York, Philadelphia, Washington, and the rest of the Northeast flocked north to escape the heat. They established summer colonies from York to Hancock Point and moved up for July and August, a tradition that continues to this day. Some would even head deep into the North Woods to climb Mount Katahdin, which Percival Baxter gave to the people of Maine in 1932. These visitors "from away" were among the first to bring automobiles to Maine. The opening of the Maine Turnpike in 1947 accelerated both the tourism industry and the pace of change in Maine. Automobiles would become the preferred way to get here as passenger rail slowly ground to a halt beginning in the 1950s.

After the Second World War, rural electrification projects began another great change, bringing power to outlying areas. By the 1960s and 1970s, a great influx of "back to the landers" began in a lot of these quiet small towns, introducing the bohemian to the backcountry. In 1962 summer resident Rachel Carson published the landmark book *Silent Spring*, helping to galvanize these newcomers—and Mainers everywhere—into an environmental movement that would become

i Anyone interested in Maine history will want to check out www.vintage maine.images.com. A project of the Maine Historical Society, it's a gold mine of venerable Down East photos, prints of which can be purchased.

among the strongest in the nation. It helped to bring an end to the logging drives, which polluted rivers, and fought the development of Maine Yankee, a nuclear power plant that was built in 1972 only to be dismantled less than 30 years later.

The 1970s and 1980s brought with them a lot of suburban growth—especially in southern Maine and Greater Portland—and that helped launch retail booms at the Maine Mall in South Portland, in Portland's Old Port, and in outlet towns like Kittery and Freeport. More and more summer vacationers, too, were moving up permanently, building homes all along the coast. This development has prompted many Mainers to worry about the small-town life that has so long been tradition here.

The 20th century continued the political traditions begun after the Civil War in Maine. Despite its relatively small population, the Pine Tree State has had a large impact on the nation's politics. Maine has produced scads of top-level politicos since the late 1800s, when Mainers were represented in Washington by a vice president, a secretary of state, a Speaker of the House, and a Senate majority leader. That tradition continued into the 1950s, when Margaret Chase Smith was elected to fill the House seat left vacant by her late husband, going on to become the nation's first female senator, delivering her famous "Declaration of Conscience" speech, which helped derail McCarthyism. About the same time, Democrat Edmund Muskie was elected governor back in

Maine, breaking the Republican stranglehold on state politics, and he'd go on to a distinguished career, serving as President Jimmy Carter's secretary of state after years in the Senate. George Mitchell and William Cohen, a Democrat and a Republican, respectively, both rose to prominence in the 1980s and 1990s, when Mitchell served as Senate majority leader and Cohen as secretary of defense during the Clinton administration. These days, Maine is known for its two dynamic senators, Olympia Snow and Susan Collins, both Republicans.

THE 21ST CENTURY

Through the years, tourism has remained a constant. Today visitors to the state and the jobs they spin off account for $5.4 billion. Though still more dependant on natural resources than some places, Maine has seen the same economic cycles as the rest of the nation. Manufacturing has dwindled, with even the mighty paper industry gasping in the past several decades, and high-tech has moved in with the emergence of telemarketing. Maine has one of the best infrastructures for communications in the nation, with a network of fiber-optic cable that is second to none at 80,000 miles long. Health care has been another growing sector. Retail and service industries, especially as they relate to the massive influx of summer visitors, remain important as well.

ACCOMMODATIONS

Maine has been a tourist getaway now for more than a century, so it has its fair share of places to stay. In fact, there's a remarkable array of lodging choices available to visitors, depending upon where you want to be and when you want to visit. You can pitch a tent on a cliff top way Down East, enjoying completely unspoiled vistas all to yourself, or stay in a luxurious suite at a South Coast beach town resort, with hundreds of other guests. There are inexpensive motels with never-ending sea views in the Boothbay area, cool cottages in Machias, farm bed-and-breakfasts in Jefferson, grand old hotels on Monhegan Island, and urban high-rise(ish) hotels in Portland. Take your pick.

A few things to keep in mind when considering accommodations: Hotels are generally limited to the cities and resort towns, and there are only so many true resorts in Maine and fewer overnight spas. Cottages, motels, inns, and bed-and-breakfasts can be found along the length of the coast. Cottages are the way to go if you want an extended stay and don't mind doing your own cooking and cleaning. There are hundreds up and down the coast. Check in the phone book or with a Realtor in the area you want to be in.

Likewise, there are zillions and zillions of B&Bs in Maine now—500 or more at last count—and Mainers like to joke that after visiting the state in the summertime, every other tourist wants to move to the coast and open his or her own place. Bed-and-breakfasts can be great for new visitors, though, because they tend to be run by personable hosts who are very familiar with their area and can be your personal guide. Of course, some of these eager innkeepers can be overbearing, too.

You can find a searchable database of places to stay at the Maine Innkeepers Association (305 Commercial Street, Portland; 207–773–7670; www.maineinns.com). It's a handy resource.

That covers the where.

The when is a bit easier these days than it used to be. Maine tourists used to leave as soon as the leaves fell, and consequently so did all the innkeepers, closing up their shops until spring returned. More places are open year-round now, but there are still many that close for at least some part of the winter, so it's best to call ahead and check. The slowdown of the tourist season can be a boon to visitors, though—rates at many fine inns and hotels can be slashed dramatically in the fall and winter, making a stay at a swanky spot affordable for the average traveler.

Wherever you decide to stay, and whenever you decide to go, make a reservation ahead of time so you won't be disappointed.

Price Code

Except where noted, prices represent the average rate or range for a double-occupancy room in the high season. Most inns, bed-and-breakfasts, motels, and resorts offer a range of pricing options based on the size of the room, the view, and the amenities. Prices do not include taxes, parking, phone usage, room service, or any other added-on costs. Most hostelries also offer bargain and package rates in the off-season.

$. . . . . $90 or less
$$ . . . . $91 to $150
$$$ . . . . $151 to $199
$$$$ . . . . $200 or more

SOUTH COAST
Kittery and Surrounding Area

Portsmouth Harbor Inn
and Spa $$–$$$$
6 Water Street, Kittery
(207) 438–4040
www.innatportsmouth.com

As you might surmise from its name, this distinctive brick inn is a great launching pad for exploration of nearby Portsmouth (you can hoof it from here), as well as a fine place to rest between trips to the outlets. Of course it's a very pleasant place to simply be, to sit on the porch, look at the garden, or indulge in any number of treatments (facials, massage, body work) in the spa on the premises. The inn's owners have individually decorated its five guest rooms, which have private bathrooms, air-conditioning, cable TV, and dataports, and they've thoughtfully added things like beach chairs and bikes. The inn is open all year.

Academy Street Inn
Bed and Breakfast $
15 Academy Street, South Berwick
(207) 384–5633

The academy in question is Berwick Academy, which used to use this gracious grand colonial for its faculty, but you don't have to be a headmaster to stay here anymore. Since 1990 the

i The chambers of commerce in resort communities like Ogunquit, Kennebunkport, and Boothbay Harbor got so used to visitors to the area coming in exasperated after an unsuccessful search for a room in high summer that they began to keep lists of beds available for any given evening. Now many chambers up the coast provide this service. If you don't have a reservation, the local chamber is often a good place to find out what's available. Many chambers of commerce—the one in Wells is a good example—keep track of longer-term rental properties, too.

five-room inn has been a bed-and-breakfast with Victorian flair. Each of the five rooms here has a private bath, and there's a nice fireplace in the parlor for taking the chill off. The 60-foot porch is ideal for sitting, but there's plenty to do in the area, from the historic home museums of South Berwick, hometown of Sarah Orne Jewett, to the beaches on the coast. The inn is open all year.

The Yorks

Dockside Guest Quarters $$–$$$$
Harris Island, York Harbor
(207) 363–2868 or (888) 860–7428
www.docksidegq.com

This complex—a main house and a series of condo cottages—sits on seven seaside acres on York Harbor and began as a marina back in 1953. So many visiting skippers would ask about a room that the owners, the Lusty family, decided to renovate the derelict 1895 house on the property. With its wraparound porch, sweeping lawn, and chairs on the shore, the main house is now a white clapboard classic. The Lookout, Crow's Nest, Quarterdeck, and Captain's Quarters cottages are clustered along the shore, making good use of sliding glass doors and banks of windows. You can choose from a variety of floor plans—suites with kitchenettes, studios, and individual rooms are available—but everything comes with a private deck, water view, and air-conditioning. Also on the property is the Dockside Restaurant, a well-liked eatery where you can fill up on seafood.

Stage Neck Inn $$$–$$$$
8 Stage Neck Road, York Harbor
(207) 363–3850 or (800) 340–1130
www.stageneck.com

If wraparound panoramas of the open Atlantic, an indoor pool, your own private beach, and exceptional dining are the sorts of things you're looking for during your Maine stay, the Stage Neck Inn is for you. A sprawling resort complex, the 58-room inn is a self-contained vacation, with two good restaurants, a fitness center, an outdoor pool, a Jacuzzi, tennis courts— just about everything you need for a getaway. Harbor Beach, which has no public parking so is all but inaccessible to the public, is right next door, and the famous York Cliff Path is, too. York Harbor's tiny downtown is a stroll away.

Pack a jacket and tie with your bathing suit, though, because Harbor Porches, the dining room, is formal. The Sandpiper Grille, the cafe on premises, isn't, however, so you won't have to dress up to dine. The rooms are nice in a resorty kind of way, but what you really want are the views, and they're ever present.

Sunrise Motel   **$$–$$$**
Long Beach Avenue, York Harbor
(207) 363–4542
www.sunrisemotel.net
When you stay at a place like this boxy, three-story motor inn, you're not looking for the high-end fineries, just a spot to lay your head between visits to the beach, which is right across the street. And if you go in with that in mind, the place is fine. It has nice balconies overlooking the crashing surf and simple rooms with bright carpeting, equipped with air-conditioning, microwaves, and clean, private baths. You probably won't even remember the inn, but you will remember the week you spent at the beach.

York Harbor Inn   **$$–$$$$**
Route 1A, York Harbor
(800) 343–3869
www.yorkharborinn.com
The new hotels and inns that have been popping up along the coast in recent years could learn a thing or two from this old place. Everything is done with taste and attention to detail, from the 300-year-old common area to the 54 guest rooms to the dining room. The inn feels old—and when your lobby dates back to the 17th century, that helps—and its rooms are outfitted with antiques and reproductions to give you that New England country inn vibe. But all the conveniences modern travelers want are mixed right in, from private baths and Jacuzzis to phones, Internet access, and

air-conditioning, to ensure that you're comfortable. The inn is divided into several distinct sections—the Main Inn, the Yorkshire Building, Harbor Hill, and Harbor Cliffs Bed and Breakfast—offering varying degrees of luxury. Many of the rooms have decks with views out to the harbor; some have fireplaces. The main dining room is generally excellent and has received high marks from the likes of *Food and Wine* magazine, serving a lot of local seafood, creatively prepared. There's a pub here, the Ship's Cellar Pub, with drinks and less expensive fare as well. The inn is right across from a neat park, and the Harbor Beach is a skip away, too. The inn has periodic Internet specials to fill vacancies at the last minute, and they can include some great deals.

Anchorage Inn   **$$$–$$$$**
265 Long Beach Avenue, York Beach
(207) 363–5112
www.anchorageinn.com
Put the word motor in front of inn and you get a better idea what this sprawling gray complex is like. It's more motel than inn and has more than 100 rooms with water views, three swimming pools, and all the modern conveniences. The location of the Anchorage on Long Beach Avenue puts you right across the street from Long Sands Beach, which means you're right in the middle of the York Beach hullabaloo, like it or not. There's a fitness center on-site, the rooms are nice if not posh, and the new pool in the atrium is a cool, hourglass-shaped indoor wonder. Some rooms have whirlpools, and all have private baths, color TVs, and air-conditioning. With its grassy lawn and gray shingles, the Anchorage is a step up from most of the other motels that line the beach here, but not a gigantic step up. (It's one of the rare places open year-round, however.) Rates vary widely depending upon room and season.

Union Bluff Hotel   **$$$–$$$$**
8 Beach Street, York Beach
(207) 363–1333 or (800) 833–0271
www.unionbluff.com
This big, white hotel dates back to 1868 and

Close-up

Maine Farm Vacation B and B Association

Farm vacations came into vogue in the 1990s, and Maine has close to 20 agricultural bed-and-breakfasts now, with a half dozen on or near the coast. The idea behind farm B&Bs is this: You spend your vacation at a working farm, enjoying country living, helping out with the chores if you feel like it, and getting back to the land. You learn something, enjoy the "real Maine," meet some interesting Mainers, and help preserve open space while you're at it. "Our primary product is peace and quiet," says the association—and who doesn't want some of that? It's a great hands-on experience, especially for kids. For details visit www.mainefarm vacation.com.

The coastal members of the Farm Vacation B and B Association are:

Quaker Tavern B and B Inn
377 Gray Road, Falmouth
(207) 797-5540
www.quakertavernbb-inn.com

Blueberry Hill Farm
101 Old Madden Road, Jefferson
(207) 549-7448
www.mainefarmvacation.com/
blueberry

The Jefferson House Farm
95 Washington Road, Jefferson
(207) 549-5768
www.jeffersonhousebb.com

Black Locust Farm
15 Old County Road, Washington
(207) 691-1431
www.blacklocust.com

Shalom Orchard
158 Eastbrook, Franklin
(207) 565-2312
www.shalomorchard.com

Bass Cove Farm
312 East Side Road, Sorrento
(207) 422-3564
www.basscovefarm.com

Inn at Schoppee Farm
RR 1, Machias
(207) 255-4648
www.schoppeefarm.com

imparts a little class to the honky-tonk atmosphere of York Beach, towering over rocks not far from the sands—at least from the outside. All white clapboards, balconies, and turrets, it's reminiscent of the grand hotels of yore. The rooms are not as nice as all that—they tend toward the modern motel end of

things—but they're comfortable enough, and the views out across the water are superb. There are more than 60 rooms, with a variety of amenities. Some have fireplaces, others whirlpools, but all have private bath, cable TV, and air-conditioning. Family-style eats are available at the Beach Street Grill, and the hotel has access to local golf courses in season. It's not a bad place to stay at all, but it's not the cheapest.

Ogunquit and Wells

Beachmere Inn $-$$$$
Beachmere Road, Ogunquit
(207) 646–2021 or (800) 336–3983
www.beachmereinn.com

Another one of those old seaside Victorians, complete with turrets, the Beachmere was a private home that just kept expanding, and it's now a multilevel, multiporched wonder. The main building is just one of the many options at the inn, which has several cottages, off-site houses, and a motel unit. But the big old manor is the grandest, lording over expansive lawns and a rocky shore, and it has its own little beaches and access to the oceanfront walking path called the Marginal Way. The rooms are pleasant and several have fireplaces or kitchenettes in addition to balconies that look out over the Atlantic. All have private baths. They have wireless Internet and cable TV as well, but you're going to want to watch the beach instead. Many rooms are large enough to accommodate Mom, Dad, the kids, and maybe an extraneous grandparent, aunt, or uncle.

Cliff House $$$-$$$$
Shore Road, Ogunquit
(207) 361–1000
www.cliffhousemaine.com

Talk about your compounds—Maine resorts don't get any more "resorty" than the Cliff House, which sprawls across a bold, 70-acre headland on the way in to Ogunquit. Things look a little different here today than they did when Elsie Jane Weare opened a hotel on the site in 1872 and charged guests $6.00 for a week of rest, relaxation, swimming, fine dining, and hikes around Bald Cliff. (Costs a bit more, too.) Today on the site of the original hotel is a full-service spa, where you can have interesting things done to you with flora and fruit, like rose body wraps and blueberry facials. You can work out in the fitness mezza-

nine over the 75-foot indoor pool, maybe play tennis in the pine grove, then head outside for a swim in the outdoor pool. All of the gazillion guest rooms feature bay windows and decks with absolutely stunning views of the open sea, as well as private baths, modem lines, air-conditioning, coffeemakers, and all the conveniences. Dining remains a hallmark, much as it was when Elsie Weare was doing the cooking. The menu is thoroughly New English, with lots of seafood, and everything presented with a special twist. As nice as the Cliff House is, though, you'll pay for it—rates are high.

Grand Hotel $$$-$$$$
276 Shore Road, Ogunquit
(207) 646–1231 or (800) 806–1231
www.thegrandhotel.com

You have to be somewhat confident to call yourself the Grand Hotel, and this place certainly makes a statement (with a lot of gilding thrown in). Right in the thick of things in Ogunquit, between Perkins Cove and downtown, the Grand has 28 well-appointed suites from which to choose, all of them with a living room, private deck, full bath, and bedroom, and each with a fridge, VCR, cable TV, and air-conditioning. The third-floor penthouse suite comes with a fireplace and grand-size deck, and its indoor heated pool and hot tub are fairly attractive. The underground parking garage is a good idea in a place like Ogunquit.

Juniper Hill Inn $$-$$$
196 Main Street, Ogunquit
(207) 646–4501 or (800) 646–4544
www.ogunquit.com/juniperhill

Not to be confused with the Pine Hill Inn, this Main Street hostelry is more motel than inn, but it does a good job and is within walking distance of downtown and the beach. Five whole acres of space and comfortable rooms with fridges and cable TV, a fitness center, indoor and outdoor pools, newspapers and coffee, and golf privileges at the Cape Neddick Country Club, a semiprivate club, are just some of the amenities. The Juniper is the recipient of a AAA Three Diamond rating, which suggests it's better than your average motel. And it is.

Marginal Way House $–$$$$
Wharf Lane, Ogunquit
(207) 646–8801
www.marginalwayhouse.com

Can't have an inn in southern Maine without adding "motelly" units, and that's the story at this big gambrel-roofed colonial, which has been welcoming guests since the 1920s. If you have a location like this one—right in the village and a short stroll from the beach, with the water ever present—you might as well take advantage of it. There are now lodging options in five buildings here at the end of an anonymous lane. The main house has 12 rooms and three suites, each with private bath, cable TV, Wi-Fi, and air-conditioning (except for rooms 4 and 6). Many of these rooms have views and/or private balconies. The Wharf House setup is somewhat similar with five rooms and a common living area, and the Dockside Motel has six more rooms, even closer to the drink. There are also seven efficiency apartments (available at $1,010 to $1,670 per week) for longer stays. Open from mid-April through late October.

The Morning Dove $–$$$
13 Bourne Lane, Ogunquit
(207) 646–3891
www.themorningdove.com

The gardens are very appealing at this big white Victorian farmhouse, which feels quiet and sedate but is within walking distance to Perkins Cove. The full breakfast is served on the porch. There are five rooms, with king- or queen-size beds topped with handmade quilts. Minimum stays required in high summer.

Riverside Motel $–$$$
50 Riverside Lane, Ogunquit
(207) 646–2741
www.riversidemotel.com

From the road, this long, low-slung carriage house–looking motel is pretty unassuming, like any other motor inn on the South Coast.

But this baby backs right up to Perkins Cove, where much of the Ogunquit action goes down. You can walk from your room to the foot drawbridge the cove is famous for and enjoy the restaurants and shops without having to worry about parking, which is an absolute nightmare in these parts. There are 41 basic rooms in total, each with cable TV and a small fridge, and many have balconies with the million-dollar view. Breakfast, included in the price of the room, is offered in the lobby. There is an adjacent cottage built in 1874 with four additional rooms appropriate for families or groups.

Sparhawk Oceanfront Resort $$–$$$$
85 Shore Road, Ogunquit
(207) 646–5562
www.thesparhawk.com

The Marginal Way, Ogunquit's hugely popular oceanfront walking path, starts right outside this Shore Road favorite. That and the gardens alone are worth visiting for. But there is much more to like. The Sparhawk has 51 rooms, 35 suites, and a cottage, so it's comfortable for a longish stay, and it sits on six acres overlooking the booming surf. The grounds are expansive and pleasant to wander, there are tennis and shuffleboard courts, there's a heated pool for dipping, and everything in town is within walking distance—from the beach and the shops to Perkins Cove. You can even get a guest membership to the local golf course. The rooms are varied; some are motelish, some are more innlike, so you're certain to find what you're looking for. The Sparhawk has been welcoming guests in some incarnation for more than a century, and you'll understand why if you choose to stay here. There's a one-week minimum stay required in high summer, but you can get good deals in the shoulder seasons when it's more pleasant to be in Ogunquit anyway.

Studio East Motel $–$$$
Main Street, Ogunquit
(207) 646–7297
www.studioeastmotel.com

Clean rooms, good rates, and a great location are the appeal of this motel right on Main Street. You can walk downtown, to the beach, to restaurants, and forget about parking your car, which can be a nightmare in Ogunquit. (Hop on the trolley if you need to travel any distance.) The rooms are basic motel rooms, maybe a step up from average, and you can even get suites. All units feature private bath, cable TV, climate control, and a fridge; some come with kitchenettes. The motel is open from April through mid-December.

Yardarm Village Inn $–$$
406 Shore Road, Ogunquit
(207) 646–7006 or (888) YARDARM
www.yardarmvillageinn.com
The first thing you'll likely notice at this white-clapboard B&B is the big old porch. Every New England inn should have one, and this one is a beauty. The inn doesn't have a water view, but it's within an easy stroll of all the shops and restaurants of Perkins Cove, and it's far enough away to be quiet. So the veranda makes for good sitting, maybe with a glass of wine and some cheese and crackers, both of which the innkeepers sell in a little shop on the first floor. The five rooms and five suites are comfortable if not exceptional, and they're clean and outfitted with quilts. All of the units have a private bath, air-conditioning, refrigerator, and Wi-Fi, in addition to the ubiquitous cable TV. Perfect as a launching pad for Perkins Cove explorations, the inn also has its own sailboat and offers charters to guests, a nice surprise.

Beach Farm Inn $–$$
97 Eldridge Road, Wells
(207) 646–8493
www.beachfarminn.com
Wells is known for its salt marshes, and this pretty, 19th-century farmstead used to be a saltwater farm. A sunny breakfast porch, a plum-colored dining room, antique furnishings, and an inviting pool are among the many amenities. There are eight guest rooms, several of which have a shared bath, and they are

ⓘ There is a bed-and-breakfast garden tour every June in the Kennebunks, which can be a great way to get a tour of many of the area's B&Bs in one fell swoop—so you can pick the one you want to stay at next year. Check with the local chamber of commerce at (207) 967–0857 to find out this year's date and time.

decorated with thoughtful details like damask curtains, satin moiré bedcovers, and hand-stitched pillows. The third floor is cooled with air-conditioning. Rates are extremely reasonable for a place this nice. Two cottages are also available for weekly rental.

Belle of Maine Vacation Village $–$$
1139 Post Road, Wells
(207) 646–2668 or (800) 943–5222
Seven new cottages were added to this little "village," but you'll want one of the funky older ones with pine paneling on the walls and varnished cabinets over the sink. Reminiscent of the old Maine and a whole lot of fun, these places are almost like going to camp! The cottages, with their clapboard sides, red roofs, and porches, cluster around an inground pool, with the marshes of the Rachel Carson National Wildlife Refuge and the ocean in the distance. They come in a variety of configurations, all heated and air conditioned—you can choose a cottage with one or two bedrooms, and they all come with a kitchenette. Gas grills are also available. (There are motel units as well.) And the trolley stops out front to trundle you off to the beach.

The Kennebunks

Lake Brook Bed and Breakfast $–$$
57 Western Avenue, Kennebunk
(207) 967–4069
www.lakebrookbb.com
This four-room inn has what you call curb appeal. The grayish farmhouse dating back to the turn of the 20th century is set beside a saltwater marsh on a quiet road in Kennebunk, with overflowing gardens and wraparound

porch. The rooms are comfortable, with country furnishings and local art, and there are three of standard size and one suite, which also has a kitchenette. One of the area's best restaurants, On the Marsh, is across the street. Though it feels like the country, the shops and restaurants are a quick stroll away.

Waldo Emerson Inn $$
108 Summer Street, Kennebunk
(207) 985–4250 or (877) 521–8776
www.waldoemersoninn.com
Don't go thinking this big old colonial is where Ralph Waldo Emerson came up with his transcendental ideas—this house, Kennebunk's oldest, was built by his great-uncle, who made his fortune in the local shipbuilding trade. (Of course, little Ralphie was a visitor in summers.) Subsequently owned by other shipbuilders (they liked it because the Kennebunk River is out back), it went up in 1753, when Kennebunk was a thriving shipbuilding port. The inn's history is still written in the architecture and details—there are heavy hand-hewn beams overhead as you enter, there's the big working fireplace from the 1770s, which is still used to take the chill off at breakfast, and there are wide pine planks on the floors of some guest rooms. The white picket fence out front is charming, and there's a nifty quilt shop in one of the outbuildings. The rooms are cozy in a decidedly old-fashioned way, but they do have private baths, and there is a living area for guests with books, cable TV, and games.

The Cottages at Cabot Cove $–$$$$
7 South Maine Street, Kennebunkport
(207) 967–5424
www.cabotcovecottages.com
No, this little inlet isn't from the TV show *Murder, She Wrote*. The cottage campus hard by the shore of Chick's Cove did take its name from the show, but don't hold that against it. The 16 cottages here are great fun in a family-good-times-at-grandma's-cottage-by-the-shore sort of way. The walls are pine, the furnishings wicker, the kitchenette cute, and they all have private baths. The April 2006 issue of *Cottage*

Living magazine proclaimed them "the cutest cottages ever," and one has to presume the magazine knows cottages. The grounds are fantastic with everything Mom, Dad, and the kids need for a week on the water—rowboats, canoes, badminton, croquet, horseshoes, a jungle gym, and a grill for cooking out. But you can also walk to Dock Square without too much difficulty.

Cape Arundel Inn $$$$
208 Ocean Avenue, Kennebunkport
(207) 967–2125
www.capearundelinn.com
You can't really talk about the Cape Arundel Inn without mentioning the fact that it stares out at Walker Point, the home of the Bush family. All but two of the inn's rooms have a view of the presidential compound jutting out into the open Atlantic, and the wraparound porch takes it all in, too. Built as a summer cottage in 1895, the inn is a shingle-style showplace, with its own turret, and it's been run since 1997 by Jack Nahil, the innkeeper who made a world-class facility out of the White Barn Inn, so you know it will be comfortable. The dining room is one of the area's best, and the rooms are right up there. Seven are in the main house itself, and they all have sitting areas. On the side of the building is Rockbound, a "motelly" spot built in the 1950s, where there are six large rooms with handcrafted furnishings, and there is also the Carriage House suite, on the second level of the carriage house, which has its own private deck. The main house rooms don't have TVs, but the others do; all have direct-dial phones and Wi-Fi, and all have private baths. The gardens are beautiful, and the white Adirondacks on the lawn are inviting.

Captain Jefferds Inn $$$–$$$$
5 Pearl Street, Kennebunkport
(207) 967–2311 or (800) 839–6844
www.captainjefferdsinn.com
We should all get wedding presents like this. This absolutely beautiful Federal was built in 1804 and given to Captain William Jefferds and his bride, Mary, by her father in 1805. It was

converted into an inn in 1982 and has been lovingly restored by its current owners. There are 15 rooms, several of which—the Santa Fe, the Assisi, and the Chatham—outclass most everything else around. Many places claim to be decorated with antiques and reproductions, but the Captain Jefferds Inn truly is and puts them to fine, extremely tasteful use, placing four-posters just so on hardwood floors beneath high ceilings and before original fireplaces. Several rooms have claw-foot tubs or tile showers or even, in one case, a whiskey barrel whirlpool. Breakfasts draw raves. Highly recommended.

Colony Hotel $$–$$$$
140 Ocean Avenue, Kennebunkport
(207) 967–3331 or (800) 552–2363
www.thecolonyhotel.com

Enjoy the coast grand hotel style. On 11 acres at the place where the Kennebunk River meets the sea, the 1914 Colony Hotel harks back to Maine's golden age of tourism, when the wealthy would flock north to escape the heat of the cities and set up for weeks in simple yet classic old hotels. Yet it's got all the amenities of a modern resort—a heated outdoor saltwater pool, private beach, acclaimed dining room, poolside lunches, afternoon tea, beautiful gardens, a putting green, badminton, shuffleboard, croquet, bike rentals, and even movies in summer. You can even bring the dog. There are 124 rooms of varying degrees of luxury (none are really posh, though). They range from those in the Garden House, adjacent to Maine hotel, which are standard affairs with TV, private bath, and king, queen, or two queen beds up to the Ocean Grand Balcony level, which is a king-size room with a spectacular sea view and a shared balcony. What makes the Colony truly stand out is its environmental philosophies—it has a serious recycling program and encourages guests to reuse towels to save water. It has been the pioneer at this sort of stuff, so that people will have many more years at places like this, overlooking the sea.

1802 House Bed and Breakfast $$–$$$$
15 Locke Street, Kennebunkport
(207) 967–5632 or (800) 932–5632
www.1802inn.com

You could say that this classic 1802 colonial is away from all the action in Kennebunkport, but in this case that would be a very good thing. Rather than be in the midst of the madness that is Dock Square in summer, this graceful clapboard place feels more like a country inn, sequestered away in a residential neighborhood by the 15th fairway of the Cape Arundel Golf Course. The five guest rooms and single three-room suite here are all different, but each has a queen-size bed (most are four-posters), several have whirlpools, a couple have gas fireplaces, and some even have heated tile flooring. The Sebago suite has a private deck. Check out the big old beams in the house proper. The inn is open year-round.

Green Heron Inn $$–$$$$
126 Ocean Avenue, Kennebunkport
(207) 967–3315
www.greenheroninn.com

One of the most pleasant things about a stay at the Green Heron Inn is that you get to wake up to breakfast here. It's arguably the best in town. The 10 rooms in the inn are plenty cozy, though, not particularly fancy but with all the comforts you may want—from air-conditioning and private bath to TV. If you're vacationing with your pet, you get a special room with its own entrance. Families like the little cottage on the cove, which sleeps five and has a kitchenette and a tiny porch. The Green Heron is ideally located for exploring town because you can walk to both the beach and Dock Square. Open all year.

Kennebunkport Inn $$$–$$$$
1 Dock Square, Kennebunkport
(207) 967–2621 or (800) 248–2621
www.kennebunkportinn.com

An imposing 1890s mansion in the heart of Dock Square, this sprawling old hotel has three different sections: the main house, the

1930s-era Riverhouse, and the 1980s Federal-style addition. Each of the 49 rooms offers something different, but all have private baths and are decorated with period antiques. (If you're into history, you'll appreciate the hallway downstairs where there are neat old photos of the inn and Kennebunkport.) All of the rooms, regardless of where they are, also have air-conditioning, phones, TVs, and Wi-Fi, and many have gas fireplaces and/or river views. From May through September you can take a dip in the pool and snack at Artemesias on the patio; year-round you can dine in the Port Tavern and Grille, a steakhouse with a piano and bar.

Lodge at Turbat's Creek $–$$$
7 Turbat's Creek Road, Kennebunkport
(207) 967–8700 or (877) 594–5634
www.turbatscreek.com

A motel that's just around a quiet corner from Dock Square, this 26-room hostelry has some surprisingly nice touches for what's essentially a motor lodge. One example is the large, heated pool, another is the complimentary use of bicycles, which will get you quickly into town or to the beach without the hassle of using your car. Each room has a little deck, air-conditioning, cable TV, and Internet access, and it is furnished with either one king-size or two double beds. Certain rooms are reserved for smokers; others are available to pet owners, with advance notice.

Maine Stay Inn and Cottages $$$–$$$$
34 Maine Street, Kennebunkport
(207) 967–2117 or (800) 950–2117
www.mainestayinn.com

The sparkling 1860 Melville Walker House, all porches and white clapboards, is the very picture of what an in-town New England bed-and-breakfast should look like. On the National Register of Historic Places, the graceful home is in a residential area filled with fine old homes, but it's close enough to walk to Dock Square. There are six guest rooms inside, 11 suites tucked discreetly around to the side of

the inn, and the owners recently opened the Artist's Studio, another cottage. The rooms inside are pleasant, furnished with antiques, but the suites are knockouts with fireplaces, stuffed chairs, kitchenettes, and even whirlpools in some. They're the ultimate in privacy—you can go over to the main inn for breakfast or have it delivered.

Nonantum Resort $$$–$$$$
Ocean Avenue, Kennebunkport
(207) 967–4050 or (800) 552–5651
www.nonantumresort.com

The grounds are the nicest thing about this 115-room box of a place, which is not nearly as nice as it should be. The grass slopes down to the Kennebunk River, and there's a heated outdoor pool. There are contemporary rooms in the Portside Lodge, which have a water view, a fridge, air-conditioning, cable TV, Wi-Fi, and a private bath (kitchenettes are also available), as well as quasi-historic quarters in the Carriage House, which was built in the 1880s. Weddings and corporate gatherings happen on occasion here, and the halls can get loud and smoky. Open from May through mid-December.

Old Fort Inn $$$–$$$$
Old Fort Road, Kennebunkport
(207) 967–5353 or (800) 828–3678
www.oldfortinn.com

This 16-room inn on a quiet residential side street presents guests with an interesting scenario—it is far enough from the bustle for which the resort is known to be serene and peaceful, yet it's within walking distance of several good places to eat and even Dock Square, if you feel like strolling a bit. Very tasteful, very discreet, the former carriage house has all the comforts people have come to expect in a fine bed-and-breakfast—four-poster beds, whirlpool baths, heated pool, tennis courts, great morning eats—but it's decorated with fine Victorian furnishings and has a relaxed feel.

Rhumb Line Motor Lodge $$–$$$
Ocean Avenue, Kennebunkport
(207) 967-5457 or (800) 337-4862
www.rhumblinemaine.com

Less than a mile from the Bush compound at Walker Point in a residential area, this sprawling motel "resort" has surprises around every corner. How about a poolside restaurant? A Swedish massage or a facial? An outdoor lobster bake on the weekend? All at a motel? Four acres of woods surround the place, and the first thing motorists driving by notice is the stone building out front (that's where the trolley stops to whisk you into town or to the beach). The rooms are motel rooms, with air-conditioning, private decks and porches, cable TV, Wi-Fi, and fridges, and they come with two queen-size or one king-size bed. But it's in the amenities that this place shines—there are indoor and outdoor pools, indoor and outdoor tubs and spas, a sauna, and a well-outfitted fitness center. There are various packages and specials available, making things even more affordable than the standard rates.

The Tides Inn $$$–$$$$
Goose Rocks Beach, Kennebunkport
(207) 967-3757
www.tidesinnbythesea.com

The location of this Victorian charmer is ideally suited for beachgoers—Goose Rocks Beach is right across the street. Designed by famous shingle-style architect John Calvin Stevens, the inn used to be known as the New Belvidere, and it hosted such eminent guests as Teddy Roosevelt and Sir Arthur Conan Doyle back in the day. (It's said that original owner Emma Foss, who died many decades ago, still looks after things.) Gracious today, the inn has nice porches with fine views and 22 bedrooms, each individually decorated. These rooms are on the small side, and they don't have phones or TVs or other distractions (those are available in the lobby), but several do have absolutely stunning panoramas out their windows. Adjacent to the inn is Tides Too, a condo complex with two-bedroom suites and more modern amenities. Also on the premises

The monks at St. Anthony's Franciscan Monastery (207-967-2011, www.franciscanguesthouse.com), a fine Tudor manse, enjoy prime real estate right on the Kennebunk River, and they take in guests. It's an inexpensive way to stay in Kennebunkport and a one-of-a-kind experience, especially if you go to mass.

is the Belvidere Club, which is popular with the locals ("inn-toxicating," they say).

White Barn Inn $$$$
37 Beach Avenue, Kennebunkport
(207) 967-2321
www.whitebarninn.com

Lauded far and wide for excellence, the White Barn sets the standard in southern Maine—and, when it comes right down to it, the entire state. A member of Relais & Chateaux, that club for über inns and hotels, the White Barn has a list of accolades from major publications that could fill a book. If you can think of something you might like in an inn, this place has already thought of it, anticipating the every need of guests. There are 25 rooms in all, and several are actually smallish, but they are very comfortable. Every one is set with fresh flowers and fruit, plush terry robes, and CD systems. Many rooms have extra touches like fireplaces, and some have rain- or steam-style showers in their bathrooms with granite floors. Jacuzzis are options. Every night your covers are turned down, you can get laundry done the same day, and you may order in for breakfast if you like. If you can rouse yourself, you can get a massage poolside, and if you're really ambitious, you can get active with complimentary canoes and bikes. You can even get lunch by the pool or packed up for a picnic on the go. And the dining room is hands-down the best around (see Restaurants chapter). New cottages have been added down the road a bit, and they are every inch as nice as the inn itself, but they sit on the waterfront, which the inn doesn't. (Ironic, isn't it, that the nicest inn in Maine is not on the water?) You can still enjoy all of the amenities of the inn as well, including the full breakfast. Of course, you'll pay dearly for all this, but it's worth it.

Yachtsman Lodge and Marina $$$$
Ocean Avenue, Kennebunkport
(207) 967–2511 or (800) 992–2487
www.yachtsmanlodge.com

All 30 rooms at this riverside hostelry have French doors that allow guests to step out onto private patios overlooking the Kennebunk River and all its boats. The talents behind some of Kennebunkport's best places—the White Barn Inn and Grissini Italian Bistro—are also behind the Yachtsman, and each room has been designed to evoke the interior of a yacht, using mahogany moldings. (If you have an actual yacht, you can slide right up to a mooring in the marina outside your room; if you don't, you can rent a canoe.) The patios alone are worth the room fee, but these quarters are eminently comfortable, with much higher ceilings than you'd ever find in a yacht. Each room has private bath, cable TV, phone, and the use of a bike—or even a canoe—which is again sensible for a town like Kennebunkport. Dining packages taking advantage of the owner's fine restaurants are also available.

Ocean Park and Old Orchard Beach

Billowhouse $–$$
2 Temple Avenue, Ocean Park
(207) 934–2333 or (888) 767–7776
www.billowhouse.com

A rambling 1881 Victorian mansion on the beach—with a turret and all—this old place serves as a nice base for exploring Ocean Park, a seaside community established the same year as the inn as a religious summer colony. There are still interdenominational services, but these days the beach fun seems to have gained ground, pushing aside the Chautauqua-type lectures a bit. But it's still much tamer than Old Orchard, which many people find refreshing, and you can enjoy movies, talks,

and concerts, or simply walk around and check out all the little cottages. There are a variety of types of accommodations at the Billowhouse, from bed-and-breakfast rooms to suites to efficiency apartments, and they are well looked after. The beach is close enough that you can track sand into the house. And the rates—and your hosts—are great.

Nautilus by the Sea $–$$
2 Colby Avenue, Ocean Park
(207) 934–2021 or (800) 981–7018
www.nautilusbythesea.com

Another Victorian fronting the 7 miles of Ocean Park beach, the 1890 Nautilus has 12 rooms. Most have views of the sea, which is just out the window. The amenities vary from room to room—some have shared baths, some full-size or queen-size beds, some king-size beds, some patios, some TVs, some fridges. All are clean and comfortable and the rates are eminently reasonable.

The Atlantic Birches Inn $–$$
20 Portland Avenue, Old Orchard Beach
(207) 934–5295 or (888) 934–5295
www.atlanticbirches.com

This attractive Victorian inn, built in 1903, seems a bit above the fray in Old Orchard, more tasteful and refined than most of the area's hostelries. A five-minute walk from the beach and just around the corner from shops and eateries, the Atlantic Birches has five guest rooms, a heated inground pool, and a very nice wraparound porch shaded by those birch trees. An adjacent cottage has five more rooms, two with kitchen facilities. All of the rooms have unique decor, private baths, and names like the Old Orchard House, the Velvet, the Fisk, and the Abbot, taken from the grand hotels of the resort's turn-of-the-20th-century golden age, when this inn was built. You can select among canopied and four-poster beds, king-, queen-, and twin-size, and several rooms are well outfitted for families. A nice escape from the hurly burlesque this town is known for.

Ocean Walk Hotel $$–$$$$
197 East Grand Avenue,
Old Orchard Beach
(207) 934–1013 or (800) 992–3779
www.oceanwalkhotel.com

A big modern motel complex at the north end of Old Orchard Beach, this place presents lodgers with rooms in a variety of configurations. You can get a tiny studio with a double Murphy bed all the way up to an oceanfront suite with a full kitchen and sliding glass doors out onto a deck overlooking the water. The rooms are bright and open and fairly straightforward. Open April through October.

Old Orchard Beach Inn $$–$$$$
6 Portland Avenue, Old Orchard Beach
(207) 934–5834 or (877) 700–6624
www.oldorchardbeachinn.com

This old inn is a recreation of the Ye Old Staples Inn, which was supposedly the first hotel in Maine. Built in the 1730s, it began taking in guests in the 1830s when it was one of four buildings in town. Expanded several times over the centuries, it's now an 18-room inn, with a lot of history still in its walls. There's a big porch out front. Some of the rooms have nice beams and old floors, others antique beds and quilts. Each room has the modern conveniences, though: air-conditioning, TV, phone, Wi-Fi, and private bath. The third-floor suite has a full kitchen. As Old Orchard goes, this is a relatively fine, tasteful place, and it's within walking distance of the pier.

GREATER PORTLAND

Prouts Neck

Black Point Inn $$$$
510 Black Point Road, Prouts Neck
(207) 883–2500 or (800) 258–0003
www.blackpointinn.com

At the Black Point Inn they like to say that the inn will remain as you remembered it, meaning it isn't going to change much from year to year. And here, at the point where Winslow Homer found his inspiration, that's a very good thing. Tradition is everything at this history-steeped shingle-style inn—it even has its own crest. Built in 1878, the Black Point was originally called the Southgate, and it still has many antiques that date back to its early days. The inn has so many amenities, it can be difficult to keep track of them all. Foremost is probably service, so you can easily get help sorting out all the options. There are 84 rooms in total, including several luxurious guest houses. Gardens seem to flow every which way, and there are nice walking paths that meander here and there. Two beaches welcome swimmers, as do indoor and outdoor heated pools, and there are whirlpools, a sauna, and massage available. (There's even a salon on the premises.) The exclusive enclave of Prouts Neck surrounds the property, and it's the sort of place where they'll have your car towed if you even attempt to slow down. A stay at the Black Point allows you to go anywhere you like, from Homer's studio to the Cliff Walk, a private seaside walking path. You can also use the Prouts Neck golf course. There's also a full slate of activities for children, something that's relatively new at the inn, which has not welcomed little ones in the past. You won't find finer accommodations in the Portland area, and that isn't likely to change for a long time.

Scarborough

Higgins Beach Inn $$
34 Ocean Avenue, Scarborough
(207) 883–6684 or (800) 836–2322
www.higginsbeachinn.com

Built as a summer place back in 1897, this three-story "colonial revival" institution began life as an eight-room home. The enterprising man who originally owned it, Edward Higgins, quickly realized people would pay to visit the nearby beach, and he put a 25-room addition on and turned it into an inn. Guests have been coming here ever since, looking to escape the annoyances of everyday life by spending time on the beautiful strand just a short walk from the inn's porch. There are 24 rooms, 14 of which have private baths, and they are simple and basic and just right in a visiting-Grandma's sort of way. Well looked after by Bob Westburg and Diane Garofalo, they are always tidy and pleasant without being at all fancy. Likewise, the eats served up in the dining room are straightforward family favorites, with a hint of Sicily, but they're good enough to earn four stars from the *Portland Press Herald*. Comfortable and homey is the word, and the reasonable rates make the inn a great deal.

Cape Elizabeth

Inn by the Sea $$$–$$$$
40 Bowery Beach Road, Cape Elizabeth
(207) 799–3134 or (800) 888–4287
www.innbythesea.com
From the road this modern complex has a shingle-style air to it that harks back to the halcyon days of Maine summers past, but inside it's a thoroughly contemporary facility with 43 one- and two-bedroom suites that overlook the smashing sea. A variety of choices are available—from decor to layout to view—with balconies, sunken tubs, Chippendale cherry furnishings, full kitchens, fireplaces, and all sorts of other amenities. With an excellent dining room, tennis and shuffleboard courts, an outdoor pool, bicycles, and walking paths to popular Crescent Beach, this is the sort of inn where you could happily set up for weeks. The inn has an exclusive arrangement that allows for use of the private Purpoodock Golf Course a couple miles down the road, too. You can even bring Fido if you make arrangements ahead of time. The inn can be very busy in summer, so make your plans and reservations early.

South Portland

Peter A. McKernan Hospitality Center $$$
Southern Maine Community College, South Portland
(207) 741–5672
This unusual hostelry is housed in the distinctive, turn-of-the-20th-century officers' quarters at what was once Fort Preble. What makes it unique is not this fact but that the old bastion is now part of the campus of Southern Maine Community College and that the school runs the eight-room inn. It's one of the better-kept secrets in southern Maine and a treat for anyone who books an evening here. The building itself is a pretty, 1902 brick structure, and it's surrounded by green lawns and some fantastic views of Casco Bay and the Portland skyline.

Students in the school's Hotel-Motel–Restaurant Management and Culinary Arts programs run the place, learning how to manage an inn by, well, managing an inn. The rooms are pleasant and well appointed, with individually crafted furnishings and superb scenery out the windows. The setup is win-win, with the students getting an education under actual working conditions and guests getting attentive service and fine rooms at a reasonable price.

Portland

DoubleTree Hotel $$$
1230 Congress Street, Portland
(207) 774–5611
www.doubletree.com
For a big corporate box of a place right off the highway, Portland's DoubleTree is surprisingly comfortable. The Hilton-affiliated hotel does a lot of things right. You get a warm cookie upon checking in, for one thing, and nothing makes you feel at home more than a freshly baked chocolate chipper. High-speed Internet connections are free and convenient. The service is quick and very friendly, and the price is reasonable for an above-average room. On outer Congress Street, the location isn't the best, unless you plan on using the Downeaster train service, which is right next door. But the hotel offers complimentary shuttle service to the Old Port, Maine Med, and the mall. The 149 guest rooms are plenty nice, too. Each features cable TV, an oversize desk, a coffee machine, and furnishings that are a step up from most midprice hotels. The place also has a pleasant indoor pool and whirlpool, a restaurant and lounge on the premises, and some exercise machines. Not a bad option at all if you don't need to be downtown or on the water. Business travelers especially like the DoubleTree.

Eastland Park Hotel $$–$$$$
157 High Street, Portland
(207) 775–5411 or (888) 671–8008
www.eastlandparkhotel.com

There isn't really any park at the Eastland Park Hotel. You won't find any green space for blocks, anyway. You'll know you're in Maine if you spend a night there, though, because the seagulls tend to scream at each other at the top of their lungs on the roofs of nearby buildings, echoing off all the brick and glass. The hotel here has been active since the Eastland went up in 1927, but it's changed ownership several times. Then Governor Ralph Brewster symbolically chucked the keys of the place into Portland Harbor to demonstrate that the Eastland will always be there and open, and, for the most part, it has been. All sorts of faded photographs tell the story of the place in its lobby and hallways, and they're fun to peruse. All told there are 202 rooms in the old hotel, and they come in varying degrees of poshness. At the standard level, they're not really posh at all—comfortable, simple, and with a host of amenities including Wi-Fi, cable TV, voice mail, and 24-hour room service—but their glory days seem a bit behind them. Lots of them have dents, stains, peeling paint, and loose bathroom fixtures. One nice feature is that in many rooms you can open the windows, which is rare in big hotels these days (but you still can smell cigarette smoke—even in the nonsmoking rooms—because it comes through the vents). The longer your elevator ride, the nicer your room, though, and the better your view. The luxury suites at the concierge level pamper you with plush bathrobes and evening cocktails. Be sure to make it all the way to the Top of the East, a popular rooftop lounge. It has amazing views of the city, Casco Bay, and the White Mountains in the distance.

The Eastland used to be considered the grande dame of Portland hostelries, but there are more upscale places to spend your money now. But this hotel is perfectly acceptable—and can even be a deal, if you price it right—as long as you're aware that the dame is aging and not the prettiest girl in town anymore.

Chain, Chain, Chain

Looking for the chain hotels? Most of the less expensive places are out by the Maine Mall in South Portland. That's where you'll find the AmeriSuites (303 Sable Oaks Drive; 207–775–3900), the Comfort Inn (90 Maine Mall Road; 207–775–0409), the Days Inn (461 Maine Mall Road; 207–772–3450), the Hampton Inn (171 Phillbrook Avenue; 207–773–4400 or 800–HAMPTON), the Marriott (200 Sable Oaks Drive; 207–871–8000 or 800–752–8810), the Sheraton (363 Maine Mall Road; 207–775–6161), Coastline Inn (80 John Roberts Road; 207–772–3838 or 800–470–9494), the Fairfield Inn Portland (2 Cummings Road, Scarborough; 207–883–0300), and the Hilton Garden Inn (145 Jetport Boulevard, South Portland; 207–828–1117).

Holiday Inn by the Bay $$–$$$
88 Spring Street, Portland
(207) 775–2311 or (800) 345–5050
www.innbythebay.com

As downtown hotels go, this place has about as much charm as the Civic Center across the street—it's 11 stories tall, blocky, and completely devoid of character. But that's on the outside. Once you get into a room and look out the window, your impression will change, and that's where you're going to spend your time anyway. This place must have the best views of any Holiday Inn, overlooking a Casco Bay panorama that is something to see. It's a prospect that few lodging establishments in town can come close to. And while the 239 rooms and two suites themselves are not beautiful, they're comfortable enough, and the amenities here are fairly extensive—air-conditioning, dataports, cable TV, Wi-Fi, an indoor pool, saunas, fitness center, and did we mention the views? The hotel is also well located for exploring the city—it's an easy walk downtown and an easy walk to the Old Port and the waterfront.

Inn at Park Spring $$–$$$
135 Spring Street, Portland
(207) 774–1059 or (800) 437–8511
www.innatparkspring.com

The Portland Peninsula is a very walkable place—just 3 miles across—and this 1835 town house is well situated to explore it all. The historic West End, the Portland Museum of Art, and Congress Street are all handy, and even the Old Port is only 10 minutes away. The six-room inn has an urban charm that belies its small size, and while it behaves a lot like a bed-and-breakfast—it has nice touches like personal service, fireplaces, sitting chairs, fresh flowers, and a smashing breakfasat—it also has the private baths, privacy, and efficiency of a small hotel. One example: You can sleep in and have your breakfast served in bed rather than in the sunny dining room. You don't want to sleep too late, though, there's so much to do just out the door.

Inn at St. John $–$$$
939 Congress Street, Portland
(207) 773–6481 or (800) 636–9127
www.innatstjohn.com

This 40-room hotel has been one of the better bargains in Portland for the past decade. Built in 1897, it's among the oldest hostelries in the Forest City, and it sits down near the bus station on Congress Street. The place isn't much to look at from outside—and the usual bus station transients in the neighborhood can make you nervous, especially at night—and its inexpensive price might make you think you're getting into something sketchy, which is what makes it such a surprise to find the rooms themselves eminently comfortable and tasteful even, in a European sort of way. They're furnished with antiques and period reproductions and are complemented by the usual amenities—air-conditioning, cable TV including HBO, Wi-Fi, coffee, and breakfast—but you may have to

share a bathroom. Downtown Portland is several blocks up the road, but with rooms as cheap as they are here, you can afford a cab.

Pomegranate Inn $$$–$$$$
49 Neal Street, Portland
(207) 772–1006 or (800) 356–0408
www.pomegranateinn.com

Housed in an 1884 Italianate mansion, this eight-room B&B shines. Another hostelry in the West End, it is proximate to everything downtown—and from there it's a short walk to everywhere else. The decor is colorful and fun, with you've-got-to-see-it-to-believe-it wall painting and fresh flowers beside the bed. Several rooms have gas fireplaces, and all have private baths. No children under age 16.

Portland Harbor Hotel $$$–$$$$
468 Fore Street, Portland
(207) 775–9090 or (888) 798–9090
www.portlandharborhotel.com

Right smack-dab in the middle of the Old Port, the Portland Harbor Hotel has an enviable location, and for the most part it makes good use of it. Relatively luxurious by Portland's standards, the hotel's rooms overlook Casco Bay, the city's streets, or its own garden; they come as deluxe single units or two-room suites; and they have amenities aplenty—concierge service, wireless Internet, nightly turndown, granite bathrooms with their own sound systems and European-style showers, plush robes, Starbucks coffee, two TVs in some rooms, and hot tubs. The lobby has a nice fireplace, and the courtyard area is a pleasant spot to sit and eat or read. The dining room, Eve's, is well regarded. Run by Hart Hotels, the place has a corporate feel to it, but the setting and amenities are hard to argue with.

Portland Regency Hotel $$$–$$$$
20 Milk Street, Portland
(207) 774–4200 or (800) 727–3436
www.theregency.com

Once the default downtown hotel in Portland, the Regency now has a lot of competition. (It will probably always have its partisans for its location and many amenities.) Housed in an 1895 armory right in the Old Port, 2 blocks from the waterfront, the hotel has 95 rooms. After serving for more than half a century as a place of munitions (trouble was brewing with Cuba when it was built) and municipal uses, it opened in 1987 as a hotel to complement the newly revitalized Old Port. It pretty much functions as an urban hotel should, with every convenience you could want (except windows in some rooms). There is a dining room that serves all three meals, as well as a fully equipped gym and spa, and valet service. Local phone calls are free, newspapers complimentary, and every room has air-conditioning and a minibar. Shuttles are available to whisk you across the city, so there are no parking hassles, and service is generally pretty good.

Freeport

Freeport Inn $$
Route 1, Freeport
(207) 865–3106 or (800) 99VALUE
www.freeportinn.com

This place always looks so appealing to travelers motoring up I-95, sitting on a hill overlooking the tidal Cousins River. And it is, with 25 acres to wander, a nice pool, a great little on-site cafe, and rental canoes to explore the river and salt marsh. More motel than inn, it's now a Best Western and features 80 rooms, which have been spruced up lately, and they're plenty comfortable, with private baths, cable TV, air-conditioning, phones, Wi-Fi—some even have water views. Pets are allowed in many rooms, and there's a kids' play area outside, which makes the place a nice option for families. The cafe is very popular with the locals, serving breakfast all day. The Muddy Rudder, another popular eatery, is just on the other side of the river, and the shops of Freeport are moments away up Route 1. Open all year.

Harraseeket Inn $$$$
162 Main Street, Freeport
(207) 865–9377 or (800) 342–6423
www.harraseeketinn.com

CondeNast Traveler named this old downtown

beauty to its Top 700 places to stay in the world, and anyone who likes shopping will certainly agree. It's but 2 blocks to L. L. Bean and the center of outletville (you could even carry heavy shopping bags that far). Actually, anyone who likes classic comforts and appreciates good taste and country inns will feel comfortable in this Federal-style hostelry. There are 84 rooms in all—as well as nine town houses designed for longer stays—and they are nicely appointed with details like actual antiques and canopy beds as well as cable TV, phones with dataports, and Jacuzzis and wet bars in some rooms. Other amenities include an attractive pool and two nice dining rooms—the elegant formal room with its white linens and Windsor chairs, where you can get one of the best brunches in the state on Sundays, and the Broad Arrow Tavern, a more casual place decked out like a North Woods lodge, complete with snowshoes and an overhead canoe. The inn is run by the Gray family, and they do a bang-up job.

Kendall Tavern Bed & Breakfast $$–$$$
213 Main Street, Freeport
(207) 865–1338 or (800) 341–9572
www.kendalltavern.com

A pretty yellow farmhouse with a fine porch, restored barn, and acreage to wander, this 200-year-old place is within walking distance of downtown Freeport but feels more like a country inn. There are seven rooms inside, each tastefully done with warm colors, sitting chairs, quilts, and four-poster beds in some cases. Fireplaces warm the parlors, where you can set up with a book or simply relax on the porch.

Maine Idyll Motor Court $
1411 Route 1, Freeport
(207) 865–4201
www.maineidyll.com

Visible from I-95, this complex of 20 white cottages is very evocative, harking back to the motor courts of the 1950s. Very cute little clapboard-sided camps with wood-paneled interiors, they are set in a grove of trees, providing shade and atmosphere. They can accommodate couples or families and, despite their antique look, they have modern baths, color TV, and kitchenettes. Outside are play sets, picnic tables, and some trails through the woods. Pets are welcome. Rates are truly amazing for a place with such character just a few miles north of downtown.

MIDCOAST
Brunswick and Surrounding Area

Brunswick Bed and Breakfast $$–$$$
165 Park Row, Brunswick
(207) 729–4914 or (800) 299–4914
www.brunswickbnb.com

The town green in Brunswick has always been one of the community's best attributes, wide open and lined with graceful historic homes. This picket-fence beauty is one of them. It's got a nice location, within walking distance of Maine Street and everything downtown and Bowdoin College in the other direction. There are 15 guest rooms from which to choose, and they all have little extras like terry robes in the private baths, desks with wireless Internet access, and quilts atop the beds. The suites are private and make for nice longer-term stays. The porch out front is what every porch should look like, and the fresh flowers at breakfast are a nice touch. The innkeepers, Steve and Mercie Normand, also have other properties that can be rented on a weekly basis, including a cottage with a neat spiral staircase, in the garden behind the inn, and town house accommodations that are large enough to sleep a family.

Captain Daniel Stone Inn $$$$
10 Water Street, Brunswick
(207) 725–9898 or (877) 573–5151
www.captaindanielstoneinn.com

This sprawling inn—it's a stately Federal built in 1819 with a long wing added in keeping with the original style—has 30 rooms and four suites. For such an attractive old inn, these quarters are comfortably modern in use if not design. They have phones, TVs, private baths, and whirlpools in some cases, and the on-site restaurant Narcissa Stone sets a fine breakfast.

Holland House Cottage $$$–$$$$
Mere Point, Brunswick
(207) 729–0709 or (877) 609–0809
www.hollandhousecottage.com

A nice little cottage that sleeps four, the Holland House sits right on Middle Bay on the south side of town. The setting is quiet, in a wood overlooking Birch Island, and there's a pleasant patio from which to take it all in. The master bedroom and pullout sofa sleep four, and there's a kitchenette (with washer-dryer) where you can do your cooking and a gas fireplace to keep you toasty on a cool August night. Pets are welcome, and a mooring is available. The cottage can be rented by the weekend, week, or even longer.

The Parkwood Inn $$–$$$$
Route 24, Cooks Corner, Brunswick
(207) 725–5251 or (800) 349–7181
www.parkwoodinn.com

This big white modern box of a place likes to bill itself as Brunswick's Crown Jewel, which is a bit of a stretch, but it's got 68 perfectly acceptable guest rooms. (The inn's literature also mentions the "high-security" property, which is ominous sounding but must have something to do with the Naval Air Station, which has housing in this area.) These rooms are a step up from your average motel quarters and have Jacuzzis and fireplaces in some cases, as well as large TVs with cable, fridges, Wi-Fi, and complimentary morning copies of *USA Today*. The suites have a bit more space to them, divided up in some cases, and have microwaves. There's also an indoor heated pool and fitness center for your use.

The Captain's Watch $$–$$$
Bed and Breakfast and Sail Charter
926 Cundy's Harbor Road, Harpswell
(207) 725–0979

On the New Meadows River, Cundy's Harbor is a classic fishing village, right in the middle of the Midcoast but away from all the bustle. From the harbor you can see this stunning old Greek Revival home, up a rise with its cupola towering over nearby homes. The cupola is only one of the fine features of the place (two guest rooms have access), which dates back to 1862. Another nice one is the *Symbion,* the house sloop, available to take you out on the water. The rooms have private baths and are in keeping with the rest of the house with their antiques and quilts, and all have water views. Breakfast can be enjoyed in the formal dining room or on a tray outside. The Captain's Watch is a fine old place in a spectacular setting.

Little Island Motel　　　　　　$$
44 Little Island Road, Orrs Island
(207) 833–2392
www.littleislandmotel.com
On its own two-acre peninsula, this small motel has nine rooms and a fantastic setting. Each unit has a TV and is comfortably outfitted. Guests can make use of bikes and the motel's boats and private dock for splashing around offshore. There's even a little beach. Rates include the buffet-style breakfast.

The Log Cabin: An Island Inn　　$$–$$$$
Bailey Island
(207) 833–5546
www.logcabin-maine.com
Part of the fun here is simply selecting a room—you can check out pictures on the Web. The variety among the nine guest quarters at this rustic retreat is cool, going from fairly modern-feeling spaces with big bay windows overlooking Casco Bay to funky retro rooms like the Wiseman where you can lie on the bed and look up at the knotty pine rafters. You could be comfortable and content in any one of them, and the amenities here are plentiful—bay vistas are common, and all have private baths, TVs, phones, and decks. Some have woodstoves, some Jacuzzis, and four have either a full kitchen or a kitchenette. An outdoor pool with views of the bay is available for dipping. Breakfast is included and is served

in the dining room from 8:00 to 9:30 A.M. from a set menu—juice, coffee, tea, fresh fruit, pastries, and an egg dish or French toast or pancakes. Dinner, which is not included, happens between 6:00 and 7:00 P.M.; it's a surf-and-turf affair with a full bar.

Other Accommodations in the Brunswick Area

A nice 19th-century Federal-style B&B, the **Black Lantern** (6 Pleasant Street, Topsham; 207–725–4165; www.blacklanternbnb.com) gets you up close to Topsham's pretty, historic district. The **Middle Bay Farm Bed and Breakfast** (287 Pennellville Road, Brunswick; 207–373–1375; www.middlebayfarm.com) dates to the 1830s and has four guest rooms and a cottage with six more rooms on the bay. **Driftwood Inn and Cottages,** old-style cottages, simple and shingled, with exceptional views (Bailey Island; 207–833–5461). The **Harpswell Inn** (108 Lookout Point Road, Harpswell; 207–833–5509 or 800–843–5509; www.harpswellinn.com) is a three-story inn dating to 1761 with twelve guest rooms.

Bath and Surrounding Area

Benjamin F. Packard House
Bed and Breakfast　　　　　　$–$$
45 Pearl Street, Bath
(207) 443–6004 or (866) 361–6004
www.mainecoast.com/packardhouse
A sea captain's home on a quiet side street, the Packard House is a Georgian mansion built in 1790. The Kennebec River is only a block away. The inn has three large rooms and one suite available, and each has a private bath. The suite has a sitting room. No children under age 10. Rates include a full breakfast. There's a two-night minimum stay required in season. Open year-round.

Fairhaven Inn　　　　　　　　$–$$
188 North Bath Road, Bath
(207) 443–4391 or (888) 443–4391
Unlike most of the other bed-and-breakfasts in Bath, the Fairhaven is not downtown. Rather it's about a half mile out in the Kennebec river-

side North Bath area. This location is great for visitors who prefer quietude and a bit of acreage in their hostelry. The Fairhaven sits on 16 acres of meadows and woods, with views of the river, and it's a rambling old farmhouse with weathering shingles. Inside are eight guest rooms, most of which have private baths, and a couple of common rooms perfect for lounging. Golfers will find the Bath Country Club nearby, and the grounds are pleasant to wander.

The Inn at Bath $$–$$$
969 Washington Street, Bath
(207) 443–4294 or (800) 423–0964
www.innatbath.com

Bath's Washington Street is a graceful old avenue, and it's thanks to houses like this 1810 Greek Revival beauty. The City of Ships is filled with fine sea captains' homes, and the area surrounding the inn is rich with them. The inn itself has eight rooms and a suite, each individually decorated and some—like the yellow Sail Loft, with its four-poster, and the Lavender Room, with its canopied full-size bed—that feel more historic than others. All have private baths, cable TV, Wi-Fi, and air-conditioning. Some have fireplaces, Jacuzzis, writing desks, and outdoor entrances. There are various specials and packages to choose from.

Grey Havens $$–$$$
Seguinland Road, Georgetown
(207) 371–2616 or (800) 431–2316
www.greyhavens.com

This is the place you picture in your mind's eye when you think of a Maine vacation. A shingle-style castle with turrets on either end, it was built in 1904 by the man who gave the people of Maine the land for Reid State Park, which is just up the road. The vistas from its wrap-around porch are overwhelming, staring out across Sheepscot Bay. The owners of the place have left the old inn as untouched as possible, while making it comfortable for the guests of today, and it is a rustic beauty, from the rockers on the porch to the fieldstone fireplace to the simple, whitewashed wood-paneled rooms. All

of the 13 rooms have a private bath (which wasn't the case when this place opened with 26 rooms and two baths). Four of them are in turrets with 180-degree views that are just stunning, and the lobby and sitting area downstairs hark back to simpler times. Not where you want to come if you like your vacations to be all TVs and bustle, Grey Havens is an escape from all of the annoyances of modern life, a restful spot to relax and refresh. Read a book in an Adirondack chair on the lawn, play a board game, paddle the canoe out to a nature preserve for a walk, or head on down to the beach. The inn is open from May through October. No children under age 12.

Rock Gardens Inn and Cottages $$$–$$$$
Sebasco Estates
(207) 389–1339
www.rockgardensinn.com

On its own peninsula, the Rock Gardens complex has 10 cottages with living rooms, fireplaces, private baths, and porches—just about everything you need to enjoy a spell on the shore. Decorating is kept simple and comfortable like Grandma's cottage. The main inn has an airy dining room, a living room with a fireplace, and a TV room, and on the grounds are a heated swimming pool and access to golf and tennis. A clambake on the water's edge is a Rock Gardens tradition.

Sebasco Harbor Resort $$$$
Route 217, Sebasco Estates
(207) 389–1161 or (800) 225–3819
www.sebasco.com

With its own tour boat, golf course, kayak and sailing lessons, fishing, evening theater—indeed, its own village—Sebasco is a full-service resort unlike most others in Maine. There are umpteen rooms here on the 575-acre compound, and they are divided into three types. There are 37 rooms in the Main Lodge, which, with its rocking chairs and screened-in porch, has an old-fashioned feel. Views here are of the village, the golf course, and Wat Tuh Lake (no lie). The four-story lighthouse, an unofficial sentinel built as a beacon for boaters by the resort's original owner, has 10 more rooms, most with a grand prospect out over Casco Bay (those that don't get a view with their room can take a peek out the cupola-like observation room at the top of the building). Then there are the 22 cottages, scattered here and there, many with kitchenettes and fireplaces and with as many as 10 bedrooms available, and the deluxe new Harbor Village Suites. Some cottages are sequestered away for privacy. There are packages available taking advantage of the three dining rooms.

Squire Tarbox $$–$$$
1181 Main Road, Westport
(207) 882–7693 or (800) 818–0626
www.squiretarboxinn.com
Many inns and B&Bs like to use the word farm in their name to convey a bucolic image, but this Federal-style farmhouse, built in 1763, is the real deal, with dairy goats, laying hens, and other barnyard animals on a peaceful setting on Westport Island between Woolwich and Wiscasset. The 11 guest rooms are country comfortable, with their fireplaces, antique beds, and braided rugs, and the grounds are very nice to stroll, with paths that lead down to a bend in a saltwater river. Mountain bikes and a rowboat are available for adventuring, and the dining room is first-rate. The shops and restaurants of Wiscasset, Boothbay Harbor, Bath, and Damariscotta are all easy drives away. Open from April through December.

Wiscasset and Surrounding Area

Marston House $$
Main Street, Wiscasset
(207) 882–6010 or (800) 852–4157
www.marstonhouse.com
Mainers like to joke that every other person who visits the coast wants to return and open a bed-and-breakfast—and the rest want to open antiques shops. At the Marston House, the proprietors apparently couldn't decide between the two, so they've done both. In the front of their Main Street building is an antiques shop, specializing in smalls, folk art, painted furniture, and textiles. At the back are

two very fine guest rooms with fireplaces, queen-size beds, private baths, and private entrances. Sunlit and airy, they're as tasteful as the goods in the store. Breakfast can be served in room if you like. Rates are quite reasonable—extremely reasonable, really, for such a nice place. Open from early May through October.

Snow Squall $$–$$$
Route 1 and Bradford Road, Wiscasset
(207) 882–6892
www.snowsquallinn.com
The theme of clipper ships carries through this 1850s-era inn—the Snow Squall was a famous clipper, and each of the seven guest rooms is named after other vessels. All of the rooms have private baths and phones. Two have working fireplaces, all but one are air-conditioned, and a few have private decks. They're all well appointed, featuring a king- or queen-size bed, and the suites have accommodations fit for families. Enjoy a spell in a rocker on the porch or in one of the cushy chairs in front of the fire in the living room. Rates include a full breakfast.

Other Accommodations in the Wiscasset Area

Sheepscot River Inn (306 Eddy Road, Wiscasset; 207–882–6343 or 800–437–5503; www.sheepscotriverinn.com) used to be home to the Muddy Rudder, just over the bridge from Wiscasset, overlooking the Sheepscot. **Wiscasset Motor Lodge** (596 Bath Road, Route 1; 207–882–7137 or 800–732–8168; www.wiscassetmotorlodge.com) is a pleasant motor inn on Route 1.

Boothbay Harbor and Surrounding Area

Blue Heron Seaside Inn $$–$$$$
65 Townsend Avenue, Boothbay Harbor
(207) 633–7020 or (866) 216–2300
www.blueheronseasideinn.com
Just a skip from downtown, the Blue Heron backs right out onto the bay. The 19th-century colonial has been lovingly restored by owners

Laura and Phil Chapman, and its balconies take in the whole show on the harbor. Each of the six units has a water view, and you can choose between smaller first-floor rooms and larger suites with panoramic views on the third. No matter, you'll always get air-conditioning, fridge, microwave, phone, cable TV, and private bath. The flowers that line the walks out front are something to behold, and there is a dock out back for your boat.

Boothbay Harbor Inn $$–$$$
31 Atlantic Avenue, Boothbay Harbor
(207) 633–6302 or (800) 533–6302
www.boothbayharborinn.com
A sprawling white inn right on the water, this full-service hotel dominates the quiet side. There are 60 rooms inside the blocky place, each with air-conditioning, color TV, and private bath. Most also have a balcony or patio that hangs right out over the water. The interior decorator should be run out of town, but you can't beat the views from the private decks, some of which take in the harbor, some the whole waterfront. There are several levels of rooms and packages from which to choose. Windows on the Harbor Restaurant provides just that and serves up traditional New England fare with a small submenu of Caribbean cuisine, a nice treat.

1830 Admiral's Quarters Inn $$–$$$
71 Commercial Street, Boothbay Harbor
(207) 633–2474 or (800) 644–1878
www.admiralsquartersinn.com
Lester and Deb Hallstrom have a nice location for their B&B—sited on a hill, they overlook the waterfront and Squirrel Island, taking in much of what makes Boothbay Harbor so picturesque—and yet they're within walking distance of anything and everything in town. The rooms are unusually comfortable and commodious. Five of them are suites—almost like two-room apartments, really—and two are smaller; all have private baths and their own entrances, which allows you to be as private or sociable as you feel like. Nice gardens, ample windows to take in the views, a warm

fireplace, and great hosts who know how to be available without being overbearing all make for a recommended stay.

Fiddler's Green $–$$$
15 Atlantic Avenue, Boothbay Harbor
(207) 633–9965 or (888) 633–9965
www.thefiddlersgreeninn.com
On the quieter side of the harbor, right next to the Boothbay Harbor Inn, this sweet little B&B used to be called the Footbridge Inn, due to its proximity to the bridge across the harbor. Under new ownership these days, it has four units: two guest rooms and two suites, each of which has a private bath. Several have picture windows looking out on the water, some have decks. Other amenities include air-conditioning, kitchenettes in three rooms, and nice feather pillows. Guests rave about the three-course breakfast.

Harborage Inn $–$$$
75 Townsend Avenue, Boothbay Harbor
(207) 633–4640 or (800) 565–3742
www.harborageinn.com
Boothbay Harbor seems to have a corner on the B&B market. Every block there's another one. This 1869 colonial has been a guest house since the 1920s, making it one of the oldest inns in the harbor, if not the oldest. The water is right off the backyard, and the wraparound porch—just what you want—takes it all in. The rooms are decorated a la Laura Ashley, whose floral designs are either to your taste or not, and all of them have private baths. They also have their own discrete entrances from the porch, which is welcome if you value quietude and privacy. Some are one-room affairs, others suites. Try the Blueberry Bay Suite, which has wood paneling and wraparound windows that frame the bay. The harborfront hot tub is a hoot.

Spruce Point Inn $$$–$$$$
Atlantic Avenue, Boothbay Harbor
(207) 633–4152 or (800) 553–0289
www.sprucepointinn.com
Smart Money magazine named the Spruce

Point Inn in Boothbay Harbor as one of the 12 best getaways—not in Maine, not in New England, but in the entire country. And, as gamblers know, you always have to follow the smart money. If budget is not a concern, this is *the* place to stay in the Boothbay area, perhaps even in the entire Midcoast. The gardens alone are incredible. The inn sits on its own 57-acre peninsula, and it's more of a resort than an inn, with the main building, condos, and little shingle-style cottages—each with various levels of luxuriousness—to choose from. It began life as a 19th-century hunting and fishing lodge and expanded and added on until it reached its current 101-unit status. Every room has a private bath, private deck, fridge, and cable TV, and many also have a fireplace, whirlpool, and kitchenette. On the grounds there are almost too many amenities to list, from the expected pools (saltwater and heated freshwater), tennis courts, and fitness center to the neat touches like hammocks for Mom and Dad, a kids' program and play area, massage therapy, and a private pier. You can dine fancifully at the inn's award-winning formal dining room ("smart casual dress") or enjoy more relaxed fare at Bogie's Hide-away. Service, anywhere you go on the premises, is great, a Spruce Point hallmark. The inn is open from late May through mid-October. Get your reservations early because it tends to fill up fast.

Linekin Bay Bed and Breakfast $$
East Boothbay
(207) 633–9900 or (800) 596–7420
www.linekinbaybb.com

Former Lewiston cop Larry Brown and his wife, Marti Booth, are the gracious hosts of this fine old inn. The couple have painstakingly restored an 1878 white clapboard gem into a fine four-room B&B right on Linekin Bay in the quiet village of East Boothbay. They left the old floors but made sure each room had a water view, private bath, fireplace, plush chairs, and nice touches like stenciling and clawfoot tubs. Good muffins, too. One of the Boothbay area's excellent preserves is within easy walking dis-

tance across the street, and Brown and Booth can steer you toward all of the famed resorts sites.

Ship Ahoy Motel $
Route 238, Southport
(207) 633–5222
www.shipahoymotel.com

A room on the waterfront in the Boothbay area with a private seaside deck for only $79? That's the story at this motel complex a few miles outside of Boothbay Harbor. The rooms may be typical motel fare, but they all have color TV, private bath, air-conditioning, access to the nice freshwater inground pool, and better still, a direct line to a quiet section of Southport waterfront where there is a dock from which you can fish or launch boats. Unbelievable, really. The Ship Ahoy campus has four motel options on it now, each with varying degrees of comfort, none of which costs more than $79, and some of which can be had for $49—and that's in high season. And the setting is truly spectacular.

Newagen Inn $$–$$$$
Route 27, Cape Newagen
(207) 633–5242 or (800) 654–5242
www.newagenseasideinn.com

Truly a breath of fresh air in the Boothbay area, the Newagen is like the grand hotels of yore—they call it "understated elegance," and it is all that: unpretentious, unfancy, but timeless and classic. This is the sort of place that the wealthy rusticators of Maine's golden age might have come to in the summer for a month or two. Set on a 19-acre, spruce-covered property at the tip of Southport Island, the inn has magnificent views of sea all around. Park yourself in one of the whitewashed Adirondack chairs overlooking the briny sea, and you may never want to leave. There are 30 guest rooms in all, with varying degrees of luxuriousness, as well as the option of staying in a cottage, which can be rented by the week. The amenities are so many that you could indeed stay for weeks and not even have to leave the property. They include a heated outdoor pool, an oceanside hot tub, tennis, boating, biking, nature trails, candlepin bowling, billiards and Ping-Pong, croquet and horseshoes, volleyball and badminton, a library of books, and those Adirondack chairs set before a sparkling Atlantic panorama. The dining room is very pleasant, with banks of windows lining the wall, and serves a broad range of well-prepared surf and turf. This is the stuff of a truly memorable vacation.

New Harbor and Pemaquid Point

Bradley Inn $$$–$$$$
3063 Bristol Road, New Harbor
(207) 677–2105 or (800) 942–5560
www.bradleyinn.com
An absolutely beautiful inn on Pemaquid Point, this rambling, 16-room, turn-of-the-20th-century hostelry has fine views and a variety of lodging options. Choose from among rooms in the main inn, with four-poster beds, period furnishings, views, and private baths; in the Carriage House Suite, which occupies an old barn; or in the Garden Cottage, with its fieldstone fireplace and screened-in porch. Dining here is exceptional, and the rooms are very well appointed.

Hotel Pemaquid $–$$$
Route 130, Pemaquid Point
(207) 677–2312
www.hotelpemaquid.com
This funky old place—all towers, veranda, and dormers—welcomed its first guests in 1888, and it's been keeping guest registers ever since. You can read them (people like the inn). Anyone with a strong arm can practically throw a stone at Pemaquid Light from the inn, but it doesn't have water views of its own. No matter, it's a really fun venerable sort of place where you can just feel the happy ghosts of summers past. Neat decor—fieldstones and stained glass—and the rooms are comfortable, with private baths, cable TV in some cases. Accommodations range from cottages to suites to simple quarters with twin beds.

Newcastle

Flying Cloud Bed and Breakfast $$–$$$
45 River Road, Newcastle
(207) 563–2484
www.theflyingcloud.com
Once the home of sea captain George Washington Tukey, who set a world speed record in 1851 in his clipper, the *Flying Cloud,* this pretty white clapboard Greek Revival sits across the street from the Damariscotta River. The five guest rooms are named for the ports visited by Captain Tukey in his ship, and four of them have views out across the water (the other looks over the garden). All have private baths, and they are each tastefully appointed, with details like a claw-foot tub here, gas fireplace there, a four-poster bed, and pumpkin pine floors. The porch out front is delightful, and the screened-in breakfast area is a treat as well. Rates include the great breakfast.

Newcastle Inn $$$–$$$$
River Road, Newcastle
(207) 563–5685 or (800) 832–8669
www.newcastleinn.com
Known as much for its food as for its 15 rooms and suites, the Newcastle Inn sits right on the Damariscotta River with nice views back at the village of Damariscotta. The dining room is considered among the best in Maine; the guest rooms are each uniquely decorated, many with antiques, lace curtains, canopied beds, and unusual touches, like the doll collection in the Seguin Island Room. Some have fireplaces, and all have private baths. Choose from options like Jacuzzis, private entrances, and queen- or king-size beds. Rates include breakfast.

Waldoboro

Blue Skye Farm $$
1708 Friendship Road, Waldoboro
(207) 832–0300
www.blueskyefarm.com
One of the many architectural delights of the Friendship Road in Waldoboro, Blue Skye Farm is a distinctive Federal-style home built in 1775

and surrounded by acres of meadows. It is brimming with old details, from stenciling most likely done by the famed Moses Eaton to perfectly preserved rooms with aged fireplaces and quilts. Jan and Peter Davidson run the six-bedroom inn, and they have restored the historic charmer in loving fashion, saving the beams, the creaky floors, and period furniture (check out the four-posters), but tastefully blending in thoroughly modern comforts like private baths in four of six rooms. Guests have the run of the place, including the kitchen and dining room—the Davidsons live next door—but you'll want to have a chat with the couple, who hail from Kent, England, but obviously know and love the area.

Tenants Harbor

East Wind Inn $$–$$$$
Tenants Harbor
(207) 372–6320 or (800) 241–8439
www.eastwindinn.com
The porch at the East Wind alone is worth the price of a room. It's a fine wraparound veranda overlooking Tenants Harbor. You could happily spend days just taking it all in. The majority of the 26 rooms inside have private baths (all but seven), and they are simply furnished but country inn comfortable with water views. Rates include full breakfast. The inn also has apartments and suites.

Port Clyde

Ocean House $–$$
Port Clyde
(207) 372–6691 or (800) 269–6691
www.oceanhousehotel.com
It doesn't get much more charming than this venerable 1830s-era hotel. Port Clyde, of course, is one of the principal jumping-off points for trips out to Monhegan, and people often stay in one of the 10 rooms here in order to easily catch the early boat. The rooms are comfortably old-fashioned, with their lace curtains and mirror-topped dressers, and many have views out onto the water.

Monhegan Island

Island Inn $$$$
Monhegan Island
(207) 596–0371
www.islandinnmonhegan.com
An impressive shingle-style castle of a place, this gray beauty dates back to 1816, or at least part of it does. It sits on a rise overlooking Monhegan Harbor and Manana Island, and it has two types of accommodations inside. There are 34 rooms and suites, some of which share baths, and the rooms have nice painted floors and down comforters for those cool September evenings. The inn's dining room is arguably the island's best, and its wraparound porches and Adirondack chairs are fine places to while away a day.

Monhegan House $–$$
Monhegan Island
(207) 594–7983
www.monheganhouse.com
Monhegan has a handful of places to overnight, and they all have different things to recommend them. The Monhegan House is just plain classic, the oldest continuously operated place on the island, dating back to the 1870s and with 33 rooms on its four floors. Everything about the boxy old inn is comfortable, from the long porch out front, topped with rockers, to the spare, quiet, breezy rooms. The floors creak underfoot, the bedspreads are the white nubby ones your grandmother used to use, and there are big leather chairs in the lobby for lounging. Some people are bothered by the fact that bathrooms are shared—all of the showers and toilets are grouped together on the second floor—but it is very clean and almost has a summer camp vibe, making it a fun adventure. Right near the center of the village, the porch has traditionally been a center of activity on the island, so spend any time on it and you'll quickly feel tuned in to local goings-on. Rates include breakfast. Open from mid-May to mid-October.

Trailing Yew $$
Lobster Cove Road, Monhegan Island
(207) 596–0440 or (800) 592–2520

If you had an eccentric grandmother with an island cottage, it might feel a bit like the nifty Trailing Yew. The simplest and least formal of all of the island's lodging options, the place is actually a compound of four weathered cottages clustered around a hilly courtyard. There are 35 rooms to choose from, and electricity is scarce. Baths are shared, and only some have electricity. Dining here is an experience, with meals served family style so that you're literally rubbing elbows with strangers. But everyone is having such a good time, it's a pleasure. Not fancy, this place, but fun. Don't forget your flashlight.

Spruce Head

Craignair Inn $–$$
Clark Island, Spruce Head
(207) 594–7644 or (800) 320–9997
www.craignair.com

In the 1920s, Clark Island was a bustling place with stonecutters carving granite out of the earth to be used in the Brooklyn Battery tunnel and the Library of Congress. This inn dates back to 1928, when it was built to house these quarry workers, and it became an inn in the 1940s. There are 21 guest rooms, some of which have private baths and most of which have jaw-dropping views of the island and the sea. People love to walk Clark Island, and there are trails all through it to explore. Check out the old quarries or hike to the far side where there are nice views out to the islands of Two Bush Channel. Open year-round.

Vinalhaven

Tidewater Motel $$
12 Main Street, Carvers Harbor, Vinalhaven
(207) 863–4618
www.tidewatermotel.com

You can certainly watch the tide if you stay at this thirtysomething Vinalhaven motel. Built in 1970 by the parents of current owner Phil Crossman, the place is just feet above the ocean. The rooms are typically "motelly" but have decks that extend right out over the water, and if you leave your windows open, you can let the ocean's swells sway you to sleep. You'll be awakened by the activity that keeps the working harbor alive, and you'll be able to see most of the goings-on right from your room. Some rooms have kitchens, all have cable TV and a private bath. The Tidewater is open year-round.

Rockland

Berry Manor Inn $$$$
81 Talbot Avenue, Rockland
(207) 596–7696 or (800) 774–5692
www.berrymanorinn.com

On a quiet residential side street, the Berry Manor Inn is one impressive place—it's one of the finest old homes in all of Rock City and arguably the place to stay. (The place is also the only historic inn in the Midcoast to receive a Four-Diamond rating from AAA and was called the "Outstanding Inn of the Northeast" by BedandBreakfast.com in 2005.) Built in 1898 as a giant Victorian wedding gift, the inn is quite luxurious by local standards, with a dozen large rooms split between the original home and the adjacent carriage house. All but one of the guest chambers has its own fireplace, each has a private bath, and they are furnished and decorated in grand style with all sorts of fancy flourishes like sleigh beds, four-posters, and antique rockers. But not at the expense of comfort: Owners Cheryl Michaelsen and Mike LaPosta, exactly the kind of B&B hosts you want, made sure to incorporate such contemporary necessities as stuffed chairs and cozy robes. Downtown Rockland and its great restaurants are only a few blocks away—but you might not want to ever leave your room. Great reduced rates in the off-season.

Captain Lindsey House Inn $$–$$$
5 Lindsey Street, Rockland
(207) 596–7950 or (800) 523–2145
www.rocklandmaine.com

The yellow brick Lindsey House was built in 1837 and sits just off Main Street within easy walking distance of most everything in the

Penobscot Bay city. The innkeepers also own the schooner *Stephen Taber* and the Water Works Pub, right next door, and they've turned this place into a nice, small downtown hotel. The nine rooms all have bright color schemes, air-conditioning, phones, TVs, private baths, and down comforters. Rates include breakfast.

Limerock Inn $$–$$$
96 Limerock Street, Rockland
(207) 594–2257 or (800) 546–3762
www.limerockinn.com
In a residential neighborhood within walking distance of downtown, the Limerock is a lime-colored Queen Anne mansion with eight very comfortable guest rooms inside. Each has a private bath, some have whirlpools, one has a fireplace. Guests are welcome to enjoy the formal parlor and the porch with its wicker chairs. Rates include a well-regarded breakfast. Be sure to visit the gardens.

Navigator Motor Inn $–$$
520 Main Street, Rockland
(207) 594–2131 or (800) 545–8026
www.navigatorinn.com
A Rockland mainstay for more than 30 years, the Navigator is just across the street from the Maine State Ferry Terminal. There are 86 rooms and suites inside, as well as bar that's a favorite watering hole among locals. Rooms are fairly standard motel fare, and many have a balcony and a fridge along with cable TV and private bath.

Old Granite Inn $$–$$$
546 Main Street, Rockland
(207) 594–9036 or (800) 386–9036
www.oldgraniteinn.com
This place is indeed old and made of granite, and it has been lending a bit of class to the north end of Rockland's Main Street since the mid-19th century. A Federal style building, it's made of stone quarried a few towns over in St. George, and it sits right across from the ferry terminal. There are eleven rooms, each with its own wallpaper pattern and private bath. Try room 4—and smell the roses.

Rockport

Samoset Resort $$–$$$$
220 Warrenton Street, Rockport
(207) 594–2511 or (800) 341–1650
www.samoset.com
The Samoset sprawls across 230 acres right on Rockland Harbor, and it features 178 guest rooms and suites. Each has a marble bath, big TV, Wi-Fi, coffeemaker, and balcony or terrace overlooking sea or the Samoset's golf course. As of 2006, these chambers were undergoing a $3-million makeover, including new moldings, fixtures, lighting, window treatments, and down bedding. A full-service place, the Samoset has a fitness center, two pools (one indoor, one outdoor), basketball and tennis courts, massage, a formal dining room, and a couple of less fancy options, the Breakwater Café and the Clubhouse Grille. You can sleep in and get breakfast delivered to your door if you like or have a candlelit dinner served on your terrace.

Camden

The Belmont $$–$$$
6 Belmont Street, Camden
(207) 236–8053 or (800) 238–8053
www.thebelmontinn.com
A charming Edwardian inn on a quiet side street in Camden, this place has been providing lodging since the 1920s. Its six guest rooms are just perfect, with nice amenities like gas stoves, window seats, and views of Mount Battie. Try the Jo Spiller room with its big mahogany sleigh bed and Oriental rug. Rates include a full breakfast.

Camden Harbour Inn $$$–$$$$
83 Bayview Street, Camden
(207) 236–4200 or (800) 236–4266
www.camdenharbourinn.com
Built in 1874, this big white inn commands one of the best views in town, set on a hill looking out across both the harbor and the mountains. There are 30 guest rooms here on three floors, and they're furnished with Victorian-era antiques. Many feature fireplaces, patios, or

decks, and all have private baths, TVs, phones, and dataports. The porch is instantly relaxing.

Country Inn $$$
Route 1, Camden
(207) 236–2725 or (888) 707–3945
www.countryinnmaine.com

The little things add up at the Country Inn. The staff is very accommodating for one, making sure everyone is comfortable, and the 47-unit inn has nice features like tea and cookies in the library in the afternoon. And the play area in the grass outback. And the private decks. And an Internet station. And nice group spaces for gatherings and get-togethers. The suites are well appointed, there's an indoor pool and fitness center, and downtown Camden is only a couple minutes up the road.

Hartstone Inn $$–$$$$
41 Elm Street, Camden
(207) 236–4259 or (800) 788–4823
www.hartstoneinn.com

The dining room here draws raves, and the same attention to detail that makes it exceptional goes into the rooms. Each of the guest quarters in the 1835 Mansard-style showplace is air-conditioned and furnished with heirlooms and antiques. Claw-foot tubs, down comforters, fresh flowers, and chocolate truffles all make it a step up from your average B&B. Breakfast is good, and the afternoon cookies are nice. Spring for a package that includes dinner. Open year-round.

Lord Camden Inn $$$–$$$$
24 Main Street, Camden
(207) 236–4325 or (800) 336–4325

This downtown favorite is a unique place with four floors of rooms upstairs above Main Street storefronts. It manages to do a nice job, though, of making people comfortable in nontraditional rooms among the hurly-burly. All rooms have air-conditioning, private baths, phones, and Wi-Fi, and several have big balconies. Whichever one you choose, you can give yourself an instant upgrade by laying down a bit more scratch for the "in-room

extras," which are gift baskets. (Wine and cheese, taste of Maine, and "ra-ra-romance" are the themes for the $65 goodies.) You can't get any closer to downtown.

Maine Stay $$–$$$
22 High Street, Camden
(207) 236–9636
www.mainestay.com
www.camdenmainestay.com

The Maine Stay has been the very definition of a bed-and-breakfast in Camden for years. The Greek Revival house is in relatively new hands now, but it remains a gem, the second oldest of all of the 66 homes in its National Register of Historic Places district. Built in 1802, the inn has eight bright and airy rooms, each with its own bath and decorating scheme. The Smith-Robson Room has an antique brass bed and was named in honor of the inn's previous owners, who became well known for their hospitality. The two acres of grounds, with their blooming gardens, are pleasant to wander, and it's an easy walk into town. You'd have a hard time finding a better B&B for miles.

Norumbega Inn $$$–$$$$
63 High Street, Camden
(207) 236–4646
www.norumbegainn.com

Europeans traveled up the Penobscot River in the 16th century looking for the mythical city of Norumbega, a place of gold and luxury. Today travelers drive up Route 1 along Penobscot Bay to lay their heads at Norumbega, where they'll certainly pay a lot. The original owner of this big stone showplace traveled throughout Europe researching castle design, and he incorporated his favorite elements. There's no question that the 1886 inn is striking and beautiful, but its 12 rooms and suites are awfully expensive for what you get. Still, it's pleasant just to get inside this landmark to see the fancy design. Guest quarters have private baths, TVs, phones, and dataports, and they come furnished with antiques. A full breakfast is included in the price of the room.

Whitehall Inn $$–$$$
52 High Street, Camden
(207) 236–3391 or (800) 789–6565
www.whitehall-inn.com

The classic old Whitehall has gotten a lot of mileage out of the fact that Edna St. Vincent Millay got her start here, reading her famous poem "Renascence" to appreciative guests. That's all very nice, but there's plenty more to like about the inn, which dates back to 1834. Start with the porch, a graceful veranda topped by rockers. Then there are the dining room, which is an underappreciated treat, and the rooms, which are simple in the best, most relaxing way. No noise, no TVs, no ringing phones, just peaceful and pleasant spaces with antiques, grandfather clocks, and lace curtains that dance with the afternoon sea breeze. Some rooms have shared or "hall" baths. Make sure you get what you want. Tariffs—and they're tariffs here, not rates, mind you—are fairly reasonable.

Lincolnville

Cedarholm Garden Bay Inn $$$–$$$$
Route 1, Lincolnville
(207) 236–3886 or (800) 361–3886
www.cedarholm.com

There are a lot of cottage villages along the coast, and this is the cottage villager's cottage village. No pine-paneled roughing it here— these are fairly luxurious little affairs with whirlpools, tile showers, stone fireplaces, waterside desks, and wet bars. A romantic little byway takes you from Route 1 down to shore, and the gardens on the 16-acre property are something to see. For privacy, views, and uniqueness, you can't beat these cute cottages, and they've won accolades from the national media again and again.

Spouter Inn $$–$$$
Route 1, Lincolnville
(207) 789–5171 or (866) 787–5171
www.spouterinn.com

Built in 1892, this expansive inn has been lovingly restored. Across the street from Lincolnville Beach and Penobscot Bay, it has five rooms, each of which provides a good look at the water. They're well appointed and spotless, and each has a private bath. Some have fireplaces, and the Captain's Quarters has a Jacuzzi, too. Very pleasant, and all of the restaurants and shops of Lincolnville—and the Islesboro ferry—are handy by. Fantastic bargain for the quality and location.

Islesboro

Dark Harbor House $$–$$$$
Islesboro
(207) 734–6669
www.darkharborhouse.com

On the island of Islesboro, Dark Harbor is another one of those exclusive enclaves where you'd better be old money and old family or you might as well leave—which is what makes the Dark Harbor House a treat. You can pretend to be these things and enjoy the same beautiful sights and experiences as the wealthy summercators who have been coming here for close to a century. The Georgian Revival stunner was built in 1896 for a Philadelphia banker, and it's supremely tasteful. There are 11 guest rooms, each with private bath and heat or air-conditioning. Some have fireplaces, some porches, balconies, or private gardens. All are picture-perfect, like walking into a magazine photograph.

Belfast and Surrounding Area

Harbor View House $$
213 High Street, Belfast
(207) 338–3811 or (877) 393–3811
www.harborviewhouse.com

Formerly the site of one of Belfast's better galleries, this antique Federal sits high atop Primrose Hill with views out toward Belfast Bay. Renovated with utmost care, the inn has pumpkin pine floors, pretty fanlights, 10-foot ceilings, and six quiet guest rooms with fireplaces, private baths, and down comforters. Guests are welcome to use the back deck with its glorious prospect, and should they be feeling stressed out, they can arrange to get a massage from innkeeper Trish Jakielski, a professional masseuse. (Which makes one think maybe all innkeepers should be required to be a little more hands-on.) Downtown Belfast is just down the hill.

The White House $$–$$$
1 Church Street, Belfast
(207) 338–1901 or (888) 290–1901
www.mainebb.com

It would be understandable if this Greek Revival mansion were so named simply because it's white and undeniably imposing. But it's actually the James P. White House, and takes its title from the man who built it more than a century and a half ago. A Belfast landmark that everyone who passes by wonders at, it's just as impressive on the inside, with marble fireplaces and ornate molding. Rooms have private baths and phones. The inn has bikes to tour beautiful Belfast and can even pack you a box lunch for a picnic in town.

Homeport Inn $–$$
East Main Street (Route 1), Searsport
(207) 548–2259 or (800) 742–5814

This is one of the old sea captains' homes that catches everyone's eye as they motor up Route 1 through Searsport. It was built shortly before the Civil War and has nice acreage sloping down to Penobscot Bay. A widow's walk sits atop the house, and there are 10 rooms inside, some with private baths, others shared. Fresh flowers, down comforters, and fancy toiletries greet guests. The inn also maintains cottages right on the water that are perfect for longer stays. *Victorian Homes* magazine gave the place the nod, which tells you a lot right there.

Other Belfast Accommodations

The **Belfast Harbor Inn** (91 Searsport Avenue; 207–338–2740 or 800–545–8576; www.belfastharborinn.com) is a modern motel on six oceanfront acres in East Belfast. The **Alden House** (63 Church Street; 207–338–2151 or 877–337–8151; www.thealden house.com) is an 1840 brick mansion with seven B&B rooms not far from downtown.

Castine

Castine Harbor Lodge $–$$$$
147 Perkins Street, Castine
(207) 326–4335
www.castinemaine.com

Castine has a lot of nice lodging options, but it doesn't have any hotels on the water—except this one. A rambling 1893 cottage, the inn has a turret, magnificent Penobscot Bay views, and 250 feet of porch to enjoy them on. There are 16 guest rooms, and they all have water views, antique beds, and couches and sitting areas.

Castine Inn $$–$$$$
Main Street, Castine
(207) 326–4365
www.castineinn.com

Gardens and water views are two of the attractions at this 1898 inn a block from the harbor. There are 17 guest rooms inside the big old place, on the second and third floors. Each has a private bath and is simply furnished. Many have views of Penobscot Bay or the inn's own gardens. Pretty porches out front. And the dining room is one of the best in Castine. Breakfast is included in the price of the room. Open from May through October.

Pentagoet Inn $–$$$
26 Main Street, Castine
(207) 326–8616 or (800) 845–1701
www.pentagoet.com

Castine's oldest summer hotel, built in 1894, the Pentagoet is a gracious place, with its turret, window box, and bunting. The 1894 Queen Anne–style mansion has 16 rooms inside, each with nicely aged furnishings, vintage lithographs, and a private bath. Dining here is good as well. Rates include breakfast and use of the inn's bikes to see what there is to see in this historic town.

Deer Isle–Stonington

Pilgrim's Inn $$–$$$
Main Street, Deer Isle
(207) 348–6615 or (888) 778–7505
www.pilgrimsinn.com

A gambrel-roofed barn of a place centrally located in Deer Isle village, this 1793 inn is on the National Register. Rooms are comfortable and commodious, and they offer water views, private baths, and their own sitting areas. Each has a different decor scheme, but they typically have Oriental or braided rugs and pretty, old antique beds, and Deer Isle granite, of course. The inn also has three two-bedroom cottages with kitchenettes and private decks. The inn's dining room is top-shelf. Open mid-May through mid-October.

Goose Cove Lodge $$–$$$
Goose Cove Road, Sunset
(207) 348–2508 or (800) 728–1963
www.goosecovelodge.com

How do we love Goose Cove Lodge? Let us count the ways. On Goose Cove near Stonington, the lodge sits on 22 stupendously beautiful acres of woods and waterfront, and it has a real natural bent. Guided nature walks, mountain biking, kayaking, stargazing parties, bird-watching, and more are an everyday part of life here. The lodge is a neat old rustic place with a huge fieldstone fireplace and wood paneling everywhere, and there are 21 guest accommodations, from cottages to suites to rooms. The cottages are exceptional, with fireplaces, decks overlooking the cove, kitchenettes, and private baths. Any nature lover who's come to visit Maine and is in need of a room would be foolish not to hole up here.

Boyce's Motel $–$$
Main Street, Stonington
(207) 367–2421 or (800) 224–2421
www.boycesmotel.com

Comfortable rooms with access to a deck overlooking Stonington Harbor are offered at this circa 1960s motel. Guest quarters are equipped with cable TV, fridges, phones, air-conditioning, and in-room coffee, and all have private baths. Some even have kitchenettes and private decks, and there are apartments available as well with fine views of one of Maine's most picturesque harbors. Everything in town is within walking distance. No matter where you stay, you can use the motel's sun-

deck and stare at the harbor to your heart's content—and that alone is worth the price of admission. Rates are eminently reasonable.

Inn on the Harbor $$–$$$
Main Street, Stonington
(207) 367–2420 or (800) 942–2420
www.innontheharbor.com

The name says it all at this attractive downtown hostelry—it's on the harbor to such a degree that the water actually passes under some rooms. Long known as the Captain's Quarters, the inn was purchased and revamped in the 1990s, and it's now a very pleasant place to stay on Deer Isle Thorofare. More of a compound than anything else, the place is made of a few buildings from the 1880s—a mansard-roofed classic with a few adjacent storefronts—joined by walkways and decks. There are 13 rooms in all, 10 of which face the waterfront, with its working boats and all its islands, and many have private entrances. Named after vessels in the state's windjammer fleet (the Mary Day, for example, which has overstuffed chairs, a king-size bed, and a large bath), these quarters are comfortable and homey without a lot of froufrou, and there are a lot of thoughtful touches, from binoculars with which to watch the activities in the harbor to fresh flowers. A breakfast of fruit and muffins comes with the room fee.

The Keeper's House Inn $$$$
Robinson Point Lighthouse Station, Isle au Haut
(207) 460–0257
www.keepershouse.com

The Keeper's House is truly one of a kind, an inn in an old light station on a stunning peninsula on as beautiful an island as you'll find. Hosts Jeff and Judi Burke have transformed the place into a romantic hideaway with instant appeal to lighthouse fans, nature lovers, Acadia National Park explorers (the Isle au Haut section of the park is just down the road), and anyone else who would enjoy a few nights at a fine island inn with truly extraordinary sea views. The inn doesn't have all-the-time power, which means each of the four rooms is lit by gas lights, candles, and kerosene lanterns, and each of these simply furnished guest quarters has a sensational view. If it's available opt for the Oil House, a small cottage right on the water with its own private deck and outdoor shower. The menu is so good it's been featured in *Gourmet* magazine. The rooms are pricey, but the enchanting experience is worth it.

Trenton

Sunrise Motor Inn $
952 Bar Harbor Road, Trenton
(207) 667–8452
www.sunrisemotorinn.com
Views of the mountains of Acadia, a heated outdoor pool, and a room with air-conditioning, cable TV, phone, private bath, and coffeemaker—for $80 or less, even in high season? That's what the Sunrise offers. The rooms are no great shakes, but they'll sleep you for the night at a rate that will allow you to stay in the area twice as long as you might if you picked a Bar Harbor room. It's typical motel fare but at an untypical price point.

ACADIA AREA
Bar Harbor and Surrounding Area

Balance Rock Inn $
21 Albert Meadow, Bar Harbor
(207) 288–2610 or (800) 753–0494
www.barharborvacations.com
Few hostelries survived the great fire of 1947, which swept through Bar Harbor, leveling everything in its path. This is why the Balance Rock Inn is such a pleasure. Built in 1903 by a Scottish rail baron, the century-old place continues the area's genteel tradition. You might even feel like a rusticator. An easy walk to town, the shingle-style manse has a country-estate feel, with pretty lawns, privacy, and quietude. The Shore Path, a spectacular seaside footpath, curls around the grounds. Frenchman Bay seems out every window. The rooms are comfortable and, while decorated with

reproduction wallpaper and furnishings, they have the amenities of today with private baths, decks, whirlpools, and phones.

Bar Harbor Inn $$$–$$$$
Newport Drive, Bar Harbor
(207) 288–3351 or (800) 248–3351
www.barharborinn.com
It would be hard for the Bar Harbor Inn to get much closer to the harbor without falling in. The eight-acre compound is right on Frenchman Bay, and many of its rooms have balconies with a real good look at it. Because the inn is so huge, with more than 150 units in three buildings, there are a wide variety of rooms to choose from. But all have, at the very least, air-conditioning, free HBO, and Wi-Fi. They're comfortable enough without being posh.

Ledgelawn $$–$$$$
66 Mount Desert Street, Bar Harbor
(207) 288–4596 or (800) 274–5334
www.ledgelawninn.com
One of Bar Harbor's last summer cottages (the others burned), this turn-of-the-20th-century, red-shingled house has 23 rooms inside its main section and another 2 in an added carriage house. All rooms have private baths (some with whirlpools), some have saunas, and many have fireplaces. Open mid-May through October.

Mira Monte Inn $$$–$$$$
69 Mount Desert Street, Bar Harbor
(207) 288–4263 or (800) 553–5109
www.miramonte.com
The 13 rooms at this 1864 estate may have a bit much froufrou, but the gardens are pretty amazing and have been featured on Home and Garden TV and in national magazines. Make sure you get out into them. Room rates on the high end of the range are for those chambers with whirlpools, fireplaces, and private decks. The breakfast, served from 8:00 to 10:00 A.M., seems unending.

The Tides $$$$
119 West Street, Bar Harbor
(207) 288–4968
www.barharbortides.com

There are only three suites and one room in this 1887 Greek Revival home, but that allows for a lot of attention to detail. Every unit has a fantastic view of the bay, private bath, fireplace, and even a formal parlor. With tiled baths, damask sofas, and French sitting chairs, the Tide has many amenities for a small inn. With your back to the inn, looking out at Frenchman Bay across its acre and a half of lawn, it's easy to forget you're right downtown.

Ullikana Bed and Breakfast $$$–$$$$
16 The Field, Bar Harbor
(207) 288–9552
www.ullikana.com

Bed and Breakfast and Country Inns of New England, a popular guidebook, calls this quiet inn "one of the secret treasures of Bar Harbor," and it's right. The 27-room hostelry provides guests with the best of two worlds. On the one hand, it is out of the way and a tad hard to find, giving it a quietude and serenity uncommon in the hurly-burly of Bar Harbor. On the other hand, it is only a few hundred yards from the point where Cottage and Main Streets meet—in other words, the epicenter of downtown. How can that be? The inn is buffered by the huge Field, a broad meadow not too far from Frenchman Bay that wraps around Ullikana, so the location is truly remarkable. And so are hosts Helene Harton and Roy Kasindorf, who know just how to be helpful and available without being the kind of on-top-of-you-all-the-time innkeepers that get annoying. They bought the 1885 Tudor-style cottage, said to be the first cottage in town, in 1990 and have made the rooms very comfortable with touches old and new. Several have fireplaces and/or private porches, all have private baths, and the breakfasts that Harton cooks are exquisite. (They might include chocolate crepes with ricotta cheese or lemon soufflé pancakes.) The couple later added six more rooms in the neighboring Yellow House, beginning an empire. It's hard to find a better place to stay in Bar Harbor, which is saying a lot.

Otter Creek Inn $–$$
Route 3, Otter Creek
(207) 288–5151 or (800) 845–5852
www.ottercreekme.com

If you stay here, you want one of the housekeeping cabins. It's not that there's anything wrong with the rooms in the inn, it's just that the cabins are such fun tiny cottages. They each have a bedroom, private bath, and a kitchen/living area. All of the units here—cabin or inn—have private bath, fridge, cable TV including HBO, and access to laundry and picnicking facilities. The rates include breakfast. Otter Creek is perfectly located for explorations of Mount Desert, surrounded by Acadia but away from the madness of Bar Harbor. An added benefit is proximity to Otter Creek Market, owned by the same folks, which is a neat little grocery where you'll find everything you forgot to bring.

Other Accommodations in Bar Harbor

Bar Harbor Regency Hotel (123 Eden Street; 800–23–MOTEL; www.barharbor regency.com) is a big corporate resort with its own marina. **Manor House Inn** (106 West Street; 207–288–3759 or 800–437–0088; www.barharbormanorhouse.com) is an 1887 manse within easy walking distance of Bar Island. The **Primrose** (73 Mount Desert Street; 207–288–4031; www.primroseinn.com) is a 10-room inn where you can bring your pooch.

Northeast Harbor

Asticou Inn $$$–$$$$
Route 3, Northeast Harbor
(207) 276–3344 or (800) 258–3373
www.asticou.com

Living is good at the Asticou, a turn-of-the-20th-century inn overlooking Great Harbor in tony Northeast. The 47 rooms and suites all have private baths, but they don't make too many concessions to the times. Most are cozy and bright, with nice views and relatively straightforward furnishings, comfortably old-fashioned. Some adjacent spots are ideal for families. Many rooms are booked long in advance by the same people using them now. Asticou is famous for its azalea gardens, so make it a point to wander through them. The inn also has clay tennis courts, a heated outdoor pool, and easy access to Acadia—trails head into the park from right across the street. Service is a hallmark, of course.

Harbourside Inn $$–$$$$
Northeast Harbor
(207) 276–3272
www.harboursideinn.com
A short walk from downtown Northeast, this 1888 shingle-style cottage is set against a woody hillside and isn't really on the harbor, but you can see it through the trees. There are 11 guest rooms and three suites spread across three floors here. Though they retain a simple, venerable style, the rooms have private baths, and some have working fireplaces and even kitchenettes. Breakfast is taken on the bright and airy wood-paneled porch—all floor-to-ceiling windows and wicker—every day between 8:30 and 9:30 A.M.

Southwest Harbor

Captain Bennett House $–$$
385 Main Street, Southwest Harbor
(207) 244–9627 or (800) 743–9627
www.captainbennett.com
The five rooms here are more comfortable than those in your average bed-and-breakfast and they are kept "shipshape." (Lots of nautical terms and touches here.) Rooms in the old inn are air-conditioned, have private baths, and have reading lamps, a nice feature that so many places overlook. Look for the white picket fence as you drive through town.

The Claremont Hotel $$$–$$$$
Claremont Road, Southwest Harbor
(207) 244–5036 or (800) 244–5036
www.theclaremonthotel.com

The rambling old Claremont offers accommodations in the grand hotel style of Maine summers past—not fancy, mind you, but classic, tasteful, simple. Amenities are plentiful for an old-fashioned place, and they tend toward the old-fashioned as well—clay tennis courts, croquet courts (this place is famous for its croquet tournaments), bikes, rowboats, library, concerts, lectures, and afternoon tea. A favorite are simply the Adirondack chairs lined up on the grounds with a fantastic Southwest Harbor panorama spread before them. The 24 rooms in the main hotel have recently been renovated and they are comfortable but spare, and the Phillips House has six more, two with fireplaces. And then there are 14 cottages of varying styles and degrees of luxury, from split log to contemporary, which all have fireplaces and living rooms. Dining is in the Boathouse in the summer. If you want to relax, this gracious old inn is the place. Open from late May to late October.

Clark Point Inn $$–$$$
109 Clark Point Road, Southwest Harbor
(207) 244–9828 or (888) 775–5953
www.clarkpointinn.com
Three stories of 1883 colonial charm are to be found at this old inn across from the town dock. The three rooms are all decorated to a theme—maritime, Venice—and have water views, private baths, queen-size beds, cable TV, and phones. There are also two third-floor suites with living rooms and fireplaces. Make sure to spend some time with Alfie, the resident cat.

Inn at Southwest $$–$$$
371 Main Street, Southwest Harbor
(207) 244–3835
www.innatsouthwest.com
An extraordinary 1884 Victorian overlooking Southwest Harbor, this seven-room inn is very tastefully appointed with nice touches like sleigh beds, four-posters, wrought iron beds, down comforters, sitting rooms, and gas stoves. Some have a bit of a water view, and all have private baths. Breakfasts are served

on the wraparound porch or patio in nice weather; they're highly regarded and might include cheesecake crepes, rhubarb crunch, or Belgian waffles with raspberries.

Seawall Motel and Restaurant $-$$
Route 102A, Southwest Harbor
(207) 244–9250 or (800) 248–9250
www.seawallmotel.com

No doubt what the principal attraction is here—the famous seawall of Southwest Harbor, an expanse of rocky shore that seems to be holding back all of the Atlantic when the waves hit hard. It's right across the street from this motel complex, and the lagoon created by the wall is adjacent, with all its birdlife. Eagles, seals, muskrats, and a range of ducks and other shorebirds are commonly spotted, and Acadia wraps around the back of the motel. Rooms are simple motel units, clean and smoke-free, with phones and Wi-Fi. The room rate includes the continental breakfast. You can hop on the Island Explorer shuttle right here and enjoy everything on the island without having to worry about driving and traffic. Open year-round. Rates are reasonable in summer and a real bargain in the off-season—which might be as early as the end of June.

Other Accommodations in Southwest Harbor

The **Birches Bed and Breakfast** (Fernald Point Road; 207–244–5182; www.thebirches bnb.com) is a pleasant B&B on five acres just 350 feet from the golf course. The **Yellow Aster** (53 Clark Point Road; 207–244–4422 or 800–724–7228; www.yellowaster.com) has four rooms and organic breakfasts. The **Moorings Inn** (P.O. Box 744, Southwest Harbor 04679; 207–244–5523 or 800–596–5523; www.mooringsinn.com) has 11 rooms in the inn and 9 more in nearby cottages, and it's famous for its views.

DOWN EAST
Hancock

Crocker House $$-$$$
967 Point Road, Hancock Point
(207) 422–6806 or (877) 715–6017
www.crockerhouse.com

Built in 1884 as part of one of the great hotels that catered to vacationers at the turn of the 20th century, the inn has been thoughtfully restored over the years, and it's quite comfortable in a country sort of way, with quilts, and antiques, and private baths. There are 11 guest rooms in its three stories, each of which has been newly redone, and common areas for hanging out. Dinner here is an event (not included in room rate), with the public flocking in, but Sunday brunch is the real treat. Don't miss it.

LeDomaine $$$$
Hancock
(207) 422–3395 or (800) 554–8498
www.ledomaine.com

It's still hard to fathom this place—so good yet seemingly so far from everything. The dining room at LeDomaine has people driving in from miles around, but the three rooms and three suites are worth the trip beyond Ellsworth as well. They, too, bear the hallmarks of innkeeper Nicole Purslow's French upbringing (she grew up here, but her mother was from France). The rooms have a Provencal touch to them with select furnishings and fabrics, and they have all the niceties, down to the heated towel racks and plush robes. Rates include breakfast. You'd be remiss if you didn't spring for dinner as well.

Winter Harbor

Main Stay Cottages $-$$
66 Sargent Street, Winter Harbor
(207) 963–2601

On the way down to the Schoodic section of Acadia, these five cottages each offer guests a different experience. The 150-year-old Boathouse, for example, is one of the original structures in Winter Harbor, a small, weathered gray building on pilings right over the water. It offers views of Mark Island Light from the deck and a queen bed, kitchenette, and gas fireplace to keep you cozy inside. Ledgelawn Cottage is a more contemporary option, about 20 feet from the water, with one bedroom, a living room/kitchenette, and water views. For the best experience, though, reserve the Molasses Pond Cottage, which is down the road in Eastbrook, right on the water with its own private beach. It features two small bedrooms, a kitchenette, and endless entertainment in the Down East woods.

Milbridge

Guagus River Inn $–$$
376 Kansas Road, Milbridge
(207) 546–9737
www.guagusriverinn.com
This thoroughly modern, six-room inn sits on 14 acres on the Narraguagus River in Milbridge. The guest rooms are decorated in a woodsy theme—named after Maine wildlife—and they are comfortable if not spectacular. The indoor lap pool, however, is very nice, as is the Jacuzzi in the Moose Room. The room with the Jacuzzi requires a two-night minimum stay.

Addison

Pleasant Bay Bed and Breakfast $
West Side Road, Addison
(207) 483–4490
www.pleasantbay.com
A working llama farm, this three-room, one-suite inn is a real charmer, overlooking the very pleasant Pleasant River in the tiny village of Addison. Owned by Leon and Joan Yeaton, the home sits on 110 acres of waterfront, and there are nice trails that skirt the bay. The rooms are nicely laid out with views and with hope chests, quilts, and rocking chairs, and the suite has a kitchenette. The porch is set before some nice vistas of the tidal river, and there's a fireplace inside to take the chill out of the late summer air. The Yeatons are quite familiar with the area and can give you good tips on exploring, from Moosehorn National Wildlife Refuge to Campobello, and they wel-come you to even help out with the llamas if you like. And the river is right there, just waiting for your canoe or kayak. *Homey* is the word.

Machiasport

Micmac Farm $
Route 92, Machiasport
(207) 255–3008
www.micmacfarm.com
Micmac Farm is better known as a restaurant than as a place to stay, but that may change once people spend a night in one of the three guest cabins behind the farm. Set in a forest overlooking the Machias River, these camps are straightforward affairs, with board and batten siding, pine-paneled interiors, two double beds, and a kitchenette. Sliding glass doors allow you to step out onto the back deck to enjoy the views of the river, and there are paths through the grass down to the water. The accommodations tend toward the inexpensive side, and they're a great bargain for it.

Eastport and Surrounding Area

Kilby House Inn $
122 Water Street, Eastport
(207) 853–0989 or (800) 853–4557
www.kilbyhouseinn.com
A nicely restored Queen Anne, the Kilby House has five pleasant bedrooms inside. Each has its own unique style and is furnished with antiques and heirlooms, some of which are from the Kilby family who originally lived here. Some have water views, and downtown Eastport is within walking distance. Breakfast is "full," all right.

Motel East $–$$
23A Water Street, Eastport
(207) 853–4747
Sitting just up the road from the downtown, Motel East has the blue expanse of Passamaquoddy Bay as its backyard, and it makes good use of it with broad picture windows in each room. Motel fare, but with an inspired vista, Wi-Fi, and easy access to all that Eastport has to offer.

Home Port Inn $–$$
45 Main Street, Lubec
(207) 733–2077 or (800) 457–2077
One of the bright spots on Lubec's down-at-the-heels Main Street, this 1880s bed-and-breakfast has seven rooms, each with a private bath. Several overlook Cobscook Bay and Eastport across the way. Some have four-posters and antiques, others handpainted tiles and sitting chairs. Very pleasant, and the dining room here is recommended as well.

CAMPING

There's nothing quite like sleeping under the stars when you're in Maine. The state is, of course, famous for its fresh air, natural beauty, and piney woods, and sleeping in a tent allows you to get away from the hustle and bustle and enjoy the "real Maine" at its most real. Literally hundreds and hundreds of campgrounds are spread across the state—from the truly primitive to the RV park—and there are just too many to list here. What follows are the best of the private camping areas. You'll find the state parks listed in the Green Space chapter.

The Maine Campground Owners Association publishes a 100-page directory—the Maine Camping Guide—on an annual basis, and it's a very useful resource for finding and comparing new campgrounds. Get your copy at a chamber of commerce, state visitor center, or by calling (207) 782–5874. Or visit the Web site www.campmaine.com.

South Coast

Recompence Shores
Freeport
(207) 865–4469
www.freeportcamping.com
If you run into a problem with your gear while tenting at this seaside park, you can just zip up the road to L. L. Bean. These 100 tent sites astride Casco Bay are only a few minutes from the giant outfitter, down a quiet peninsula near Wolfe's Neck State Park. Run by Wolfe's Neck Farm, an agricultural operation known for its beef and environmental consciousness,

---

i The state of Maine has a very useful Web site for making campground reservations. You can find all the information you need on camping in the state parks—from maps, rules, and fees to general visiting information—at www.campwithme.com.

---

the campground is one of the best in southern Maine and certainly the best in Greater Freeport. A network of trails makes for good hiking, too.

Midcoast

Hermit Island
Phippsburg
(207) 443–2101
www.hermitisland.com
Hermit Island is a Maine classic, one of those places where you have to work to get a site, because so many people begin planning their trip for the next year before they've even gone home. Right on Small Point Harbor in Phippsburg, the campground is an oceanfront resort of sorts and it offers some of the best oceanfront camping in the state. It's been there for decades. A total of 275 sites occupy the 255-acre island; they're spaced for privacy and set up to accommodate tents, small pop-up trailers, and pickup campers but not RVs. Many are just steps from the ocean, others are in spruce or birch groves, and some face the camping area's harbor. All are a pretty easy walk to white-sand swimming beaches. Amenities here include a camp grocery (yes, fresh lobster), boat rentals and launching sites, pay phones, drinking water, and warm showers. The campground is quite the village in mid-summer, with teens doing their mating dance, families having reunions, and anglers spinning their reels, but it is big enough that you can get away from it all if you want. The most obvious appeal of Hermit Island is for beach lovers—the island's own or Popham, just a few miles down the road—but kayakers, sailors, and hikers enjoy stays here, too. Look into reservations sooner than later.

Medomak Family Camp
178 Liberty Road, Washington
(207) 845–6001 www.medomakcamp.com
Don't you wish you could still go to summer camp, maybe bring the whole family this time? At this fine camp in the inland town of Washington (30 minutes from Rockland), hard by the shore of Washington Pond, you can. The motto here is "relive the best summer of your life," and it certainly gets you started with many of the hallmarks you remember from your summer camp days. There's the cabins, the meals in the lodge, swimming in the lake, arts, crafts, canoeing, fishing, games, new friends—everything you'd find at a traditional summer camp; you just don't have to be 12 to enjoy it. (Oh, and there's lobster dinner once a week.) You might be too old to sneak over to the girls' camp, though. Sessions run for a week at a time from the end of June through mid-August. Call or check the Web for this year's dates.

Acadia Area

Mount Desert Campground
516 Sound Drive, Somesville
(207) 244–3710
www.mountdesertcampground.com
Sitting right at the end of Some Sound, the only fjord for miles, suffice it to say, this quiet campground has a rather ideal location. And it has built up a loyal clientele with its policies of serenity and for limiting the size of hulking RVs. Tenters particularly are drawn to the spot, though motor homes of 20 feet or less are welcome, too, but it isn't any sort of wilderness. Electric hookups, showers, and a store known for its muffins and ice cream are all available. Many of the campground's sites are right on the sound, and boat launching ramps make it easy to jump in, an attractive feature for kayakers.

Down East

Ocean Wood
Birch Harbor
(207) 963–7194
Owner Michael Brunton hasn't done much advertising for this extraordinary seaside camping area, mostly because he wants to keep it a quiet, special place. And quiet and special it is. Run primarily as a nature preserve, the 70-site campground wraps around a peninsula that pokes into the cold Atlantic Down East, and there is plenty of space between sites, making it serene and cozy. Brunton doesn't allow radios or partying, and there are a bunch of sites that are walk-in only, which further removes you from the noise. Many bivouacs are right smack on the shore, and there's a large seawall of a beach for enjoying by those on an inland spot. Perhaps best of all, the sights of the Schoodic Peninsula are less than 5 miles away. It's truly a remarkable campground. So don't tell anyone about it; just call for reservations.

RESTAURANTS

Yes, we have lobster. Everyone knows that, and probably two-thirds of the state's visitors indulge in a little red crustacean when they're vacationing on the Maine coast. The Pine Tree State also boasts a lot of other homegrown delicacies, though, from blueberries to potatoes, and it's home to a wide variety of restaurants, from the eclectic to the ethnic to the family style. Some cosmopolitan types from away, in fact, are surprised by both the quantity and quality of fine restaurants that can be found here. You won't go hungry traveling up Route 1, that's for sure.

The best places to go looking for a great meal are Greater Portland and the resort communities. In the late 1990s, Portlanders claimed that they had more restaurants to choose from—per capita—than any other city outside of San Francisco. Whether or not that is the case, it might as well be, and it seems that since then things have just gotten better with more and more eateries opening up. The state's largest city is a foodie's paradise, with a dizzying array of great places, from the hip and of the moment to the tried-and-true.

The resort communities tend to be a little more straightforward—more seafood, less inventive, fewer ethnic options—but that's not always the case. There's great Japanese food to be had in Camden and Rockland (thanks to Oh! Bento), and Kennebunkport's Hurricane is nothing if not creative. The same is true in Bar Harbor at George's.

Maine chefs have access to great raw ingredients—in the form of locally grown produce and the freshest of seafood—and the best of them put it to excellent use. Look around, and you won't be disappointed.

Price Code

Except where noted, prices represent the cost of a single adult dinner entree, not including tax or tip, and are intended to convey a general idea of how expensive the restaurant may be. Total cost will vary depending on type and quantity of additional food and beverages ordered, such as appetizers, desserts, coffee, or wine. Lunches are usually cheaper than dinners. The prices at many seafood restaurants fluctuate greatly due to changes in the market.

$. . . . . $9.99 or less
$$ . . . . $10.00 to $15.99
$$$ . . . . $16.00 to $24.99
$$$$ . . . . $25.00 or more

SOUTH COAST
Kittery and Surrounding Area

Bob's Clam Hut $$
315 Route 1, Kittery
(207) 439–4233
www.bobsclamhut.com
Founded in 1956 by Bob Kraft, Bob's Clam Hut has been steaming clams for generations of southern Mainers. The tasty little bivalves are the staple here and are served every which way, but people come for a host of other seafood treats, from scallops to shrimp to oysters to calamari. If it's edible and from the sea, you'll find it here at prices that are easy to take. Used to be Bob's was just a hut, now it's a sit-down eatery as well. Good stuff.

Chauncey Creek Lobster Pier $–$$$
16 Chauncey Creek Road, Kittery Point
(207) 439–1030
www.chaunceycreek.com
The creek and the pier make the beautiful backdrop for shore dinners at this classic Maine lobster house. You can select a "bug" from the tank, sit back and enjoy the views of the saltwater river while it boils, and then make a mess. They may call it lobster in the rough,

but it's not too hard to take. Steamers are excellent as well, and you can even get raw oysters if that's your thing. Open May through September from 11:00 A.M. to 7:00 P.M.

Other Dining Options in Kittery

Cap'n Simeon's Galley (Route 103, Pepperrell Cove; 207–439–3655; www.capn simeons.com) and **Warren's Lobster House** (1 Water Street; 207–439–1630; www.lobster house.com) are both very popular for seafood.

The Yorks

Flo's Steamed Dogs $
Route 1, York
www.floshotdogs.com
Expect to wait in line at Flo's, which has been pulling in the crowds since it opened in 1947. Open only from 11:00 A.M. to 3:00 P.M., the York institution has six stools that fill up fast and a secret hot sauce that keeps people coming back. Hot dogs, chips, soda, and milk— that's all Flo wrote. Closed Wednesday. (Flo's has since expanded into new locations—198 Post Road in Moody and at the Kittery Trading Post, and their secret sauce is now available at retail locations across southern Maine.)

York Harbor Inn $$$–$$$$
Route 1A, York Harbor
(800) 343–3869
www.yorkharborinn.com
One of the best inns in the Yorks serves one of the finest meals around as well. *Food and Wine* magazine gave the dining room here the nod, and locals have always liked its creative uses of local seafood. Lobster lovers will want to try the Yorkshire Lobster Supreme (lobster stuffed with scallops and shrimp with thermidor-style sauce), the lobster-stuffed breast of chicken, or the ravioli and lobsters. Others might like the roast rack of lamb, the filet mignon, or the vegetable melange. Service is generally very good. Brunch is a favorite on Sundays, and reservations are always wise. Open nightly for dinner from 5:30 to 9:30 P.M. and from 9:30 A.M. to 2:30 P.M. for Sunday brunch.

Windbreakers/Mimmo's Restaurant $$–$$$
243 Long Sands Road, York Beach
(207) 363–3807
Traditional Italian fare served with fun flair is what you'll find at this York Beach favorite. Right in the hurly-burly of the summer community, it's a family style place, and Chef Mimmo Basileo is a character. Kids will like the plain old spaghetti, Mom and Dad might try something more adventurous, like the calamari. The place hops, so a reservation is a good idea. Open daily for dinner from 5:00 to 10:00 P.M.

Cape Neddick Lobster Pound $$–$$$
Harborside Restaurant
Shore Road, Cape Neddick
(207) 363–5471
www.capeneddick.com
Like the best of the state's lobster pounds, Cape Neddick has a deck where you can sit and watch the action in the harbor as you tear apart your crustacean. The dining area inside is open and bright from big windows that shine over the simple wooden tables, and there's a bar where the locals like to gather. Fare is a tad broader than you might expect from a pound, with the lobsters, of course, but also with small-plate items like smoked Maine shrimp ravioli, scallops wrapped in applesmoked bacon, and fried calamari. Seafood is obviously the draw, but there are grilled options, too, in the form of steak and chicken. You can't beat the view.

Clay Hill Farm $$$
220 Clay Hill Road, Cape Neddick
(207) 361–2272
www.clayhillfarm.com
Leave time for wandering the grounds when you visit Clay Hill Farm. The restaurant sits on 30 acres, and it is the only restaurant in the country (so it says) to be certified by the National Wildlife Association as wildlife habitat. Chef Melissa Ettinger calls her cuisine "New American" or "American Fusion," both of which seem about right. Entrees might include roast half duckling, chicken piccata, grilled lamb chops, and Haddock Maison, which

comes topped with a lobster soufflé. Open year-round. The restaurant was voted No. 1 for most romantic restaurant in the local paper's Best of the Best 2006, so you may want to bring your sweetie.

Frankie and Johnny's Natural Foods $$
1594 Route 1, Cape Neddick
(207) 363–1909
www.frankie-johnnys.com

An unassuming place on Route 1, this dinner spot gets creative quickly when you step inside. The menu is known for its vegetarian fare, but you can get carnivorous if you like. Everything is made from scratch with fresh ingredients, from the signature crustolis—which are French bread rounds topped with goodies like a pizza—to the smoked lobster salads to the blackened pork Demonico. You can get as wacky as you like here, in terms of the cuisine, or keep it fairly traditional (baked chicken), and you'll always go home happy. There's a bit of a Mediterranean flavor to Frankie and Johnny's, and the candlelight is a nice touch. Oh, and bring cash—plastic is not "natural," and they don't accept it here.

Other Dining Options in the Yorks

Fazio's (38 Woodbridge Road, York Village; 207–363–7019; www.fazios.com) is where you'll find good traditional Italian food.

Ogunquit

Arrows Restaurant $$$$
Berwick Road, Ogunquit
(207) 361–1100
www.arrowsrestaurant.com

The accolades that this 18th-century farmhouse has garnered are fairly astounding. How about one of the top 50 restaurants in America? That's what *Gourmet* magazine said in its October 2006 issue. Or one of the 10 most romantic restaurants in the country? That's *Bon Appetit* speaking. Or "hands down the best dining in the area"? That would be the influential Zagat Survey. The place is indeed very, very good. (It also happens to have a savvy press person.) And the goodness starts in the garden. Arrows is now famous for its produce, which it grows right on-site (guests are welcome to wander the grounds). The menu tends to favor whatever's in season, and every element on the plate is integral. Main courses—and there are usually only about a half dozen choices—might include grilled veal rib chop and crispy Arborio rice–coated veal sweetbreads with bacon-wrapped fennel, baby parsnips, garlic chives, bell pepper purees, and an enriched veal stock sauce; Alaskan wild king salmon wrapped in papillote with spring leeks and black truffles, champagne *glaçage* (glaze), baby endive salad with pancetta and crispy baby squid, and roasted potatoes; or Maine lobster and sautéed jumbo Maine sea scallops with a ginger noodle pillow, spring vegetables, and a rhubarb, pinot blanc, and Sichuan peppercorn sauce. There's a tasting menu as well. Be sure not to wear shorts or you won't be seated—guests are encouraged to dress up. Reservations are a good idea. Open at 6:00 P.M. for dinner Wednesday through Sunday in June and September, Tuesday through Sunday in July and August. Hours are reduced in the off season.

Barnacle Billy's $–$$$$
Perkins Cove, Ogunquit
(207) 646–5575 or (800) 866–5575
www.barnbilly.com

You wouldn't expect a place with a name like Barnacle Billy's to have valet parking, but that's become the necessity in the Perkins Cove of today, where you can circle for hours—days, it seems—before finding a spot to ditch the car. Famous for its seafood dinners, Barnacle Billy's has been at it for ages, serving up tons of lobster to eager diners. You can get it boiled, on a roll, in a salad, in a sauté, in a stew, by the pound, you name it. Other seafood stand-bys—from tuna salad to steamed clams to crab rolls—are also available, but you can find some turf options as well, including a great barbecued chicken. This is all at the original Barnacle Billy's—as opposed to Barnacle Billy's Etc., which is a fancier seafood place right next door. The original is a better deal for much the same fare.

Old Village Inn $$$
30 Main Street, Ogunquit
(207) 646–7088
www.oldvillageinn.com
Long the only game in town for a fancy off-season dinner, the Old Village Inn now has competition even when the days begin to get dark, but its five dining rooms still turn out some of the better meals to be found in the resort community. The comfort foods are there, but you can try something new in this 1833 clapboard in the center of town. The cuisine is a fine mix of surf and turf, sometimes with a twist, from pork porterhouse chops to salmon with a ginger soy glaze. But you can still get classics like lobster bisque or rack of lamb. Ambiance is nice—each of the dining rooms has its own theme and decorative style—and the service is fine, too.

Village Food Market $–$$
230 Main Street, Ogunquit
(207) 646–2122 or (877) 646–2122
www.villagefoodmarket.com
If you're in town for a while, don't feel like waiting in line at a restaurant, or just want a nice dinner in, get thee to this downtown market, which has a great selection of prepared meals. Soups, salads, grilled meats, fish—take your pick. Grab a bottle of wine, a blueberry pie, and some scones for breakfast, and you're ready to go.

Other Dining Options in Ogunquit

98 Provence (262 Shore Road; 207–646–9898; www.98provence.com) is a good bet for rustic French foods. **McPerkins Cove** (Shore Road; 207–646–6263; www.mcperkinscove.com) is the new venture by the team behind Arrows, so you know it's good. People like the french fries at Charlie's (127 Beach Street; 207–646–8280). The **Cliff House** (Bald Hill Cliff; 207–361–1000), the famed resort and spa, has an upscale dining room with fancy views and great food. The breakfasts at **Egg and I** (501 Main Street; 207–646–8777; www.eggandibreakfast.com) have been voted the best in southern Maine, which is a stretch, but they're very good. The northern Italian fare at **Roberto's** (200 Shore Road; 207–646–8131; www.robertos.com) packs them in. **Raspberri's**, the dining room at the Gorges Grant Hotel (449 Main Street; 207–646–7003), is another good breakfast option, known for its waffles.

The Kennebunks

Cherie's $
7 High Street, Kennebunk
(207) 985–1200
www.cheriesbakery.com
Cherie's got its start as a fun, funky bakery with a checkerboard floor, and it has since expanded into a fine dining room that became popular quickly. Today it's mostly doing breakfast and lunch. Try the barbecue chicken or the grilled tuna steak if you want a treat. And be sure to stop at the bakery on the way out for desserts to travel miles for—they're what first put Cherie's on the map. The chocolate flourless torte is a favorite.

The Clam Shack $–$$
Lower Village Bridge, Kennebunk
(207) 967–2560
A writer once joked that the state should pass a constitutional amendment to keep this bridge-side take-out stand open year-round, and many locals sigh a sad sigh when it closes in the fall. Clams are obviously the appeal here, and they are very good, with a homemade tartar sauce, but the place turns out a mean lobster roll as well. At least that's what Martha Stewart thought. And *Coastal Living* magazine. And *Travel and Leisure*, which called it the best in Maine in its August 2006 issue. Pick up a copy of the Maine Lobster Roll Kit, which contains freshly picked lobster meat, traditional rolls, the shack's own mayo, and the recipe, all packed into a tiny lobster trap. Open May through September.

Hurricane Restaurant $$$$
Dock Square, Kennebunkport
(207) 967–9111
www.hurricanerestaurant.com

A Maine original, the Hurricane in Ogunquit may have closed, but its sibling in Dock Square is going great guns and remains as good as ever, turning out plate after plate of superbly crafted surf and turf. Try one of the small entrees—the crispy crab cakes ($15), the Bento box ($22), or the Prince Edward Island mussels ($10). Or step up to a larger plate like the fettucine Alfredo ($16), the yellowfin tuna burger ($11), or the pièce de résistance—baked stuffed Maine lobster with scallops, shrimp, and crabmeat stuffing ($45). The place is always busy, but you'll be glad you put up with the hassles. Be sure to make a reservation.

Joshua's Restaurant　　　　**$$$–$$$$**
1637 Post Road, Wells
(207) 646–3355
www.joshuas.biz
Having your own organic vegetable garden seems to be a recipe for success among Maine restaurants. It's the practice at two longtime favorites, Arrows in Ogunquit and Chase's in Belfast, and it's also the plan at the new Joshua's Restaurant in Wells. Chef/owner Joshua Mather grew up in a beautiful 1774 house on an organic farm 6 miles from his new dining room, and his dad provides the vegetables for his restaurant. The chef's plan is not to do too much to what his dad, and his other suppliers, bring to him, and his menu is fairly simple—pork tenderloin, duck, haddock, rack of lamb, filet mignon—but expertly crafted, and with some unusual combinations. The chicken is stuffed with shrimp, the ravioli filled with lobster, the scallops come with a pumpkin risotto. The young chef's attention to detail has the place already thriving. The *Boston Globe* calls Joshua's "fabulous," and *Travel and Leisure* recommends that people "keep an eye on this guy." We'd have to agree.

Windows on the Water　　　　**$$$–$$$$**
Chase Hill, Kennebunk
(207) 967–3313
www.windowsonthewater.com
This old standby actually has a mission state-

i　A lot of people are unaware that the breakfast at the Green Heron Inn (126 Ocean Avenue, Kennebunkport; 207–967–3315) is open to the public—it is, and it's arguably the best in town.

ment: "to offer our guests award-winning specialties at moderate prices." People seem to be buying it—the dining room has been voted the most romantic in York County by the readers of the local paper several years running—and the kitchen here has actually won some of the accolades it promised to when it opened with that mission statement in 1985. In 1997 the Culinary Guild of the Americas presented it with an Epicurean Plate Award. What's all the fuss? Start with the windows, floor-to-ceiling panes that overlook the harbor. Then add good service, and finally add such delicacies as lobster ravioli, prime filet mignon, seared ahi (tuna), and Thai-style lobster. Open year-round for lunch and dinner.

Alisson's Restaurant　　　　**$$–$$$**
11 Dock Square, Kennebunkport
(207) 967–4841
www.alissons.com
Arlo Guthrie should write a song about this Dock Square stalwart. (Its name was actually inspired by his classic "Alice's Restaurant.") The place has been an anchor in the square for more than 30 years, and everybody loves it. The atmosphere is very comfortable and casual—with the ball game going on the TV over the bar—but it's the food that brings people back. The chowder has been voted southern Maine's best, the fried clams have their own partisans, and the menu is fairly long with seafood, steak, chicken, and sandwich options (try the prime rib sandwich). Especially good for lunch. Open daily, year-round, for lunch from 11:00 A.M. to 5:00 P.M. and for dinner from 5:00 to 9:00 P.M., with the hours cut back a bit in the off-season.

Cape Arundel Inn $$$$
Ocean Avenue, Kennebunkport
(207) 967–2125

People flock to Kennebunkport to get a look at the Bush compound on Walker Point, and the summer home of the presidents forms much of the view of this fine dining room. (George the First occasionally even sups here, so you can get a real close look.) The food, however, should be the real attraction. After establishing the White Barn Inn as *the* place to stay and eat in Maine, Jack Nahil sold the famous hostelry and turned his attention to this new project. The cuisine is thus exceptional, with seafood and continental favorites done with ingenious twists, like crab cakes with a sweet sesame rémoulade, for example, or grilled Atlantic salmon with a roast tomato vinaigrette. Quite aside from the views of crashing surf and Secret Servicemen out the windows, the dining room is very comfortable, with its candles and white linens, and the service is exceedingly professional. Open Monday through Saturday for dinner from mid-April through December.

Grissini Italian Bistro $$–$$$$
27 Western Avenue, Kennebunkport
(207) 967–2211
www.restaurantgrissini.com

"Quintessential Tuscan cooking with a New England accent" is how this fantastic bistro describes its fare, and that about sums it up. Featuring some of the talents who have made the White Barn Inn world famous, the kitchen here turns out absolutely delicious northern Italian fare using fresh local fish and just the right spices. Try the grilled tuna with sun-dried tomato, the salmon with sautéed shiitake mushrooms, or the half grilled chicken with cipollini onions. Guaranteed you won't forget Grissini if you eat here. It has a nice downstairs bar, big fireplace, and patio. Just great. Open nightly for dinner from 5:30 to 9:00 P.M. On Saturday they open at 5:00 P.M.

On the Marsh $$$–$$$$
46 Western Avenue, Kennebunkport
(207) 967–2299
www.onthemarsh.com

The Salt Marsh Tavern used to be one of the finer restaurants in this resort community, and when Denise Rubin purchased it in 2000, she only made it better. Much better. Retrofitted into an old farm and barn, the eatery was completely redone, and it is sparkling, from the twinkling lights outside to the candles inside. The menu likewise was reborn, and it is a comfortable mix of classics done with artful twists. The filet mignon has a wild mushroom ragout, for example, and the pork tenderloin comes with roasted shallots. Not only immensely flavorful, but the presentation is a treat for the eyes as well as the palate. Those in for a real spectacle can be seated in the kitchen, where they can watch the chefs at work. Another intriguing note: If you really like the unique antique sculpture on the wall near your table, you can buy it—the dining rooms are filled with art, furnishings, and collectibles that are for sale. Neat idea.

White Barn Inn $$$$
37 Beach Avenue, Kennebunkport
(207) 967–2321
www.whitebarninn.com

You could spend almost an hour reading all the accolades written about the White Barn. *Food and Wine* magazine calls it one of the top 50 hotel restaurants in the nation, *Conde-Nast Traveler* puts it atop its "gold" list, *New England Traveler* calls it a "most notable gem," the *Maine Sunday Telegram* deemed it "perfect" and "otherworldly," and the kudos go on and on, literally dozens worth. Suffice it to say the place is good, and in a way that outclasses just about everywhere else in Maine. Its dining room is five-diamond good, the only recipient of AAA's highest honor in the whole state.

Actually built into a pair of 19th-century, timber-framed barns—heavy beams, rafters, hayloft, and all—the inn's dining room is both rustic and fancy, with candlelit, white-linen-covered tables, cushy chairs, ample flowers, and picture windows overlooking gardens. The country feel puts you completely at ease and ready to savor four courses of prix fixe excellence. Chef Jonathan Cartwright's menu changes weekly but always draws inspiration from the seasons, Maine seafood, and European traditions. Beef, veal, lamb, and fowl are generally options, and house specialties include delicacies like lobster spring rolls, forest-mushroom soup, saffron-scented Maine shrimp, and seared Quebec foie gras. Everything is presented as a form of art, and service is as good as it gets in Maine. The desserts are astonishing, like the vanilla goat cheese timbale and raisin compote. You'll be back. Open Monday through Thursday from 6:00 to 9:30 P.M. and Friday through Sunday from 5:30 to 9:30 P.M. Jackets required.

Lucas on 9 $$–$$$
62 Mills Road, Cape Porpoise
(207) 967–0039
www.lucasonnine.com
The team behind the ever-popular Fisherman's Catch in Wells, the Lane family, has purchased and renamed the old Lobster Pot in Cape Porpoise, one of the few real villages left in southern Maine, so the people who show up here will probably be expecting seafood. And that's largely what they'll get, in the form of baked stuffed flounder with Newburg sauce, and spicy tuna with kiwi. But you can also get baby back ribs, chicken, and other meats. The menu is actually quite long and well-rounded, with both swimmers and walkers. You could happily fill up on a couple of smaller plates or go home with a doggie bag by ordering an entree. Worth a stop.

Nunan's Lobster Hut $–$$
Mills Road, Cape Porpoise
(207) 967–4362
Lobsters come right off the Nunan's own boat here, not too far from Kennebunkport. The menu of this dinner-only place is pretty straightforward, from steamers and lobster stew to boiled lobsters and shrimp rolls. And people tend to rave about the blueberry pies as well, so you've got it all. A staple for ages—since 1953, actually—the place inspires real devotion among lobster lovers (some have been known to drive three hours from Vermont just to eat here). Open daily at 5:00 P.M. from mid-April through mid-October.

Other Dining Options in the Kennebunks

Along with being the best big hotel in town, the **Colony** (Ocean Avenue, Kennebunkport; 207–967–3331) also sets one of the best tables, heavy on the seafood. **Mabel's Lobster Claw** (Ocean Avenue, Kennebunkport; 207–967–2562) is famous for its stuffed lobster, lobster stew, and one of the best lobster rolls you'll find. **Bartley's Dockside** (By the Bridge, Kennebunkport; 207–967–5050) is the place to turn for blueberry pie. And **Federal Jack's Restaurant and Brew Pub** (8 Western Avenue, Kennebunk; 207–967–4322; www .federaljacks.com) is where you'll find great beer brewed on the premises and good pub food.

Saco

Rapid Ray's $
179 Main Street, Saco
(207) 282–1847
Everything about Rapid Ray's feels classic, from the diner exterior to the simple menu of burgers, dogs, lobster rolls, onion rings, and similar fare. The place has been at it for more than 40 years and is still going strong. You walk in, make your selections from the list near the ordering window, get your chili dog or clam cake burger with fries in a little box, and eat it at the thin, wraparound counters. Best of all, most items on the menu will set you back only a few bucks—even the seafood. The lobster roll is great, and it costs half of what you'd pay just up the road in Kennebunk.

GREATER PORTLAND
Scarborough

Anjon's Fine Italian Food $$–$$$
521 Route 1, Scarborough
(207) 883–9562
www.anjons.com

John DiSanto's grandparents, Ann and John DiSanto, opened Anjon's Italian Food in 1957 on the strength of Ann's marinara sauce. They transformed an old seafood shack into an Italian food institution, and Greater Portland residents have been eagerly digging into DiSanto family recipes ever since. (Grandma DiSanto's sauces are now sold in stores under the Anjon name.) Rocco DiSanto was 10 when his grandmother first showed him how to make her sauce, and he's continuing the fine family tradition in the kitchen to this day.

The menu is long and deep, with dozens of entree options, from traditional Italian delights—ravioli, pasta primavera, fettucine Alfredo, and lasagna—to Maine-spun dishes like lobster stew and haddock marinara. There are a dozen of these Down East–by-way-of-Roma choices in the "Taste of Maine" section of the menu, and they inform the appetizers (Italian-style steamers, Maine steamers) as well. It's a delicious merging of cultures. The setting can't be beat, either—sitting, as the restaurant does, on the edge of Scarborough Marsh.

Clambake Seafood Restaurant $$–$$$
Route 9, Scarborough
(207) 883–4871
www.clambakerestaurant.com

Not far from Pine Point Beach, this seafood joint has both a cafeteria-style sit-down dining room and a takeout, which is nice because you can grab a pint of fried clams and head to the beach. There is seating for 700 here, which all but eliminates any waiting, and many tables have nice views of Scarborough Marsh. Always busy in midsummer, the Clambake is a favorite among Greater Portland seafood fans, and it's popular with tourists as well. The menu is deep with seafood, but you can get grilled chicken if you must. Start with some chowder and follow it up with a twin lobster dinner. All dinners are served with choice of potato, Caesar salad, coleslaw, and bread. You won't go home hungry.

Dunstan School Restaurant $$
Route 1, Scarborough
(207) 883–5261
www.dunstanschoolrestaurant.com

All you-can-eat buffets in a classic brick schoolhouse built in the mid-1940s are what to expect here. The chalkboards are still hung where they were when the last classes left here in 1980, and you'd better behave or you'll get a detention. (Just kidding.) The food is better than average buffet fare, thanks to a lot of homemade items, like breads and pies. Locals seem to like the breakfast, which is served daily in July and August and on weekends in June and September. There are over 100 items to choose from, including Maine classics like baked beans and corned beef hash.

Cape Elizabeth

Audubon Room $$$–$$$$
Inn by the Sea
40 Bowery Beach Road, Cape Elizabeth
(207) 767–0888
www.innbythesea.com

The great dining room at the Inn by the Sea often gets overlooked by diners who are unaware that the Audubon Room is open to the general public and not just inn guests. It is, and those in the know take advantage of the fine fare. The place gets its name from the genuine Audubon prints that line its walls, which enhance the white linen, English bone china, and crystal ambience. Many tables have views of the water in the distance, and the service is good, but it's the New American cuisine that's the real attraction. Fresh local greens and seafood make their way into favorites like lobster bisque, crab cakes, grilled salmon with orange-basil vinaigrette, and wild mushroom risotto. Breakfast is a real treat as well. Reservations are required.

The Good Table $

527 Ocean House Road (Route 77), Cape Elizabeth
(207) 799–4663

A devastating 2002 electrical fire didn't stop this local favorite—it rebuilt in no time, bringing Greater Portland residents the "honest food and honest prices" they want. The family-style fare is a mix of hearty comfort foods with Greek overtones here and there (spanakopita, gyros). The turkey dinner is pretty much perfection, the lobster roll is fine, and the desserts are tempting. Sunday brunch here fills up fast. Open Tuesday through Friday from 11:00 A.M. to 9:00 P.M., Saturday 8:00 A.M. to 9:00 P.M., and Sunday 8:00 A.M. to 3:00 P.M. Closed Monday.

Lobster Shack $$

225 Two Lights Road, Cape Elizabeth
(207) 799–1677
www.lobstershack-twolights.com

You don't have to be a fan of seafood to enjoy a visit to the Lobster Shack, just below the twin towers that give the Two Lights area of Cape Elizabeth its name. The view of the open Atlantic from the picnic tables outside the small eatery is simply jaw-dropping, and it alone is worth the trip. It certainly helps if you enjoy fried clams, haddock, shrimp, lobsters, or scallops, though. (No fear, landlubbers—fried chicken, hot dogs, and hamburgers are also "specialties.")

South Portland

Barbara's Kitchen $$–$$$

Cottage Road, South Portland
(207) 767–6313
www.barbaraskitchen.com

This cool little neighborhood cafe can be difficult to find—South Portland is a notorious tangle of streets—but it rewards the effort. Barbara Winthrop has been filling the old Willard Square drugstore with creative soups, sandwiches, burgers, and salads since 1995, and it's a neat place, with high tin ceilings, groaning floors, and big bay windows on the street. Locals flock to Barbara's and are often leaning from one table to another to talk to

friends. Lunch is particularly good here, and it's little more than what you'd pay for fast food. Try the french-roasted in-house turkey sandwich or the crab cake salad. Breakfasts also have a following, with made-to-order omelets a specialty, but dinner does quite well, too. The rosemary focaccia that starts things off is superb. See for yourself. Open for lunch Tuesday through Sunday from 8:00 A.M. to 2:00 P.M. and for dinner Wednesday through Saturday from 5:00 to 9:00 P.M.

Joe's Boathouse $$$

Spring Point Marina, South Portland
(207) 741–2780
www.joesboathouse.com

The many masts and sparkling waters of Spring Point Marina are out every window at this South Portland favorite. And a patio gives you an even better look out onto Casco Bay. Some say the views here are among the best of any Greater Portland restaurant, and the fare holds its own. Lunch and dinner are popular with the boating crowd, and people make the drive over from Portland to sit at one of the 45 seats here and enjoy them. The Sunday brunch, though, is the real treat, with Port Harbor pancakes, Peaks Island French toast, and corned beef hash and eggs.

One Fifty Ate $$$

158 Benjamin W. Pickett Street
South Portland
(207) 799–8998

A neat little eatery—it seats 25—this happening spot has reinvigorated Spring Point and made SoPo seem almost an appropriate moniker for the southerly neighbor of Maine's largest city. *Relaxed* is the word, from the creaky floorboards of this old boatbuilder's shed to the group of friends who own the place. The menu is decidedly eclectic and might include tomato pie one day and trout and succotash the next—simple yet creative fare that shows that these kids learned something when they worked at places like Street and Company and Fore Street. Recommended, as are reservations.

Ricetta's Brick Oven Pizzeria $$
29 Western Avenue, South Portland
(207) 775–7400
www.ricettas.com

If you can't get a table at Ricetta's, you can always take out. This beloved pizzeria in a South Portland strip mall has become so popular that it's often difficult to even get in the door, and people become resigned to getting their pies to go. Diners consistently vote the thin-crust, gourmet pizzas here the best in the Portland area, and they are eminently customizable. A nice way to experiment is to visit during the lunchtime buffet, so you can sample several varieties. Various other entrees—from pasta to soups to calzone—are on the menu, but you likely won't even notice. Ricetta's has expanded into Falmouth now, and its second restaurant is hard to get into, too.

Other Dining Options in South Portland

Imperial China (220 Maine Mall Road; 207–774–4292), located in the uninspired confines of the Mallside Plaza, is often called the best Chinese place in Maine. Much-better-than-average pub fare and great beer are available at **Sebago Brewing Company** near the mall (150 Phillbrick Avenue; 207–879–2537; www.sebagobrewing.com). **Mr. Bagel** (Mall-side Plaza; 207–773–3238; www.misterbagel .com) has great—you guessed it, bagels—including a lobster bagel. And **Cap'n Newick's Seafood Restaurant** (740 Broadway; 207–799–3090) is legendary for its lobster, clams, and sheer massiveness. **Beale Street Barbeque** (90 Waterman Drive; 207–767–0130; www.mainebbq.com) is exceptional for barbecue and blues.

Portland

Back Bay Grill $$$–$$$$
65 Portland Street, Portland
(207) 772–8833
www.backbaygrill.com

It isn't all that uncommon for Portland visitors to enjoy a restaurant on one vacation only to return a year later and find it long gone. There's been a lot of turnover in the city, but here is one eatery that has managed to survive and thrive since the late 1980s. And this despite its unlikely location on a side street in a neighborhood that is if not sketchy then at least far from trendy. The food—inventively done takes on tried-and-true American favorites—simply keeps people coming back. Try the filet mignon with Roquefort, the lamb with potato gnocchi, or the Scottish salmon. The seafood is fresh, the produce organically grown, the wine list strong. Restaurateur Larry Matthews puts a premium on comfort and service.

Becky's $
Hobsons Wharf, Commercial Street, Portland
(207) 773–7070
www.beckys.com

Everyone seems to love Becky's, from the fishermen who catch the seafood for the diner's famous chowders, to *Gourmet* magazine, to lawyers in suits and ties, to those tourists lucky enough to find the place. Well-prepared diner fare—heavy on the seafood—is what you can expect here, at very reasonable prices. Try the fried haddock with fries and slaw or the clam cakes and slaw. You can even get a hot dog. The ambience and staff are just right, and, for all the accolades, the place is still real. Look for the red awning on Commercial Street.

Bibo's Madd Apple Café $$$
23 Forest Avenue, Portland
(207) 774–9698

When the Portland Performing Arts Center's calendar is in full swing, so is Bibo's. It's a favorite among the theatergoing set. The colorful place sports an eclectic menu from a world of flavors—it has Asian, Italian, and French influences—served up with flair in a brightly painted dining room a few steps from Congress Street. Everything begins with bread, which is served with olive oil and *dukka*, a nut blend. Entrees include salmon with sesame vinaigrette and pork tenderloin with avocado and lime. The wine list has many fans.

Caiola's
58 Pine Street, Portland
(207) 772–1110
www.caiolas.com

Besides simply providing the city with great food, Portland's two culinary institutions, Street and Company and Fore Street, have done the city—the state even—a great service by spinning off so many other great restaurants. Alums of the two titans have been opening up new restaurants all over the place. This comfy West End eatery is a case in point. Chef Abby Harmon worked for years as the top chef at Street and Company before opening her own place, and she continues the high standards set there. Here she's set up a European-style bistro featuring simple peasant foods done exactly well. The menu changes daily and might include anything from a Caesar salad with fried oysters to a bacon-cheeseburger to paella to bouillabaisse, all served on handcrafted wood tables in warm little spaces divided by walls with rustic murals. Opened in the winter of 2005–2006, the place is already filling its seats, and the plans are to expand with cafe seating outside.

DiMillo's Floating Restaurant $$–$$$
Long Wharf, Portland
(207) 772–2216
www.dimillos.com

A tourist staple on the Portland waterfront, DiMillo's is a restaurant retrofitted into an old car ferry. It's big enough at 260 feet to avoid the swells when the seas get to rocking, but it still provides a great window onto the harbor, and out-of-towners eat it up. Grab a table outside on one of the decks if you can. As you might expect, seafood takes up much of the menu that comes out of the galley, but steaks, poultry, the occasional Italian dish, and other

landlubber fare are also available. The cuisine isn't going to win any awards, but the views make it a worthwhile lunch or dinner option.

Federal Spice $
225 Federal Street, Portland
(207) 774–6404

Federal Spice has a lot of the angles covered. The small joint across the street from the post office serves up healthy fare with unique tastes, it's inexpensive, and it's hip to boot. All that has made it a go-to place, a default lunch spot for many Portlanders. The eatery serves a world of flavors in the form of wraps, and they're the best in the state. Try the curry chicken and Asian slaw, the smoked turkey and green onion quesadilla, or the Chinese mako shark. You get delicious chips with your wrap as well, and you can eat inside or cafe style on the sidewalk. (Avoid the upstairs on hot days in summer—it's suffocatingly hot.) You won't be disappointed. Open for lunch and dinner.

Fore Street $$$
288 Fore Street, Portland
(207) 775–2717
www.forestreet.biz

After a decade, this place is still setting the standard for Portland. Since it was founded in 1996, chef Sam Hayward's Old Port enterprise has been packing people in with its grilled peasant food. Walk in and you can smell the delicious seared aroma of the grill, and you can watch food roasting on the soapstone hearth from your table. Seafood is a staple, but there are plenty of tasty meat dishes as well, from the turn-spit roasted pork to the

---

i If you know you're going to be around awhile and you enjoy a bargain, the Portland Dine-Around Club (207-775-4711; dineportland.maine.com) is a great deal. Annual membership is $29.95, and it gets you discounted meals and more, usually a two-for-one entree arrangement. Eat out a couple of times and it pays for itself very quickly.

marinated hanger steak. People swear by the roasted mussels. Hayward is painstakingly good—the eminent James Beard Foundation named him Best Chef in the Northeast in 2004—and his people scour the fish markets and farmstands for the freshest and best organic ingredients. This has won the place a devoted following. Some would say that the only place that might be better in Portland is Street and Company, which is part of Hayward's empire, along with Standard Baking Company and Two Fat Cats Bakery.

The Front Room $–$$
73 Congress Street, Portland
(207) 773–3366
www.thefrontroomrestaurant.com

Portland's Munjoy Hill, traditionally a down-at-the-heels sort of neighborhood, has been enjoying a bit of a renaissance lately, and places like this comfortable eatery are among the reasons why. An old Victorian apartment building on the Eastern Prom is the setting for a restaurant that chef/owner Harding Lee Smith hopes will become a community gathering place. All three meals are offered daily, and the menu is described as "New American comfort food," which means the kinds of macaroni and cheese, burger, BLT, grilled meatloaf, and lamb pot roast that won't scare off the natives. But you also get the occasional twist—such as corned hake, cedar-planked salmon, or Casco Bay scallops in mustard sauce. It's a fine combination, and the dining room is a place you can return to several times a week.

Gilbert's Chowder House $$
Commerical Street, Portland
(207) 871–5636

Right on the waterfront, Gilbert's is about as salty an eatery as you'll find in Portland, and it serves up a raft of good seafood dishes in addition to its famous chowders. (Clam, corn, seafood, and super seafood, these chowders come the best way—in bowls made of fresh bread.) Not the least bit pretentious, it's where fishermen and lawyers sit at adjacent tables, hungrily digging into clam cakes, lobster stew,

fried haddock, and scallops. The food is prepared by Ed Gilbert, who runs the place with his brother Jim, and everything comes in a fairly large portion for a fair price. The lobsters and fish are literally just off the boat, sometimes even that morning, and Ed Gilbert has attributed the success of the venture to this freshness. Great word of mouth doesn't hurt, either.

Hugo's $$$$
88 Middle Street, Portland
(207) 774–8538
www.hugos.net

Dana Street has been very complimentary of Rob Evans, chef at this longtime restaurant on Franklin Arterial. No small thing, considering that Street runs two of Portland's best and most popular eateries, Fore Street and Street and Company. Evans bought the restaurant from founder Johnny Robinson several years back, and he's truly put his stamp on the bistro. He was the chef at the old Hugo's, before leaving to study at cooking schools, and when he returned to buy out Robinson, he really got things going, combining French and Italian accents with the culinary traditions of New England in a way that was amazingly original. Try the Vermont quail breast, the Casco Bay cod, or the Maine gray sole. Delightful.

Local 188 $$–$$$
188 State Street, Portland
(207) 761–7909
www.local188.com

Guidebooks don't know where to put this Portland hipster hangout. By day it's an art gallery. By night it's one of the city's more interesting restaurants. The young and happening like to visit regularly because the staff is made up of artists, writers, and musicians worth knowing. Other cool kids are always there, and foodies and fans of good wine are right behind them, hankering for the tapas cooked up Jay Villani. The food is as good as anything else being served in the city, and Villani and his staff have expanded the once tapas-only menu to include larger entrees. Staples include paellas, pastas with *romesco* sauce, and creatively prepared meat dishes. Try the pork tenderloin with mashed potatoes and apples or the vegetarian soups, like the split-pea and curry with leeks and carrots and peppers. The price-portion ratio allows for sampling several dishes and sharing, the service is great, and there is always something interesting to look at, from cutting-edge art to cutting-edge people.

Natasha's Restaurant $$$
82 Exchange Street, Portland
(207) 541–3663

Natasha Durham has been on the Portland restaurant scene for more than a decade, which is an achievement in itself in the city's everchanging culinary landscape. Since 1997 she's run her own show, first on Portland Street and now at this location on the upper end of the Old Port's Exchange Street. She attracted a lot of attention by offering free—or nearly free, depending upon their situation—lunches to the homeless in her old spot, and she continues to make a name for herself with fine cuisine that manages to fuse Asian and Italian influences into her own style. You could choose from among the Laos crispy orange whitefish, the Korean vegetable pot stickers, eggplant Napoleon, or northern Italian fish pie. Everything is exactingly crafted using produce the whimsical Durham might have picked up on her way in to the "office." A meal here can be costly with wine and tip, but it's worth every penny.

Norm's Bar and Grill $$
617 Congress Street, Portland
(207) 828–9944

Eager diners will occasionally walk into Norm's on the east side of Congress Street only to find that they're in the wrong place. They've walked into Norm's Downtown Lounge, which is not to be confused with Norm's Bar and Grill. That Portland favorite—formerly in this location—has moved across the street. Seems this Norm fellow is taking over the city. Now there are three outlets for his talents. (Norm's East End Grill, a barbecue hot spot, is over on

Middle Street.) The Bar and Grill still has the red walls and the checkerboard floors, the booths of burgundy pleather (faux leather), the bar with the ball game on, about a dozen tables, and, thankfully, the menu filled with grilled items, urban eclectic pub food, not-really tapas, and good beers and wines. Try the baked meat pie, the fried sea scallops, or the grilled barbecue shrimp wrapped in bacon.

Pepperclub $$
78 Middle Street, Portland
(207) 772–0531

When you've had your fill of lobster rolls and fried clams, head over to this beloved eatery, just a few blocks from the Old Port across the Franklin Arterial. Readers of the local alternative weekly have tabbed the restaurant as the place with the best food for under $10 in years past, but prices have gone up a bit. The fare is still indisputably good, though. It's a smorgasbord of cosmopolitan, nouvelle flavors inspired by eats from all over the globe, and you order off a chalkboard covered with colors. You might find on any given night Moroccan chicken, sesame vegetable spring rolls, curried organic beef pie, or lamb in phyllo with Greek salad. Everything comes recommended, and the knowledgeable staff will help you sort things out.

Portland Flatbread Co. $–$$
72 Commerical Street, Portland
(207) 772–8777
www.flatbreadcompany.com

This isn't your grandfather's pizza place. Another of the more "happening" eateries in the city, this Commercial Street pizza house serves up all-natural pizzas baked in "primitive," wood-fired clay ovens. Part of a small chain, the eatery has a nice spot on the Portland waterfront, and there are views of the harbor visible from its wooden booths. The flatbread—or crust—is made of organic wheat, and one is large enough to feed two people. Choose from the nitrate-free pepperoni; the Casco Bay community flatbread, which comes with caramelized onions, organic mushrooms, cheeses, and herbs (exactly like the Amesbury community flatbread, in Amesbury, Massachusetts); or the vegan, which has caramelized onions, kalamata olives, garlic oil, and herbs. Portlanders seem to be into this joint, and there can be a wait.

Ri Ra $$$
72 Commercial Street, Portland
(207) 761–4446

One of the hotter things in town for a while, this Irish place enjoys good word of mouth for its brews, bands, bonhomie, and Emerald Isle–inspired fare. Yet somehow it doesn't seem quite so special—the hometown pub spirit is diminished—when you find out it's part of a chain with pubs in Providence, Burlington, and as far south as North Carolina. You might begin with some tasty Irish potato leek soup, which comes with brown bread and Guinness butter, then move onto the Linguine Galway, which combines shrimp, mussels, tomatoes and white wine with spices on a bed of linguine; Dublin Fisherman's Stew, which combines lobster, mussels, and fresh fish in a light seafood broth with garlic, spinach, and fennel (yes, that's Maine lobster); or Emigrants Corned Beef, which consists of braised beef, cabbage, and boiled potatoes. Or go with the fish and chips or shepherd's pie. Plenty of Guinness by the pint as well. Fun stuff, though a franchise, and at least here on the Portland waterfront on a foggy day, you could imagine you were in County Cork.

The Roma Café $$$
769 Congress Street, Portland
(207) 773–9873
www.theromacafe.com

With its chandeliers, heavy drapes, and white linens, this Congress Street favorite has a decidedly old-school feel, and it is, in a classic sort of way. The Roma has been feeding Portlanders since 1924 with fine Italian-accented continental fare. It's the sort of restaurant where you take that special someone on that special occasion, when a little romance is required (Roma puts the *roma* in romance—it's been voted Portland's most romantic restaurant several years running). The 1887 Rhines mansion serves as the setting, the service is known for being impeccable, and the fare is prepared with supreme care. You won't soon forget the Roma seafood lasagna, the chicken and Maine shrimp fettuccine, or the roast pork tenderloin.

Silly's $
40 Washington Avenue, Portland
(207) 772–0360

Silly's enjoyed its 15 minutes of fame a few years back when famed pranksters, the Jerky Boyz, called the little restaurant up to ask them what was going on there that was so silly. Portlanders already know the answer. The funky eatery has become known for a "silly" array of items—the place's burgers are called the city's best by some. Others hail the jerk chicken, the pizza, and the milk shakes. It's also famous for vegetarian options. The atmosphere is kooky, the staff fun, and everything is inexpensive. As the slogan goes: EAT AT SILLY'S.

Street and Company $$$–$$$$
33 Wharf Street, Portland
(207) 775–0887

Along with Fore Street (with which it shares owners), this place has been setting the standard in Portland since 1989, and it's surprisingly informal. The specialty is grilled seafood, and nobody does it better. Entrees come right out of the kitchen and onto your table, often in the skillet they were cooked in. Specialties include lobster *diavolo* and scallops in Pernod and cream, but everything is excellent. Space has always been a concern—the restaurant is so popular, there's often a wait, and expanded seating and outdoor dining have been added. Still, best to make a reservation.

Susan's Fish and Chips $–$$
Morrill's Corner, Portland
(207) 878–3240

The garage facade of this Portland eatery may

be discouraging to some tourists, but locals know that they'll find some of the best inexpensive food in the city inside the old service station. Susan's has been a regular winner of local polls for its lobster roll and fried clams, the place has built up legions of regulars, and even *Gourmet* magazine has taken notice. (Some fishermen actually bring in their own fish and have Susan fry it for them.) Place your order at the counter, choosing from a wide variety of delicately fried fishies, clams, and shrimp, from chowders served in bowls of bread, or from delicacies like the Down East Reuben, a haddock burger with coleslaw and cheese, and then take a seat at one of the picnic tables inside. You can look at all the funky nautical kitsch while you wait—lobster traps, fishing nets, and the like. When the food arrives, and with it the tartar sauce in a mason jar, you'll understand the accolades.

Village Café $$$
112 Newbury Street, Portland
(207) 775–5320
www.villagecafemaine.com

The Village has been an East End Italian staple since 1936. The Reali family welcomes mostly families, and their menu is comfortably traditional—linguine, ravioli, and other pastas—but adds Maine favorites like fried clams, lobster stews, bisques, and more, and prime rib on the weekend. The dependable if not exceptional fare has been very popular among Portlanders for ages, so there can be a wait. Some foodies would argue that there are better places to spend your $18 for an entree, but the loyal hordes that the Village draws can't all be wrong.

Walter's Café $$$
15 Exchange Street, Portland
(207) 871–WALT
www.walterscafe.com

Since 1990 Walter's has been showing the world what can be done with pasta and seafood, and the restaurant, right smack in the heart of the Old Port, has developed a loyal following in the process. (Apparently

Springsteen is a fan.) Very pleasant, with its windows onto the street, exposed brick, tin ceilings, and cozy tables, the cafe melds a wide variety of culinary cultures on its menu— from the Caribbean across the globe to the Mediterranean. Dinner might start with the crackling calamari, a Walter's specialty, and move on to shrimp and lobster skillet pie, another longtime favorite here. Or it might include the pan-seared salmon with pineapple crab salsa or angel lobster, which mixes the Maine ingredient with scallions, mushrooms, and a marsala cream and tops it off with Parmesan. Seating for large parties is available upstairs. Dress may be casual but the fare isn't. Reservations are a good idea, as the place is popular.

Other Dining Options in Portland

The **Old Port Sea Grill and Raw Bar** (93 Commercial Street; 207–879–6100; www.the oldportseagrill.com) is a new place where you can down uncooked oysters in yupscale environs while watching TV. At **Standard Baking Co.** (75 Commercial Street; 207–773–2112) you can pick up a loaf of what is arguably Maine's best bread along with a host of desserts. Stop by **Harbor Fish Market** (9 Custom House Wharf; 207–775–0251 or 800–370–1790; www.harborfish.com) to buy lobster and fish fresh off the boats; it's the kind of salt-steeped place where people walk around in rubber boots. **Granny's Burritos** (420 Fore Street; 207– 761–0751) serves up the best burrito in New England and is a great, inexpensive lunch or dinner option. **Cinque Terre** (36 Wharf Street; 207–347–6154; www.cinqueterremaine.com) receives raves for its traditional Italian fare. **Hi Bombay** (1 Pleasant Street; 207–772–8767) makes some of the best Indian curries in town—try the Friday lunch buffet. **Sala Thai** (1363 Washington Avenue; 207–797– 0871) is your best bet for Thai food. Fuji (29 Exchange Street; 207–773–2900) and **Benkay** (2 India Street; 207–773–5555) are generally regarded as the places to go for Japanese and sushi. The **Cafe at Pat's** (484 Stevens Avenue; 207–874–0706;

http://cafeatpats.com) is garnering raves for its European comfort food.

Falmouth

O' Naturals $$
240 Route 1, Falmouth
(207) 781–8889
www.onaturals.com
Don't be surprised to see this fast-food joint taking over the country. Founded by some of the folks behind popular Stonyfield Yogurt, the eatery provides a healthy alternative to the greasy, processed McGrub at your chain burger joints. The menu is built around soups, sandwiches, salads, noodle dishes, and, yes, burgers made with organic and local produce, free-range meats, and no preservatives, additives, or "multiple-syllable stuff that you find in processed foods." How's it taste, though? Great. Try the miso noodles, the curried chicken, the spicy peanut salad, the *chap chae* Korean noodles, or the hoisin portobello sandwiches on flatbread—all delicious and prepared on demand for you in woks and grills by an eager young staff. Amazingly, it comes out just about as quickly as it does at the Golden Arches across the street. The ambience is nice—like a comfortable cosmpolitan coffee bar, with its art deco lights and exposed industrial piping. Opened in the late 1990s, the place has already expanded three times—it now has restaurants in Portland's Old Port and in Acton, Massachusetts—and with food this good and an idea this sensible, it's sure to grow again soon.

Chebeague Island

Chebeague Island Inn $$$
61 South Road, Chebeague Island
(207) 846–5155
www.chebeagueislandinn.com
Floating in Casco Bay just to the south of Yarmouth, Chebeague Island is a treat to visit. It's the largest of the bay's isles at 5 miles long and 3 miles wide, and it's great fun to walk, bicycle, and explore. And, now, to eat. The Island Inn has relatively new owners, and they've transformed their dining room into a

showplace—white tablecloths, fieldstone fireplace, and all. The menu's not going to surprise anyone, featuring the expected upscale surf and turf, but it's very nicely done. And the whole package—the boat ride, the romantic old inn, the fine fare—makes for a memorable outing.

Yarmouth

Royal River Grillhouse $$–$$$
106 Lafayette Street, Yarmouth
(207) 846–1226
www.royalrivergrillhouse.com
The restaurateur behind this local favorite learned his trade from Sam Hayward, the chef at the extraordinarily popular Fore Street in Portland. Which is a good thing, when you consider that he's running a grill where seafood is prominent on the menu. This place has gotten popular quickly, getting people talking about dishes like wood-grilled yellowfin tuna, sautéed Prince Edward Island mussels, fresh Maine crab cakes, and warm spinach and Maine shrimp salad. The menu changes nightly. Everything is presented in a nice dining room overlooking the Royal River, and there are tables on the deck in summer. Open daily from 11:30 A.M. to 9:00 P.M. Reservations are a good idea.

South Freeport

Harraseeket Lunch and Lobster $–$$
Main Street, South Freeport
(207) 865–4888
You'll never believe you're still in Freeport as you stare out at this working waterfront on Casco Bay. Fresh lobster, well prepared, is on the docket at the lunch half of this equation, and it can attract crowds (which might remind you you're in Freeport). The other half—Harraseeket Lunch—is where you'll find all sorts of fried seafoods, sandwiches, chowders, and desserts. Try the fried clams, and follow it up with a whoopie pie. See why the Food Network stopped by.

MIDCOAST
Brunswick and Surrounding Area

Danny's and Pops Dogs $
Brunswick Mall, Brunswick

Call it a dogfight—these two hot dog stands sit right next to each other on the town green in Brunswick, duking it out for the attention of wienie lovers. It's been that way for ages, and people like them both for different reasons. Try them and see for yourself.

Great Impasta $$
42 Maine Street, Brunswick
(207) 729–5858
www.thegreatimpasta.com

Though some might be tempted to call it the Good Impasta, this place certainly has staying power—it's been a local favorite for ages. The specialty here is pasta—obviously—with a mix of seafood, veal, chicken, and veggies on top. Try the Pollo Spinaci, which is chicken sautéed with fresh spinach, or the manicotti, the primavera Alfredo, or Melanzana Parmigiano, which is sliced baked eggplant stuffed with smoked mozzarella.

Richard's Restaurant $$–$$$
115 Maine Street, Brunswick
(207) 729–9673

Richard's is a find, if only because you can indulge in a little bratwurst, Wiener schnitzel, or Rheinischer sauerbraten (Rhineland-style marinated roast beef) right there in downtown Brunswick. This Maine Street classic is a house divided—on the one hand, you can get good old New English favorites like shrimp and scallops, steak, and sautéed chicken breast, and on the other hand, you can enjoy genuine Deutsch delicacies. German beer is also on tap. Open Monday through Saturday from 11:00 A.M. to 2:00 P.M. for lunch and 5:00 to 9:00 P.M. for dinner (Friday and Saturday till 9:30 P.M.). Closed Sunday.

Scarlet Begonias $
212B Maine Street, Brunswick
(207) 721–0403
www.scarletbegonias.org

This small eatery has all the hallmarks of your neighborhood pizzeria, from the college kids behind the counter to the regulars picking up their to-go pies, but it's much more than that. Typical, Scarlet Begonias is not. Start with the flowers on every table, the local artworks on the walls, the words of high praise from the naval air squadron down the street. Then move to the menu, from which you can order a pizza, yes, but it might be topped with broccoli or hot cherry peppers or even corn. Try the Simon Says, which adds sausage, chicken, peppers, mushrooms, and corn to your average pepperoni. Or try pasta, like the Scarlet Harlot, a classic *putanesca* with garlic, olives, and fresh herbs over penne. Sandwiches and salads abound, and they too are a step up from the usual. How about the terrapin tuna sandwich, for example, which has cheddar, tomato, and Bermuda onion in addition to the fish, on pizza bread? The choices go on and on.

Shere Punjab $–$$
46 Maine Street, Brunswick
(207) 373–0422
www.sherepunjabmaine.com

It's amazing that this Indian eatery at the end of Maine Street is not more popular. If people knew better the quality of the curries, chutneys, and especially the samosas served here, they'd be lining up and fighting over the handful of tables inside. But the small restaurant is rarely full, and you often have the place to yourself. You can usually get one of the tables set up in the window, which is a nice spot to take in all the colorful goings-on out on the street while you wait to feast on nan, dal, and chicken vindaloo. Service is good, food is great, and the menu is deep and long with rice, seafood, chicken, lamb, and vegetarian "delights," so everyone should be able to find something. Prices are probably the catch; they're a little more expensive than other area Indian dining rooms. But they often have specials, and they have a more affordable lunch menu, too.

Star Fish Grill $$$
100B Pleasant Street, Brunswick
(207) 725–7828
www.starfishgrill.com
This eatery is another great find, situated as it is on Pleasant Street, a boulevard also known as Route 1 that is neither particularly pleasant nor anyplace you'd go looking for a grill with inventive cuisine. Crazy with traffic, it's more the province of convenience stores, car dealerships, and fast food. But there in a small, unassuming strip mall, next to a video shop, is the Star Fish Grill. Run by Alyson Cumming, a woman who learned her chops at one of the best restaurants in Portland, Street and Company, the grill has become known for its fanciful seafood, entrees like Cajun blackened salmon, crab cakes, mussels and calamari in green curry, and lobster paella. With blue painted walls and surf on the windows, the decor is fun and whimsical, and the menu is just as entertaining.

Wild Oats Bakery and Café $
149 Maine Street, Brunswick
(207) 725–6287
What a great place this is. First you have to arrange to meet someone here, because this is one of the town's community gathering places. Second, order up a sandwich, a bowl of soup, or some salad and take it to the tables outside, if it's nice, or to the overstuffed chairs in the Tontine Mall, if it's not. The baked goods section—date bars, pecan bars, strawberry snickerdoodles, plus a zillion other cookies and brownies—is amazing. The salad sandwiches—curried chicken, tuna, egg—are fantastic, and every day brings with it a new type of bread. A half sandwich will fill most everybody's belly.

Cooks Lobster House $$$
Off Route 24, Bailey Island
(207) 833–2818
When an ad agency went looking for an authentic Maine lobster pound for the Visa "It's everywhere you want to be" campaign, it settled on Cooks. Not hard to understand why.

In business since 1955, it's everything a lobster pound wants to be: a neat old dining room of varnished pine booths with a wraparound panorama of the green-blue waters of Casco Bay. Obviously the lobster is the main attraction here, and you can get it baked, stuffed, stewed, Newburged, or plain-old boiled. A raft of other choices are there for the picking as well, from oysters to clams to fried fish. Cooks does lobster right, and they'll even ship some home for you by overnight air if you just can't get enough.

Other Dining Options in the Brunswick Area

Great German food can be found at the **Old Munich Biergarten** (6 First Street, Topsham; 207–729–1688). **Fat Boy Drive-In** (Old Route 1, Brunswick; 207–729–9431) has to be one of the last restaurants around with carhops, and its burgers, fries, and prices are great. **Bangkok Garden Restaurant** (14 Maine Street, Fort Andross, Brunswick; 207–725–9708) is a fine place to turn for pad Thai. Great seafood abounds in the area, especially down in the Harpswells. Try the **Dolphin Marina** (South Harpswell; 207–833–5343) or **Block and Tackle** (Cundy's Harbor Road, Harpswell; 207–725–5690) for an indoor, sit-down meal, and **Estes Lobster House** (Route 123, South Harpswell; 207–833–6340) for waterside lobster in the rough.

Bath and Surrounding Area

Beale Street Barbecue $$
Water Street, Bath
(207) 442–9514
www.mainebbq.com
The staff at this exceptional barbecue joint wear T-shirts that read "It's a long way to Memphis," which is where the real Beale Street is. But like that avenue, famed for its food and its blues, BSB serves up good eatin' and music, and Midcoast residents are thankful for it. The business got its start when owner Mark Quigg opened a roadside barbecue stand in Freeport but found himself working a catering job in Bath for the crew of the

Close-up

Lobsterbakes

Many Mainers contend that there's only one real way to eat a lobster—someplace close to the water it came out of and with the salt air on your face. Lobsterbakes are a Maine tradition, and there are innumerable catering outfits that will take you and a group of friends out, usually to an island or rocky stretch of coast, or come right to your yard, and cook you a mess of bugs you'll never forget. Here are a few recommendations.

Foster's Downeast Clambake
Route 1A, York Harbor
(207) 363–3255
www.fostersclambake.com

The Great Maine LobsterBake Co. of the Casco Bay Islands
P.O. Box 15412, Portland 04112
(207) 828–6374
www.cascobaylobsterbake.com

Sam's Lobsterbakes
1281 Forest Avenue, Portland
(207) 797–6719
www.samslobsterbakes.com

Cabbage Island Clambakes
P.O. Box 21, East Boothbay 04544
(207) 633–7200
www.cabbageislandclambakes.com

Coastal Critters Clambakes
551 Atlantic Highway, Northport
(207) 338–3384
www.coastalcrittersclambakes.com

Lobster done right. MAINE OFFICE OF TOURISM

1996 Harvey Keitel–Cameron Diaz feature film *Head Above Water.* Quigg liked the little city and thought it could use a barbecue joint, so he and his brothers went in on the place, and now they fill the parking lot behind Reny's department store with the most delicious aroma from their smokers. The menu is deep with barbecue choices, from pulled chicken sandwiches served on corn bread to jambalaya to the grilled fish of the day. The coleslaw is great, the baked beans even better, and the fries have a spice all their own. The portions can satisfy even the hungriest iron workers.

The Cabin $$
552 Washington Street, Bath
(207) 443–6224
Arguably serving the best pizza in Bath, the Cabin is an institution, a gathering place of lots of locals and hungry shipbuilders—the restaurant sits across the street from the massive yards of Bath Iron Works. The dimly lit restaurant has been packing them in for more than 30 years, and it is always busy. Its wooden booths are filled shortly after they're emptied, and takeout is ever popular. There's a nice outdoor courtyard as well. The pizza is great, with

a tangy sauce that has just the right combination of spices and a crust that is baked to perfection. If you're in the area and have a hankering for pizza and beer, this is the spot. It's an especially nice option if you're in town and it's late—the Cabin stays open until 11:00 P.M. Thursday through Saturday and until 10:00 P.M. during the rest of the week. Open year-round.

Osprey Restaurant   **$$–$$$**
Robinhood Marina, Robinhood
(207) 371–2530
This place used to be quite good when Michael Gagne was the chef. These days it's still serving decent seafood but with less flair. Still, it's generally a busy place, so calling ahead is wise. The Osprey offers nice views of the marina and the waterfront and a fairly traditional menu with the expected seafood dinners—lobster and fried clams, for example—as well as rack of lamb and filet mignon. Open from May through September.

Five Islands Lobster Co.   **$$**
1447 Five Islands Road, Georgetown
(207) 371–2990
www.fiveislandslobster.com
Food with a view is what you'll find at this Midcoast staple. A long wharf extends out into the island-studded drink south of Bath, and there are tables atop it at which to enjoy a traditional lobster dinner. Local fishermen help run the place—they're usually hard at work on the other side of the wharf—so you know the bugs have just arrived, but there are plenty of other options, too. You'll find excellent fried clams, made from a secret family recipe, as well as mussels, shrimp—you name it, as far as seafood goes—and locally famous onion rings.

Robinhood Free Meetinghouse   **$$$$**
Robinhood Road, Georgetown
(207) 371–2188
www.robinhood-meetinghouse.com
Chef Michael Gagne made quite a name for himself at the old Osprey Restaurant on the Georgetown peninsula in the early 1990s, and when he opened this beautiful eatery in the spring of 1996, a lot of people followed him. He's built a larger clientele since, making the Robinhood Free Meetinghouse into one of the state's finest dining rooms. That's no small feat, as this is a tiny village far from the usual corridors of tourist traffic. Gagne's menu is a diverse and worldy affair, with as many as 40 different dishes on any given evening. You might try the Szechuan rib eye, the grilled duck breast with shiitake soy broth, or the haddock Oscar with Maine crabmeat. And he manages to pull it off admirably. The setting is as pretty as they come, too. Built in 1855, the restaurant's home is one of the state's distinctive old meetinghouses, a post-and-beam structure that's all white clapboards on the outside, 16-foot ceilings and 10-foot windows on the inside. As fine as dining comes in Maine and well worth the drive. Reservations are a good idea.

Solo Bistro   **$$$$**
128 Front Street, Bath
(207) 334–3373
www.solobistro.com
Modern food, contemporary taste. That's how this hip joint in downtown Bath bills itself, and by the standards of Victorian downtown Bath—Midcoast Maine, even—it rises to the occasion. The cuisine, as you might guess, is on the nouvelle end of the spectrum. It features New American stuff like grilled hanger steak with carmelized onions and hand-cut pasta in a squash ragout. Everything is done very well and the wine list is obviously a specialty. People seem to be digging the place and it's bringing a cachet to the City of Ships.

Squire Tarbox Inn   **$$$$**
1181 Main Road (Route 144),
Westport Island
(207) 882–7693 or (800) 818–0626
www.squiretarboxinn.com
A lot of people like to spend a few minutes with the goats when having dinner here, and they are a charming bunch. Meals are served

in a 1763 saltwater farm, which is run as a dairy of the goat variety these days, and many of the nice touches during the prix fixe dinner are goat derived. The cheeses are delicious, and the warm buns, made with whey (a cheese by-product), have become a signature dish. Entrees might be rosemary roasted rack of lamb with garden mint sauce, filet mignon, sauteed giant shrimp, or Maine sea scallops. If you can't get enough, you can stay in a room at the inn. Reservations required.

Other Dining Options in the Bath Area

The **Kennebec Tavern and Marina** (119 Commercial Street, Bath; 207–442–9636; www.kennebectavern.com) serves fairly good surf and turf right at the side of the river. **Maryellenz Cafe** (15 Vine Street, Bath; 207–442–0960; www.maryellenz.com) is enjoying good word of mouth for its Italian fare. Lunch fare is a treat at **Star Light Café** (15 Lambard Street, Bath; 207–443–3005), and the lunch pail crowd—read, Bath Iron Works workers—lines up at the **Sandwich Shop** (45 Vine Street, Bath; 207–442–7858). For lobster and seafood try **Spinney's Restaurant** (Route 209, Popham; 207–389–1122), **Lisa's Lobster House and Grill** (Five Islands Road, Georgetown; 207–371–2722), and the **Water's Edge** (75 Black's Landing Road, Phippsburg; 207–389–1803; www.thewatersedge restaurant.com).

Wiscasset

LeGarage $–$$$
Water Street, Wiscasset
(207) 882–5409
When they built the garage here in the 1920s, they gave it a remarkable view of the Sheepscot River. Now it's a restaurant, which puts the panorama to good use—walls of glass on the porch frame the scene nicely. LeGarage is known for its lamb and its finnan haddie (which Mainers line up for), but it has plenty of seafood and vegetarian options as well. Try the lobster pie. Sit on the porch. Open for lunch and dinner and for Sunday brunch.

Red's Eats $$
Water and Main Streets, Wiscasset
(207) 882–6128
This tiny red shack on Route 1 is now legendary for its lobster rolls—they've been voted the best in Maine many times over and been featured in innumerable magazines and newspaper articles from coast to coast. And deservedly so. These hot-dog-roll delicacies aren't exactly cheap, but they're worth every penny. More than one whole lobster supposedly goes into them, and you can choose the amount of mayo or butter you want to add. Other options include plain ol' dogs, fried shrimp, and fried clams. Classic.

Sarah's Cafe $$
Route 1, Wiscasset
(207) 882–7504
www.sarahscafe.com
Many Maine restaurants have trouble staying open in the off-season, when the hordes of tourists leave and take their wallets with them. This has never been a problem for Sarah's. Yes, things do slow down considerably after school goes back into session, but Sarah Hennessey has built up such a loyal local clientele that her cafe on the Sheepscot never seems to suffer. In fact, Sarah's has been expanding ever since she first went into business in Boothbay in 1982.

People used to travel for miles then to tuck into some of Sarah's thick-crust pizza, and eventually the legions of these folks, coupled with all the tourists that found the place, filled her restaurant to overflowing. A few years later she expanded into an old hardware store on Wiscasset's busy Main Street. Sarah's menu has expanded too, incorporating Mexican-via-Maine favorites (haddock burritos, chili boats, etc.), along with seafood courtesy of Sarah's fisherman brother, and her now-famous soups. Area residents will come one night for her beloved pizza and be back again that same week for soup—with trips to the bread bar—or a Whaleboat, her own version of a calzone. She's been serving breakfast for a few years now as well. The atmosphere is extremely comfortable, with wooden booths, tables topped with nautical charts of the area, and seating on a deck overlooking the Sheepscot. All told, it's one of the more memorable dining experiences you'll have in the Midcoast. For her efforts Sarah was awarded the Restaurateur of the Year in 2002 by the Maine Restaurant Association.

The Sea Basket $
Route 1, Wiscasset
(207) 882–6581
www.seabasket.com

Residents of Greater Wiscasset all but cry when this local institution closes its doors in December with another season behind it. Some people from the area have been known to take more than one meal here a day, and others make sure to slide into one of the orange, Formica-topped booths at least once a week. You'll get an inkling of how good the place is as you wait for your order to come up—several framed articles on the wall from the likes of the *New York Times* attest to the Basket's greatness. The name of the eatery pretty much says it all—the majority of people order platters of fried haddock, clams, shrimp, or scallops that come with fries and coleslaw. It's simple but delectable, and the restaurant's method of frying, using soybean oil and a high-tech convection system, cuts down on absorbed fats and is cholesterol-free, so it isn't even as sinful as it tastes. Other recommended options include the clam chowder, the lobster roll, and the lobster stew. (Landlubbers have a few choices as well.) Think of the Sea Basket as a fishy diner and you have the right idea, both of the type of food and the atmosphere.

Other Dining Options in the Wiscasset Area

Bintliffs Ocean Grill (Route 1, Edgecomb; 207–882–9401) sets a decent brunch table—with jazz. **Treats** (80 Main Street, Wiscasset; 207–882–6192; www.treatsofmaine.com) is a great gourmet market at which you can provision for a fine meal.

Boothbay Harbor and Surrounding Area

Baker's Way $
89 Townsend Avenue, Boothbay Harbor
(207) 633–1119

A big yellow building with ample parking out front, this place looks for all the world like your average bakery—and then you see the little sign that says VIETNAMESE FOODS. Step inside and you'll find all the doughnuts, bagels, pastries, and croissants of a traditional bakery, but you'll also discover a menu that is long and deep and filled with traditional Vietnamese dishes like yellow curry (excellent), stir-fried beef, stuffed rice pancakes, and stir-fried lobster. If the TV inside bothers you, step out back into a little garden where there is seating cafe style ringed by greenery. A visit here has a Tourist in Wonderland feel to it—so incongruous is the idea of a great Vietnamese restaurant hidden in a Boothbay bakery—but you'll be glad you went in.

Bet's Fish Fry $
Town Square (off Route 27),
Boothbay Harbor

This is the kind of place you want to find on your vacation—a take-out lobster shack at the side of the town green, owned by a real character, and serving delicious inexpensive lunches. The haddock sandwiches turned out by Bet Lauriat look like the cartoon eats that Shaggy from Scooby-Doo digs into—a real tower of goodness. Another option is the fish and chips. Bet's been at it since the early 1990s, delicately frying away, to the delight of locals and the tourists lucky enough to stop here and dine at one of the funky, cafe-style tables out front. The sign on the side of the place always says jokingly FREE BEER TOMORROW, and may it ever be so.

Andrew's Harborside Restaurant $$–$$$
12 Bridge Street, Boothbay Harbor
(207) 633–4074

If you were to conjure up a seafood restaurant in a Maine resort town in your mind's eye, it would probably look a lot like this eatery just above the harbor. But it'd be better than you think. Known around town for its breakfasts, the place turns to seafood for lunch and dinner, serving up dishes like blackened salmon Alfredo over pasta, lobster in a puff pastry with lavender butter, and pepper-crusted yellow tuna with a wild mushroom risotto.

Kaler's Crab and Lobster House $$
48 Commercial Street, Boothbay Harbor
(207) 633–5839
www.kalers.com
You could come here just for the views—just about every table looks out at the harbor. With its weathering shingles and varnished pine walls and gingham-checked tablecloths, this place has the tourist lobster house look nailed, and the eats fit, too. Seafood served baked, fried, stewed, grilled, and sautéed makes up most of the menu, but you can get steak and chicken as well. People have been known to wax enthusiastic about the fried clams. Kids like the touch tank. Open daily at 11:30 A.M.

Lobstermen's Co-op $$–$$$
97 Atlantic Avenue, Boothbay Harbor
(207) 633–4900 or (800) 996–1740
www.mainelobstercoop.net
USA Today singled out this eatery, run by area lobstermen, as one of the best places to find a "New England Lobster Roll," and whether the editors of "the nation's newspaper" know much about seafood, they're right in this instance. Among the reasons are the ample amount of meat the cook here crams into a bun. Their lobster bake on a platter—boiled bug, a couple ears of corn—is great, and it's nice to know you're directly supporting area fishermen and not some middleman. It also doesn't hurt that the tables look out on the quiet side of the harbor.

Thistle Inn $$$
55 Oak Street, Boothbay Harbor
(207) 633–3541
www.thethistleinn.com
A notorious place for rowdy bikers in the 1960s, the Thistle has been transformed into a

i If you're staying in the Boothbay area and have access to a kitchenette, you can get great seafood deals by shopping at the fish markets and lobster pounds on the east side of the bridge.

very pleasant dining room. The menu is heavy on seafood, and main courses might include grilled salmon, seared Hawaiian ahi (tuna), and scallops in a bed of mascarpone lobster risotto, but you'll also find rack of lamb and chicken Madeira. The atmosphere is "authentic nineteenth century"—sort of—and there is outside dining on the porch. Open for dinner daily at 5:00 P.M. from June through mid-October.

Upper Deck Café $
By-Way at the Footbridge,
Boothbay Harbor
(207) 633–7447
Another reliable place to turn for seafood, the Upper Deck is a good lunch option. Try the Crabmeat Monty Melt, which combines Maine crabmeat with melted Monterey jack cheese and bacon on an open-faced English muffin, or grab a lobster roll or a bowl of the Downeast Seafood Chowdah. Lunch only.

Lobsterman's Wharf $$
Route 96, East Boothbay Harbor
(207) 633–3443
This is the place where the locals get their seafood, so you know it must be good. The tourists tend to stick to downtown Boothbay Harbor, but area residents know they'll find consistently good lobster dinners on this rambling wharf right on the water. Picnic tables overlook the harbor, with all its activity, and they're topped with traditional shore platters, complete with crustaceans and corn, with lobster rolls overflowing with meat, with clam chowder, and with bowls full of steamers, all done with a bit more flair than your average lobster pound. The regulars have been coming here for 38 years—always a good sign.

Robinson's Wharf $$
Southport
(207) 633–3830

Watch lobsters being hauled on Townsend Gut, a stretch of saltwater that gets busy with lobster boats, while you wait to haul your own. Lobster is served any number of ways, and those allergic or immune to the charms of red crustaceans can dig into burgers and fries. The fish chowder has its fans, and people like the crabmeat roll as well. *Yankee* magazine called this a "must"-visit eatery when in Maine. Open daily from mid-June through Labor Day.

Other Dining Options in the Boothbay Harbor Area

Don't forget the fine dining available at the area inns—the **Newagen** and **Spruce Point** (see Accommodations chapter)—they're among the best meals you'll find in town. The **Ocean Point Inn Restaurant** (East Boothbay; 207–633–4200) is popular for its Black Angus steaks. **McNab's Tea Room** (Back River Road, Boothbay; 207–633–7222; www.mcnabstea .com) and **Tea by the Sea** (18 Sunset Rock Road, East Boothbay; 207–633–9996) are British tearooms and fun for it. Despite its name, **Dunton's Doghouse** (40 Sea Street, Boothbay Harbor; 207–633–2403) is known for its seafood. If you can't get enough lobster, try the **Lobster Dock** (Footbridge East, Boothbay Harbor; 207–633–7120; www.thelobsterdock .com).

Damariscotta and Surrounding Area

Augustine's Backstreet Grill $–$$
Elm Street, Damariscotta
(207) 563–5666

This longtime favorite in Damariscotta pays for its exceptional view—some people have a hard time finding the place, which is tucked behind Main Street on a little back alley right on the river. Locals would be just as glad if the tourists stuck to the eateries on Main, as they've always filled the dining room here—they call it by its old name, Backstreet Landing—coming back often for soups, sand-

wiches, and seafood. Try the barbecued ribs or the sautéed shrimp. Open daily year-round from 11:30 A.M. to 2:30 P.M. for lunch and 5:00 P.M. till closing for dinner.

The Breakfast Place $
Main Street, Damariscotta
(207) 563–5434

Homey is the word at this corner shop in downtown Damariscotta. The coffee cups are kept on a neat hutch that seems taken from your grandmother's, the waitress may well call you "dear," and every table has a rooster lamp atop it. So the place is very comfortable, and the fare is good, solid, morning comfort food. If you want something more adventurous than bacon and eggs or pancakes, you can try the McRoss, the house special. It's a French toast sandwich with egg and bacon or sausage. Or order up the broccoli and cheese omelet or the corned beef hash with a single poached egg. The bread is homemade, the coffee has a kick, and the service is just right. Open daily from 7:00 A.M. to 1:00 P.M.

King Eider's Pub $$
2 Elm Street, Damariscotta
(207) 563–6008

This Damariscotta watering hole has a cool cartoon logo, good beer, and a nice selection of pub foods—its burgers are a favorite. The ball game will be on above the bar downstairs, the waitresses will be friendly, and the desserts are not to be missed. Opened in 1996, the place became popular for Culinary Institute of America–trained chef Stephanie Redfern's local oysters on the half shell and fish and chips.

Paige's Deli $
Main Street, Damariscotta
(207) 563–1999

Formerly the site of the ever-popular sandwich shop Zecchino's, this joint is still a good lunch bet. Order at the counter—maybe a crab cake sandwich, a veggie melt on a wrap, or a chicken Caesar wrap—and take it out onto the deck not far from the point where the

Damariscotta River flows by. Or enjoy views of the river from the round, varnished, picnic-style tables inside—if you can score one. This is where the locals grab lunch on the go. Not open for dinner.

The Newcastle Inn $$$$
River Road, Newcastle
(207) 563–5685 or (800) 832–8669
www.newcastleinn.com

The six-course meal at this area institution elicits raves, beginning with appetizers that might include duck livers with mustard greens, moving on to salad with organic greens and a lemon anchovy vinaigrette, then to one of a handful of entrees that might include Atlantic salmon with cucumber-ginger coulis, roasted duck breast with braised bacon and chicken of the woods mushrooms, or hanger steak with a red wine reduction sauce. If cuisine like this served before the fireplace in the fine dining room of a classic New England inn appeals, this place is for you. A prix fixe meal is offered. Open Tuesday through Saturday.

Bradley Inn $$$–$$$$
3063 Bristol Road, New Harbor
(207) 677–2105 or (800) 942–5560
www.bradleyinn.com

A real find, this turn-of-the-20th-century inn serves up some fantastic Pemaquid oysters (the Damariscotta region is famous for the little bivalves). Seafood is prominent on the menu, from salmon to halibut. Try the tasting menu to sample several different flavors and see if you agree with some that the inn's dining room is among the best in the state. Open year-round.

Other Dining Options in the Damariscotta Area

Right downtown the **Salt Bay Café** (Main Street, Damariscotta; 207–563–3302) fills up at lunchtime. A big-time lobster fishing area, the Pemaquid Peninsula has no shortage of lobster pounds. Try **Shaw's Wharf** (Route 32, New Harbor; 207–677–2200), **Muscongus Bay Lobster** (Round Pond; 207–529–5528),

Round Pond Lobster Co-op (Round Pond; 207–529–5725), or **Pemaquid Fisherman's Co-op Harbor View Restaurant** (Pemaquid; 207–677–2801; www.pemaquidlobster co-op.com).

Waldoboro

Borealis Breads $
Route 1, Waldoboro
(800) 541–9114
www.borealisbreads.com

Bodacious, baby. In 1993 Borealis launched under the name Bodacious Breads before discovering that a company of the same name already existed in California. So owner Jim Amaral changed the name to its current, northerly moniker. But the bodacious spirit still animates the bright yellow headquarters kitty-corner across Route 1 from Moody's. Fifteen varieties of freshly baked breads are made here—pick up a loaf of the salty rosemary or the French peasant—and they all have their fans. The real secret, though, is that you can get one of the best inexpensive sandwiches you're ever going to find at lunchtime here. "The Van Gogh of Dough" is the Borealis slogan, and you gotta think old Vincent would be stopping by for lunch if he were vacationing in the Midcoast. There's another retail store in Wells, and Borealis is sold in stores across the state.

Moody's Diner $–$$
Route 1, Waldoboro
(207) 832–7785
www.moodysdiner.com

The sign above the door says simply EAT and under it MOODY'S DINER in bright neon, and people seem to take the message to heart, swinging in off Route 1 as if they have no choice. Moody's is the single most famous restaurant in the state, the L. L. Bean of diner cuisine, and a visit is all but obligatory. Rare are the moments when its parking lot is empty. The Moody family has been feeding generations of Mainers—and their hungry guests—since they opened for business on the old Atlantic Highway in 1927. Back then the road was longer and the ham-and-egg sandwich cost 20 cents. Over the years the humble diner has gained wide acclaim for its fare, especially for its pies and muffins—*Gourmet* magazine asked for the recipe for the walnut pie, *Saveur* named the Moody's whoopie pie a 1999 "food find," and the Culinary Hall of Fame gave the blueberry muffins top honors. Plenty of locals eat at Moody's on a weekly (or even daily) basis, and the eats are dependably good. You'll find all the usual diner suspects—burgers, fries, shakes, turkey sandwiches, tuna melts, but with several Maine twists, like chowders and corned beef hash. You may have to wait a few minutes, though. Pick up a T-shirt that says, "I'm a Moody Person" on your way out the door.

Other Dining Options in Waldoboro

Morse's Sauerkraut (3856 Washington Road; 207–832–5569; www.morsessauerkraut.com) has been selling its famous sauerkraut since 1918, and people go out of their way to make the pilgrimage.

Monhegan Island

There are a surprising number of dining options for such a tiny isle. For fine food you might want to start at the **Island Inn** (207–596–0371), a huge, shingle-style castle of a place with windows overlooking Monhegan Thorofare. The fare here tends toward well-prepared American favorites, heavy on the seafood—a traditional lobster spread, prime rib, and roast duck, that sort of thing ($15–$30). The **Monhegan House** (207–594–7983) is another choice for seafood and steaks, and people like it for its breakfast omelets as well ($15–$25). Dinner at the **Trailing Yew** (207–596–0440) isn't about the food—not that it isn't good—but for the fun. Meals here are on a weekly schedule—Monday is roast beef, Saturday, of course, is hot dogs and beans—and they're taken family style, so you get to know your fellow islanders. Lunch might take you to **Fish & Maine** (207–596–0041), a low-slung place in the village at the site of the old Periwinkles. Here

you'll find burgers, salads, sandwiches, and desserts; the **North End Market** (no phone), the primary pizza place on the island; or the **Barnacle** (207–596–0371), which is near the ferry landing and is a good source for carryout items for the boat ride home, like premade sandwiches, coffees, and cookies. To cool off in the afternoon, take a short walk out behind the Monhegan House and pick up a cone at the **Novelty** (no phone), a small take-out window—if it happens to be open.

Thomaston and Surrounding Area

Silver Lane Bistro $$–$$$
1 Silver Lane, Warren
(207) 273–6464
www.silverlanebistro.com

You can hardly drive around the Midcoast without hearing an ad for this up-and-comer on the radio. Built into an old barn on a side road off Route 1, the small place serves a globe-trotting mix of surf and turf. One day you might want the shrimp scampi, the next the Asian trout, the beef tenderloin with chimichurri sauce, or the duck a l'orange. The dining room is cozy and the desserts worth sticking around for. The place is open for dinner Thursday through Monday. Reservations are a good idea.

Thomaston Café and Bakery $$$
154 Main Street, Thomaston
(207) 354–8589
www.thomastoncafe.com

Herbert Peters, owner-chef of this downtown favorite, got a nod from *Gourmet* magazine for his fish cakes, so you may want to order those. Everything in this small cafe is good, however, and made from scratch. Ingredients tend toward organic, and the fish is not long off the boat. The menu is small but inventive, with a lot of traditional favorites done with flair, like lobster ravioli with fresh oyster sauce or Frenched lamb chops. The fish chowder comes highly recommended as well, and the soups are always a good selection. Quiche, pasta, and sandwich options change on a regularly basis. The seating area is casual, comfortable and bright, and lunch is fairly inexpensive for food of this quality. Recommended.

Waterman's Beach Lobster $$–$$$
South Thomaston
(207) 596–7819

The actual eatery here might not be large, but its reputation certainly is. And the salty panorama is pretty huge, too. Waterman's is in a section of South Thomaston that's off the radar of your average tourist, not that travelers are exactly beating a path to South Thomaston anyway. But to get there you have to swing off the main thoroughfare in these parts, State Route 73, onto Spruce Head Road, turn again onto Waterman Beach Road, and then make your way down a fire road. When you do, though, you find yourself staring out at island-dotted Mussel Ridge Channel and are happier for it. Then you get a taste of the lobster and understand what the fuss is about. It's prepared a variety of ways—grilled, on a roll, in a pie—and they're all worth the calories. Waterman's won a James Beard Award, that culinary stamp of greatness, which is not granted to lobster shacks every day. It was called one of the state's "10 Best Lobster Shacks" by *Travel and Leisure* as well.

Other Dining Options in the Thomaston Area

Dave's Restaurant (Route 1 South, Thomaston; 207–594–5424) is well known and well loved locally for home-cooked seafood. The **Dip Net** (Port Clyde; 207–372–6307; www.dip netrestaurant.com) has a loyal following for its soups, salads, and seafood. For seafood consider **Miller's Lobster Company** (Off Route 73, Spruce Head; 207–594–7406; www.millers lobster.com) or **Cod End** (Tenants Harbor; 207–372–6782; www.codend.com).

Rockland

Amalfi $$–$$$
421 Main Street, Rockland
(207) 596–0012

Amalfi promises diners "the brightest flavors of the Mediterranean with all the freshness of the Maine coast," and it largely delivers. The house specialties include paella, tapas, and seafood dishes, especially oysters, and on any given night there might be a dozen or more entrees to select from in addition to the tapas, salads, soups, and appetizers like Moroccan meatballs and manicotti. From the steamed mussels to the pan-seared Atlantic salmon to the braised shank of lamb, the grilled strip steak to the scallops St. Jacques, everything is uniformly good. The wine list draws praise for its quality and affordability, too. The atmosphere is pleasant and intimate, with classy wooden built-in booths festively painted and small tables in a cozy space. A tiny bar separates the dining room from the kitchen, and the smells are delectable. The bread that comes out first goes quickly, and the desserts that cap the meal—the crème brûlée is a favorite—have gained themselves quite a following. The service tends to be excellent. All told, a very fine dining experience. Reservations are a good idea.

Brown Bag $
606 Main Street, Rockland
(207) 596–6372

A lunch spot par excellence, the Brown Bag used to be so popular that locals would avoid it in summer. You simply couldn't get a parking spot, never mind a table in the restaurant's pretty brick confines. Things seem a little better these days, but it isn't because the food has gotten worse. The fare is still the same: great, made-from-scratch sandwiches, soups, and specials, fresh comfort food of the finest kind. Roast turkey—cut right off the bird—has always been a particular specialty, and you can get it a number of ways: in sandwiches, in pie, in soups, and in wraps. Seafood is big as well. Everything comes with chips and a pickle. Don't forget to stop in the bakery on your way out.

Café Miranda $$–$$$
15 Oak Street, Rockland
(207) 594–2034
www.cafemiranda.com

The pink flamingos stuck in the window boxes

out front should give you the idea that Café Miranda is a kooky place, and it is, but in a very good way. The building used to be a men's club—the Owls Fraternal and Benevolent Club—but you'd never guess it now. The waitstaff is cool to a person, the ambience is fun—you'll feel part of the hip crowd because of all the interesting artsy types who eat here regularly—and there are endless neat touches, like the whimsical salt and pepper shakers on each table, the over-the-top Elvis-themed bathroom, and the colorful slang names for the items on the menu. These entrees, of course, are the real reason for seeking the place out. There's a genuine danger of filling up on the focaccia before you even get to them, though—the salty flatbread here ranks among the best ever—but you gotta resist it in order to enjoy the saucy, wood-grilled dishes that owner-cook Kerry Alteiro serves up. The menu is extensive and covers both sides of a legal-size sheet of paper with small, handwritten entries. (It changes often.) The fare is an eclectic, inventive, international mélange, heavy on the seafood and with a slight Italian slant. From the dozens of appetizers you might try the roasted leek pâté or the oyster mushrooms or the fish tostada. Entrees could be panfried haddock and kimchi, barbecued brisket, chili pork posole, seafood in green sauce, or veal scaloppine. And each comes highly recommended.

The place is dinner only, but Miranda has served lunch on its patio in the past, and it's worth checking to see if that is currently an option. Many good restaurants have popped up in Rockland since Café Miranda first lit its neon sign in 1993, but there are few that are more fun. Loincloths and tool belts are discouraged.

Oh! Bento $$

10 Leland Street, Rockland
(207) 593–9216
www.ohbento.com
From its exuberant name to the tempting Japanese cuisine set before you inside, Oh! Bento is a gem of an eatery on an anonymous side street in Rockland. Bay Bigelow built a devoted following for his sushi and smiles in both Rockland and Camden before selling to Keuth and Karen Olson. Oh! Bento got its start in Camden, offering Japanese box lunches, and those are still a staple, but the menu has expanded with the move to a sit-down restaurant in Rockland. Now a whole slate of lunch and dinner choices, bigger and more complex options, are available as well. The menu has everything from chicken teriyaki to sole tempura, which come with side dishes and rices, as well as a handful of rice bowls, noodle dishes, seven sushis, and six veggie rolls, in addition to soups and salads. You can eat in or call ahead and take out.

Primo $$$$

Route 73, Rockland
(207) 596–0700
www.primorestaurant.com
When Primo opened in April 2000, the buzz was so hot—thanks to reviews in such high-profile magazines as *Esquire, Gourmet, Town and Country, O, Food and Wine,* and *Wine Spectator*—that you almost had to know somebody who knew somebody or be willing to wait a long time to get a table. It's a little better than that now, but you're still going to want a reservation. What's all the excitement about? Call it pedigree. The principal players at the restaurant, Melissa Kelly and Price Kushner, came from the Old Chatham Sheepherding Company, an upstate New York dining room that is frequently considered one of the nation's best, and executive chef Kelly had won the James Beard Foundation's American Express Best Chef for the Northeast award as well as a nod as an upcoming chef from *Food and Wine.* Luckily for Midcoast Mainers, she wanted to open her own place and to do so on the coast of Maine, where she's been visiting for years. Primo, retrofitted into an old Victorian house south of Rockland, is the result. The food has Italian and French overtones, and Kelly uses as much farm-fresh produce and newly landed seafood as she can get. Try the roast breast of Foggy Ridge pheasant, the

grilled wild striped bass, or the Weskeag oysters "Rockefeller Style." Pizzas make for a relatively affordable lunch. Open year-round for dinner Thursday through Monday at 5:30 P.M.

Rockland Café $
441 Main Street, Rockland
(207) 596–7556
www.rocklandcafe.com

This downtown Down East diner has a devoted following—many people eat here several times a week. The family-style menu is filled with seafood options. A lobster roll and fries is a favorite, or you might want to try the homemade fish chowder. From hot pastrami sandwiches to burgers to tuna melts, all the usual suspects can be found here. The specials board is always leaned against the entrance so it can be read from the street. Open year-round daily from 6:00 A.M. to 9:00 P.M. (closes at 8:00 P.M. in winter).

Thorndike Creamery $–$$
385 Main Street, Rockland
(207) 594–4126

When Michael and Shelley Kushner made noises about closing this popular Main Street ice-cream parlor and pizzeria for the winter to go to Florida, Michael had to offer to give the regulars keys to the place so they could still get their pizza fix. And he was only half joking. That's the kind of guy he is and the kind of place this is. The pizza, which Kushner calls New York-style and which comes by the slice or by the pie, is arguably the best in the Midcoast. It's a thin crust, with a nice tangy sauce and just the right spices. There are plenty of locals who keep coming back for it. The ice cream (Annabelle's of New Hampshire) is good, and the hot dogs and Philly-style cheesecakes are not bad either, but what you really want is that slice. Highly recommended.

Wasses Hot Dogs $
2 North Main Street, Rockland
(207) 594–7472
www.midcoastmaine.net/wasseshotdogs/

Wasses Hot Dogs are legendary in Knox and Waldo Counties, especially in Rockland, where there are two locations: this, the original one, and one on the south side of town. The outfit has one of those McDonald's-inspired TWO MILLION SOLD signs, and it's not hard to believe when you see the lines of eager people at the counter on the average workday and figure that most people buy more than one dog. (You can easily do so for under $5.00.) You can smell the grilling onions even before you park your car here, and it's takeout only. There are now four Wasses stands—one in Thomaston and the other in Belfast, in addition to the two in Rockland—and the locales aren't particularly inspired. You'll usually find the little shacks in parking lots. But the hot dogs are as good as they come, grilled in peanut oil, topped with onions, and served on a warm roll. There are a handful of choices—your basic dog, bacon dogs, cheese dogs, chili dogs, and kraut dogs, and combinations of the aforementioned. Keith Wass was studying psychology when he opened the first stand in 1972, and he apparently understands the human psyche—at least where weiners are concerned.

Rockport

Market Basket $
Routes 1 and 90, Rockport
(207) 236–4371

The Market Basket has had a full parking lot seems like forever. Ostensibly a specialty foods store—known for its gourmet groceries and good selection of wine—the cheerful green barn of a building at the corner of U.S. Route 1 and Route 90 becomes a lunch counter at midday and serves up a host of inventive and delicious ready-made dinners in the late afternoon. Diners can choose from a variety of cellophane-wrapped sandwiches in the coolers off to one side or custom-order one on homemade bread or baguette with choices of meats and toppings. There are always a couple of soup options—often tasty and exotic, like African chicken stew or Shaker chicken—as well as a variety of creative salads and deli counter specials. Made from roast turkey, stuffing, and cranberry sauce, the Thanxgiving Sandwich is recommended, as are the Indian chicken salad and the Caesar salad with chicken. There's usually a wait involved with a visit here, but it's always worth it.

Prism Glass Cafe $$
297 Commercial Street, Rockport
(207) 230–0061
www.prismglassgallery.com

When this purple place opened on Route 1, people at first didn't know what to make of it. Was it a gallery? Or a cafe? Turns out it's actually both, combining "high-design glass art" with high-design food art. The *Boston Globe* has called it a "one-of-a-kind experience," and it's that, too. The fare injects traditional New England foods—read seafood and steak—with Italian tastes, so you might find swordfish puttanesca one day and Tuscan meatballs marinara on another. Lobster is well represented, but meat-and-potatoes people should have no fear. The entrees are quite artful themselves, and the glass is fascinating to look at, making a meal here as much a visual as a gustatory treat. The combination of glass gallery and cafe is unique, but it works.

Rockport Corner Shop $
Main and Central Streets, Rockport
(207) 236–8361

This is the sort of cool diner you wish you had in your hometown, the kind where they still sling hash, friends meet over a real burger and fries, and the coleslaw's good. Open only for breakfast and lunch, the place serves up some good eggs and French toast, and lunchtime brings BLTs, grilled cheese, tuna melts, and a wide variety of diner favorites. Good milk shakes, good service, good times. Good people watching, too, when the Maine Photographic Workshops are in session across the street.

Other Dining Options in Rockport

The banks of windows and fine dining make for a nice experience at the Samoset Resort's

Marcel's (Samoset Resort; 207–593–1529); just be sure to bring a jacket.

Camden

Boynton McKay Food Company $
38 Main Street, Camden
(207) 236–2465
www.boynton-mckay.com

When Boynton McKay pharmacy filled its last prescription not too long ago after more than a century in downtown Camden, local residents were worried that the distinctive 1890s drugstore would become another T-shirt shop or other tourist magnet of some sort. So they were pleased to learn that the building would be saved by a group of business owners, its interior preserved, and would become a cafe serving excellent meals year-round. The place still has its cool tin ceilings, soaring glass cases full of pharmaceutical oddments, and old counter, where you can get a coffee or a delicious dessert, and six booths have been added on the opposite wall. (There are a couple of bars with stools, too.) Up above, clocks tell the time around the world, but it's always Coffee Time in Camden. You place your order with the cooks at the back of the shop, choosing from an eclectic menu that might include chicken chimichangas, wraps, fajitas, gazpacho, stir fries, Thai chicken on skewers, and a wide variety of sandwiches and salads. Boynton McKay is very popular with the morning crowd—exceptional coffees, you see—and breakfast items are available all day long. The prices combined with the creativity of the cuisine make this arguably Camden's best lunch bet. Again, expect a wait for a booth (in summer). Open for breakfast and lunch.

Camden Bagel Café $
Mechanic Street, Camden
(207) 236–2661

For breakfast on the go, pop into the old Brewster Mill, find the Camden Bagel Café, and grab one of its freshly baked bagels. You'll find an array to choose from—salt to onion to pumpernickel—and tofutti to slather on top. There are several booths and tables if you feel like lingering, coolers to get your OJ, and a slew of coffees. You may end up standing in line for a few minutes, but you'll feel a part of the local crowd and might even learn something about the community. The bulletin boards inside are among the better in town and you can quickly see what's going on.

Camden Deli $
37 Main Street, Camden
(207) 236-8343
www.camdendeli.com

Half the reason to eat at the Camden Deli is the view of the falls where the Megunticook River meets Camden Harbor. The water goes right under the restaurant and tumbles spectacularly down a bank on the other side. Windows in the dining area overlook it all—and the panorama of the harbor itself isn't too shabby, either. The other reason to visit is simply the extensive list of sandwiches—more than 40—and soups, which are fairly traditional but always good. The eatery was completely remodeled in 2003 and looks classier than ever.

Francine Bistro $$-$$$
55 Chestnut Street, Camden
(207) 230-0083
www.francinebistro.com

Chef/owner Brian Hill has quite the résumé, having cooked at Olives in Boston and in L.A., Hawaii, and New York, and he puts everything he's learned into good use at this cafe up the road from the post office. He also grew up on an organic farm, though, and so he brings to his menu both a sophistication and an understanding of fresh food, plundering the local farmer's market for produce and getting his meats at area farms. Perhaps this explains why he's less seafood-oriented than most of his Midcoast neighbors. You might find braised pork chops with turnip fondue or seared duck breast with a plum sauce, but you can find salmon as well. Dinner here is cozy and hip (Hill used to be a rock star) and something of an event, too. Open Tuesday through Saturday from 5:30 to 10:00 P.M., and reservations are a good idea.

French and Brawn $
Main Street, Camden
(207) 236-3361
www.frenchandbrawn.com

Every town ought to have a grocery like French and Brawn. The store manages to cram a little bit of everything into a relatively small space in downtown Camden, complete with a meat counter, produce section, and small bakery. It's the sort of neighborhood market where the staff knows all the customers, you're always bumping into friends and acquaintances, good local gossip goes around, and there's even an old-fashioned credit system if you're sticking around a while. Besides carrying your average grocery store items, the place has a good selection of gourmet items, as well as premade sandwiches, salads, soups, and even sushi at the back, which you can pick up to go and eat in one of the many parks in town. Makes for a nice picnic option.

Hartstone Inn $$$$
41 Elm Street, Camden
(207) 236-4259 or (800) 788-4823
www.hartstoneinn.com

Wow. Would that every Maine B&B could wine and dine like this Camden sleeper. Like any other inn in town from the street, the Hartstone becomes a world apart when you sit down for a meal cooked up by chef Michael Salmon. Once the head of a staff of 200 cooks turning out meals for hundreds of diners, Salmon now concentrates on pleasing the appetites that can be seated in the dining room of the old Victorian inn. Call it more refined. His influences range from the Caribbean to Europe to Asia, and his menu changes based on what's fresh on any given day. Dishes might include Ducktrap smoked salmon and Maine crabmeat terrine with capers, roasted duckling cannelloni with caramelized onions and a port wine reduction sauce, Chinese five-spice quail, or lobster and asparagus quiche. Desserts are just as appetizing. The inn was lovingly restored and is elegant in a white-linen-and-candles sort of way, and the service is impeccable. Reservations are essential as word is getting out about the place.

Natalie's at the Mill $$$$
43 Mechanic Street, Camden
(207) 236–7008

The Knox Mill in Camden has been many things: major employer, woolen mill, credit card company, and now home to this new eatery. You'll often have to wait here, and some question whether it's worth it. The food is good, more fanciful surf and turf, like grilled poussin with spinach, pan-fried crab cakes, and pan-roasted halibut, and the atmosphere is nice enough, with the Megunticook River plunging by outside. But the place is getting a reputation for being bigger than its britches, with very high prices and service that can be great one day and snooty the next. So you might want to ask around for opinions before you make a reservation. Open for dinner Tuesday through Saturday from 5:30 to 9:00 P.M.

The Waterfront $$
Bayview Street, Camden
(207) 236–3747
www.waterfrontcamden.com

The name says it all here. The Waterfront has cafe-style dining under umbrellas right at the side of Camden Harbor, where you can watch the megayachts parade ostentatiously in and wish for a moment that you could be a reef. The fare is among the more dependable in town, trending toward the seafood. Dinner might be a sesame-seed-seared salmon or blackened haddock with cilantro marinated cukes; lunch could be an herbed salmon burger or a grilled panini sandwich. There's plenty of seating inside the cedar-shingled building, but it's really nicest out on the deck on a sunny day. The Waterfront doesn't take reservations and can fill quickly, so keep that in mind when making your plans.

Other Dining Options in Camden

Cappy's Chowderhouse (Main Street; 207–236–2254; www.cappyschowder.com) is a family favorite for a cup of chowder with a slice of anadama bread. **Atlantica** (1 Bay View Landing; 207–236–6011; www.atlantica restaurant.com) is the yuppie's choice for upscale seafood.

Lincolnville and Lincolnville Beach

Youngtown Inn $$$
Route 52, Lincolnville
(207) 763–4290 or (800) 291–8438
www.youngtowninn.com

The Youngtown Inn is the very picture of a New England country inn, a three-story, white-clapboard, 1810 colonial that used to be part of a dairy farm, but the delectable dishes it presents in its white-linen dining room are straight from France. Owner-chef Manuel Mercier hails from Paris, where he learned to cook, and his menu combines fresh Maine ingredients with French culinary traditions. When your waiter brings out your entree—say, the Faisan Perigourdine (grilled farm-raised pheasant breast with foie gras and brandy), the Loup de Mer au Safran (marinated striped sea bass with saffron broth), or the Filet d'Autruche au Poivre (grilled ostrich with black pepper and brandy), you'll wonder why it was so easy to get a table. The service is first-rate, the dining room is beautifully done, and the wine list is highly recommended. The inn has six rooms upstairs should you decide you need to eat here more than once, and it's only 4 miles from Camden on a spectacular stretch of road pinched between the cliffs of Mount Megunticook and the lake of the same name.

The Lobster Pound $$
Route 1, Lincolnville Beach
(207) 789–5550
www.lobsterpoundmaine.com

The staff at this Midcoast landmark probably spends a lot of time cleaning sand out of the entryway—it's literally steps from the beach. Crowds throng here for its reliably good seafood, especially the shore dinner. The surprise is that you can also get a good turkey dinner or a well-done steak. Exceedingly comfortable, the restaurant can seat large groups and has tables on a patio overlooking the water. Service is friendly and relatively efficient. The parking lot fills quickly, and reservations are highly recommended during the blush of summer.

Other Dining Options in Lincolnville Beach

Chez Michel (Route 1; 207–789–5600) is a favorite for its French food. **Whale's Tooth Pub** (Route 1; 207–789–5200; www.whalestoothpub.com) is a great seaside pub with better-than-average pub fare and a nice woodstove.

Northport

Dos Amigos $–$$
Route 1, Northport
(207) 338–5775
You can always tell when this pink Mexican restaurant just south of Belfast opens for the season—the parking lot overflows with loyal regulars who just couldn't wait for the place to get hopping once again. Dependably good Mexican fare—the nachos are *grande* and the margaritas not small; try the fried ice cream—is what you'll find here in this cozy place. Open mid-March through the end of November.

Belfast

Bay Wrap $
20 Beaver Street, Belfast
(207) 338–9757
Belfast has its own healthy and delicious alternative to fast food in Bay Wrap, a flatbread wonderland retrofitted into an old pharmacy on a side street in the Penobscot Bay city. The original sandwich material, flatbreads have been a staple of on-the-run foods for centuries, and Bay Wrap uses them to good effect, loading them up with a variety of flavors. Anyone could find something on the eatery's globe-trotting menu. If you're hungry for barbecue, order up the Ayuh, It's BahBQ, which combines chicken or steak with barbecue sauce, jasmine rice, roasted zucchini, and Asian slaw. Perhaps you're feeling Japanese?

Try the Samurai Salmon, a mix of grilled salmon, nori, sprouts, cukes, avocado, scallions, and jasmine rice with a wasabi vinagrette. There's also Yeh Man!, a jerk seasoning-based wrap, and The Mexican, which combines chicken or tofu with avocado in a chipotle-spiced tomato sauce.The choices go on and on, and there are soups and salads and bowls of noodles as well. Eat in or take out. All this for just a bit more than a trip to McDonald's. The place has been so successful that it recently spun off an Augusta franchise.

Chase's Daily $$
96 Main Street, Belfast
(207) 338–0555
Tables can be hard to come by at this vegetarian hot spot in downtown Belfast. Waldo County residents—and plenty of people from farther afield—are wild about the creative fare served here. Though everyone just calls it Chase's, the proper name is Chase's Daily, and that's how frequently many people seem to visit. Breakfast is arguably the best in Belfast, lunch is usually packed, and dinner is now served on Fridays and Saturdays in the summer. Veggies come from the family farm in Monroe, and they make their way into an array of innovative and eclectic dishes. Soft tacos; curried fried rice with fresh vegetables, herbs, nuts, and tofu; sandwiches like the fresh tomato, mozzarella, and basil on a baguette; and specialty salads like the all-tomato salad, which features four types of the red fruit with basil and oil, are all regularly featured. There are daily soups and daily pastas and daily breads. The decor is very comfortable with tin ceilings above, wide boards below, and brick everywhere, and you'll rub elbows—sometimes literally, as the tables are close together—with the Greater Belfast "hipoisie." You'll often find produce being sold farm style at the back; get there by noon if you want fresh breads to go or inexpensive bouquets of cut flowers.

i Clams don't have to cost a lot of clams these days, especially if you dig them yourself. The state allows you to pick up to two pecks for personal use, as long as you dig in areas that aren't restricted. Equipment is widely available, and you'll get the hang of digging right quick. It's backbreaking work, but you'll feel like a Mainer—and your dinner will taste better somehow.

Darby's $$
155 High Street, Belfast
(207) 338–2339
www.darbysrestaurant.com
This old eatery used to be the default restaurant in Belfast. There weren't many dinner options back before the arrival of Chase's and Seng Thai and the Twilight Café, and Darby's was always dependable. If you wanted pad thai, you went to Darby's. If you wanted a Cajun chicken sandwich, you went to Darby's. If you wanted a drink after the movies . . . you get the idea. Food has been served at this locale since the Civil War—check the beautiful tin ceilings—and the kitchen here continues to turn out good, unusual fare. In fact, the travel Web site Visiting New England gave the award for "most eclectic restaurant" to Darby's, praising the fact that it mixes Thai, Mexican, and good old Maine cuisines with aplomb. Try the crab cakes or the fish and chips.

Dockside Restaurant $
Main Street, Belfast
(207) 338–6889
A favorite of locals and the travelers who wander down Main Street to the waterfront, the Dockside is your typical Maine family-style, seafood-place diner but with the focus on the fish and crustaceans. Wooden booths, vinyl seating, big portions, friendly staff—it's all very comfortable and familiar. The lobster stew is a crowd-pleaser and, even though it's an appetizer, it's almost a meal in itself, stuffed as it is with meat. You can still get a traditional turkey dinner if you like, but it's the seafood that you'll remember.

Other Dining Options in the Belfast Area

Three Tides (2 Pinchy Lane, Belfast; 207–338–1707; www.3tides.com) is the best place around for bar food and bar fun. **Seng Thai** (Route 1, East Belfast; 207–338–0010) gets raves for its tasty Thai food. **Young's Lobster Pound** (Mitchell Avenue, East Belfast; 207–338–1160) is a lobster-in-the-rough classic. And the **Belfast Co-op** (123 High Street, Belfast; 207–338–2532), a grocery-store-size cooperative that caters to the organic and proud crowd, has great lunches in its cafe, and is a good Belfast microcosm. **Bell the Cat** (Reny's Plaza, Route 3, Belfast; 207–338–2084) was once a downtown cafe—now it's the eatery in Mr. Paperback bookstore, and it's a great sandwich place.

Searsport

Rhumb Line Restaurant $$$–$$$$
200 East Main Street (Route 1), Searsport
(207) 548–2600
www.therhumblinerestaurant.com
Finally, fancy-pants dining comes to Searsport. Waldo County foodies, especially those north of Belfast, have been rejoicing about this place, a fine restaurant on the left as you head out of town—reservations are a must in summer. The chef-owners of the Rhumb Line, Charles and Diana Evans, formerly ran an eatery on Martha's Vineyard, and they bring their talents to this pretty old farmhouse. Their menu is creative American fare, making good use of produce from the inn's own garden, which might include entrees like spicy seared medallions of pork tenderloin, grilled rack of lamb, or curried Contessa shrimp. Desserts are knockouts.

Bucksport

MacLeod's Restaurant $$
Main Street, Bucksport
(207) 469–3963
There are simply not a lot of dining options in Bucksport—this is the tried-and-true place. Family comfort foods, heavy on the seafood,

are what make up the long menu. Choose from among MacLeod's own baked meat loaf, the baked scallop strudel, or the grilled lemon chicken. Everyone in town goes here, sometimes several days a week. Open for lunch and dinner, year-round.

Blue Hill and Surrounding Area

Arborvine $$$
Main Street, Tenney Hill, Blue Hill
(207) 374–2119
www.arborvine.com

Named for the vine that arcs around the front door of its 1823 Cape, the Arborvine has been offering fine dining to residents of the Blue Hill area since summer 2000. The house has been lovingly restored, with the beams and floorboards and fireplaces left in place, which lend the dining rooms a quiet elegance, and the landscaping is classic as well. The menu is traditional New English fare, heavy on the meats, which might be anything from noisettes of lamb *chasseur*, tenderloin steak with three peppercorns, or fresh fish in season. Make sure to allow space down below for the desserts, like the crème caramel. You might recognize proprietors John and Beth Hikade—they used to own the ever-popular Fire Pond.

Brooklin Inn $$$
Route 175, Brooklin
(207) 359–2777
www.brooklininn.com

If you're into wine you're going to want to stop at this Victorian inn. *Wine Spectator* has called the line up of vino here "one of the most outstanding wine lists in the world." Order a bottle and sit down for a menu that changes daily but might include peeky-toe crab cakes, coq au vin (naturally), sesame seared scallops, and finnan haddie with lobster. The produce tends to be organic and in season, the seafood fresh, and the poultry free-range and local. Served in a nice dining room with well-worn floors, Oriental rug, sashed windows, and French doors, it all amounts to an exceptional dining experience.

Morning Moon Café $
Route 175, Brooklin
(207) 359–2373

A local breakfast and lunch favorite, this cafe sits right in Brooklin village proper. The pizza here is quite good—actually everything's pretty good, from the soups and salads to the sandwiches. To-go options are available. In summer you also can order pizza from 5:00 to 8:00 P.M.

Oakland House $$–$$$
435 Herrick's Road, Brooksville
(207) 359–8521 or (800) 359–RELAX
www.oaklandhouse.com

This classic old inn—a mansard-roofed Maine beauty—has been serving dinner for more than 50 years, and it sets a beautiful table, with candles, Blue Onion china, and flowers. Traditional fare with contemporary twists peppers the menu and comes in five courses. Try the prime rib, the Arctic char with tomato and pesto, or the wild salmon. On Thursdays in summer the inn serves a lobster bake on the beach; in the spring and fall the dining room moves to the Shore Oaks Seaside Inn. Very nice.

Other Dining Options in the Blue Hill Area

Set at the reversing falls, **Bagaduce Lunch** (Route 176, North Brooksville; 207–326–4729) dishes up take-out seafood you can take to a picnic table overlooking the water. **Pain de Famille** (Main Street, Blue Hill; 207–374–3839) is a great bakery where you can get all sorts of carryout items, from soups to salads.

Castine

Bah's Bakehouse $
Water Street, Castine
(207) 326–9510

Bah's is the sort of place you hope to find in every town you visit, that comfortable eatery with great food, delightful personnel who remember you, entertaining locals, and prices that allow you to return several times during your stay. Baked goods are the staple here, but people often start their day at Bah's with coffee, return at lunch for one of the area's best sandwiches, and maybe pick up some wine on the way home. Open daily 7:00 A.M. to 2:00 P.M. in summer; during off-season hours are reduced.

Castine Inn $$$–$$$$
Main Street, Castine
(207) 326–4365
www.castineinn.com

Chef Tom Gutow has been praised all over for his culinary talents. He was the Maine Governor's Lobster Chef of the Year in 1998, the Castine Inn was chosen as one of the nation's 50 best by *Food and Wine* magazine, and countless magazines have weighed in with their approval. What's the fuss? Again, creative use of fresh local ingredients and, yes, a way with seafood. Try the Penobscot Bay mackerel with green peppercorn pickled onions, the loin of lamb with pickled fiddleheads, and farm-raised striped sea bass. He even offers cooking classes if you want to understand the source of the magic. The 1898 inn with wraparound porch serves as a perfect backdrop. Open for dinner, May through October.

Dennett's Wharf $
15 Sea Street, Castine
(207) 326–9045
www.dennettswharf.com

On pylons over Castine Harbor, the seating area at Dennett's Wharf puts you right out on the water, almost like dining on a boat. It's a great place to watch the action on East Penobscot Bay, especially in high summer, when the windjammers are running. The fare is made up primarily of stuff that's recently been pulled from that very same drink—oysters are a specialty, as are steamers. Try the boiled Stonington lobster, the roasted chicken, or the grilled barbecued salmon brochettes. If you feel like you've eaten too much, rent one of Dennett's bikes or kayaks and work it off. Open daily from 11:00 A.M. to midnight, from May through Columbus Day.

Other Dining Options in Castine

The **Manor Inn** (Battle Avenue; 207–326–4861) and the **Pentagoet** (Main Street; 207–326–8616; www.pentagoet.com) both open their dining rooms to nonguests and have nice, high-end menus. The **Castine Variety Store** (Main Street; 207–326–8625) is a good bet for crab rolls, of all things.

Deer Isle and Surrounding Area

Goose Cove Lodge $$–$$$$
Route 15A, Sunset
(207) 348–2508 or (800) 728–1963
www.goosecovelodge.com

The setting at this nifty inn is positively magical, overlooking the cove of the same name (you're going to want to get a gander at this Goose), which is an inlet on East Penobscot Bay. Isles and islands, spruce forests, and shimmering sea everywhere you look, and you have to travel some off-the-beaten-track byways to get there. There's dining on the deck or in the dining room known as the Point, with wood grain all around. Surf and turf with occasional Mediterranean influences comprises the menu. Try the porterhouse steak, the Mediterranean seafood stew (lobster, clam, mussels, shrimp, scallops and fish in an orange fennel broth), or grilled Italian sausage served over penne pasta. (See if you can weasel your way into an invitation to stay at the stargazing parties that often occur here in summer.) No kids' menu. Full bar. Open from mid-June through mid-October. Reservations advisable.

Fisherman's Friend $
School Street, Stonington
(207) 367–2442

This place surely must be a friend to fishermen. It serves so much seafood, it must keep half the local fleet in business. The classic Down East–style diner with its varnished booths, low ceilings, plywood paneling, good fresh fish, and pies serves a lot of fishermen breakfast or dinner, too. The chowders and lobster are fan favorites, but you'll also find a turkey dinner with homemade stuffing that's no slouch, either. Portions are hearty enough for a day at sea, prices very fair, and the service very friendly. Definitely save room for the pies or you'll regret it.

Other Dining Options in the Deer Isle Area

Café Atlantic (Main Street, Stonington; 207–367–6373) has great views to go with its good seafood. **Eaton's Lobster Pool** (Deer Isle; 207–348–2383; www.eatonslobsterpool .com) has the same. **Sisters Restaurant** (Little Deer Isle; 207–348–6115) and **Lily's Café** (Route 15, Stonington; 207–367–5936) are great for lunch. **Penobscot Bay Provisions** (West Main, Stonington; 207–367–5177) has exceptional picnic fare.

Ellsworth

The Bangkok Restaurant $–$$
321 High Street, Ellsworth
(207) 667–1324

This place is a real find—some of the best Thai food on the coast served in a small restaurant attached to a motor lodge. Who'd guess? On the hill as you head out of town, Bangkok serves up traditional fare, from great pad Thai to delectable drunken noodles. Prices are reasonable, to boot.

Cleonice Mediterranean Bistro $$$$
112 Main Street, Ellsworth
(207) 664–7554
www.cleonice.com

Now, this is the stuff. The tastes of southern Italy and Spain in a pretty, old downtown landmark in a small Maine town. Cleonice pairs good Maine ingredients—of the land and sea—with the spices and tastes of Europe in a delectable way, offering what it says are the only tapas served north of Portland. The menu is deep and long, with a half-dozen specials per night complementing just as many seasonal entrees and at least a dozen tapas. Try the lamb and pumpkin tagine Marrakesh or the "symphony of seafood," or make a meal of two or three tapas for a feast of flavors. It all adds up to a very welcome addition to the Ellsworth scene. Foodies Down East must be doing backflips.

Maidee's $$–$$$
156 Main Street, Ellsworth
(207) 667–6554

Worldly fare, a 1932 Worcester Deluxe diner tucked inside, and a jungle's worth of foliage make this place an interesting visit, to say the least. Entrees might be anything from a vegan fusion stir-fry to prime rib au jus to sautéed shrimp and salmon with black and white bean cakes. Soups might be seafood chowder or gingered chicken wonton soup. You really never know with this place, except that it will be good. Wine and beer are available, and locals enjoy the bar. Open Monday through Saturday from 4:00 P.M. to close. Closed Sunday.

The Mex $
185 Main Street, Ellsworth
(207) 667–4494
www.themex.com

Mexican fare done well has kept this place hopping since 1980. Atmosphere is fun—nice stuccoed walls, cozy rooms, wooden booths, and beaded curtains—the service is good, and the menu both has some wit to it and is well rounded. Try the chile relleno, the chimichanga, or the enchilada salad. Margaritas, frozen daiquiris, and Mexican beer are readily available. Open daily for lunch and dinner.

Riverside Café $
151 Main Street, Ellsworth
(207) 667–7220

A longtime favorite in Ellsworth with the breakfast and lunch crowds, this is truly a pleasant cafe. The chowder is very good, the omelets are recommended (try the State Street, with spinach, Swiss cheese, mushrooms, and onion), and there are plenty of sandwich, burger, and even vegetarian options. Breakfast is served all day—and people seem to like that—and the Sunday brunch is a local event. Open all year, seven days a week, from 6:00 A.M. to 3:00 P.M.

Union River Lobster Pot $$
8 South Street, Ellsworth
(207) 667–5077
www.lobsterpot.com

Tucked away on the river behind Rooster Brothers, this seafood staple serves up a mean lobster dinner, complete with drawn butter, french fries, coleslaw, and homemade biscuits. That's just the beginning. From clam chowder, lobster stew, and steamers to fried scallops, clams, shrimp, and fish—all the usual suspects are here, served cafe style along the river. Open from mid-June through September.

Trenton

Trenton Bridge Lobster Pound $$
Route 3, Trenton
(207) 667–2977
www.trentonbridgelobster.com

Hard to resist to anyone driving by on Route 3 en route to Acadia, this restaurant places its cookers right outside by the road—and you just know what's inside: fresh lobster. They've been at it since 1956, making this pound one of the oldest in the state, so you know they must be doing something right.

ACADIA AREA
Bar Harbor and Surrounding Area

Ben and Bill's Chocolate Emporium $
66 Main Street, Bar Harbor
(207) 288–3281 or (800) 806–3281
www.benandbills.com

Lobster ice cream may be the confection that turns heads at this Bar Harbor staple, but there is so much more to like here than that acquired taste. From truffles to brittles to fudges to suckers, the place is colorful as a cartoon and smells like heaven. You can watch the machines at work at the back while you try to decide between homemade ice cream or a piece of thick fudge. Ben and Bill's retains the ambience of an old-fashioned candy store, but it's very much a part of the Bar Harbor of the present, serving up ice cream and goodies to crowds and open until midnight in summer.

Café This Way $$$
14½ Mount Desert Street, Bar Harbor
(207) 288–4483
www.cafethisway.com

Everything about this place is imaginative and whimsical, from the burgundy walls to the shelves full of books to the eclectic menu. Sit by the fireplace and order up the Bibimbap, a Korean vegetable stir-fry, or the lemon vodka lobster and be prepared to be delighted when your entree arrives. Or come for breakfast and sit on the deck and try Kit's burrito or the Harney, which is This Way's own corned beef hash. You'll remember which way it is to This Way, and you'll surely be back for more.

Havana $$$–$$$$
318 Main Street, Bar Harbor
(207) 288–CUBA
www.havanamaine.com

Who ever would have thought that Cuba would be such a big draw in Bar Harbor, past home of capitalist barons and now filled every summer with middle-class tourists? You can hardly get a seat in this Main Street eatery, with its ruby-red walls and hip wicker chairs. If you do get in, you can enjoy island drinks at the newly expanded bar or outside in the rock garden while you wait for your "innovative American cuisine with Latin flair"—which could mean crab cakes with roasted corn and cilantro cream or lobster in a quesadilla with charred jalapeño and corn salsa or sole roulades. The menu changes frequently. Open daily from 5:00 to "9:00-ish."

Mache Bistro $$$
135 Cottage Street, Bar Harbor
(207) 288–0447
www.machebistro.com

An intimate space on the main drag, Mache is a true bistro, comfortable and cozy and a place where you feel compelled to linger. The chef here once worked at Portland's famed Fore Street, and his menu is highly regarded for its inventiveness and use of fresh local products. There's a French country influence. Try the seared foie gras, the polenta cakes, or the waterzooi, a fish and shellfish stew. The wine list is impressive as well. Open for dinner nightly in season starting at 5:00. Closed Monday and Tuesday in the winter.

Maggie's Restaurant $$–$$$$
6 Summer Street, Bar Harbor
(207) 288–9007
www.maggiesbarharbor.com

Maggie O'Neil knows her way around seafood, having shucked scallops on a commercial dragger back in the mid-1970s and worked in the fish marketing business. She personally selects the fish that she now serves at her Bar Harbor restaurant, and she also grows many of her vegetables. Even the beef and poultry are local. So things tend to be good and fresh at Maggie's. The menu changes weekly and is heavy on the seafood, but the chefs here do artful vegetarian dishes with all that produce. Try the Maine crab cakes with mustard-caper remoulade, the lobster crepes, the crab enchiladas, or the seafood Provençale. Open Monday through Saturday for dinner, June through October.

Poor Boy's Gourmet $$
300 Main Street, Bar Harbor
(207) 288–4148
www.poorboysgourmet.com

You'll find this place by the gardens out front, which bloom colorfully and all but obscure the porch. Your best bet here is the early-bird extravaganza, an all-you-can-eat pasta smorgasbord with 10 or so options, from baked stuffed farfalle to linguine with clam sauce to linguine with pesto. Sample all you like, but be sure to leave room for the famous cheesecakes. The a la carte menu is extensive, with lobster 10 different ways as well as steak, chicken, and vegetarian choices. Open seven days a week.

Reading Room Restaurant $$$$
Bar Harbor Inn
Municipal Pier, Bar Harbor
(207) 288–5331

Once was, you had to be some sort of mag-
nate or nabob to dine at the Reading Room—during the golden age of Bar Harbor it was a gentlemen's club of the rich and famous. Today you don't even need to wear a jacket (dress is informal). The views of Frenchman Bay from the big bay windows, though, are still extraordinary. Fare is fairly traditional New English—boiled lobster and lobster pie are specialties, and seafood dominates the menu, with charbroiled swordfish and Frenchman Bay bouillabaisse being another pair of options. Terra firma is represented by selections like the Dijon roasted rack of lamb and the citrus grilled breast of chicken. Sunday brunch is a good time to visit, as is lunch any day, when you can enjoy the Reading Room's menu at the Terrace Grille, an outdoor cafe overlooking the bay. Open for breakfast from 7:00 A.M. to 10:00 P.M., terrace from 11:30 A.M., and dinner from 5:30 to 9:30 P.M.

Rosalie's Pizza $$
46 Cottage Street, Bar Harbor
(207) 288–5666

This is the place for pizza on Mount Desert Island, and it's one of the best pizza joints in all of Maine, frankly. Unless you get here early, you'll have to stand in line with the locals and tourists for a table. Enjoy the 1950s kitsch while you do. The homemade pies come in four sizes, and the sauce and spices are exactly how you want them. Worth the wait—or call in an order and picnic by the water. Beer and wine are served.

The Rose Garden $$$$
Bluenose Inn
90 Eden Street, Bar Harbor
(207) 288–3348

Across from the College of the Atlantic, the dining room at the Bluenose Inn features a three-course prix fixe menu of "contemporary American regional cuisine." (That's steak and seafood to you.) You might start with petite crab cakes, locally smoked salmon, or chilled mango soup with jumbo shrimp, then move on to grilled salmon with a spinach potato terrine, Maine lobster out of the shell with pepe pasta, or rack of lamb. Desserts could be sweet potato crème brûlée or white chocolate and raspberry mascarpone cheesecake. If you don't wear "dressy casual" attire (button-down shirts and no jeans), you might feel out of place. Open daily from 5:30 to 9:30 P.M.

Rupununi $$
119 Main Street, Bar Harbor
(207) 288–2886
www.rupununi.com

This place right downtown is always spirited. The name is from Guyana, but the cuisine doesn't really show any one strong influence other than Maine seafood. There are hints of the Mediterranean in the Porcelli's veal piccata and the lobster fettucine and a little bit of the South in the bourbon pork chops and Louisiana gumbo. A raw bar appeals to oyster lovers; others like the burgers, from beef to veggie, ostrich to buffalo. A fun spot, and there is often live entertainment happening. Open from 11:00 A.M. to midnight daily.

Burning Tree $$$
Route 3, Otter Creek
(207) 288–9331

The specialties at this excellent eatery are gourmet seafood and vegetarian fare, and people routinely make the 5-mile journey out of Bar Harbor to get a table here. An open and airy place, it tries to utilize seafood newly arrived from the boats and produce from its own gardens. The menu is witty and fun. Try the blueberry lavender soup, which comes chilled, or the squash blossoms stuffed with goat cheese. Entrees might include sautéed halibut in a Parmesan crust or salmon grilled over sweet corn bread pudding. Yum. Reservations are a good idea.

Other Dining Options in Bar Harbor

Michelle's (194 Main Street; 207–288–0038) at the Ivy Manor Inn is an elegant pairing of French and New English. **Lompoc Café and Brewpub** (36 Rodick Street; 207–288–9392) is Bar Harbor's oldest brewpub and has a beer garden with boccie. **Jack Russell Brew Pub**

(102 Eden Street; 207–288–5214) is another go-to place for suds. **Jordan's Restaurant** (80 Cottage Street; 207–288–3586) is the place to get breakfast.

Northeast Harbor

Colonel's Deli Bakery $$
Main Street, Northeast Harbor
(207) 276–5147

A favorite for breakfast, this unpretentious place also has good pizzas with homemade crust and a nice selection of beer and wine. You can fashion a pretty fine picnic from the sandwiches, snacks, and pies here or eat a seafood dinner that holds its own with other more expensive options across the island. Open from 6:30 A.M. to 9:00 P.M. from April through October.

Docksider Restaurant $
14 Sea Street, Northeast Harbor
(207) 276–3965

People rave about the lobster served at this straightforward place not far from the chamber of commerce, whether it be the traditional boiled version or the lobster roll. Locals and visitors line up for it. The chowders have their fans, too, as do the crab cakes, and there are plenty of salads and burgers for those who prefer not to eat seafood. Open from 11:00 A.M. to 9:00 P.M. daily for lunch and dinner.

Other Dining Options in Northeast Harbor

Don't forget the inns. The **Asticou** (Route 3; 207–276–3344) has an elegant dining room. For more picnic fare try the **Pine Tree Market** (Main Street; 207–276–3335), an excellent little grocery.

Southwest Harbor and Surrounding Area

Beal's Lobster Pier $$
182 Clark Point Road, Southwest Harbor
(207) 244–3202
www.bealslobster.com

Right next to the local Coast Guard base, this

lobster pound has an incredible view, overlooking Southwest Harbor and the mountains of Acadia. Beals have been working the waterfront here for generations, and the seafood at their restaurant is newly landed. Chowders, clams, and lobsters a variety of ways are the specialties, and they're done right. If you fall in love, you can ship whatever you want home via next-day air.

Fiddler's Green Restaurant $$$
411 Main Street, Southwest Harbor
(207) 244–9416
www.fiddlersgreenrestaurant.com

Like the best of Maine's restaurants, this place makes fine use of fresh local fish and seasonal ingredients. The chef here makes everything possible on the premises, smoking the fish, stuffing the ravioli, baking the breads. The menu changes frequently, and guests in the eatery's three dining rooms can choose from a half dozen specials in addition to the nightly fare, which might be smoked rainbow trout, seared and roasted duck breast with pomegranate glaze, or grilled and marinated rib-eye steak. Extensive wine list. Open Friday to Sunday from 5:30 to close, May through October.

Little Notch Café $$
Main Street, Southwest Harbor
(207) 244–3357

The name of this place suggests a small alpine eatery sandwiched between tall peaks. But it actually comes from the notch in the side of Acadia's Western Mountain, which cafe owner Arthur Jacobs grew up looking at. The Seal Cove native left Mount Desert for cooking school and returned to open this great lunch spot smack in downtown Southwest Harbor. The gourmet pizzas, sandwiches, salads, and soups attract a whole host of regulars, and the smartly decorated cafe, with its picture windows looking out on the street and wrought-iron chairs, has enough curb appeal to attract passersby. Pizzas are topped with an array of original flavors, like turkey sausage, prosciutto, hot chili peppers, and artichoke hearts. The sandwiches are just as creative—sweet Italian sausage with Parmesan, say, or roasted broccoli, onions, and cheddar—and they come on delectable focaccia. Open from 11:00 A.M. to 8:00 P.M.

Restaurant XYZ $$
Shore Road, Manset
(207) 244–5221

It's hard to decide which is more stunning, the view from the dock here or the fact that this place exists at all. The X, Y, and Z of the name stand for Xalapa Yucatan Zacatecas, and the small eatery serves foods of the Mexican interior, the sort of cuisine you might find in a mid-size city in Mexico. This might be *mole poblano,* which is chicken mole; *lengua mexicana,* which is beef tongue; or *camarones ajo,* which is tiger shrimp. Entrees are served with flour tortillas and a salad. Everything is made right here from scratch, with imported chilies from Mexico, and the degree of spiciness is left up to the diner. There are the expected margaritas and Mexican beers as well. What a wonder this place is.

Other Dining Options in the Southwest Harbor Area

Beech Hill Farm (Beech Hill Road, Somesville; 207–244–5204) is a fine source for organic produce, locally made breads, meats, and gourmet items. **Sawyer's Market** (344 Main Street, Southwest Harbor; 207–244–3315) is an upscale market with a gourmet deli. For lobster try **Thurston's Lobster Pound** (Steamboat Wharf Road, Bernard; 207–244–7600).

DOWN EAST
Hancock Point

Crocker House $$$–$$$$
Hancock Point Road, Hancock Point
(207) 422–6806
www.crockerhouse.com

One of the best places to stay Down East is also one of the best places to dine. A country inn in exclusive Hancock Point, the Crocker House serves up a fairly traditional menu that is exceedingly well done. Try the house special—Crocker House scallops, which are served with a lemon wine sauce—the broiled swordfish, or the shrimp scampi. Veggies come straight from the garden, desserts are homemade and fresh. Fine food is hard to find the farther you go down the coast—this place holds its own with just about anyone. Open daily from mid-April through October and weekends in the off-season.

LeDomaine $$$$
Route 1, Hancock
(207) 422–3395 or (800) 554–8498
www.ledomaine.com

Less than 10 miles from Ellsworth, this inn feels a world away, and part of that is due to Nicole Purslow's exquisite French country cuisine. The place is warm and welcoming with its Provençal fabrics and fireplace (the lobby and bar have been recently renovated), and when you sit down, you'll not believe the dishes that come out of the kitchen. Traditionally French, the entrees make use of fresh ingredients, and they might be Coquilles St. Jacques Saute Provençale, which are Maine sea scallops pan-seared; Filet Mignon Bordelaise, which is steak in a rich bordelaise sauce; and Le Charlotte d'Agneau aux Aubergines, a braised lamb dish. The desserts are fantastic, especially the house's special bread pudding Le Domaine, and there are 5,000 French wines in the wine cellar. Many Maine guidebooks simply end here when writing about dining on the Down East coast, because it doesn't get any better. Inn guests have a reserved table, and you'll be wanting to make a reservation so you don't drive all the way out here to find the dining room full. Open Tuesday through Sunday from 6:00 to 9:00 P.M.

Other Dining Options in the Hancock Point Area

For lobsters in the rough, you can't beat the **Tidal Falls Lobster Pound** (Off Route 1, Hancock; 207–422–6457). **Ruth and Wimpy's Kitchen** (Route 1, Hancock; 207–422–3723) serves sandwiches.

Winter Harbor

Fisherman's Inn Restaurant $$–$$$$
7 Newman Street, Winter Harbor
(207) 963–5585

The irony at this Winter Harbor staple is that there is no inn. No matter, the food cooked up by award-winning chef Carl Johnson is reason enough to visit. (Plus, it's on the way to the Schoodic Point section of Acadia National Park.) Johnson was the Maine chapter of the American Culinary Association's selection as the 2002 Chef of the Year, and if you sit down for a meal here, you'll understand why. Seafood is prominent on the menu, with native lobster showing itself in a variety of ways, but you can often find a delectable filet mignon, which makes for interesting eating in a community better known for its views than its culinary options.

Other Dining Options in the Winter Harbor Area

West Bay Lobsters in the Rough (Route 186, Prospect Harbor; 207–963–7021) lives up to its name. For sandwiches try the **Downeast Deli** (Routes 186 and 195, Prospect Harbor; 207–963–2700).

Jonesboro and Surrounding Area

The White House $
Route 1, Jonesboro
(207) 434–2792

Like Moody's Diner down the coast, this Down East restaurant has achieved legendary status (though mostly to residents of Washington County). And again like Moody's, a lot of the esteem in which people hold the place is due to the pies it serves. People swear by them. The parking lot here is filled most of the time with diners interested in the pies, the seafood platters, the fish chowder, and the breakfast, which begins at 5:00 A.M. Try the homemade molasses doughnut, the corned beef hash, or the waffles. Just about everyone has a different favorite, from the eggs to the pancakes, so it must be good. Sit down at the counter or one of the tables, and you can say you've had breakfast, lunch, or dinner at the White House.

Other Dining Options in the Jonesport-Jonesboro Area

Joshy's Place (8 High Street, Milbridge; 207–546–2265) is a tiny takeout with great crab rolls.

Machias

Helen's Restaurant $–$$
32 Main Street, Machias
(207) 255–6506
This family favorite has become legendary Down East for its pies—try the blueberry. The fare is best described as "Maine seafood dinery" and consists of a lot of fried fish, stews (excellent), and the usual assortment of burgers and dogs. But what you really want is a piece of pie. Open from 6:00 A.M. to 8:00 P.M. daily year-round.

Riverside Inn $$
Route 1, East Machias
(207) 255–4134
www.riversideinn-maine.com
Machias is not brimming with creative eateries, which makes the dining room at the Riverside Inn a treat. Here you'll find entrees like chicken Milan, pistachio-crusted pork medallions, lobster and scallops in Champagne sauce—you know, the kind of stuff you're not supposed to find outside of cities and resorts and certainly not in remote fishing villages. Your table overlooks the Machias River, so you can enjoy views while you take your meal. Nice.

Whole Life Natural Market $
80 Main Street, Machias
(207) 255–8855
www.wholelifemarket.com
This funky co-op is exactly the sort of thing a small Down East college town needs. You've got your natural and gourmet products, your supplements, your bulk items, and a neat little counter where you can pick up a garden burger, garden salad, or tofu, hummus, or vegetarian wrap. Very nice in a seafood-and-potatoes town like Machias.

Lubec

Home Port Inn $$–$$$
45 Main Street, Lubec
(207) 733–2077 or (800) 457–2077
www.homeportinn.com
Lubec isn't exactly bursting at the seams with fine restaurants, and this place is the best of them. The dining room is in a pretty old 1880s inn, tastefully done, and the menu is slanted toward seafood. You might start with some cold smoked salmon, move on to Down East scampi, flounder, or steak au poivre, and finish up with some blueberry shortcake. Reservations are advisable. Open from 5:00 to 8:00 nightly.

Other Dining Options in Lubec

Murphy's Village Restaurant (126 Main Street; 207–733–4440) has good homemade pies.

Eastport and Surrounding Area

WaCo Diner $
Water Street, Eastport
(207) 853–4046
Don't let the locals intimidate you away from this legendary diner dive on the waterfront (they like to turn and give newcomers a menacing stare). It actually isn't even dark and smoky anymore, thanks to a new expansion that has made way for a deck over the water and a face-lift to the exterior (due to its status as an extra in *Murder in Small Town X*, perhaps?). WaCo stands for Washington County, and this place has been a fixture since the 1920s. Breakfasts are great, and there are all your favorite diner foods from the roast turkey dinner to good burgers. And, of course, plenty of seafood. Open year-round.

Lobster Crate $–$$
Route 190, Perry
(207) 853–6611
One would think that great seafood would be easy to come by Down East, but it's actually more difficult to locate than you might think. Quality control at some lobster shacks just

isn't what it should be, and the meals you end up taking can be less than satisfactory if you stumble into the wrong place—which is why Mainers and travelers alike are thankful for the Lobster Crate, not far from Route 1 on the way down to Eastport. It's got the neodiner ambience that is so common in the Pine Tree State, with simple booths and plastic trays and ordering at the counter, and takeout is also available. The food is far from ordinary, however. The clam chowder is a particular favorite—it must be close to a quart—and the lobster roll is recommended as well. The fish is fresh, and the restaurant has the hallmark of any good Maine place—it always fills up with locals.

Other Dining Options in the Eastport Area

Eastport Chowder House (167 Water Street, Eastport; 207–853–4700) has great, yep, chowders.

Robbinston

**Katie's on the Cove (aka
Katie's Chocolates)** $
Route 1, Robbinston
(207) 454–3297
www.katieschocolates.com
Who knew there even were chocolate recipes from "Down East candy makers of the past"? Lea and Joseph Sullivan have been using those old-fashioned notions to make some of the best chocolates you'll ever find. They're hand formed and hand dipped and so popular they get mailed out around the globe. It's hard to find better fudge and truffles and barc anywhere.

Calais

Bernardini's $–$$
89 Main Street, Calais
(207) 454–2237
One of very few reasons to go to Calais to eat, Bernardini's is a fairly straightforward Italian place with all the expected pastas and marinaras. But Marilyn Bernardini is a gifted

enough chef to win the Maine Restaurant Association's Restaurateur of the Year of award in 1999. Try one of her soups or even the lobser rolls, which were pleasant surprises. The place is comfortable, with its checkerboard walls and glass-topped tables, but not fancy. Open year-round from 11:00 A.M. to 8:00 P.M. Monday through Saturday; closed Sunday.

Other Dining Options in Calais

Chandler House (20 Chandler Street; 207–454–7922) serves very well-prepared seafood. **Sandwich Man** (206 North Street; 207–454–2460) has reliably good subs.

ICE CREAM

Lobster ice cream? It seemed inevitable that someone would come up with the idea of combining the favorite dinner of Mainers with one of their favorite desserts. (Ben and Bill's Chocolate Emporium in Bar Harbor has the crustaceanary cream if you're interested.) Ice cream is indeed one of the preferred snacks in Maine, second maybe to whoopie pies in the estimation of the state's residents, and it's available all along the coast at various stands and shacks. You can get a wealth of flavors, soft serve and hard packed varieties, edible cones, and toppings galore. But there are a handful of places that make ice cream that transcends, crafting dairy art out of a few ingredients. Those are listed here.

South Coast

Brown's Old Fashioned Ice Cream
232 Nubble Road, York Beach
(207) 363–1277
You'd figure that Ben Cohen, of Ben and Jerry's fame, might know a thing or two about ice cream, so when he goes nominating an ice-cream stand as one of the 10 best in the nation, it must mean something. He did just that for this low-slung brown ice creamery near the Nubble Light, calling it "the quintessential summer ice cream stand" in the pages of *USA Today*. Not bad for the neighborhood

favorite that has been scooping out cones since 1967. Try the Maine Survivor flavor. To be fair, Ben goes on to say that the ice cream here is good, but the view is the real treat. Still, the cold stuff holds its own.

The Goldenrod
York Beach
(207) 363–2621
www.thegoldenrod.com
Best known for its saltwater kisses, the century-old York Beach favorite also makes 135 flavors of homemade ice cream dished up at an old-fashioned marble soda fountain, as it should be.

Viking Ice Cream and Candy
Main Street, Ogunquit
(207) 646–3982
Select from among 30 to 40 flavors here while putting together your own sundae, salad-bar style.

Big Daddy's Ice Cream
Route 1, Wells
(207) 646–5454
A favorite for decades, Big Daddy's can have lines well after 9:00 P.M., thanks to excellent homemade dairy goodness. Some 30 flavors are available, from the usual—vanilla and chocolate—to more exotic treats like ginger and coconut and strawberry cheesecake. Summer in Wells wouldn't be the same without it.

Shains of Maine
1491 Main Street, Sanford
(207) 324–1449 or (800) 324–0560
www.shainsofmaine.com
Besides being one of the best and brightest wholesalers of ice cream in Maine, Shain's supplies the Portland Sea Dogs baseball team with their delicious "dog biscuits." And they have a retail operation in Sanford where you can tour the factory and sample the more-than-100 flavors the company turns out. Delightful.

Greater Portland
Beal's Famous Old-Fashioned Ice Cream
Scarborough
(207) 883–1160
There's nothing too special about Beal's ice-cream stands—they look like any other small roadside takeout—but when the staff person opens the window and hands you a homemade "Swiss" cone filled with rich, creamy, cold, and sweet vanilla, you know you've found something special. Beals serves up 150 homemade flavors.

Q's Ice Cream
505 Fore Street, Portland
(207) 799–0552
A funky spot on the fringes of the Old Port, Q's produces an astonishing 200 varieties right there on the premises. Try the triple chocolate delight.

Midcoast
Downeast Ice Cream
Pier One, Boothbay Harbor
(207) 633–3016
Ice cream with a view is the focus here (of course, you can get seven frozen yogurt, sherbet, and sugar-free cones, too).

Wannawaf
At the Footbridge
Under the Harborside Restaurant, Boothbay Harbor
(207) 837–1274
This take-out stand would be better served listed under a waffle heading, but since there isn't one of those, it goes here. Since the late 1980s this spot has been the site of an ice-cream stand, and for the past few it's been home to Wannawaf, which combines ice cream with hot Belgian waffles. Try the Maine Squeeze, which adds blueberry ice cream, blueberries, blueberry syrup, and whipped cream to a waffle, or the Classic, which is a waffle with vanilla ice cream, strawberries, and whipped cream. Decadent.

Round Top Ice Cream
Business Route 1, Damariscotta
(207) 563–5307
Round Top not only sells its 52 flavors in stores across the Midcoast, but it sells them in an ever-expanding gambrel-roofed stand on the way out of Damariscotta. In business since 1924; people still flock here regularly.

Dorman's Dairy Dream
Route 1, Thomaston
(207) 594–4195
Sure, the name has a preciousness to it, but this roadside ice-cream stand is the real deal, having been a hugely popular institution for more than 50 years. Kendrick Dorman started serving homemade ice cream out of a little white building on the Rockland Thomaston town line, back before Route 1 was even Route 1. His brother, William, was doing the same thing down the road, making cones from ice cut on northern Maine lakes. Sugar shortages during the Second World War forced the pair to combine their efforts, and their enterprise as it stands today was born. Family members still run the shop, dishing out 22 flavors of homemade goodness, and crowds line up for it, particularly the pistachio. Good to see it survive all the development occurring in the neighborhood.

FARMERS' MARKETS

Farmers' markets are still a big deal in Maine—from roadside stands to small shops to once-a-week parking lot gatherings, they're the source of produce for a lot of Mainers. The food is fresh, and the farmers are often fun characters. They give you an excuse to venture out into the countryside, and by spending your money at the source, you help preserve both sustainable agriculture and open space, by preserving family farms.

Oftentimes, the veggies are even less expensive at farm stands than they are at the grocery store, and they're a lot less work than doing it yourself. (Some residents of Knox and Lincoln Counties don't even bother to plant gardens anymore because they know the produce is better at the legendary Beth's Farm Market in Warren.) Many farmers are organically certified, and many markets carry much more than greens and corn. Some have meats, ciders, honeys, jams, yarns, and cut flowers. If you're in Maine for any length of time and have access to cooking facilities, farmers' markets are the way to go for good, cheap meals.

South Coast

South Berwick Farmers' Market
Central School, Main Street,
South Berwick
(207) 384–2093
Open Thursday from 4:30 to 7:00 P.M. from mid-July through August.

Springvale/Sanford Farmers' Market
Rite Aid parking lot at Routes 109 and 11A, Springvale
Parking lot next to Sanford Institution for Saves (SIS), Route 109, Sanford
(207) 324–0331
Open at Springdale Wednesday and Saturday from 8:00 A.M. to noon and at Sanford Friday from 8:00 A.M. to noon from May through October.

Gateway Farmers' Market
Greater York Region Chamber of Commerce, Route 1, York
(207) 363–4422
www.gatewaytomaine.org
Open Saturday from 9:00 A.M. to noon from Memorial Day through mid-October.

Wells Farmers Market
Wells Town Hall, Route 109, Wells
(207) 646–5926
www.wellsfarmersmarket.org
Open Wednesday from 2:00 to 6:00 P.M. from May through mid-October.

Farmers' markets are a great source of fresh blueberries. JENNIFER SMITH-MAYO

Kennebunk Farmers' Market
Municipal Parking Lot, Route 1, Kennebunk
(207) 646–5926
www.kennebunkfarmersmarket.org
Open Saturday from 8:00 A.M. to noon from
May through mid-October.

Saco Farmers' and Artisans' Market
Saco Valley Shopping Center, Saco
(207) 929–5318
www.sacofarmersmarket.com
Open Wednesday and Saturday from 7:00 A.M.
to noon from mid-May through October.

Greater Portland

Maine Mall Farmers' Market
Just off Gorham Road, Maine Mall, South
Portland
(207) 929–3248
www.mainemallfarmersmarket.org
Open Friday from noon to 5:00 P.M. from early
May through mid-October.

Portland Farmers' Market
Monument Square and Deering Oaks Park,
Portland
(207) 883–5750

Open Wednesday from 7:00 A.M. to 2:00 P.M. at Monument Square and Saturday from 7:00 A.M. to noon at Deering Oaks Park from late April through mid-November.

Falmouth Farmers' Market
Shops at Falmouth Village, Route 1 and Depot Road, Falmouth
(207) 846–4405
Open Wednesday from 3:30 to 7:00 P.M. from late May through mid-September.

Cumberland Farmers' Market
Greely Green, Main Street,
Cumberland Center
Route 1, at Wal-Mart, Falmouth
(207) 865–9539
www.cumberlandfarmersmarket.org
Open Wednesday from 2:00 to 5:00 P.M. at Falmouth and Saturday from 8:30 A.M. to 12:30 P.M. at Cumberland Center from mid-June through late September.

Midcoast

Brunswick Farmers' Market
Brunswick Mall, Maine Street, and Crystal Springs, 9 Pleasant Hill Road, Brunswick
(207) 966–2363
www.brunswickfarmersmarket.com
Open Tuesday and Friday from 8:00 A.M. to 3:00 P.M. at Brunswick Mall and Saturday from 9:00 A.M. to 12:30 P.M. at Crystal Springs Farm from early May through the end of November.

Bath Farmers' Market
Bath Waterfront Park, Commercial Street, Bath
(207) 582–2213
www.bathfarmersmarket.com
Open Thursday and Saturday from 8:30 A.M. to 12:30 P.M. from May through October.

Boothbay Farmers' Market
Town Common, Route 27, Boothbay Harbor
(207) 563–1076
Open Thursday from 9:00 A.M. to noon from mid-May through October 5.

Damariscotta Area Farmers' Market
Damariscotta River Association, Belvedere Road, Damariscotta
(207) 737–8834
Open Monday and Friday from 9:00 A.M. to noon from mid-May through October.

Rockland Farmers' Market
Public Landing, Rockland
(207) 594–8644
Open Thursday from 9:00 A.M. to 1:00 P.M. from the end of May through mid-October.

Camden Farmers' Market
Colcord Street (across from Tibbet's Industries)
(207) 722–3112
www.camdenfarmersmarket.org
Open Wednesday from 4:30 to 6:30 P.M. from mid-June through September and Saturday from 9:00 A.M. to noon from mid-May through October.

Islesboro Cooperative Farmers' Market
On the grounds of the Island Lodge, Main Road, Islesboro
(207) 323–3656
Open Thursday from 9:00 A.M. to 1:00 P.M. from early June through mid-August.

Belfast Farmers' Market
Municipal Parking Lot, Lower Main Street, Belfast
(207) 649–0831
www.belfastfarmersmarket.org
Open Friday from 9:00 A.M. to 1:00 P.M. from May through mid-November.

Belfast New Farmers' Market
Reny's Parking Lot, Routes 1 and 3, Belfast
(207) 338–2895
Open Tuesday, Friday, and Saturday from 9:00 A.M. to 1:00 P.M. from May through October.

Bucksport Riverfront Market
Main Street, Bucksport
(207) 469–7368
Open Saturday from 9:00 A.M. to 1:00 P.M. from the end of May through September.

Blue Hill Farmers' Market
Blue Hill Fairgrounds and Congregational
Church parking lot, Blue Hill
(207) 374–5273
Open Saturday from 9:00 to 11:30 A.M. from
Memorial Day to mid-August at the fair-
grounds and from Labor Day through mid-
October at the church.

Stonington Farmers' Market
Stonington Community Center parking lot,
Deer Isle
(207) 326–4741
Open Friday from 10:00 A.M. to noon from mid-
May through September.

Ellsworth Farmers' Market
Maine Community Foundation parking lot,
245 East Main Street, Ellsworth
(207) 667–9212
Open Monday and Thursday from 2:00 to 5:30
P.M. and Saturday from 9:30 A.M. to 12:30 P.M.
from June through mid-October.

Acadia Area

Eden Farmers' Market
YMCA parking lot, Main Street, Bar Harbor
(207) 223–2293
Open Sunday from 9:00 A.M. to 1:00 P.M. from
Mother's Day through October.

Northeast Harbor Farmers' Market
Huntington Road across from Kimball
Terrace Inn, Northeast Harbor
(207) 223–2293
Open Thursday from 9:00 A.M. to noon from
the end of June through the end of August.

Down East

Milbridge Farmers' Market
Milbridge Market parking lot on Route 1,
Milbridge
(207) 546–2395
Open Saturday from 9:00 A.M. to noon from
early June to mid-October.

Machias Valley Farmers' Market
Route 1 across from Helen's Restaurant,
Machias
(207) 483–2260
Open Saturday from 8:00 A.M. to noon from
early May through October.

Sunrise County Farmers' Market
Next to Raye's Mustard, Eastport
Perry Municipal Building, Route 1, Perry
Across from library on Union Street, Calais
(207) 454–3896
Open Tuesday from 11:00 A.M. to 3:00 P.M.
(Calais), Thursday from 11:00 A.M. to 2:00 P.M.
(Eastport), and Saturday from 9:00 A.M. to
noon (Perry) from the end of June through
October.

SHOPPING

A fellow by the name of Leon Leonwood Bean put Maine on the retail map back in 1912, and credit-card-toting visitors have been pounding their way along the coast ever since in search of good values. In terms of shopping, Maine is really about three things: bargains, antiques, and fine arts and crafts. The outlets that have sprouted up around the store that L. L. Bean founded in Freeport and those located down in Kittery are among the best in the nation. And the state also has some native job lot favorites like Marden's and Renys, discount department store chains where trucks pull in from all over carrying everything under the sun at sometimes ridiculously low prices. Some people have an almost devotional attachment to these places and visit daily, and houseguests always want to get to one of them during their stay.

Because Mainers have long been pack rats and the state has its share of historic homes, and simply because there's tourist demand, Maine has quite the antiques culture—it's no surprise that one of the biggest and best national periodicals on the subject, Maine Antique Digest, got its start here and that some of the region's largest antiques shows happen here. Auctions, a great place to find older items at affordable prices, are a Maine tradition, too—some people go just for entertainment. Antiques lovers will find a lot to love just by staying on U.S. Route 1, and they'll

> **i** Anyone interested in antiques would be wise to grab a copy of the *Maine Antique Dealer's Directory*, which lists many of the state's biggest and best shops and is available for $2.00 at many stores and chambers of commerce. Or you can order a copy by calling (207) 872–5849.

want to be certain to hit Wells, Wiscasset, the Damariscotta area, and Searsport, all of which have developed reputations as repositories of the good and old.

And craftspeople, aware of the "Made in Maine" mystique, have turned the Pine Tree State into a nice place to hunt for more high-end items as well. Visit Camden, for example, if you're looking for fine jewelry, as there is an unusually high concentration of gold- and silversmiths in that Penobscot Bay town and its neighbors. Deer Isle is a good place to go if you're looking for ceramics, thanks to the Haystack School of Arts and Crafts, and Greater Portland has finely made furnishings.

There are a few towns, such as Kittery and Freeport; a few districts, like Portland's Old Port and downtown Bar Harbor; and even a few legendary stores, like the Big Chicken Barn in Ellsworth, that are absolutely can't-miss with shoppers. But there are many lesser-known gems scattered along the coast in unexpected places, which makes shopping in Maine always an adventure.

Most shops are open from 9:00 A.M. to 5:00 P.M. Monday through Saturday and closed Sunday, except the big chain stores and the Maine Mall, which tend to be open from 9:00 A.M. to 9:00 P.M. Monday through Saturday and 9:00 A.M. to 5:00 P.M. Sunday. Good luck.

SOUTH COAST

Kittery

Anyone entering Maine gets a look at the back of Kittery's famous outlets, sitting there next to Interstate 95 enticingly flashing sale signs. And the handful that can be seen from the road are just the beginning. Kittery's outlet row is home to more than 120 stores and sprawls for more than a mile in strip malls along Route 1—the local business association calls it "America's Maine Street for Shopping"—but you don't want to walk on this Main Street. You'll need wheels. (And you should proceed with caution everywhere you go, because people here are tourists who don't know the place and spend more time looking up at store names than they do paying attention to where they're driving.)

You'll find all of the big-name brands along this miracle mile—Banana Republic, Ralph Lauren, J. Crew, Old Navy, Tommy Hilfiger, Reebok, Calvin Klein, Gap, Timberland, Eddie Bauer, Brooks Brothers, Coldwater Creek, Bass, Geoffrey Beene, Brookstone, Skechers, Crate and Barrel, and on and on. Some amazing deals await in town—if you can remain patient enough to navigate the crowds.

The stores collaborate a lot to keep the registers ringing. Most keep the same hours: 9:00 A.M. to 8:00 P.M. Monday through Saturday and 10:00 A.M. to 6:00 P.M. on Sunday in summer. You can buy gift certificates good all over town, and there are special sale periods that most outlets participate in. These include mid-June around Father's Day, mid-August for back-to-school shopping, Labor Day, and Columbus Day. You can find out the exact dates, see a list of stores, find maps, and discover all sorts of interesting poop at the Web site www.thekitteryoutlets.com. Or call (888) KIT–TERY for more information.

Kittery Trading Post
301 Route 1, Kittery
(888) KTP–MAINE
www.kitterytradingpost.com
Kittery Trading Post plays a role in Kittery similar to the one L. L. Bean plays in Freeport—the outfitter is a bit of real, old Maine made good, a one-room shack turned into a 42,000-square-foot outdoor empire that more than holds its own against all the chains from away. Where L. L. Bean has gone soft, selling more clothes and "lifestyle" goods than tents and packs, Kittery Trading Post has remained true to the sporting goods it began with when it was founded in 1938. Blood sports remain a staple—hunting

and fishing rule much of the store, and it even claims the largest selection of top-quality firearms on the East Coast. But you'll also find acres of camping gear, canoes, kayaks, bikes, backpacks, boots, and apparel. Open Monday through Saturday from 9:00 A.M. to 9:00 P.M. and Sunday 10:00 A.M. to 6:00 P.M.

The Yorks
Bell Farm Antiques
244 Route 1 South, York
(207) 363–8181
With its red picket fence, curving walkway, and red, cupola-topped shop, Bell Farm is an inviting place. The sign above the porch simply reads antiques, and you'll find plenty of them. Rex and Judy Lambert run a group shop with two whole floors of Victorian and country furniture, rugs, quilts, art, silver, stoneware, dinnerware, and early glass. Flow blue china, a Maine favorite, is here, too.

Salmon Falls Stoneware
2 Route 1, York
(207) 351–2588
www.salmonfalls.com
Functional salt-glazed pottery is the specialty of Salmon Falls Stoneware, which has outlets in both York and Dover, New Hampshire. The pots, cruets, mugs, casserole dishes, plates, lamps, even piggy banks here are turned the old-fashioned way, with clay on a wheel, much as it was done in the mid-19th century. They're handpainted with a variety of designs (blueberries are popular) and once done, are ready for use like any other serving and dinnerware, safe for both the dishwasher and microwave. Just over the town line from Kittery, the shop sells both first-quality pieces and seconds, which can be real bargains, like the outlet deals found just up the road. Open every day from 9:00 A.M. to 5:00 P.M.

Stonewall Kitchen
Stonewall Lane, York
(207) 351–2712 or (800) 207–5267
Once sold in a farmers' market stall, Stonewall Kitchen's delicious specialty foods—jams, jel-

lies, mustards, chutneys, relishes—can now be found all across Maine, and there are company stores in Portland and Camden. But it all began right here in York. The business's headquarters is right next to the York Chamber of Commerce, and it is perpendicular to the road you hop onto when you take the York exit, so you can't miss it. A big, colonial-looking complex of buildings with nice courtyards and gardens, Stonewall has an outlet where you can shop, ask questions, and taste products. The company sells an array of cookbooks, packed into a built-in bookshelf against one wall, as well as some housewares, in addition to its now-famous condiments. There's also a viewing area next door, where you can watch employees in aprons and hats working machines and conveyors, filling, capping, labeling, and packing the bottles. Stonewall has even expanded into home and garden products. Quite the little empire.

Woods to Goods: Maine Prison Product Outlet
891 Route 1, York
(207) 363–6001 or (888) 966–3724
The Maine State Prison store on Route 1 in Thomaston has become well known as a place to buy kitschy prison-made items, and this small York emporium is much the same but farther off the radar of your average tourist. Inside you'll find all sorts of wares made in the wood shop by inmates—imprisoned from Maine to Oregon—from furniture to lamps to boat models and ship wheels. You'll find jewelry, kitchenware, toys, and birdhouses, and they also carry Prison Blues jeans.

Gravestone Artwear
250 York Street, Lower Level,
York Village
(800) 564–4310
www.gravestoneartwear.com
Gravestone rubbing is an age-old New England tradition, and Cassandra and Paulette Chernack have taken rubbing to the next level by screen-printing old burial-ground art onto note cards, stamps, soaps, window decals, coffin boxes, and a whole line of clothing. The mother-and-daughter team have combed the cemeteries of New England in search of cool designs, and they have found them aplenty. They've taken these artistic engravings and transferred them to velvet scoop-neck tops, dresses, cloaks, pouches, and scarves, but it's their T-shirts that are the most fun, with artful displays both somber and humorous (Time Cuts Down All, Both Great and Small, and Happy Valley Cemetery Pit Crew, for example). They have shirts inspired by Shakespeare, H. P. Lovecraft, and Ichabod Crane of *Sleepy Hollow* fame, and many have cool border designs on them. Most are available only in black. Ingenious stuff, and very good-looking to boot.

Knight's Quilt Shop
1901 Route 1, Cape Neddick
(207) 361–2500
www.mainequiltshop.com
Quilters in southern Maine make frequent pilgrimages to Michelle Knight's Route 1 Cape in search of all their stitchery necessities. With more than 3,000 bolts, she has the area's largest inventory of quilt fabrics, from the simple to the designer. And of course she carries all the supplies that one would need to do the job, including batting, stencils, pattern books, thread, and other notions. The service can't be beat.

Ogunquit

Ogunquit Round Table
24 Shore Road, Ogunquit
(207) 646–2332
An old cape on Shore Road houses this fine independent bookseller. Thoughtfully laid out and well stocked, it's eminently browsable, and there's even a reading group to join, if that's your thing. Open year-round.

Ogunquit Wooden Toy
19 Chestnut Road, Ogunquit
(207) 646–3718
www.ogunquitwoodentoy.com
Could there be a more appropriate name for a wooden toy builder than William John Woods?

Or a better street than Chestnut for him to locate his studio? That's where you'll find Woods and his Ogunquit Wooden Toy, which features all manner of playthings crafted from maple and walnut and cherry. There are cars and helicopters, tractors and boats, all curvaceous and colorful. (Woods incorporates plantation-grown redheart, purpleheart, and cocobolo for contrast.) Each toy is finished with walnut oil and buffed with beeswax to give it a soft feel. In this day of plastic everything, these wooden toys are a delightful throwback any kid could love.

Out of the Blue
1 Beach Street, Ogunquit
(207) 646–0430
Ogunquit is filled with gifty shops. This one at least has some neat stuff in it, jewelry especially. There are fanciful "jewelry as art" earrings by Holly Yashi and Old Pool Glassworks. Lots of frames and photos and that sort of thing as well as stained glass.

Swamp John's
Perkins Cove, Ogunquit
(207) 646–9414
Fine art, blown glass, and jewelry are the stuff here, and much of it is impressive. Graceful glass roses, wrought-iron candleholders and statuary, beach glass jewelry, a blue heron desk light of granite and steel—the place is filled with goods by artisans who make use of natural resources in whimsical and arty ways.

Wells

The Arringtons
1908 Post Road, Route 1, Wells
(207) 646–4124
If you're looking for a first edition of some obscure World War II epic, you'll probably find it at this bookstore. The Arringtons has long been the go-to place for military titles. They stock everything else—more than 3,000 general titles are here, too—but it's in war books that the place really shines, especially for those interested in the American Revolution,

"Made in Maine" mean anything to you? If you're like a lot of people, those three words have become synonymous with excellence and quality. The state has a mystique and a reputation for a reason—traditions of craftsmanship, hard work, and high standards. You can find lists of a variety of made-in-Maine items—and find out where to buy them—at www.mainemade.com.

the Civil War, the two world wars, and particular unit histories. Practically across the street from Hardings, it makes for a good twofer.

Douglas N. Harding Rare Books
2152 Post Road, Route 1, Wells
(207) 646–8785
www.hardingsbooks.com
Legendary in Maine's antique book circles, Hardings has an enormous inventory—as many as 100,000 books at any given time—as well as maps and prints, and if they don't stock the title you're looking for, they can probably get it for you. A family-owned operation in business since 1960, Harding's has particularly strong selections of Maine, New England, maritime, and Americana titles. You could spend hours, days even, perusing the shelves—and many people do. A great rainy-day option.

R. Jorgensen Antiques
502 Post Road, Route 1, Wells
(207) 646–9444
www.rjorgensen.com
One of the better antiques shops in a town known for them, Jorgensens is a sprawling operation, stuffing two whole buildings with 18th- and 19th-century furnishings and accessories, both American and European. And you'd hardly know it driving by, because the place is mostly obscured by hedges. Make the turn into the driveway and you'll be glad you did.

MacDougall-Gionet Antiques
2104 Post Road, Route 1, Wells
(207) 646–3531
www.macdougall-gionet.com
An old red barn serves as the home of close to 70 dealers at this South Coast staple, which specializes in antique furniture, fine, formal, and country, as well as smalls and folk art. Just don't show up on Monday when the place is closed.

Marden's
1247 Main Street, Sanford
(207) 324–1239
www.mardenssurplus.com
Mickey Marden was definitely on to something when he opened his first store in Fairfield in the 1960s. He bought job lots, stuff from bankruptcy courts, flood and fire sales, factory overruns—anything that needed to go soon and cheap—and built the largest surplus and salvage empire in Maine. Now the store that bears his name, Marden's, has a dozen stores and more than 700 employees. And more than that, Marden's has become like a religion to bargain-conscious Mainers. Many people stop by almost daily to see what has arrived on the Marden's trucks, and they never know what they might find. One day it may be the contents of a Radio Shack store, the next Armani suits, the next a software bonanza. There are also stores on the coast in Portland, Ellsworth, and Calais, as well as a whole fleet inland, and they all stock everything from books to electronics to clothes to furniture in their many departments, but every week brings something new, so it's always an adventure.

The Kennebunks

Kennebunk Book Port
10 Dock Square, Kennebunkport
(207) 967–3815
www.kbookport.com
The shelves full of new books are only part of the charm at this second-floor shop in the heart of "K'port." Owners Rick and Ellen Chasse are the kind of genial, knowledgeable proprietors every good bookstore should

have—and they've tucked a zillion thoughtfully selected titles into the loft of an old rum warehouse. You're sure to find that perfect vacation book here, as well as signed books, a fine selection of Maine titles, and some children's classics.

Lovell Designs
17 Ocean Avenue, Kennebunkport
(207) 967–8534
www.lovelldesigns.com
Ken Cantro's jewelry is handcrafted in pewter, sterling, and gold plate, and it picks up themes from both Maine and the natural world. Truly classic stuff that transcends age and style—it's liked by everyone, from Goth kids to grandmothers. There are Lovell stores in Freeport, Portland, Portsmouth, and then this place, one of the better spots to spend your dollars in Dock Square.

Marlow's
64 Main Street, Kennebunk
(207) 985–2931
www.marlows-maine.com
This nifty department store is sort of a case study in how to grow a small retail store into a local institution. The company began in the early 1980s as a 500-square-foot shop in an old mill, where you could buy stationery. Every few years the place would add products—usually whole departments at a time. In 1994 Marlow's moved and quadrupled its size, and it doubled it again with another move in 1999. What does all this mean to you? Well, it means that you can now find home furnishings, garden items, bath and body products, toys, jewelry, gourmet foods, candles, and, yes, stationery at the little retailer that could.

Old House Parts
One Trackside Drive, Kennebunk
(207) 985–1999
www.oldhouseparts.com
Any fan of *This Old House* will want to wander around here. Now located off Route 35 (Summer Street), about a half mile from its old location, this is one of the state's best architectural

salvage operations, and you'll have your choice of old doors, windows, stained glass, doorknobs, balustrades, moldings, and all sorts of architectural oddments from the 18th to the early 20th centuries. While of most interest to people owning houses that predate World War II, the goods here can add a bit of character to any home. Prices can be a bit steep, though.

Tom's of Maine Natural Living Store
Storer Street, Kennebunk
(207) 985–3874 or (800) 985–3874
www.toms-of-maine.com

The story goes that when American troops invaded Manuel Noriega's home in Panama in 1989, they found some Tom's of Maine toothpaste among the notorious general's toiletries. If he likes Tom's earth-friendly line of products, he'd go crazy at the company's factory store in an old mill in downtown Kennebunk. Toothpastes, soaps, herbal goods, tote bags, and more by Tom's and select others are all available at greatly reduced prices. Ask about the tour of Tom's factory across town. (Legendary in Maine for its eco-friendly, socially conscious business practices, Tom's broke a few hearts in 2006 when it became part of the Colgate-Palmolive empire.)

Wallingford Farm
21 York Street, Kennebunk
(207) 985–2112
www.wallingfordfarm.com

Anyone with a home, garden, or taste for Maine delicacies will find something to like about this neat store housed in a sprawling 19th-century barn on Route 1. The place is a country store in the truest sense, stocked practically to the exposed rafters with farm-related goods, from local produce to Maine-made foods, flowers to garden tools, handmade soaps to books on landscaping. The goal of owner Charles Godfrey has been to supply area residents with reasonably priced specialty items they can't get at supermarkets, and he's done a great job at it. Worth a detour.

Saco

Stone Soup Artisans
228 Main Street, Saco
(207) 283–4715
www.societyofsouthernmainecraftsmen.org

Not to be confused with the Portland restaurant of the same name, Stone Soup is a co-op gallery sponsored by the Society of Southern Maine Craftsmen. More than 30 artisans—including potters, jewelers, glass and fabric artists—consign their work to be sold here, and they staff the place as well.

GREATER PORTLAND
South Portland

Maine Mall
364 Maine Mall Road, South Portland
(207) 774–0303

Mainers have a love-hate relationship with "the Mall." They love the ease, convenience, and selection that more than 140 stores in one place afford, but they hate the traffic, congestion, and tackiness that go along with it. The state's largest shopping center, the Maine Mall is anchored by Sears, Macy's, Best Buy, and JCPenney, and inside are the kinds of stores you expect to find in a major mall: Gap, Victoria's Secret, Olympia Sports, Eddie Bauer, Abercrombie, and WaldenBooks. In recent years, this one-level mall has turned a bit yupscale, though, with the addition of Pottery Barn and Williams Sonoma. Several other retail plazas have sprung up all around the mall, as well as chain eateries like Olive Garden, Macaroni Grill, and Pizzeria Uno, and movie theaters. There's a big Borders bookstore in the parking lot. The food court is open Monday through Saturday 9:30 A.M. to 9:00 P.M., Sunday from 11:00 A.M. to 6:00 P.M.

Portland

Amaryllis Clothing Co.
41 Exchange Street, Portland
(207) 772–4439
www.amaryllisclothing.com

Maine designers Jill McGowan, Kendra Haskell,

and Cindy Hanley contribute their creative works to this, Portland's best women's clothing store. Inspired and often whimsical contemporary fashions, formal wear, jewelry, and accessories are offered for sale.

Apple Bee Company
370 Fore Street, Portland
(207) 772–8940
www.applebeecompany.com
If you have a youngun with a taste for books, get thee to this Fore Street favorite. ABC specializes in classic children's book characters—not Harry Potter but Pooh, Curious George, Madeline, Eloise, Olivia, Thomas the Tank Engine, and their peers. There are Raggedy Ann and Andy jewelry boxes, Clifford the Big Red Dog and Snoopy dolls, pictures of Lily, Curious George pinball games, Eloise board game, and Pooh tea sets. And that's just the beginning. The company has lines and lines of teacher's aids, learning toys, books, and children's wear. There are all sorts of items to spark a child's intellectual curiosity.

Book Traders
561 Congress Street, Portland
(207) 773–1840
Quality paperbacks are the staple at Book Traders, an unassuming storefront on Congress. Lots of contemporary fiction, a good selection of mysteries, and pop culture titles occupy the shelves along with 35,000 books and videos.

Books Etc.
38 Exchange Street, Portland
(207) 774–0626
www.mainebooksetc.com
Arguably downtown Portland's best store for new books, Books Etc. has been a popular destination on Exchange Street, thanks to a good selection of contemporary fiction, Maine books, and pop culture titles. They now have a store in Falmouth, too.

Browne Trading Company
262 Commercial Street #3, Portland
(207) 775–3118
www.browntrading.com
The Browne family has been in the seafood biz for generations, specializing in caviar, and fancy chefs all across the country currently turn to Browne's for fresh seafood. And you can, too. The company has its retail store just steps from the docks the fish come in on, and you can find everything from Casco cod and monkfish to Jonah crabs and scallops. (Lobster too, of course.) And that's just the local stuff. Browne also offers sole from France, tai snapper from New Zealand, and arctic char from Iceland. Then there are the innumerable caviars the place stakes its reputation on. . . . Anyone with a jones for seafood will want to make the pilgrimage. You can even buy beef and wine, cheese, and bread while you're at it.

Bull Moose Music
151 Middle Street, Portland
(207) 780–6424
www.bullmoose.com
Maine's native record-store chain, Bull Moose was born in the early 1990s by a Bowdoin student in Brunswick, but this is the best-stocked of the company's nine stores. Not as good as it once was, Bull Moose remains the place to turn in downtown Portland for CDs by underground and independent artists. You can find Top 40 stuff, too, and the prices are guaranteed to beat your mega–chain stores. The pierced and tattooed employees will order whatever they don't have on hand.

Carlson-Turner Books
241 Congress Street, Portland
(207) 773–4200 or (800) 540–7323
At the Munjoy Hill end of the Forest City's old retail corridor, Carlson-Turner has arguably the biggest selection of used books in town—more than 70,000 titles—with specialties in antiquarian, Maine, Civil War, and "unusual and eccentric" books. Great fun to peruse.

Casco Bay Books
151 Middle Street, Portland
(207) 541–3842
www.cascobaybooks.com
In the same building as Bull Moose Music, Casco Bay Books brims with new and used contemporary fiction. Whether the spine has been cracked or not, they're shelved together, making for a treasure hunt. With good selections of zines and magazines, genuine bookworms on staff, and a refined hipster quality to the shop—Ikea-looking chairs, track lighting, chai, Italian sodas, and teas—it's a pleasant place to browse. The place often hosts readings by cool cartoonists, zinesters, and authors as well.

Casco Bay Wool Works
10 Moulton Street, Portland
(207) 879–9665
www.cascobaywoolworks.com
An Old Port staple for more than a decade, Casco Bay Wool Works has become known for its fine wool capes and shawls, but it also turns out fishermen's sweaters of Shetland wool, refined women's sweaters, blankets and throws, all of which make perfect sense for Maine winters—or even a late summer boat ride.

Catwear
399 Fore Street, Portland
(207) 772–2668
www.catwear.com
Not the clothier for kitties that its name implies, Catwear is a warm, fuzzy company that makes women's clothing out of fleece. These are cardigans and vests and pullovers that have more in common with couture than with fleece jackets as we've known them. Nice stuff, and nice people, too. They also have a store in Kennebunkport.

The Clown
123 Middle Street, Portland
(207) 756–7399
www.the_clown.com
A French country table from the 1880s. A Dutch butcher's block from the early 1900s. Woodcuts by Maine artist Siri Beckman. Wines from Chile's Casablanca Valley. These are the sorts of things you'll find at the Clown, a small chain with shops in Portland, Blue Hill, and Stonington.

The Clown receives regular shipments of antique furnishings from Europe, and they are displayed in the front of the cosmopolitan gallery, with its soaring ceilings, track lighting, brick walls, and window on the street. The inventory changes, but you might find anything from a French walnut armoire circa 1840 to an English pie chest table circa 1800.

At the back is an art gallery featuring a selection of up-and-coming Maine artists as well as the work of a few painters from away. And downstairs, logically, is the wine cellar with ports and Chiantis from all over the globe. On the first Thursday of every month, the shop hosts wine tastings.

The Clown purports to "Celebrate Life's Finer Arts," and the folks here do a good job at it. Life's fineries are not cheap, though, so you'd best bring your wallet.

Cunningham Books
188 State Street, Portland
(207) 775–2246
Cunningham's is a favorite in the city's Longfellow Square area, with some 50,000 titles to explore on its shelves, all thoughtfully organized by shopkeeper Nancy Grayson.

Decorum
231 Commercial Street, Portland
(207) 775–3346
www.decorumonesource.com

Portland Architectural Salvage
131 Preble Street, Portland
(207) 780–0634
www.portlandsalvage.com
The Forest City's best bets for architectural salvage are these two shops on opposite ends of the peninsula. You'll have a hard time maintaining a sense of decorum if you visit Decorum, on Commercial Street, so excited

will you be. It's a great place to look for bathroom fixtures, lighting, and details like knobs, switches, and drawer pulls. It specializes in specialty hardware, and the selection is amazing. Very inventive, fun, and inspiring stuff. Portland Architectural Salvage, newly located on Preble Street, is a better bet for larger pieces, old built-ins, doors, windows, posts, and cabinets—more than 12,000 square feet of the stuff on four floors. They'll even track items down for you, with their personal shopper service. Enticing places both, for the old-home owner.

Fetch
195 Commercial Street, Portland
(207) 773–5450
www.fetchorama.com

It'd be hard to find a store in Portland that's more fun than Fetch—especially if you have four legs. A spirited supply store for cats, dogs, and their people, it brims with wit and whimsy. Dog packs, travel bowls, feed bags, tents, sleeping bags, sunscreen, bug spray, laser play toys, place mats, sock toys—these sorts of goods fill a pretty old building on Commercial Street.

This isn't a superstore like PetCo but a mom and pop with spunk. They regularly host events—Wednesday is Pug Night, for instance, and they seem as enthusiastic about pet toys as a pug puppy.

Folia
50 Exchange Street, Portland
(207) 761–4432

Folia used to be called Fibula, and it's long been a favorite place among shoppers looking for inventive, creative, one-of-a-kind jewelry. A group of local jewelers is behind the place.

Green Design Furniture
267 Commercial Street, Portland
(207) 775–4234
www.greendesigns.com

You're going to be wanting to take some of this stuff home with you. Douglas Green's black cherry furniture is fantastic—updating and contemporizing Shaker and Mission-

inspired designs. His new pieces have clean and curvaceous lines, and they are all very functional. Open Monday through Saturday from 10:00 A.M. to 6:00 P.M.

LeRoux Kitchen
161 Commercial Street, Portland
(207) 553–7665

Formerly known as the Whip and Spoon, this kitchenware store makes amateur chefs gaga. From creative colanders to crazy cookbooks, brilliant bread machines to bagel cutters, anything and everything a cook could want can be found here. The store also has specialty foods and one of the city's best wine selections. The owners host cooking classes at the rear of the place.

Maine Potters Market
376 Fore Street, Portland
(207) 774–1633
www.mainepottersmarket.com

Several pottery co-ops exist in Maine, and this is the largest and arguably the best, representing the work of 32 craftspeople from across the state. Founded in 1978, the shop is right in the heart of the Old Port, and the works within are unique and functional. Each potter has a unique style.

Mexicali Blues
9 Moulton Street, Portland
(207) 772–4080
www.mexicaliblues.com

Maine seems to have a particular fondness for jam bands and the neohippie phenomenon— Phish has played some of its largest gigs here, and shows by Strangefolk and Moe are always well attended—and that support has kept this Old Port emporium busy since 1987. (There's another store on Route 1 in Newcastle as well.) All the requisite tie-dye, batik, flowing dresses, drums, incense, patchouli, beads, jewelry, and wall hangings can be found inside. The shop's owners cruise the globe— from Bali to Baja—to track down unique items, and they have their own lines as well. A convenient, one-stop shop for the whole happy hippie family.

Yes Books
589 Congress Street, Portland
(207) 775-3233

For more than a decade, Yes Books was located downtown on Danforth Street, but owner Pat Murphy moved into Congress Street digs when his landlord decided to turn his old spot into office space. By relocating, Yes has helped turn Congress—at the heart of the city's Arts District—into a book lover's lane. Murphy's shop is a good place to turn for countercultural titles, art books, and general nonfiction, but it doesn't stock much fiction outside of a selection of classics and neoclassics. If you're looking for books by the Beats, titles from the hippie era, punk tomes, or cyberpunk futurism, this is your store. Want a copy of Brautigan's *Revenge of the Lawn* or Gerard Malanga's *Three Diamonds*? Step inside.

F. O. Bailey Antiquarians
35 Depot Road, Falmouth
(207) 781-8001
www.fobailey.com

Long the name in Portland antiques—it claims to be Maine's oldest business, founded in 1819—F. O. Bailey specializes in fine furniture, rugs, and art, and the place hosts auctions regularly as well. Now off peninsula in Falmouth.

Yarmouth

DeLorme Map Store
2 DeLorme Drive, Yarmouth
(800) 642-0970
www.delorme.com

Stop at the DeLorme Map Store in Yarmouth on your way north—you can't miss it, it's the place with the three-story, glowing globe—and you won't get lost during your Maine travels. Famous in the state for its indispensable Maine Atlas and Gazetteer, DeLorme sells that book of maps and so many others in the store at its headquarters. You can buy maps for every state, travel guides, globes, world maps, GPS accessories, software, and more. Plus you

can check out Eartha, reportedly the world's largest rotating globe.

Maine Cottage Furniture
Lower Falls Landing, 106 Lafayette Street, Yarmouth
(207) 846-3699
www.mainecottage.com

You know that feeling of relaxation and contentment you get when you hit the cottage by the shore for a week's vacation? Somehow Maine Cottage Furniture has managed to distill that and paint it onto their line of colorful, whimsical home furnishings. From beds to desks, dining tables to wicker, the company's "spirited furniture" is fun and stylish and reminiscent of lazy days on the coast. You might not feel as good when you see the prices, though.

Freeport

While Kittery is a place where the automobile rules, Freeport is much more walkable and retains the appeal of a Maine village. The presence of one of the more desirable anchor stores any one could ever want—a little outfitter called L. L. Bean—attracted dozens of major retailers to downtown Freeport, creating one of the nation's biggest outlet bazaars—there are 170 stores clustered in a handful of blocks. Step along its sidewalks, and you'll pass a who's who of American retailing, heavy on the clothes—Polo, Levi's, J. Crew, Brooks Brothers, Patagonia, Anne Klein, the North Face, Cole Haan, Gap, Banana Republic, Maidenform, Jockey, Jones New York, Burberry, Coach, Samonsite, and too many more to count. There are plenty of crafts, gifts, and housewares packed onto the town's side streets, but it's apparel where Freeport truly shines. Contact the Freeport Merchant Association (207-865-1212; www.freeportusa.com) for a list of stores, events, and dining and lodging options.

A handful of Maine stores have been able to carve out their own niches in town. Some of the more notable ones follow.

Abacus American Crafts
36 Main Street, Freeport
(207) 865–6620 or (800) 206–2166
www.abacusgallery.com

Mainers love Abacus, a functional arts store in a few locations along the cost (they can also be found in Kennebunkport, Portland, and Boothbay Harbor). As much an art gallery as a store, it's been purveying kooky, fun, and often beautiful furnishings, jewelry, pottery, and blown glass since 1971 and has been voted one of the top 10 retailers in the country by *Niche* magazine.

Cuddledown
475 Route 1, Freeport
(888) 235–3696

Begun in the early 1980s as a home business making down comforters, Cuddledown has grown and grown into one of the nation's leading makers of bedding. Their outlet store in Freeport stocks all the exquisite goose feather puffs they've become famous for as well as sleepwear, rugs, pillows, sheets, mattress pads, and all sorts of other housewares.

L. L. Bean
Bow Street, Freeport
(800) 559–0747
www.llbean.com

By now just about everyone knows about L. L. Bean and its customer-friendly policies—the store's open 24 hours a day, 365 days a year, and everything you buy inside is unconditionally guaranteed. While the store has turned more toward lifestyle goods—apparel, housewares, etc.—you'll still find plenty to like in the outdoors sections on the first floor.

L. L. Bean Factory Store
Depot Street, Freeport
(207) 552–7772

Locals remember when Bean sold its seconds and discontinued items out of the warehouse down the road, but everything's been neatly displayed in this emporium for years. The deal on the imperfect items found here is the same as it is on the perfect ones on Bow Street—

everything's satisfactory or your money back—which is why it's a good idea to start at the Factory Store first before heading to the main store. If you do find what you're looking for here, which is a good possibility, you'll pay up to 60 percent less than what you might just a few blocks away. Open seven days a week from 9:00 A.M. to 10:00 P.M.

Thos. Moser Cabinetmakers
Mallet Drive, Freeport
(207) 865–4519 or (800) 708–9041
www.thosmoser.com

Don't be confused by the name. Thos. Moser makes a lot more than cabinets. Since 1973 the fine wood craftsman—along with his sons—has turned out beautiful hardwood furnishings inspired by Shaker, Pennsylvania Dutch, and Queen Anne designs. In the beautifully restored 19th-century home that serves as the company's only Maine showroom, you'll find two floors full of tables, chairs, beds, and desks, each an heirloom in the making.

MIDCOAST

Brunswick

Brunswick Bookland
Cooks Corner Shopping Center, Brunswick
(207) 725–2313
www.booklandcafe.com

The once mighty Bookland chain fell to competition from book megastores and bad accounting years ago, going from 13 shops down to this one and filing for bankruptcy in 2000. This is one of two left, managing to stay afloat with a great selection of magazines, discounted best sellers, lots of remainders, several racks of used books, and a cafe that encourages lingering.

Cabot Mill Antiques
14 Maine Street, Brunswick
(207) 725–2855
www.cabotiques.com

Fort Andross, an imposing old mill building on the Androscoggin, is the nicest antique at this 15,000-square foot showroom. But there are

Close-up

Bath Antiques

Downtown Bath is both an antique itself—it dates back to the 1890s—and is brimming with antiques shops. Among the best of them are **Front Street Antiques** (190 Front Street; 207–443–8098), which is a group shop specializing in books, Victorian wares, glass, and china, and **Pollyanna Antiques** (182 Front Street; 207–443–4909), which is a good place to turn for vintage clothing and old tools. Also try **Brick Store Antiques** (143 Front Street; 207–443–2790) for country and formal goods and **Cobblestone and Company** (176 Front Street; 207–443–4064) for antiques, art, and accents.

plenty of furnishings and collectibles to like, too. More than 140 displays are here to peruse, filled with china, Oriental rugs, decorative items, porcelain, bottles, Victorian furniture, and more. There are flea markets at Fort Andross on summer weekends. Open seven days a week from 10:00 A.M. to 5:00 P.M.

Day's News
143 Maine Street, Brunswick
(207) 729–3131
The best selection of magazines downtown line the walls of this variety store on Maine Street.

Gulf of Maine Books
134 Maine Street, Brunswick
(207) 729–5083
One would think that as a college town, Brunswick would have some truly great bookstores. The community disappoints a bit, but Gulf of Maine is the standard-bearer downtown, with a diverse selection heavy on the environmental and countercultural titles. Owner Gary Lawless is a legend in his own right—he's a poet with a regional reputation and is the publisher behind Blackberry Books, among other things—and the place is definitely worth a visit, especially if you're into poetry or literature with a conscience.

Other Shopping in Brunswick

For more music stop in the original **Bull Moose Music** (151 Maine Street; 207–725–1289), though this isn't the site where it was born.

Bath and Surrounding Area

Bath Goodwill
Bath Shopping Center, Route 1, Bath
(207) 443–4668
A certain internationally known outfitter based a few towns over sends this thrift store its seconds and blemished items, and you can often score some great finds on the racks and racks of clothing here. Just a hint. Proceeds benefit people with disabilities.

Halcyon Yarn
12 School Street, Bath
(207) 442–7909 or (800) 341–0282
www.halcyonyarn.com
More than 100 varieties of yarn and a host of wools, merinos, felts, kits, books, videos, and classes make Halcyon Yarn into a haven for knitters, spinners, and fabric artists of all sorts.

Bath Cycle and Ski
Route 1, Woolwich
(207) 442–7002
www.bikeman.com

An excellent full-service bike and ski shop with a gondola out front, this place has been around for ages. You'll find mountain and road bikes; kids' bikes; downhill, cross-country, and telemark skis; snowboards; snowshoes; and a great staff inside. Open Monday through Friday from 9:00 A.M. to 6:00 P.M. (till 8:00 P.M. Thursday) and 9:00 A.M. to 5:00 P.M. Saturday, year-round.

Montsweag Flea Market
Route 1 and Mountain Road, Woolwich
(207) 443–2809

In 1976 Norma Scopino lost her bookkeeping job, and she set up a little bazaar on her front lawn to take advantage of tourist traffic. That yard sale has grown into one of the state's biggest—and certainly most widely known—flea markets. More than 100 tables are now part of the action, some of them semipermanent, like the tool area, and they are topped with everything from CDs and books to antiques and old toys. On Wednesdays the focus becomes antiques and collectibles, but on weekends it's a free-for-all. Always fun to explore.

Wiscasset and Surrounding Area

Big Al's Super Values
Route 1, Wiscasset
(207) 882–6423

Another job-lot-type emporium, Big Al's has plenty of its own partisans. Most of the merchandise here is of the cheap, made-in-China, plastic variety, but here again you never know what you'll find—quality paper products of late—and people love to paw through Al's bins. There's even a free gift for everyone on the way out.

Edgecomb Potters
727 Boothbay Road, Edgecomb
(207) 882–9493
www.edgecombpotters.com

Specializing in porcelain and known for their glazes, Edgecomb Potters have been at it since 1977, when Richard and Chris Hilton opened shop in an old schoolhouse. Today they have more than 30 employees and three galleries—here in Edgecomb, and ones in the Old Port and Freeport—each filled with artfully crafted shell bowls, ikebanas, vases, glass works, and even jewelry. And they always seem to be expanding their base (recently adding a 25,000-square-foot storage building).

Margonelli Fine Furniture
780 River Road, Edgecomb
(207) 633–3326

David Margonelli's showroom is all but obscured by the foliage on the River Road, but you're going to want to turn into the drive and have a look. The contemporary furniture here is exquisite—handmade and known for clean lines, elegant curves, and a classic simplicity—and it's often constructed with Margonelli's Flexure system, which allows for curving pieces to be interchanged for different looks and flexible uses. Open 10:00 A.M. to 5:00 P.M. or by appointment.

Sheepscot River Pottery
Route 1, Davis Island, Edgecomb
(207) 882–9410
www.sheepscot.com

When people are looking for wedding presents and Christmas gifts, this is one of the places they frequently turn. While lovingly glazed pottery with Maine themes is the staple, on everything from vases to tiles and sinks, you'll also find rugs, artwork, and other gifts at this showroom on the banks of the Sheepscot. Another store is in Damariscotta.

Boothbay Harbor

McKown Square Quilts
14 Boothbay House Hill Road,
Boothbay Harbor
(207) 633–2007

Seven rooms in this old farmhouse are brimming with handcrafted quilts, clothing, and boutiquey gifts. Peruse purses and scarves and custom-order a quilt from the 1,500 fabrics in stock.

Close-up

Wiscasset Antiques

The old town of Wiscasset, on the Sheepscot River, has long been known for its antiques shops, and there are many—about 20 at last count. Here are a few you shouldn't miss. **Marston House** (101 Main Street; 207–882–6010) specializes in 18th- and 19th-century painted furniture as well as textiles, rugs, toys, and French pottery. **Parkers of Wiscasset** (Route 1; 207–882–5520) is a group shop with a wide-ranging inventory. **Lilac Cottage** (Route 1; 207–882–7059) has a lot of American and English furniture and decorative items. American country painted furniture, hooked rugs, quilts, and folk art are among the specialties at **Patricia Stauble Antiques** (Pleasant and Main Streets; 207–882–6341). **James H. Welch Antiques** (207–529–5770) carries 19th-century country furniture and folk art.

Mung Bean
37 Townsend Avenue, Boothbay Harbor
(207) 633–5512
In the same spot since 1977, this gift shop is a tourist favorite, and inside you'll find all manner of crafts and souvenirs. You can find the balsam pillows and the handpainted slate welcome signs you might expect in a Maine resort town gift store, but you'll also come across some items that are a step up from that, like Anne Kilham's always tasteful cards, cool wooden toys, and some nice jewelry. So it's worth a peek on a rainy day.

Palabra Shop
53 Commercial Street, Boothbay Harbor
(207) 633–4225
The Palabra has been going strong in Boothbay for decades, and it claims the "World's Largest Collection of Moses Bottles," which were created for the grand opening of the Poland Spring Hotel in 1876. Ten rooms here are filled with primitives, nautical items, Shaker boxes, fine art glass and china, and estate jewelry. Just don't bump into anything.

The Ritz
33 Townsend Avenue, Boothbay Harbor
(207) 633–6484
The Ritz specializes in estate jewelry, and they have cases and cases full of the stuff. Lots of vintage gold and silver and diamonds, some of it gaudy—like the $4,500 eight-diamond ring in the window that you could imagine on a gangster—some of it stunning—like the 1.01-carat American brilliant cut diamond in a 14K gold solitaire setting, which would make a perfect engagement ring for someone. They don't make it like they used to, as they say.

Salt River Gallery
Route 27, Boothbay
(207) 633–0770 or (877) 725–8748
www.saltrivergallery.com
Another one of those nifty co-op stores that's owned and run by a group of artists, Salt River brims with handmade home furnishings, the sorts of lamps and benches that elevate simple household items to the level of art. Each of the nine artisans has a specialty and seems to excel at it; simply finding so many talented individuals in one spot makes this a rewarding stop.

Other Shopping in Boothbay Harbor
Don't forget **Sherman's** (5 Commercial Street; 207–633–7262), the great old Maine bookstore. **Westwind Design Gallery** (36 Sea

Street; 207–633–3787) has a large collection of art, antiques, Oriental rugs, and decorative items. **A Silver Lining** (17 Townsend Avenue; 207–633–4103) is a shop run by metalsmiths with a large selection of original jewelry; **Slick's Boutique** (27 Townsend Avenue; 207–633–7426) has women's contemporary clothing that will make you look, well, slick.

Damariscotta Area

Maine Coast Book Shop
Main Street, Damariscotta
(207) 563–3207

One of those local-business-makes-good success stories, this Damariscotta bookseller was so popular, it moved out of its small old store into a former supermarket, which it has filled with a great selection of children's books and Maine titles. You can find the best sellers, of course, but you can also pick up signed Down East titles. The staff is what makes the place great.

Pine Tree Yarns
Main Street, Damariscotta
(207) 563–8909
www.pinetreeyarns.com

Maine has all kinds of yarn makers, but there are a few whose fibers and colors seem to transcend. Elaine Eskesen's company, Pine Tree Yarns, which operates out of the historic Nathaniel Austin House, is one of them. Eskesen has wool that she dyes herself, as well as yarns and natural fibers from around the state. At Pine Tree Yarns you can pick up a colorful skein to knit your mom a sweater—or buy her the sweater instead. There are kits for dyeing, books, hats, mittens, gloves, and scarves, as well as all sorts of knitting knickknacks and accessories. You'll be "yarning" before you know it.

Reny's
33 Main Street, Damariscotta
(207) 563–5757
www.renys.com

Mainers have quite the love affair with Reny's.

These small neighborhood department stores are brimming with an amazing variety of goods—from jeans to DVD players to vitamins—and they inevitably have things cheaper than anywhere else if they have them. Usually a great deal cheaper, thanks to the chain's pipeline of brand-name suppliers, who send them their seconds and refurbished items. Just about every neighborhood has one now, it seems. Reny's are spread across the state in Bath, Belfast, Biddeford, Bridgton, Camden, Damariscotta, Dexter, Ellsworth, Farmington, Gardiner, Madison, Pittsfield, and Saco. This store is the flagship, though. Actually it's two stores that sit on opposite sides of Main Street, one for clothes, the other with everything else. You'll inevitably leave with something. It's that good.

Scottish Lion Wrought Iron
1486 Route 32, Round Pond
(207) 529–5523 or (866) 896–1806
www.scottishwroughtiron.com

Any excuse to visit the stunning hamlet of Round Pond is a good excuse, and this smithy is just that. The shop features the work of Andrew Leck, who forges all manner of household items, from the expected—fireplace tools and towel bars—to the unique—shelf stands for plates and bowls, birdbaths, beam racks, and lamps. Leck's Christmas stocking hooks are nicely formed and keep you from having to make holes in your mantle. Beautiful stuff, in a beautiful place.

Weatherbird
74 Courtyard Street, Damariscotta
(207) 563–8993

A sort of yupscale country store, Weatherbird has an inventory that's difficult to classify. A small grocery and specialty food store greets you as you walk in off the street; it's filled with wine, teas, and gourmet foods of all varieties. A small nook filled with neat toys then leads you to a section of nice, creative women's clothes. Tucked here and there are housewares, rugs, mobiles, and soaps.

Other Shopping in the Damariscotta Area

The **Come Again Shop** (65 Main Street, Damariscotta; 207–563–5863) is where you can pick up cards and gifts for your grandmother; the **Puffin's Nest** (36–40 Main Street, Damariscotta; 207–563–1815) is where you can grab novelty gifts and souvenirs (balsam pillows, lobster bibs) for your friends back home; **Two Fish** (Main Street, Damariscotta; 207–563–3559) has nice women's apparel and jewelry. Try the **Art Mart** (Main Street, Newcastle; 207–563–2220) and **Brush and Easel** (Main Street, Newcastle; 207–563–3559) for art supplies.

Waldoboro

Well-Tempered Kitchen
122 Atlantic Highway (Route 1), Waldoboro
(207) 563–5762
www.welltemperedkitchen.com
An old barn here is filled with a stupendous array of kitchenwares for the gourmet cook—not necessarily what you'd expect to find on the outskirts of Waldoboro. Cookbooks, pots, pans, cutlery, tableware, and unique cooking gadgets are all here. Quite a surprise, and it's even better than it sounds.

Wooden Screen Door Company
3542 Route 1, Waldoboro
(207) 832–0519
www.woodenscreendoor.com
Nothing says summer in Maine like the *thwack* of a screen door slamming shut. Somehow only a good one made of wood will provide that resounding sound, which will take you back to Grandmother's house and summer camps past. This small outfit has about a dozen designs to choose from, and it will customize to your specs. A variety of themes are available, and they evoke the Maine coast, from canoes to fish, from schooners to blue herons, and the doors are built of weather-resistant Honduran mahogany. They run from $400 up to about $1,000.

South Thomaston

Art of the Sea
Route 73, South Thomaston
(207) 594–9396
www.artofthesea.com
Owner Joan Woodhull has joked that her museumlike gallery of nautical art makes up two-thirds of beautiful downtown South Thomaston, and she's right. Also known as the Old Post Office Gallery, the shop is about the biggest thing going in this hamlet on the fantastically picturesque Weskeag River, encompassing 10 rooms on two huge floors of the building. Scores of paintings by some of the biggest names in the world of maritime art are on the walls—names like John Stobart, William Bishop, Michael Karas, and Marlene Evans—fetching thousands of dollars, and they're complemented by photographs by Mainers like Peter Ralston and Benjamin Mendlowitz. Ship models, books, prints, lamps, scrimshaw, instruments, and various other nautical items fill cases and floor space. It's a remarkable collection that would seem more appropriate in a resort community than in a small, salty hamlet. You don't even have to have salt in your blood to appreciate it, and it's a great excuse to see this neat Maine fishing village.

Rockland

Archipelago
386 Main Street, Rockland
(207) 596–0701
www.thearchipelago.net
What an appropriate name for the gift store of the Island Institute. The shop looks more like a gallery and brims with arts and crafts from the Maine islands (more than 100 artisans). Check out the granite vases from Island Granite Works ($25).

Black Parrot
328 Main Street, Rockland
(207) 593–9370
www.blackparrotonline.com
This staple on Main is primarily known for its tasteful women's clothes, but it also carries an

assortment of accessories and housewares and even products for the home and office. If you want a high-end duster or a nice hand cream or a whippa (Maine-speak for "great") journal, you'll find it here. The shoes are funky and unique, and there is always a lot of neat knitwear.

Grasshopper Shop
400 Main Street, Rockland
(207) 596–6156

One store in a small chain, the Grasshopper Shop has nice enough women's clothes to keep the ladies from having to drive to Portland for their blouses, skirts, and shoes. It also carries jewelry and accessories, some unique toys, several lines of housewares, and a really good selection of cards. Check the other shops in Searsport, Stonington, and Bangor, too. Open all year.

Harbor Beauty Bar (HBB)
395 Main Street, Rockland
(207) 596–9913 or (800) 958–9913

Perhaps no other storefront downtown is more emblematic of the change Rockland has undergone in the past 10 years than is this chichi place. Two decades ago a spare and cosmopolitan salon such as this, selling Skyn skin-care products from Iceland, Gucci fragrances, and Bliss and Fekkai bath and body wares, and featuring a whole section devoted to high-end men's skin-care products by companies like Clarins, would never have been possible. Men's fragrance in Rockland? That would be *eau de fish guts*. But not anymore, thanks to HBB. Admittedly, even today the store seems a little forward-thinking, but in the Rockland of the future it just might make it.

Planet Toys
318 Main Street, Rockland
(207) 596–5976

As much an experience as a store, Planet Toys is an offshoot of the Planet World Marketplace, a gift store in Camden (which has great toys itself). It's the kind of overwhelming toy store you expect to find in cities, not small

Maine communities. It sells everything under the sun, from plastic Playmobil sets to homemade wooden whirligigs. The store has a great kids' books section, hosts all sorts of special events, and can amuse even the oldest kids.

Second Read
328 Main Street, Rockland
(207) 594–4123

Rockland's hip bookstore and coffee shop is the place to find good used books in Rock City, and what a pleasant destination it is. Open and airy, with big windows overlooking Main Street and a series of clocks telling you what time it is around the world, comfortable chairs for sitting, and an Internet connection, it makes searching for books and beans a whole lot of fun. The titles are all thoughtfully chosen and are a really good deal for relatively new titles in good condition. There is a fine selection of coffees, cappuccinos, lattes, and espressos—including the local Rock City brand—and there are yummy sandwiches and salads. The staff is great, and there are occasional shows by jazz and folk artists.

Other Shopping in Rockland

Caravans (429 Main Street; 207–594–0293) has a really nice selection of worldly women's wear and jewelry. **Huston Tuttle** (365 Main Street; 207–594–5441) has all the art supplies you'll ever need and a nice gallery upstairs. The **Black Parrot** (328 Main Street; 207–594–9370) is filled with more boutiquey women's clothing. **Trillium Soaps** (68 Crescent Street; 207–594–5003) has handmade soaps that you can smell from the street.

Rockport

Maine Sport Outfitters
Route 1, Rockport
(207) 236–8797
www.mainesport.com

A gigantic outfitter, this Midcoast staple recently finished another expansion and now has 30,000 square feet of space. It fills it with a good selection of outdoor products, from tents to packs to canoes, but the place has a reputation for being expensive (and you don't get the unconditional guarantee here that you do at L. L. Bean).

Michael Good Designs
Rockport
(207) 236–9619
www.michaelgood.com
Anticlastic raising—this guy is synonymous with it. If you want anticlastic raised jewelry, you want Michael Good's designs. What is it? It's a jewelry-making process taken from hammered sheet metal, and it's characterized by twisted and flattened pieces. Good has made a big mark in the field. See his Spirit Sun pendant; it's truly beautiful.

State of Maine Cheese Company
461 Commercial Street, Rockport
(800) 762–8895
www.cheese-me.com
There's a lot more going on at this Route 1 store between Rockland and Camden than simply cheese making. The company expanded a while back and opened a 9,500-square-foot space where they both make their Katahdin cheddar, Saint Croix black pepper, Casco Bay garlic jack, and variety of other flavors—you can watch the production from windows in the store—and where they sell a slew of Made in Maine items. You can load up on cheeses, condiments, jellies, coffees, mustards, pickles, honeys, even chocolates, bringing home the tastiest souvenirs you ever did buy, or fashion a gift basket for friends and family back home. Open Monday through Friday from 9:00 A.M. to 5:30 P.M., Saturday from 9:00 A.M. to 5:00 P.M., and Sunday from noon to 4:00 P.M. in season.

Sweet Sensations
315 Commercial Street (Route 1), Rockport
(207) 230–0955
www.mainesweets.com
This is the pastry store of all pastry stores in the Midcoast. Great cakes and pies—by the slice!—cookies, macaroons, brownies, and sweets of all sorts fill a nice old Cape on Route

1. Certified pastry chef Steven Watts also does wedding cakes and custom orders.

Other Shopping in Rockport
Timothy Whelan Photographic Books and Prints (25 Main Street; 207–236–4795) is a tiny place with an extraordinary collection of photographic titles.

Camden

ABCD Books
23 Bayview Street, Camden
(207) 236–3903 or (888) 236–3903
www.abcdbooks.com
The go-to place for book collectors in Camden, this classic shop has an extensive collection of used and rare books—good Maine section, too—and is a pleasure to browse. You can spend a day here contentedly. Open year-round.

Josephine
39 Mechanic Street, Camden
(207) 236–2123
www.ejosephine.com
Not every store in Maine has personal shoppers—you'd be hard-pressed to find them anywhere—but this boutique in the old Knox Mill is not every other store. Either Eliza or Erin or Vanessa is available every day from 10:00 A.M. to 6:00 P.M. to help you make stylish choices from the simply chic women's wear—lines like Theory, Michael Stars, Vince, Joes, and Citizens of Humanity—or from the accessories and unique furnishings. Inspired by the empress of France, the shop is filled with everything from earrings to linens and it promises "to save seasoned shoppers a trip to Boston or New York." It's certainly a start, and should you find yourself overwhelmed by all the "elements of style," you can arrange for help.

Once a Tree
46 Bayview Street, Camden
(207) 236–3995
www.onceatree.net
If it's made of wood, you'll find it here, as this

Close-up

Camden Jewelers

The resort town of Camden must have more jewelers—genuine gold- and silver-smiths—than it does barbers, and not every community can say that. Since the 1980s more and more fine jewelry makers have settled in the Camden-Rockport area, and many of them have a national or even international reputation. Looking for wedding rings or a one-of-a-kind anniversary gift? This is the place to come. Here are a few ideas.

Camden Jewelry Co.
4 Bayview Street, Camden
(207) 236–8124
www.camdenjewelry.com
Ensconced on Bayview Street for ages now, this goldsmith's shop has cases filled with goodies, like their trademark gimmal rings, interlocking hoops of contrasting metals, or their Munsteiner tourmaline necklaces, which break into smaller, wearable pieces (one can be worn as a pendant or a brooch).

Etienne Fine Jewelry
14 Sea Street, Camden
(207) 236–9696
www.etienne.com
Known for his work with diamonds, Etienne Perret comes from Swiss stock, and he incorporates a lot of European sensibilities into his designs. His pieces are sold from coast to coast. He has won two Diamonds of Distinction awards and his designs are now selling in the millions. Check out the starlight bands, which are gold rings with a constellation of diamonds.

Thomas Michael Designers
7 Bayview Landing, Camden
(207) 236–2708
www.thomasmichaels.com
You've most likely seen this guy's stuff in fashion magazines. His store on Bayview Landing requires you to be buzzed in. Known for jewelry, Michael and his wife, Nora, craft contemporay rings and fine items like titanium cuff bracelets and elevate them to art levels.

shop's slogan goes, "from grandfather clocks to alphabet blocks." Bowls and canes and kitchen utensils and cutting boards and fanciful fish—it's all in this attractive shop on the waterfront. Hours are 9:00 A.M. to 10:00 P.M. daily in summer. Open year-round.

Planet World Marketplace
10 Main Street, Camden
(207) 236–4410
Planet is a huge, eclectic department store with the best toys around (lots of good learning games), a nice selection of decorative

accessories (bowls, place mats, frames, and candleholders), a small section of men's clothes, and a great bunch of gag gifts near the counter.

Unique One
2 Bayview Street, Camden
(207) 236–8717 or (888) 691–8358
www.mainesweaters.com
Original sweaters handmade by native knitters are the appeal of this longtime Bayview Street favorite. Yarns come from Maine sheep farms (and there's a selection here of yarn as well), and the sweaters are beautiful and one-of-a-kind. They can run you as much as $110, but they'll wear for ages—and look good doing so. Some cutesy moose designs, yes, but a lot of classics like the snowflake pullover. If you see something you like but they're out of your size, you can order one and have it shipped. They also carry patterns, needles, books, and other knitting-related items. Open Monday through Saturday from 9:00 A.M. to 5:00 P.M. and Sunday from noon to 4:00 P.M.

Other Shopping in Camden
For lingerie try **Theo B. Camisole** (24 Bayview Street; 207–236–0072). **Heavenly Threads** (57 Elm Street; 207–236–3203) resells clothing, and in a tony town like Camden you can make some real finds. **Foreside Company** (6 Main Street; 207–236–0998) has attractive and affordable housewares. **Wild Rufus** (22 Main Street; 207–236–2263) is actually rather tame, but it's your best bet for CDs for miles around.

Lincolnville

Monroe Saltworks
Route 1, Lincolnville Beach
(207) 338–3460
Begun in the tiny town of Monroe, inland from Belfast, this pottery emporium has grown exponentially, and it now ships its cool, grainy, salt-glazed wares across the country (there are stores in Copley Place, Boston, and Arlington, Massachusetts, as well as here and in Ellsworth). You can get seconds here on their plates, bowls, serving platters, and mugs,

which makes things affordable. Check out the crow line. Open year-round.

Belfast and Surrounding Area

Belfast Co-op Store
123 High Street, Belfast
(207) 338–2532
www.belfastcoop.com
Not every small Maine town can support a grocery-store-size co-op filled with organic produce, natural meats, enviromental magazines, green health and beauty products, organic snacks and chips, and on and on, but Belfast isn't every Maine town. The Co-op is a meeting place—it has a nice little cafe—and an important grocery to many who live in Waldo County. It's been at it for 30 years now. You may fall in love with a product, though, only to have it never available again. That happens here. Open daily from 7:30 A.M. to 8:00 P.M.

Brambles
Main Street, Belfast
(207) 338–3448
You don't have to have a garden to appreciate this Main Street favorite. While the store specializes in upscale garden goods—tools, ornaments, statuary, planters, herb markers, and on and on—it also carries fanciful housewares and gifts, note cards, soap, and ribbon. It's a can't-fail place to buy Mother's Day presents and housewarming items for your friend with the new cottage.

Cherished Home
Route 1, Belfast
(207) 338–4111
www.thecherishedhome.com
If you're like 30 million other people, you remember the 1981 wedding of Luke and Laura on ABC's General Hospital. The "it" couple's nuptials drew the largest daytime audience in history. People still ooh and ah at Laura, but today they do so in East Belfast, Maine. That's where actress Genie Francis and her husband, Jonathan Frakes (known to Trekkies everywhere as Commander Riker of

Star Trek: the Next Generation), run this fancy housewares store on busy Route 1. Inside you'll find furnishings of all sorts—new and antique, rugs and end tables and linens and table settings and even robes—anything that might "make a house into a home." And you might find Laura herself; Francis not only runs the place, which is set up in an 1890 home overlooking the harbor, but has poured herself into it, having long been interested in interior design. If not, you'll discover manager Lynn Doubleday, a Belfast resident who has a keen eye herself. Either way it's worth a stop.

Coyote Moon
54 Main Street, Belfast
(207) 338–5659

Coyote Moon is something of a reflection of Waldo County. It has all the funkiness and whimsy you might expect of a boutique catering to ex-hippies and back-to-the-landers and then some, with dresses from India, crazy cool mobiles hanging from the ceiling, neat turquoise jewelry, and gifts and accessories. And it's somehow managed to thrive for more than a decade while other stores on Main Street boarded up or changed hands long ago.

The Green Store
71 Main Street, Belfast
(207) 338–4045
www.greenstore.com

This place bills itself as the general store for the 21st century, and we can only hope that people will be as forward-thinking as the Green Store. From health and beauty products to rugs to clothing to solar technology, the store has environmentally sustainable goods galore. Check out the horse tire swing, the Audubon birdcalls, the natural cotton baby slings, and the rack of environmental magazines. This is the flagship of a small chain that includes shops in Damariscotta and Brunswick. Open year-round.

Liberty Tool
Main Street, Liberty
(207) 589–4771

This is the sort of funky old place where you can get happily lost for hours. Four stories of second-time-around tools fill this creaky old building on Main Street, as well as a mixture of antiques, junk, and books. It's always fun to peruse the electric hand tools, axes, drill bits, and dusty shelves here, and few people leave without buying something.

Other Shopping in Belfast

Perry's Nut House (Route 1; 207–338–1630), the once legendary, strange gift store, is not quite the same anymore. The **Good Table** (68 Main Street; 207–338–4880) carries an astonishing array of kitchenwares. **Colburn Shoe Store** (79 Main Street; 207–338–1934) is the nation's oldest shoe shop (or so it claims). The **Fertile Mind Bookshop** (105 Main Street; 207–338–2498) is an independent bookseller with not a lot of books. **Mr. Paperback Music and Café** (Reny's Plaza; 207–338–2735) has a mediocre selection of books but a surprisingly good selection of music.

Searsport

Penobscot Books
Route 1, Searsport
(207) 548–6490

Art books are the specialty at this lemon-yellow bookshop a mile shy of Searsport, and there are several rooms filled with them, from obscure titles about the Middle Ages to more recent tomes about current painters. There are so many books, in fact, that owners Howard and Kate La Rue have made floor maps to guide you through. You'll also find good sections on religion, poetry, cartography, and Maine subjects, all personally selected by your hosts.

Bucksport

Book Stacks
71 Main Street, Bucksport
(207) 469–8992

Bucksport isn't exactly a bookish town, but it

certainly has a great bookstore in this place. Proprietor Andy Lacher does a bang-up job, with a good selection and a pleasant atmosphere.

Castine

Compass Rose Bookstore and Café
3 Main Street, Castine
(207) 326–9366
www.compassrosebooks.com
At this longtime favorite they take bookselling seriously. You can get great recommendations, peruse well-selected shelves (especially the Maine and maritime titles), linger over a cup of tea at the Linger Longer Café, and order whatever you can't find. You'll quickly see why the place has a loyal following.

Leila Day Antiques
53 Main Street, Castine
(207) 326–8786
Leila Day has been at it here since 1978, and she has a nice selection of antique furniture, both formal and country. You'll find nautical accessories, folk art, and fine art as well, all housed in the pretty old Parson Mason House on Main. Open daily in summer, by appointment in the off-season.

M & E Gummel Chairworks
600 The Shore Road, Castine
(207) 326–8122
www.gummelchairworks.com
How do you make a historically accurate chair? You use historically accurate tools. That's one of the secrets at this fine furniture maker in Castine, a place that knows a thing or two about history. Known for their Windsor chairs, the father-and-son team here turns out fanbacks, spindle backs, bow backs, and continuous-arm chairs as well as dining tables and wooden bowls, and they do it all by hand, at benches, using hand planes, spokeshaves, and drawknives. The results are exquisite, colonially correct furnishings that would look appropriate in any old house. Prices range from about $550 to $2,000. The shop is in a neat old barn. Call for hours.

Harborside

Architectural Antiquities
Harborside
(207) 326–4938
www.archantiquities.com
At it since the 1980s, this fun shop seeks out all the distinctive architectural salvage it can find, cleans it up, organizes it, and fills its showroom with mantles and columns, stained glass and lighting, hardware and fixtures. Victorian-era items are a specialty. If you don't see the perfect piece for your old home, ask, and they'll keep an eye out for you. Great stuff.

Blue Hill

North Country Textiles
Main Street, Blue Hill
(207) 374–2715
www.northcountrytextiles.com
This Main Street staple has all sorts of gifts—candles, wooden utensils, wind-bells—but it is the textiles that got the place started that are the real attraction. The throws, rugs, baby blankets, and shawls are extraordinary. The folks here have been at their looms since 1976, making most everything themselves but carrying some items made by other area talents. Open all year.

Rowantrees Pottery
Union Street, Blue Hill
(207) 374–5535
Named for the mountain ash trees nearby, the Rowantrees Kiln dates back to 1934 in Blue Hill. And it's been turning out pitchers, cups, vases, and plates since, covering each one with its signature glaze. Quite a tradition in Blue Hill—and a quite a place. Open Monday through Saturday from 8:30 A.M. to 5:00 P.M. in summer, Monday through Friday from 8:30 A.M. to 3:30 P.M. in winter.

Other Shopping in the Blue Hill Area

Peninsula Weavers (Route 172, Blue Hill; 207–374–2760) turns out beautiful woven items, like rugs and scarves. **Blue Hill Books** (Pleasant Street, Blue Hill; 207–374–5632) is your source for reading material.

Little Deer Isle

Harbor Farm
Route 15, Little Deer Isle
(207) 348–7737 or (800) 342–8003
www.harborfarm.com
The selection of housewares, pottery, blown glass, and especially handmade tiles here is truly impressive—you'd think you were in Portland. It's especially nice to visit at Christmastime (they have a thing about it and sell some of the best wreaths around).

Ellsworth

Big Chicken Barn
Bucksport Road (Route 1), Ellsworth
(207) 667–7308
www.bigchickenbarn.com
On the way to Acadia, the Big Chicken Barn is just that, a large and long former chicken barn, and it's brimming with books and antiques of all sorts—we're talking 21,600 square feet of stuff. Dozens of dealers show their wares in the downstairs, divided into booths. The upstairs is practically groaning under the weight of thousands upon thousands of books and magazines. You could return each day of your weeklong vacation and not make it through everything here. And people do. Great for rainy days—great for any day.

ACADIA AREA

Bar Harbor

Alone Moose Fine Crafts
78 West Street, Bar Harbor
(207) 288–4229
www.finemainecrafts.com
The name may be cutesy, but the wares certainly are not. Proprietors Sherry and Ivan Rasmussen put the work of prospective artisans through an application process much like a juried competition, so not much second-rate stuff shows up on their shelves. You will find an array of fine arts and crafts—sculpture, pottery, photography, furniture, and jewelry.

Bark Harbor
200 Main Street, Bar Harbor
(207) 288–0404 or (877) 462–2659
www.barkharbor.com
Be sure to visit this kooky shop when you bring Fido to Acadia. From gourmet treats to "paw-tery" dog bowls, you'll discover a lot of neat stuff for man's best friend here. Leashes, collars, doggie towels, and breed-specific T-shirts for you—it's all here.

Dunn and Powell Books
The Hideaway, Bar Harbor
(207) 288–4665
www.dpbooks.com
You have to do some serious sleuthing to find this gem of a mystery book store. The place is open only by appointment, but any fan of noir thrillers and whodunits will want to track down owner Steve Powell and check out his collection of close to 10,000 rare and hard-to-find titles. Together with his partner, William Dunn, who runs a shop in Connecticut, Powell has access to 20,000 more books, so if there is an obscure gumshoe you're into, you'll likely be able to find the tome here. And if you can't, Powell will surely know how to get it. Bar Harbor itself has a history with the mystery—they've been written in town since before the turn of the 20th century and continue to this day with the works of Janwillem van de Wetering. Powell deals in mysterious cinematic materials as well. Worth the detective work.

Get Clocked
119 Main Street, Bar Harbor
(207) 288–1149
www.getclocked.com
This must be where Father Time shops. Every imaginable timekeeping device is stocked here, from cuckoos to fancy marble clocks. You'll never be late again. Open daily from 9:00 A.M. to 9:00 P.M. (check your watch).

Sherman's Books and Stationery
56 Main Street, Bar Harbor
(207) 288–3161 or (800) 371–8128
www.shermans.com
There are not many Bar Harbor businesses

Close-up

Uncle Henry's

While not a store per se, *Uncle Henry's* is something every Maine shopper should be familiar with. The Augusta-based weekly swap-it-or-sell-it guide is a genuine phenomenon in the state. The digest-size book of classifieds has transcended ordinary usefulness and become something of a bible for thousands of Mainers, and it's undoubtedly the most-read periodical Down East. Everything one can imagine has been sold in its 400-or-so pages, from snakes to fire trucks, houses to guitars, and people read it carefully cover to cover. It comes out on Thursdays, and the good stuff inside is often gone by the weekend. Still, there are some truly great deals to be had in its newsprint pages, and even if you're not in the market for something, it's an entertaining read simply for the craziness of some of the ads. You can find out more by logging on to www.unclehenrys.com or by picking up a copy at the local convenience store.

that can claim to have been founded in 1886, but that's exactly the case at this favorite, which has rescued generations of vacationers from rainy days. Bill Sherman opened up that year, printing the local paper and selling books. They just sell books now, and they have a nice selection; there's a good Maine section and a fine lineup of maps and trail guides. A visit to Bar Harbor just wouldn't be the same without Sherman's, and there are now stores in Freeport, Boothbay Harbor, and Camden as well.

Other Shopping in Bar Harbor

Willis' Rock Shop (69–73 Main Street; 207–288–4935) is the best place to turn for rocks and beach stone bracelets. **Window Panes** (74 Cottage Street; 207–288–9555) has a great selection of housewares. The **Alternative Market** (16 Mount Desert Street; 207–288–8225) is your gourmet grocery and hipster hangout.

Somesville

Port in a Storm Bookstore
Route 102, Somesville
(800) 694–4114
www.portinastormbookstore.com
Port in a Storm seems just that—a quiet haven

for real readers among the tempest that is the Acadia area during summertime. A two-story shop on an inlet of Somes Sound, the East Coast's only fjord, the bookseller has garnered quite a following since it opened in 1993 and has become known for having a very good selection. Nature and children's books are particularly well represented, but it's one of those bookstores where just about every title on the shelf looks like something you might like. And it's the kind of store that inspires lingering, with its cats, couches, and easy chairs. Housed in a cool old ship chandlery, where 19th-century tall ships would pull up to provision, Port in a Storm even has resident eagles, which perch just outside its broad picture windows. They recently opened a satellite shop in tiny Bernard.

DOWN EAST

Gouldsboro

Bartlett Maine Estate Winery
Off Route 1, Gouldsboro
(207) 546–2408
www.bartlettwinery.com
Maine's most famous winery, this is where to turn for local favorites like blueberry wine. Specializing in fruits other than grapes, the

owners have won many national and even international awards for their vino.

Perry

45th Parallel
Route 1, Perry
(207) 853–9500
www.fortyfifthparallel.com
Housed in an old elementary school, this home furnishing store calls itself the answer to the question "Where in the world did you find that?" And it's apt, both because you'll be very surprised to find a shop this fun and funky in Perry, Maine, and because proprietors Philip and Britani have filled their shop with cool and creative oddments from all around the globe. "Exotic" antiques, nautical items, architectural pieces, souvenirs, and unique decorative accessories—neat stained glass, candlehold-ers, funky lamps, artful clocks. It's an intriguing mix of stuff, and you'll hardly believe you're still Down East. Open daily from May through October and weekends in November and December.

Eastport

The Eastport Gallery
74 Water Street, Eastport
(207) 853–4166
www.eastportgallery.com
Few Eastport shops have a lot of staying power, but this downtown gallery has been around a while. The 27 area artists repre-sented here are affiliated with the great local Eastport Art Center, and this gallery is where you can buy their work. You'll find painting, sculpture, and photography. There's a gift shop as well. Open seven days a week from June through September.

Raye's Mustard Mill
Route 190, Eastport
(207) 853–4451 or (800) 853–1903
www.rayesmustard.com
Eastport's most famous attraction, Raye's has been grinding out mustards for more than a century. Their mustards come in more than a dozen flavors, and you can get a gift pack at their Pantry Store. Try the smooth Down East Schooner or the Hot and Spicy. You can also get coffee and a tour of the factory here, and it's a fascinating slice of Maine history. Open daily from 9:00 A.M. to 5:00 P.M. in season.

Other Shopping in the Eastport Area

Passamaquoddy baskets are available at Pleas-ant Point—try **Theresa Neptune Gardner** (207–853–4623) or **Clara Neptune Keezer** (207–853–4322).

ATTRACTIONS

Whether you like your culture of the high variety or the pop, you'll find what you're looking for on the coast of Maine. Thanks to its age, the state is home to a vast number of historic house museums—often the headquarters of the local historical society. We have two truly exceptional art museums, the Portland Museum of Art and the Farnsworth Art Museum, and any number of eclectic collections, from vintage autos to butterflies. We also have a couple of sports franchises in Portland with legions of fans. And there's plenty more to discover. Just turn the pages and read on.

Price Code

Except where noted, prices represent cost per person for admission, not including tax. In cases where donation is listed, there is no mandatory admission fee, but a donation is appreciated and recommended to support upkeep of the facility.

$	$5.99 or less
$$	$6.00 to $12.99
$$$	$13.00 to $19.99
$$$$	$20.00 or more

MUSEUMS

South Coast

Ogunquit Museum of American Art $
543 Shore Road, Ogunquit
(207) 646–4909
www.ogunquitmuseum.org
It stands to figure that Ogunquit would have a good art museum, as it earned a national reputation as an art colony a long time ago. But it's still surprising that such a tiny town would have such a fine museum. Dedicated to 20th-century American art, the collection here includes more than 1,300 works by such talents as Marsden Hartley, Edward Hopper, and Walter Kuhn, and many other internationally famous artists. Built in the early 1950s due to the hard efforts of Ogunquit painter and scenester Henry Strater, it opened in 1953 and grew impressively thanks to a lot of donations by big-name artists. Floor-to-ceiling windows frame ocean views like living paintings, and they are as beautiful as anything on the walls. The museum hosts rotating exhibits and has lectures and workshops in the summer. Open from 10:30 A.M. to 5:00 P.M. Monday through Saturday and 2:00 to 5:00 P.M. Sunday from July through October. Free for children 11 and under.

Wells Auto Museum $
Route 1, Wells
(207) 646–9064
More than 80 classic cars are on display here, including a Stanley Steamer, a Stutz Bearcat, and a 1908 Baker Electric Car once owned by John D. Rockefeller. (Check out the 1940 Bombardier snowmobile.) And strangely the museum isn't just about wheels—there is collection of nickelodeons and toys as well. Of course, the cars are why you come to this warehouse on Route 1, and you can even get a ride in a vintage car. The museum is open from 10:00 A.M. to 5:00 P.M. daily from Memorial Day through Columbus Day.

Brick Store Museum
117 Main Street, Kennebunk
(207) 985–4802
www.brickstoremuseum.org
Four pretty old commercial buildings—basically one block in downtown Kennebunk—serve as the headquarters for this local institution. The collections here are a mixed bunch, showcasing the history of the Kennebunks. The museum

ℹ️ Maine Archives and Museums is a consortium of museums, historic homes, historical societies—all manner of venerable institutions, really—and it has a handy Web site. Visit www.maine museums.org and you can find everything from museum locations and hours to interesting historic tidbits, like the fact that two Civil War engagements happened Down East.

dates back to 1936, and it's known for its decorative arts but also for maritime artifacts, and even exhibits about the Bush family, who have summered for ages in Kennebunkport. Some spaces look like rooms in an old home, others more like museum galleries. Nice quilts and shipbuilding tools. The Brick Store hosts rotating exhibitions, educational programs, and walking tours (see Close-Up). Open year-round Tuesday through Friday from 10:00 A.M. to 4:30 P.M. and Saturday from 10:00 A.M. to 1:00 P.M. Donation.

Kennebunkport Maritime Museum $
125 North Street, Kennebunkport
(207) 967-4195

Tiny compared to some of the state's other nautical museums, this collection is housed in the former boathouse of author Booth Tarkington, and it's where he did much of his writing. You'll find what's left of his schooner, *Regina,* as well as some scrimshaw and maritime artifacts, but it's the building itself, a neat place of weathered shingles right on the river, that is the real attraction. The museum is open from mid-May through mid-October from 10:00 A.M. to 3:00 P.M. every day except Wednesday.

Seashore Trolley Museum $-$$
195 Log Cabin Road, Kennebunkport
(207) 967-2800
www.trolleymuseum.org

Trolleys have been a part of summer in the South Coast for ages, and this fine museum explores every aspect of them. This is the oldest and largest electric railway museum in the world, dating back to the 1930s, and it includes more than 225 vehicles. Favorites are the snow sweepers, like the 1920 Russell Car and snow sweeper with its big bristle brushes, and the ones from Maine, like the 12-seat, red, open-air car from Biddeford-Saco. Rides along a 4-mile loop happen regularly from 10:00 A.M. to 4:15 P.M., and they are noisy good fun. If you're really into this sort of thing, consider the Be a Motorman program. Pony up $50 and you can drive one of these babies. The museum is open from 10:00 A.M. to 5:00 P.M. daily in summer and on weekends only in May and September. At 7:30 P.M. every Wednesday and Thursday in July and August, the museum conducts sunset and ice-cream trolley rides that are popular with families.

Saco Museum $
371 Main Street, Saco
(207) 283-3861
www.sacomuseum.org

A distinctive brick building downtown, this colonial revival place looks like a library from the street, but it's actually a little-known gem of a museum. (The building was designed by noted architect John Calvin Stevens in 1926 to house Maine's third-oldest museum, which dates back to 1866.) Five period rooms serve as the backdrop for a fine collection of early American furnishings, artworks, and artifacts. Some of the more notable pieces are the 850-foot-long Panorama of Pilgrim's Progress, one of few surviving 19th-century panoramas, and paintings by John Brewster Jr., Charles H. Granger, and Gideon Bradbury, as well as a daguerreotype camera that was the first of its kind in the country and a re-created colonial revival kitchen. The museum frequently hosts lectures, workshops, classes, and walking tours. Open Monday, Tuesday, Wednesday, and Friday from noon to 4:00 P.M. and Thursday from noon to 8:00 P.M. year-round and weekends in summer.

Greater Portland

Portland Harbor Museum $
Fort Road, South Portland
(207) 799–6337
www.portlandharbormuseum.org
Once known as the Spring Point Museum, this
neat little repository of Casco Bay history is
housed in a building that once served as Fort
Preble's Ordnance Machine Shop. The
grounds, part of the Southern Maine Technical
College Campus and right next to the Spring
Point Ledge Light (see Lighthouses chapter)
and the Spring Point Walkway, are alone reason to visit. But the museum, founded in 1985
to conserve the bow of the *Snow Squall,* the
only surviving remnant from the glory days of
American clipper ships, has a nifty collection
of nautical items. Among them are more than
500 glass plate negatives that tell the compelling story of the harbor, and there are still
more photos that depict the building of the
South Portland Liberty ships, which help
turned the tide in World War II. The small
museum regularly hosts changing exhibits that
explore the history of the great bay out its
doors. Open daily from 10:00 A.M. to 4:30 P.M.
from Memorial Day through mid-October, and
on a limited basis in the off-season.

Museum of African Culture $
122 Spring Street, Portland
(207) 871–7188
www.tribalartmuseum.com
That you can wander among tribal masks from
Nigeria, sacred carvings from Ghana, and
bronze statuary from Benin in Portland, Maine,
is pretty astounding. But it's the result of Oscar
Mokeme and Arthur Aleshire's dream to preserve tribal artworks. The small museum—it
has more than 500 artifacts but is feeling
pinched for space—is the only place in New
England to see sub-Saharan tribal art. It was
founded in August 1998 and has a variety of
educational programs like Discover Africa,
which it takes into communities to help shed
light on a region of the world with which many
Mainers are unfamiliar. The museum is open
Tuesday through Friday from 10:30 A.M. to

4:00 P.M. and Saturday from 12:30 to 4:00 P.M.;
closed Monday.

Portland Museum of Art $$
7 Congress Street, Portland
(207) 775–6148
www.portlandmuseum.org
The Portland Museum of Art is a major anchor
in the Forest City's Arts District, and it has
become a huge draw since it was established
more than a century ago. Housed in an
impressive, award-winning I. M. Pei–designed
building at the upper end of Congress Street,
the museum has a fine collection of American
and European art and regularly welcomes
major traveling exhibitions. Maine is well rep-
resented in the American collection, especially
in the Elizabeth Noyce collection, which was
given to the museum by the late Intel heiress
and includes works by Andrew and N. C.
Wyeth, George Bellows, Mary Cassatt, Freder-
ick Childe Hassam, and Fitz Hugh Lane, among
others. The European collection includes
works by such greats as Edgar Degas, Claude
Monet, Henri Toulouse-Lautrec, and Pablo
Picasso.

The newer LDM Sweat Memorial Galleries
are home to the museum's collection of paint-
ings by Winslow Homer, who lived for many
years just a few miles down the coast at
Prouts Neck. And the PMA also has a decora-
tive arts showcase on the lowest floor that
includes more than 2,000 pieces of glass and
artistic housewares.

Educational opportunities abound at the
PMA, and there are frequent talks and work-
shops. The cafe here has a decent reputation
as well, and you can get an array of good
titles, including several related to Maine, at the
gift shop. The museum is open Tuesday
through Sunday from 10:00 A.M. to 5:00 P.M.;
it's open until 9:00 P.M. on Friday and is free to
visit after 5:00 P.M. that day.

Portland Observatory $
138 Congress Street, Portland
(207) 774–5561
In the early 1800s scouts used to climb this

86-foot tower atop Munjoy Hill to look for ships coming into Portland Harbor. They'd then use coded flags to alert merchants about arrivals so warehouses could prepare wharves and line up stevedores. (They didn't have cell phones, remember.) The vista from atop the octagonal red structure was extraordinary—and it still is today. On a clear day you can see miles out to sea and as far as the White Mountains of New Hampshire, and tourists and schoolkids love to climb it to do just that. The observatory is the only remaining marine signal tower in the nation, and children find it particularly entertaining. But there are few people who don't enjoy the view. Open Memorial Day to Columbus Day from 10:00 A.M. to 5:00 P.M. daily.

Salt Gallery for Documentary Field Studies
110 Exchange Street, Portland
(207) 761–0660
www.salt.edu

Dedicated to field journalism—photography is the specialty—Salt has a fine gallery on the corner of Exchange and Federal Streets where you can see work by students and faculty of the Salt Institute. Often black-and-white but occasionally in color, these shows explore places and themes with genuine intimacy and gritty reality. Shows change about four to six times a year. The gallery is open from 11:30 A.M. to 4:30 P.M. Tuesday through Friday year-round; closed weekends. Free.

Midcoast

Bowdoin College Museum of Art
Walker Art Building, Bowdoin College, Brunswick
(207) 725–3275
www.bowdoin.edu/art-museum

One of the great surprises here is the world-class collection of classical items, including pieces from ancient Greece, Rome, and Asia. But you'll also find a worthy assemblage of American and European paintings, sculpture, drawings, and photographs. The beautiful old Charles McKim–designed building is currently being renovated in order to expand exhibit space; check the Web site for details. Open Tuesday through Saturday from 10:00 A.M. to 5:00 P.M. and Sunday from 2:00 to 5:00 P.M. year-round. Donation.

Maine Maritime Museum $$
243 Washington Street, Bath
(207) 443–1316
www.mainemaritimemuseum.org

The City of Ships is where you'll find the state's largest nautical museum, right on the Kennebec River and just downriver from the massive shipyard of the Bath Iron Works. People around here know boats, and you can tell by strolling through this excellent collection. Just about anything you ever wanted to know about ships is here in this incredible complex of buildings. There's the big brick Maritime History building, which brims with paintings, models, pieces of boats, documents, and other artifacts—reportedly more than a million pieces—and has permanent displays on fishing, canning, and, of course, shipbuilding. If you can't get enough about this last, simply step outside and venture over to the famous Percy and Small Shipyard, the nation's only remaining yard devoted exclusively to wooden vessels. The largest wooden ship ever built, the six-masted schooner *Wyoming*, was constructed right here. You'll get hungry if you step across the square to the Lobstering and the Maine Coast exhibit, where you can see dioramas of a Down East fishing village, learn the natural history of the lobster, and see a 1950s-era documentary about lobstering narrated by author E. B. White. Walk on over to the Maine Watercraft Exhibit, and you can see a variety of small vessels straight out of the state's history, from rowing boats to canoes to bateaux. And if you feel like actually getting out on the water, you can do that, too. The museum sponsors excursions all summer long, which leave right from its own pier (see Lighthouses chapter's Close-up on Lighthouse Cruises). You could easily spend a few days here (and eat at the cafe in Long Reach Hall). Open from 9:30 A.M. to 5:00 P.M. daily.

Morris Farm
156 Gardiner Road (Route 27), Wiscasset
(207) 882–4080
www.morrisfarm.org

In 1994 it looked like Wiscasset was going to lose a bit more of its precious open space. A 60-acre local farm was up for sale and could have well become condominiums or another convenience store. But a group of concerned citizens built a nonprofit corporation, purchased the land, and thus Morris Farm was born. Today it's a working farm and educational center set up to celebrate an agricultural way of life that's becoming endangered in Maine (and everywhere else, for that matter). Children come for summer camp; there's a great farm store with Morris Farm's own organic milk, free-range eggs, broilers, and turkey at Thanksgiving; garden tours are hosted; educational seminars are scheduled; and the public is welcome to stroll the grounds with its barns, meadows, woods, and waterfall from dawn to dusk. You'll want to move back to the land. Free.

Musical Wonder House $$–$$$$
18 High Street, Wiscasset
(207) 882–7163
www.musicalwonderhouse.com

A strange and fascinating collection of music boxes, player pianos, mechanical musical instruments, and melodious oddments make up this museum on a quiet Wiscasset side street. Austrian-born Danilo Konvalinka assembled the collection, and it fills an 1825 sea captain's home. Check out the musical candy dishes in the Green Room or the shadow box with sailing ships and windmill in the Red Room. Guided tours are offered, and they're the best way to get a handle on it all. You can get the abbreviated standard tour, which lasts 35 minutes; the standard tour, 1 hour, 15 minutes; or the be-all and end-all, the Grand House Presentation, which lasts for an exhausting 3 hours. Open daily from 10:00 A.M. to 5:00 P.M. from Memorial Day through October 15.

Wiscasset, Waterville, and Farmington Railway Museum $
Cross Road, Alna
(207) 882–4193
www.wwfry.org

This is another museum devoted to the unique Maine 2-foot railroad, a diminutive cousin to the railroads across the nation. In their heyday, these rails, 2-feet wide as the name suggests, traversed 200 miles of track in Maine, running dozens of trains, hauling thousands of passengers and tons of freight. The museum here is a nonprofit dedicated to restoring the operation of these trains in the Sheepscot Valley, and it's done a fine job since opening in a small way in 1989. There's a small museum on site that tells the story of the trains and actually takes you out for rides on Saturdays and Sundays. The trains run every 45 minutes from Sheepscot station, from Memorial Day to Columbus Day, beginning at 10:00 A.M. and ending at 4:45 P.M. It's a neat jaunt through the woodlands along the Sheepscot and a bargain at $5.00.

Boothbay Railway Village $$
Route 27, Boothbay Harbor
(207) 633–4727
www.railwayvillage.org

This museum re-creates an old Maine village, down to the narrow-gauge working train that runs through and around it. See the Kidstuff chapter for a more detailed description.

Thompson Ice House
Route 129, South Bristol
(207) 644–8551

Many people forget that before the advent of electric refrigeration, people used to get the ice cubes for their drinks from icehouses like this one south of Damariscotta. Ice harvesting began at Thompson Pond in 1826 and continued through to the 1980s. A museum exploring the commercial ice business was established on site in 1990, and it's a cool place. Ice is still cut here for demonstration purposes, using antique tools, and the big blocks are stored under sawdust and salt marsh hay and can last months and months.

The museum is open Wednesday, Friday, and Saturday from 1:00 to 4:00 P.M. in July and August. Free.

Farnsworth Art Museum $$
356 Main Street, Rockland
(207) 596–6457
www.farnsworthmuseum.org

These are renaissance days for the Farnsworth, and we're not talking Florentine painting. No, one of the best collections of Maine art has a nicely redone home that's enjoyed considerable expansion and refinement since the 1990s. And it's never been more popular. Established in 1948, the museum was once hard for some tourists to find, sequestered away on a side street in downtown Rockland. But the museum built a Main Street gift shop and entrance in the 1990s, which has doubled the number of visitors and touched off a downtown revitalization that has breathed a lot of life into the city on Penobscot Bay.

The Farnsworth's campus now includes five buildings, among them the Wyeth Center in Maine, which houses the works of the dynastic First Family of American Art. In a pretty, restored church across the street from the main Farnsworth building, the Wyeth Center is where you'll find paintings by patriarch N. C. Wyeth, the famed illustrator, and Jamie Wyeth, his grandson. (Most of the museum's collection of egg tempera paintings and drawings by son Andrew Wyeth are in the Farnsworth proper.) Entrance is free with the purchase of a ticket to the museum.

The Farnsworth had interesting beginnings. Reclusive Rockland resident Lucy Farnsworth left $1.5 million behind when she died for the establishment of a museum and library and the preservation of her family home. But she had never shown any interest in the worlds of arts or letters, so the 1935 gift was a complete surprise. Boston Museum of Fine Arts advisor and Farnsworth agent Robert Bellows roamed far and wide in search of good buys in the 1940s and came back with loads, from the likes of Andrew Wyeth,

Winslow Homer, Maurice Prendergast, and Eastman Johnson. Over the years the collection evolved, becoming ever more Maine-centric and featuring significant pieces by many of the greats to live and work here, from George Bellows, Rockwell Kent, and Robert Indiana to Neil Welliver and Alex Katz. The best of these works can be found in the exceptional permanent exhibition Maine in America, which showcases the considerable impact the state has had on the art world for the past two centuries. Also on continuing display are many pieces by local favorite Louise Nevelson, who emigrated to Rockland and lived in town for years before going on to world fame as a sculptor. All told there are more than 6,000 works in the museum's collection. The Farnsworth owns the old Farnsworth homestead, as well as the Olson House, which served as the backdrop for one of the most famous American paintings of all time, Christina's World. The site of many Wyeth paintings, the Olson House is open to tours.

You can always tell when people have been to the Farnsworth—they usually end up wearing the colorful little admission sticker all around town. The little round Day-Glo badge is proof that they've visited one of the nation's best regional museums and arguably the best collection of Maine art in the state. Open daily from 10:00 A.M. to 5:00 P.M. from Memorial Day through Columbus Day, and Tuesday through Sunday from 10:00 A.M. to 5:00 P.M. during the remainder of the year.

Project Puffin Visitor Center
311 Main Street, Rockland
(207) 596–5566
www.maineaudubon.org/explore/centers/
projectpuffin.shtml

The puffin is one of the more beguiling characters on the coast of Maine, and the story of the birds is an epic one. The colorful feathers of the small sea parrots were valuable commodities in the 19th century—ladies liked them in their hats—and the birds were hunted to the point of extinction Down East. Though puffins once inhabited six islands along the coast, there was only one pair left nesting at Matinicus Rock by 1902. Around the turn of the century, public outrage about the decline of sea bird populations led to the passage of legislation protecting our feathered friends. By the early 1970s there were two small puffin colonies left in Maine, the one on Matinicus Rock and another on Machias Seal Island. But the bird hadn't returned to the other islands it once called home. Project Puffin was begun by the National Audubon Society in 1973 to help puffins take back their neighborhoods. The society transplanted young puffins from New-foundland to Eastern Egg Rock in Muscongus Bay, hoping they'd take root. They did. In 1981 four pairs nested on the rocky isle. By 2006 there were 80 pairs. Another colony was established at Seal Island National Wildlife Refuge in outer Penobscot Bay. Audubon used techniques it learned in Project Puffin to help endangered roseate terns in Maine—and 40 other species of seabirds in 12 countries around the world. You can learn the whole tale at this new Project Puffin Visitor Center on Main Street in downtown Rockland, where there are interpretive maps, murals, displays, photographs, and even video cameras you can operate yourself. It's open daily from 10:00 A.M. to 5:00 P.M. and Wednesday until 7:00 P.M. from May through October.

Owls Head Transportation Museum $$
Route 73, Owls Head
(207) 594–4418
www.ohtm.org
There's hardly a weekend between May and October when something isn't going on at this Rockland-area institution. From vintage car meets to air shows, the museum's calendar is chock-full of events, and they're almost more interesting than the goings-on inside the big building. The museum has more than 100 vehicles on display—planes, cars, bikes, motorcycles, and carriages—all of them intriguing in one way or another. From one of the earliest bicycles, the colorfully named 1868 Veloci-pede Boneshaker, a brutal, suspensionless ride in those days of rutty roads, to the 1953

Whizzer Sportman, a protomotorcycle, from the carriagelike 1885 Benz automobile to the Model T–based 1926 Ford Snowmobile, the collection is fascinating. Car, airplane, and motorcycle buffs travel from around the globe to visit, but there is plenty to enjoy if your world doesn't revolve around engines. Plenty of educational opportunities are offered here as well as well as guest lectures and work-shops. And don't miss the air show. Open daily from 10:00 A.M. to 4:00 P.M. (until 5:00 P.M. in summer).

Penobscot Marine Museum $–$$
5 Church Street, Searsport
(207) 548–2529
www.penobscotmarinemuseum.org
Long ago, Searsport, Maine, used to boast more sea captains than any other community in the country, and several of their homes—and many of the treasures they brought back from around the globe—are on display at the Penobscot Marine Museum. The maritime museum occupies a campus right in the cen-ter of town, which includes an even dozen buildings. Inside are all manner of nautical art and artifacts, chronicling the rich seafaring his-tory of Maine and particularly of Penobscot Bay and the Down East coast. Paintings, mod-els, vessels—the collection numbers more than 10,000 pieces. And the very buildings they are housed in are themselves antiques, furnished much the same way they were when 19th-century salts called them home. The museum hosts a slate of changing exhibits as well as workshops and programs. Not long ago it built a Main Street gift shop, which is pleasant to visit and actually helps you find the place. Open Monday through Saturday from 10:00 A.M. to 5:00 P.M. and Sunday from noon to 5:00 P.M. from Memorial Day through mid-October.

The Good Life Center $
372 Harborside Road, Harborside
(207) 326–8211
www.goodlife.org
A celebration of the lives and simple-living

The Olson House is the site of Andrew Wyeth's iconic Christmas world. LISA MOSSEL VIETZE

philosophies of Helen and Scott Nearing, the Good Life Center occupies the old homestead that the couple built by hand. Authors of the famous book *The Good Life,* which advocated a back-to-the-land lifestyle and became a handbook for a generation of new Mainers who moved to rural areas and began farming, the Nearings were famous for welcoming interested visitors to their homestead. That tradition continues with the work of the center. Tours of the couple's gardens and the stone home they built are offered from September through June along with a calendar full of workshops and programs. Open from 1:00 to 5:00 P.M. every day except Wednesday in summer and Tuesday in the off-season.

Deer Isle Granite Museum $
Stonington
(207) 367–6331
Stonington takes its very name from the bedrock of granite on which it sits, and the community was the site of quite the quarrying industry in the late 19th century. Stone slabs from this picturesque village made their way into some American landmarks, from the George Washington Bridge to Rockefeller Center to the Smithsonian, and you can learn all about it at this small museum. An 8-by-15-foot working model depicts what Stonington and nearby Crotch Island, where stonecutting continues to this day, looked like in the golden age of granite. Open in July and August. Call for hours.

Stanwood Homestead Museum $
High Street (Route 3), Ellsworth
(207) 667–8460
www.birdsacre.com
Former home of noted ornithologist, photographer, and author Cordelia Stanwood, the museum features an impressive collection of mounted bird specimens and eggs, too. Real live birds flock to the wooded nature trails on the 160 acres outside. It's an incredible bit of green on the notoriously overdeveloped strip-mall stretch east of downtown Ellsworth. The grounds are open year-round during daylight

hours and the museum is open daily from June through September from 10:00 A.M. to 4:00 P.M.

Acadia Area
Abbe Museum $$
26 Mount Desert Street, Bar Harbor
(207) 288–3519
www.abbemuseum.org
The Abbe Museum was always much bigger than its 2,000-square-foot confines at Sieur de Monts Spring in Acadia National Park. The collection, representing 10,000 years of Native American life Down East, numbered some 50,000 pieces assembled over the museum's 75-year history, and it just didn't fit in such a small space. People used to visit and go away yearning for more than the single exhibit the museum was able to host. Not anymore. In 1997 the museum bought the old YMCA building in downtown Bar Harbor and set about transforming it into a first-class exhibition space. Designed by Schwartz/Silver Architects of Boston, the 17,000-square-foot museum opened in 2001, and it is just what the Abbe needed. There is now room for multiple exhibitions at a time, and the museum can show a lot of the collection that was packed away in storage, items like Micmac quill boxes and woven sweetgrass baskets, Penobscot pottery, and a 3,000-year-old flute made from the bone of a swan. It also allows the museum to host a full schedule of educational programs—and remain open year-round. The old octagonal building at Sieur de Mont will still be used, too. Open daily from 9:00 A.M. to 5:00 P.M. Hours are reduced during the winter months, so call ahead.

George B. Dorr Natural History Museum $
College of the Atlantic, 105 Eden Street, Bar Harbor
(207) 288–5015
www.coamuseum.org
A fine collection of flora and fauna indigenous to the Acadia area is on display in a relatively new home on the campus of the College of the Atlantic. Kids like the indoor tide pools. Even if

whalebones, stuffed puffins, and student-designed nature dioramas are not your thing, the museum is a good excuse to pay a visit to COA, always ranked highly among the most beautiful college campuses in the country. Open Monday through Saturday from 10:00 A.M. to 5:00 P.M. from mid-June through Labor Day.

Great Harbor Collection Museum $
Main Street, Northeast Harbor
(207) 276–5262
Another one of Maine's eccentric museums, this Northeast Harbor institution collects Mount Desert Island memorabilia on two floors of an old fire station. Old fire engines, sleighs and carriages, and boating-related displays chronicle the rich and interesting past of the summer colony. Call for hours.

Seal Cove Auto Museum $
Pretty Marsh Road, Mount Desert Island
(207) 244–9242
www.sealcoveautomuseum.org
Definitely worth a look-see if it's open when you visit, this eccentric museum boasts more than 100 old autos and more than 30 antique motorcycles in a collection known around the world. Some of these beauties date back to the turn of the 20th century. Check out the 1911 Thomas Flyer or the 1907 Chadwick. They're in pristine condition, all shiny and gleaming, and some evoke Chitty Chitty Bang Bang. Others are of relatively recent vintage (1973 Toyota Land Rover, 1974 Volkswagon Bug). Open from 10:00 A.M. to 5:00 P.M. from June through mid-September.

HISTORIC HOMES AND SITES
South Coast

Kittery Historical and Naval Museum $
Rogers Road, Kittery
(207) 439–3080
This cool maritime history museum has a lot in the works. It's close to its fund-raising goal to erect a new wing, which it will use to house a rebuilt garrison that stood on a hill overlooking Brave Boat Harbor in the 1720s. But there's plenty to like here now. The small collection, which grew out of a bicentennial project in 1976, features all sorts of nautical items, from ship models and replicas (including the USS *Ranger,* made famous by John Paul Jones) to a permanent shipbuilding display, as well as intriguing objects like the light from Boon Island, site of a disastrous shipwreck that led to cannibalism. Anyone interested in Kittery or nautical history will find enough to while away an hour or two. Open Tuesday through Saturday from 10:00 A.M. to 4:00 P.M. from June through late October.

Hamilton House $$
40 Vaughns Lane, South Berwick
(207) 384–2454
www.spnea.org
Maine doesn't have a lot of mansions, but this is one of them, a distinctive three-story Georgian on the sleepy Salmon Falls River. Built in the 1780s, the home was purchased in 1898 by a mother-daughter combo, and they restored it beautifully, furnishing it with antiques and country items in keeping with the house's history. The grounds are just as lovely as the home, beautifully landscaped and featuring formal gardens. The property is now owned by the Society for the Preservation of New England Antiquities, and tours of the place are offered on the hour between 11:00 A.M. and 4:00 P.M. daily in summer. There's also a concert series on the gracious lawns. Open Wednesday through Sunday from June through mid-October; the grounds are open from dawn to dusk.

Sarah Orne Jewett House $
5 Portland Street, South Berwick
(207) 384–2454
www.spnea.org
Former home of celebrated 19th-century author Sarah Orne Jewett (she of the environmental classic *The Country of the Pointed Firs*), this old place—circa 1774—looks much the same as it might have when Jewett lived here. It is a pretty Georgian with period furnishings

collected by Jewett and her sister. The pair were friendly with the family that owned the Hamilton House nearby, and Jewett helped make sure that home was preserved. This is also a Society for the Preservation of New England Antiquities property, and it's open Friday through Sunday from 11:00 A.M. to 5:00 P.M. from June 1 through October 15. Tours are given on the hour between 11:00 A.M. and 4:00 P.M.

Old York Historical Society $–$$
207 York Street, York Village
(207) 363–4974
www.oldyork.org

It seems fitting that one of the state's most historic communities should have one of the best historical societies. A very active bunch, the Old Yorkers keep seven venerable properties hopping throughout the summer. They provide guided tours—in costume—and living history demonstrations, and they set up self-guided walks of their antique buildings. Mixed right into downtown York Village, these buildings include the society's headquarters at Jefferds Tavern, a watering hole on the route between Portland and Portsmouth that dates back to 1750. (It's painted an unfortunate brown color.) Then there's the Old Gaol, which, built in 1719, is considered one of the oldest British public buildings in the country. Better than that, it's a fascinating look at the treatment of prisoners in the colonial area— you wouldn't have wanted to be one. It's a favorite among visitors, as is the Old Schoolhouse, a one-room school from 1754. Other stops to check out are the John Hancock Warehouse, where you can see a displays depicting York's maritime heritage, and the Wilcox House, a 1742 picket-fenced beauty with more displays of York history inside. These buildings are open every day but Sunday from 10:00 A.M. to 5:00 P.M. from June through Columbus Day. Also plan to hit the Museum Store, which has the same hours. Children 3 and under free.

Sayward-Wheeler House $
9 Barrell Lane Extension, York Harbor
(207) 384–2454
www.spnea.org

Another property maintained by the Society for the Preservation of New England Antiquities, this 1718 gem has its original furnishings—and a nice view of the York River. It was once the home of a Loyalist who served in the Massachusetts legislature, and it was opened to tours as far back as the 1860s to show how people used to live in the colonial era. Open from 11:00 A.M. to 5:00 P.M. on the first Saturday of the month from June 1 through October 15. Tours are offered on the hour between 11:00 A.M. and 4:00 P.M.

Historic Meetinghouse Museum $
Buzzell Road, Wells
(207) 646–4775

The town of Wells's original meeting place serves as the home of the historical society's collection of nautical and local memorabilia and a trove of genealogical information about area families. Open Tuesday through Thursday from 10:00 A.M. to 4:00 P.M. and Saturday by appointment from mid-May through mid-October.

Wedding Cake House
104 Summer Street, Kennebunk

All white spires and over-the-top Victorian gingerbread, the Bourne house was built as a wedding present, and it's become known far and wide as the Wedding Cake House. It's the stuff of a million postcards and Maine photographs. (The story behind the name is based in legend, but it was said that the man who did all of the ornate handmade carvings did so on a ship at sea because he had to leave his new wife before he even had a chance to eat his wedding cake.) Privately owned now and not open to the public, it's still a favorite photo op among visitors.

Richard A. Nott Memorial House $
Kennebunkport
(207) 967–2751
www.kporthistory.org

A Greek Revival mansion decorated with original furnishings, the Nott house is known locally as White Columns for the distinctive Doric columns that wrap around. Built in 1853, it's an example of the prosperity that shipbuilding brought to this community on the Kennebunk River. Be sure to hit the gift shop in the carriage house. Open Tuesday, Wednesday, and Friday from 1:00 to 4:00 P.M. and Thursday and Saturday from 10:00 A.M. to 1:00 P.M. from mid-June through mid-October.

Greater Portland

Neal Dow Mansion
714 Congress Street, Portland
(207) 773–7773

Neal Dow was the mover and shaker who made Maine the first state to outlaw alcohol, and his 1829 mansion has been the home of the upstanding teetotalers of the Maine Women's Christian Temperance Union for years. Dow came of age when Portland was a port in the rum trade from the West Indies and drunkenness and disorder were not uncommon. Dow was bothered by that, and he crusaded to get booze banned. He was also an ardent abolitionist who commanded a regiment of volunteers and rose to the rank of brigadier general in the Civil War. Whether or not you agree with his politics, he was an interesting fellow, and his house is fun to explore. Open Monday through Friday from 11:00 A.M. to 4:00 P.M. Free.

Tate House $
Westbrook Street, Portland
(207) 774–9781
www.tatehouse.org

This Georgian was built in 1755 by the colonial mast agent for the British navy. Restored at the turn of this century, the home has historic landscaping and an 18th-century herb garden among its attractions. Now owned by the National Society of the Colonial Dames of

America, it is the only pre-Revolutionary home that's open to the public in Greater Portland. The furnishings are something to see—check out the cool fireplace in the kitchen with its crane and cast iron pots. Open June 15 through mid-October, Tuesday through Saturday from 10:00 A.M. to 4:00 P.M., and the first Sunday of every month from 1:00 to 4:00 P.M.

Victoria Mansion $–$$
109 Danforth Street, Portland
(207) 772–4841
www.victoriamansion.org

How did an ornate—overwrought, even—New Orleans–inspired Italian villa end up in Yankeeville? Also known as the Morse-Libby House, this Victorian showplace was built in the 1850s by Ruggles Morse, a Mainer who made his fortune running New Orleans hotels and pumped a good deal of his money into his Maine summer home. Morse hired almost 100 highly skilled craftsmen to work on this brownstone to make it a place his wife would want to be, and the result is an extraordinary, head-spinning treasure trove of Victoriana complete with intricate wall painting, soaring staircases, elaborate stained glass, angels and gilding everywhere, and even a Turkish smoking room. The house included such contemporary comforts as central heating, hot and cold water, and a call system for servants, which were unusual for the day. Today 90 percent of the furnishings and details are still intact, making this into one of the finest examples in the nation of how the ultra-affluent lived prior to the Civil War. Gaudy is the word. Perhaps the best time to visit is during the city's Victorian holiday celebration at Christmastime, when the mansion is richly decorated for the yuletide.

The museum is open from 10:00 A.M. to 4:00 P.M. Tuesday through Saturday and 1:00 to 5:00 P.M. Sunday from May through October and again for the holidays. Tours of the mansion are 45 minutes long and are given at quarter past and quarter 'til the hour. Holiday hours vary, so call ahead. Children 5 and under free.

Wadsworth-Longfellow House $–$$
Congress Street, Portland
(207) 772–1822
www.mainehistory.org

Part of the Center for Maine History complex right downtown, this 1786 colonial set back from the street right in the heart of Portland was the boyhood home of famed poet Henry Wadsworth Longfellow. Opened as Maine's first historic house museum in 1901, it underwent considerable renovation in 2002 and is now in grand form. Many of the original furnishings used by little Henry and his family are still intact, and the shaded gardens out back are a nice sanctuary of quiet from the hubbub of Congress Street. Tours of the house, which will fill you in on this fascinating family and the ways of life in 19th-century Portland, are offered on the hour. Open Monday to Saturday from 10:00 A.M. to 5:00 P.M. and Sunday from noon to 5:00 P.M. from May through October, and sporadically during the holidays. The Center for Maine History is right next door.

The Fifth Maine Regiment Community Center $
Peaks Island
(207) 766–3330
www.fifthmainemuseum.org

You don't have to be a Civil War buff to enjoy a visit to this old hall, but it certainly helps. Built in 1888 as a meeting place for veterans of the Fifth Maine, the small museum brims with memorabilia from the Civil War. Exhibits rotate in and out, there's a gift shop, and programs are hosted during the summer months. Many people get married here, too. Open from 11:00 A.M. to 4:00 P.M. from June through September and on a limited basis in the off-season.

Midcoast

Joshua Chamberlain House $
226 Maine Street, Brunswick
(207) 729–6606

If you wonder what it might have been like to stand in Joshua Chamberlain's boots during his star turn at Gettysburg, you can see for yourself at his former residence, across the street from Bowdoin College in Brunswick. The very boots he wore at Bull Run are right there (of course, you can't actually try them on), along with original furnishings and other war memorabilia. Interesting stuff, and a fine tribute to one of the state's proudest sons. Open Tuesday through Saturday from 9:00 A.M. to 4:15 P.M. from late May to October.

Peary-MacMillan Arctic Museum $
Bowdoin College, Brunswick
(207) 725–3416

Admiral Robert Peary was the first man to reach the North Pole. That's what you'll learn at this collection, which is stuffed with diaries, letters, and photographs of the trip he took with his assistant, Donald MacMillan. In these days of Gore-Tex, it's interesting to look at some of the gear they used, and the museum has displays on the peoples and environments they found up there. Inquire about Peary's summer home on Eagle Island. Open Tuesday through Saturday from 10:00 A.M. to 5:00 P.M. and Sunday from 2:00 to 5:00 P.M. year-round.

Pejepscot Museum/Skolfield Whittier House
161 Park Row, Brunswick
(207) 729–6606

The history of Brunswick is the big draw at this local landmark. On the one side you can see how Midcoast residents might have lived in the Victorian age—there are original furnishings, down to the spice rack—and on the other you can see the story of the larger community told through exhibits and 19th-century memorabilia. The museum is open Tuesday through Friday from 9:00 A.M. to 5:00 P.M. (Thursdays to 8:00 P.M.) and Saturday from 9:00 A.M. to 4:00 P.M. The house is open to tours Tuesday through Saturday from the end of May to October at 10:00 and 11:30 A.M. and 1:00 and 2:30 P.M. Free.

Castle Tucker and the Nickels-Sortwell House $
Wiscasset
(207) 882–7169
www.spnea.org

Close-up

Walking Tours

Kennebunk

Kennebunk wears its history well—it's written in clapboard and cupola all across town. The architecture of the well-aged community ranks among the finest in all of Maine, and there's a great guided walking tour put together by the Brick Store Museum that shows off much of it. It's concentrated on Summer Street between the Kennebunk and Mousam Rivers, a gallery of early American home design with scads of historic places on the National Register. There's the Hartley Lord House (1885) designed by famed Boston architect George Meacham; the Huge McCulloch House (1782), once home to the secretary of the treasury under Presidents Lincoln, Johnson, and Arthur; as well as the famous Wedding Cake House, a piece of Victorian gingerbread that looks good enough to eat. Most of these homes housed sea captains and shipbuilders, merchants, and barons, and they tell interesting stories—your guide will fill you in on what you're seeing. All told, the walk is a little less than a mile, costs $5.00, and takes place from mid-June through the end of August. Call the museum at (207) 985–4802 for more information.

Kennebunkport

Kennebunkport had a fairly rich history long before anyone who summered here became president. The community is filled with distinctive old structures, many of which are now on the National Register of Historic Places. The local historical society (207–967–2751) conducts tours each Thursday and Saturday from July through September and on Saturday only through mid-October. Cost is $5.00 per person.

Here is another pair of buildings kept up by the Society for the Preservation of New England Antiquities. Castle Tucker was built in 1807 and remodeled shortly before the Civil War, and many of the furnishings of the bright yellow showplace are original. Also dating to 1807, the Nickels-Sortwell House is a Federal mansion of unique architectural details and a lot of antique furnishings—just one look at the place and you'll understand quickly how well some of the more prosperous sea captains lived. Both are open Friday through Sunday from 11:00 A.M. to 5:00 P.M. from June 1 through October 15. Tours are given on the hour between 11:00 A.M. and 4:00 P.M.

Old Lincoln County Jail and Museum $
Federal Street, Wiscasset
(207) 882–6817
www.lincolncountyhistory.org
In a residential area packed with old homes is this old penitentiary—the state prison until the one in Thomaston was built—and woe be to anyone who got stuck in here. The jail dates back to 1809–1811 and was in use until the 1950s. In its history it has been home to your usual thieves and murderers, but it was also used to imprison French sailors, back when privateering was happening off the coast, as well as British POWs. The interior consists largely of big, cold granite blocks with barred

Portland

Greater Portland Landmarks has long been the best friend an old building could have, and the preservation organization hosts walking tours of the Old Port daily from 10:30 A.M. to noon from July through September. The outfit does a variety of other themed tours of Portland and the islands as well. The tour leaders are well versed in the history and lore of the city and put on a good show. Call (207) 774-5561 for more information.

Bath

The local historic preservation group, Sagadahoc Preservation, hosts a tour of the history-rich City of Ships every Tuesday and Thursday in summer at 2:00 P.M., beginning at the Winter Street Church. Call (207) 443-2174 for details.

Belfast

Some people have called the architecture in this Penobscot Bay city the finest in Maine, and from the Gothic downtown structures to the many neighborhoods of colonial, Greek Revival, and Italianate homes, it certainly ranks up there. Pick up a self-guided walking tour map of the city's exceptional Museum in the Streets at the chamber of commerce.

Eastport

One of the more attractive of Maine's old towns, this Passamaquoddy burgh was once a bustling place of sardine canneries and shipping. It's a lot quieter today—but no less pretty or interesting. You can look for buildings that served as the setting for the Fox TV series *Murder in Small Town X* while you walk along this self-guided tour. Maps are available at businesses across town.

---

windows and iron doors, and there is still some neat graffiti—ships, names, dates, and poetry—scratched on the walls. Open from 10:00 A.M. to 4:00 P.M. Tuesday through Saturday in July and August and with varying hours in the off-season.

Fort Edgecomb State Historic Site $
66 Fort Road, Edgecomb
(207) 882-7777
An octagonal blockhouse built in 1809 to protect Wiscasset Harbor, Fort Edgecomb is the best-preserved fort of the period in the nation, and its grassy slopes overlook the Sheepscot River. The old bastion is a fairly

simple affair made of blocky wood, and you can run through it in no time, reading the interpretive panels and peering out through the musket holes. But the grounds offer some of the best picnicking you're going to find in the area. Try not to look at the power plant offshore, and concentrate on the scenic coves instead. You may see circling osprey or bobbing seals. The fort is just a skip from Route 1, so you can wait out Wiscasset's infamous traffic if you like. Open daily from Memorial through Labor Day.

Chapman-Hall House $
Main Street, Damariscotta
(207) 563–3176

A fine old cape, this Damariscotta institution has been sitting at the top of Main Street since the 1750s, making it one of the state's most venerable buildings. It was built by Nathaniel Chapman, who was part of the family that settled the area, and inside you'll find period furnishings and historical memorabilia of the area. Many examples remain of the way the place was constructed, and there are famous herb beds and 18th-century roses outside. Hours of operation vary from year to year.

Colonial Pemaquid State Historic Site $
Pemaquid
(207) 677–2423

One of Maine's oldest settlements was here at the end of the Pemaquid Peninsula, where the English arrived in the 1620s. Over the years a village took shape that once included many houses and 1692 Fort William Henry. The remains of this compound are being excavated by archaeologists today in one of the longest-running digs in the state, and visitors are welcome and typically fascinated. Several cellar holes scattered about show exactly how the compound was laid out, and they've yielded a lot of finds to archaeologists. Little interpretive pedestals sit next to them, and they tell the story of the village, which grew when a pair or merchants from Bristol, England, acquired patent rights to the area and began recruiting settlers. By 1665 it's estimated that there were 30 homes by the water here, but this was on the outskirts of British territory then, and Pemaquid residents were beset with raids by the French and Indians—hence Fort William Henry. Though it was a big and impressive bastion for those days, with walls close to 40 feet high, 20 cannons, and 60 soldiers, the fort was overrun by the French and Indians only four years after it went up, and the Brits decided not to rebuild. (The current fort is a replica of a section of the original.)

Visitors today can learn about all this early history by stepping into the museum and visi-

tor center and perusing the more than 75,000 artifacts that have been unearthed here. From tools, hardware, and pipe fragments to fine china and ceramics from across Europe, these items—and the other displays nearby—paint a compelling picture of life in the early days of Maine settlement. There are so many various elements here—the fort, sea vistas, the museum, the excavations—that everyone finds something of interest. The museum is open daily from 9:00 A.M. to 5:00 P.M. from Memorial Day through August.

Old German Church $
Route 32, Waldoboro
(207) 832–5100

The story behind this landmark house of worship is as compelling as the unique box pews found inside. German immigrants migrated to Waldoboro in 1740 with the idea that they would be moving to a thriving city. Instead they "found nothing but wilderness." (Seems town father Samuel Waldo may have exaggerated a bit when he did his recruiting.) The Germans decided to stay and make the best of things and built a village here, erecting this pretty old church in 1772 on the Medomak River. (They hauled it across the ice to its current site in 1794.) It's one of the oldest houses of worship in the state and has several remarkable meetinghouse features, like the hanging pulpit. Open daily from 1:00 to 4:00 P.M. in July and August.

Montpelier General $–$$
Knox Mansion
High Street, Thomaston
(207) 354–8062
www.generalknoxmuseum.org

This grand white mansion lords over Route 1 as it heads north after Thomaston. (Unfortunately so does the Dragon Cement plant behind it.) Though it looks straight out of the colonial era, it is a reconstruction of the former estate of Henry Knox, George Washington's secretary of war—the original was torn down to make room for the Thomaston railroad station. But the Daughters of the American Revolution thought that Knox deserved a tribute and worked tirelessly to have this exact replica built in the 1930s. The inside has been designed to replicate even the minutest of details, and the house is filled with antiques and some furnishings rescued from the original. The museum and gift shop are open from 10:00 A.M. to 4:00 P.M. Tuesday through Saturday from late May through late September and opened occasionally afterward for special occasions. Tours are given on the hour and half-hour from 10:00 A.M. to 3:00 P.M.

Farnsworth Homestead $$
Rockland
(207) 596–6457
www.farnsworthmuseum.org

When Lucy Farnsworth left her fortune for the establishment of a museum, she also specified that a portion of the monies be used for upkeep of her family home. This Greek Revival building, adjoining the Farnsworth Art Museum, is the result. Many original furnishings remain, depicting the life of a Victorian businessman and his family in the Penobscot Bay area. Open daily from 11:00 A.M. to 4:00 P.M. from Memorial Day through Columbus Day. Admission includes the Farnsworth Art Museum.

Old Conway Homestead and
Mary Meeker Cramer Museum $
Route 1, Camden
(207) 236–2257
www.crmuseum.org

A restored 19th-century farm serves as the centerpiece for this historical society headquarters. The Old Conway Homestead is furnished as it might have been when it was home to the old Conways, and the surrounding buildings are filled with antique carriages, tools, sleighs, a blacksmith shop, and a maple sugar house, where displays of sugaring occur each spring. The Cramer Museum is a contemporary building that serves as a repository of local history, from photographs to apparel to guns and swords. Open Monday through Thursday from 10:00 A.M. to 4:00 P.M. in July and August.

Fort Knox State Historic Site $
711 Fort Knox Road, Prospect
(207) 469–7719 (in summer)

Not to be confused with the U.S. Treasury and mint, this Fort Knox was named for Henry Knox, George Washington's secretary of war, and it's Maine's largest fort. Built of granite and an imposing presence looming large over the Penobscot River across from Bucksport, the roughly pentagonal bastion was begun in 1844, when tensions were great over the Maine-Canada border. It never took a bullet, either—but it was capable of raining shot down on the river from 69 cannons. Fascinating to explore, especially the underground bunkers (bring a flashlight). And the grounds are impressive, with a fair prospect. Nice picnicking as well. This is the state's most visited historic site—renovated a few years back by an excellent friends group—and it's a must if you're in the area. Open May 1 through October 30.

Fort George
Battle Avenue, Castine

Not much is left of this fort built in 1779, but it saw its share of action back in the day. The British erected it, lost it to the upstart Americans, gained it back, and lost it again. This was the last post surrendered by the defeated redcoats at the close of the Revolutionary War, but they took it again a few decades later during the War of 1812. Legend has it that you can hear the sounds of a ghost drummer boy if you visit during August. It's mostly grassy hills and picnicking facilities here now, but placards tell the site's rather amazing story. Free.

John Perkins House $
Court Street, Castine
(207) 326–9247
www.wilsonmuseum.org

The town of Castine is a treasure trove of American architecture, and this is the only pre-Revolutionary building left in town, a white clapboard classic, built in 1763. It has all the details of an early American home, from handsplit, feather-end clapboards on the outside to

Fort Knox lords over Bucksport Harbor. JENNIFER SMITH-MAYO

the beautiful timber framing on the inside. The furniture is accurate to the period. Open in July and August on Wednesday and Sunday from 2:00 to 5:00 P.M.

Wilson Museum
Perkins Street, Castine
(207) 326–9247
www.wilsonmuseum.org
All of Castine feels like a museum, so historic and well-preserved is the old village. The former home of John Howard Wilson is an actual museum, though it's as eccentric as Wilson must have been. The anthropologist first came to town in 1891 and over the years amassed a unique collection of everything from Native American artifacts to ship models to antique tools to rocks to seashells to firearms. It's an amazing assortment of unusual items and spreads across two floors. Open from the end of May to the end of September, Tuesday through Sunday from 2:00 to 5:00 P.M. Donation.

Holt House $
3 Water Street, Blue Hill
(207) 326–8250
An 1815 Federal-style home, the Holt House was one of the early homes built at the head of Blue Hill Bay. Home of the Blue Hill Historical Society, it's become known for its period stenciling and is furnished with antiques reflecting the town's history. Note the four chimneys, eight fireplaces, and wide plank flooring. Open Tuesday and Friday from 1:00 to 4:00 P.M. and Saturday from 11:00 A.M. to 2:00 P.M. from July 1 through mid-September.

Jonathan Fisher House $
Route 15, Blue Hill
(207) 374–2459
Jonathan Fisher was quite the renaissance man. His motto was "Let every hour be filled to the brim," and he did his best to achieve it, working as a preacher, carpenter, artist, scientist, surveyor, teacher, and writer. The Calvinist parson was given 300 acres, a barn, $200

annually, and help in building his home when he moved here in the late 18th century, according to a local history. He built his house in 1796 and added to it in 1814, and the addition is what is left standing today. It's an interesting testament to an interesting fellow, with its built-in Fisher-made grandfather clock in one corner and paintings here and there. It was renovated using the parson's own detailed notes. Open Tuesday through Saturday from 2:00 to 5:00 P.M. from July through mid-September.

Daniel Merrill House
Sedgwick
(207) 359–4447

Built in 1795, this straightforward two-story (plus) home was named after the Reverend Daniel Merrill, the first clergyman to serve the area. The townspeople had it constructed for the minister as part of his compensation package; today it serves as the local historical society and is open for tours. Open on Sunday in July and August from 2:00 to 4:00 P.M. Free.

Colonel Black Mansion $–$$
Route 172, Ellsworth
(207) 667–8671
www.woodlawnmuseum.com

As nice an example of Georgian architecture as you're going to find in Maine, the Black Mansion was named for Colonel John Black, and it went up in the early 19th century. Sometimes called Woodlawn, sometimes the Black House, it is filled with original furnishings and has been open as a museum since 1930. Be sure to check out the amazing spiral staircase as you wander through. Also leave time to wander the grounds, which are known for their gardens and incorporate more than 2 miles of woodland trails. Tours are offered on the hour. Open Tuesday through Saturday from 10:00 A.M. to 5:00 P.M. and Sunday from 1:00 to 4:00 P.M. from May through October.

Acadia Area

Mount Desert Historical $
Society Museum
Route 102, Somesville
(207) 288–3723

Many people find their way to this Mount Desert Island collection only because of the famous bridge that sits out front. In the center of town, the photogenic footbridge, whitewashed and gracefully arcing over the lily pads of a mill pond, has been the subject of countless calendar photos, and visitors often will stop to grab a snapshot and drive off without visiting the little museum adjacent. Their loss. The displays inside the 1981 building chronicle the very rich and colorful history of the island, from its world-renowned summercators and their mansion "cottages" to the great fire that ate up much of the island in 1947. As is the case with many historical society museums, the collection here is so large that many interesting items have to be in storage. Exhibits rotate in and out. Open Tuesday through Saturday from 10:00 A.M. to 4:00 P.M. from mid-June through September. Children free.

Down East

Ruggles House $
Columbia Falls
(207) 483–4637
www.ruggleshouse.org

Welcome to Plantation 13. That's what this part of Maine was called when Thomas Ruggles moved here in the early 19th century. His home, an 1820 Federal showplace known for

> **i** The Bar Harbor Historical Society has a lot to work with, as the history of Mount Desert Island is rich. Its home at 33 Ledgelawn Avenue (207–288–0000) brims with early photographs, paintings, exhibits on landscape architect Beatrix Farrand and architect Fred Savage, and even a milk bottle collection from former island dairies.

Close-up

Portland Sports

The term sport has a different meaning in Maine than it does elsewhere. (Here it refers to people who hunt and fish.) And sports fans in the state don't have a lot to cheer about—there are only a handful of professional teams in Maine. But two of them are in Portland—the Double-A Portland Sea Dogs baseball team and the American Hockey League's Portland Pirates.

The Sea Dogs are a farm club for the Boston Red Sox, and they play at the nifty 6,500-seat Hadlock Field, right off Interstate 295. City residents have really gotten behind the team in the course of a decade, and the Sea Dogs do a good job of marketing themselves with promos—re-creating the Field of Dreams cornfield, for example—special events, and inexpensive seats. The stands consequently fill up quickly, especially when the Dogs are winning, as in 2006, when they won their first Eastern League championship. General admission seats are only $6.00 for adults and $3.00 for kids (reserved seating is just a buck or two more), which makes going to a Dogs game a lot more affordable than going to a Sox game. Call (207) 879–9500 or (800) 936–3647 for tickets or visit www.portland seadogs.com.

The Portland Pirates do their skating at the Cumberland County Civic Center, a big ugly box on Free Street. They're the farm team for the Washington Capitals of the NHL, and they've also been in town since the early 1990s, taking up where the beloved Maine Mariners left off. They took home the Calder Cup in the 1993–94 season, and had a banner year in '05–'06, when they won the Atlantic Division and set 11 franchise records. They average about 4,400 fans a game (Civic Center capacity is 6,733), so it's pretty easy to get tickets. Tickets range from $7.00 to $20.00 for adults. Call (207) 775–3458 to get yours or visit www .portlandpirates.com.

its suspended, or "flying," staircase and its carved paneling, is testament to the riches he made as a timber baron. Neat antiques, like a tall old spinning wheel, are spread throughout. Open Monday through Saturday from 9:30 A.M. to 4:30 P.M. and Sunday from 11:00 A.M. to 4:30 P.M. from June 1 through October 15.

Burnham Tavern $
Route 192, Machias
(207) 255–4432
www.burnhamtavern.com
When rebels were looking for a place to plot their attacks on the British during the Revolutionary War, they settled down for a pint at this tavern, built in 1770. It's the oldest building Down East and is still furnished much the way it was during its heyday in the 1770s. After the war's fateful first naval battle, the injured were treated here. Open Monday through Friday from 9:00 A.M. to 5:00 P.M. from mid-June through late September.

SPORTS
Greater Portland

Beech Ridge Motor Speedway
Scarborough
(207) 885–0111
www.beechridge.com

This 1/3-mile oval is a well-known short-track facility and home to stock car races several times monthly. Events run from April through mid-September and might be truck rallies or NASCAR races. Check the Web or give a call to find out the schedule. Admission fees vary with the race.

Scarborough Downs
Scarborough
(207) 883–4331
www.scarboroughdowns.com
Here is another racetrack in the southern Maine town of Scarborough, but this one is of the harness variety. For more than half a century the half-mile track has been hosting horse and chariot races, and it's one of the few things that can be bet upon in Maine. Races run from late March through late December and are usually held on Wednesday, Friday, and Saturday in the summer, with post times at 7:00 P.M., and Sunday at 2:00 P.M. Good luck. Admission fees vary with the race.

Midcoast

Wiscasset Raceway
West Alna Road, Wiscasset
(207) 882–4271
www.wiscassetraceway.us
An antidote to the slow-going Route 1 traffic this town has become famous for, the Wiscasset Raceway—the biggest and fastest asphalt oval in the state—holds events on most week-ends from May through mid-October. These might be anything from monster truck rallies to the Friday night racing series. It's noisy and fast and everything you want regional stock car racing to be. Tickets range from $5.00 to $20.00, depending upon the races.

Great Maine Lumberjack Show
Route 1, Trenton
(207) 667–0067
www.mainelumberjack.com
Timber Tina, the vibrant woman behind this Acadia-area attraction, has won logging titles from Australia to South Africa. A world champion lumberjill (as opposed to lumberjack), she can chop, saw, and roll logs with the best of them, and she's been featured in National Geographic and Sports Illustrated, on ESPN, and even on MTV. Summers she can be found here on the way to Acadia, hosting nightly exhibitions of logging sports. The events are the kinds of activities that were—and are to a certain extent—prevalent in Maine's North Woods, and they make for some rousing entertainment. At a show you can watch as contemporary woodsmen and women— mostly students who compete in collegiate lumber meets—throw axes, roll logs, and climb 65-foot poles, among other things. And you'll also get a good dose of Maine lumbering history, which is fascinating stuff. Shows are nightly at 7:00 P.M.

LIGHTHOUSES

Maine's lighthouses were built to be beacons for sailors, keeping them safe from the state's serrated shoreline, but they might as well have been put up to attract tourists. The state's sentinels seem to have a gravitational pull on visitors, drawing them in with their blinking beams. There are dozens upon dozens of them—more than 60—and these stoic icons of the sea are ever-popular among people from away.

The lighthouse has been an evocative symbol of the Maine coast ever since the tall towers started going up in the 18th century, and they now adorn everything from the state quarter to T-shirts to key rings to car commercials. Their endlessly tracking lights and lowing horns have kept generations of mariners safe, allowing the Maine coast to be a thing of beauty rather than something to be feared. Which might explain why many Mainers have a soft spot for them, too, creating preservation organizations and friends groups whenever a light seems to be in need of help.

Maine's lights are certainly nice places to visit, if only because they sit on some of the finest acreage in the state—on rocky promontories, headlands, islands, and other scenic settings. Lighthouses are perfect for picknick-

ing, and they offer up just the right amount of history for the average visitor. Stir in a little fog and you have instant romance.

Most are fairly accessible, serving as the centerpieces of many a state park or owned by local trusts that allow visitors. Some have attendant museums, others nearby trails, and some are even free to visit. What follows are the most notable of Maine's lighthouses. Look for others offshore on your drive up the coast or click over to www.visitmaine.org and look up lighthouses in the search box.

SOUTH COAST

Cape Neddick Light
Nubble Road, York
(207) 363–1040
Built in 1879, this 41-foot, cast-iron tower is formally known as Cape Neddick Light, but it's popularly called the Nubble, the name given to the point it sits on by fishermen long ago. The great irony of the Nubble is that while it's one of the state's best-known lights—and one of the most photographed in the world—it sits on a small isle offshore and is all but inaccessible to the public.

Originally red, the tower was painted its white color in 1902 and was automated in 1987. The town of York owns the property and maintains the Sohier Park Welcome Center on the mainland within full view of the light. The center has restrooms and lighthouse memorabilia, but you might have to wrestle for a parking space in high summer. The center is open from Memorial Day through Columbus Day from 10:00 A.M. to 8:00 P.M.

Boon Island Light
Off York
Six miles out to sea, this 133-foot gray tower is

ℹ The Lighthouse Depot on Route 1 in Wells and now at One Park Drive in Rockland is a must for lighthouse fans, featuring books, maps, gifts, ornaments, and on and on. If you need more information or memorabilia, this is the place. The owners also publish a monthly magazine devoted to beacons—*Lighthouse Digest*—have a thick catalog, and run an excellent Web site, www.lighthousedepot.com. Call (800) 758–1444 for details.

Lighthouse Cruises

Several organizations on the Maine coast offer lighthouse cruises, pleasure boat rides that take in one or more beacons. Two notable ones to consider are the trips offered by Maine Maritime Museum in Bath and by the Elms Inn in Camden.

Maine Maritime has three regularly scheduled options in the summer: a cruise down the Sasanoa River to Boothbay Harbor for viewings of four lights; a cruise up the Kennebec River, passing by five lights; and another trip up the Kennebec to see the sentinels at sunset. These cruises range from an hour to two and a half hours long and cost as little as $19.95 per person. Call the museum at (207) 443–1316 or visit the Web site www.mainemaritimemuseum.org for details.

The Elms Inn in Camden hosts similar jaunts, taking in the lights of Penobscot Bay. A pleasant hostelry on Elm Street, the Elms has an arrangement with the local passenger boat the *Lively Lady Too*, and together they provide a daylong journey to area lights on Sundays, shoving off at 8:30 A.M. and returning at 3:30 P.M., stopping for lunch along the way. There are four different routes to choose from, stopping at as many as seven lighthouses, and each costs $50 per person. Cruises are open to nonguests as well. Call (207) 236–6060 or (800) 388–6000 for more information.

Hosted by knowledgeable guides, these cruises not only get you up close to some of the more scenic lights on the coast, but they also provide a wealth of information about each one.

Lighthouse cruises are a fun way to see the coast's impressive beacons. MAINE OFFICE OF TOURISM

no tourist favorite. But it sits on an island with an interesting history. All but submerged in storms, the isle is considered one of the most dangerous pieces of rock on the state's coast, which is why the light was originally built during the War of 1812. In 1710 Boon Island was the site of one of the most grisly episodes in Maine history, during which a group of British sailors got marooned on the island after the wreck of their ship, the *Nottingham,* and ended up resorting to cannibalism in order to survive. The story is recounted in Kenneth Roberts's famous book, *Boon Island.* And the light here is the subject of a poem by the daughter of a lightkeeper, Celia Thaxter, one of the more beloved of Maine's writers. It can be seen from a few mainland points on Cape Neddick.

Goat Island Light
Pier Road, Cape Porpoise
Somehow the hamlet of Cape Porpoise in Kennebunkport has managed to remain a little fishing village even as the southern Maine coast booms with development all around it. Goat Island Light, a 25-foot tower built in 1833, is a pretty landmark offshore. Inaccessible to visitors, it's still photogenic.

GREATER PORTLAND

Portland Breakwater Light
Bug Light Park, South Portland
Called Bug Light affectionately by its neighbors, this short tower stands guard over the west side of Portland Harbor. It was built in 1855, and though it's inactive today, it was restored in 1990 and is on the National Register of Historic Places. The surrounding park is popular with strollers and Frisbee throwers and has a fine view of the harbor and the city of Portland.

Spring Point Ledge Light
Southern Maine Technical College, Broadway, South Portland
Not as well known as some of Maine's sentinels, the Spring Point Ledge Light should be

more popular. The 54-foot tower looks like a spark plug set down in Portland Harbor. A 1,000-foot breakwater connects the 1897 beacon to the mainland and invites walkers. The view of the city of Portland and the harbor from the tip is fantastic. If that isn't enticement enough, the Spring Point Walkway, a very pleasant 3-mile greenway along Casco Bay, passes right nearby. The Portland Harbor Museum, a must-visit for people interested in maritime history (see Attractions chapter), is a short walk away, too. The museum (207–799–6337; www.portlandharbormuseum.org) occasionally offers tours of the light in summer.

Portland Head Light
Shore Road, Cape Elizabeth
(207) 799–2661
www.portlandheadlight.com
When people picture a Maine lighthouse in their mind's eye, this is probably the one they conjure up. Like the Nubble, the Portland Head Light is one of the most painted and photographed lighthouses in the world and is among the most-visited lighthouses in the country. It's also often called the oldest beacon on the Atlantic Coast, and whether or not that's true, it has to be close, built by order of George Washington in 1791.

The light itself is a 58-foot conical tower built of white fieldstone and rising above a restored keeper's house. Since the light was automated in 1989, this pretty building has been converted into an excellent little museum, telling the story of this sentinel, Portland Harbor, and the surrounding area. It's open from 10:00 A.M. to 4:00 P.M. daily from Memorial Day through Columbus Day and weekends only from mid-April to the Sunday before Memorial Day and between Columbus Day and Christmas. Admission is $2.00 for adults, $1.00 for children age seven or older, and free for youngsters age six or younger.

The grounds on which the light sits are truly magnificent, looking out over the open sea in one direction and back toward Portland Harbor in another. The surf rages here, and several ships have wrecked on the rocks below the light, even when the light was working. The worst was the *Annie C. Maguire,* which went aground on its way from Buenos Aires to Quebec in 1866. The crew of 15 was saved by the quick actions of Portland Head's fabled lightkeeper, Joseph Strout, but the ship was bashed into splinters.

People have been flocking here ever since poet Henry Wadsworth Longfellow used to walk over from his home in Portland to enjoy the views. Ninety-four-acre Fort Williams Park wraps around the headlight and is the place where Portlanders take their houseguests—to the tune of nearly a million people a year. It's particularly popular among picnickers and kite flyers and features a beach and tennis course in addition to sweeping lawns.

MIDCOAST

Seguin Island Light
Phippsburg

At 180 feet above the sea, the Seguin Island Light is a fairly dramatic lighthouse, and the view from its tower is exceptional, taking in Portland, Mount Washington, and Monhegan Island all at once. Relatively few people ever get to see it, though, because of the fact that Seguin Island is 2 miles from the end of the Kennebec River and is deserted for most of the year. Visitors are welcome to climb the 1795 lighthouse tower, and there's even a three-room museum on the island filled with lighthouse memorabilia. Captain Howie Marston of Kennebec Charters makes the 20-minute crossing from Popham in the Old Duff. It's worth the effort, and runs $50 for the boat, which accommodates up to six people. Call (207) 389–1883 for more information.

Pemaquid Light
State Route 130, Bristol
(207) 677–2494

When storms threaten to batter the Midcoast, many residents will make a trip down to this 32-foot fieldstone tower because the surf here is always impressive. Pemaquid is among the most popular lighthouses to visit in Maine, and

with its ample parking, public grounds, and adjacent museum, it's very welcoming.

The light has one of the more romantic settings of any lighthouse in Maine, sitting at the end of the Pemaquid Peninsula south of Damariscotta and overlooking open sea. The tower went up in 1827, was replaced in 1835, and in 1934 became the first Maine beacon to be automated. In the former keeper's house is the Fishermen's Museum (207–677–2494), run by the town of Bristol. Open daily in summer from 1:00 to 5:00 P.M., it's a good excuse to get inside a keeper's house. The museum also houses a collection of artifacts that shed light on the fishing industry in Maine. No admission fee.

Monhegan Light
Lighthouse Hill, Monhegan Island
(207) 596–7003
www.monheganmuseum.org

There are many reasons to plan a visit to Monhegan Island (see Area Overview chapter), 10 miles off the Midcoast, and one of them is this 47-foot tower. A dull gray granite, it isn't the most impressive of the state's beacons, but its location most certainly is. The light is set high atop a hill where the island meets the sky, and it lords over both Monhegan and Manana Island, its uninhabited sister isle across Monhegan Harbor. The place is so grand you could sit on the lawn here for the better part of a day and never get tired of it. If you visit only one lighthouse in Maine, make it this one.

The light was automated in the late 1950s, and the grounds and buildings surrounding the tower were sold to the local island association. Today there is a very fine museum in the keeper's house that documents the natural and cultural history of the island. It includes exhibits that explore the fishing industry and early island life, and it features works by some of the nation's most famous artists, many of whom—George Bellows, Rockwell Kent, Jamie Wyeth—came here to live and paint. In recent years some of the collection was moved to the renovated and climate-controlled assistant keeper's house, making the museum twice as

A pretty old light in a stunning setting, Monhegan Light provides a fantastic view of the harbor.
LISA MOSSEL VIETZE

impressive. It's open daily from 11:30 A.M. to 3:30 P.M. from July through September. Admission is free, but a donation is encouraged.

Marshall Point Light
Marshall Point Road, Port Clyde
(207) 372–6450
www.marshallpoint.org
Marshall Point is another one of Maine's oft-photographed lighthouses, thanks to its distinctive footbridge. The white tower protects the south entrance to Port Clyde Harbor, and it was built in 1832 at a time when the small community was an important Maine port thanks to its granite quarries, shipbuilding yards, and canneries. Today the town owns the light, and its grounds are open to strollers and picnickers. There's also a small museum on the premises that tells the story of this light and a few others in the area. It's open Sunday through Friday from 1:00 to 5:00 P.M. and Saturday 10:00 A.M. to 5:00 P.M. from Memorial

Day through September. Admission is free, but donations are appreciated.

Rockland Breakwater Light
Jameson Point, Rockland
The lighthouse here is not the primary attraction. An 18-foot-tall square tower, it sits on a fog signal house and is pleasant enough, but the real appeal is the breakwater itself, a granite cribwork that stretches for close to a mile into Rockland Harbor. Put in place to protect the harbor from crashing waves, the breakwater was built across the span of 18 years, a massive undertaking that took close to 700,000 tons of the area's famed granite. Walkers, anglers, photographers, hand-holding couples—everyone loves the result, as it affords a magnificent view of the city of Rockland, Penobscot Bay and its islands and tall schooners, and the Camden Hills in the distance.

Owls Head Light
North Shore Road, Owls Head

Owls Head Light serves as the centerpiece of Owls Head Light State Park, just south of Rockland. This little-known green space occupies a pretty headland overlooking Rockland Harbor and the open blue of Penobscot Bay. The prospect is fine, and there are nice picnicking facilities and a little pebble beach.

The light is a 20-foot, white-brick tower that was built to protect mariners heading into the harbor in 1825, when the lime trade brought many vessels to Rockland and Thomaston. One local history recounts how a spaniel here named Spot learned to pull a rope and ring the fog bell when he saw ships coming into view, saving the day on a few occasions.

Both the light and the keeper's house are closed to the public, but the grounds alone make this beacon worth visiting.

Curtis Island Light
Curtis Island, Camden

Many things make Camden Harbor dramatic—the rounded green backs of the Camden Hills towering above, the pretty brick town below it, and Curtis Island at the harbor's entrance. A small, piney isle, Curtis is home to a 26-foot sentinel, built for $4,500 in 1896 on the order of President Andrew Jackson.

The island is reachable by kayak or dinghy, and it is now a public park owned by the town of Camden. Respectful visitors are always welcome. If you don't have a boat, the light is easily viewed from a variety of Camden points, including Bayview Street, the Public Landing, and the tops of Mount Battie and Mount Megunticook.

Fort Point Light
Fort Point Road, Stockton Springs
(207) 567-3356

Many of the roads that take a right off coastal U.S. Route 1 and wend their way down peninsulas hold little-known treasures on them, and Fort Point State Park in Stockton Springs is one such place. The 120-acre state park features a mile of shoreline at the point where the Penobscot River floods into the ocean, a 200-foot pier for fishing, trails for exploring, the earthworks that remain from historic Fort Pownall, and Fort Point Light.

The 31-foot, square white tower was erected in 1836 (and rebuilt in 1857) by order of President Andrew Jackson to provide safe passage for boats bound for Bangor, at that time a major timber port. Besides the keeper's house and other outbuildings, the complex here includes a cool 1890 bell tower in the shape of an obelisk that's on the National Register of Historic Places. The park is open from Memorial Day through Labor Day.

Dice's Head Light
Battle Avenue, Castine

Castine positively looks historic, with its white clapboard homes, tidy streets, brick downtown, and all-American campus, and Dice's Head Light certainly doesn't detract. The old town sits at the end of an ax-head-shaped peninsula, dangling into East Penobscot Bay, and the lighthouse itself occupies a headland at the top cutting corner of that ax, with panoramic views all around. It was built in 1828 to help guide ships to the opening of the Penobscot River, not far away, and the stone tower was once wrapped with a wooden

---

i Any lighthouse lover would be foolish to pass by the new Maine Lighthouse Museum at the Maine Discovery Center in Rockland. The collection here used to be housed up the road at the Penobscot Bay city's popular Shore Village Museum, and it includes the largest assemblage of lighthouse lenses in the world. It has an important collection of lighthouse memorabilia and Coast Guard artifacts as well. It's located in the same building as the Lighthouse Depot at One Park Drive and is open daily (except Sunday in winter), so it's an instant "two-fer" for buffs. Admission is $5.00. Call (207) 594-3301 or visit www.mainelighthouse museum.com for details.

Close-up

Lighthouse Living

Ah, romance. It's hard to get more romantic than a lighthouse inn on a picture-perfect Maine island. That's the scenario at the Keeper's House, the only lighthouse inn Down East, sequestered away down a piney road on the island of Isle au Haut off Stonington. You can truly imagine what life must have been like for the lightkeepers of yore when you spend a night in the Keeper's Room, which stares out at Robinson's Point Light, attached by a boardwalk, and the green waters of Isle au Haut Thorofare beyond. Make that a very well taken care of keeper. The food here is exceptional; the rooms rustic and cozy, with oil lights and no phones or electricity; and the owners, Jeff and Judi Burke, are gracious hosts.

Built in 1907, this white tower is still operational, and guests are welcome to tour it. Standing on the walkway to the beacon, lighthouse aficionados can take in a total of four lights winking in various directions. The Burkes entertain guests aboard their boat, *Pax*, several times a week, and the rest of the island is truly stunning, with a white clapboard fishing village on one end and the small peaks, forests, and trails of Acadia National Park on the other. Access is by mailboat only (see our Getting Here, Getting Around chapter).

The inn is open from late May through late October, and rooms are a bit pricey—in the $300 range. Call (207) 460-0257 to make reservations.

---

frame. The site is owned by the town and is no longer operational, but a neat set of stairs leads down to the rocks on the shore below where there is a small working beacon built to replace Dice's Head.

ACADIA AREA

Bass Harbor Head Light
Lighthouse Road, Bass Harbor
Bass Harbor resides on the "quiet side" of Mount Desert Island, the end of the island opposite Bar Harbor and Acadia National Park and thus much less visited. Still, many people make their way over to this small village each summer, and Bass Harbor Head Light is one of the reasons why. Though privately owned, the lighthouse is among the most accessible lights in Maine, and it certainly adorns its share of calendars.

Erected in 1858 to mark the eastern flank of Blue Hill Bay, the white brick tower is set on a small cliff and hidden from mainland viewers by a stand of spruce. The adjacent keeper's house has traditionally been home to the commander of the Coast Guard station in Southwest Harbor and thus is closed to the public. But there are paths through the forest here and walkways that take you down to the shore where viewing of the light is most impressive. And just up the road are two of Acadia's best secrets, the Ship Harbor and Wonderland trails, shore paths that take you to beautiful prospects.

Mount Desert Rock
Open Atlantic
Far from the radar of most visitors to the Acadia area, Mount Desert Rock is still a fascinating place. Eighteen miles southwest of the

island, the rock is just that—a small, wave-battered ledge amid the constant swells of the Atlantic. The light is a 58-foot, gray granite tower, and it is routinely thrashed by storms. Back when keepers lived here, they attempted to plant vegetable gardens, and each one was washed away by late fall.

Early lights here burned on whale oil. Today the rock is a research station for the Bar Harbor–based College of the Atlantic and its Allied Whale program, which has been monitoring and cataloging whale populations for decades and now has the largest collection of photo-identified humpback and finback whales in the world.

DOWN EAST

West Quoddy Light
West Quoddy Head Road, Lubec
(207) 733–0911 (in season) or (207) 941–4014 (winter)
West Quoddy Light has a lot of unique distinctions: It sits on the easternmost point of land in the United States, it presides over the most dynamic tides in the nation, and it's Maine's only red-and-white-striped tower. The pretty light station was built in 1808 on the order of Thomas Jefferson and is the focal point of Quoddy Head State Park, one of the more breathtaking of the parks in the state's system. The views that stretch before it are absolutely astonishing.

The light itself is positioned near some of the tallest cliffs in Maine and overlooks all the world, it seems. On the horizon, across the Grand Manan Channel, is Grand Manan Island, a tall, arcing isle in New Brunswick, Canada. Whales frequently swim through the channel and can be spotted from the lighthouse grounds often enough in summertime that people like to sit here and look for them. The tides below swing as much as 24 feet in and out.

The light was built in 1808 and rebuilt 50 years later, and its beacon still shines through its original Fresnel lens. The lightkeeper used to have to ring a fog bell by hand to warn approaching vessels; later a steam-powered foghorn was put in place. The light was automated in 1988 and became part of Quoddy Head State Park.

Because the property is state owned, you can get right up and have a close look. Then you'll want to wander the 4.5 miles of trails here, which skirt 100-foot cliffs, splinter off to amazing overlooks, wend through cool bogs, and more. Very worthwhile. Quoddy Head State Park is open from May 15 through October 15.

BEACHES

For a state famous for its rocky coast, Maine has its share of wide, sandy beaches. The rocks don't really begin to rule until after Portland; the South Coast is a place of fine strands, great swimming, and a genuine beach culture. People flock to Ogunquit and Old Orchard and Goose Rocks and Scarborough beaches like seagulls to the snack bin, and whole communities have been built to cater to these sun worshippers. At the other end of the spectrum are the beaches east of Ellsworth, which tend to be rockier, quieter—and colder, if that's at all possible. From quiet neighborhood beaches to big amusement-park-style strands, you can find whatever you're looking for in Maine.

SOUTH COAST
Kittery

Fort Foster Park
Pocohontas Road, Kittery
(207) 439–2182
This old bastion on Gerrish Island was put in place to protect the entrance to Portsmouth Harbor in 1872 and was in use through World War II, when an antisubmarine net was stretched from here to Fort Stark across the way in New Hampshire. There are enough ruins of fortifications scattered across this 90-acre park to amuse history buffs, but you don't have to worry about U-boats much anymore. The island has a few swimming areas as well as places for windsurfing and scuba diving. When you're done splashing, you can eat at the picnic tables, play in the grass, or enjoy the playground. It's a nice family destination because there are shallow stretches and gentle waves. Nice views as well of Whaleback Light. The park is open from 10:00 A.M. to 8:00 P.M. from Memorial Day through Labor Day. Admission is $10 per car.

Seapoint and Crescent Beaches
Seapoint Road, Kittery
These two beaches lie on either side of Seapoint, a small peninsula in the state's southernmost town between Gerrish Island and Brave Boat Harbor. The pair are adjacent to a marshy area known for its wealth of birdlife, so it isn't uncommon to see binocular-toting birdwatchers as well as beer-cooler-toting beachgoers. Both beaches are in the 600-yard range, small by southern Maine standards. Facilities are limited, parking is scarce, and you have to look out for yourself—no lifeguards. Kids have been known to party here, to the consternation of area residents, so you might want to head out by dinnertime.

The Yorks

Harbor Beach
York Harbor
(207) 363–4422
Harbor Beach is truly a stunner, but good luck finding parking. There isn't any at the parking area nearby (it's all reserved), so your best bet is to try to leave your car up on the street in one of the spots across from the York Harbor Inn and right next to Hartley Mason Park. They go very quickly, however, on a fine August day.

The beach is a little cul-de-sac with gentle surf backed up to rocks and the Stage Neck Inn's massive resort. You can set up your towel, enjoy the swells and the pebbly sands, and then go climb along the cool Cliff Path, if you want. Portapotties are here, and lifeguards will look after you from the end of June through Labor Day.

Long Sands Beach
Route 1A, York Harbor to York Beach
Not many of Maine's beaches have a designated surfing area, but there's the sign at Long

Sands in York, imploring dudes to hang ten. And they actually gather here when the waves are rolling. Of course, everyone, it seems, comes to this southern Maine favorite on a hot summer afternoon. The beach here stretches for about 1.5 miles, paralleling U.S. Route 1A as it travels between York Harbor and York Beach. When the tide's out, it exposes about a half mile of sand, and the slope is very gradual, making it a good place to take children. The beach is the heart of a summer colony, and motels line the road for much of its length. Across the street from all of these is metered parking, which goes fast. Lifeguards stand on duty in July and August, and there are both bathhouses and restrooms.

Short Sands Beach
Route 1A, York Beach
On the other side of Cape Neddick from Long Sands Beach, Short Sands is just that, a petite crescent compared to its lengthy sibling. The sands are so short here, in fact, that the beach completely disappears when the tide is high. So make sure you check the tide charts before you pay a visit. Like Long Sands, Short Sands has metered parking off Route 1A, bathhouses, restrooms, and lifeguards in high summer. All of the amusements of York Beach—the stores, the amazing Goldenrod candy store, York's Wild Kingdom, the playground, the arcades, the basketball courts—are within easy walking distance, so families tend to like the beach here.

Ogunquit

Ogunquit Beach
Ogunquit
The natives called Ogunquit a "beautiful place by the sea," and 3.5-mile-long Ogunquit Beach—all fine white sands and clear surf—is a large part of what makes this community attractive. Residents made a real effort to preserve the sanctity of the strand, pleading with the state legislature to cede the area between the beach and the river to the town, and they did a good job—most of the commercial activity in town is kept at bay, but there are a cou-

ple of snack shacks handy when you get hungry. You can easily walk into town if you've forgotten sunscreen or your smokes.

The beach is unbelievably popular in summer, so forget about parking anywhere nearby—best to take the trolley in; it makes trips to both ends of the beach three or four times an hour—and it's divided into a variety of sections. There's Footbridge Beach, the large section known as plain old Ogunquit Beach, and Moody Beach up by Wells. The Ogunquit River slides in behind the beach, separating it from the main, and kids often like to splash in the warmer, protected basin the river creates.

Ogunquit is a very gay-friendly town, so don't be surprised to see his-and-his and hers-and-hers couples. A cool sand-castle-building contest is held here every summer, so you can try your hand at that château you've always wanted.

You're in good hands when you do your swimming here, too—the lifeguards of Ogunquit Beach have placed high in the state's lifeguard contests for years running. There is parking for a fee, if you can find a spot, and there are changing areas as well.

Wells

The community of Wells is one long beach, basically, from the town line near Ogunquit to the border with Kennebunk. There are several small, lesser-known beaches, which are worth seeking out, as well as Wells Beach proper, a lengthy beauty on a long, narrow peninsula separated from the mainland by the Webhannet River. Wells Beach is by far the most popular. The sands sit across the road from a line of cottages—this is a big summer resort community—which spill bathers out onto the strand all day long.

Crescent Surf Beach
Wells
The tides put the squeeze on these sands, eliminating most of the beach when the water is high. The facilities are fairly limited—no lifeguards, no picnic areas, no ice-cream

stands—so if you want to make a day of it, you should bring your own lunch and be prepared to watch the kids. Portapotties are it as far as relief is concerned. Everyone enjoys the tide pools here, which can be rife with life and can entertain for hours, and the bird-watching is good as well, because of more National Wildlife Refuge marshes. Parking is available at the Gold Ribbon Drive lot, accessible from Webhannet Drive.

Drakes Island and Laudholm Beaches
Wells

This pair sit adjacent to one another, and combined, they sprawl for about 1,000 yards. Drakes is the second largest of Wells's beaches, behind Wells Beach proper, and it's framed by dunes, sea grass, and seawalls, sitting at the end of Drakes Island Road near another little cottage village. There are far fewer distractions near the sands here than there are at Wells Beach, with its summer homes and boardwalk, but the ice-cream truck appears occasionally in summer. Everybody loves the ice-cream guy.

Erosion has been a concern here, and the Army Corps of Engineers has pumped dredged sand onto the beach to offset the gradual removal by natural forces. It's still beautiful, though, and naturalists dig the eastern end of the beach, because it's adjacent to more Rachel Carson National Wildlife Refuge lands. Fishermen take to the stone jetties. There is some public parking just before you get to the beach, which will cost you $7.00 per person, and there are restrooms and lifeguards.

You can walk to Laudholm Beach or drive down to the Wells Reserve/Rachel Carson Wildlife Refuge. Enjoy the sands or hop onto the network of trails that thread through the reserve. Laudholm is a truly beautiful beach because it's been protected as part of the reserve. The area is home to rare least terns and piping plovers, which run about in packs and streak down to the water, comically touching their toes in and racing away.

Wells Beach
Wells

Besides simply being one of the finer stretches of sand and surf on the coast—4,000 feet of fun and sun—Wells Beach offers some interesting bird-watching, thanks to the Webhannet Marsh, where there are often waders, shorebirds, and migrating waterfowl of all sorts. But it also has many of the hallmarks of resort beaches, those conveniences and superficial delights that seem to grow up wherever there is a natural wonder—an arcade, playground, take-out stands, and restrooms. Lifeguards patrol all summer long. Parking is limited, so you might consider paying to put your car in a lot.

Kennebunk and Kennebunkport

The sands just continue to roll from the Wells town line all the way through the famed Kennebunks. There are a slew of small beaches along the way. Parking is by permit only at many of these spots, and you can get a pass at the chamber of commerce, the town hall, the police station, or, depending where you're staying, area motels and inns.

Cleaves Cove Beach
Off Ocean Avenue, Kennebunkport

A small strand off Ocean Avenue, Cleaves Cove has no parking, no lifeguards, no restrooms, just a very private little arc of sand.

Colony Beach
Off Ocean Avenue, Kennebunkport

Right across the street from the grand Colony Hotel, this vest-pocket beach sits at the mouth of the Kennebunk River. All of 150 feet, it is best reached by foot or bike, because there is very limited parking. No lifeguards, either.

Goose Rocks Beach
Kings Highway, Kennebunkport

The Goose Rocks are a little archipelago of tiny isles in Goosefair Bay, and you can see them from this picturesque beach. Backed up to the larger village of Goose Rocks, the sands

stretch for 3,600 yards here and have a reputation for being soft and friendly to the feet of
those who walk along them. As southern
Maine beaches go, Goose Rocks is relatively
unspoiled, quiet, and scenic, with both dunes
and tide pools. Endangered birds nest here,
and at one end is another marsh with good
bird-watching. The sandy slope is gradual, so
it's good for kids and hesitant swimmers. Parking is by permit only—$10 per day, $20 per
week, and $50 for the season—and the per-
mits only allow you to park; they don't guarantee you a spot.

Kennebunk Beach

All told, the sands of Kennebunk Beach are
among the longest in Maine, and they're
divided into three sections. Parking is by permit only—again $10 per day, $20 per week—
so taking the trolley is a good idea.

Mother's Beach: A short section of Kennebunk Beach on the west end of Beach
Avenue, off Routes 9 and 35 near Lords Point,
Mother's is within walking distance of the
Lower Village if you feel like stretching the
gams a bit. (Might be a half mile.) Parking is
limited, so it might be easiest to take the trolley. Though it's only 750 feet or so, Mother's
Beach has many of the amenities of the super
strands, including a playground, public restrooms, and lifeguards.

Middle Beach: The central section of Kennebunk Beach, between Mother's and
Gooch's, Middle Beach is a 1,200-foot rocky
strand with black stones. (Some locals call it
Rocks Beach.) This is where you want to go if
your idea of going to the beach includes
Rollerblades—there's a sidewalk that runs
along the top. No lifeguards here.

Gooch's Beach: The largest stretch of
greater Kennebunk Beach at 3,346 feet,
Gooch's Beach is well within view of many of
the condos and hotels of Kennebunk, which
makes it not as pretty as some of Maine's
beaches. The fine, fine sand almost makes up
for it, though, and attracts big crowds. This is
the most popular stretch of Kennebunk Beach,
and it can be swarming with sunbathers,

surfers, picnickers, and castle builders on a
hot summer day. You can watch the pleasure
boats cruise down on the Kennebunk River,
which empties into the Atlantic nearby. Lifeguards are on duty in high summer.

Biddeford and Saco

Biddeford Pool Beach
Off State Route 208, Biddeford

Biddeford Pool was created by the movement
of barrier beaches, with sand and sediment
sifting in from the nearby Saco River. It
seemed like prime real estate for summer
home development when cottages began to
go in, but since then hurricanes and tidal
swings have made the ground shift under
some properties, and city officials wonder
whether it made sense to build here in the first
place. Still, these sands make for a pretty
beach. Lifeguards patrol the beach, and there
are restrooms. Parking is by permit only, and
the $50 stickers can be picked up at Biddeford
City Hall.

Fortune's Rocks Beach
Fortune's Rocks Road, Biddeford
(207) 284–9307

This 3,740-foot gem curves up and away from
Kennebunkport toward the summer colony of
Biddeford Pool. It's open to the full force of the
Atlantic, facing the sea unprotected. The
sands are long, and there are lifeguards and
restrooms. Parking for the season is by permit
only (you can pick up the $50 permits at the
Biddeford city hall).

Ferry Beach State Park
Bay View Road, Saco
(207) 283–0067

Maine's state parks sit on some prime real
estate, and this preserve named for the old
ferry across the nearby Saco River is perhaps
the best example. Its 1,700 yards of white-
sand waterfront and 117 acres of property sit
in booming southern Maine, where houses are
going for millions these days. The views out to
sea are fantastic, the sands warm. There are a
bunch of trails through unique woodlands

Close-up

Old Orchard Beach

What can one say about Old Orchard Beach? It's the beach of beaches in Maine—if you like big beach culture, you'll like Old Orchard. The 7 miles of sand here are more a phenomenon than anything else, backed up to a pier with arcades and greasy fried foods, to an amusement park with screaming rides, and to a village of pizza joints and souvenir shops with cheap T-shirts and plastic stuff from China. People stroll around in scanty Speedos and sometimes less, and there can be tens of thousands on a hot day, making the beach into the biggest "city" in Maine. Volleyballs get smacked around all day, and bands play at night. Motels sprawl for miles behind the waterfront, and some inns can be found on side streets. The big strand is consistently voted best beach in the state by readers of the local newspaper. Old Orchard is the closest thing Maine has to a Coney Island, a Jersey Shore, or an Ocean City, and there are free concerts, fireworks, and all sorts of scheduled amusements on a weekly basis. Bring change for the parking meters, patience, your swimsuit, perhaps a French dictionary (the beach has long been a favorite of the French Canadians), and be prepared for some serious people-watching. Lifeguards will be watching you, and you can change up at the bathhouse on West Grand Avenue. For more information contact the local chamber of commerce at (207) 934-2500. You can park at Memorial Park across the street for $4.00 to $7.00, depending on the day of your visit.

(where you'll find tupelo trees, which are rare this far north), and there's even a freshwater pond for fishing. And it's all yours to use. There are restrooms, changing rooms, and picnic areas. The rangers even provide guided nature tours. Open from Memorial Day through Columbus Day. Admission is $2.00.

GREATER PORTLAND

Scarborough

Ferry Beach and Western Beach
Off Route 207, Scarborough
A Prouts Neck neighborhood beach, Ferry Beach here is not to be confused with Ferry Beach State Park in Saco. This one is much smaller and much more difficult to get onto, as there is very limited parking. Still, between Ferry Beach and neighboring Western Beach, there are 1,700 yards of sand to be enjoyed.

Ferry faces the outlet of the Scarborough River and the summer colony of Pine Point; Western looks out at Pine Point. You won't think you're on a deserted isle here—despite some good bird-watching, the vistas tend toward the heavily developed. No lifeguards and limited facilities.

Grand Beach (Pine Point Beach)
East Grand Avenue, Scarborough
This is the spot where the beaches of York County meld into the beaches of Greater Portland (it connects to the end of Old Orchard), and it is indeed a grand beach, 2,500 yards of fine white sands. Good swimming, nice views of the tony cottages of Prouts Neck, and there's a rocky breakwater where people like to fish. There's a snack bar, changing area, and some parking.

Higgins Beach
Off Spurwink Road (Route 77), Scarborough

The beach used primarily by the summerca-tors who have cottages in the small village of Higgins Beach, this strand is about 900 yards long and has nice dunes and tide pools. Park-ing is not available anywhere unless you stay in one of the cool inns nearby. Residents of Higgins Beach have been concerned with all the traffic the area sees and have had erosion concerns as well, but it's a very pleasant strand if you can find a place to put your car. Surf is good for riding.

Scarborough Beach State Park
Route 207, Scarborough
(207) 883–2416

Prouts Neck has been a very exclusive enclave for more than a century, the province of the wealthy and a place where no one would dare to park without permission. Scarborough Beach is the great equalizer, one of the best beaches in Maine, 2,060 yards of fine sands just a short walk up the road from Prouts Neck. The great barrier beach protects the outlet of Scarborough River and the wild estu-arine oasis of Scarborough Marsh. You can park and enjoy the sands and facilities here—there are changing rooms and lifeguards—and walk down Black Point Road to see the sum-mer colony or do some beach hopping and take your towel to Ferry Beach. You'll still need to arrive early if you want a parking spot, and while it's technically a state park, it's run by the town, so you can't use your state park pass here.

Cape Elizabeth

Crescent Beach State Park
Route 77, Cape Elizabeth
(207) 799–5871

There are several popular Maine beaches called Crescent Beach, but this is probably the best, a 1,560-yard expanse of fine sand not too far from Portland. As such, it's always busy in summer. Because it's a state park, there are plenty of amenities—a playground, a picnic area, a snack bar, a group site, nature trails, and a bathhouse with cold showers—which makes it a good option for families. The water is maybe even a tad warmer here than at other beaches, which is a welcome benefit. There's even a boat launch, but it requires a permit from the Cape Elizabeth Public Safety Office (on State Route 77). The park is techni-cally open from Memorial Day through Colum-bus Day, but the state welcomes skiers and hikers in the winter and even folks just out for a walk in the off-season. Admission is $4.00 for anyone age 12 or older.

South Portland

Willard Beach
Willow Street, South Portland
(207) 767–7651

In one of the city of South Portland's residen-tial neighborhoods, Willard is maintained by the local parks and recreation department. It's a nice sand beach with a good look at Spring Point Lighthouse, a few Casco Bay forts, sev-eral islands, and scads of pleasure and work-ing boats—including massive oil tankers on their way to the tanks on the Fore River. A con-cession area, outdoor showers, and a play-ground make it popular with kids; lifeguards please the parents. Because it's a city beach, you may wonder about the cleanliness of the water, but it's tested twice weekly.

Portland

East End Beach
Eastern Promenade, Portland

This small beach is the city's only public strand, and it's located—you guessed it—on the eastern edge of the Portland Peninsula underneath the Eastern Prom. On the rocky side, it affords a spectacular gander at the myriad delights of Casco Bay—forts, islands, lighthouses, and boats galore. Trails connect with the fine network laid out by Portland Trails, and there is a boat launching area for getting out onto the bay. Changing areas and restrooms are available.

Yarmouth

Sandy Point Beach
Cousins Island, Yarmouth

Not too many people know about this short stretch of sand on Casco Bay's Cousins Island, part of the town of Yarmouth and attached by a bridge. Right below where the bridge meets the isle, there's a beach good enough for dipping. A small parking area is available here, as is a boat launch. Not much, but it gets increasingly more difficult to find beaches from here to Popham Beach State Park.

Freeport

Winslow Memorial Park
Staples Point Road, Freeport
(207) 865–4198

What a find this 90-acre park is. Owned by the town of Freeport, it has stupendous views of the Harraseeket River and Casco Bay and its islands, and there's a small tidal beach that makes for good swimming. (Get here two hours before or after high tide.) The facilities include picnic areas large enough for groups, a nature trail, a boat launch site, and a playground. Good stuff and only minutes from all the shopping downtown. You can even set up camp in one of the 100 sites here if you bring your tent. Admission is $1.50 per person. Open Memorial Day weekend through Columbus Day.

MIDCOAST

Brunswick

Thomas Point Beach
Thomas Point Road, Brunswick
(207) 725–6009
www.thomaspointbeach.com

A small, privately run beach on Thomas Bay, an inlet of the New Meadows River, this 290-yard strand is a beachgoer's paradise, if only because it's one of the rare Midcoast beaches open to the public. The water is tidal, so make sure you check the charts before packing the car. The facilities are pretty lavish as beaches go, with hot showers, picnic areas, lawns to explore, playgrounds, fireplaces to cook at, an arcade, a snack bar, and lifeguards. It's a great choice for functions or family get-togethers, and there are special events here all summer long, like the Thomas Point Bluegrass Festival. Open from 9:00 A.M. till sunset daily. Admission is $3.50 for adults, $2.00 for kids age 12 or younger.

Freshwater Alternatives in Brunswick

Brunswick's parks and rec department runs **Coffin Pond** (River Road; 207–725–6656), an artificially created basin very popular in the summer. Also busy is **White's Beach** (Durham Road; 207–729–0415), a 9-foot-deep pond that's part of a campground but open to the public. Small fees are charged at both places.

Georgetown

Reid State Park
375 Seguinland Road, Georgetown
(207) 371–2303

Now, all of Maine's beaches front some famously frigid water, but Reid State Park has a reputation for being the coldest. The inviting, bodysurfable breakers here offer bathers swimming that often results in an all-over ice-cream headache sort of feeling. Mainers, of course, call this invigorating. People from away consider it just shy of arctic and spend most of their time at this mile-and-a-half beach just testing the water with their toes, as if they can't believe it. The saving grace of the place for these people, and for kids, is the lagoon, a strip of sand that is protected from the freezing water by a sandbar and fronts a small pool that is noticeably warmer.

Reid State Park covers about 700 acres of remarkably varied terrain, with the beach, the lagoon, and marshes, ledges, pine forest, and some of the rare sand dunes in the state. The land was donated to the people of Maine by the gentleman it's named after, Walter E. Reid, in 1946, making it the first state-owned saltwater beach Down East. And it has a fairly colorful history; it was used by fighter planes for target practice in World War II—unexploded ordnance has been found in the sands as recently as the 1990s—and was the setting for a mock, cold-weather U.S. Navy invasion in the 1970s (citizens sued to stop the exercise, but the courts decided the environmental damage done by 900 marines, seven amphibious tractors, several howitzers, and some helicopters would be "insignificant"). Today the sand dunes—uncommon in Maine—are the site of a critical nesting habitat for endangered least terns and piping plovers, which can often be seen running down to the water and darting away from it in flocks, as if they don't care much for the 50-degree water temps, either. Sections of beach are occasionally closed to allow the birds to multiply. Striper fishing is another biggie down in these parts.

Along with Popham, about 4 miles away by boat, Reid serves up the big one-two punch of Midcoast beaches—there are a few sandy strands east of here, but they're much, much smaller. Consequently the pair are extraordinarily popular. The bathhouses are crawling with people, and you usually have to wait for a while at the snack bar. Bring your own hot dogs and burgers for the grills in the picnic area if you don't want to wait. You'd better arrive early if you want a parking spot. Open year-round. A small fee is charged.

Phippsburg

Head Beach
Small Point Road, Phippsburg

On the same peninsula as Popham Beach, Head is a sand beach of 360 yards that's a bit of a local secret. Parking is the problem here, but you can pay a small fee and leave your car after the gate on the peninsula and walk over. Hand Beach is a nice strand facing the beautiful eastern edge of Casco Bay.

Popham Beach State Park
10 Perkins Farm Lane, Phippsburg
(207) 389–1335

Sitting on an elbow-shaped peninsula between the Kennebec and Morse Rivers, Popham Beach is a wonderland of sand and surf. The grainy expanse sprawls for 3 miles, by far the longest beach in the Midcoast, and it's got a

i If you plan on visiting Popham Beach, call the tide and parking hotline at (207) 389–9125 or visit the Web site www.pophambeach.com to find out tide, weather, and sunset information. The site is updated every 15 minutes.

little of everything—ledges, tide pools, offshore islands, nearby lighthouses, great shell collecting, picnicking facilities, and on and on. People even ride the fast current of Morse River like a waterslide (Popham's well known for its riptides and strong underwater pulls, so be careful if attempting these sorts of activities). And beachgoers will often walk across the sands to Fox Island when the tide's right. Schedule a full day here or you'll be disappointed.

Whenever the sun makes an appearance during the warm-weather months, from the time the park opens in mid-April until it closes in October, there will be people at Popham—lots of them. The beach is the most popular strand north of Portland and south of Acadia, which means the parking lot is almost always full—cars line the approach road for miles on a hot summer weekend. But the beach is so long, it can absorb the thousands who show up, and you can almost always find an uncrowded spot to sit.

Pemaquid Peninsula

Pemaquid Beach Park
Route 130, Bristol
(207) 677–2754

Facing Johns Bay to the south, Pemaquid is a nice sandy strand of about 600 yards not too far from popular Pemaquid Lighthouse. It's really your only chance for a day at a saltwater beach between Reid and Popham and the Penobscot Bay area. Backed up to sea grasses and woods and looking out at Johns Island, the beach is thus understandably popular in summertime with locals and tourists. People truly care about the swimming area, too. Local groups check water quality weekly and have started dune protection programs. There is a snack bar, as well as coldwater showers, toilets, and picnic tables.

Freshwater Alternatives in the Pemaquid Peninsula Area

Damariscotta Lake State Park (Route 32, Jefferson; 207–549–7600) is a popular choice for lake swimmers, with its sand beach, picnic area, and lifeguards, several miles inland from Damariscotta in the pretty old town of Jefferson. **Biscay Pond** (Biscay Road, Damariscotta) is another local favorite.

Owls Head and Rockland Area

Birch Point State Park
Ballyhac Road, Owls Head
(207) 941–4014
One of the state's newest parks, this 220-yard arc of sand and stones is known locally as Lucia Beach, and it's long been a place to go for a quick dip in the Rockland area. The state officially protected 5.5 acres here with funds from the Land for Maine's Future program in 1999. They put up a big brown sign at the entrance, improved access a bit, put in a couple of pit toilets, and otherwise didn't change much. It's still free, there are still great views out across Mussel Ridge Channel, and the water is still absolutely frigid. For privacy, locals like to crawl into their own crannies in the rocks that flank the beach. You can usually find parking somewhere down here.

Crescent Beach
Owls Head
About 1,100 yards of rare Midcoast sand beach can be found here south of Rockland, staring at Sheep Island. Just below a summer community, these great grains can be very popular in summer, and parking is notoriously hard to come by.

Freshwater Alternatives in the Rockland and Camden Areas

North of Owls Head, **Johnson Memorial Park on Chickawaukee Lake** (State Route 17, Rockland) fills up fast with swimmers. Not the prettiest place, but it'll cool you off. **Shirttail**

Point (State Route 105) in Camden is a good place for kids to splash around in the sandy Megunticook River. An even better spot in Camden is **Barrett's Cove** (State Route 52), under Maiden's Cliff on a cove of Lake Megunticook.

Lincolnville

Lincolnville Beach
Route 1, Lincolnville
This beach must be one of Maine's easiest to find, sitting right off U.S. Route 1 within full view of everyone charging north to Acadia. Across the street are the handful of gift shops and restaurants of the village known as Lincolnville Beach; down the sand a bit is the large pier where the state's ferry to Islesboro docks. The beach is relatively short—850 yards—and skinny, and some people find it a little awkward to be frolicking in front of all the drivers passing by and the diners at the Lobster Pound restaurant, which is right next to the sands, and with the local residents going to the post office across the street. If you can get used to that and can deal with parking hassles and crowds, you'll enjoy this little beach. You can take in the nice views of Penobscot Bay, you can watch the ferry run to and from Islesboro 3 miles offshore, and when you get hungry you can wander across to the Beach Store. Free parking if you can find a spot, and there are portapotties.

Ducktrap Beach
Off Route 1, Lincolnville Beach
Locals try to keep this point where the Ducktrap River pours into Penobscot Bay a secret (you didn't hear about it here). Turn onto the Fire Road just before the bridge after Lincolnville Beach. Not the best place to lay down a towel—it's very rocky—but it's always pleasant to swim here. It's relatively private, set back from Route 1 down a dirt road. It's got a nice view of the Ducktrap Bridge, and you can swim on either side of a little peninsula—or ride the current between the two basins. Fun stuff, and free.

Searsport

Sandy Point Beach
Searsport

Despite the fact that this 1,370-yard beach is less than half a mile off Route 1, few tourists find this strand tucked away in the quiet old colony in Sandy Point between Searsport and Bucksport. The sands here sit just above the point where the Penobscot River meets Penobscot Bay. Fine swimming and nice views of Verona Island. Parking is fairly limited, though, as are the facilities.

ACADIA AREA

Lamoine Beach
State Route 184, Lamoine
(207) 667–4778

Some people feel that the real appeal of Lamoine Beach isn't the beach at all but the jaw-dropping views of the mountains of Acadia National Park that you can see while standing on its sands. Mount Desert Island is just across Eastern Bay, and the 2,740 yards of fine beach give you an ideal prospect. But it's hard to argue with this much sand beach in a part of the state where you're not supposed to find any. The facilities are limited—picnic tables and a boat ramp—but you can find more (showers, bigger play areas, larger picnicking spots) up the way a bit at Lamoine State Park.

Sand Beach
Acadia National Park Loop Road, Bar Harbor

Not the most original name, but the sand here is literally it for miles around, so at least it's apt. There are 290 yards of the precious stuff here, and it is extremely popular. There are not really many other places to get into Acadia's famous seas. The water is positively bone-chilling, but the views of Great Head, a bold headland, on one end of the beach and of the Beehive, a cliff face, on the other are fantastic. Parking goes very quickly, so be sure to arrive early. You'll have to pay the park entrance fee to get in. It's always fun to scale Great Head and look back down, and there are some cool marshes in the area to check out as well. You might recognize the beach from photographs and from movies like 1999's *The Cider House Rules*, in which Tobey Maguire and Charlize Theron frolic here.

Freshwater Alternatives in the Acadia Area

Echo Lake (State Route 102 near Somesville) is by far the most popular place to swim on the island outside of Sand Beach. Lifeguards will look after you. **Lake Wood** (Park Road, Mount Desert) is known as a nudie spot.

DOWN EAST

Sandy River Beach
Off State Route 187, Jonesport

Though the parking can be difficult, the sands rocky, and the water icy, this 500-yard natural wonder—sands Down East?—is always busy because it's all there is. Nice views of Roque Island and the neat tidal river.

Roque Bluffs State Park
145 Schoppee Point Road, Roque Bluffs
(207) 255–3475

This Down East park is unusual in several ways. First, it's a fairly large sand and pebble beach at 910 yards. Second, there is a big freshwater basin right behind it, so you can swim in the sea and then wash off the salt in the 60-acre pond. And finally, as Maine state parks go, it sees few visitors for the beauty of the spot. The park covers a total of 274 acres, and there's plenty of space for picnicking, with tables and grills. There's a bathhouse for changing and a playground for the kids. All the amenities you could ever want in a Maine beach are here, and then some, without all the commercial distractions and superficialities of those found in southern Maine.

ON THE OCEAN

Many people say that a Maine vacation isn't quite complete unless you've gotten out onto the ocean, felt the sea spray on your face, smelled the rich brine, and seen the state from the deck of a boat. And plenty of options for seagoing await, whether they be climbing aboard a classic schooner for a six-day sail, heading out on a half-day nature cruise in search of whales and puffins, dropping a line from a deep-sea fishing boat, sliding into a kayak and exploring coves, or donning a wet suit and diving under for an hour.

The best places to start your search for offshore adventure are resort communities like Kennebunkport, Boothbay Harbor, Camden, and Bar Harbor or the state's largest city, Portland, where there is an infrastructure for tourism. These towns are where excursion boats are most concentrated and most easily found, but even tiny Cutler and Jonesport have their boat rides. If you're interested in kayaking, your options multiply, as that graceful sport has exploded in Maine since the 1980s, and it's hard to find a town without a sea kayak outfitter.

While heading out on a windjammer cruise will set you back some serious change—some boats are more than $100 a day—there are plenty of ways of getting afloat that won't sink your bank account. An afternoon kayak tour can be as little as $25, and there are sunset cruises and half-day sails that are eminently reasonable.

Many vessels offer more than one type of trip, maybe whale watching one day and deep-sea fishing the next. They're listed in this chapter by their primary specialty. We tried to include excursion boats with regular schedules rather than charter vessels.

WINDJAMMER CRUISES
Berthed in Rockland

The timbers of the tall old ship creak and sway with the waves. The sails luff and flap overhead. The sea sparkles in the sun, while dolphins do loop-the-loops off the bow. You can almost imagine the year is 1854. Welcome aboard a Maine schooner. More than a dozen of these historic vessels offer tours of the Down East coast, some putting together weeklong packages where you sleep in a small berth, help out on deck if you wish, eat the fleet's famous food, and enjoy spectacular sunsets and star shows as you travel to quiet coves and gunkholes along the coast. Each vessel is unique and has its own story to tell, but several boats are genuine antiques and are National Historic Landmarks. The captains and crews, too, come from all sorts of backgrounds, but they all tend to be charismatic, outgoing, and some of the more interesting people you'll meet. Most provide a raft of options, from half-day to three-day to weeklong cruises, and rates tend to be in the same ballpark for all of them, about $550 for a three-day cruise, up to $900 for a week. Some welcome children, others don't. Many of these boats are represented by the Maine Windjammer Association (P.O. Box 1144, Blue Hill 04614; 800–807–9463; www.sailmainecoast .com), which is a great resource for one-stop shopping.

American Eagle
North End Shipyard, Rockland
(207) 594–8007 or (800) 648–4544
www.schooneramericaneagle.com
The 92-foot *American Eagle* was launched in 1930 and was the last fishing schooner in the famous Gloucester fleet. It made its final fish-

ing trip in 1983, was completely rehauled in 1986, and is now a Historic Landmark. Captain John Foss offers primarily three- and six-day cruises.

Heritage
North End Shipyard, Rockland
(207) 594–8007 or (800) 648–4544
www.schoonerheritage.com
Built right in Rockland's North End Shipyard in 1983, the *Heritage* was designed along the lines of the coasters of the 19th century. It accommodates 30 people, and Captains Doug and Linda Lee have been gracious hosts for as many years. These days they offer four- and six-day excursions.

Isaac H. Evans
North End Shipyard, Rockland
(877) 238–1325
www.midcoast.com/~evans
The *Isaac Evans* was built in Mauricetown, New Jersey, in 1886 and spent years in the oystering trade on Delaware Bay. Rebuilt in 1973 to carry passengers, it's now a Historic Landmark. Captain Brenda Walker offers three-, four- and six-day cruises.

J&E Riggin
136 Holmes Street, Rockland
(207) 594–1875 or (800) 869–0604
www.mainewindjammer.com
The *J&E Riggin* is another old oystering vessel, built in Dorchester, New Jersey, in 1927. It is 90 feet long on deck, was granted Historic Landmark status in 1991, and is captained by Jon Finger and Anne Mahle. They provide three- to six-day jaunts and spice things up with sailing concerts and kids' cruises.

Nathaniel Bowditch
P.O. Box 459, Warren 04864
(207) 273–4062 or (800) 288–4098
www.windjammervacation.com
Another speedy schooner, the *Nathaniel Bowditch* was built in East Boothbay in 1922 to be a racing vessel. It hauled its 82-foot frame to special-class honors in the Bermuda

i Bring a sweater. It's always a lot cooler on the water than you expect, even in August.

Race of 1923 and served in the Coast Guard during World War II before being rebuilt for windjamming in the 1970s. Captain Owen and Cathie Dorr welcome passengers aboard for two-, three-, four-, and six-day sails.

Stephen Taber
70 Elm Street, Camden
(207) 236–3520 or (800) 999–7352
www.stephentaber.com
Built in 1871, the *Stephen Taber* is the oldest continuously operating sailing vessel in the United States, and it's another National Landmark. At 68 feet, it accommodates 22 passengers, and it's become famous for its food, with its own cookbook, *The Taste of the Taber*. It offers an eight-day extravaganza, among other options.

Summertime
115A South Main Street, Rockland
(800) 562–8290
www.schoonersummertime.com
The only pinkie schooner in the Maine fleet, the *Summertime* was locally built in 1986 on designs that replicate the classic New England pink. Popular as mackerel fishing vessels, pinks have been in use in the Gulf of Maine since the 1700s and got their name because of their uplifted, or "pinked," stern. The 53-foot *Summertime* does a lot of day sails during the summer and heads for three-, four-, five-, six-, and seven-day excursions as well. The ship accommodates seven people.

Victory Chimes
P.O. Box 1401, Rockland 04841
(207) 594–0755 or (800) 745–5651
www.victorychimes.com
Built in Delaware in 1900 as a work vessel, the *Victory Chimes* is the largest American passenger sailing vessel at 132 feet. It's the only original three-masted schooner on the East

Coast and is now a National Historic Land-mark. Captains Kip Files and Paul DeGaeta will even let you barter for your trip, especially if you have World War II collectibles or a spare MG lying around.

Berthed in Camden

Angelique
P.O. Box 736, Camden 04843
(207) 785–6036 or (800) 282–9989
www.sailangelique.com
The *Angelique* was built specifically to work the windjammer trade, launched in 1980. Ketch-rigged, with beautiful maroon sails, it's 95 feet long and was modeled after English fishing schooners of the 19th century. Captain Mike and Lynne McHenry offer whale watching and other nature cruises.

Grace Bailey
Maine Windjammer Cruises
P.O. Box 617, Camden 04843
(207) 236–2938 or (888) 692–7245
www.mainewindjammercruises.com
The flagship of the Maine Windjammer Cruise fleet, the *Grace Bailey* got its start hauling tim-ber and granite to the West Indies. A 123-foot coaster, it was built in 1882. Captain Ray and Anne Williamson offer weekend and five-day cruises.

Lewis R. French
P.O. Box 992, Camden 04843
(207) 236–2463 or (800) 469–4635
www.schoonerfrench.com
The *Lewis French* was bestowed National His-toric Landmark status in 1992, and it's about time, since it was launched in 1871 in Christ-mas Cove and is the oldest schooner in the Maine windjammer fleet. The ship is 64 feet long and previously served as a working ves-sel, hauling lumber, bricks, granite, lime, and Christmas trees—all those classic Maine exports. Captain Garth Wells runs three-, four-, and six-day getaways.

Mary Day
P.O. Box 798, Camden 04843
(207) 785–5670 or (800) 992–2218
www.schoonermaryday.com
The schooner *Mary Day* was built in the 1960s with the aim of being a comfortable passenger vessel—and it succeeds. Ninety feet long, it was the first pure sailing schooner built in Maine since the 1930s, and it's known as a very fast vessel, perennially winning the Great Schooner Race. Captains Barry King and Jen Martin are first-rate hosts, and they offer light-house cruises, naturalist trips, foliage tours, and even a folk-music outing.

Mercantile
Maine Windjammer Cruises
P.O. Box 617, Camden 04843
(207) 236–2938 or (888) 692–7245
www.mainewindjammercruises.com
This was the ship that started it all in 1942, back when legendary captain Frank Swift started taking people out on cruising vaca-tions and thus founded the Maine windjammer trade. The 115-foot *Mercantile* dates back to 1916 and served its prepassenger life as a cargo ship, toting barrel staves, salt fish, and firewood. Today it offers three- and four-day cruises.

Mistress
Maine Windjammer Cruises
P.O. Box 617, Camden 04843
(207) 236–2938 or (888) 692–7245
www.mainewindjammercruises.com
The *Mistress* is the specialty boat in the Maine Windjammer Cruises fleet, built on the lines of a coasting schooner but laid out like a yacht belowdecks, allowing for more room and pri-vacy for passengers. It's 60 feet long, accom-modates just six passengers, and can be chartered.

Berthed in Rockport

Timberwind
P.O. Box 247, Rockport 04856
(207) 236–0801 or (800) 759–9250
www.schoonertimberwind.com

The *Timberwind* is unique among the state's windjammers in that it's never left Maine, fitting for a boat that now represents the state on its official quarter. It was constructed in 1931, served as the harbor pilot boat in Portland Harbor for 38 years, and has berths for 20 passengers. Owners Robert and Dawn Tassi are especially eager to have you aboard, and, unlike many of the other windjammers, welcome families with children age 6 or older for their three-, four-, and six-day cruises.

BOAT RIDES AND DAY SAILS

Almost inexhaustible options await those looking for boat rides and day sails on the Maine coast—you could head out on all 14 days of your two-week vacation and do something different every day. From types of vessels—old lobster boats, car ferries, and yachts—to the kinds of trips available, *variety* is the word. Ship out for a breakfast cruise, go lobstering, sail to lighthouses, watch for seals, cruise to museums, explore islands, enjoy the sunset—there's plenty to do and see.

South Coast

Finestkind Cruises
Barnacle Billy's Dock, Perkins Cove, Ogunquit
(207) 646–5227
www.finestkindcruises.com
Finestkind is a Down East term for "the best," and this company certainly ranks very highly, having been cruising the coast since 1956. The Finestkind vessels—there are now three—make 15 trips daily out of Perkins Cove, offering breakfast outings ($15), trips to the Nubble Lighthouse ($18), cocktail cruises ($12), and genuine lobstering jaunts ($12), where you can see what it's like to pull a trap.

Bellatrix
Nonantum Resort, Ocean Avenue, Kennebunkport
(207) 590–1125
www.sailingtrips.com
"Captain Jim" and his 37-foot yacht *Bellatrix*

are based on the Kennebunk River behind the Nonantum Resort, and they do two or three sails daily depending upon weather and the tides. The three-hour tours are $50, and they're limited to six people, so calling ahead is a good idea, especially in high summer. These pleasant runs are a good way to get a gander at the Bush compound on Walker Point without having to worry about crowds.

Eleanor
Arundel Wharf, Ocean Avenue, P.O. Box 572, Kennebunkport 04046
(207) 967–8809
One of the prettier day sailers you're going to find, the schooner *Eleanor* is a modern vessel, launched in 1999 and built by its captain, Rich Woodman. The 55-footer has the gaff rigging and the traditional lines of a classic Herreschoff windjammer and yet boasts all the comforts and security of a contemporary cruiser. *Eleanor* leaves Arundel Wharf one to three times daily for two-hour trips (it can be chartered, too). Passage is $40 per person, and reservations can be made by calling ahead or by stopping by the Schooner Shack on the wharf.

Greater Portland

BayView Cruises
184 Commercial Street, Portland
(207) 761–0496
Seal cruises, harbor lunch cruises, lighthouse cruises, sunset cruises, even "attitude adjustment" cruises—BayView Cruises of Portland offers them all on a daily basis, June through

i When Portland area residents have houseguests in town who are interested in going for a boat ride, they know just where to send them—the Casco Bay Lines mail boat run, which services the populated Calendar Islands. It's a three-hour trip around the bay for the fee of $13. There's no better deal on the coast. Contact Casco Bay Lines, Commercial Street, Portland; (207) 774–7871; www.cascobaylines.com.

September. The tours vary in length from an hour to two hours, but they all take you out onto the waters of Casco Bay, giving you a look at Portland Harbor and all its boats, forts, and nearby islands. You can also charter the 117-foot sightseeing vessel if you need more time than that and want to bring along 89 friends. Look into the lobster bake option, which can be added to any of these trips at a moment's notice.

Eagle Island Tours
Long Wharf Commercial Street, Portland
(207) 774–6498
www.eagleislandtours.com
Eagle Island Tours provides passengers with the usual one-and-a-half-hour tour of Portland Harbor and Casco Bay—seals, lighthouses, etc.—which is all good fun, but the really cool thing they do is a trip out to Eagle Island, former home of Admiral Robert Peary, the first person to reach the North Pole. There's a nifty museum on the island documenting the explorer's feats. The Eagle Island cruise ($24) departs Long Wharf at 10:00 A.M. on Tuesday, Thursday, Saturday, and Sunday from June 15th through Labor Day.

Mainely Tours
3 Moulton Street, Portland
(207) 774–0808
www.mainelytours.com
A sightseeing company known for its trolley tours of Portland, Mainely Tours also offers a 90-minute lighthouse lover's cruise on the bay, taking in seven beacons, plus all the islands and seals you can count, which is packaged in a Land and Sea tour. Trolley-buses and boats head out three or four times daily, and the combo tour will set you back $25.

Downeast Duck Adventures
177 Commercial Street, Portland
(207) 774–DUCK
www.downeastducktours.com
It's a boat! It's a bus! It's a Downeast Duck! So goes the marketing behind Maine's only amphibious tours. And they're amusing stuff.

The open-air blue Ducks take you on a quick-and-quacky tour of Portland's history before driving right into the harbor for a jaunt around the city's working waterfront. The "Duckaneer" trips run $22, and, as Portland is inextricably tied to Casco Bay, they're arguably the best way to get a quick-and-dirty—and entertaining—feel for the city.

Atlantic Seal Cruises
25 Main Street, South Freeport
(207) 865–6112
Most visitors to Freeport are unaware the famous outlet town even has a waterfront, let alone a cruise company offering seal and osprey watches, foliage cruises, lobstering trips, and excursions to Eagle Island to see the former home and museum of Admiral Robert Peary, the first man to the North Pole. But there's Captain Tom Ring, owner of Atlantic Seal Bed and Breakfast, shoving off from the Freeport Town Wharf on a daily basis in summer (late May through October).

Midcoast

Sea Escape Charters
P.O. Box 7, Bailey Island 04003
(207) 833–5531
www.seaescapecottages.com
Captain Les McNelly will take you out on a two-hour tour of Casco Bay and the Bailey Island area whenever you're ready. He does sunset and seal-watch cruises as well as trips to Eagle Island, on an on-demand basis. And he also takes people out after mackerel, striped bass, and bluefish aboard his *Sea Escape Too*. If you can't get enough, you can hole up for the night at one of McNelly's cottages—they're fantastic—and go out again the next day. Two-hour tours are $70 per person for two people, $40 each for four.

Yankee
Hermit Island, Small Point
(207) 443–2101
Hermit Island is one of the best oceanfront camping areas in Maine, and every afternoon and evening the campground's 50-foot boat,

Maine Maritime Museum

The best of the state's nautical museums, Maine Maritime Museum at 243 Washington Street in Bath is a full-service kind of place, scheduling a variety of boat cruises in the summer months in addition to its great collection of art, artifacts, and ship models and its working shipyard. These tours shove off from the museum's waterfront site on the Kennebec River, just downriver from Bath Iron Works, and venture out to the world of waterways to which the Kennebec connects. Some visit lighthouses like the one at Seguin, some stop over at isles like the one to Admiral Peary's old place on Eagle Island, others head to nature preserves and marine wildlife habitats, and one even goes to the Boothbay Harbor aquarium. They're narrated, start in June and run into the autumn on an almost weekly basis, tend to last a few hours, and cost anywhere from $25 to $50 per person. Visit www.mainemaritimemuseum.com or call (207) 443–1316 for the year's schedule.

Yankee, makes a nature or sunset cruise on which noncampers are welcome. While the trips are fun, one look at Hermit Island and you'll be making a reservation for next year.

Balmy Days Cruises
Pier 8, Commercial Street,
Boothbay Harbor
(207) 633–2284 or (800) 298–2284
www.balmydayscruises.com
Balmy Days has a veritable cruising empire in Boothbay Harbor, one of the best outfits on the coast. A family business run through the years by Captains Bob and Bill Campbell, Balmy Days has four vessels and as many options, taking passengers aboard for trips to Monhegan Island, day sails, harbor tours, and mackerel fishing. Rates vary with the nature of the trip but are reasonable.

Cap'n Fish's Cruises
Pier 1, Wharf Street, Boothbay Harbor
(207) 633–6605 or (800) 633–0860
www.capnfishs.com
Cap'n Fish is the other biggie on the scene in Boothbay Harbor, offering all manner of boat rides. The schedule is exhaustive, and some of

its highlights include seal watches, Kennebec River journeys, Damariscove Island tours, a Pemaquid Lighthouse cruise, and a few mix-and-match options. Call or see the Web site for the complete lineup.

Hardy Boat Cruises
Shaws Fish and Lobster Wharf,
Route 32, New Harbor
(207) 677–2026 or (800) 278–3346
www.hardyboat.com
One of the companies that provide service to enchanted Monhegan Island, Hardy Boat also offers any number of trips on a daily basis aboard its 60-foot excursion vessel, *Hardy III*. Among the highlights is the one-hour lighthouse cruise, a sunset ride that departs New Harbor at 7:30 P.M. daily in summer and heads to Pemaquid Light to watch it and a handful of other beacons blink on with the coming darkness. Reservations are recommended for the $12 trip. Another good one is the fall foliage cruise past the islands of Muscongus Bay, a 90-minute ride where you can see the glows of red and orange against a backdrop of dark sea and black spruce. Spectacular. That cruise goes out daily through September (better

viewing is the latter half of the season), and on Wednesdays and weekends after that. The trip is $15 for adults, $10 for children.

Appledore
Bayview Landing, Camden
(207) 236–8353
www.appledore2.com

The last schooner custom-built by the well-known Harvey Gamage shipyard in South Bristol using age-old shipbuilding methods, the 86-foot *Appledore* was launched in 1978. It works both Key West and Camden now, offering two-hour tours of Penobscot Bay four times daily in spring, summer, and fall, including a sunset cruise. You can help raise the sails and even take a turn at the wheel if you like, all while taking in vistas of islands, mountains, birds, and seals. Rates are $30 per person.

Betselma
Bayview Landing, Camden
(207) 236–4446
www.betselma.com

The 30-foot *Betselma* was once a working lobster boat and now takes passengers where the hauling used to be done. Captained by Les Bex, it leaves the public landing in the Camden harbor on one-, two-, and three-hour cruises around Penobscot Bay and its islands, with the captain narrating away. He has 35 years of experience and will fill you in on the lobster industry, the three lighthouses you pass, the seabirds and seals you see, and local history. Rates are $10 an hour per adult, half price for kids.

Olad
Bayview Landing, Camden
(207) 236–2323
www.maineschooners.com

The schooner *Olad* sails from Camden Harbor five times daily, beginning at 9:45 A.M., but the trip you shouldn't miss is the one that pushes off at 5:00 P.M. every day from mid-June through mid-August for a two-hour sail about Penobscot Bay. The sun falling behind the round, green heads of the Camden Hills is a

sublime sight. So is the *Olad*, for that matter. The graceful 57-foot, two-masted schooner is a classic wooden windjammer, and it once whisked Walter Cronkite about. Passage is $29 per person.

Surprise
Bayview Landing, Camden
(207) 236–4687
www.camdenmainesailing.com

The oldest of Camden's day-sailing windjammers, the schooner *Surprise* was built in 1918 to be a racing yacht, and it was granted Historic Landmark status in 1991. A 57-foot beauty, Surprise putters out of Camden's photogenic harbor for two-hour sails four times daily from July 1 through mid-September (three times daily after that through October 15) before hauling sails and running with the wind. Rates are $30 per person, and smoking is not allowed.

Schooner Heron
Rockport Harbor, Rockport
(207) 236–8605 or (800) 599–8605
www.woodenboatco.com

Not to be confused with *Wooden Boat* magazine, Wooden Boat Co. is a boatbuilding outfit in Rockport. They constructed the beautiful 65-foot *Schooner Heron,* launching it in 2003. They offer a variety of cruises on a daily basis on the graceful vessel, including a lobster lunch ($50), a lighthouse-and-wildlife sail ($38), and a sunset hors d'oeuvres cruise ($50); the latter is a fine cap to a day spent on the Midcoast.

Isle au Haut Company
Sea Breeze Avenue, Stonington
(207) 367–5193 or 367–6516
www.isleauhaut.com

The *Miss Lizzie* navigates Deer Island Thorofare on a daily basis as the ferry and mail boat to the island of Isle au Haut, so it knows these island-dotted waters better than most—which is what makes a sightseeing cruise aboard the local institution a pleasure. That and the captain's narration about marine life, the many islands, Mark Island Lighthouse, and the history of granite quarrying in the area. The boat leaves Stonington Dock daily at 9:00 A.M. and 2:00 P.M.

Old Quarry Ocean Adventures
130 Settlement Road, Stonington
(207) 367–8977
www.oldquarry.com
Half- and whole-day trips aboard the 38-foot lobster boat *Nigh Duck* are Captain Bill Baker's specialty. With more than a quarter-century on the water, he's a wealth of information about the seabirds, sights, and history of the Stonington area. You can even try your hand at sailing if you like. Morning cruises sail from 9:00 A.M. to noon, and afternoon trips are from 1:00 to 4:00 P.M. The rates are $37.

Acadia Area

Bar Harbor Whale Watch Co.
1 West Street, Bar Harbor
(207) 288–9800 or (888) 533–WALE
www.whalesrus.com
A multifaceted excursion boat company with a whole fleet of vessels, Bar Harbor Whale Watch does two-hour lighthouse and nature tours of Frenchman Bay. These trips take you to the seal haul-outs and tall beacons off Mount Desert, with naturalists narrating all the while. They head out at 10:00 A.M. and 1:15, 3:30, and 6:00 P.M. daily from July 1 through the end of August and two or three times a day in the off-season. Call for the full schedule.

Downeast Windjammer Cruises
Bar Harbor Inn Pier, Bar Harbor
(207) 288–4585 or 288–2373
www.downeastwindjammer.com
At 151 feet, with four masts and nine deep-red sails taking in 4,800 square feet of wind, the *Margaret Todd* is an impressive vessel. It's the only four-master to cruise New England waters in a half century, and perhaps more than any other of Maine's schooners, it seems to be sailing right out of history when it comes in off the harbor—which is quite ironic, because it was

launched in 1998. Named for Captain Steve Pagels's grandmother, the ship sets sail three times daily—morning, afternoon, and sunset cruises—plying the waters of Frenchman Bay. Eagles, seals, porpoises, and even whales might be spotted, and the ship passes before a lot of the "cottages" that made Bar Harbor famous. Plus it gives you a prospect of Mount Desert and Acadia, mountains soaring high above, that every visitor should see. Tickets are $32 per person. Captain Pagels also offers trips across the bay to the other Acadia—the Schoodic Peninsula in Winter Harbor—narrated by national park rangers. Inquire about the schedule or see the Web site.

Rachel B. Jackson
Bar Harbor Regency Resort, Bar Harbor
(207) 288–2216
www.downeastsail.com
Built to resemble an 1890s schooner, the *Rachel B. Jackson* has quite an interesting history. It has circumnavigated the globe, been the state of Maine's representative in the Tall Ships 2000 race, served as a whale research vessel for the National Geographic Society, and been used to train student sailors as a Sail Training Association ship. The salient point to you, though, is that this 67-foot beauty takes passengers out on cruises around Frenchman Bay daily in summer at 10:00 A.M. and 1:00, 4:00, and 6:30 P.M. You might see porpoises, ospreys, eagles, and seals, and even if you don't, you'll enjoy breathtaking vistas of Acadia, Bar Harbor, the bay, and its islands. Passage is $30 per person.

Sea Princess
Municipal Pier, Sea Street,
Northeast Harbor
(207) 276–5352
www.barharborcruises.com
Somes Sound is the only true fjord—a place where mountains plunge directly into the sea on both sides—on the eastern seaboard, and perhaps the best way to get a look at this magnificent natural spectacle is aboard the 75-foot *Sea Princess*. The boat makes a

Close-up

Sailing Schools

Ahoy! Some people assert that the Maine coast is among the best sailing grounds in the world, if not *the* best. And there are any number of places along it where you can learn to sail, acquiring the skills to safely get out among it all. These range from free outfits like CFAIR in Rockland, which is done as a community service, to adventure schools like Outward Bound, also in Rockland, where you learn to sail as part of a deeper exploration of yourself. Some programs operate by the day, others overnight. Here are a few examples.

School of Ocean Sailing
www.maine.sailingschool.com
This is a 10-day course that takes you from Portland to Yarmouth, Nova Scotia, and back, all the while providing you with an in-depth course in seamanship.

Sail Maine
58 Fore Street, Portland
(207) 650–7878
www.sailmaine.org
A nonprofit, Sail Maine is devoted to support sailing at the grassroots, community level, and to that end it offers basic classes to both adults and children.

Sawyer's Sailing School
Harpswell
(207) 783–6882
www.hometown.aol.com/sailabob/index.html
Captain Bob offers basic ASA-certified courses in coastal cruising and keelboat sailing out of the Brunswick area.

CFAIR Sailing School
SBI Marine, Rockland
(207) 594–2891
www.by-the-sea.com/saltys/saltsail.html
The initials stand for Citizens for an Improved Rockland, and this extraordinary group of volunteers believes that

90-minute circuit from the town dock in Northeast Harbor well up into the sound on a daily basis. Sights include Acadia, Norumbega, and Saint Sauveur Mountains, tumbling Man-O-War Brook, the working waterfront of Southwest Harbor, Bear Island Lighthouse, Hall Quarry, and all of the wildlife that lives in this valley of sea. The boat also makes daily trips to the beautiful Cranberry Isles, one of which is narrated by a ranger from Acadia, and a sunset cruise as well.

Island Cruises
Little Island Marine, Shore Road, Bass Harbor
(207) 244–5785
www.bassharborcruises.com
The Strauss family runs the Bass Harbor outfit, Island Cruises, motoring from the hamlet of Bass Harbor to Frenchboro Island for a walk and lunch and simply out nature watching through Blue Hill Bay. Their boat, the *R. L. Gott,* a 41-foot vessel named for a family friend, putts out past Bass Harbor Light and across the way to Frenchboro, pausing long

sailing is a fine way to do just that. It's a pay-it-forward operation—someone once taught these folks to sail, so all that they ask is for you to try, to be on time, and to pass on what you learned to someone else. Classes take place on evenings and weekends and are intended for those age 13 and up.

Outward Bound
Rockland
(866) 467–7651
www.outwardboundwilderness.org
The nation's leading outdoor adventure program has several sail-training-based exercises each year, where you'll gain a basic understanding of seamanship—and your own self.

Sailing the Maine coast. JENNIFER SMITH-MAYO

enough on this small island of about 50 year-rounders for lunch at the local eatery and a guided tour of the village. Reservations are necessary for the three-and-a-half-hour trip. Passage is $25.

Down East

Captain Laura Fish
Kelley Point Road, Jonesport
(207) 497–3064
The personable Captain Laura Fish takes as many as six passengers out on the 23-foot *Aaron Thomas* on a daily basis in summer

from Jonesport harbor. Her three-hour tour takes in many of the sights in Moosabec Reach, from Great Wass Island, where there's a Nature Conservancy preserve noted for its wildflowers, to the colorfully named Mistake Island. Reservations are necessary.

Sylvina W. Beal
Downtown Eastport
(207) 853–2500
www.eastportwindjammers.com
For years, the classic schooner *Sylvina W. Beal* sailed out of Boothbay Harbor, but it has ven-

tured Down East and now calls the city of Eastport home. Built in East Boothbay in 1911, the 84-foot vessel is a knockabout schooner, which means it doesn't have a bowsprit, and it served years as a fishing boat. Movie buffs might recognize the *Sylvina W. Beal* from its roles in *Amistad* (1997) and *The Age of Innocence* (1993). These days the schooner takes passengers out on two daily cruises: a whale-watching trip (1:30 P.M.) and a sunset sail (7:00 P.M.) under the experienced hand of Captain Butch Harris. This is the prettiest way to see whales on the coast. Rates are $25 to $35 per person.

WHALE AND PUFFIN WATCHING

Maine is prime whale-watching country, especially in spring and fall, when the gentle giants migrate north and south. Humpbacks and finbacks are the most commonly spotted, but minkes and rare right whales also swim the Gulf of Maine. Whale-watching companies are so certain of spotting these leviathans that most offer some sort of guarantee (usually a voucher good for another trip). Sightings can be very up close, as whales swim up to the boat for a bit of mammal bonding, but more typically you get to see their fins and flukes as they come up for air. There's something truly transcendental about the experience.

South Coast

Deborah Ann
Perkins Cove, Ogunquit
(207) 361–9501
www.deborahannwhalewatch.com
Built in 1994, the 40-foot *Deborah Ann* is one of the smaller boats in the whale-watching fleet, and because it's based in Ogunquit, it's closer than many other outfits to the prime whaling grounds of Jeffrey's Ledge, so you get an intimate experience. Reservations are a good idea for the four-and-a-half-hour trips, which leave at 8:00 A.M. and 1:30 P.M. Rates are $45 for adults, $40 for seniors, $30 for children.

Indian Whale Watch
The Landing Restaurant, Ocean Avenue, Kennebunkport
(207) 967–5912
Indian departs the Landing Restaurant at 10:00 A.M. from July through September, and this outfit offers sunset trips in July and August. Expect to see dolphins, sharks, and seals, as well as the whales you're after, Ishmael.

First Chance Whale Watch
4 Western Ave, Lower Village, Kennebunk
(207) 967–5507 or (800) 767–2628
www.firstchancewhalewatch.com
Like the other vessels in the southern Maine whale-watch fleet, First Chance travels to Jeffrey's Ledge for its whale hunt. The very comfortable 80-foot *Nick's Chance* makes the journey on a daily basis at 9:00 A.M. and again at 2:30 P.M. in July and August. In late May and from September through mid-October, the boat sails only on weekends. Passage is $40 for adults, $25 for children.

Greater Portland

Olde Port Mariner Fleet
Long Wharf, Commercial Street, Portland
(207) 775–0727
www.marinerfleet.com
Portland's finest, Olde Port Mariner Fleet sends boats to both Jeffrey's Ledge and Sagadahoc Grounds in search of humpbacks and finbacks, and they've reported seeing sei and blue whales, North Atlantic white-sided dolphins, basking sharks, ocean sunfish, sea turtles, and tuna as well. The company's day trips run from 10:00 A.M. to 3:00 P.M. daily from June through August and on weekends only from late May through mid-October. Adults are $40, children $30.

Midcoast

Boothbay Whale Watch
Pier 6, P.O. Box 547, Boothbay Harbor 04538
(207) 633–3500 or (888) WHALE–ME

Every Boothbay Whale Watch tour begins with a narrated trip through the harbor itself, during which the naturalist on the 100-foot *Harbor Princess* discusses the homes, lighthouses, islands, and wildlife seen on the way out to the whales' feeding grounds. Then it's all hands on deck—or rather, all eyes on the water—as the search begins for finbacks and humpbacks. The boat sails twice daily from July through Labor Day at 9:30 A.M. and 1:30 P.M., and it goes out once daily at 11:30 A.M. during the off-season.

Cap'n Fish's Cruises
Pier 1, Wharf Street, Boothbay Harbor
(207) 633–3244, (207) 633–2626, or (800) 636–3244
www.capnfishs.com or
www.mainewhales.com

Whale-watching expeditions are a daily occurrence at Cap'n Fish's in Boothbay Harbor. The Boothbay legend claims to have the fastest vessels around, which gets you out to the whales quicker and allows for longer sightings when you're out there. This outfit also makes trips to National Audubon Society's puffin colony on Eastern Egg Rock. Call for the complete schedule.

Hardy Boat Cruises
Shaws Fish and Lobster Wharf, Route 32, New Harbor
(207) 677–2026 or (800) 278–3346
www.hardyboat.com

Best known as a ferry to Monhegan Island, the folks at Hardy Boat also make daily runs to Eastern Egg Rock to see the crazy puffins there, and they have a trip that goes to Monhegan first and then to the puffins, combining two Maine favorites. Puffin watches leave New Harbor at 5:30 P.M. and last an hour or so every day from mid-June through late August, and on Wednesday, Saturday, and Sunday from mid-May through mid-June. Fare is $20 for adults, $12 for kids.

Acadia Area
Bar Harbor Whale Watch Co.
1 West Street, Bar Harbor
(207) 288–9800 or (800) 533–WALE
www.whalesrus.com

Bar Harbor Whale Watch Co. boasts that its *Friendship V* is the fastest catamaran whale-watch boat in the United States, which may or may not be the case. But at speeds of 40 mph, it moves right along, getting you out to the whaling grounds off Mount Desert Island in no time. It also has a galley to keep you fat and happy while you're combing the waves for flukes and fins. The company's boat the *Helen* also does whale watches, and the outfit has other vessels for seal and puffin watching, so its schedule is packed. Check the Web site or call for details.

Down East
Barna B. Norton
118 Main Street, Jonesport
(207) 497–2560
www.machiassealisland.com

Puffins may be charismatic critters, with their cute sea-parrot faces, but they've got nothing on Captain Barna B. Norton of Jonesport. You want to meet a character, a genuine old-time Maine boat captain, venture Down East to Jonesport and you'll find Barna. He's single-handedly taken on the Canadian government, fighting for rights to access Machias Seal Island, one of the few Maine isles with a breeding puffin colony. Our northerly neighbors may erect a maple-leafed flag on the island, but that doesn't stop Norton and his son, John, from staking a Maine claim to the island and taking guests out there aboard the Chief to see the little, feathered Maine icons. Marlin Perkins of *Wild Kingdom,* famed bird-watcher Roger Tory Peterson, *National Geographic,* and just about every worthy magazine and newspaper in the land all have ventured offshore with Barna—you should, too. He makes the 80-minute crossing to Machias Seal Island daily at about 7:00 A.M. from Memorial Day through the end of August and gives you a few hours on the island to take pictures. He recommends calling the night before you expect to make the trip to establish the exact time he's heading out. The cost is $100 per person.

Bold Coast Charter Company
P.O. Box 364, Cutler 04626
(207) 259–4484
www.boldcoast.com
The hamlet of Cutler is one of the finest Maine communities you're ever going to find, a few houses and some fishing boats sitting on the Little River way Down East. One of these boats belongs to Captain Andrew Patterson, who offers cruises out to see the puffins of Machias Seal Island, the largest colony of the cute bird on the coast of Maine. Patterson makes the trip to the island on the *Barbara Frost*, a lobster boat, on a daily basis from May through August. He shoves off at seven or eight in the morning for the five-hour round-trip, and reservations are recommended. (Call the night before to find out what time the trip will commence.) The cost is $80 per person.

Harris Whale Watching and Fishing
Downtown Eastport
(207) 853–2500
www.eastportwindjammers.com
There are so many reasons to recommend a whale-watching trip out of Eastport. First, the city is handy to the Bay of Fundy, an oceanic region known for its large whale population. Second, you have to cruise past the Old Sow, a legendary whirlpool, on your way out to the whaling grounds. And finally, you're most likely going to be aboard the *Sylvina Beal*, a graceful windjammer. Most whale-watching vessels are boring new motorized craft, but Captain Butch Harris's ride is a pretty knockabout schooner. The trip is three hours, and the sightings often include puffins, seals, dolphins, ospreys, and eagles as well. The ship sails at 1:30 P.M., and passage is $35 for adults, $18 for kids age 12 or younger.

SCUBA TOURS

With its dark waters and cold temperatures, the Maine coast hasn't developed the sort of reputation that the Caribbean has when it comes to scuba diving. There are no azure vistas of coral reefs, no garishly colored fishies or bathwater-warm lagoons. You have to be a hardy type to enjoy diving here, but if you are, there is plenty to see, from seals and porpoises, lobsters and skates, to shipwrecks and seawalls. You just have to know where to look. Several dive outfitters know just that and will take you out on an undersea excursion. Here are a few ideas.

Seafari Charters
7 Island Avenue, Kittery
(207) 439–5068
www.seafaricharters.com
The *Seafari* may be a 44-foot sportfishing boat, and it may do mostly fishing charters these days, but it was custom-built as a dive platform for scuba diving. It's available for charters to such fantastic diving locales as Boon Island, site of a grisly stranded-island tale; Nubble Light; the Isles of Shoals; and Fort Foster. Call or visit the Web site for a rate schedule.

Divers Locker
460 Old North Berwick Road, Lyman
(207) 985–3161
Diver Mike Bridges, owner of the Divers Locker in Lyman, will give certified divers a guided tour of the wreck of the steamer *Wandby*, which went aground off Kennebunkport in 1921—among other great Maine dives—and you can rent gear from him if you don't want to tote yours along.

Sea Ventures Charters
Saint George
(207) 685–4693
www.divefishmaine.com
Divers will find a lot to like about Sea Ventures Charters, based in Saint George. The small outfit provides all types of certification courses—from beginner to advanced stuff like

nitrox and ice diving—and they do several cool charters as well. The most notable perhaps are the shark dives offered in August, when Maine waters are busy with 12-foot blue sharks (they sometimes even see big and scary makos). Divers are sent down in a cage, the waters are chummed, and they get an up-close-and-personal visit with these menacing predators. It can be spine-tingling, and it's available to anyone with basic certification because the cage, while in 500-foot-deep waters, is only 10 feet below the surface. The company also regularly dives off Monhegan Island, a treat because of the unusually rich sea life and great underwater terrain, as well as to the *Scottish Pride,* a 44-foot fishing boat wrecked in 115 feet of water. Deep-sea fishing is another option from these guys. Prices vary per trip and are based on six people participating; they can be $540 for an open-water dive to $1,080 for shark dives. Call or visit the Web site for full details.

Downeast Diving
1267 Route 1, Perry
(207) 263–8251
www.downeastdiving.com
Some say that the best diving in the state is along the Down East coast—and that's just where you'll find Dennis Dorsy's scuba outfit. Downeast Diving will take you out for simple shore dives or more technical stuff like ice and night and wreck diving. They even do a shark trip (and yes, there are sharks in Maine). If you don't know how to dive, they can help you with that, too. Check the Web site for details.

FISHING

Thanks to years of overfishing, the fisheries in Maine might not be what they once were—early English explorers described cod practically jumping into the boat—but they're still healthy enough to support an afternoon of deep-sea angling. Boats the length of the coast will take you out for mackerel, bluefish, stripers, cod, cusk, haddock, and more, for reasonable sums. Here are few places to start.

Bunny Clark
P.O. Box 837, Ogunquit 03907
(207) 646–2214
www.bunnyclark.com
The term *bottom feeder* is usually considered derogatory, but not when it comes to fishing the Maine coast. The bottom is where the cod, pollock, halibut, haddock, hake, cusk, redfish, monkfish, and wolffish can be found, and Captain Tim Towers of the legendary *Bunny Clark* knows how to find them. Not only can you catch an award-winning fish aboard the 40-foot fiberglass boat—it's seen a lot of record-breaking fish—but the captain and crew will even filet your catch for you to take home. The *Bunny Clark* is built for fishing, with seats and rods on deck, and its captain is one of the more experienced of the Maine deep-sea fleet. All gear is provided. Half-day, full-day, and "marathon," or 12-hour, trips are available daily from April 1 through November 13 for $45, $70, and $145, respectively.

Ugly Anne
Perkins Cove, Ogunquit
(207) 646–7202
www.uglyanne.com
There's nothing unattractive about the *Ugly Anne,* a 44-foot red-and-white wooden vessel that takes anglers out of Perkins Cove to plumb the depths for cod, pollock, halibut, hake, haddock, cusk, and wolffish. It offers two four-and-a-half-hour trips daily from mid-June through Labor Day, with the morning boat departing the docks at 8:00 A.M. and the afternoon boat leaving at 1:15 P.M. Daylong outings occur in the offseason. The half-day trips are $45 per person.

Captain Satch Deepsea Fishing
Town Dock, Wells Harbor
(207) 337–0716 (boat),
(207) 324–9655 (home)
http://captainsatch.tripod.com
Captain Satch McMahon and his sons Whit and Dennis welcome guests aboard a pair of vessels on a daily basis in summer: the *Gath III,* a classic 33-foot lobster boat that does

inshore runs for striped bass, and the *India Marie*, a 32-foot Cape Islander that heads off-shore for cod. The most popular excursions are their 4-hour ($70) and 6-hour ($90) inshore fishing expeditions, using light lines for stripers, mackerel, and bluefish, but they also do 2-hour introductory outings as well as 10-hour marathons in the course of their season, which runs from the end of April through the end of October.

Olde Port Mariner Fleet
Long Wharf, Commercial Street, Portland
(207) 699–2988
www.oldportmarinefleet.com
Known for its whale-watching and sightseeing cruises, the Olde Port Mariner Fleet also does deep-sea fishing runs from late April through early October. Full-day trips are $63; half-day are $28. Call or see the Web site for the schedule.

Sea Escape Charters
P.O. Box 7, Bailey Island 04003
(207) 833–5531
www.seaescapecottages.com
Mackerel, striped bass, and bluefish are what Captain Les McNelly is after when he takes anglers out on the *Sea Escape Too*. (See the earlier Boat Rides and Day Sails section of this chapter for details on his operation.)

Balmy Days Cruises
Pier 8, Commercial Street, Boothbay Harbor
(207) 633–2284 or (800) 298–2284
www.balmydayscruises.com
Mackerel fishing from the back of the *Miss Boothbay*, a converted lobster boat, is just one of Balmy Days Cruises' many offerings (see Boat Rides and Day Sails section earlier in this chapter). Two-hour angling adventures are offered four times daily from Pier 8 in Booth-bay Harbor. The experienced captains know where to drop anchor, the scenery is fine, and all tackle is provided. The trips are $20 for adults, $12 for kids age 11 or younger.

Bingo Deepsea Fishing
100 Commercial Street, Boothbay Harbor
(207) 633–3775
From the pier behind the Tugboat Restaurant in Boothbay Harbor, the 52-foot *Bingo* chugs 60 miles out to sea before anchoring in 300-foot water and dropping 10-ounce diamond jigs in search of good old staples like cod, pollock, haddock, and cusk. The fishing is usually very good, and being this far out, you often see whales and porpoises as an added bonus. If you get lucky, the crew will dice up your dinner for you on the 90-minute trip back into port. The boat goes out daily, and reservations are a good idea. The daylong trip is $125.

Janna Marie
Bar Harbor Inn Pier, Bar Harbor
(207) 288–4585 or 288–2373
www.downeastwindjammer.com
Part of Captain Steve Pagels's armada, the 56-foot *Janna Marie* sets out on four-hour trips in search of cod, cusk, pollock, mackerel, cunner, sculpin, black sea bass, and redfish at 8:00 A.M. and 1:00 P.M. daily in summer. Trips are limited to 35 anglers, and all bait and tackle is provided. Passage is $39.50 per person.

Harris Whale Watching and Fishing
Downtown Eastport
(207) 853–2500
www.eastportwindjammers.com
Captain Butch Harris has quite the excursion boat empire in Eastport, and his 35-passenger *Quoddy Dam* is the deep-sea representative. Eastport is ideal for deepwater fishing because, as the second-deepest natural seaport in North America, it sits only minutes from 300-foot waters rather than the hours required by most Maine boats—which means longer fishing for you. Bald eagles, porpoises, seals, and whales may be your companions. Four-hour trips leave daily at 8:00 A.M., and gear is provided. The fee is $25 per person.

LOBSTERING

Maine lobstermen have been called the cow-boys of the sea, rugged independent types who ride the waves, spending all day outdoors and risking rough conditions so that they can have their freedom. Tourists tend to buy into this image, seeing the romance of life on the glorious coast of Maine—out at sea all day, breathing the salty air, enjoying the sunshine and the views. And lobster fishing is all that, but it's also difficult, backbreaking work with uncertain results; you never know what's going to be in your traps when you haul them up—they might well be empty—and you have that expensive boat and all the gear to pay for. Still, most lobstermen will fish until they can't anymore. Several current and former lobstermen take passengers out on their boats in summer, showing them the ins and outs of hauling traps, from bait to catch. Don't plan your trip for a Sunday, though, because it's against Maine law to lobster on Sunday (gives the fishery a breather). Here are a few ideas.

Finestkind Cruises
Barnacle Billy's Dock, Perkins Cove, Ogunquit
(207) 646–5227
www.finestkindcruises.com
Providers of the best known of Maine's lob-stering trips, perhaps because they're in bustling Ogunquit, Finestkind Cruises offers hour-long jaunts five times daily from July 1 through Labor Day—10:30 and 11:30 A.M. and 1:00, 2:00, and 3:00 P.M.—and four times daily in the shoulder seasons. Fee is $12.00 for adults and $7.00 for kids, who tend to get a big kick out of the whole thing.

First Chance
4 Western Avenue, Lower Village, Kennebunk
(207) 967–5507 or (800) 767–2628
www.firstchancewhalewatch.com
Kylie Chance's lobster cruise has quite the pedigree, having been written up in *USA Today* and featured on the *Today Show*. The tour takes passengers down the Kennebunk River, past the Bush family compound on Walker Point, and out to the open Atlantic, stopping to haul traps. As the captain and crew bait and haul traps, you'll learn about the lifecycle of lobsters, their habits, loves, and hates, as well as the fishing industry and its importance to Maine. Added bonuses are trips to Bumpkin Island to see seabird colonies and fat seals, and a bit of lore about Kennebunk-port to boot. All for $18. The hour-and-a-half runs ship out at 10:00 A.M. and noon, 2:00, and 4:00 P.M. daily from Memorial Day through Columbus Day.

Lucky Catch
170 Commercial Street, Portland
(207) 761–0941
www.luckycatch.com
They don't come out of the water red. That's one of the many things you'll learn on a cruise with the *Lucky Catch,* a 37-foot lobster boat that works out of Portland Harbor, carrying passengers in summer and lobstering in the winter. The appeal of these 90-minute tours is that they trace a variety of scenic routes while stopping to pull and reset 10 or so traps. The 10:30 A.M. and 2:00 P.M. tours head over to Portland Head Light, the 12:15 and 3:45 P.M. go to ledges known for their seal populations, and in July and August there's an additional run to White Head. The trips are $20 for adults, $12 for kids, and perhaps best of all, if you call ahead, you can buy a "mess of bugs" (lobsters) for your dinner.

Atlantic Seal Cruises
25 Main Street, South Freeport
(207) 865–6112
Captain Tom Ring hauls a trap on his narrated tour of Casco Bay, just one of the many offer-ings of Freeport-based Atlantic Seal Cruises (see the section Boat Rides and Day Sails ear-lier in this chapter). Tours are offered on a daily basis in summer (late May through Octo-ber).

Lobstering has long been a way of life in Maine. LISA MOSSEL VIETZE

Lively Lady Too
Bayview Landing, Camden
(207) 236–6672

A former biology teacher, Captain Alan Philbrick knows his way about the marine environment, and he offers passengers aboard his lobster boat, the *Lively Lady Too*, a lively question-and-answer session while checking traps on the magnificent waters of Penobscot Bay. Binoculars and cameras are recommended on this trip, as seals, eagles, ospreys, sea ducks, and other seabirds are often spotted. Three trips are done daily in summer.

Old Quarry Ocean Adventures
130 Settlement Road, Stonington
(207) 367–8977
www.oldquarry.com

Lobstering aboard the *Nigh Duck* is just one of the zillions of trips and tours offered by Old Quarry. Help haul traps if you like—or just sit back and watch, learn, and enjoy the spectacular scenery off Stonington. The boat heads out at 9:00 A.M. sharp and returns at about noon on Monday, Tuesday, Thursday, Friday, and Saturday. Adults are $37, children age 11 or younger $22.

Lulu Lobster Boat Ride
Golden Anchor Pier, Bar Harbor
(207) 963–2341 or (866) 235–2341
www.lululobsterboat.com

Lobster boxing? Captain John Nicolai will explain what that is if you step aboard *Lulu*, his traditional lobster boat based in Bar Harbor, for a cruise out into Frenchman Bay. He'll explain all sorts of neat facts about everyone's favorite crustaceans—that they smell with their leg hairs, for example—while hauling and baiting traps. The trips clock in at close to two hours, they're very informative, and they're the only lobstering cruises out of Bar Harbor.

From June 14 to August 19 they depart daily at 8:00 and 10:30 A.M. and 1:00, 3:30, and 6:00 P.M., and while they are still offered on Sundays, no actual traps are hauled. Fare is $25 for adults, $22 for seniors, $15 for kids age 11 or younger.

SEA KAYAKING

It's surprising that the sea kayaking explosion in Maine took until the 1980s to happen, because the long, skinny vessels are perfect for navigating the myriad coves, inlets, salt marshes, and island-studded bays Down East. But boom it did, and now kayak outfitters are ubiquitous, almost as common as lobster shacks on the state's shoreline. You can buy boats, rent boats, and, if you're new to the sport, learn how to paddle properly at locales from Kittery to Calais. And a host of guide services take guests out on tours. The state requires that kayak guides be licensed, and thus all of your hosts will be genuine Registered Maine Guides, who have to pass tough written and oral exams to earn their red-and-green badges. The tours they offer might be two-hour get-to-know-me harbor paddles for beginners, half-day expeditions, or overnight voyages. There are few better ways to experience the Maine coast than being right down in it.

South Coast

Kittery Trading Post
Route 1, Kittery
(888) 587–6246
http://kitterytradingpost.com
Maine's other great outfitter (besides L. L. Bean) offers one-day kayak excursions focused on the basic skills. You'll learn proper techniques and strokes, types of boats, tides and currents, safety, and exits, all while spending the whole day in the cockpit of a kayak. The course takes place in Little Harbor, New Hampshire (just south of Portsmouth), a protected haven where the waters are not rough. Cost for the seven-hour seminar is $85. Call for details.

Harbor Adventures
P.O. Box 345, York Harbor 03911
(207) 363–8466
www.harboradventures.com
Based in York Harbor, Harbor Adventures explores the coast from New Hampshire to the Kennebunks. This outfitter regularly schedules two-hour turns around York Harbor ($39), half-day tours ($53), lobster luncheons ($65) up Chauncey Creek, sunset tours ($32), and full-moon paddles when the lunar cycle and the weather agree ($40). The company also does four-hour introductory courses ($70) that focus on types of boats, strokes, safety, and rescue.

Excursions Coastal Maine Outfitting Company
Route 1, Cape Neddick
(207) 363–0181
www.excursionsinmaine.com
"Wanna get paddled?" That's the slogan of Coastal Maine Outfitting Company in York, and to that end it offers a weekend getaway kayaking excursion into Casco Bay. For two days you'll paddle among the islands, coves, and rivers of the great southern Maine inlet, spending the evening in between playing Swiss Family Robinson and camping on a deserted isle. All gear and meals are provided. You can shove off on this particular adventure ($250); try their coastal explorer trip, a 5- or 6-mile, half-day excursion; or you can customize a trip of your own.

World Within Sea Kayaking
746 Ocean Avenue, Wells
(207) 646–0455
www.worldwithin.com
With the great Rachel Carson National Wildlife Refuge marshes in its backyard, World Within has great grounds to explore. The most popular outing here is the Ogunquit River Plantation tour, which is designed for novice kayakers and doesn't venture out onto the open ocean, but the company also does sunrise, sunset, and full-moon trips. The plantation tour is $70 per person.

Gone with the Wind
524 Pool Road, Biddeford
(207) 283–8446

Frankly, you'll give a damn about Gone with the Wind's kayak tours, especially if you are at all hesitant about kayaking, intrigued by the sport but maybe a little nervous. The guides here take clients out in small groups, they use "umiaks," very stable open-topped kayaks, and they paddle in the protected waters of Biddeford Pool in Saco, which are usually placid. Favorite routes include trips to Wood Island Light, a beacon built in the early 1800s, and to Beach Island, where there is a colony of charismatic seals.

Greater Portland

Maine Island Kayak Company
70 Luther Street, Peaks Island
(207) 766–2373 or (800) 796–2373
www.maineislandkayak.com

Tom Bergh is the kind of guy you want to go to sea with. He's been a guide for most of his life (mountaineering, backcountry skiing, river running, and hiking), and since 1986 he's been ensconced on Casco Bay's Peaks Island, where he runs Maine Island Kayak Company, aka MIKCO, among the biggest and best outfitters in the state. His slate at MIKCO is amazingly full: Bergh and his guides offer all manner of sea kayak trips, from half-day introductory paddles to full-on expeditions to points east. Amazing stuff. MIKCO also has its own Ocean School, where you can learn all things kayak.

L. L. Bean Outdoor Discovery Schools
3 Bow Street, Freeport
(888) 552–3261
www.llbean.com/outdoorsOnline

Who better to take you out sea kayaking than L. L. Bean, which practically invented the outdoors? As part of its Outdoor Discovery program, Bean provides half-, one-, and two-day kayak schools, as well as three-day trips on Casco Bay, where you'll paddle in tandem kayaks by day, learning your way around the sport, and spend evenings at the company's base at Wolfe's Neck Farm in Freeport. Fee is

$450. Call or visit the outfitter's excellent Web site for all of the options.

Midcoast

Seaspray Kayaking
New Meadows River, Brunswick
(888) 349–SPRAY
www.seaspraykayaking.com

Based on the stunning New Meadows, Seaspray has a whole raft of kayaking options, among them bed-and-breakfast tours, moonlight paddles, and introductory splashabouts. But their coolest trip might be the one they do in search of the Midcoast's famed stripers, or striped bass. That's right, fishing from a kayak. You cast and catch right from the cockpit, and all tackle and techniques are provided. These tours are $75 per person, which includes a half-day kayak rental. See the Web site for details.

H2Outfitters
P.O. Box 72, Orrs Island 04066
(207) 833–5257 or (800) 205–2925
www.h2outfitters.com

One of the oldest and best outfits on the kayak scene, H2Outfitters has its "galactic headquarters" on Orrs Island south of Brunswick (with satellite outposts in Connecticut, New Jersey, Pennsylvania, and North and South Carolina). H2O provides anything and everything you could want in the way of sea kayak instruction as well as multiday voyages along the coast. One of the more unique offerings is the Bed and Breakfast Trip, during which you stay at the funky Black Friar Inn in Bar Harbor and paddle a variety of coves, bays, and islands around Acadia over the course of three days. This package costs $1,195 per person, based on double occupancy, and occurs several times during the summer. Call or visit the Web site for the complete list of adventures.

Dragonworks Inc.
Stevens Road, Bowdoinham
(207) 666–8481

Merrymeeting Bay is a place like no other in Maine, a 9,000-acre delta just above Bath

Close-up

Maine Island Trail

Often referred to as the Appalachian Trail of the sea, the Maine Island Trail was founded in 1987, a 325-mile ocean corridor from Portland to Machias. More than 70 islands lie along the route, and, by arrangement with state and local officials and with private citizens, they can be used as overnight stops, allowing boaters to hop from one to the next almost the length of the Maine coast. The trail is principally used by sea kayakers, who make voyages both long and short along it, paddling by day, camping out by night like so many Robinson Crusoes, and enjoying a quasi-wild go of it. There's nothing quite like waking up amid the peaceful pines of a small, uninhabited island and basking in the serenity of the shore.

The Maine Island Trail Association (MITA), a nonprofit conservation organization, governs the use of the trail and publishes the only guide that lets you know which islands are open to the public. The outfit was founded to try to mitigate the overuse and abuse of islands by boaters, and it has imposed some guidelines to prevent such occurrences, from restricting the use of certain spots during seabird nesting seasons to encouraging low-impact camping. It's a worthy cause, and in recent years, despite the best efforts of MITA, there's been ever-growing concern that paddlers and boaters are loving the islands to death.

For more information contact the Maine Island Trail Association at P.O. Box C, Rockland 04841; (207) 596–6456. Membership, which gets you a copy of the trail guide, is $40 a year.

---

where six major rivers converge, and Ed Friedman knows it better than most. He offers informal, on-demand tours of the great bay in his own line of kayaks, guiding guests through this unique estuarine ecosystem famous for its ducks. You can learn to paddle, learn to roll, learn whatever you're interested in under his knowledgeable guidance. Stops may include freshwater flats and sandbars where wild rice and pickerel weed grow. Fascinating stuff. Rates depend upon the length and type of tour.

Frozen Paddler
271 Old Bath Road, Wiscasset
(207) 882–9066
www.frozenpaddler.com
A spirited explorer who's out in all kinds of weather, Kurt Geib specializes in custom fitting tours to clients. He'll take people on half-day

tours on the Sheepscot River, full-day paddles around Midcoast islands, or anywhere else you'd like to explore. He'll tote along some food, too, and he'll bring "other types of toys to play with." Two-hour tours, which he recommends for families, are $35, four hours are $75, and daylong outings are $95. As he says, "We have some ideas, but yours might be better. Let us see what we can come up with." Geib's a neat character. He might even quote some Zappa for you.

Tidal Transit
18 Granary Way, Boothbay Harbor
(207) 633–7140
www.kayakboothbay.com
Tidal Transit's been at it since the late 1980s, and it has a handful of fine offerings. Based in Boothbay Harbor, the outfitter's guides paddle out to Burnt Island Lighthouse, where they

stop for a stroll ($35); they venture into prime marine mammal and bird territory in search of seals, herons, ospreys, and eagles on the Wildlife Tour ($40); and they paddle against a backdrop of lovely reds and yellows at the dimming of the day on the Sunset Tour ($35). Most of these paddles are in the two-hour range, and all gear is included. Reservations are required, so call ahead.

Sea Spirit Adventures
Business Route 1, Damariscotta
(207) 563–5732
www.seaspiritadventures.com
Muscongus Bay is a favorite among Maine sea kayakers, a place of islands and coves and birdlife, and that's where Sea Spirit is located. Stewart and Suzanne Blackburn do a variety of trips on the bay on a daily basis in summer, from their two-hour introductory tour ($35) to their nighttime tour ($40), another two-tour paddle done under the stars. They also spend a lot of time on the nearby Damariscotta River and host lessons for kayakers of all levels. Check the Web site for all of their trips.

Breakwater Kayak
Boat Barn at the Public Landing, Rockland
(207) 596–6895 or (877) 559–8800
www.breakwaterkayak.com
Founded by Mark DiGirolamo, Breakwater Kayak specializes in natural history tours, using Penobscot and Muscongus Bays as their campus. When he's not guiding, DiGirolamo spends his time working on birding projects for the Maine Department of Inland Fisheries and Wildlife or teaching in the local schools, so he knows of what he speaks when he takes you out for his daylong natural history tour. Birds are an obvious interest, and you can expect to spot ospreys, eagles, and warblers, as well as seals, and the trip always includes an exploration of the intertidal zone. The natural history tour pushes off at 9:00 A.M., returns at 4:00 P.M., and costs $100 per person. Breakwater Kayak also takes paddlers out to the mile-long breakwater for which it's named, to Owls Head Light, and around busy Camden

Harbor. Camping excursions are another possibility.

Maine Sport Outfitters
Route 1, Rockport
(207) 236–8797 or (800) 722–0826
On any given day in summer, the parking lot at Maine Sport is chock-full, and many of these cars belong to people out kayaking somewhere. Maine Sport has been guiding since 1976 and is single-handedly responsible for introducing thousands of people to the wonderful world of paddling. This outfitter has a calendar full of options. Some of the more popular outings include the Camden Harbor tour, a paddle around the protected haven known for its mountain views, lighthouse, windjammers, megayachts, and summer homes ($35); and the Harbor to Harbor Tour, which takes you from Rockport Harbor, once home of Andre the Seal, on up to Camden Harbor, stopping at Curtis Island for a picnic lunch ($75). Multiday trips, like the two-day island cottage trip to Muscongus Bay ($295), are another possibility, and there is no end to the instruction available. Visit Maine Sport online or in person for all the details.

Ducktrap Sea Kayak Tours
Route 1, Lincolnville
(207) 236–8608
The guides at this oldie but goody push off from Ducktrap Beach for tours out into the wilds of Penobscot Bay. They'll follow the coast to Belfast, work back Camden way, or head out into the deep water toward the long green island of Islesboro. Dolphins, seals, and loons are common paddling companions. Families with young children are often taken to the more placid waters of Megunticook Lake. Reservations are required and rates vary. Call for details.

Belfast Kayak Tours
Belfast Public Landing, Belfast
(207) 382–6204
The tours offered by Harvey Schiller on Belfast Harbor are instructional and designed for

Kayak outfitters are now as common as lobster shacks along the coast. JENNIFER SMITH-MAYO

novice paddlers, but anyone would enjoy heading out onto Penobscot Bay with the gregarious guide. Belfast is where the tugs that work the bay are located, and everybody likes to have a look at those, and there are always interesting goings-on in the harbor. Schiller uses wider, more stable boats, making for an easy paddle even for the absolute beginner. He has an informal setup at the Public Landing in the hip city, working from 9:00 A.M. to 6:00 P.M. every day except Wednesday and, while reservations are always a good idea, they're not necessary. Fees vary depending on the size of the group.

Water Walker Kayak Tours
State Route 52, Belfast
(207) 338–6424
www.touringkayaks.com
Registered Maine Guide Ray Wirth likes to give paddlers a lot of choices, and he has quite the menu to select from on his Web site. Two- or three-hour trips ($40) might include paddles around Belfast or Rockport or Blue Hill Harbor, Sears Island, or Camden's Lake Megunticook. Half-day trips ($45) might be outings to Moose or Fort Points; to Flat, Ram, Seal, or Warren Islands; or to Camden or Owls Head. Full-day outings ($85) could be excursions to Islesboro, Great Spruce, Butter, or the Muscle Ridge Islands, or an exploration of Muscongus Bay. It's all up to the client, and Wirth is an accommodating and accomplished host.

Castine Kayak Adventures
Dennett's Wharf, Castine
(207) 326–9045
www.castinekayak.com
Castine Kayak Adventures are worth seeking out if only because they bring you to Castine, one of Maine's prettiest towns. Of course, these trips are quite something in and of

themselves. Castine Kayak's overnights are particularly appealing, and they have three itineraries to choose from and are willing to customize, too. You might try the one- or two-night Exploration of Bagaduce Estuary, an inner waterway known for its reversing currents, islands, and seal haul-outs (this trip even features paddles to several restaurants), or the more ambitious 3-mile Paddle to Warren Island, a crossing of Penobscot Bay to the state park on Warren Island. These trips are $125 per person per day. Castine also does half-day tours around Castine Harbor, full-day paddles, sunset tours, you name it. Call or look them up on the Web for full details.

Old Quarry Ocean Adventures
130 Settlement Road, Stonington
(207) 367–8977
www.oldquarry.com
The 60-island archipelago off Stonington is the seascape worked by the guides of Old Quarry. An outdoor institution on Deer Isle, Old Quarry has a campground, provides sail and motorboat charters, rents bikes, and even does camping trips. The outfitter also offers full-day ($105) and half-day ($55) outings in single and tandem kayaks from June through September.

Granite Island Guide Service
66 Dunham Point Road, Deer Isle
(207) 348–2668
www.graniteislandguide.com
Maine has so many great stretches of coastline to paddle, but it's hard to beat the Stonington area for sheer jaw-dropping beauty. The armada of islands offshore, the rugged granite, the dark spruce spires along the coast, the hills that rise above the water—it's all quite breathtaking. Granite Island Guide Service explores it on a daily basis in summer. Dana and Anne Douglas offer morning, afternoon, and sunset trips out among it, as well as the Day on the Bay tour ($90), which makes a round-trip from Stonington to Isle au Haut or circumnavigates Little Deer Isle. The couple also does overnights that incorporate a genuine lobster bake. Call them for all the details.

Acadia Area
Coastal Kayaking Tours
48 Cottage Street, Bar Harbor
(207) 288–9605 or (800) 526–8615
www.acadiafun.com
You can't walk down a street in Bar Harbor without bumping into someone toting a kayak paddle these days. Coastal Kayaking is one of the companies responsible for the proliferation of the sport, and the folks here take kayakers out like clockwork to paddle the pristine waters around Acadia National Park. Their half-day tour ($45) is popular, covering about 5 miles of coastline and featuring narration about the natural and geological history of Mount Desert Island, but you might also consider the two-hour harbor tour ($37), the 10-mile full-day tour ($69), or even the solo tour, which is a personalized outing geared toward improving paddling skills ($59). There are many other options as well. Call or see the Web site to find out more.

National Park Sea Kayak Tours
39 Cottage Street, Bar Harbor
(800) 347–0940
www.acadiakayak.com
The name says it all with National Park Sea Kayak—though not officially affiliated with Acadia National Park, the outfitter uses the waters off the park as its playground. Depending upon the weather conditions and tides, the company's half-day or sunset tours might explore 5 or 6 miles of Frenchman, Western, Eastern, and Blue Hill Bays or Somes Sound. Departure times for the four-hour tours are at 8:00, 9:00, and 10:30 A.M. and 1:00, 2:30, and 4:00 P.M. The outfitter has a sunset paddle in the evening, too, and occasionally offers multiday expeditions. This is one of the oldest outfitters on Mount Desert, and it has gotten sea kayaking down to a science.

Maine State Sea Kayak Guide Service
254 Maine Street, Southwest Harbor
(207) 244–9500 or (877) 481–9500
www.mainestatekayak.com
A couple of major magazines (*National Geo-*

graphic Adventure and *Travel and Leisure*) have given this outfit the nod in the past, and its good reputation might be due to 20-plus years of experience. Its specialty is introducing new paddlers to this graceful game, and its guides use the waters off Southwest Harbor to that end, regularly paddling five or six different routes, depending upon weather, tides, and clients. Half-day trips, giving you four hours of kayaking and instruction—a good taste—are $46 per person. They're available from mid-May through mid-October.

Down East

Mooselook Guide Service
Route 186, Gouldsboro
(207) 963–7223
www.mooselookguideservice.com
Though its name makes it sound more like an up-country outfit, Mooselook is actually based in the pretty coastal town of Gouldsboro, and while the guides here do offer canoe trips down the Narraguagus River, they do most of their work in the Schoodic area. The big blue expanse of Arcadia National Park, with its spruce-topped isles, pink granite ledges, seals, dolphins, and seabirds, is the setting for their half-day trips, which are open to novices as well as experienced paddlers. Individual or tandem kayaks can be used. Mooselook also offers some unique kayak-camping options, from the Honeymoon Special—during which a guide will paddle you out to a quiet island, make you dinner, and then leave you to your own delights, returning to make you breakfast—and a two-day, two-night trip for those interested in more time in the cockpit. Mooselook works every day in summer. Call for a reservation.

GREEN SPACE

The Maine coast may be largely developed these days, but thankfully, a lot of shoreline has been preserved over the centuries. From Kittery to Quoddy, there are miles and miles of forest to explore, many mountains to hike, routes to bike, gardens to enjoy, and unique nature preserves to visit. Outdoor adventurers will find no end of things to do and will have to come back again and again before they begin to see half of what the state has to offer.

Some of the finest stretches of green space on the coast are managed by the federal government or by the state, either as parks or public lands. There are 19 coastal state parks, and they provide visitors with truly great hiking (see Camden Hills or Quoddy Head in this chapter), exceptional swimming and sunbathing (see earlier Beaches chapter), and fine picnicking on the shore. The U.S. Fish and Wildlife Service has a handful of reserves along the waterfront, including the Rachel Carson, Petit Manan, and Moosehorn National Wildlife Refuges.

Other great recreation areas are overseen by conservation outfits. Maine Audubon has several properties, as does the Nature Conservancy. Even small local groups like the Damariscotta River Association, the Boothbay Region Land Trust, and the Georges River Land

Trust have made their marks on the state, saving spectacular parcels of land from becoming condo communities or making arrangements with landowners to allow public use. All of this effort has resulted in an array of nature preserves and gardens.

You'll surely run out of time before you run out of places to explore.

ISLES OF SHOALS

Nine miles off the coasts of Maine and New Hampshire lie these nine islands, the site of early fishing activity in the 1600s and later divided up between the two states (Maine got five, New Hampshire four). Among the more romanticized islands off the Pine Tree State, they're remote, largely unchanged, and hard to get to, but Star and Appledore Islands once had grand hotels on them, were colonized by Unitarians, and allow limited visitation. Appledore was home to famed poet Celia Thaxter, who built beautiful gardens and entertained the literati, and people make the pilgrimage out to see her blooming beds. The Isles of Shoals Steamship Company (315 Market Street, Portsmouth; 603–431–5500 or 800–441–4620) cruises to the islands all summer long.

PARKS, PATHWAYS, AND PRESERVES
South Coast

Vaughn Woods State Park
28 Oldsfields Road, South Berwick
(207) 384–5160
Famed writer Sarah Orne Jewett grew up not too far from these woods, and one has to wonder how often the nature-loving author wandered the 250 acres here along the

> **i** With the price of gas spiraling ever upward, the East Coast Greenway will surely take on a new urgency. The trail will eventually link Maine to Florida, connecting bike paths and walkways and providing walkers, joggers, and cyclists with a "superhighway" of sorts, free of automobiles. Maine already has several sections in place. Find out more at www.exploremaine.org/bike/greenway .html.

Salmon Falls River. If she were here today, she'd find much hasn't changed—at least at this small spot. The old-growth stands of pine and hemlock are still standing tall, and there are still nice looks at the Salmon Falls River. Handy to the Yorks, Ogunquit, Kittery, and points in New Hampshire, Vaughn Woods is, just as its name suggests, a woodland preserve, and it's rarely crowded, used more by locals than tourists. The spot makes a nice diversion or picnic setting when visiting the historic sites in the Berwicks—like Jewett's home.

Cliff Walk
York Harbor
The equal of Ogunquit's famous Marginal Way or Bar Harbor's well-known Shore Path, the Cliff Walk is an extraordinary footpath that walks the fine line between the distinctive old summer homes of York Harbor and the crashing surf. It's never become as widely talked about as other paths because it has frequently been closed to the public. The walkway, you see, goes right through the backyards of some of the nicest homes in York, ducking under banks of bay windows, passing flower beds, and skirting rows of shrubs, and on occasions in the past, public use has been curtailed due to complaints over vandalism or property rights. But the Cliff Walk is once again open, and it's something to see. You can make the jaunt in less than an hour round-trip, beginning at Harbor Beach and walking to the pebble shore at which the path ends. The panoramas of open sea and smashing surf are as good as you'll see anywhere, and you can scramble along the rocks, peer into tidal pools, and have a very up-close look at some fine homes. About 50 feet above the serrated shoreline in some places and broadside to the open sea, the path threads through bird-filled bushes and little groves of trees, and much of the going is paved or gravel. It's open from 5:00 A.M. to 6:00 P.M. No dogs allowed, and don't even think about dropping that candy wrapper—there's a $1,000 fine for littering.

Mount Agamenticus
Off Mountain Road, York
(207) 363–1040
This 572-foot peak is more of an uppity hill than any sort of self-respecting mountain, but however you look at it, Agamenticus is by far the tallest thing around. As such it makes for a great playground for residents of the South Coast. In summer hikers enjoy the trails up its sides; in autumn, leaf peepers enjoy the prospect from its summit; and in winter it attracts sledders, skiers, and snowboarders galore. The town of York owns the property now, and there's a tangle of antennas at the top, but it's still plenty fun to scramble up.

Steedman Woods
Old Mill Road, York Village
Reached by the famous Wiggly Bridge, a suspension span that is indeed wiggly, this 16-acre preserve is owned by the excellent Old York Historical Society, and it's a beauty. Spread across a peninsula between the saltwater Barrells Mill Pond on one side and the York River on the other, the preserve was given to the town's historians by the man it's named after, Charles Richard Steedman, with the proviso that it be kept "forever wild." (He borrowed a page from beloved Maine governor Percival Baxter.) A little plaque on site explains that the area was "the focal point of much of York's history for the first 300 years," and you can understand why early settlers were drawn to the spot. It's very beautiful, and a few trails run around its circumference, allowing for some fine water views and connecting with paths into York Harbor and York Village. You could walk the whole peninsula in a half hour or so, but it's also a nice place to sit and read a book or take a picnic.

Marginal Way
Ogunquit
The best way to get between Perkins Cove and downtown Ogunquit in summer is this mile-long walkway. Forget about driving. Even this path can get elbow to elbow, but it's a lot easier to take the traffic here than it is out on the

street, thanks to fresh sea air and unparalleled vistas of the open ocean. When the going here is quiet, it's positively magical. Try it early in the morning, late at night, or in the off-season. You can get on the path behind the Sparhawk Resort downtown and at Perkins Cove. Along the way you'll see crashing breakers, rocks for scrambling, and tide pools. There are benches where you can pause to catch your breath.

Rachel Carson National Wildlife Refuge
321 Port Road, Wells
(207) 646–9226
http://rachelcarson.fws.gov

Rachel Carson is often credited with helping to bring environmental consciousness to the average American with the publication of her landmark book, *Silent Spring*. Less known is the fact that Carson spent many years working for the U.S. Fish and Wildlife Service. That same organization honored her years ago by naming its sprawling southern Maine reserve after the author, who did a lot of her work in Maine. Ten parcels on about 5,000 acres of coastline comprise the reserve, spread across towns from Kittery to Cape Elizabeth. (It hopes to be 9,125 acres when current land acquisition projects are completed.) Most are fairly small, purchased to help protect estuarine ecosystems important to migrating birds. A few of these preserves have trail networks and make for good visits. You can pick up a trail guide at the reserve headquarters and get started right here on a mile-long walk through the salt marsh.

Wells National Estuarine Research Reserve
342 Laudholm Farm Road, Wells
(207) 646–1555
www.wellsreserve.org

One of the last remaining saltwater farms in southern Maine, Laudholm Farm was saved by local residents years ago, and it now serves as the centerpiece for this 1,600-acre research sanctuary. Seven miles of trails wander through a wide diversity of ecosystems—from forest to sea dunes to beach to meadow to marsh, and they're open for the public to use every day from 7:00 A.M. to sunset. Bird-watchers especially love the place, which is habitat to an array of seabirds. Trail maps can be picked up at the entry kiosk or at the visitor center, which is located in the old farm and has exhibits and informational displays. They'll show you where to find the scenic overlooks and how to get to the beach. The informative visitor center is open Monday through Friday from 10:00 A.M. to 4:00 P.M. in the off-season and on weekends also from May through October.

Massabesic Experimental Forest
Lyman and Alfred
(207) 324–7000

Even though it's a sprawling piece of land open to recreation in the most congested part of the state, most tourists never find this 3,600-acre woods. Split into two halves of approximately the same size in Lyman and Alfred and riddled with old woods roads and trails, the forest is perfect for mountain biking, hiking, bird-watching, and fishing, and it's owned by the USDA Forest Service. Critters are fond of the vernal pools and wetlands, and there are some unique species like Atlantic white cedar, which doesn't grow much farther north. But most people never find it.

Waterboro Barrens
Buff Brook Road, Waterboro
(207) 729–5181

Close to 3,000 acres of pitch pine barrens and scrub oak blanket this unique preserve in the inland town of Waterboro. Just 20 minutes from the coast—Waterboro is next door to York County seat Alfred—the barrens are among the best examples of pitch pine vegetation in the world, and they're owned and managed by the Nature Conservancy. Three trails loop through the scruffy ecosystem, which was caused by poor soils and glacial outwash. Rare and endangered species are concentrated here—an array of turtles, moths, and butterflies, especially near Round and Little Teeny Poverty Ponds—but you'll also see deer, grouse, and, if you're lucky, maybe even a moose. You'll also likely have the trails to yourself as the preserve is one of the least-visited of the Nature Conservancy's properties. It's open year-round, sunup to sunset, and is free.

Kennebunk Plains
State Route 99, Kennebunk
(207) 729–5181
The Nature Conservancy owns these 2,000-some subtly beautiful acres, and the conservation outfit tends to be particular about the properties it preserves, so you know it must be special. And it is. Besides being the largest sand plain grassland in New England, it is habitat for a variety of birds that are rarish to endangered in Maine and elsewhere—grasshopper sparrows, horned larks, upland sandpipers, and vesper sparrows. These feathered friends intrigue birders, of course. Anyone who visits in autumn will be impressed by the vast plains of purple that occur when another rare species, the northern blazing star, puts on its September show—acres upon acres of vibrant hues. This used to be commercial blueberrying land, too, so you know a few tasty berries will be around if you time your visit right (that'd be August).

Starfield Observatory
Off State Route 35, Kennebunk
www.asnne.org
The home of a southern Maine stargazing club, the Astronomical Society of Northern New England, this cool, relatively new observatory is free and open for the public to use. Housed in a 512-square-foot building with a peel-back roof, it's equipped with two impressive telescopes on long-term loan from Bowdoin College: a 12.5-inch reflector used to see into deep space and a 6-inch reflector used to focus on closer-up items like the moon and the planets. The club, now at it since 1982, is a welcoming lot, and its members enjoy sharing their hobby with guests. They regularly host events open to the public. Check the Web to find out when the next gathering is.

Butler and Marshall Preserves
Off the Old Port Road, Kennebunkport
(207) 985–8734
These two green Kennebunk Land Trust reserves frame the lower Kennebunk River. Forested gems, they're reachable by boat or by land. You can paddle a canoe downriver from town or take the Old Port Road 1.7 miles from Kennebunkport to the woods road on the right, which is marked with a KENNEBUNK LAND TRUST sign. Park there and walk in. A nice loop trail will link you to Picnic Rock, a popular spot for just what its name implies (and swimming) in the Butler Preserve, which is covered in red and white pine back from the river. The much larger 181-acre Marshall Preserve is accessed from the River Road in Arundel.

East Point Sanctuary
Lester B. Orcutt Boulevard, Biddeford Pool
(207) 781–2330
www.maineaudubon.org
At the very tip of Biddeford Pool, jutting out into the Atlantic, this Audubon Sanctuary is a must-visit among Maine birders. The 30-acre property is a mixture of open meadow and low shrubs on the shore, and a trail takes you along the waterfront. Commonly spotted birds include gannets, red-throated loons, sea ducks, alcids, and terns. People also often see harbor seals. Open sunrise to sunset, year-round.

Saco Heath
Buxton Road, Saco
(207) 729–5181
One of the biggest bogs in Maine—and the southernmost raised peat bog in North America—this 1,000-acre wetland has a lot to recommend it. First, it's simply a bit of open space in a part of the state where that is increasingly difficult to find. Second, it's home to a bunch of rare and endangered species. This is the only place where Atlantic cedar is known to grow in a domed heath, and it's home to the Hessel's hairstreak, an uncommon butterfly, a bunch of cool shrubs and car-

nivorous plants, and even moose, which are usually found much farther north in Maine. Finally, a mile-long boardwalk makes it all accessible in a way that it never used to be, and the Nature Conservancy, which owns the property, provides maps for a self-guided tour that is worth doing. Autumn is a particularly good time to visit, thanks to glowing expanses of mountain holly and highbush blueberries.

Greater Portland

Scarborough Marsh
Route 9, Scarborough
(207) 883–5100

The largest salt marsh in Maine lies in one of the most booming towns in the state, the Portland suburb of Scarborough, a place where shopping centers and subdivisions grow like Topsy. So the 3,000-acre estuary is something of a wild oasis. A half dozen small rivers converge in the marsh, making it rich habitat for birds and wildlife, especially during the spring and fall migrations. The Maine Audubon Society manages the site and maintains trails and a nature center where you can rent canoes ($15 per hour for nonmembers). Paddling is really the best way to see the marsh, and it truly rewards anyone who launches a boat. Naturalists lead 90-minute tours daily at 10:00 A.M., which is a great introduction to the estuary, and the center hosts a whole slate of cool programs, like moonlit paddles and early-morning bird tours. The marsh is open to the public from dawn to dusk, year-round.

Scarborough River Wildlife Sanctuary
Route 9, Scarborough

When you start off down the trail here, just up

> **i** If you're up for a bit of outdoor recreation but can't convince others in your party to come along or are alone, look up the Maine Outdoor Adventure Club in Portland. A big outing club, MOAC sponsors trips several times a week and welcomes newcomers. Call the activity hotline at (207) 828–0918 for a list of upcoming events.

State Route 9 from the wide green expanse of Scarborough Marsh, all you can hear is cars going by and orders being called out at Ken's Place, a seafood joint, across the street: "One-thirty-nine, please, one-thirty-nine." After a few minutes of walking, though, the traffic noise fades to a quiet hiss—like a waterfall in the distance—and it's eventually replaced by wind in the grass, birdcalls, and the singing of the trees. Then things get very pleasant. The town-owned 56-acre nature preserve is threaded with 1.5 miles of trails—grass, gravel, and dirt—none of which seems particularly well used. Little interpretive signs lead you through an array of habitats, from the meadow in which the trails begin, to the edge of the marsh, to mixed forest, and back to fields. These tiny posts point out some rather obvious sights—eastern white pine, old cement walls—as if walking you through the southern Maine that once was. (You almost expect one to read "Open space, now extinct.") But that's what's so refreshing about this small sanctuary—it isn't the most spectacularly beautiful nature walk in Maine, and it won't take you more than an hour to fully investigate, but it is an oasis of undeveloped land in a part of the state where such a thing is rapidly going the way of the elm. The nicest part of a hike through the area is the front seat it gives you on Scarborough Marsh, the state's largest estuary and a truly stunning little bit of sea. Green ocean grasses, swirling rivers of salt water, and the open ocean beyond it fill your field of vision, and you actually have to look around a bit to find signs of civilization. You're sure to see a variety of birds, and perhaps something exotic. Open all year, sunrise to sunset.

Two Lights State Park
66 Two Lights Road, Cape Elizabeth
(207) 799–5871

You can look awfully hard for the pair of lighthouses that lent Two Lights State Park its name, but you won't find them in the 41-acre preserve. The first twin lighthouses built on the Maine coast, going up in 1828, they're down a nearby road and are inaccessible. What people will find on this rocky headland are sweeping vistas of Casco Bay, the ruins of a World War II fort, picnic tables, and some trails along the shore. The park is very popular among picnickers, Frisbee tossers, Portland houseguests, and hand-holding couples, and it's just a skip from Crescent Beach State Park. Hard to beat its prospect of the bay and the open Atlantic.

Fort Williams Park
Shore Road, Cape Elizabeth
(207) 799–2868

If you have houseguests and you live in Greater Portland, chances are you'll all end up here at some point. Surrounding Portland Head Light in Cape Elizabeth, town-owned Fort Williams Park is the go-to place for visitors to the area (the place sees nearly a million visitors a year). Ninety-four acres of fun are what we're talking about, a Frisbee thrower's dream. Expansive lawns, some of the best ocean views in Greater Portland, a small waterfront, neat ruins of forts, perfect picnicking facilities, tennis courts, and ball fields—the park has a lot to like. And more than a million people a year take advantage of it.

Commissioned in 1894, Fort Williams was integral to keeping Portland Harbor safe in the Second World War, but it was deemed unnecessary in the wake of the conflict and was decommissioned in 1963. The town purchased it shortly thereafter. What's left of the actual fortifications are interesting to explore. Hardly a day goes by, year-round, that someone isn't having fun at Fort Williams.

Spring Point Shoreline Walkway
Southern Maine Community College,
Broadway, South Portland

Some of the best looks you'll get at Portland Harbor and Casco Bay can be found along this 3-mile seaside path on the campus of Southern Maine Community College. The trail connects some of the finest things South Portland has to offer. It begins at the Spring Point Ledge Light on one end and ends at Willard Beach on

the other, going through the Spring Point Arboretum and connecting to the South Portland Greenway, from which point you can go just about anywhere. You'll get a self-guided tour of what's left of Fort Preble, see more forts and islands in the bay, and have a great prospect on the Portland skyline. Tourists don't generally find the walkway, but they probably should.

Back Cove Trail
Portland

Not exactly a park, Back Cove Trail is a 3.5-mile, multiuse path that rings the city's Back Cove. Used by hundreds daily for walking, jogging, and biking, it is paved and it offers a great look back at the skyline of the city. Thanks to the good works of Portland Trails (see Close-up), it also connects to other great trail networks. Park in the Forest Avenue Hannaford parking lot.

Baxter Woods
Forest Avenue, Portland

A 30-acre sanctuary between Forest and Stevens Avenues, Baxter Woods was donated to the city by former governor Percival Baxter—the same man who gave the state its wilderness treasure Baxter State Park. This place is no Katahdin, but its short trails are pleasantly shaded by some white oak and hemlock, which are good examples of the Forest City's early forest. A nice place to walk yourself and your dog. Contact Portland Parks and Recreation department (207–874-8793) for more information.

Deering Oaks
Park and Forest Avenues, Portland
(207) 874–8793

Portland's nickname is the Forest City, and the 51 acres of Deering Oaks Park make the name at least a little bit fitting. The city's best-known park, Deering is a classic, and there are more than 1,000 trees on its grounds, including stands of red and white oaks, and three giants—a pin oak, a Siberian elm, and a yellowood—on the state's list of big trees. A swath of green space between the highway and downtown, the park wouldn't be confused with a real forest, composed mostly of wide open lawns. With its grassy spaces, ponds, fountains, and recreation areas, it's the picture of a city park and has been voted best place to recreate many times by the readers of local papers.

And people recreate here en masse. Quite aside from the usual park entertainments of strolling, dog walking, and Frisbee tossing, there are a host of things to do. Eleven tennis courts, several basketball courts, and a ball field beckon to athletes; paddleboats and ducks attract children; there are rose gardens and a Saturday farmers' market to appeal to adults; and there are regularly scheduled events, from weekly concerts to the Deering Oaks Family Festival, that take place here every summer. In winter, of course, there's skating—just ask Denzel Washington and Whitney Houston, who did figure eights in Deering Oaks for the 1996 film *The Preacher's Wife*. But like other city parks, Deering takes a more shadowy cast at night and isn't anywhere you want to be after dark.

Eastern and Western Promenades
Portland

Flanking the Portland Peninsula are two long grassy open spaces—the proms. Both loft up over the city's waterfront, the Eastern Prom offering exceptional views of Casco Bay and its islands and forts and the Western Prom overlooking the Fore River and beyond it the White Mountains. The pair are pleasant to walk, and there are some fine trails along the Eastern Promenade as well as access to Fort Allen Park, another nice place to mosey and relax.

i Get halfway around the 1.5-mile trail that circumnavigates Mackworth Island, and you'll hardly believe you're just outside of Portland. Reached by a causeway off U.S. Route 1, the Falmouth island is a fantastic place to hike and enjoy Casco Bay.

The Western Prom, the street that fronts the green, is rightly famous for its Victorian architecture.

Fore River Sanctuary
Congress Street, Portland

A beautiful spot where the Fore River begins to get marshy, this 85-acre preserve is owned by the Maine Audubon Society (207–781–2330), and it's popular with walkers and birds. Three and a half miles of walking trails meander along an estuary where hawks and warblers and seabirds can often be seen. Another treat is Jewell Falls, an actual waterfall within the city limits, which is something to see. Park at the Maine Orthopaedic Center, where Portland Trails has carved out access.

Gilsland Farm
20 Gilsland Farm Road, Falmouth
(207) 781–2330

It's somewhat surprising to find such a peaceful sanctuary in the town just to the north of the state's largest city, but then these 65 acres are the headquarters of Maine Audubon Society, so it makes a certain amount of sense. Still, 2.5 miles of trails wandering through woods and meadows and along the banks of marshes isn't what you expect scant minutes from downtown Portland. The beauty of the former cow farm is the diversity of habitats—visitors can tromp through fields, explore woods, skirt a pond, and stand on the edge of a salt marsh. There are three primary trails—the West Meadow Trail, a .75-mile loop that goes up onto a rise overlooking the Presumpscot Estuary and offers views of Portland's skyline; the Pond Meadow Trail, which is a little more than half a mile and goes through a hardwood forest, past an apple orchard, to a pond known for its birdlife; and the longest, the North Meadow Trail, which makes a wide, 1.2-mile circuit through fields. Also on-site is the Gilsland Farm Environmental Center, where the society maintains three classrooms, and the Nature Store, where you can pick up those great Audubon field guides. The property is open from dawn to dusk, seven days a week,

Close-up

Portland Trails

Portland Trails at 1 India Street is the best friend a Portland outdoorsperson ever had. A dynamic conservation outfit dedicated to creating greenways in the state's largest urban area, Portland Trails is responsible for many of the best places to walk in the Forest City. The group was founded in 1991, and it picked up where turn-of-the-20th-century urban planners left off. Former mayor James Phinney Baxter had hired the Olmsted brothers, the famed landscape architects, to come up with drawings connecting several of the city's parks with walkways. The project never was finished. Portland Trails is doing the work now.

And what a job they've done. In only a decade they've accomplished 14 miles of greenways, helping to establish a network of 23 trails in town. Ever-popular Back Cove is now linked to a trail along the Eastern Promenade, you can even cross a footbridge over into Falmouth, and they've helped create the trails on the 60-acre Presumpscot Preserve. The Portland map is all green and squiggly with their handiwork. The organization's goal is to create a 30-mile network of trails that allows people to walk clear across the city—and beyond. You can find maps, trail descriptions, plans for the future, and more on the group's Web site, www.trails.org, or call (207) 775–2411.

year-round. The center is open Monday through Saturday from 9:00 A.M. to 5:00 P.M. and Sunday from 1:00 to 4:00 P.M. year-round. Free.

Mill Creek Preserve
Route 88, Falmouth
(207) 729–5181
Along with the neighboring preserve owned by the town of Falmouth, the Nature Conservancy's Mill Creek property protects some 50 acres of marsh on Casco Bay. There are trails on the town side, which make for great hiking through the woods and down to the water. Popular with great blue herons and snowy egrets, the preserve is enjoyed by those people savvy enough to find it. Take State Route 88 past the Falmouth Pumping Station and park in the next parking lot.

Basket Island Preserve
Off Falmouth and Cumberland
(207) 729–5181
Just off Falmouth, this nine-acre isle is owned by the Nature Conservancy, and it's a popular place to visit in summer among the yachting and kayaking crowds. Nice to walk the beaches and check out the remains of an old lighthouse, but leave your sleeping bag at home—it's closed to camping—and be careful with fire, because the island already burned once. You can access it fairly easily by small craft from the Falmouth Town Landing, off Route 88 in Falmouth Foreside.

Pineland Public Reserved Land
Gray Depot Road, Gray
(207) 778–8231
Greater Portland kids were once creeped out by Pineland, which used to be a mental institution in the town of New Gloucester. Combined with the novels of Stephen King, some of which took place not far away in Durham, you had the grist for some preadolescent nightmares. The center closed years ago, and the state subsequently turned the 600 surround-

ing acres into a reserve for outdoor recreation. Thank goodness it did. Three miles of trails explore the old farm pasture and forest along the Royal River here, a refuge for deer, fox, hare, grouse, and a wide variety of other birds, and it's become something of a haven for walkers and hikers, too. A very pleasant place to walk, and not all that scary, either.

Bradbury Mountain State Park
528 Hallowell Road, Pownal
(207) 688–4712

Bradbury Mountain isn't much of a mountain. At 462 feet, it's really a tall hill, and you can practically run up to its summit. But the little peak here, set between Lewiston and Portland and a skip from Freeport, has a truly great panorama at its top. Look in one direction and you can take in the distant seas of Casco Bay, turn in another and enjoy a look at the White Mountains of New Hampshire. For the amount of effort you expend getting to the top—the trail is less than a half mile—the vistas are incredible.

The park in which the mountain sits is a 590-acre gem, one of Maine's original state parks, founded in 1939. Forty-one bosky sites await campers; there are ball fields and a playground for kids, picnic sites and shelters that often cater to large groups of families and friends, and even trails open to riders of horses and mountain bikes. Fall is an especially good time to pay the park a visit, when the leaves are radiant and hawks are migrating, but it's always a good diversion from the crowded streets of Freeport. Bradbury Mountain State Park is open all year, 9:00 A.M. to sunset.

Mast Landing Sanctuary
Upper Mast Landing Road, Freeport
(207) 781–2330
www.maineaudubon.org

An Audubon sanctuary, this 140-acre refuge is popular with walkers and nature lovers. There are 3.5 miles of trails that thread through open fields, apple orchards, hemlock forest, and alder lowlands, and Mill Stream pours over an old dam and mill site. The preserve was so named because the Royal Navy used to use it as a source for its ship masts. Today you'll find few mast agents but a lot of songbirds and, if you visit in summer, a lot of schoolkids, who go to a day camp here. Open sunrise to sunset.

Wolfe's Neck Woods State Park
425 Wolfe's Neck Road, Freeport
(207) 865–4465

One of the best-kept secrets in Freeport, Wolfe's Neck Woods is a marked departure from the retail madness of Bow and Main Streets downtown, and relatively few of the town's visitors ever find it. A forested preserve of 230 acres overlooking Casco Bay, the park is a fine mix of woods and water, with tide pools and salt marsh and estuaries. Five miles of trails—try the Casco Bay or Small Bog Trails—explore the beautiful meeting of sea and shore, along both the bay and the Harraseeket River, and interpretive signposts at various points clue you in on what you're seeing. Nearby Googins, Eagle, and Cousins Islands can be spotted, and there is an active osprey colony on Googins that's fun to scope out. Bird-watchers often search for seabirds here, and it's popular among families and picnickers.

Given to the state by Mr. and Mrs. Lawrence Smith of Freeport in 1969, Wolfe's Neck is an exceptional spot to take a breather from the retail madness this town is known for. Bring a picnic or pick up some seafood at Harraseeket Lobster Pound in South Freeport, and then enjoy the smell of the sea and the pine. Rangers run a variety of workshops and programs here during the summer as well. Officially open from April through October, the park allows skiing and snowshoeing in the winter.

Midcoast

Androscoggin River Bicycle Path
Water Street to Cooks Corner, Brunswick

When this 2.5-mile paved walkway was opened in 1998, town officials had no idea that it would be so successful. Right along the

Androscoggin River, the path enjoyed heavy use from the outset and became a national model for other community paths. People use it to commute to and from work, to walk or jog, to sit on the benches and scan the skies for eagles, or even to, yes, bicycle. Fourteen feet wide, it's perfect for that. You can hop on at Water Street or Grover Lane.

Boothbay Region Land Trust Preserves
Boothbay Area
(207) 633–4818

It can be hard to find just a moment of qui-etude in Boothbay Harbor in summer, when the community is swarming with people. There are a handful of nature preserves, though, where you can enjoy a bit of peace among the madness. Six refuges are available on the mainland—there are a couple offshore as well—and they protect some 700 acres of prime real estate. Each has its own character, and all are within 10 miles of the busy harbor. The Ovens Mouth Preserve is the biggest at 150 acres, spread across three peninsulas where the Cross River meets the Back River, and you can look out at tidal coves and salt marshes from its network of trails. The Linekin Preserve is also on a river, the Damariscotta, and is home to 2.5 miles of trails. There's a small beach on the Sheepscot River at the Porter Preserve. The Kitzi Colby Wildlife Pre-serve, once the site of both saltworks and ice-works, is now a great birding area, thanks to its marsh habitat. You can pick up a map with information about all the preserves at the chamber or call the land trust and they'll hook you up.

Hamilton Sanctuary
Fosters Point Road, West Bath
(207) 781–2330
www.maineaudubon.org

These 74 acres were given to Maine Audubon by local resident Millicent Hamilton. A 1.5-mile system of trails explores the peninsula on which the sanctuary sits, surrounded by the New Meadows River. These paths will take you across meadows, through a pine forest, past a

former ice pond, and out to the river, known for its populations of ospreys, blue herons, snowy egrets, and horseshoe crabs. Open all year from sunrise to sunset.

Josephine Newman Sanctuary
Route 127, Woolwich
(207) 781–2330
www.maineaudubon.org

Twenty interpretive signs lead you along 2 miles of trails through this 119-acre preserve, pointing out all of the natural features you pass, from glacial erratics to reversing falls. A mature mixed forest covers much of the prop-erty, but you'll also find a beaver pond, brooks, a cattail marsh, and the tidal shore of Robin-hood Cove. A booklet called *Forest, Fields, and Estuaries* will inform your self-guided hike if you pick up a copy ahead of time. Contact Maine Audubon. Open year-round, from sun-rise to sunset.

Montsweag Preserve
Montsweag Road, Woolwich
(207) 729–5181

On the shore of Montsweag Brook, this nifty 45-acre preserve is owned by the Nature Con-servancy. A 1.5-mile loop trail wanders through the rectangular property, which begins as meadows and ends as waterfront on the brook, skirting a large salt marsh in the interior. Very pleasant walking and often nice waterfowl watching at the water's edge. Open from sunrise to sunset.

Robert P. Tristram Coffin Wildflower Sanctuary
Route 128, Woolwich

Known by hardly a soul, this 180-acre preserve owned by the New England Wildflower Society is a wonderland filled with 200 species of flow-ers, grasses, trees, and shrubs. The sanctuary was named in honor of the Brunswick-born poet, who won a Pulitzer for his 1936 book *Strange Holiness*. Quite aside from the pretty flowers, the preserve features some nice walk-ing in cobbled coves and hemlock stands.

Hiking trails abound on Hog Island. LISA MOSSEL VIETZE

Damariscotta Lake State Park
8 State Park Road, Jefferson
(207) 549–7600 or (207) 941–4014 off-season
Sand beaches come in many shapes and sizes in Maine. This fine little strand isn't a salty one on the coast in Damariscotta; rather, it's on the very long lake of the same name. Drive State Route 213 inland to the neat village of Jefferson, and you'll find the big brown state park sign marking the entrance. The park itself is tiny—only 17 acres—but it's very popular, especially with families. The swimming is good in the cul-de-sac of a lake, lifeguards are on duty to look after bathers, there are picnic tables and grills set up for après-dip dogs and burgers, and a field and playground provide a place for the kids to romp. Good, basic summer fun.

Damariscotta River Association
109–110 Belvedere Road, Damariscotta
(207) 563–1393
www.draclt.org
Founded in 1973, this little conservation organization has done a fantastic job helping to preserve the finest parcels of open space in the Damariscotta area, and it now manages more than 2,000 acres and 18 miles of shoreline. Many people have heard of the Damariscotta Shell Middens, big heaps of oyster shells discarded centuries ago by natives on holiday, but few have visited them. Step along on the Salt Bay Heritage Trail, and soon you'll find yourself staring up at them. Even if you have no interest in archaeology, the trail, which begins across from the Lincoln County Publishing Building, a skip from the Damariscotta exit off Route 1, is a beautiful 3-mile walk that skirts photogenic Great Salt Bay. On the other side of the bay is the Salt Bay Farm Heritage Center, a pretty old farm on Belvedere Road that serves as the River Association's headquarters, and there are miles of trails through the surrounding 100 acres of hills and meadows and down to the river behind it. It's open from dawn to dusk. Finally, off of old Route 1, just up the road from Hannaford, is the Whaleback Park,

another great walk through eight acres of wide-open fields and down by the water.

Dodge Point Public Reserved Land
River Road, Newcastle
(207) 778–8231
The state acquired these 521 acres on the Damariscotta River in 1989, and people have been flocking to Dodge Point ever since. Why? The Damariscotta is a very scenic, wide saltwater river, and this piece of property has more than a mile of frontage. A few trails and an old woods road go here and there on lands that used to be an old tree farm, and they make good use of the river and its pocket beaches. Also of interest are a freshwater pond and a variety of habitats for wildlife watching. Mostly used by locals for quiet walks or jogs, the site is worth a visit. Open from dawn to dusk.

Audubon Camp at Hog Island
11 Audubon Road, Bremen
(207) 781–2330
www.maineaudubon.org
Ever wanted to go to summer camp? If you have—and you enjoy the natural world—you might consider spending a week on Hog Island, an Audubon camp a quarter mile off Bremen in Muscongus Bay. Every summer the environmental organization sponsors a variety of workshops on its cool campus on the 330-acre island. You stay in an old cottage-style dorm and spend your time in the field studying whatever it is you signed up for. (Classes might include birding, drawing with nature, natural history of the Maine coast, or naturalizing by kayak.) At night you eat together in the rustic dining hall. Every week there are excursions to puffin outposts and special treats like slide shows and a lobster bake. Great fun, and you might actually learn something.

Rachel Carson Salt Pond and
La Verna Preserves
State Route 32 New Harbor, Bristol
(207) 729–5181
These two Nature Conservancy properties

protect 189 acres along Muscongus Bay. The Carson preserve is where the famed environmental author did some of the research for her book *The Edge of the Sea*. Tides leave much of the quarter-acre pond exposed, making for some of the best tide-pool hopping in the state. Seaweed here is slick, of course, and it's best to leave those who live in the area (the shells, mussels, crabs, periwinkles, starfish, sea urchins, and other creatures) in their native habitat. La Verna lies about 2 miles north, 119 acres along the bay. Woods, marshes, a tamarack swamp, and old cellar holes are what you'll find here, as well as some nice saltwater vistas when you reach the shore. A trail bisects the parcel.

Weskeag Marsh
Buttermilk Road, South Thomaston
Birders in particular like this smallish salt marsh on the Weskeag River, because it attracts a whole lot of migrating waterfowl and shorebirds, among them teal, wigeon, ruddy turnstones, pintail, harriers, and killdeers. You'll find the dirt parking lot off Buttermilk Road, which is in turn off Route 1 not far from Dragon Cement.

Camden Hills State Park
Route 1, Camden
(207) 236–3109 or (207) 236–0849
off-season
Mount Battie and Mount Megunticook provide the dramatic green backdrop for the town of Camden, and they also serve as the tall centerpieces of Camden Hills State Park, a green playground on Penobscot Bay. Both are fairly easy climbs, topping out at 1,380 feet, and the views from their summits seem never to end—downtown Camden, all white steeples and brick, is tiny down below, and the blue waters of Penobscot Bay wash to the horizon, interrupted by the black-green of several islands. A road scales Mount Battie, so you don't even have to sweat to take in the prospect, but it's preferable to walk through the forest.

Some visitors are surprised to learn that

there are 30 miles of trails within the park—it's deceptively large, stretching inland behind the mountains for a few miles into neighboring Lincolnville. One of the best climbs is little-known Bald Rock Mountain, an 1,100-footer that is reached via Youngtown Road in Lincolnville (you'll see the parking lot). It's always a pleasant hike, beginning as an old logging road and becoming a narrow trail at the summit. And surprisingly few people discover the fine picnic area right across the street from the main section of park. A mix of woods, grass, and looping roads, it slopes down toward the bay, providing some good ganders.

The 107 campsites at Camden Hills accommodate RVs as well as tents, and they're always busy. Motorists zipping up the coast often can see people grilling outside their behemoth mobile homes from Route 1. These sites are like the rest in the state park system, with fire rings and picnic tables, but the park does have flush toilets and hot showers.

The sites are only $20 ($15 for residents), and, if you can handle hustle and bustle and the sound of cars passing by on Route 1, they're the best deal going for an overnight in busy Camden. They also make for a good place to rest your head if you're interested in other area outdoor pursuits—like hiking the exceptional Georges Highland Path, rock climbing on Maiden Cliff, or kayaking out on Penobscot Bay. Open from May 15 through October 15. Admission is $3.00 for adults.

Lane's Island Preserve
Vinalhaven
(207) 729–5181
Forty-five acres of wide-open windswept moors, surrounded by rocks and beach, are what you'll find at this astonishingly beautiful isle off Vinalhaven. Because it was used for sheep pasture for ages, it's got an almost British Isles quality to it, grand and sweeping and romantic. All sorts of birdies favor the spot—including ospreys, great blue herons, spotted and least sandpipers, merlins, kestrels, and marsh hawks. Rough trails criss-

cross the entire island, and you can peek at the small cemetery, where generations of Lanes have been buried. Whether you just want a walk—it's 15 minutes or so from the ferry landing on Vinalhaven—to bird-watch, or to spend some time on the edge of the sea, it's a small paradise.

Georges Highland Path
Route 17, Rockport
(207) 594–5166
www.grlt.org

A few years ago Rockland-based Georges River Land Trust (207–594–5166) began to make deals with landowners to allow public access to many of the Camden Hills. Up until that point, most of these picturesque peaks—and there are dozens trundling inland from the coast—were off limits to hikers. Not anymore. Dedicated to preserving the rural heritage of the St. George River Valley, along which many of these peaks lie, the ambitious conservation organization has opened more than 30 miles of trail along some of the finest acreage in the Midcoast. Ultimately the group hopes to establish a trail that runs the length of the St. George watershed, from Frye Mountain in Montville to the coast at Thomaston, and it's making good progress.

None of the hills of the Highland Path are particularly high—Camden's Ragged Mountain is probably the tallest at 1,300 feet—but because they lord over the coast, the river, lakes, and bucolic countryside, they provide some astonishingly good views. Trails now climb Bald Peak and Ragged Mountain in Camden, as well as Pleasant and Spruce Mountains in Rockport and Warren, and they are all exceedingly pleasant hikes. Some are more rugged than others. The Georges River Land Trust has also been quietly building preserves all over the Camden-Rockport-Lincolnville area. Pick up a map at the trailhead and parking area on State Route 17 in Rockport on Mirror Lake.

Fernald's Neck
Fire Road 50, Lincolnville
(207) 729–5181

Locals don't want you to know about this fine little preserve off State Route 52. Managed by the Nature Conservancy, the Neck is a long peninsula that fingers out into the middle of Lake Megunticook, and it's topped by a beautiful pine forest. The conservancy owns 315 acres of it, and walking paths wander through the trees, across meadows, and along 60-foot cliffs above the water. They skirt more than 3 miles of undeveloped shoreline. Once a part of a private farm, the preserve is a mix of habitats that appeal to deer, moose, all manner of small animals—and people. Maps are available in a kiosk at the outset. Open from dusk to dawn.

Tanglewood 4-H Camp
1 Tanglewood Road, Lincolnville
(207) 789–5868

On the pretty, salmon-laden Ducktrap River, Tanglewood is busy with campers all summer long. In winter, though, the 830-acre woodland is a cross-country skier's dream—a free-to-use, virtually groomed, well-marked, and very beautiful 10-mile system of woods trails. So many skiers use it that you never have to break trail yourself, yet it's never so busy you feel overwhelmed. It's just perfect.

Warren Island State Park
P.O. Box 105, Lincolnville 04849
(207) 941–4014

The state describes an overnight at its 70-acre Warren Island park as "Robinson Crusoe-esque," and if Crusoe had a nice log lean-to to retire to at night, docks and moorings for his getaway boat, and fresh drinking water, then it might be something like it. One of the best of the campgrounds in the state park system, Warren Island is a fantastic retreat for a serene stay on a wild isle, and because you need your own boat to get there, it's quieter than most parks. Ten campsites and two Adirondack-style shelters provide the accommodations, and the sea and spruce island is wide open for

ℹ️ Mainers have always been leaders in reusing and recycling—Yankee ingenuity, ya know—and the rails-to-trails phenomenon is a fine example of this. Local outdoors and conservations groups have taken old and unused trailbeds and turned them into great hiking and biking paths. Many of these are in the northern parts of the state, but several are up and running along the coast. Details can be found at http://members.fortunecity.com/railtrails/ME/index.htm.

exploration. The much larger isle of Islesboro is only a quarter mile away, and camping here allows you to get over there for a look-see without shelling out large dollars for one of Islesboro's fancy inns. (Camping is $19 a night.) You can easily reach Warren Island via canoe or kayak from Islesboro, so one idea is to take the ferry over to the big island and make the easy paddle from there. It's so simple, you won't need Man Friday.

Frye Mountain State Game Management Area
State Route 137, Montville

This 5,111-acre game preserve is better known to snowmobilers than hikers, but it shouldn't be. Astride the Knox-Montville town line in rural Waldo County, it is only 20 minutes away from Belfast but feels a world apart from the racket of Route 1. The area was once home to a farming community, which followed better times elsewhere, and it has sort of a ghost town vibe, especially when you stumble on old cemeteries and cellar holes. What most people come for, though, are the vistas from atop Frye Mountain, a small peak that offers a commanding look at the surrounding hills and valleys. A fire tower sits at the summit, and it lofts you up good and high to take in the scene. The setting is great for a picnic, and it's a pretty easy climb, too, because drivable old tote roads take you very close to the top. After your ascent, take time to walk the fields and meadows that meander all over the preserve.

Moose Point State Park
310 West Main Street, Searsport
(207) 548–2882 or (207) 941–4014, off-season

Believe it or not, moose are occasionally spotted along Route 1 in the vicinity of Moose Point. Not often, but sometimes. This small park on the coast between Belfast and Searsport isn't exactly known for its large population of bullwinkles—they tend to habitate much farther north—but they've been seen in the area enough times for the DOT to install moose crossing signs. (Maybe those are just there to inspire people to stop at the park?)

What people really come to this 183-acre parcel for—those savvy enough to find it, anyway—is its Penobscot Bay panorama. The views are drop-dead gorgeous from the grassy lawns that comprise much of the park, and they're even better from the short hiking trail that meanders through a pine grove along the bay's edge. Looking out you can see the northern end of Islesboro, the mountains of Acadia, and the town of Castine, 6 or 7 miles away across the water. Tide pools and rocks are the more immediate focus, and they are fun to explore, too.

The facilities are limited to a few picnic tables and outhouses, but the fields are big enough for a group to gather on, or to host a ball game, and they're plenty pleasant to picnic upon or simply stroll. Visitors who need to stretch their legs for a while on their drive up to Acadia would be foolish not to stop here.

Lake St. George State Park
State Route 3, Liberty
(207) 589–4255

Another great swimming lake not too far inland from the coast, Lake St. George can get busy on a warm day. The water here is on the coolish side compared to other lakes, since it's spring fed, but that doesn't stop people from splishing and splashing under the watchful eyes of lifeguards. The 360-acre park is about halfway between Belfast and Augusta, 19 miles from the Penobscot Bay city, and it's well worth the trip out.

The grounds were once a pretty farm, and the old homestead and some barns are used by the rangers. There are 38 campsites—many of them right on the shore of the 1,017-acre lake—with hot showers, and flush toilets, to boot. The sites can fill up quickly with locals, who like to swim and fish and use the boat launch and play areas here. The only drawback to camping is the proximity of Route 3, the primary thoroughfare between Belfast and the capital, and cars and big trucks whiz by at all hours. Across the street from the lake is the bulk of the park's property, and there are some hiking trails that thread through the woods. The park's open from May 15 through September.

Swan Lake State Park
100 West Park Lane, Swanville
(207) 525–4404 or (207) 941–4014 off-season

Swanville is not Maine's prettiest town, and Swan Lake is not the state's most attractive lake, but somehow Swan Lake State Park manages to transcend its surroundings. It's a fine little park—and little it is at just 67 acres. Located 6 miles north of Belfast at the north end of Swan Lake, it is far enough away from the overdeveloped sections of waterfront and the depressing hovels on the roads on either side of the lake.

The focus here is on swimming and picnicking, and there are changing areas and lifeguards for the former and grills and tables for the latter. The bathing area is a sandy horseshoe backed up to a section of woods. Groups will also find a large shelter for gatherings as well as facilities for volleyball and other family-reunion-type games. The park's open from Memorial Day through Labor Day, 9:00 A.M. to sunset.

Holbrook Island Sanctuary
172 Indian Bar Road, Harborside
(207) 326–4012

Cape Rosier could hardly be more beautiful, sticking out into the island-studded expanse of Penobscot Bay—and then you find Holbrook Island Sanctuary. The state owns just over 1,000 acres in Brooksville, looking out at the island the preserve's named after, and it's a fine meeting place of sea and shore. The sanctuary itself protects an array of ecosystems, from woods to marsh to meadows, and all the wildlife that live in such places. And the views of the bay are never ending. There are facilities for launching canoes and kayaks, trails for hiking, perfect picnic grounds, and all the makings of a great afternoon.

Crockett Cove Woods Preserve
Off Whitman Road, Stonington
(207) 729–5181

This sanctuary covers 100 acres of lush woods—fog forest, as Mainers call it—and four trails wind through it past a wide variety of lichens and mosses. The area is covered with spruce and fir and is rich with birdlife. You'll find tree beard lichen draping many trees and tamarack and cedar in the wet areas toward the middle of the preserve. The Nature Conservancy owns the property, and a brochure describing what you'll see is available at the trailhead. Open from sunup to sundown.

Lamoine State Park
23 State Park Road, Ellsworth
(207) 667–4778 or (207) 941–4014 off-season

People clamor to get into the campgrounds of Acadia National Park and the private camping areas in Bar Harbor, going a little crazy to pack themselves in, while Lamoine State Park, about a half hour away under the same mountains and on the same sea, often has empty spaces in the evening. The savvy few who make it to these 55 acres in Lamoine have it good.

This is the sort of campground you won't find near the state's only national park. First off, it has fantastic views of the park's peaks, out across the glistening waters of Frenchman Bay, something you can't see when you're right underneath them at Seawall or Blackwoods. Lamoine is not usually overcrowded, there's a pebble beach, and, perhaps best of all, it's quiet and even has a sense of privacy, which are rare in Bar Harbor in summer. So the park definitely rewards those who seek it out.

Most people miss Lamoine because they stick to Route 3 en route to Bar Harbor. Jog left in Ellsworth onto State Route 184, follow signs, and you'll end up on a seahorse-shaped peninsula that juts into Eastern Bay, an arm of Frenchman. Sixty-one sites are congregated here on the shores of the bay, and they have pleasant woods buffers between them. Accommodating both RVs and tents, they are simple spots with picnic tables and fire rings, but the campground also sports hot showers and flush johns. Anglers like the park's pier, boaters appreciate the boat launch, and nearby is Lamoine Beach, a popular swimming area, so there's plenty to do right here. Most people, though, use the park as a launching pad to explore Acadia, and it's perfectly suited for that. Lamoine State Park is open from mid-May through mid-October.

Acadia Area

Indian Point–Blagden Preserve
Off Indian Point Road, Bar Harbor
(207) 729–5181
Another Nature Conservancy property, this 110-acre parcel protects stands of trees that escaped the great fire of 1947, and it includes 1,000 feet of frontage on Western Bay. There is a seal haul-out just off the northwestern corner of the preserve, and you can watch them from the shore (be respectful). Paths thread through the sanctuary. Trail brochures and bird-watching checklists—you could see black-backed three-toed woodpeckers, ruby-crowned kinglets, and boreal chickadees—are available at the caretaker's house. Open from sunup to 6:00 P.M. year-round.

Down East

Donnell Pond Public Reserve
T10 SD, between Franklin and Cherryfield
(207) 827–1818
Donnell Pond has a reputation as being a party zone, a place where kids—and many adults,

too—go to drink, boat, and camp. And it is that. But this wild swath of public reserve land 12 miles east of Ellsworth covers more than 15,000 acres, and much of it is woods, so there's plenty to enjoy away from the yahoos on the lake. In fact, the state owns frontage on Tunk and Spring River Lakes as well, and most of Schoodic, Black, and Caribou Mountains. The landscape here feels almost like the North Woods, rugged, piney, largely undeveloped. Not to be confused with the Acadia property of the same name, Schoodic offers enviable vistas of the mountains of Acadia and is accessed by old logging roads and a trail. Those grown-over tote roads wander here or there, making for easy hiking, and a network of trails climbs Black Mountain, which is a little over 1,000 feet. Primitive campsites are available on all of the bodies of water.

Maine Coastal Islands National Wildlife Refuge
P.O. Box 279, Milbridge 04658
(207) 546–2124
www.fws.gov/northeast/mainecoastal/
This sprawling "refuge" is actually a series of preserves, as it contains more than 47 islands as well as three mainland pieces. Intended as wildlife habitat first—and in this case that largely means birds—the refuge formerly known as Petit Manan has some nice hiking trails on its lands, especially at Petit Manan Point in Steuben. The best of these paths might be the Holingsworth Trail, a 1.5-mile loop through woods, across meadows, and down to cobbled beaches, with interpretive signs that fill you in on what it is you're looking at. The signs won't tell you what animals you'll see, but a wide variety of critters might be about as well. The preserve is open from sunup to sundown.

Great Heath Public Reserved Land
Columbia
(207) 827–1818
The Great Heath is one of the many wonders of Maine's natural world—it's the largest raised bog in the state at 6,000-some acres and

seems like remotest Africa at points. Scruffy, flat, desolate, it occupies a huge chunk of land along the Pleasant River in Hancock County and is unlike anything else around. The state owns most of the territory here, but there are no facilities to speak of, and it's primarily of interest to canoeists, bird-watchers, and, well, heath lovers. Myriad birds, bears, moose, and beavers, who'll splash at your canoe with their tails, are frequently found here, and its flat water is easy and fun to paddle. Bring a map, though, or you'll never find the place. It's located on unmarked dirt roads in blueberrying country and requires a bit of cartography to locate. But it's worth it for sheer uniqueness and excellent canoeing.

Great Wass Island
State Route 187, Beals
(207) 729–5181
Yet another Nature Conservancy property, Great Wass is the largest island in an archipelago at Beals, south of Jonesport, and it's known for a couple of things: birds and wildflowers. There are some 104 species of the former, including spruce grouse, boreal chickadees, barred owls, and blackpolls, warblers that nest in the peat lands and coniferous forest. As for flowers, there are many varieties, which turn the island into a riot of color in spring and early summer. All told the preserve sprawls for about 1,600 acres, and there are a couple of popular trails that cover about 5 miles of fairly rugged terrain. The hiking can get a bit squishy after a rain.

Rocky Lake Public Reserved Land
State Route 191, T18 ED BPP
(207) 827–1818
The East Machias River has long been a favorite canoeing and fishing spot among Down East outdoorsfolk, and some years back, the state obligingly purchased 11,000 acres around the river and its neighboring lakes, ponds, and streams. It's another public reserve prize, a big wildland full of prime canoeing, camping, fishing, and exploring opportunities. You'll hardly guess that you're

just 10 miles from Route 1 and downtown Machias—it feels a world away. Facilities are limited to a handful of boat launches and some primitive campsites.

Cutler Coast Public Reserved Land
Route 191, Cutler
(207) 827–1818
Though it's a much quieter place than the rest of Maine, the Bold Coast of Washington County is still fairly well settled along the shore. Large tracts of undeveloped land are increasingly rare. But there is one stretch of wild woods that traces cliffs for close to 5 miles that was preserved by the state and turned into a public land. The parcel is one of the largest undeveloped expanses remaining on the East Coast.

You'll find it hard to believe that the Cutler Coast Unit isn't crawling with people when you stand atop one of its high cliffs overlooking Grand Manan Channel with the picture-perfect isles of the Canadian Maritimes floating offshore. A loop trail cuts across the roughly rectangular, 12,000-acre parcel and then follows the shore for more than 4 miles, hugging the cliffs, climbing through forests of spruce and fir, meandering through meadows, and passing all sorts of secret pocket beaches that you'll vow to return to. At the far end of the unit are three primitive campsites on headlands overlooking the sea. The views are truly spectacular.

Shackford Head State Park
Route 190, Eastport
(207) 941–4014
Shackford Head is a state park just like Reid or Popham or Sebago Lake, but you'd never know it. In fact, you'd probably never find it, unless you got directions from a kindly Washington County resident. A 90-acre green spot on Moose Island at the far right-hand corner of Maine, the tall headland lifts you up to fantastic views over Eastport after a simple 1-mile walk. But hardly anyone outside of Eastport knows it's there. The park is tucked away behind the "Boat School" (aka Washington

County Technical College) on the edges of the attractive old burgh in a neighborhood where you wouldn't think to go looking for natural wonders. There it is, though, a woodsy nub with a fantastic prospect, overlooking Cobscook Bay, Lubec, and Campobello. There isn't much to the place beyond the hill, the woods, and the trails up the mountain and along the shore, but that's all you need. The hike up the headland is easy, and the vista will knock you out—you can see right out into the salmon pens for which this part of Maine is famous. The trail to the shore is a little more challenging—you have to time it right with the tides—but is equally rewarding. Nice autumn fare, and you'll most likely have it all to yourself.

Moosehorn National Wildlife Refuge
R.R. 1, Box 202, Baring 04694
(207) 454–7161
http://moosehorn.fws.gov

Someone once likened a visit to this U.S. Fish and Wildlife property to going on a Down East safari. The 23,000 acres here are prime country for moose, bear, coyote, and all manner of birdlife, from impressive eagles to twittering woodcocks to cute and charismatic gray jays. The preserve is the easternmost national refuge on the Atlantic Flyway, and more than 220 species of birds have been identified on its grounds. Moosehorn is divided into two sections, or units. The largest part is a 17,000-plus-acre stretch of dense woods near Calais. The other is a 7,200-acre parcel on Cobscook Bay. Both make for fine exploring. More than 50 miles of roads and trails crisscross through these refuges, and maps are available at the preserve's headquarters on the Charlotte Road in Baring. Most of the reserve can be accessed by automobile, unfortunately, but there are wilderness sections. For easy hiking try the 1.25-mile Habitat Trail, which is an interpretive walk through woods that starts near the headquarters. When venturing into the backcountry, be sure to bring a map, compass, and plenty of food, water, and clothing. The refuge is open daily, year-round, from dawn to dusk.

Cobscook Bay State Park
R.R. 1, Box 127, Dennysville
(207) 726–4412

That people cram themselves into camping areas at Acadia and Sebago Lake is hard to understand when you visit this spacious Down East gem. Word is getting out about the myriad delights of Cobscook Bay State Park, especially among kayakers, but it is still far less traveled than parks in the Midcoast and in York and Cumberland Counties. You can still get a reservation on a whim for the 106 sites here, even in the summer, which is unheard of in points south, and for a good site, no less.

Just about all the sites at Cobscook are good. The park sprawls for 888 acres across a peninsula on the shore of the bay, and the camping area is ringed by the brine. Many sites are a skip from the water—so close, in fact, that campers arriving late at night have awoken to find salt water lapping at their tents. (The tides swing 24 feet here.) There's plenty of space at each site, and a nice buffer of spruce forest between them—Cobscook's famous for its privacy. Tenters have their pick in one area, RVs in another, and walk-in sites allow for real quietude. Kayakers like to push off right from their bivouacs, but there are proper boat launching sites. Swimming is not allowed, thanks to the undertows caused by the huge tidal rotation.

Hot showers, a wealth of birdlife in the park and next door at Moosehorn National Wildlife Refuge (200 species have been spotted in these parts), meadows of wildflowers, digging for clams, and a great launching pad for explorations of Eastport, Lubec, Machias, the rest of Washington County, and Canada, too—what more could anyone want in a park? Open from mid-May through mid-October.

Lubec Flats
South Lubec Road, Lubec

On the northern side of West Quoddy Head, this is a great spot to see birds getting ready to make their long-distance flight across North America. Visit in the fall, and you'll see a wide variety of shorebirds preparing to head out, including black-bellied and semipalmated plovers, dunlins, greater and lesser yellowlegs, and red knots.

Quoddy Head State Park
Box 1490, Lubec
(207) 733–0911 or (207) 941–4014 off-season

West Quoddy Head Light is the biggest attraction at this, the nation's most easterly state park, but nature lovers know that the real treats here are the soaring cliffs and jutting headlands overlooking the Bay of Fundy and Grand Manan Island. Grand is the word. The lighthouse located just outside the park's grounds is nice and all, in a tall, red-and-white-striped kind of way, but the shoreline that it protects is nothing short of astonishing. Rising above the highest tides in the country, these cliffs approach 100 feet tall, lording over waters often frequented by spouting whales.

A trail wanders along the cliffs for close to 2 miles, occasionally letting out onto rocky ledges that are great for tide pooling or simply watching the crashing surf and the seabirds. The going is of moderate difficulty, climbing and falling through a dense, pleasantly scented pine forest, and benches are set at the outset of the walk and at a few places here and there along it. A little over a half mile from the outset is Gulliver's Hole, a frothy sea pocket that's worth checking out. All told, there are 4.5 miles of trails, including a board-walk that leads inland to a mossy bog, where there are signs identifying this heath and that fern. Fun to peruse, it's a National Natural Landmark.

Near the light, there are picnic tables where you can enjoy a fine spread before a world-class backdrop. But you want to get out on that trail—the nice thing is, relatively few people make it more than a few hundred feet down it, so you'll have it all to yourself. The park is officially open from May 15 through October 15 but allows snowshoers and nature walkers in the winter, too.

PUBLIC GARDENS AND LANDSCAPE ART

Gardeners in Maine take to planting flowers like sunbathers take to the beach because they know their time is short. The results are show gardens up and down the coast. There are so many noteworthy garden and land-scape sites in the state that the Maine Department of Agriculture decided to put together a map and tour of horticultural hot spots. Get your copy by calling (800) 782–6497. Here are several landmark landscapes sure to appeal to green thumbs—and anyone else who appreciates beauty. Admission is free unless otherwise stated.

South Coast

Hamilton House
Vaughn's Lane, South Berwick
(207) 384–2454

One of the state's best-known historic homes, this 1785 manse has a colonial revival garden that reportedly dates back to 1898. It was renovated in the late 1990s and is something to see. Walking trails thread through 35 acres of attractive grounds here (not all garden, of course), and they overlook the pretty Salmon Falls River. Admission is $8.00 and includes house and grounds.

Hartley Mason Estate
112 Main Street, Kennebunk
(207) 985–2173

This children's garden—including a touch-and-sniff section as well as flowers and herbs—was designed by the Seacoast Garden Club, and it has won some awards. *Whimsy* is the word.

St. Anthony's Shrine and Franciscan Monastery
Beach Avenue, Kennebunk
(207) 967–2011

What a nice place to be a monk. The grounds here were designed by the Olmsted brothers, famous landscape architects of the early 20th century who did a lot of work in Maine, and it's become known for its rhododendrons. A walking path explores the 25 acres here, and includes a boardwalk and a pavilion on the Kennebunk River.

Sanford Parks
Main Street, Sanford
(207) 324–9130
Not usually considered the state's most picturesque community, this mill town nonetheless has two parks designed by famed Boston landscape architect Arthur Schurcliff in the 1930s: Gowen Memorial Park, where you'll find a cool stone gazebo, and Central Park, where there's a statue of one of the men who built this town, mill owner Thomas Goodall.

Greater Portland

Spring Point Arboretum
Southern Maine Technical College, South Portland
(207) 767–7670
It's hard to concentrate on the trees at this one-acre arboretum thanks to the magnificent views of Casco Bay that sit just beyond them. Planted by the city of South Portland in 1981, the tree garden features 70 species of trees, shrubs, vines, and groundcovers, and there are little interpretive signs telling you what you're looking at. The Spring Point Walkway connects, making for a surprisingly fine afternoon.

Evergreen Cemetery
672 Stevens Avenue, Portland
(207) 874–8300
A National Register of Historic Places green space in Portland, this 300-acre park was laid out in 1854, and it's very popular with strollers and joggers. Quite aside from being a nice place to take the dog, it is pleasantly landscaped.

Longfellow Arboretum
Payson Park, Portland
If you're curious what trees don't grow in Maine, visit this three-acre park in the Forest City—it was planted in 1976 and includes species not native to the state. The Longfellow

Garden Club established the green with the help of the City of Portland.

Post Office Park
Corner of Exchange and Middle Streets, Portland
(207) 874–8300
Postage-stamp park might have been a better name for this in-town square. Trees and shrubs native to the state of Maine were planted here on the site of the city's first post office, and they are joined by a boulder display representing the Calendar Islands of Casco Bay. You can hang out with the exhausted shoppers, soapbox speakers, and punk rockers while you take it all in.

Wadsworth–Longfellow House Gardens
489 Congress Street, Portland
(207) 774–1822
While the gardens here at the boyhood home of the great American poet Henry Wadsworth Longfellow (you remember him from English class, right?) are pleasant, the opportunity to find a moment's quiet and sit in the middle of downtown Portland is almost as fine. This green space went in in the 1920s, and the city continued to grow up around it.

Harrington House
45 Main Street, Freeport
(207) 865–3170
This circa 1830 Federal is the home of the local historical society's gift shop, which is particularly well done. But so are the gardens of antique roses and perennials to be found outside it.

Pettengill Farm Gardens
45 Main Street, Freeport
(207) 865–3170
Historic wild roses, lilacs, old-fashioned perennials, and cedars are among the draws at this 1810 saltbox in the state's famous outlet village. Antique apple orchards, woods, and salt marshes sit on the 140 acres here, which border the Harraseeket River and are run by the local historical society.

Tidebrook Conservation Trust
38 Bartol Island Road, Freeport
(207) 865–3856
A 45-acre conservation easement has allowed the gardens here to grow undisturbed, and the old orchards bloom with wildflowers, native and ornamental flowering shrubs, and the plantings of a more formal garden.

Midcoast

Heather Garden at Walker Art Building
Bowdoin College, Brunswick
(207) 725–3000
This museum should be visited more often than it is, and the same might be said of the heath and heather gardens that sit outside it.

City Park
Summer Street, Bath
(207) 443–5143
A William Zorach sculpture might have been the most talked-about element of this five-acre park—it was the source of controversy in the 1960s—but the Victorian landscaping, pond, and fountain are certainly worthy of note, too. It's a nice place to sit or stroll.

Nickels-Sortwell House
Route 1, Wiscasset
(207) 882–6218
If Wiscasset is the "Prettiest Village in Maine" (which, despite its claim, it probably isn't), it is pretty old houses like this one that are the reason why. The 1807 house museum sits on a plot that was landscaped in 1926 by noted architect Charles Eliott II and it's a National Historic Landmark.

Sunken Garden
Corner of Main and Federal Streets, Wiscasset
(207) 882–6218
Literally steps from Route 1, this perennial garden sits in the cellar hole of the old Hilton House. It was a gift from a gentleman to his wife in the 1910s and is now open to the public. It's a nice place to sit, even if you don't like flowers.

Coastal Maine Botanical Gardens
Off Barter's Island Road,
Boothbay Harbor
(207) 633–4333
A lovely work in progress, these gardens have been under construction since the 1990s, but there's already plenty to see on 128 acres. Some 300 native species have been planted, and there is a library and visitor center where you can find out about the long-term plans for the gardens. A mile of tidal shorefront doesn't hurt.

Christina's Garden at the Olson House
Hathorn Point Road, Cushing
(207) 354–0102
Andrew Wyeth spent more time painting this house and its denizens than he did the small annual garden on the premises kept by Christina Olson. Nonetheless, the Farnsworth Museum, which now owns this famous property, has re-created the beds here from historical research.

Farnsworth Art Museum
352 Main Street, Rockland
(207) 596–6457
Most people visit this exceptional museum for the artworks inside, logically enough, but they shouldn't miss the two small gardens outside. Both were built during the museum's grand renovations of the late 1990s, and one is Victorian in style while the other features native plants and perennials.

Vesper Hill Children's Chapel
Chapel Road (off Calderwood Lane), Rockport
(207) 236–0603
You have to practically wrestle to get a wedding scheduled for this nondenominational chapel nestled in the woods on Beauchamp Point, so popular is the site. The gardens that surround the rustic meeting place, which overlooks the sea, are part of the reason why.

Camden Public Library
Route 1, Camden
(207) 236–3440
One of the state's more distinctive libraries, perched on a hill underneath Mount Battie and above the harbor, the library has a beautiful spread out front. Some call it the finest institutional garden in the state, and it is pretty all season long. The amphitheater designed by Fletcher Steele in 1929 is another reason to visit (as is the park across the street, which was laid out at the same time by the Olmsted brothers).

Merryspring Horticultural Nature Park
Conway Road, Camden
(207) 236–2239
Truly an oasis of serenity amid the madness of summertime Camden, Merryspring can't be more than a mile from Route 1. But you'd never know it, stepping onto the preserve's 60-some acres. Lush woodlands, singing birds, trails overlooking the Camden Hills, gardens, interactive nature-trail displays, the place has a little of everything. The fairly complex network of trails takes walkers through an array of environments—marshes, shrubs, an arboretum, exposed ledges—and the Merryspring gardens are a treat for any green thumb. Hostas, perennials, roses, and heathers compete for the eye's attention. Step into the Ross Center, a visitor facility and library, to find out about all of the organization's classes, workshops, and programs. Or simply explore and be amazed that the whirl of Camden feels so far away.

Amen Farm Garden
Naskeag Point Road, Brooklin
(207) 359–8982
The attraction here, quite aside from the nifty community of Brooklin itself, is the arboretum, planted with 150 trees. They're all rare or uncommon to Maine.

Colonel Black Mansion
81 West Main Street, Ellsworth
(207) 667–8671
One of the better house museums Down East, this 1824 showplace has a fine formal garden. Originally laid out in 1903, it was restored in the 1990s from the original plans. The house also has 185 other acres worth seeing, if only to wander the walking trails.

Acadia Area

College of the Atlantic
Eden Street, Bar Harbor
(207) 288–5015
What would Eden be without gardens? (That's the paradisiacal name by which Bar Harbor used to be called.) The library grounds at this progressive learning institution include terraces that were designed by noted landscape architect Beatrix Farrand, a legend in these parts.

Jordan Pond House Flower Gardens
Park Loop Road, Bar Harbor
(207) 288–3338
People typically flock to the Jordan Pond House for its tea and popovers, but they should make sure to check out the perennial beds filled with dahlias, monkshood, delphiniums, and scads of other colorful flora.

Asticou Azalea Garden
Route 198, Northeast Harbor
(207) 276–5130
The azaleas are the real draw here, obviously, but their springtime bloom is only one of the many reasons to visit. Others include the rhododendrons, the laurels, and the Oriental touches. Architect Charles Savage designed the gardens here, and he used many plants rescued from Beatrix Farrand's famed Reef Point estate.

Japanese Garden at Yourcenar
South Shore Road, Northeast Harbor
(207) 276–3940
Better known for her books, Marguerite Yourcenar kept a garden at her Northeast Harbor home that is full of wild flowers, fruit trees, and walking paths. Yourcenar is one of the few women elected to the prestigious Academie Française, and her house-museum is open by appointment.

Thuya Garden
Route 3, Northeast Harbor
(207) 276–5130
Another garden designed by famous landscape architect Charles Savage and inspired by Beatrix Farrand, the semiformal, English-style perennial garden here is a true stunner, set against a backdrop of woods on a hill in Northeast Harbor.

Down East

Cottage Garden
North Lubec Road, Lubec
(207) 733–2902
Two acres of old-fashioned roses, delphiniums, and other flowers sit at this public garden against the backdrop of beautiful Cobscook Bay. Orchards are all around.

BIKING

Despite its narrow, winding roads, Maine is a favorite among the two-wheel set because of its country byways and ocean vistas. Road biking has long been popular, and mountain biking has been growing in recent years. Options for the road are fairly limitless—you can pedal from one end of the coast to the other if you like, as long as you stay off the Maine Turnpike (U.S. Route 1) and I–95—and many communities are making themselves more attractive to bicyclists by creating dedicated bike paths like those in Portland and Brunswick or simply adding bike lanes onto current roads. Mountain bike trails are a little bit harder to find, but they're there if you look for them. The great paperback book *Mountain Bike Maine* (Menasha Ridge Press, Birmingham, AL) lists scads of places for fat-tire freaks to find some doubletrack.

The state has very active biking clubs and groups helping to make the East Coast Greenway—that bike and walking path from Florida to Maine—a reality Down East. And there is also a lot of work going on in the state to transform old, unused railroad tracks into bike and walking paths. Forward-thinking motel owners in places like Kennebunkport now offer bikes as ways to get around to avoid the congestion of cars, and you can find rentals up and down the coast. Resort communities are the best places to look—Kennebunkport, Ogunquit, Bar Harbor, Camden—but you'll find rentals even in tiny spots like Chebeague Island. In fact, island biking continues to grow because most islands are relatively flat, the views are grand, and traffic is minimal. Ferries will transport your bike. (And, for that matter, the Downeaster train now has provisions for bikes as well.)

So it's a good time to be a cyclist on the coast. Just remember to wear your helmet—it's the law if you're age 15 or younger, and it's just plain smart if you're not.

Riders' Resources

The best friend Maine bicyclists have is the Bicycle Coalition of Maine, a two-wheelers advocacy group. Its Web site—www.bikemaine.org—is a great help to anyone interested in pedaling in the state. You'll find information on the outfit's political and educational work as well as a lot of links of interest to bikers, from races to group rides.

The Maine Department of Transportation also has some helpful bicycling information on its Web site, including a great list of pedaling routes, trip planning resources, and links to clubs and shops. You can find it at www.state.me.us/mdot. Just type the word *bike* in the search box.

CANOEING

Most people think of canoeing as an up-country activity, best done in the state's wild interior. That's where you'll find the Allagash and the Saint John, Maine's two famous canoeing corridors, as well as places like Northeast Carry, which was named for portaging canoes. But there are several good places to paddle along the coast. (You can rent canoes at sporting shops up and down Route 1.) Here are a few ideas—DeLorme's ubiquitous *Maine Atlas and Gazetteer* has several more.

Saco River

This lazy river washes down from Crawford Notch, New Hampshire, to the sea in Saco, putting in 84 miles in Maine, and it's one of the most popular places to paddle in the state. A lot of people get their first taste of canoe camping on the Saco, paddling by day and sleeping in the campgrounds that line the river at night. Most people put in at Fryeburg up on the border, but there are plenty of places to launch for shorter trips closer to the coast. Try the section from Salmon Falls down. You can rent boats at **Two Rivers Canoe** (24 Hubbard Avenue, Limington; 207–637–2169).

Royal River

Considering that you're paddling through the suburbs of Greater Portland, this 6-mile route has a nice, bucolic feel to it, and you don't see that many homes when you're in the middle of it. Put in on Route 9 in North Yarmouth and take out at West Elm Street in Yarmouth proper. Allow yourself a few hours for a leisurely go of it. Rent canoes in Portland.

Sheepscot River

A nice trip here could take you the better part of a day. Put in at North Whitefield and paddle to the dam at Head Tide, a 12-mile run that will take you through some Class I and II rapids. Portage at Whitefield, and travel to the incredibly scenic village of Head Tide, where you portage at the dam. From there you can paddle to Sheepscot Village and take out at the bridge. This is a nice route with a variety of environments, woods, hamlets, fields, and farms, and a mix of water types. You can rent canoes at **Trading Post Canoe and Kayak Rental** in Wiscasset (Route 1; 207–882–9645), which is 15 minutes from the takeout in Sheepscot Village.

Pemaquid River

On the Pemaquid Peninsula this quiet river runs between Pemaquid Harbor and Pemaquid Pond, flowing through 22 miles of lakes and ponds. It's flat-water paddling, and there is a launching point at Bristol where you can hop on and head north to Biscay Pond or beyond. The going is easy, the riverside quiet and woodsy, and there are always frogs sunning and turtles swimming in water so clear you can see them 4 feet down. There are plenty of places to pull out and take a swim or spread out a blanket for a picnic. Rent a canoe at **Pemaquid River Canoe Rental** (207–563–5721) just above the dam in Bristol Mills. You can put in and take out right here or hire a kayak at Maine Kayak in New Harbor (866–624–6352).

St. George River

A very picturesque paddle through the rural countryside of Knox and Waldo Counties, this route begins in Searsmont at the bridge and flows to Appleton Village. Typically run in the spring, it requires high water because of the boniness of the river through here. Lots of beaver dams, bird nesting areas, and stretches of quiet water, but there can be some Class III rapids. Portage the old dam—or paddle it if you dare. Rent canoes at **Maine Sport Outfitters** (Route 1, Rockport; 207–236–8797) 20 minutes south of Appleton.

Machias River

This is one of the biggies in Maine and is usually run only by experienced paddlers or people with guides. The section from Third Machias Lake to Whitneyville will take you some 50 miles through wild country, with many stretches of Class III rapids. You need to do a lot of scouting and several portages, and there is primitive camping at the river's edge. Rent canoes—or hire a guide—at **Mooselook Guide Service** (Schoodic; 207–963–0995).

ACADIA

The single biggest attraction Down East and the state's only national park, Acadia is the reason more than two million people a year visit Maine. It has been called the crown jewel in the National Park system, and it's truly a stunner. Occupying much of Mount Desert Island and a few other nearby points, Acadia is a geologic marvel, an Atlantic wonderland of sea and surf and summits. The park sprawls for close to 50,000 acres, including miles of dramatic shoreline, the only genuine fjord in the Lower 48, several lakes, 26 peaks, 120 miles of trails, and innumerable ponds. As such, it's an outdoor lover's paradise, with exceptional hiking, biking, walking, swimming, climbing, and kayaking. And there's plenty to see from a car window, too.

Acadia dominates the Mount Desert Island map, spread on either side of the island, which is divided in two by the sea, split by scenic Somes Sound. The heaviest concentration of parklands—and the most popular sites—are on the east side, where the resort town of Bar Harbor is also located. This is where you'll find the Park Loop Road, and where Thunder Hole, Otter Cliffs, Great Head, Sand Beach, Jordan Pond, Blackwoods Camping Area, and Cadillac Mountain all reside. Across the sound—a glacially carved fjord—is what is known as the island's "quiet side," a place that sees far less tourism than does Bar Harbor but that can still get busy in the full blush of summer.

Bar Harbor is all about tourism, the very picture of a resort community (see Area Overview chapter). It has all the restaurants, shops, and B&Bs anyone could ever want, all attractively packaged into the tidy brick streets and venerable lanes of one of the oldest summer colonies in the country. Several painters of the Hudson River school made their way to the island in the mid-1800s,

among them Thomas Cole and Frederic Church, and the paintings they made here attracted many early vacationers. By 1880, there were 30 hotels on the island, and, not long after that, the captains of American industry began to summer over, building huge mansions and calling them "cottages." Originally drawn here to escape the heat of New York and Philadelphia, the Carnegies and Rockefellers, Vanderbilts and Astors soon remade the island in their own image, creating an exclusive community of estates, parties, and all the luxurious trappings.

Thankfully, though, these wealthy folks from away also had the foresight to see that the mountains and sea that they loved needed to be preserved for future generations. One of them, textile heir and conservationist George Dorr, devoted more than 40 years to making that happen. Dorr worked on his affluent friends and neighbors until they relented, donating land piece by piece. John D. Rockefeller himself helped acquire nearly a third of the park's acreage, and Harvard president Charles Eliot was instrumental as well. The land was then turned over to the federal government, and in 1919 Acadia National Park opened to the public (though it was originally called Lafayette National Park, in 1929 the name was changed to Acadia, derived from the term the French used for these lands, L'Acadie) as the first national park in the East.

i The name of the national park on Mount Desert Island is pronounced *Uh-cay-dee-A*, not *AR-cay-dee-a*. While Bar Harbor was once known as Eden, Acadia is not to be confused with Arcadia, the pastoral setting for the poetry of ancient Greece. Innumerable visitors get the name wrong. Don't be one of them.

Acadia's been extraordinarily popular since. Unfortunately, most people who visit miss the good stuff. They content themselves with a drive along the two-lane Park Loop Road, the 20-mile byway that circuits the eastern half of Acadia, and then head into Bar Harbor. And while the Park Loop Road is truly spectacular—an Atlantic Coast highway of sorts, passing underneath mountains, alongside cliffs, and a skip from the surging sea—there is so much more to the park than that. To best enjoy Acadia, you have to leave the car behind and get out into it.

SOURCES OF INFORMATION

Hulls Cove Visitor Center
State Route 3, Hulls Cove
(207) 288–3338
www.nps.gov/acad
This is the primary information clearinghouse for Acadia National Park, and it sits very close to the best access point for the park's main thoroughfare, the Park Loop Road. Open from mid-April through October, the center brims with relief maps, natural history displays, and other guides to the goods on Acadia. You can pick up maps and postcards, watch a film about the park, and get answers to all your questions here.

Acadia National Park Headquarters
State Route 233, Bar Harbor
(207) 288–3338
This is the place to turn for information in the off-season, when the visitor center is closed but the park isn't.

i Many Acadia visitors enjoy their vacation without ever picking up a copy of the park's newsletter, the *Beaver Log* (so named because of the abundance of the toothy rodents throughout the park). That's too bad for them, because it's filled with a wealth of handy info, from the schedule of ranger-led programs to tide calendars. Grab your copy at the park information center.

GETTING AROUND THE ISLAND

Island Buses
Islandwide
(207) 667–5796
www.exploreacadia.com
When the Island Explorer bus service was first proposed as a way to alleviate the traffic headaches that can tie up Acadia on a hot summer day, there were a lot of naysayers. People are too tied to their vehicles to want to climb aboard propane-fired buses, they argued. They were proved spectacularly wrong. The buses turned out to be a great success—they carted 285,000 park visitors around the island in 2005, or more than 4,000 a day in summer—linking hotels, restaurants, campgrounds, boats, and ferries to the national park. Eight routes crisscross the island, taking passengers to popular destinations like downtown Bar Harbor and Sand Beach and traveling as far as the Schoodic Peninsula. They run as often as every 15 minutes, they're on time and efficient, and they'll take you virtually everywhere you might want to go on Mount Desert. And best of all they're free, thanks to support from the National Park Service, the U.S. and Maine Departments of Transportation, local businesses, Friends of Acadia, and L. L. Bean (which donated a grant to allow the buses to run through Columbus Day). Quite aside from the environmental benefit the fleet provides—taking all those cars off the roads and using the less-polluting propane gas—they take all the headaches away from drivers. The buses start to roll as early as 6:45 A.M. downtown and continue to do so until 11:00 P.M. Pick up a copy of the schedule at a variety of spots downtown, call, or visit the Web site for full details.

PARK LOOP ROAD

The primary thoroughfare through Acadia National Park, the Park Loop Road makes a 20-mile circuit on the east side of Mount Desert Island. Not only the best way to see the sights if you only have a day or so, it's also how you'll

Close-up

Ranger-Led Programs

Acadia has an exceptional series of ranger-led programs designed to help visitors get the most out of their time in the park. These workshops and seminars run the gamut from hikes to boat rides, and they're hosted by knowledgeable park staff. A complete list of offerings is available in the park's newsletter, the *Beaver Log*. A sampling follows.

Life between the Tides
This two-and-a-half-hour tour explores the natural world from the edge of the forest to the waterline. The walk takes you a little over a mile and is of moderate difficulty.

Trails through Time
Discover the history of some of the park's beloved hiking trails as you walk along a few of them. This two-and-a-half-hour program takes you 2.5 miles over some strenuous terrain.

Animals of Acadia
This hour-and-a-half program serves as an introduction to the charismatic critters you might meet during your trip to the park, from deer to turtles to, yes, beavers.

Acadia's Birds
More than 200 avian species have been spotted on Mount Desert Island, and during this easy, three-hour trek you'll look for and learn about many of them. Binoculars are a good idea.

Discover Acadia
An easy half-mile hike takes you to Cadillac Mountain for an introduction to the natural and cultural history of Acadia.

Mr. Rockefeller's Bridges
John D. Rockefeller helped create the 45 miles of gravel carriage roads in Acadia, many of which feature beautiful old bridges. Learn their history on a two-and-a-half-hour, 2-mile walk on these genteel old paths.

Frenchman Bay Cruise
Climb aboard a 151-foot schooner for a tour of the island's wildlife and history.

get wherever you're going in the park, as it links most of the major points. There are a few spots to get on, but it becomes a one-way route after Sand Beach. Driving the loop is practically mandatory to Acadia visitors. Vehicle passes good for a week are $20, and you'll be stopped and asked to pay at the tollbooths on the Loop Road. Many people get on in Bar Harbor and drive south, passing underneath the cliffs of Champlain Mountain and skirting the shore below Sand Beach. The road continues past the booming Thunder Hole, Gorham Mountain, and Otter Cliffs, and it hugs the water past Otter and Western Points before heading back inland toward Jordan Pond and Cadillac Mountain. The views of relentless surf, pine and birch forests, pretty ponds, and greenbacked peaks don't get much better than this. A handy map available at the park's visitor center will inform your drive and make a neat self-guided tour.

Cars are a constant all day long on the Loop Road, and bicyclists enjoy it, too. The speed limit is 35 mph, and drivers often have a hard time maintaining that thanks to traffic, lollygaggers, and all of the comings and goings at the scenic pull-offs and parking areas. Pedestrians cross at a variety of points as well, and you might even bump into a film crew (they love to make car commercials here). Best to be patient and enjoy the views or to get up early or visit in the off-season to have time by yourself.

ACADIA NATIONAL PARK TOURS

One of the better ways to get a broad overview of Acadia and all it offers is to hop aboard the green-and-white buses run by Acadia National Park Tours (www.acadiatours .com). They host two-and-a-half-hour trips through the park twice daily, at 10:00 A.M. and 2:00 P.M. The bus drivers are full of knowledge and trivia, and they'll fill you in on all the backstory, from the rusticators of yore to the fledgling falcons of today. These tours are billed as being ideal for "nature lovers, history buffs, and photographers," and they make either a good starting point for your trip or an informative rainy-day option. They're offered daily from May through October for $25 for adults, $10 for kids age 12 or younger. Call (207) 288–0300 or look for the buses across from Testa's Restaurant on Main Street.

Oli's Trolleys
Cottage Street, P.O. Box 784,
Bar Harbor 04609
(207) 288–9899
Another option for a motor coach–based excursion is Oli's Trolleys, which offers one-hour and two-and-a-half-hour tours of Bar Harbor and Acadia in its colorful, open-windowed, ersatz trolleys. Like the bus tours, these trips combine a bit of cultural history—stories of old Bar Harbor as you pass by the venerable "cottages"—with visits to the more popular

scenic spots in the park itself. Reservations are recommended, and tickets can be purchased at One Harbor Place (next to the Town Pier) an hour before the tours.

CARRIAGE ROADS

If the Park Loop Road will take you to most of the major points in the park, the 57 miles of carriage roads that John D. Rockefeller helped establish in 1913 will get you just about everywhere else. Sometimes referred to as "Mr. Rockefeller's Roads," for the 27 years the philanthropist put into their creation, these wide, gentle, crushed-rock byways wend and wander deep into the interior of the park, linking everything from Jordan Pond and the Bubbles to remote ponds. They pass by lakes, climb to scenic overlooks, and get you well up some of the park's peaks. Perfect for an afternoon amble, for mountain biking, and even horseback riding, these roads are laid out in a well-organized network, and maps are available at the park's information centers. A visit to Acadia wouldn't be complete without a stroll along one. Try the network near Jordan Pond; it's especially scenic, rising high above the little basin and looking out at the green bonbons of the Bubbles.

Wildwood Stables
Park Loop Road, Box 241, Seal Harbor
(207) 276–3622
www.acadia.net/wildwood
What more perfect way to appreciate the carriage roads of Acadia than by a horse-drawn carriage? Wildwood Stables, a privately run livery, is located on the Park Loop Road not far from Jordan Pond and offers a variety of outings in open-air carriages. You might want to try the Day Mountain Tour, a one-hour trip that takes you from forest to peak and back again; the two-hour Tea and Popover Carriage Ride, which explores the terrain around Jordan Pond, stopping at the teahouse there for its famed popovers; or the beautiful two-hour Sunset Tour in the evening. Reservations are a good idea. Find out more at the Web site.

HIKING

Acadia is a day hiker's dream, with more than two dozen peaks, plenty of shore paths, and 120 miles of hiking trails of varying degrees of difficulty. You can do everything from climbing vertical ladders on the sheer faces of cliffs, like those on the Beehive and the Precipice, to simply trekking through pretty boreal forests just steps from the sea. Cadillac Mountain is the tallest peak on the island—in fact, it's the tallest peak right on the eastern seaboard at 1,530 feet—and most of Acadia's mountains are in the 1,000-foot range, so we're not talking Everests here, more like ambitious hills. Eager hikers have been known to do two or three in a day, because the climbs can be fairly easy, the peaks are often close together, and the trails are interconnected. Just about all of the mountains offer stunning prospects from their summits, though, a patchwork of green forest and blue sea and often other peaks in the distance. The trails themselves can be works of art—intricate stone stairways and ladders are common—making the view at your feet interesting, too. This is arguably the best way to see the park, and comprehensive maps and trail guides are available at the park information centers. Here are a few to get you started.

Cadillac Mountain

There are many ways up the island's tallest peak, including an automobile road, but the South Ridge Trail will make you feel like you earned it. One of the longest hikes on the island at 3.5 miles, it starts across from Blackwoods Campground and climbs steadily northward through mixed forest. At about a mile there are good lookouts to the east and southeast at Eagles Crag; much of the climbing is done on exposed granite ledges, and the views just keep getting better and better. You might be annoyed at the commotion you find at the top—cars, crowds, and a gift shop—after the peace you found on the way up, but the astounding views in all directions will more than make up for it.

Ship Harbor and Wonderland

Twin trails on the island's quiet side, Ship Harbor and Wonderland are both relatively short, easy walks, coming in at under 1.5 miles each. They both get their starts on Route 3 in Southwest Harbor and head through bosky woods to end at the water. Birders particularly love them, but they are fun for anyone who wants a peaceful nature walk or a few private minutes at the ocean's edge.

Great Head Trail

Great Head is the tall green peninsula that wraps protectively around the far side of Sand Beach. It rises 145 feet from sea level and is among the highest headlands on the East Coast. The trail here makes a circuit from Sand Beach that climbs steeply at first and then levels off when it reaches the top of the head, circling around the promontory and skirting cliffs. Views of the open ocean, the Beehive, and Schoodic Point are magnificent, and the going is fairly easy. The hike takes you 1.6 miles. Park at the Sand Beach parking area on the Loop Road.

Beech Cliffs

There are few hikes in Maine that rival Beech Cliffs when it comes to the views you're rewarded with for the effort you make. The half-mile trail takes you only a few minutes to walk and deposits you atop Beech Cliffs. The vistas here are terrific, overlooking Echo Lake. Other trails will connect you to the summit of Beech Mountain (839 feet) and nearby Canada Cliffs. This is a great hike for a picnic lunch, as these trails are much quieter than those on the other side of the island. Take State Route 102 through Somesville and turn onto Beech Hill Road.

Beehive Trail

The Beehive is a whole lot of fun for anyone who is not afraid of heights. It is a very steep climb, though, and you cross narrow ledges from which some people have fallen. So due caution and respect are in order. This was the first piece of Acadia purchased back when the park was being founded, and it's a cool, craggy cliff face that rises up on one side of Champlain Mountain. The ledges here have a sort of honeycomb look to them (hence the name), and they are exposed for almost the entire ascent. The trail switches back and forth along them, using iron ladders for climbing sheer cliff faces at points. It'll get your heart pumping and will afford you a great prospect of Sand Beach, Great Head, Otter Cliffs, Gorham Mountain, and the open sea from the top. Other trails leave from the summit. Park at the Sand Beach parking area.

Precipice Trail

This is the be-all and end-all trail for adventure seekers at Acadia, a vertical ascent up a cliff face on Champlain Mountain. After a half mile of walking, the trail goes straight up for 500 feet, using iron rungs that were hammered into the mountain granite. It's downright terrifying for those afraid of verticality and should not be attempted by anyone under 5 feet tall, who might have difficulty reaching the ladders. Not for the faint of heart, for sure, and a place where it is essential that you stick to the designated trail. The views from the top are breathtaking, though, and you'll have earned bragging rights. There's a parking area off the Park Loop not far from the base of the trail.

Penobscot and Sargent Mountains

This pair rank among the loftiest on Mount Desert Island—Sargent is second to Cadillac, Penobscot fifth tallest—and the ridge linking them rises above the tree line for much of the way, making for fine views. The trail leaves from near Jordan Pond (park in the parking area there) and climbs up over Penobscot before descending to Sargent Pond and heading back up over ledges to the top of Sargent Mountain. The views of Jordan Pond, the Bubbles, Cadillac Mountain, and the sea in the distance are truly special. The hike from the start to Sargent summit is about 2.5 miles.

The Bubbles

A pair of cute green hills with perfectly rounded tops, the Bubbles hunker at one end of Jordan Pond in a most photogenic way—in fact, these twins make one of the most frequently photographed images in Acadia. Neither North nor South Bubble is a particularly difficult climb, topping out at 872 and 766 feet, respectively. You can park right below them on the Park Loop Road and scale either one in no time. People frequently do both in an afternoon, and you might still have the energy to hook up with the Jordan Pond Shore Trail or the Eagle Lake Trail, too. You'll get nice peeks at Jordan Pond and Penobscot and Pemetic Mountains from the tops of the Bubbles.

Champlain Mountain

The easternmost mountain on Mount Desert Island, Champlain is best known as the home of the Precipice, but there is a really nice trail on the other side of this long, sprawling thousand-footer that begins on Route 3. The Beachcroft Trail is one of the more elaborately designed of Acadia's hiking paths, following a carefully built stone staircase up the face of Huguenot Head, switching back and forth as it climbs like something out of a fairy tale. Once you've climbed the steps, you're on a false summit, overlooking the Tarn and Dorr Mountain, and you have to go another half mile or so, down into a bosk, and then climb up steeply to reach the actual peak. It's windswept and wide open and quite scenic. There is parking near the base of the trail at the Dorr parking lot.

Gorham Mountain

Gorham is one of the smaller of Acadia's peaks, but it is an exceedingly pleasant hike and provides good viewing of Sand Beach, Great Head, the Beehive, and the open sea. Some say it offers vistas unparalleled on the island. The trail begins in the Gorham Trail parking lot, just down the Loop Road from Sand Beach, and climbs for a ways through a pine woods before reaching ledges of exposed bedrock. There's the option of taking the Cadillac Caves Trail at .3 mile, which is a worthwhile loop that takes you through some boulder-strewn, above-ground caves before rejoining the trail. (This option requires a bit of scrambling.) Then it's up over more open terrain to the panoramas that wait up top. This is a relatively easy hike that will keep your camera snapping.

ROCK CLIMBING

Acadia Mountain Guides Climbing School
198 Main Street, Bar Harbor
(207) 288–8186 or (888) 232–9559
www.acadiamountainguides.com.
A 60-foot seawall, Otter Cliffs is the most popular of all of Maine's rock climbing sites. On any given day, these pink granite walls are snaked with colorful lines and crawling with people, many of them experienced climbers but many just learning the ropes, too. The best bet for instruction and advice is Acadia Mountain Guides Climbing School, run by seasoned vet Jon Tierney. His outfit offers day and half-day climbs on the cliffs along with a full slate of more advanced courses. Cost for a half-day climb is $90 for up to four people, and all gear—including those silly shoes—is provided.

CAMPING

If you're planning on staying overnight in Acadia, you'd better bring your tent—the only accommodations in the park are at two campgrounds, Seawall and Blackwoods, and a few remote campsites on Isle au Haut. The fee is $20 per site, per night, which is about the best deal you'll find for a place to stay on MDI during the summer. Seawall is on the Southwest Harbor side of the island, not far from the artificially created seawall from which it takes its name. Despite the fact that it has more than 200 sites, the place fills up quickly in summer on a first-come, first-served basis. It's a good idea to show up before 8:00 A.M. if you want to

lay your head here. The amenities are limited—just restrooms and dumping stations—but the campground makes a good jumping-off point for explorations of the quiet side of the island by bike, boat, or foot. Rangers lead entertaining nature programs at the amphitheater here on summer evenings.

Blackwoods is the more popular of the two Mount Desert Island camping areas, with 300-some sites and a reservation policy good between May 1 and October 31 (800–365–2267). Just up the road from Bar Harbor on Route 3, it is divided into a few loops, and the sites are pretty tightly packed together. But the shore is an easy walk across the road and through a bit of woods, and you have easy access to Bar Harbor and most of the park. It too has an amphitheater at which rangers hold nature talks in the evenings.

Most people who visit Acadia do so unaware that the park owns a large parcel on Isle au Haut, reached by way of a mail boat from Stonington, many miles up the coast from Bar Harbor. Like the rest of the park on Mount Desert, the Isle au Haut section is a stunning place of peaks, cliffs, and sea, but it has a decidedly wilder feel enhanced by dense woodlands and the fact that access is limited to only 48 people on any given day. Those lucky few who find it (something like 5,000 people a year) tend to keep going back, though, which makes getting a site at one of the five lean-tos at Duck Harbor Campground a bit of a challenge. The sites are available from May 15 through October 15 and can be reserved for five nights at a time maximum.

i Visit Acadia in the off-season—May or November, say—and you'll have the place to yourself. The vast majority of the park's visitors come during high summer and when the foliage turns. If you plan your vacation at any other time of the year, the park will be wide open to explore and free to use (in winter). There also will be good deals at those inns and motels that are open year-round in Bar Harbor.

The gorgeous views are endless at Acadia National Park. MAINE OFFICE OF TOURISM

Call Acadia for a reservation form (207–288–3338) and return it to Acadia National Park, P.O. Box 177, Bar Harbor 04609 prior to April 1 to request a space. Be sure to list alternate dates. It may be tough to get in here, but it is very definitely worth the effort.

SCHOODIC PENINSULA

Some of the best views to be found of Mount Desert Island are not even on the island. Seven miles away, as the boat rows, is Schoodic Point, a headland in Winter Harbor on which Acadia owns 2,000 acres. While three million people visit the Bar Harbor area every year, only a few thousand ever make their way down this rugged, remote point of land to enjoy the parcel of parkland at its tip. The drive to get here is more than an hour from Acadia, but it's very worthwhile, especially if the Mount Desert crowds are getting you down. In 2003 the Island Explorer bus service began offfering free rides on Schoodic in conjunction with the Bar Harbor–Winter Harbor ferry (which isn't free and costs $27.50 for adults, $17.50 for kids under 12).

Schoodic Point is much like the rest of Acadia, only a bit more raw. It has its own Park Loop Road, which passes through woods of pine and spruce and under hills before arriving at the shoreline, where the surf booms and the look back at the mountains of Acadia is jaw-dropping. Bring a picnic (watch out for the brazen seagulls—they'll take your chips), park in the big lot at the end of the road, and revel in the rocks and sea. If the tides are high or the seas are stormy, the crashing surf is particularly impressive.

A few trails explore the forest of Schoodic, but it's definitely more of an automobile and bicycle friendly section of the park. Try the trek up Schoodic Head, the woody, 440-foot hill that crowns the point. The loop trail will take you a couple of hours to complete.

To get to Schoodic, take Route 1 to Gouldsboro and hang a right onto State Route 186 to Winter Harbor. Then follow signs for the park.

BIKING

Cyclists have been smitten with Acadia for a century, and a mountain bike just might be the most perfect mode of transportation for a visit. With the carriage roads, the Park Loop Road, and back roads on the island's quiet side, there are plenty of extraordinary avenues to pedal. Some crazies even like to ride down the auto road on Cadillac Mountain, a winding road with precipitous drop-offs. Rentals are available at a variety of locations in Bar Harbor, and fees tend to be about $18 to $25 a day for a bike, a lock, and a helmet. Try **Bar Harbor Bicycle Shop** (141 Cottage Street; 207–288–3886), **Acadia Outfitters** (106 Cottage Street; 207–288–8118), or **Acadia Bike** (48 Cottage Street; 207–288–9605).

SWIMMING

With all that sea about, you'd think there'd be a lot of places to throw on the suit and get into it. There is actually only a single saltwater beach at Acadia, the crescent-shaped strand known as Sand Beach. When Charlize Theron and Tobey Maguire aren't here (the pair shot a scene for the 1999 film *The Cider House Rules* on the empty sands), the beach is thronged. The parking lot fills up quickly on a hot August day despite the fact that the water is absolutely frigid. This is the only sandy stretch of oceanfront for many miles in any direction, though, so many just come to sunbathe and ogle. There are restrooms and a bathhouse on-site and lifeguards on patrol.

If you prefer to cool off in freshwater, you have a few options: The park's Echo Lake swimming area is another popular one, staffed with lifeguards and always busy. There's a parking area on Route 102, and people often like to sneak into the woods—they're full of footpaths—to private spots; just be respectful of the trees and other swimmers. Lake Wood, a small pond on the north side of Mount Desert, is a favorite clothing-optional site, and people also frequently swim in Somes Pond or at Round or Seal Cove Ponds.

Close-up

Acadia Literature

Countless books have been written about Acadia, and there are several really good ones that will enlighten and entertain you as you enjoy the park. Here are a few ideas:

AMC Maine Mountain Guide
Not specifically about Acadia, this handy little book fits into the pocket of a backpack and includes the best trail descriptions of Acadia's peaks going. It also has a great foldout map of the trails of Mount Desert. 352 pages, $18.95.

A Pocket Guide to Paddling the Waters of Mount Desert by Earl Brechlin
Slim and handy, this paddler's handbook was written by Earl Brechlin, Registered Maine Guide and editor of the local newspaper for years, so it's got the inside poop on boating on and around the island. 64 pages, $7.95.

A Pocket Guide to the Carriage Roads of Acadia National Park by D. Abrell
Another small and slender guide, this will help you more fully enjoy the carriage roads. 40 pages, $4.50.

A Walk in the Park: Acadia's Hiking Guide
A great resource for trekkers on the island, and part of the proceeds go to help the very worthy Friends of Acadia. 144 pages, $11.95.

Lost Bar Harbor by G. W. Helfrich and G. O'Neil
A compelling look at old Bar Harbor, the luxury resort of the late 19th and early 20th centuries, before it was decimated by the great fire of 1947. 125 pages, $9.95.

Mr. Rockefeller's Roads by A. R. Roberts
This very pleasant volume chronicles the creation of Acadia's fabled carriage roads by John D. Rockefeller. 184 pages, $17.95.

NATURE TOURS

Down East Nature Tours
P.O. Box 521, Bar Harbor 04609
(207) 288–8128
www.downeastnaturetours.com
Michael Good has been a guide for years and has about 30 years of experience studying birds. He'll take you on a four-hour tour of Mount Desert's avian species—focusing on bald eagles, ospreys, peregrine falcons, shorebirds, and warblers—or set up photography or camping trips. Rates vary according to the trip.

FRIENDS OF ACADIA

We should all have friends as dedicated and devoted as Acadia does. Friends of Acadia (FOA) is a membership organization whose mission is to help preserve and protect the natural resources of the park. Love it though they might, three million visitors can be hard on a place—even one made out of granite. FOA puts together work parties to shore up trails, raises funds to help defend Acadia against external threats, lobbies on behalf of the park when political issues arise, and does so much more. The Friends built the Great Meadow Loop, connecting Bar Harbor to Acadia, and they do maintenance projects all summer long with their Acadia Trails Forever Program; they helped fund and manage the Island Explorer bus service; and they contribute almost a quarter of a million dollars to help maintain the carriage roads, along with myriad other good works.

The Friends of Acadia appreciate all the help they can get, both fiscal and physical. They accept donations and collect $35 annual membership dues, and they organize work parties three times a week that help get things done that the cash-strapped federal government can't seem to afford. These outings take place from 8:30 A.M. to 1:00 P.M. on Tuesdays, Thursdays, and Saturdays from June through November, and they're a fun way to meet people and give something back. Call the work hotline at (207) 288–3934 for the meeting place.

For more information on Friends of Acadia, call (207) 288–3340 or (800) 625–0321 or visit the Web site www.friendsofacadia.org.

GOLF

Golfers in Maine tend to be a lot like gardeners. Because their season is cut short by snow and ice, they take to their hobby with a passion not found elsewhere. It's not uncommon to see Maine golfers hitting the links very early in the morning, playing through rain and flurries, and pushing the season as long as possible.

Their zeal is understandable. Who wouldn't want to spend their days on some of the finest acreage in the state? Maine courses sit on prime property, on headlands overlooking the sea, tucked under mountains, along rivers. There are more than 120 in all—many of them on the coast—and they range from neat neighborhood greens like those at the tiny Northport Golf Club to upscale country clubs like Cape Arundel Golf Club to some of the oldest and toughest holes in the nation, like those at Kebo Valley in Bar Harbor.

I've listed the Maine courses that are public or semiprivate and open to nonmembers. These courses tend to be very busy in summer, so it's not a bad idea to call ahead about tee times. Greens fees vary wildly, depending upon the course and the time of week you go; best to ask when you call ahead to reserve a tee time.

SOUTH COAST

Links at Outlook
State Route 4, Berwick
(207) 384–4653
www.outlookgolf.com
Designed "in the Scottish tradition," the links here nonetheless feel thoroughly New English, built as they are on the grounds of an old Maine farm—there's still a big, beautiful red barn on the premises (see if you can hit the broad side of it). The 18-hole course was designed by Golf World magazine's Architect of the Year 1999, Brian Silva, and its bent grass greens and fairways are thoughtfully laid out on 140 acres of rising and falling meadows. Here and there these grasslands are punctuated by sand bunkers and rolling dunes. Its 6,500, par 71 yards are very open and photogenic, and they play nicely, too. The season here starts in May and runs through autumn, and there are attractive off-season rates ($37 for 18 holes on a weekday, say, in foliage season). The Links also offers Twilight All You Can Play times after 4:00 P.M. during summer, where $40 (weekday) or $45 (weekend) will get you as many hours of golf as you want. Then wind down on the patio with something from the bar. Find the latest golf fashions in the pro shop, sign up for instruction, or plan your wedding on the course—it's a full-service place. Rentals, practice green, and a driving range with targets at 100, 150, and 200 yards all await.

Highland Links Golf Club
301 Cider Hill Road, York
(207) 351–2727
Just inland in the southern Maine community of York Village, this is about as close to the entrance of the Pine Tree State as a golf addict's going to get. The nine holes here were built in 1995, and they're arranged into a fairly short course of 5,599 yards. The setting is pleasant, and golfers will find just about all they need: a pro shop, snack bar, club and cart rentals, a driving range, a practice green, a practice bunker, and instruction to boot. Reserving tee times is a good idea during the high season.

Close-up

More on Maine Golf

A great source for additional golf information is the Maine State Golf Association. It has a handy Web site—www.mesga.org—which lists member clubs, golf-related events and tournaments, and other helpful links, and provides details on its member discount card, a bargain for people who log a lot of time on the fairways. If you want to know who the point leaders in Maine are or find out the Web address of your favorite club, this site is a good place to start.

The Ledges Golf Club
One Ledges Drive, York
(207) 351–9999
www.ledgesgolf.com
The Ledges was voted the best new public course in New England by *Golf Magazine* in 1999, and it's indeed an impressive place. Eighteen holes are laid out across a hilly landscape (views of the Piscataqua River between Maine and New Hampshire can be dramatic at points), and it's not uncommon to see a critter or two during your round. Water plays a role on a few holes—the par-three 8th, the par-three 11th, the par-four 15th, and the par-five 18th—and there are islands of forests all around the fairways. The porch on the clubhouse is a particularly pleasant feature, and the food is good in the dining room. The pro shop has got what you need, there's a driving range and a practice green and bunker, and you can rent whatever gear you don't want to bring. All very nice. Tee times are recommended.

Cape Arundel Golf Club
19 River Road, Kennebunkport
(207) 967–3494
www.capearundelgolfclub.com
Established in 1896, Cape Arundel is a semiprivate, 18-hole course that President Bush the elder is fond of playing (his grandfather is a past club president), so it's not surprising that it's a tad exclusive—no jeans or sweatshirts—and no nonmembers between 11:00 A.M. and 2:30 P.M. It's a Scottish-links course, and water

comes into play on 13 holes. Caddies are available upon request. The season runs from mid-April through mid-November, and tee times are necessary. Greens fees are $65.

Webhannet Golf Club
26 Golf Club Drive, Kennebunk Beach
(207) 967–2061
www.kennebunkgolf.com
Yet another 18-hole semiprivate club in the Kennebunks, Webhannet was built in 1901 and is a very busy place in summer. The club offers a public tee time only once every hour, so it's definitely a good idea to call at least a day in advance. Nine holes were added to the original nine back in 1925, and now it's a 6,049-yard, par 72 course with bent grass greens, bluegrass fairways, several water hazards, 31 sand bunkers, and a snack bar on the eighth tee. The fairways are pleasant and open, with woods at their edge. The facilities are well equipped, including a pro shop, practice greens and bunkers, and club and cart rental.

President George Herbert Walker Bush has whacked the ball around here when he wasn't playing at Cape Arundel. Former secretary of state Edmund Muskie was a member. Eighteen holes are $60; nine holes, after 3:00 P.M., are $30.

Dutch Elm Golf Course
5 Brimstone Road, Arundel
(207) 282–9850
www.dutchelmgolf.com

Perhaps the most welcoming course in the Kennebunk area, Dutch Elm is in the inland town of Arundel. It is public, has rentals, and at $25 for 18 holes, its greens fees are considerably cheaper than those of the coastal courses. The facility features a pro shop, club and cart rentals, a snack bar for a goodie after the ninth hole, and putting greens. You can also reserve tee times a week in advance. The only things that aren't welcome are short shorts, groups larger than four, and metal spikes.

Pine Hollow Par 3
1486 Main Street, Sanford
(207) 324–5271
A good club for up-and-comers, Pine Hollow is a short, par 3 course, with the longest of its 18 holes a distant 80 yards. This is a great place to come and practice and hone your game. You'll also find a practice green, rental options, and instruction offered. Open from April through September.

Sanford Country Club
Route 4, Sanford
(207) 324–5462
www.sanfordcountryclub.com
Built in 1924, Sanford County Club sits on Bauneg Beg Pond and began its life as the Bauneg Beg Pond Country Club. The nine original holes were laid out by Maine course architect Alex Chisholm, and nine new holes were added in 1997 by Marvin Armstrong, when the unwieldy name was changed. The result is a popular, par 72, 18-hole championship course with four sets of tees. The facilities include a driving range, tee mats, a practice bunker, rentals, instruction, and the all-important snack bar and lounge. The course is open from April through October. Tee times are necessary and can be made a couple of days ahead of time. Eighteen holes are $41, $48 on weekends.

Biddeford-Saco Country Club
101 Old Orchard Road, Saco
(207) 282–5883
www.biddefordsacocountryclub.com

Back in 1987 the Biddeford-Saco club added a back nine to the nine holes that were originally built here in 1922 on a design by Donald Ross. Golfers here tend to be of the hardy variety, playing from April into mid-November, and it's not usually too difficult to get tee times despite the fact that these par 71 links are considered to be among the best in southern Maine. Pay your greens fee and you're a member for the day and get access to all the amenities, which are impressive. They include a full pro shop, a driving range, a practice green and bunker, cart and club rental, instruction, a locker room, and a restaurant and lounge. Find out why *Golf Digest* ranked these bluegrass fairways among the best in Maine in 1996.

Dunegrass Golf Club
200 Wild Dunes Way,
Old Orchard Beach
(207) 934–4513 or (800) 521–1029
www.dunegrass.com
One of Maine's newest courses, Dunegrass opened in 1998, and it's very popular. The *Boston Globe* has called it a "must," and word of mouth tends to bear it out. The greens fees are pretty steep to play on this 300-acre course, though. The large clubhouse features both a restaurant and a pro shop, and you can even enjoy "play and stay" vacation packages that include time at a two-bedroom condo on Fairway 1.

GREATER PORTLAND

Nonesuch River Golf Club
304 Gorham Road, Scarborough
(207) 883–0007
www.nonesuchgolf.com
Eighteen-hole Nonesuch has been lauded for preserving much of the wildlife habitat it was built amid in the woods along Scarborough's Nonesuch River. The club was designed as something of a sanctuary, and it carefully tried to keep the living space of moose, deer, wild turkeys, and foxes intact, which has made the par 70 course unique and fun to play. The fair-

ways and greens are bent grass and were constructed in the late 1990s to USGA specifications with the average golfer in mind. General manager Daniel Hourihan has been quoted as saying that what the course offers "is everything that's good about golf." There's something to that—the place is very welcoming, from the greens to the 2,500-square-foot clubhouse. Tee times are required, can be reserved a week in advance, and can even be made on the course's Web site.

Pleasant Hill Golf Club
38 Chamberlain Road, Scarborough
(207) 883–9340

A nine-hole course handy to much of Greater Portland, Pleasant Hill was built in the early 1960s. The holes here are a par 34 and stretch 2,400 yards. The course's big greens and shortish layout make it forgiving to novice golfers. There's a snack bar, and both clubs and carts are available to rent.

Willowdale Golf Club
52 Willowdale Road, Scarborough
(207) 883–9351
www.willowdalegolf.com

Willowdale is sandwiched between the horses and huff of Scarborough Downs harness-racing track and the salt marsh and seabirds of pretty Scarborough Marsh. And in the case of the latter, Greater Portland's big, beautiful estuary, that's not a bad thing. The front nine holes are open, the back nine are hugged by trees, and water separates the two but only comes into play on two holes. Because of the marsh, the par 71 course is among the most attractive in the area. The club is big on tournaments, so, depending upon when you visit, you can try your hand. There are plenty of amenities, from the modern clubhouse to the practice greens, rentals, snack bar, and lounge, and if you don't find what you want in the pro shop, you can always skip over to the Maine Mall, which is just minutes down the road. Tee times are recommended on the weekends.

Sable Oaks Golf Club
505 Country Club Drive, South Portland
(207) 775–6257
www.sableoaksgolf.com

A public course, Sable Oaks has a reputation for being challenging—both the 18 holes themselves and getting tee time. Calling ahead is required to get onto the well-loved, par 70 greens here (a week in advance would help your cause). *Golf Digest* called it Maine's eighth best public course in 1996; *Travel Golf Maine* magazine says it's "certainly the Portland area's premier daily fee layout," and people do indeed line up to play these tight fairways and fast greens. The course is hilly and woodsy, ably masking the fact that the Maine Mall and the Portland International Jetport are scant minutes up the road, and water comes into play on seven holes. The facilities are first-class, with a beautiful banquet room, a fully outfitted pro shop, a locker room, rentals, and more.

South Portland Municipal Golf Course
155 Wescott Road, South Portland
(207) 775–0005

The short nine-hole course run by the city of South Portland is known for being a good place to learn golfing. It's only 2,285 yards long, so you don't have to be Tiger Woods to be successful, and there are few hazards to worry about, just hills and trees, and pleasant ones at that. Par is 33, and you can get going early in the morning if you like. Club and pulled cart rental are available, and you can munch on goodies from the snack bar. Tee times are not necessary.

Riverside Municipal Golf Course
1158 Riverside Street, Portland
(207) 797–3524

Owned by the city of Portland, Riverside is actually two courses in one—Riverside North, an 18-hole, par 72 course, and Riverside South, a 9-hole, par 35 course. First opened to play in 1935, the 18-hole half is the more challenging setting—it hosts the Greater Portland Open—and it's among the most popular of all the courses in southern Maine. (Be thinking tee times if you want to play on the weekend.) The hills roll across its 6,406 yards, and it borders the Presumpscot River on the back part of the course. From the locker rooms and showers to the restaurant and lounge, it's a very professional operation. The facility also has a full pro shop, a driving range, practice greens, and rentals—the whole nine yards. In the winter the course becomes a popular cross-country skiing and snowshoeing destination.

Rivermeadow Golf Club
216 Lincoln Street, Westbrook
(207) 854–1625

Established in 1958, Rivermeadow is a par 35, nine-hole course in the Greater Portland mill town of Westbrook. The river in question is the Presumpscot, which helped make Westbrook into the industrious little city it is by getting things started at the local paper mill. The course is pleasant and tree lined, with water coming into play on three holes and sand and grass bunkers. You shouldn't have too much difficulty arranging a tee time, especially if you show up promptly at 7:00 A.M. The club is well outfitted, with a full pro shop, a practice green, a lounge and snacks, rentals, and instruction available.

Twin Falls Golf Club
364 Spring Street, Westbrook
(207) 854–5397

This is a tough one, thanks to woods and hills and small greens. Built in 1971 on the site of an old dairy farm in the Portland suburb of Westbrook, Twin Falls measures only 4,880 yards (par 33), but they are full of intriguing difficulties for the average golfer. The course is open from April through October, and there are club and car rentals and a snack bar. You won't find tee times necessary.

Westerly Winds Sports Park and Golf Learning Center
853 Cumberland Street (River Road), Westbrook
(207) 854–9463
www.westerlywinds.com

Yet another set of Westbrook links, this is the Johnny-come-lately on the scene, built in 1985. Two nine-hole courses compete for the attention of golfers here: the old nine-hole, par 27 pitch-and-putt Westerly Winds Course and the new nine-hole, par 35 championship Sunset Ridge Golf Links course. The former is just good fun, the latter a serious course with white birch stands and apple orchards to play through and around (and nine more holes currently in the works). If it proves too challenging, you might want to switch over to the 18-hole minigolf course or the driving range, or put down the clubs altogether and hit a few balls in the batting cage, or try your luck at shuffleboard or tennis, or take a swim in the pool. This is quite the full-service facility and should keep the whole family happy.

Gorham Country Club
134 McLellan Road, Gorham
(207) 839–3490

In the college town of Gorham—half of the University of Southern Maine is located here (the other campus is in Portland)—this is a fun course of bluegrass fairways and bent grass greens spread across a bosky, rolling landscape. The 18 holes are par 71, and water comes into play on four of them. Built in 1961 and designed by James MacDonald Sr., the course has played host to the Maine Open, and it has all the facilities to accommodate such an event. From a well-outfitted pro shop to cart and club rentals to the restaurant and lounge to the locker room and showers, everything a duffer would need is here. Unless you want to show up at 6:30 A.M. when the course opens, you might want to call ahead for tee times—and wear a shirt there, Tarzan, they're required (along with shoes).

Val Halla Golf and Recreation Center
60 Val Halla Road, Cumberland
(207) 829–2225
You won't find any Norse gods at Val Halla, but if you can avoid the brook on the 18th hole and come in somewhere around the 72 par, you might feel like one. Built in 1965 and expanded to 18 holes in the 1980s, the course is owned by the town of Cumberland, a pleasant suburb north of Portland. There's a whole complex of entertainments here, from tennis courts to a driving range to the Viking Grill. The place opens at 7:00 each morning, and you could easily fill a whole day playing 18 holes, having lunch at the grill, and then pulling on the tennis shoes. The course itself is 6,568 yards, and because it was designed in two phases, it has a different feel on the back nine. The facilities are excellent and include a well-stocked pro shop, a practice green and bunker, club and cart rental, and instruction. You can wind down with a cold beverage on the big deck off the back of the clubhouse overlooking the course.

Freeport Country Club
2 Old County Road, Freeport
(207) 865–0711
www.harrisgolfonline.com
Thanks to the fact that it's visible from Interstate 95 and less than 10 minutes from L. L. Bean, Freeport Country Club is a particularly active course. A nine-hole set of links established in the late 1960s, it's a 36 par and begins in flat fields just off the highway, ending in the woods beyond. Easily walkable, its short track makes it a good course for beginners. The facilities are set up much like you'd expect a place that sees a lot of guests to be, with a full pro shop, club and cart rentals, a practice green, and a bar at which you can grab a snack after your round. Tee times are recommended.

MIDCOAST

Brunswick Golf Club
165 River Road, Brunswick
(207) 725–8224
www.brunswickgolfclub.com
Brunswick has two interesting clubs that reflect the community. This is one of them, established in 1901 for use by Bowdoin College students. Now everybody seems to be enjoying its 18 holes on an average weekend. The course is divided into two nine-hole loops, the first original, the second added in 1970, and it's usually busy, so calling ahead is almost mandatory. There are all the major amenities, from club rental to eats to instruction, but you'll have to dress properly to enjoy them (no Bowdoin T-shirts—or tees of any kind—tank tops or cutoffs, etc). Open from April through mid-November. Eighteen holes in midsummer will set you back $65.

Mere Creek Golf Course
551 Fitch Avenue, Brunswick
(207) 921–2155
On the grounds of the local navy base, this course was for years called the Brunswick Naval Air Station Golf Club, but the Feds thought the name might be scaring away potential business. The nine holes here have been open to the public for years, but many people—especially visitors and newcomers to the area—aren't aware of it. It's a fine, open course, not too far from the runways of the navy's airport, and you get to rub shoulders with military personnel. From a full shop to a driving range to a snack bar and lounge, all the amenities are here. Club and car rentals are available. Tee times are a good idea on busy summer weekends. Because the BNAS is slated to close, it's a good idea to call ahead, anyway.

Shore Acres Golf Club
Sebasco Harbor Resort, Phippsburg
(207) 389–9060
The 9-hole course at this oceanfront resort was rebuilt in 2001, and it's open to

Virtual Golf

It's amazing that in a place like Maine, where the running joke is that there are two months of summer and the rest is winter, virtual golf hasn't become a huge phenomenon. But it's beginning to catch on. The latest and greatest golf simulators can be found at Out of the Rough Indoor Golf Club on Biddeford's Pomerleau Street (207–284–9900). There are eight of them at this indoor country club, allowing you to tee off in January if you like. You can also eat and drink at the grille on-site. Tee times are highly recommended. You can find more fair weather links (read virtual) at Harris Golf in South Portland (207–771–1975), at Portland's Fore Season Golf on Forest Avenue in Portland (207–797–8835) and at the Samoset in Rockport (207–594–2511 or 800–341–1650; www.samoset.com).

nonguests. The panoramas of Sebasco Harbor are phenomenal, and the course takes full advantage of them. Holes are set up such that rank amateurs and experienced duffers alike can choose tees that match their skill level. There's even a three–hole, regulation-size practice course for beginners. The facilities also include a pro shop, club and cart rentals, and a restaurant and lounge. The views alone are worth the drive down the Phippsburg Peninsula. Open from late April through early November.

Bath Country Club
387 Whiskeag Road, Bath
(207) 442–8411
www.skipworkplaygolf.com
These 18 holes have been renovated and expanded into an impressive course, and you should set aside a whole afternoon to play them. It's a good idea to come early for lunch at the clubhouse restaurant. There's also a pro shop on-site, along with practice greens, club and cart rental, and a lounge for bragging after the game is done. Tee times are necessary on weekends. Open from early April through October. Greens fees are a reasonable $14 for 9 holes, $20 for 18.

Boothbay Country Club
Country Club Road, Boothbay
(207) 633–6085
www.harrisgolfonline.com
Designed in 1921 by Styles and Van Cleek, the Boothbay Country Club expanded to 18 holes in 2000. The course is a scenic, rolling, par 70 affair, and the log-cabin-style clubhouse atop the first tee reminds you you're in Maine. Open from mid-April through October. The facility includes a full pro shop, a driving range, a practice green, and club and cart rental. Instruction is available.

Wawenock Country Club
Route 129, Walpole
(207) 563–3938
What would Damariscotta area duffers do without Wawenock? A lot of traveling, that's what. This is the only course for miles, and it is consequently very popular on weekends. Established in the 1920s, the nine holes here have a reputation for being fairly challenging. Par is 70 for these 6,037 yards, and the hilly, tree-lined terrain makes for plenty of tough shots. The clubhouse is located across State Route 129 from the actual links and is a neat old Victorian structure. It's fairly well stocked with a pro shop, snack bar, locker room, and

showers. You can rent clubs and carts, practice on the green or the practice bunker, or hit a few on the driving range. Tee times are a good idea on weekends in high summer and can be arranged as much as a week in advance.

Rockland Golf Club
606 Old County Road, Rockland
(207) 594–9322
www.rocklandgolf.com
An 18-hole public course established in 1942, Rockland Golf Club is open from April through October and rarely sees a day when it isn't in use by somebody. There are some nice views of the surrounding Camden Hills, as well as of Penobscot Bay from the first hole, Lake Chickawaukie from the 15th, and even some neat old lime quarries. The club serves breakfast and lunch and has a full bar, and the pro shop is well outfitted. You can rent whatever you might need. Tee times are required and should be reserved a few days in advance. A note: Be careful when crossing Old County Road; drivers are supposed to slow down due to the dramatic S curve here, but they are always zipping through. (Some have been known to toot in an attempt to throw off your swing out on the Route 17 legs of the course, too.) Oh, and leave your spikes behind.

North Haven Golf Club
Iron Point Road, Waterman Cove,
North Haven
(207) 867–2024
A public course on the exclusive island of North Haven? Yes, indeed, and an exceptionally pretty one. You'll have to walk from the ferry landing to the links, though, which isn't too far but tiring with heavy clubs. It might be best to rent on-site (clubs and carts). Penobscot Bay is the scenic backdrop for these nine holes, and it is truly spectacular. Take the ferry over from Rockland and make a day of it, playing a half day of golf and spending the other half strolling this pretty old island. Tee times are not usually needed. Open from May through October.

Goose River Golf Cub
50 Park Street, Rockport
(207) 236–8488
www.gooserivergolf.com
Many people are unaware that there is a golf course in the Camden-Rockport area, so tucked away is this gem. On a back road on the inland side of Rockport, not far from Bald and Ragged Mountains, it's listed in guidebooks with both Camden and Rockport addresses, so it's understandably difficult for the casual visitor to the area to find. But anyone with an interest in whacking a few should seek these greens out. The course is a bent grass, par 71 setup with water in play. Alternate tees make the 9-hole course almost like an 18-holer. Weekends can be busy, so tee times are necessary, and they can be reserved a week in advance. There are a snack bar and lounge on the premise for après-swing, a full pro shop, cart and club rentals, and a resident pro handy to give you tips. Open from mid-April through late October.

Samoset Golf Course
The Samoset Resort, 220 Warrenton Street,
Rockport
(207) 594–2511 or (800) 341–1650
www.samoset.com
One of the most popular courses along the coast, the Samoset has 18 holes on a stunning piece of coast overlooking both Rockland Harbor and the open ocean. These holes have been lauded up and down, called "a golfer's paradise" by *Golf Traveler,* hailed as "the seventh-most beautiful course in America" by *Golf Digest,* and ranked 26th in *Golf Digest's* listing of the country's 75 best resort courses. It's easy to understand, as 14 holes have superb views of the sea and seven actually border it. Part of the Samoset Resort, these links are available to nonguests, but the fees tend to be steep—$130 these days—and tee times are scheduled to favor guests. Still, it's worth making the effort for the views alone.

Northport Golf Club
581 Bluff Road, Northport
(207) 338–2270
Backed up against the cottage community of Bayside, just south of Belfast, the Northport Golf Club is a pleasure. Established in 1916, the course has nine holes and a par 36. It is fairly wide open with midsize greens of fast bent grass. Alternate tees are available for an 18-hole outing. The clubhouse is a nice old Victorian building, in keeping with the cool Victorian cottages of Bayside, which you should check out on your way in or out. Open from mid-April through October.

Searsport Pines Golf Course
240 Mount Ephraim Road, Searsport
(207) 548–2854
www.searsportpines.com
Built by a retiree on his family farm in 1999, this nine-hole, par 36 course is surprisingly enjoyable. The terrain is hilly and the fairways lined with pines, but it's a fairly short course at 5,766 yards, so it's not a difficult walk. The views can be very pleasant (as is the gazebo snack bar). Water comes into play on many of the early holes and then again on the ninth, where there's a large pond that undoubtedly has a bottom full of balls. Cart and club rentals are available, and tee times are recommended on the weekends.

Country View Golf Club
Route 7, Brooks
(207) 722–3161
The name says it all. Inland along State Route 7, 15 minutes from Belfast, Country View rides the backs of a series of rolling hills and offers some fantastic scenery of the Camden Hills and even the White Mountains on a superclear day. Be prepared to do some walking, as the terrain is hilly (cart rental is available). The club is family owned and friendly. Best of all, the nine holes here are not usually too busy. Open from mid-April through October.

Bucksport Golf Club
Route 46, Bucksport
(207) 469–7612
www.bucksportgolfclub.com
Bucksport bills itself as Maine's longest nine-hole course, and if it isn't, it must be close—hole 5 alone is a 502-yarder. The facility includes a pro shop, a snack bar, a driving range, cart and club rental, and two chipping greens. Open from mid-April through September, you can tee off as early as 7:00 A.M., and tee times are not usually necessary.

Island Country Club
Route 15A, Sunset, Deer Isle
(207) 348–2379
www.islandcountryclub.net
There's a lot to like at this nine-hole course. The greens were well laid out when the place was built in 1928, the clubhouse has recently been expanded, and it has a pleasant, welcoming air. You might be tempted to show up at 6:30 A.M. and play until dark after a few rounds here. The club is open from late May through mid-October. The facilities include cart and club rental, a practice green, a snack bar, and tennis courts.

Castine Golf Club
200 Battle Avenue, Castine
(207) 326–8844
Sprawling across one of the prettiest villages in Maine, the Castine club was opened in 1897, its fairways sweeping down toward the water. English designer William Parker Jr. crafted the original nine-hole layout, some of which is still the same. Open from May 15 through October 15. Instruction is available, as are club and cart rentals. There are tennis courts on-site, too, and you should make it in town to have a look at Castine, if you make it this far.

White Birches Golf Club
Route 1, Ellsworth
(207) 667–3621
www.wbirches.com

One of the more unusual courses in Maine, this par 33 18-holer is part of a motel complex right on U.S. Route 1, the main drag to Acadia National Park. One might expect minigolf here rather than 18 nice holes, but that's what lies out behind the White Birches motel. The first nine holes were built in 1983 and the second added in 2000, and the course has added a new twist to its offerings—golf under the lights. You'll feel like you're back in high school, playing the big game before the home crowd. The greens fees are eminently reasonable, and the club is well outfitted with a pro shop, practice green and bunker, and club and cart rental. And you can book a night in the motel if 18 holes during the day and another round under the lights just aren't enough. Open from April through October.

Bar Harbor Golf Club
Routes 3 and 204, Trenton
(207) 667–7505
This old favorite is not actually in Bar Harbor—or even on Mount Desert Island, for that matter. Established in 1965, the club is actually in Trenton, a few miles short of the island but with truly fantastic views of the green mountains of Acadia. The 18-hole, par 71 course gently rolls on small hills and the Jordan River plays through; other bodies of water provide challenges on a few holes, and the ocean makes itself felt, too, in the form of periodic breezes. The club is fully outfitted with a pro shop, driving range, restaurant, lounge, rentals, and a practice green. It's open from mid-April through October.

ACADIA AREA

Kebo Valley Golf Club
100 Eagle Lake Road, Bar Harbor
(207) 288–3000
www.kebovalleyclub.com
Bar Harbor is perhaps better known for its minigolf, but Kebo Valley is magnificent, one of Maine's best courses. In fact, it has a national reputation as a classic course, the eighth oldest in the nation. Built in 1891, the 18 holes here sit before some astonishing mountains-meet-the-sea vistas, which make a day on the links almost as much of a sightseeing trip as a hike in nearby Acadia National Park. Local legend has it that President Howard Taft needed 27 tries to sink the 17th hole on this par 70 course. The facilities live up to the greens and fairways, with a pro shop, rentals, instruction, club storage, a practice green and bunker, and a fine restaurant and lounge. They have a full-service caterer here, so, theoretically, you could get a tasty lunch delivered to you halfway through your round. Might be expensive, is all. The place is understandably popular, and tee times are necessary. Open daily from May through October.

Northeast Harbor Golf Club
Sargent Drive, Northeast Harbor
(207) 276–5335
Much like Kebo Valley, in that it feels old and classic, Northeast Harbor Golf Club was built in 1895 on the side of Somes Sound, the only genuine fjord in the Lower 48. Duffers enjoy 18 short, hilly, woodsy holes here, with views of beautiful Mount Desert frequent companions. The course has a full pro shop, a practice green, and club and cart rental. The driving range is for members only. Make sure to wear clothes that are appropriate—no cutoffs or halters. You can tee off as early as 7:00 A.M., and the course is open from Memorial Day through Labor Day.

Causeway Golf Club
Fernald Point Road, Southwest Harbor
(207) 244–3780
Built in 1920, this nine-hole course is considerably simpler than some others in the Mount Desert Island area. It has some nice water views, a couple of challenging holes, and a pro shop. Clubs and carts can be rented, and snacks can be had when you start to get hungry. Allow three hours to play 18 holes, and don't worry too much about tee times.

DOWN EAST

Blink Bonnie Golf Club
Route 185, Sorrento
(207) 422–3930
This little-known gem has been around since 1916, but you'd never know it. Most people remain unaware of the nine holes here (par 70), so tee times are not usually hard to come by. The layout is open, and the nearby sea factors in on a couple of holes. Open from May through September.

Grindstone Neck Golf Course
106 Grindstone Avenue, Winter Harbor
(207) 963–7760
www.grindstonegolf.com
There isn't much unpleasant about this grindstone. Duffers have been whacking them here since the 1890s, when the rusticators used to summer in the exclusive enclave of Winter Harbor. Pause for a moment before you tee off, and you'll see why they came—the scenery is extraordinary, looking out at the waves and islands of Frenchman Bay and the mountains of Acadia. Water is ever present. Par is 36 for 3,095 yards, and the course has a reputation as being fairly challenging, with tight bluegrass fairways. The fun begins each morning at sunrise, from early June through September, and tee times usually aren't necessary.

Great Cove Golf Course
Roque Bluffs Road, Jonesboro
(207) 434–7200
www.greatcovegolf.com
Ample ocean views make playing this nine-hole course a real treat. These holes were built in the 1970s, and they tend to be on the easier side of things. The amenities are not abundant—snack bar, driving range, practice green, and club and cart rental—but the setting here is the key and more than makes up for it. Tee times are not necessary, and you can play until dark on the one greens fee. Open from May through September.

Saint Croix Country Club
Route 1, Calais
(207) 454–8875
You can practice your French while you play on these nine holes—the club is bilingual, thanks to the fact that it borders the Canadian province of New Brunswick. The layout is open, and the St. Croix River comes into play on one hole. Greens are of bent grass, the fairways are of bluegrass, and par is 68 for 5,470 yards. You can tee off as early as 7:00 A.M., and when you do, chances are you'll be one of the first people to smack a ball in the United States, as this course is the easternmost in the country and gets the first rays of sun every morning. The facilities include a pro shop, club and cart rental, and a snack bar and lounge. Open from late April through late October. Très agréable.

Barren View Golf Course
1354 Route 1, Jonesboro
(207) 434–6531
www.barrenview.com
The views are anything but barren here. This nine-hole course opened in 2003 and it has panoramas aplenty; it's just that you're looking at, well, barrens—the blueberry barrens that the Down East coast is famous for. Par is 34, and you may find it easier than some to make. There are the usual amenities—clubhouse with cafe, pro shop, and rentals—and you can start playing as early as 7:00 A.M. Play all day for $36, or just the nine holes for $16.

KIDSTUFF

Maine continually ranks among the top states in the country to raise children—it was fourth best in a recent national Kids Count survey by the Annie E. Casey Foundation—and millions upon millions of people have rosy memories of childhood vacations spent on the Maine coast. Kids just love the place.

It's easy to understand why—there are endless things to do by simply stepping outside: Beaches and tide pools await explorers, trees are there to climb, hikable mountains are everywhere to be found, and swimming holes dot the landscape. The state also boasts a lot of entertainment for the smaller set, from the children's museums in Portland and Bangor, to the Maine State Game Farm in Gray, to petting zoos and amusement parks in various communities up and down the coast. Some conservation groups have great day programs for kids and families, and there are YMCAs along the length of the coast that are perfect for rainy days. Mom and Dad shouldn't have to work hard to find stuff to keep the kids busy.

This chapter features kidstuff by region, plus two sections at the end describing miniature golf courses and paintball centers along the Maine coast.

Several of the places and activities listed in previous chapters are just perfect for youngsters, too. These places include lighthouses (see Lighthouses chapter), beaches (see Beaches chapter), forts (see Attractions chap-

ter), and state parks (see Green Space chapter). Check them out for still further ideas.

Price Code

Except where noted, prices represent cost per person for admission, not including tax. In cases where donation is listed, there is no mandatory admission fee, but a donation is appreciated and recommended to support upkeep of the facility.

$	$5.99 or less
$$	$6.00 to $12.99
$$$	$13.00 to $19.99
$$$$	$20.00 or more

SOUTH COAST

The Goldenrod
York Beach
(207) 363–2622
www.thegoldenrod.com
More than a candy store, this old York Beach favorite is a veritable candy factory, and it's been at it for more than a century. Most famous for its taffy, the Goldenrod produces nine million Goldenrod Kisses a year—that's 65 tons of fun—using an 1896 recipe created by the shop's founder. (The secret science of saltwater taffy is reportedly understanding the weather.) There are 12 flavors—try the peanut butter or wintergreen—and you can watch it all being turned into sticky goodness right in the windows of the shop. The place also has a host of other treats, from fudge to barc to peanut brittle to candy corn, and there is still a penny candy counter where little suckies cost, yep, a penny apiece. Quite aside from being a sweet and aromatic stop, the Goldenrod has an anachronistic appeal, taking you back to summers long past with its old building, mar-

Close-up

Directory of Summer Camps

Maine has long been synonymous with summer camp for many people, and with good reason. There are about 100 camps in the state. Many of them are in the western mountain region, where there are woods and lakes galore, but plenty exist along the coast, too. The Maine Youth Camping Association has an extensive directory of camps, broken down by gender, and with all the pertinent information you need to decide where your daughter or son should go, from camp history to current activities and programs. The camps offered by environmental groups, religious organizations, and schools, as well as those geared toward sports or music, are all listed. It's a very handy resource. Your kids may not want to go to camp, of course, but they'll be glad they did when they get there—especially if you pick the right one. Get your copy of the directory by calling (207) 780–4628 or click over to the Web site www.mainecamps.org.

ble soda counter, and stone fireplace—classic stuff that will entertain moms and dads almost as much as the kids. York Beach just wouldn't be the same without it. There's no charge to come in and look around, but you're sure to want to buy some sweet treats. Free.

York's Wild Kingdom $$$
Route 1, York Beach
(207) 363–4911
www.yorkzoo.com

This York Beach institution is much more than a zoo. There are plenty of beasties about, sure—they number in the hundreds now, from llamas and lions to elephants and bears to camels and sloths to everyone's favorite, Rewa the Bengal tiger. But there are also go-karts, arcade games, Skeeball, haunted houses, minigolf, batting cages, bumper boats and paddleboats, rides upon rides, and all the snacks you could eat. (This place is just a short walk from York Beach.) A variety of scheduled shows—elephant shows, Wildlife Theatre educational programs, etc.—and other events occur on a daily basis, so be sure to call ahead for times. The Wild Kingdom is a full-fledged amusement park, and if you're into that sort of

thing, it's very amusing. Admission prices do not include go-kart or pony rides, which cost extra. In the high season—basically when school is out—the zoo is open daily from 10:00 A.M. to 6:00 P.M. and the park from noon to 9:30 P.M. Special rates for children.

Aquaboggan Water Park $$$–$$$$
980 Portland Road, Saco
(207) 282–3112
www.aquaboggan.com

The state's biggest water park, Aquaboggan is an endless source of fun for kids. Besides the waterslides, tubular slides, and suislides (dual high-speed cannonball runs), the facility offers an Olympic-size swimming pool, a wave pool, bumper boats, minigolf, water wars, paddleboats, go-karts, an arcade, and the Aquasaucer, a half dome of bouncy fun. Little people can—and do—spend days here before they get bored. Many of the activities, though, require that participants be over 4 feet tall. Rates vary, depending upon which rides and slides you want to try. Open daily from mid-June through Labor Day from 10:00 A.M. to 6:00 P.M.

Funtown USA $$$$
774 Portland Road (Route 1), Saco
(207) 284–5139
www.funtownusa.com
Not far from Aquaboggan, this amusement
park has been voted Maine's number one
tourist attraction, which makes one wonder
who's doing the voting (people under the age
of 14?). There is no end to the activities. They
include the state's largest and tallest roller
coaster, the Excalibur Wooden Roller Coast;
the Dragon's Descent, a free-fall ride that
drops you from 220 feet; the Thunder Falls Log
Flume ride; go-kart rides; the water park of
Splashtown; a whole slate of games; and
enough food to keep you and yours going all
day. A major water park expansion that will
double its size is scheduled to open 2007. The
park opens in mid-May and runs through mid-
September, with hours that vary upon the day
of the week (basically 10:00 A.M. to 10:00 P.M.
in July and most of August). Rates vary, too,
and are based on height rather than age.

Palace Playland
1 Old Orchard Street,
Old Orchard Beach
(207) 934–2001
www.palaceplayland.com
Palace Playland is a big part of what makes
Old Orchard Beach Old Orchard Beach—four
acres big—it's the state's only beachfront
amusement park. Two roller coasters, a log
flume ride, a 70-foot-high gondola-style Ferris
wheel, and two scary new rides—the Power
Surge, a revolving 50-foot, 360-degree turn,
and Moby Dick, on which you twist on the
whale's tale—are available for the high-thrills
seekers. And there are a host of teacup-type
rides for folks who are smaller or fainter of
heart. You can also get your palm read, visit a
fun house, and try your hand at a variety of
games of chance. This is an old-fashioned seaside carnival on the order of Coney Island, and
it has an obvious appeal to kids. Admission to
Palace Playland is free, but tickets for rides are
a dollar. Most rides require two to four tickets
each.

GREATER PORTLAND

Children's Museum of Maine $$
142 Free Street, Portland
(207) 828–1234
www.childrensmuseumofme.org
The highlight at this excellent kids' museum—
where the motto is "please do touch"—might
be the Camera Obscura, a dark room with a
lens to the outside world, where you can see
an extraordinary, 360-degree panorama of
Portland flash before you. This is absolutely fas-
cinating Renaissance-era technology, and there
are only two others like it in the nation. But
there's a lot more to enjoy here, from the Our
Town exhibit, a miniature community where
kids participate like grown-ups, to the L. L. Bear
Discovery Woods, to the space shuttle, work-
ing TV station, and the hands-on science room.
They're all very well done, and they'll keep the
kids entertained for hours. The museum hosts
birthday parties, special camps, and a variety
of events throughout the year. It's open Mon-
day through Saturday from 10:00 A.M. to 5:00
P.M. and Sunday from noon to 5:00 P.M., Memo-
rial Day through Labor Day, and during the rest
of the year the same hours except that after a
members-only time on Monday from 9:00 to
11:00 A.M., the museum is closed the rest of
the day. The first Friday of each month, it's free
to visit from 5:00 to 8:00 P.M.

Children's Theatre of Maine $$
317 Marginal Way, Portland
(207) 828–2774
www.childrenstheatremaine.org
This nifty drama outfit—the oldest continuously operating kids' theater in the country—
has kids squarely in mind. It produces shows
that are geared for younger audiences and
hosts the Maine Young Playwright's Contest—
the winner gets his or her show staged. Visit
the Web site to see the current offerings.

Maine Narrow Gauge
Railroad and Museum $–$$
58 Fore Street, Portland
(207) 828–0814
www.mngrr.org

Kids love those trains, and this neat museum has working engines that will haul them along the city's working waterfront. Open-air cars allow you to take it all in. These trains are all narrow gauge—the 2-foot-wide tracks that were big in Maine before the advent of the automobile—and the museum has a fine collection of old examples. It also has a full schedule of special transportation-oriented events. The trains run daily on the hour from 11:00 A.M. to 4:00 P.M. from mid-May through mid-October, and weekends for much of the rest of the year. The museum is open daily except for major holidays, from 10:00 A.M. to 4:00 P.M.

Portland Museum of Art $$
7 Congress Street, Portland
(207) 775–6148
www.portlandmuseum.org
The Portland Museum of Art has a variety of offerings designed to introduce kids to the world of art. Among the best are the Artsquad programs, which happen on Tuesdays. These hour-long workshops—from 4:00 to 5:00 P.M.—take kids ages 6 to 12 through the galleries of the museum and then back to the art studios, where they can make their own works of art. Another idea might be ARTREK, a five-day summer camp for kids ages 6 through 15, where they'll explore the museum and then come up with their own creations. These programs run from early July through August, and each week is geared toward a different age group. And there is always the designated Family Room at the McLellan house, where Mom and Dad and the kids can see interactive computer displays about 19th-century life, puzzles of the art on view at the museum, and a variety of games, like Go Fish using cards depicting artworks from the museum's collection.

Portland Observatory $
138 Congress Street, Portland
(207) 774–5561
www.portlandlandmarks.org
This tall signal tower has an interesting history

(see Attractions chapter), but kids don't care about that. They just like climbing its 103 steps to the top of the 86-foot tower for a view that takes in all of Portland, Casco Bay, the White Mountains, and beyond. Open daily from May through October, 10:00 A.M. to 5:00 P.M. Children 6 and younger free.

Portland Public Library Kid's Place
5 Monument Square, Portland
(207) 871–1700
www.portlandlibrary.com/kidsplace/ kidsplace.htm
The Portland Public Library is an exceptional resource for readers of all ages, and the staffers here get kids interested early with a full slate of programs for children, from story hour to bingo to finger fun for babies to family movies. Call or check the Web site for more details. Free.

Portland Symphony Orchestra $–$$
477 Congress Street, Portland
(207) 773–6128
www.portlandsymphony.com
The state's best orchestra frequently hosts Kinderkonzerts, which are designed to introduce kids ages 3 through 7 to live classical music and various families of instruments through interactive programs with symphony musicians. These fun events occur across the state. Check the Web site to see when and where the next one is.

Southworth Planetarium $$
96 Falmouth Street, Portland
(207) 780–4249
www.usm.maine.edu/~planet/
Part of the University of Southern Maine, Southworth is one of two planetariums in Maine (the other's in Orono). Every Friday and Saturday the auditorium here becomes the site of astronomy shows at 7:00 P.M. and laser light shows at 8:30 P.M. Saturdays also have matinees. The planetarium also regularly holds special programs exploring space themes.

Smiling Hill Farm
State Route 22, Westbrook
(207) 775–4818
www.smilinghill.com
Unfortunately, the barnyard at this working dairy in Westbrook is now closed due to ominous-sounding "biosecurity" reasons. Kids used to like to visit with the animals. But they can still get a cone of homemade ice cream and pet some cunning wee animals near the Dairy Store, like pygmy goats and a baby bull. The Knight family has been working these 500 acres since before the American Revolution, and they've done a great job staying with the times, selling natural milk, cheese, great lunches, and ice cream and opening the farmstead to skiing in the winter. Summer hours are Monday through Friday from 11:00 A.M. to 8:00 P.M., Saturday from 9:00 A.M. to 8:00 P.M., and Sunday from noon to 8:00 P.M. There's no charge to look around and pet the little animals, but you'll want to buy some of that delicious ice cream. Free.

Maine Audubon Society $
20 Gilsland Farm Road, Falmouth
(207) 781–2330
www.maineaudubon.org
Education has always been at the core of the Maine Audubon Society's mission, and the old conservation organization has helped generations of Maine kids gain a greater appreciation for the outdoors. The society hosts a vast array of workshops, programs, and field trips that are oriented toward families and children. These activities are open to nonmembers, and they include Star Bright: Family Astronomy Night, a tour of the night sky above Gilsland Farm; Dragonflies: Winged Jewels of Summer, an exploration of the ponds near the farm in search of dragonflies, appropriate for kids age 6 and older; and Buzzing Bees, a program looking at the lives of honeybees. There are also programs filled with nature walks, outdoor games, and songs geared toward preschoolers, as well as a raft of summer camps for young kids, teens, and family groups. Call the society and ask for the full schedule.

Maze Craze
Plummer-Motz Elementary School
State Route 9 and Lunt Road, Falmouth
The playground to beat all playgrounds, this gigantic wooden maze of a place is great fun for kids to get lost in. (They're fine; don't worry.) Schools from all over bus their children here to explore the castlelike structure, swing on the swings, slide on the slides, and make like monkeys on the monkey bars. A play area for kids with disabilities is right here, too. Open dawn to dusk. Free.

Maine Wildlife Park $
Route 26, Gray
(207) 657–4977
www.state.me.us/ifw/education/wildlifepark.htm
Formerly known as the Maine Game Farm and Visitors Center, this state-run animal rehabilitation center functions a lot like a zoo, and kids love it. Strolling around the farm, you can see bears, moose, eagles, lynx, wild turkeys, bobcats, and a host of other charismatic critters. Most of the inhabitants of the park are animals that have been injured or orphaned and are being rehabilitated to be released again into the wild, and while they're doing their physical therapy, they entertain the kids. The Maine Department of Inland Fisheries and Wildlife is in charge, and it has set up interactive displays that will teach you and yours about the various animals and their habitat—the Maine woods. You are welcome to stroll the trails of the 200-acre farm or even have a picnic. A fun outing for the whole family, it's worth the short drive inland.

Desert of Maine $–$$
95 Desert Road, Freeport
(207) 865–6962
www.desertofmaine.com
Camels, anyone? The Desert of Maine doesn't actually have any camels, but they'd feel comfortable in this 300-acre Freeport oddity. Ages of overgrazing and a sandy, arid substratum have turned this old farm into a veritable desert of giant dunes. There are guided safaris

Close-up

Why the Y?

Many Maine communities have excellent YMCAs these days, and they often have short-term or even daylong membership options that can be great for visiting families. The Boothbay Region Y, for example, has nice facilities, with its Olympic-size pool, fitness center, gym, racquetball courts, game room, and day camp at a private lake, and it offers a day membership that allows for use of everything for $8.00 per adult or $11.00 for the whole family. This membership can be a vacation saver on a rainy day. The Y here also has day-care programs in the summer, if you happen to be staying for a while. Most other Ys along the coast have similar deals. On the coast, Ys can be found in the following places:

Sanford Springvale YMCA, Sanford; (207) 324–4942
Northern York County YMCA, Biddeford; (207) 283–0100
Greater Portland YMCA, Portland; (207) 874–1111
Casco Bay Regional YMCA, Freeport; (207) 865–9600
Bath Area Family YMCA, Bath; (207) 443–4112
Central Lincoln County YMCA, Damariscotta; (207) 563–3477
Boothbay Region YMCA, Boothbay Harbor; (207) 633–2855
Penobscot Bay Area YMCA, Rockport; (207) 236–3375
Waldo County YMCA, Belfast; (207) 338–4598
Down East Family YMCA, Ellsworth; (207) 667–3086
Mount Desert Island YMCA, Bar Harbor; (207) 288–3511

of the area on the half hour, but you're welcome to explore the walking trails through the desert on your own. On a hot summer day, you'd swear you were in the Sahara (except for all the pine trees that surround). There are a gift shop, picnic area, and convenience store here where you can learn more about this freakish oasis. Kids love the place, and parents usually find it unusual enough to be worthwhile. Open from early May through mid-October. Children 4 and under free.

Wolfe's Neck Farm
184 Burnett Road, Freeport
(207) 865–4469
www.wolfesneckfarm.org
Natural foods may be all the rage these days, but this environmentally conscious farm on Casco Bay has been raising beef cattle the all-natural way since the 1950s. In keeping with its philosophies (natural, organic, pesticide-free foods, family farms, knowing where food comes from, sustainability), the farm has an educational arm and offers an array of programs to kids. Favorite activities, according to farm staff, are bottle-feeding baby pigs, going on hayrides, canoeing on the bay, and helping sell produce. Workshops may be half-day, full-day, or weeklong, like the Farm School program, where kids in third through eighth grade work on the farm, learning sustainable principles, and helping grow gardens. April and May are special months, because that's when all the baby animals are born—as many as 80 calves—and who doesn't like baby animals? Summer brings day camp activities; winter brings skiing and sledding. A visit to the farm is a rich experience and one that kids won't

soon forget. You can visit the farm for free, but a fee is charged for activities and workshops. Call for current rates.

MIDCOAST

Chewonki Foundation Summer Camps
485 Chewonki Neck Road, Wiscasset
(207) 882–7323
www.chewonki.org
The Chewonki Foundation has been involved in environmental education since 1962, and it's got its business down to a science, teaching people of all ages about the outdoors at its 400-acre center in Wiscasset and on field trips to remote locations. The outfit has a variety of offerings for kids, too, including several summer camp programs. These are fairly traditional summer camps for both boys and girls ages 8 through 15. Kids live in cabins and learn sailing, swimming, kayaking, canoeing, arts and crafts, and farm skills. There are three-and-a-half-week and seven-week sessions, and in August there are five-day adventure camps for children ages 10 through 13 that put them through challenges on ropes and in canoes and sea kayaks. Kids tend to have fun at all of these programs and walk away at the end with some new skills and, it is hoped, a new or renewed love or appreciation for the great outdoors.

Morris Farm
156 Gardiner Road (Route 27), Wiscasset
(207) 882–4080
www.morrisfarm.org
Here's another fantastic old farm in the Midcoast region where kids can learn about sustainable agriculture, pet a few cows, and sign up for workshops or courses. The 60-acre working farm has agriculture, community, and education as its basic tenets, and it's the last one that grabs the kids, even if they're having too much fun to know they're soaking up information. Since the late 1990s, when the farm was rescued from development by a group of concerned area citizens, it's made great progress. The site now features an operational

dairy, a 68-tree organic orchard, a half acre of raspberries, another half-acre market garden, yet another children's garden, a small poultry operation, and an interpretive trail through 10 acres of woodlands. The farm's school programs are operated in keeping with the state's learning standards. There are workshops like the Afternoon at the Farm series, where kids can spend several hours after school on Monday, Wednesday, and Friday and do easy and fun chores, like feeding and milking cows, feeding rabbits, gathering eggs, making cheese or butter, or putting up canned items. And in summer there are day camps where kids learn all that and more, play games, do crafts, and even do some science projects. The opportunities are many, and there are plenty of one-day programs available. You're welcome to simply visit and have a look around, too.

Boothbay Railway Village $–$$
State Route 27, Boothbay
(207) 633–4727
www.railwayvillage.org
Ten acres and 28 historic buildings provide the backdrop for train tours at the Boothbay Railway Village, an ersatz hamlet on the main route to Boothbay Harbor. The steam engine makes runs at least hourly (sometimes twice an hour) around a short, narrow-gauge rail through the village to the delight of passengers young and old. Many of the trains in the collection here date back to the heyday of train travel—the late 1800s—and there is a vintage vehicle exhibit, too, which includes all sorts of automobiles. These might include an 1885 fire pumper or a 1929 Packard Limo. In addition to the cars and trains, there is a full slate of events and programs here, from classes in steam engines to firefighters' days and a fall festival.

Maine Resources Aquarium $
McKown Point Road,
West Boothbay
(207) 633–9542
www.state.me.us/dmr/rm/aquarium/

A petting zoo of sorts resembling the Maine coast, this small aquarium opened in 1993. Kids love to lean over the side of the 20-foot-long touch tank and handle the invertebrates, feeling the sea urchin and getting squirted by a sea cucumber. And they like to peer into the 850-gallon tank filled with sharks and skates, even getting a chance to feel a shark's skin. Then there's Fritz the Lobster, who weighs close to 23 pounds. The aquarium is run alongside the Department of Marine Resources' fisheries research station, and there are occasional presentations about the state of the state's fisheries. Tours of the research facility are also available. Open daily from 10:00 A.M. to 5:00 P.M. from Memorial Day through September 4. Children 4 and under free.

Damariscotta Mills Alewives Run
Off State Route 215, Damariscotta Mills
This is a miracle of nature that's fascinating to see. Old-time Mainers used to talk about fish so thick you could walk across the river on their backs, and you'll believe them if you make it to see the spring run of alewives (tiny herring) up from Great Salt Bay to their spawning grounds in Damariscotta Lake. Every May and June—and you can always tell it's time when you see the circling seagulls and ospreys—the alewives scale a concrete fish ladder, climbing from sea level up more than 40 feet to ponds that connect to the lake. They move en masse—hundreds of thousands have been counted—and it's an epic struggle. Some make it, some don't. If you think the Maine Turnpike is bad in August, get a load of this. They wriggle, they fight, their silver bodies twist and turn, and you can watch them go for much of their run. You'll feel like you've watched Rocky again when you see them splash into the pond at the end of the ladder. Kids are transfixed. Take the Mills Road out of Damariscotta; you'll see the cars and birds if it's happening. Free.

Fawcett's Antique Toy Museum $
Route 1, Waldoboro
(207) 832–7398
Former art professor John Fawcett has filled a deceptively large colonial in Waldoboro to the brim with toys and toys and more toys. There are pictures, posters, and artifacts about toys, and actual toys themselves. Disneyana is a specialty—which is to be expected from a curator and artist whose work is in the book *The Art of Mickey Mouse*—but there are also whole sections devoted to the Lone Ranger. Also look for Peanuts, Looney Tunes, Super-man, Popeye, Pogo, Rocky and Bullwinkle, *Star Trek*—they're all represented. If it was a toy, it's in here. Geared for adults, it's a treasure trove for kids, too. Open Memorial Day through Columbus Day Thursday through Monday from 10:00 A.M. to 4:00 P.M. Open weekends only from Columbus Day through Christmas from noon to 4:00 P.M.

The Farnsworth Art Museum $$$$
356 Main Street, Rockland
(207) 594–6457
www.farnsworthmuseum.org
A favorite of grown-up visitors to Rockland, the Farnsworth hosts a few programs for kids, too. Most are art classes, in various disci-plines, for various ages. An example might be Children's Class: Drawing and Painting II, a series of classes designed to bring out the budding Wyeth in kids, teaching youngsters ages 10 through 12 the ways of the pencil and the brush. The museum also hosts afterschool programs for teens. Call or check the Web site for more information. (For more information on the museum's regular hours and its exten-sive collection, see the Attractions chapter.)

Camden Snow Bowl $
Hosmer Pond Road, Camden
(207) 236–3438
www.camdensnowbowl.com
Every community should have a ski mountain like this one. The town-owned center sits on the side of 1,300-foot Ragged Mountain on the inland outskirts of Camden. There's plenty of

skiing to be had here when the weather provides the fluffy stuff. Nine trails, most of them classified as intermediate, await schuss-boomers, so it's a good learning mountain. Better still, though, perhaps, for young kids is the tubing run at the base of the peak, which is a safe, fast, fun, and bouncy run. The Snow Bowl is also famous for its toboggan chute, a 400-foot trough that shoots the wooden sleds down the mountain at high speeds and out across Hosmer Pond. There is ice-skating on the pond as well. The well-run facility with its classic A-frame lodge is not about wearing the newest and tightest ski fashions or about zillion-dollar lift tickets, but about having an enjoyable day on the slopes with the rest of the community. In summer there is a rec program for kids between second and sixth grades that includes all sorts of sports, arts and crafts, hiking and canoeing, and day trips to beaches. There are also ball fields and tennis courts and concerts during the summer months.

MERI Center for Marine Studies
55 Main Street, Blue Hill
(207) 374–2135
www.meriresearch.org

Maine Environmental Research Institute (MERI) is a research facility dedicated to protecting the health of the Gulf of Maine, and it has a variety of outreach programs that appeal to kids. At its beautiful facility on Main Street there is a small Ocean Aquarium Room where there is a touch tank to explore. There is also a sea-themed story hour on Friday mornings from 10:00 to 11:00 and a variety of boat cruises and island walks aimed at kids. These activities run through July and August. Families pile aboard the R/V MERI for a tour out on the bay. A naturalist will point out the seals, porpoises, seabirds, and eagles encountered on the way. The Island Explorer program couples a boat ride with tide pool exploration and island ecology lessons. There are three of these programs, aimed at differing ages (6–10, 8–12, and 10–16). Costs vary depending upon the program but are in the $30 to $40 range. Admission is free.

Seacoast Fun Park $$–$$$$
Route 3, Trenton
(207) 667–3573
www.seacoastfunparks.com

One of those multifaceted amusement parks that inevitably seem to spring up near national parks, this small amusement complex 3 miles from Ellsworth has something for everyone: waterslides, minigolf, go-karts, a pool, a snack bar, an arcade, a trampoline, and even Maine's only tented paintball facility. Open daily from Memorial Day through Labor Day and weekends in the shoulder season. Admission fees vary from the all-day package passes that allow access to a variety of rides ($18 for adults, $16 for kids) to individual passes for specific activities ($8 or $6 for golf, for example, or $12 for paintball).

Dive-In Theater Tours
Bar Harbor Inn Pier, Bar Harbor
(207) 288–3483
www.divered.com

Diver Ed is a clever fellow. From the puns of his own name and business name to simply offering the throngs of people who visit Acadia a chance to see what's on the sea bottom—without even getting wet—he's on to something. The Dive-In Theater is Diver Ed's scuba tour, during which he swims to the bottom with a camera and projects video back to a large screen on the boat above to the delight of passengers. They get to virtually dive Frenchman Bay, seeing the rich array of sea life in this fertile basin, and toward the end of the two-hour jaunt, he scoops up a bagful of sea critters for the kids above to pet. Neat stuff. Diver Ed also does dive charters on his boat the *Seal*. He hosts three shows daily from Memorial Day through September 22—10:00 A.M. and 1:00 and 5:30 P.M.—and reservations are required. Tickets are $25 for adults, $15 for kids ages 5 through 11, and free for children age 4 younger.

Diver Ed amuses the kids. LISA MOSSEL VIETZE

MINIATURE GOLF

What kid doesn't love a round of miniature golf? Especially if Dad lets him or her win. Here's where you'll find some tiny links.

Wells Beach Resort
1000 Post Road, Route 1, Wells
(800) 640–CAMP
www.wellsbeach.com

Wonder Mountain Miniature Golf
U.S. Route 1, Moody
(207) 646–9655

Shakerland Golf
Route 202, East Waterboro
(207) 247–4653

Cascade Miniature Golf
955 Route 1, Saco
(207) 282–3524

Schooner Miniature Golf
58 Ocean Park Road, Saco
(207) 284–6174

Pirate's Cove
70 First Street, Old Orchard Beach
(207) 934–5086

Adventure Falls Miniature Golf
510 Warren Avenue, Portland
(207) 878–5800

**Westerly Winds Sports Park &
Golf Learning Center**
853 Cumberland Street (River Road),
Westbrook
(207) 854–9463

Long Shot Golf Center
305 Bath Road, Brunswick
(207) 725–6377

Dolphin Mini Golf
510 Wiscasset Road, Boothbay
(207) 633–4828

Treasure Island Miniature Golf
125 Townsend Avenue, Boothbay Harbor
(207) 633–6669

Mini-Golf
773 Commercial Street, Rockport
(207) 594–5211

Finest Kind
Center District Crossroad (halfway between
Routes 15 & 15A), Deer Isle
(207) 348–7714

Pine Ridge Golf Center
R.R. 15, Sedgwick
(207) 359–6788

Vokes Mini-Strokes
Bar Harbor Road (Route 3),
Ellsworth
(207) 667–9519

Whale-In-One Mini-Golf
Narrows Too Camping Resort
1150 Bar Harbor Road, Trenton
(207) 667–4300

Pirate's Cove
Bar Harbor
(207) 288–2133

PAINTBALL CENTERS

Paintball has been all the rage in Maine, especially among teenage boys. There are now several centers where they can don body armor,
pick up a rifle, and compete in war games.
Here are the coastal options.

Westside Paintball
72 Emery Street, 4th floor
(207) 324–0071
www.westsidepaintball.com
With a 25,000-square-foot course, this newly
opened facility is Maine's largest indoor paintball arena. It has all the amenities a weekend
warrior might want—a retail store, a spectator
viewing area, and even a picnic area for that
après-war pick-me-up. Open Monday through
Friday noon to close, weekends 10:00 A.M. to
close, and they'll open the space any time day
or night with 24 hours' notice.

Birch Hill Paintball
76 Birch Hill Road, York
(207) 363–6416
www.birchhillpaintball.com
All sorts of thrills await paintballers here, from
a Hyperball field to a spools field to a castle
scenario to a Woodsball field, and there is a
full-service pro shop. Rentals are $40 per per-
son. Open weekends from 9:00 A.M. to 4:00
P.M. and weekdays by appointment.

Bennett AllWeather Paintball
463 Fort Hill Road, Gorham
(207) 839–9177
www.bennettallweatherpaintball.com
This place is known for speedball, and it has
two outdoor Ultimate Airball fields and one
indoor field.

ARTS AND ENTERTAINMENT

Artists of all sorts have drawn inspiration from the Maine coast. Painters were among the first tourists to discover its beauties, and some of the biggest names in American art have worked here. The state has an unusually high number of writers who have called it home as well. And for a rural state with few urban centers, there are a surprising number of world-class classical music festivals and schools.

When the affluent summercators moved north to places like Kennebunk and Bar Harbor for the season, you see, they didn't want to leave behind all the culture they'd grown accustomed to. So they brought it with them. Summer theater, summer concerts, summer dance—all have long traditions on the Maine coast. The resort communities seem almost as busy as Portland in the summer.

The state was once famous for its art colonies in Ogunquit, Monhegan, and Bar Harbor, and that heritage is carried on today as well. There are several galleries along the coast with artworks on their walls that can compete with the big guns in New York. You just have to look.

Unfortunately, the state still doesn't have much in the way of a live music scene—there's just no comparing Portland's nightlife to places like Boston, even on a per capita

basis—but if you're lucky you might be in town when a good show is scheduled. We do have a large number of great downtown cinemas, though, where you can catch the arty films before they become national sensations, and plenty of soulless multiplexes as well.

Culture? We got culture.

THEATER
South Coast
Hackmatack Playhouse
538 Route 9, Berwick
(207) 698–1807
www.hackmatack.org
One of the nicest things about the Hackmatack theater company is the neat old barn it performs in. Every summer for decades, the company here has presented a handful of musicals and comedies aimed at family audiences. Shows are held nightly at 8:00 P.M., Wednesday through Saturday, with matinees on Thursday at 2:00 P.M.

Booth Theater
Beach Street, Ogunquit
(207) 646–8142
www.boothproductions.com
Based in Worcester, Massachusetts, this theater troupe is in residence at the Betty Doon Motel in summer and stages old standbys one after another from July through September.

John Lane's Ogunquit Playhouse
U.S. Route 1, Ogunquit
(207) 646–5511
www.ogunquitplayhouse.org
The star power that this professional theater has seen since it opened in the 1930s is staggering. The playhouse is often referred to as "America's foremost summer theater," and it

i The Maine Art Commission, a state-run, arts promotion organization, has a handy Web site—http://mainearts .maine.gov—with an events calendar, a news section, and an artist directory, which will help you find that gallery you remember visiting last time you came to Maine. It also publishes a bunch of useful guides, like the *Maine Art Museum Trail*, to various arts disciplines and organizations.

fits the bill. Shows run Monday through Friday at 8:00 P.M. and Saturday at 8:30 P.M. from late June through Labor Day. On Wednesdays and Thursdays there are matinees at 2:30 P.M.

Maritime Productions
Kennebunkport
(207) 641–2313 or (877) SEA–SHOW
www.maritimeproductions.org

Not your usual theater company, this outfit bills itself as the "world's only completely nautical professional entertainment company," which gives you a small idea of what they do. From June through October they present the award-winning show *Seafaring Legends, Haunts, and Folklore of New England and the Seven Seas,* aboard the pleasure boat *Deep Water II* out of Kennebunkport. This is their own script, and it's based on actual tales.

Arundel Barn Playhouse
53 Old Post Road, Arundel
(207) 985–5552
www.arundelbarnplayhouse.com

This young company—formed in 1997—brings a mix of old and new productions to the restored Smith Sisters barn not far from the Kennebunks. In the same season, they'll do a New England premiere—like Roger Bean's *Route 66*—and follow it up with a weathered play like *Grease.* Call or visit the Web site for this year's schedule.

Biddeford City Theater
205 Main Street, Biddeford
(207) 282–0849
www.citytheater.org

Murder mysteries, big bands, the *Rocky Horror Show,* Lazer Vaudeville—this is the rich mix you'll find at the City Theater, a great space in downtown Biddeford. It's enjoyed some revitalization since the early 1990s, after hosting such greats as Fred Astaire, Mae West, and W. C. Fields in earlier days. Active year-round.

Greater Portland

Lyric Music Theater
176 Sawyer Street, South Portland
(207) 799–6509
www.lyricmusictheater.com

This community troupe has been producing musicals since 1952. It stages four a year now at the Cedric Thomas Playhouse between September and May. Tickets are $19 for evening performances and $17 for matinees.

Portland Players
420 Cottage Road, South Portland
(207) 799–7337
www.portlandplayers.org

Arguably Maine's best community theater, the Portland Players actually work in South Portland, where they stage old standbys from September through June at the Thaxter Theater and typically do a good job of it. Tickets are in the $17 to $20 range.

Portland Stage Company
25A Forest Avenue, Portland
(207) 774–0465
www.portlandstage.com

Portland Stage is a professional troupe that presents performances from October through April at its own theater in an old Odd Fellows hall. From Shakespeare and *A Christmas Carol* to world premieres, it does a little of everything. Call or check the Web site for the current lineup.

Midcoast

Maine State Music Theater
22 Elm Street, Brunswick
(207) 725–8769
www.msmt.org

Broadway in Brunswick. That's the idea behind this Equity company, which performs in a beautifully renovated space just up the road from its old home on the campus of Bowdoin College. People turn out in great numbers for its summer season of old and new favorites. Local kids often get small parts. Summer shows are at 8:00 P.M. Tuesday through Saturday, with additional matinees on Tuesday, Thursday, Friday, and Sunday. Tickets are $30 to $49.

The Theater Project
14 School Street, Brunswick
(207) 729–8584
www.theaterproject.com
Founded in 1971, Theater Project produces innovative dramas and does a lot of work with kids. It has its own space in downtown Brunswick and works year-round.

Carousel Music Theatre
Route 27, Boothbay Harbor
(207) 633–5297 or (800) 757–5297
www.carouselmusictheatre.com
The cast will serve you from a menu that isn't half bad at this big red barn of a place. Boothbay has always loved its dinner theater, and Carousel has been entertaining area residents and visitors since 1975. After your waiter serves you dinner and a cocktail, he or she will set about singing show tunes with the rest of the cast. There's a lot of vaudeville to the act and a little bit of Broadway. Open Monday through Saturday from mid-May through mid-October. Reservations are a good idea. Tickets to the show only are $17.

Camden Civic Theatre
Camden Opera House, Main Street, Camden
(207) 236–2281
www.camdencivictheatre.com
One of the state's best community drama programs, Camden Civic Theatre has been delighting area residents since the early 1970s. One of the nicest things about its productions is the venue—the restored Camden Opera House, on the second floor downtown, is a beauty. Tickets are $12 and $16.

Belfast Maskers
Railroad Theater, Front Street, Belfast
(207) 338–9668
www.belfastmaskerstheater.com
A top-notch community theater, the Maskers

have attracted some big-name stars to the stage in Belfast. Mostly, though, it's the work of dedicated Waldo County residents that lights up the stage at the Railroad Theater: classics and premieres, locally directed. Shows are on Saturdays. Tickets are $10 to $15. Call ahead for showtimes.

National Theatre Workshop of the Handicapped
96 Church Street, Belfast
(207) 338–6894
www.ntwh.org
Belfast residents were excited when this school set up in town several years ago, and it produces several shows a year now. Look for local listings.

Acadia Area

Deck House Restaurant and Cabaret Theater
11 Apple Lane, Southwest Harbor
(207) 244–5044
www.thedeckhouse.com
Show tunes in the round are on the menu at the Deck House, where the audience eats and the waitstaff doubles as the players. Music from Broadway is the usual fare, but dance, mime, puppetry, and barbershop harmonies have happened here in the past. Reservations are recommended.

Acadia Repertory Theatre
State Route 102, Somesville
(207) 244–7260
www.acadiarep.com
More professional summer fare on the island. These guys have been at it for more than 30 years. A mix of comedies, dramas, mysteries, and children's shows make up their calendar, and the stage is at the neat old Masonic Hall in Somesville. Tickets are $22.

Down East

Downriver Theater Productions
Liberty Hall, Machiasport
(207) 255–4997
This community theater puts on musicals

every June through August. Call for current schedule.

Stage East
Washington Street, Eastport
(207) 853–4747
www.stageeast.org
When this community theater needed seats at its performance space, it went out and bought what it could afford—but the 100 new seats needed repair. So the community got involved, the local vocational school helped fix the hardware, a reupholsterer recovered them, and area residents bought them for $25 each, making it all possible. When they needed still more space, they bought the local Baptist church. This is what community theater is supposed to be about. They do several shows a year, from old standbys to new award winners.

PERFORMING ARTS CENTERS
South Coast

Ogunquit Performing Arts
Dunaway Center, School Street, Ogunquit
(207) 646–6170
This local promoter presents a chamber music fest every June with name acts at the Ogunquit Arts Collaborative Gallery and other venues.

River Tree Arts
35 Western Avenue, Kennebunk
(207) 967–9120
www.rivertreearts.org
This local outfit sponsors contra dances, summer concerts, and all sorts of arts classes for adults and children.

Greater Portland

PCA Great Performances
477 Congress Street, Portland
(207) 842–0800
www.pcagreatperformances.org
Some of the best shows to have played Portland are those that are sponsored by this vibrant outfit. Each season—from fall to summer—PCA brings about 20 performers to the

stage of Merrill Auditorium, from the hyperactive percussion of an ensemble like Stomp to the individual brilliance of an artist such as cellist Yo-Yo Ma. Drama, dance, and music are all represented, and the talents are always of the caliber that usually visit only much larger cities. Call or click over to the PCA Web site to find out this year's lineup.

The St. Lawrence Arts Center
76 Congress Street, Portland
(207) 775–5568
www.stlawrencearts.org
One of the city's more distinctive buildings, the St. Lawrence Church was in need of rescuing in the late 1990s, and a grassroots effort was undertaken to restore and preserve the 1897 stone Congregational church. The result is a really cool 110-seat, multifunctional venue for local arts and cultural organizations, including bands. Groups from around the state play the stage regularly, especially in summer.

Midcoast

The Chocolate Church Arts Center
798 Washington Street, Bath
(207) 442–8455
www.chocolatechurch.com
This 1847 Gothic church is hard to miss, both because it's big and prominent, even from Route 1, and because it's painted a rich chocolate brown. And you wouldn't want to miss anything that goes on inside. A cultural bright spot in the City of Ships, the church is a multifaceted operation, presenting an array of concerts, lectures, and performances and hosting shows at its adjacent art gallery. Check the Web site for the latest information.

Round Top Center for the Arts
3 Round Top Lane, Damariscotta
(207) 563–1507
www.roundtoparts.org
The calendar is full at the old Round Top farm year-round with performances, art classes, exhibitions, and lectures. Every summer the Portland Symphony Orchestra puts on an outdoor pops concert here, and other concerts

might range from cabaret interpretations of Kurt Weill's music to the U.S. Marine Band String Quartet to the Salt Bay Chamber Fest. Shows might be mime or vaudeville or dance. The center does a fine job of presenting a well-rounded schedule. Check the Web site to see what's coming up.

Lincoln Arts Festival
Various locations, Boothbay Harbor
(207) 633–3913
www.lincolnartsfestival.org
Since 1980 this outfit—it's a cultural organization, not any kind of fair—has been sponsoring concerts and performances in the Boothbay area, from jazz to classical to pop, primarily by regional performers. Summer only. Call or check the Web site for this year's events.

Grand Auditorium
Main Street, Ellsworth
(207) 667–9500
www.grandonline.org
Residents of towns within a 75-mile radius of this place ought to be singing their praises that it exists. From live music to theater to first-run and art films, this old space has it all. Check the excellent Web site or call for a list of upcoming events.

LIVE MUSIC—CLASSICAL AND OPERA
Greater Portland
Portland Opera Repertory Theatre (PORT)
P.O. Box 7733, Portland 04112
(207) 879–7678
www.portopera.org
Portland's resident opera company, established in 1995, PORT regularly brings big operatic productions to the stage of Merrill Auditorium. Call or check the Web site for the complete schedule.

Portland String Quartet
www.portlandstringquartet.org
Called "Maine treasures" by Colby College (the quartet members are artists in residence

there), this combo performs frequently at venues across the state. Check the Web site for its schedule.

Portland Symphony Orchestra
477 Congress Street, Portland
(207) 773–6128
www.portlandsymphony.com
In 1997 Merrill Auditorium, the home of the Portland Symphony Orchestra, was completely refurbished, transformed from a tired old city hall auditorium into a world-class concert hall. Finally the PSO had a home worthy of the house band. The 80-member orchestra has been a popular draw in the city for decades. Particular crowd-pleasers are the PSO's annual summer pops and the December-long Magic of Christmas series.

Midcoast
Kneisel Hall Chamber Music Festival
Pleasant Street, Blue Hill
(207) 374–2811
www.kneisel.org
Austrian violinist Franz Kneisel emigrated to the United States in 1885, joining the Boston Symphony Orchestra. He went on to work at the school that would become Juilliard, and he started summering in Maine. In 1902 he began bringing students to Blue Hill to study with him, and thus this, one of the oldest chamber music festivals in the nation, was born. Students still come every summer to work on their chops, and they get to watch faculty and guests put on concerts from late June through mid-August—shows are on Fridays and Sunday afternoons—and present their own recitals on several occasions as well. You might not expect to find world-class string ensembles in Blue Hill, but here they are for everyone to enjoy. Tickets are $20 to $30.

Bowdoin Summer Music Festival
6300 College Station, Brunswick
(207) 373–1400
www.summermusic.org
What do you get when you bring 200 gifted students to a Maine college to be taught for

months by some of the best known classical music teachers? A whole lot of great music at reasonable prices. There are several concert series each summer, and Midcoast residents turn out in droves. On Friday evenings there are performances by distinguished guest artists—of the world-renowned likes of Emanuel Ax, Julius Baker, and Eugenia Zukerman. Faculty members put on shows midweek, usually doing both contemporary and traditional works, and students perform at various times. Venues include Bowdoin buildings and the Brunswick high school. Tickets can be as much as $30.00 for big names, as little as $5.00 for stars to be.

Bay Chamber Concerts
Rockport Opera House
10 Summer Street, Rockport
(207) 236–2823 or (888) 707–2770
www.baychamberconcerts.org
Best known for its summer chamber music concerts, this outfit established in 1961 also hosts jazz, folk, and world music shows by acts like the Paul Winter Consort, Judy Collins, and Inca Son. They do 30 shows a year, at 8:00 P.M. every Wednesday and Thursday in summer, and half the fun is just getting inside the beautiful old downtown opera house, which has been attractively renovated (and cooled with air-conditioning). Bay Chamber also has a radio broadcast series of its archived concerts. Ticket prices vary.

Arcady Music Festival
Various Midcoast and Down East locations
(207) 669–4425
www.arcady.org
Founded in Blue Hill in 1980, Arcady presents concerts all across eastern and northern Maine, from Bucksport to Castine to Millinocket. Acts range from Arcady's Ragtime Review to the Avalon String Quartet to more worldly combos like the Mindanao Kulintang Ensemble. Summer series shows are held at St. Savior's Church in Bar Harbor. They also do a handful of concerts in winter as well. Tickets are $8.00 to $17.00.

Acadia Area

Bar Harbor Music Festival
59 Cottage Street, Bar Harbor
(207) 288–5744
www.barharbormusicfestival.com
Still more fine classical music can be found in Bar Harbor, where this annual festival has been hosting concerts since the early 1960s. But you'll also see Dixieland, opera, jazz, show tunes, and more contemporary fare as well. Concerts are at 8:15 P.M. at venues across town.

Down East

Pierre Monteux School for Conductors and Orchestra Musicians
Hancock
(207) 422–3280
www.monteuxschool.org
Here is yet another opportunity for Mainers Down East to see top-flight classical music. (This part of the state must have more shows than Portland!) Like Kneisel, the Monteux School, in business since 1943, brings budding young classical talents to Maine for the summer, but often they are on the other side of the baton—conductors. Concerts are offered by students and faculty in June and July.

Machias Bay Chamber Concerts
Centre Street Congregational Church
7 Centre Street, Machias
(207) 255–3889
Founded in 1970, this outfit could not ask for a more attractive venue for its excellent classical series, six concerts in July and early August. The church, with its soaring spires and riverside location, is a stunner, and the range of acts—from the Vermeer Quartet to the Los Angeles Guitar Quartet—is impressive as well.

LIVE MUSIC—NIGHTLIFE AND OTHER POPULAR MUSIC

South Coast

Jonathan's
92 Bourne Lane, Ogunquit
(207) 646–4777
www.jonathansrestaurant.com
How does Jonathan West manage to do it? He consistently books name acts of national repute for his small restaurant in Ogunquit, making it one of the best places to see a show north of Boston. Most are small combos, often folk or blues, but they could be anyone from protopunk troubadour Jonathan Richman to Arlo Guthrie to Cheryl Wheeler to Tom Rush. The current lineup is available on the Web.

Greater Portland

Asylum
121 Center Street, Portland
(207) 772–8274
www.asylumlive.com
It's a shame the booking agent here doesn't work a bit harder to fill the calendar. Shows by national acts are sporadic, but this is the place to turn to when you want to see a band like Wilco or the Old 97s just before they make it really big. There's a sports bar adjacent, and the floor here is often used for dancing on weekends when there's no music, which is most of the time.

Dogfish Bar and Grille
128 Free Street, Portland
(207) 772–5389
Just a few steps down from the Portland Museum of Art, Dogfish is both an eclectic restaurant and a bar where lesser-known local and national acts play. The stage is tiny, the bar a fine watering hole, and the food is good enough that you should arrive early.

i To find out what's happening in the Portland music scene, visit www.myspace.com/livenationmaine, which is hosted by the local booking agent.

Geno's
Congress Street, Portland
(207) 450–7992
Here is Portland's answer to CBGB, which is to say an age-old punk-rock dive with scuzzy decor, a lousy sound system, and a lineup of good, loud, fast young bands. A Maine classic.

The Space Gallery
538 Congress Street, Portland
(207) 828–5600
www.space538.org
One part art gallery, two parts rock club, the Space Gallery took up where the late, great Skinny left off as Portland's best place to see the newest latest bands. Most of the acts that play here are from the indie and underground worlds, whether they be local combos like Seekonk or rural electric or national performers like Richard Buckner and Bob Mould. More cosmopolitan than many clubs of its ilk, Space serves alcohol, and you can peruse the gallery with its revolving shows of up-and-coming artists. Call or check the Web site to see what's scheduled.

State Theatre
609 Congress Street, Portland
(207) 780–8265
www.liveatthestate.com
From Bob Dylan to the Foo Fighters, from Lucinda Williams to the Flaming Lips, this 1929 theater has hosted some of the best shows Portland has seen. It's the city's midsize concert hall for rock shows, staging bands too loud for the more refined Merrill Auditorium but too big for the clubs. The space is pleasant, but it can be hard to see if you're on the first level way in the back.

The White Heart
551 Congress Street, Portland
(207) 828–1900
www.thewhiteheart.com
Another restaurant-cum-nightclub, the White Heart mixes a menu of soups and salads, steaks and spuds with live music by local acts, the occasional art and poetry shows, and

deejay-supported dance. Soon to have some competition right across the road if the new Skinny is launched, which it's been attempting to do for a couple of years.

Other Portland-area Venues

Cumberland County Civic Center (207–775–3548; www.theciviccenter.com) might warrant a larger mention if it scheduled more shows. Primarily a hockey arena, "the Civic Center" hosts about seven or eight big rock acts a year, from Marilyn Manson to Cher. The **Old Port Tavern** (207–774–0444; www.oldporttavern.com) is Portland's best poolroom, and it stages local and regional acts on weekends.

Midcoast

Sea Dog Brewing Company
1 Main Street, Great Mill Island, Topsham
(207) 725–0162
www.seadogbrewing.com
One of the surviving pubs owned by the Sea Dog Brewing Company, this cool bar is a good example of what can be done to save old mill buildings. It was retrofitted into the old Topsham Mill, and it's a beautiful space right on the Androscoggin River. Brews and views are good, and there's often music on Friday and Saturday at 9:00 P.M. Open daily from 11:30 A.M. to 1:00 A.M.

Waldo Theatre
Main Street, Waldoboro
(207) 832–6060
www.waldotheatre.org
Music is but one of the offerings at this great downtown theater. Fiddle contests and folk singers and classical quartets have played here, but so have theater troupes, kids' programs, and films. Open year-round. Call or check the Web site for more information.

Camden Opera House
Main Street, Camden
(207) 236–7963
www.camdenoperahouse.com

A surprising number of good shows pop up in this beautiful, second-floor theater in downtown Camden. Singer-songwriter Iris Dement has performed here a couple of times, and even fairly big bands like Wilco have played this stage. Worth checking the Web site if you're in town.

Rockland Nightlife

A handful of venues in Rockland—mostly cafes and pubs—host live music. Try the **Time Out Pub** (275 Main Street; 207–593–9336), where you can see open mikes and often well-known blues acts. **Second Read Books and Coffee** (328 Main Street; 207–594–4123) has hosted the occasional folk show. The beautifully restored **Strand Theater** (207–594–0070; www.rocklandstrand.com) has a variety of folk and classical shows scheduled when it isn't showing art films.

Acadia Area

Carmen Verandah
119 Main Street, Bar Harbor
(207) 288–2766
www.carmenverandah.com
This local cafe has a full slate of musical offerings in the summertime, usually local and regional performers in a wide range of styles. Check the Web site to see what's coming up.

Lompoc Café
36 Rodick Street, Bar Harbor
(207) 288–9392
www.lompoccafe.com
Another cafe with music in Bar Harbor, the Lompoc books bluegrass, jazz, rock, and blues for Friday and Saturday nights. Thursdays are for open mikes. Check the Web site for the lineup.

COMEDY

Comedy Connection
6 Custom House Wharf, Portland
(207) 774–5554
www.mainecomedy.com
This Old Port staple isn't where you want to

turn for Down East "humah." But if you want to see good local stand-up—this place launched comic Bob Marley, who is now plying his trade in Hollywood—as well as some nationally known funny folks, this is the place to be. Shows play Thursday through Sunday at 8:00 or 8:30 P.M. All shows are for guests age 18 or older. Tickets range from $6.00 to $12.00.

ART GALLERIES
South Coast
York Art Association Gallery
Route 1A, York Harbor
(207) 363–4049
www.yorkartassociation.com
A nice space to see the work of area talents. Open Thursday through Sunday from 11:00 A.M. to 4:00 P.M.

Cuckle-Button Farm Gallery
Thompson Green, Ogunquit
(207) 646–1700
www.ogunquitgallery.com
Despite its cutesy-sounding name, this art showplace is the real deal. Just up the road from Perkins Cove, you'll find paintings by the likes of Charles Woodbury, John Neill, Ann Gallop, Henry Strater, and others who've made names for themselves in the once famous art colony here.

Ogunquit Art Collaborative Gallery
Shore Road and Bourne Lane, Ogunquit
(207) 646–8400
Ogunquit is a Maine art hot spot, and this gallery is among the reasons why. The Ogunquit Arts Association got its start back in the 1920s, when the fishing village was enjoying its heyday as a nationally known art colony, and the group reinvented itself in the late 1990s and renamed its showplace the Barn Gallery. It remains a first-class exhibition space and one of the best places around to see works by area artists. The gallery regularly schedules classes, workshops, and educational programs.

Mast Cove Galleries
Mast Cove Lane and Maine Street, Kennebunkport
(207) 967–3453
www.mastcove.com
Mast Cove got its start in the early 1980s with a dozen artists, and it has since evolved into the biggest of the many galleries in the Kennebunks. In fact, it claims to be the largest privately owned group gallery in all of Maine now, representing more than 100 artists. From Robert Eric Moore to DeWitt Hardy, these galleries have a lot of good stuff inside.

Greater Portland
Greenhut Galleries
146 Middle Street, Portland
(207) 772–2693 or (888) 772–2693
www.greenhutgalleries.com
Peggy Greenhut Golden has an eye for talent, and she has some really fine works in the gallery she's run since 1977. The focus is on contemporary art, and painters include regional talents like Mary Bourke, Leo Brooks, and Kathleen Galligan, whose work is showcased nicely in the bright, museum-like space. Open year-round, Monday through Saturday.

June Fitzpatrick Gallery
112 High Street, Portland
(207) 772–1961
www.junefitzpatrickgallery.com
A good selection of contemporary works are hung here across from the Portland Museum of Art. Exhibits change monthly. Hours are noon to 5:00 P.M. Tuesday through Saturday and by appointment.

Midcoast
Spindleworks
7 Lincoln Street, Brunswick
(207) 725–8820
www.spindleworks.org
Begun in the 1970s as a weaving program for people with disabilities, this creative arts organization now turns out fantastic paintings, drawings, sculpture, and poetry. And some of its artists even have New York repre-

sentation these days. The Spindleworkers show their art at various galleries across the state—and right here at their own space. There are paintings, beautiful handwoven scarves and wall hangings, prints, and a variety of other cool items. Open Monday to Friday from 9:00 A.M. to 4:00 P.M.

Wiscasset Bay Gallery
67 Main Street, Wiscasset
(207) 882–7682
www.wiscassetbaygallery.com
Here is a fine gallery specializing in 19th- and 20th-century American and European paintings, especially those by painters from Monhegan Island and throughout Maine. The gallery also represents some contemporary artists from elsewhere in New England and displays rotating exhibits.

Gleason Gallery
31 Townsend Avenue, Boothbay Harbor
(207) 633–6849
www.gleasonfineart.com
The Gleason Gallery isn't quite what you'd expect a resort town gallery to be. While many such places are filled with seascapes by second- and third-rate painters, the Gleason Gallery is full of works that might seem more appropriate on the walls of museums and can run into the tens of thousands of dollars. Housed in an 1807 brick town house right in the center of town, the gallery fills eight rooms with the handiwork of Maine and Northeast artists, particularly those associated with Boothbay and Monhegan. You might see lithographs by world-renowned Fairfield Porter; gouaches by Eleanor Parke Curtis, who painted in Boothbay in the 1920s; and watercolors by James Fitzgerald, among a handful of Monhegan painters. Depending upon when you visit, you could even pick up a Wyeth. Truly a cut above most of the rest of the state's galleries.

The Firehouse Gallery
1 Bristol Road, Damariscotta
(207) 563–7299
www.thefirehousegallery.com

Made famous by the likes of George Bellows, Edward Hopper, Robert Henri, and Rockwell Kent, Monhegan Island still has quite the artist culture, with more than 20 studios open to visits. Pick up a map and guide from the Monhegan Boat Line on your way out.

This gallery makes for a nifty visit, housed as it is in a renovated mid-19th-century firehouse. Where there was once firefighting apparatus, there are now paintings by regional talents, crafts, folk arts, ceramics, and jewelry. The gallery has rotating exhibits.

Harbor Square Gallery
374 Main Street, Rockland
(207) 594–8700
www.harborsquaregallery.com
A neat former bank with three floors of fine art, Harbor Square represents a raft of artists. Inside you'll find everything from the colorful paintings of Sharon Larkin to the jewelry of goldsmith Thomas O'Donovan, and you may be mortified, like so many others have been, to see paintings and sculpture displayed right on the street. Fine art as sidewalk sale. "Won't it be stolen?" "What if it rains?" Good questions; you'll have to find out the answers when you visit.

Nan Mulford Gallery
313 Main Street, Rockland
(207) 594–8481
www.nanmulfordgallery.com
Works in all media by contemporary local talents like Siri Beckman, Phil Schirmer, Barbara Osterman, Gretchen Dow Simpson, Mike Stiler, and Frederic Kellogg fill this nice space in downtown Rockport. Open Tuesday through Saturday from 10:00 A.M. to 5:00 P.M. and Sunday from noon to 5:00 P.M.

Bayview Gallery
33 Bayview Street, Camden
(207) 236–4534
www.bayviewgallery.com
If you buy a contemporary land- or seascape

Close-up

Rockland Galleries

The renaissance of the Farnsworth Art Museum in the late 1990s helped spawn quite the gallery scene in downtown Rockland. Gallery owners used to be scared away by the grittiness of Main Street, but several have located here rather than Camden since the Farnsworth started its expansions. It was a wise move, which has resulted in a vibrant downtown arts scene. The **Caldbeck Gallery** (12 Elm Street; 207–594–5935; www.caldbeck.com) is the best of them, and it's been here the longest (since 1982). It represents such top-flight talents as William Thon, Lois Dodd, Sam Cady, and Abby Shahn. Another fine space is the **Harbor Square Gallery** (374 Main Street; 207–594–8700; www.harborsquaregallery.com), a neat former bank where you can see the artwork of Sharon Larkin and Michael Waterman and the jewelry of goldsmith Thomas O'Donovan. More up-and-coming talents can be found at the **Gallery at 357 Main** (357 Main; 207–596–0084) and **Gallery 407** (407 Main; no phone). Rockland galleries usually have their openings on Wednesday night, and it's a nice excuse to grab something to eat downtown and wander the streets.

painting here, you can get it framed on the premises. Representing three dozen painters from Maine and away, the gallery also has made a name for itself as a custom framer. It has another location in Brunswick now (used to be in Portland).

Leighton Gallery
24 Parker Point Road, Blue Hill
(207) 374–5001
www.leightongallery.com
One of the longest-lived and, frankly, best Maine galleries, this Blue Hill institution was built into an old Maine barn. When she opened up in 1986, proprietor Judith Leighton purposefully set out to make her gallery as comfortable as can be, as opposed to the stiff and stuffy art showrooms you might find in more urban areas, and she left a lot of "barni-ness" intact when she designed her space. A few years later she built a sculpture-filled garden that alone is worth the trip, showcasing the works of Cabot Lyford, Melita Westerlund, and Elizabeth Ostrander, among others. The

lineup and presentation here are generally among the best in Maine.

Deer Isle Artists Association
13 Dow Road, Deer Isle
(207) 348–2330
www.deerisleartists.com
Deer Isle has become synonymous with crafts, thanks to the fact that the well-respected Haystack Mountain School of Crafts is located here. It seems everyone who attends the school decides to move to the island. That's an exaggeration, yes, but consider that there are 150 area artists represented at this co-op gallery where you can find fine art–quality ceramics, textiles, and more. Exhibits change every two weeks.

Acadia Area

Island Artisans
99 Main Street, Bar Harbor
(207) 288–4214
www.islandartisans.com
Also in Northeast Harbor, this crafts gallery

represents more than 75 artisans working in Maine. They have a nice collection of fiber, jewelry, blown glass, stoneware, tiles, ceramics, and basketry. (Check out the sweetgrass baskets of Abigail Goodyear and the whimsical, almost psychedelic blown-glass bowls by Linda Perrin.)

MOVIES

Great Downtown Movie Theaters

Leavitt Theatre
40 Main Street, Ogunquit
(207) 646–3123
One of the finer old downtown theaters in the state, the Leavitt has been an Ogunquit institution since 1923. First-run movies are screened nightly at 7:00 and 9:00 P.M. on a rotating schedule, unlike most cinemas. Check the listings carefully. Open May to October.

The Movies on Exchange Street
Exchange Street, Portland
(207) 772–9600
www.moviesonexchange.com
When you have the audacity to call yourself The Movies, you'd better be good. This grandaddy of independent cinema in Maine is that and more. There is only one screen (it's not even a big screen), and the seats are not the most comfortable in the world, but the people who run the show are so in tune with what's hip and worthy in the world of cinema that the fare is first-rate. You'll see the great flicks—daring foreign films, underground classics, American indies—here months before they end up on screens elsewhere. Greater Portland movie buffs look for the flyer put out by the Movies, hang it by the calendar, and circle the ones they can't wait to go see. Neat festivals, and good popcorn, too.

Eveningstar Cinema
Tontine Mall, Brunswick
(207) 729–5486
www.eveningstarcinema.com
Another one of those cool downtown theaters, Eveningstar has stayed in business

longer than just about anyone else in the tiny Tontine Mall. And it provides a good alternative to the bland multiplex at Cooks Corner for all the college students and arty types in Brunswick. Art films, indies, foreign pics, and all those great movies that come out every year that the suburban theaters can't seem to fit on their 10 screens are regularly shown here. Nice matinee programs for kids as well.

Harbor Theater
Meadow Mall, Route 27
Boothbay Harbor
(207) 633–0438
This tiny cinema used to be called Harbor Light Cinema, and it screens first-run films on a daily basis in summer. What's really neat is the premovie slide show, which features photographs of the Boothbay Region (local gardeners, for example, are invited to bring pictures of their flower beds—it's a hoot). Two shows nightly in summer—plus matinees on rainy days—and on weekends from October through May.

Lincoln Theater
2 Theater Street, Damariscotta
(207) 563–3424
www.lcct.org
A state-of-the-art showplace when it was built in the 19th century, this aging gem now shows first-run movies, one a week, in summer.

Bayview Street Cinema
Bayview Street, Camden
(207) 236–8722
www.bayviewcinema.com
Movie buffs love this second-floor theater. For a creaky old auditorium with antique seats, Bayview puts on a very nice show—the sound is surround and the screen is wide. Traditionally the movie fare has been arty, independent first-run flicks on the verge of going to video, which are much cheaper for the theater to rent, but the place is getting more up-to-date movies now. Popcorn won't set you back a day's wage, as it does at some of the big box multiplexes, and you can get all warm and

Close-up

Northeast Historic Film

The Alamo Theater on Main Street in Bucksport has always been among Maine's coolest downtown cinemas, and since 1986 it's been home to Northeast Historic Film, an organization dedicated to preserving the cinematic heritage of New England. Surprisingly there's a lot to save, and NHF has been doing a great job of it. Maine looms large in its archives, the setting, as it was, of the North Woods dramas that were so popular in the silent-film age. NHF has a fascinating series of videos available for purchase that cover a wide array of old Maine themes, from early rail history to fishing to logging to native life to Joshua Chamberlain, and they occasionally screen historic movies, in addition to the first-run fare that occupies the place in the summer. An inspired outfit. For more information call (800) 639–1636.

fuzzy watching screenings of *It's a Wonderful Life* during the holidays.

Colonial Theatre
High Street, Belfast
(207) 338–1930
www.colonialtheater.com
That the Colonial is painted aquamarine and pink and has an elephant on the roof should tell you something about the three-screen cinema. It has a lot of spunk and is a ton of fun. A celebration of moviegoing, the landmark theater has art deco detailing all over the place, a dizzying carpet of electric colors, and even ticket takers in old-fashioned costumes when big movies open. Run by Belfast mayor Michael Hurley and his wife, Therese Bagnardi, it somehow manages to snag blockbuster movies on their opening weekend, something most independent theaters can't seem to do, and screens arty pictures in the winter. Belfast filmgoers have enjoyed going to the movies here for generations, and it just keeps getting better. New seats in 2006, to boot.

Criterion Movie Theater
35 Cottage Street, Bar Harbor
(207) 288–3441
www.criteriontheater.com

This is another one of those Maine downtown cinemas that screens first-run flicks in repertory. Each week movies play for two-night runs, which allows the single-screen theater to show all sorts of offerings in the average week. Going to the movies here is worth it simply to get inside this art deco gem, circa 1932. Concerts and special events—plays, puppet festivals—happen here on occasion, too.

Reel Pizza Cinerama
11 Kennebec Place, Bar Harbor
(207) 288–3811
www.reelpizza.com
Whoever thought of pairing pizza and movies—good arty and independent movies, at that—is a minor genius. That's what's offered at this hip little spot, with its bean-bags.

Milbridge Theater
Main Street, Milbridge
(207) 546–2038
It's a good thing that this old movie house is such a pleasure, because it's the only place to see first-run films for many miles around. (Nightlife is seriously scarce Down East.) But it's great—air-conditioned and with stereo surround sound. Shows are at 7:30 P.M.

Multiplexes

Wells Five Star
75 Wells Plaza, Route 1, Wells
(207) 646–0500
A multiplex that provides a good rainy-day alternative to the beach, it shows the block-busters of the moment.

Smitty's Cinemas
420 Alfred Road, Biddeford
(207) 283–4500
Near the resorts of the coast, this eight-screen cinema is also very near the Saco multiplex. Unfortunately for moviegoers, they seem to prefer to go head-to-head rather than vary their selection of movies—both show largely the same films.

Cinemagic Saco
779 Portland Road (Route 1), Saco
(207) 282–6234
www.cinemagicmovies.com
This big multiplex is handy to the resorts of Kennebunk and Old Orchard.

Regal Clarks Pond
Clarks Pond Parkway, South Portland
(800) 326–3264
www.regalcinemas.com
Out by the Maine Mall, this big box cinema has eight screens on which to show the latest flicks. Call for the current attractions.

Patriot Nickelodeon Cinemas
1 Temple Street, Portland
(207) 772–4022
On the edge of the Old Port, this used to be the local $1.50 movie theater, where you could go see an art film for cheap. Today it still shows slightly more eclectic fare, but you gotta pay prices that you would anywhere else—admission is $7.50.

Westbrook Cinemagic 16
183 County Road, Westbrook
(207) 774–3456
The multiplex of multiplexes, this new theater opened in 2006 with stadium seating and six-

ⓘ The movie listings at the *Portland Press Herald*'s Web site are very up-to-date and comprehensive, which is nice when you're looking for some cinematic alternatives. Click over to http://movies.mainetoday.com/theater.html to see what's playing where.

teen, count 'em sixteen, screens. Modern moviegoing comes to Maine.

Regal Falmouth
Route 1, Falmouth
(800) 326–3264
www.regalcinemas.com
Formerly a Hoyt's theater, this suburban cinema has 10 screens, plenty for all the block-busters.

Regal Brunswick
19 Gurnet Road, Cook's Corner, Brunswick
(207) 798–3996
Formerly a Hoyt's, this is your standard multiplex with 10 screens.

Flagship Cinemas
Route 1, Thomaston
(207) 594–2100
Though it's poorly run, this is your only megaplex option in the Rockland-Camden-Belfast area.

Maine Coast Cinemas 2
Maine Coast Mall, Route 1A, Ellsworth
(207) 667–3251
This small theater in a strip mall screens first-run films.

Drive-In Movies

Saco Drive-In
969 Portland Road, Saco
(207) 284–1016
Drive-ins and double features right on Route 1.

Pride's Corner Drive-In
Westbrook
(207) 797–3154
The giant screen at Pride's Corner Drive-In

went up in Westbrook in 1953, and Mainers have been holding hands and making out to the bright glow of feature films ever since. While the screens in most other neighborhoods across the street have been demolished due to rising real estate values and the prevalence of videos and DVDs, the old place still fills the lot and these days usually offers two pictures in an evening. Call for the coming attractions.

DAILY NEWSPAPERS (ON THE COAST)

Bangor Daily News
491 Main Street
Bangor 04401-6862
(207) 990–8000
www.bangornews.com

Portland Press Herald/Maine Sunday Telegram
390 Congress Street
Portland 04101-3514
(207) 791–6300
www.mainetoday.com

Journal Tribune
Alfred Road
Biddeford 04005
(207) 282–1535
www.journaltribune.com

WEEKLY NEWSPAPERS

South Coast

York County Coast Star
R.R. 1
Kennebunk 04043-9801
(207) 985–2961
www.seacoastonline.com/news/yorkstar

York Weekly
17 Woodbridge Road
York 03909-1411
(207) 363–4343
www.seacoasatonline.com/news/yorkweekly

Sanford News
P.O. Box D
Sanford 04073-3016
(207) 324–5986
www.sanfordnews.com

Biddeford Saco Old Orchard Beach Courier
180 Main Street
Biddeford 04005-2598
(207) 282–4337
www.biddefordsacooobcourier.com

Greater Portland

Scarborough Leader
180 Main Street, Biddeford
(207) 282–4337
www.scarboroughleader.com

Cape Courier
P.O. Box 6242
Cape Elizabeth 04107-2419
(207) 767–5023
www.capecourier.com

American Journal
4 Dana Street
Westbrook 04092-2224
(207) 854–2577

Gorham Times
77 South Street
Gorham 04038-1715
(207) 839–8390
www.gorhamtimes.com

Forecaster
8 Fundy Road
Falmouth 04105-1431
(207) 781–3661
www.theforecaster.net

Midcoast

Times Record
3 Business Parkway
Brunswick 04011
(207) 729–3311
www.timesrecord.com

Coastal Journal
99 Commercial Street
Bath 04530-2564
(207) 443–6241
www.coastaljournal.com

Wiscasset Newspaper
Wiscasset 04578
(207) 882–6355
www.wiscassetnewspaper.maine.com

Boothbay Register
97 Townsend Avenue
Boothbay Harbor 04538-1140
(207) 633–4620
www.boothbayregister.maine.com

Courier Gazette
1 Park Drive
Rockland 04841-3437
(207) 594–4401
www.mainecoastnow.com

Free Press
6 Leland Street
Rockland 04841-3016
(207) 596–0055
www.freepressonline.com

Camden Herald
45 Mechanic Street
Camden 04843-1807
(207) 236–8511
www.mainecoastnow.com

Village Soup Times
21 Elm Street
Camden 04843
(207) 236–8468
www.villagesoup.com

Republican Journal
33 High Street
Belfast 04915-1921
(207) 338–3333
www.mainecoastnow.com

Village Soup Citizen
48 Marshall Wharf
Belfast 04915
(207) 338–0484
www.villagesoup.com

Waldo Independent
47 Church Street
Belfast 04915-1128
(207) 338–5100
www.mainecoastnow.com

The Enterprise
105 Main Street
Bucksport 04416
(207) 469–6722

Weekly Packet
13 Main Street
Blue Hill 04614
(207) 374–2341
www.weeklypacket.com

Compass Publications
69 Main Street
Stonington 04681
(207) 367–2200
www.penobscotbaypress.com

Island Ad Vantages
69 Main Street
Stonington 04681
(207) 367–2200
www.islandadvantages.com

Castine Patriot
8 Water Street
Castine 04421
(207) 326–4383
www.castinepatriot.com

Ellsworth American
30 Water Street
Ellsworth 04605-1902
(207) 667–2576
www.ellsworthamerican.com

Acadia Area

Bar Harbor Times
76 Cottage Street
Bar Harbor 04609-1441
(207) 288–3311
www.mainecoastnow.com

Mount Desert Islander
310 Main Street
Bar Harbor 04609
(207) 288–0556
www.mountdesertislander.com

Down East

Machias Valley News Observer
31 Broadway Avenue
Machias 04654-1105
(207) 255–6561

Downeast Coastal Press
Route 191
Cutler 04626
(207) 259–7751

Lubec Light
74 Washington Street
Lubec 04652-1145
(207) 733–2939

Calais Advertiser
14 Church Street
Calais 04619-1604
(207) 454–3561
www.calaisadvertiser.com

The Quoddy Tides
123 Water Street
Eastport 04631
(207) 853–4806
www.quoddytides.com

ANNUAL EVENTS

JANUARY

Annual Maine Lobster Dip
Old Orchard Beach
(800) 365–9386
Northern states everywhere have their traditional first-of-the-year "polar bear challenges," those crazy occasions when seemingly normal people jump into the ocean on a freezing winter's day. This is the same sort of idea, Maine-style. You'll certainly emerge looking like a lobster (the cooked variety, anyway), with skin that's all red and hard from the cold. Sponsored by the Portland Rugby Club, the event takes place in front of the Brunswick Hotel in Old Orchard Beach. Usually about 300 hardy souls participate, running down into the water, diving in, screaming, and running back out as fast as they can. It's probably the only time you'll see Old Orchard Beach with so few people on it. And it's for a worthy cause—it benefits Maine's Special Olympics program. Find out more at the Old Orchard Beach Chamber of Commerce Web site at www.oldorchard beachmaine.com or by calling (800) 365–9386.

FEBRUARY

Camden Conference
P.O. Box 882, Camden 04843
(207) 236–1034
www.camdenconference.org
Unusual though it may sound for a town of 5,000 far away from any major metropolis to host an influential conference on foreign affairs, that's just what happens every February in Camden. The Camden Conference got its start in 1987, drawing on the experience of retirees from the CIA and the Foreign Service, and it has evolved over the years into a real draw. High-ranking mucky-mucks turn out every year for two days of seminars and discussions on such topics as: Islam, the global environment, the world's population, and issues related to the countries of Latin America as well as Russia, China, and Japan. The whole town gets involved—area restaurants serve food, art galleries have shows, there are book discussions and concerts, and school-children do research, all on the year's theme. Definitely unique, undeniably informative, the program is worth exploring. Call or check the Web site for the current year's topic.

U.S. National Toboggan Championships
Camden Snow Bowl
P.O. Box 1207, Camden 04843
(207) 236–3438
www.camdensnowbowl.com
Where can you see the Mount Washington Morons take on the Last of the Monhegans 2 at speeds of up to 45 mph? At the U.S. National Toboggan Championships, of course. This campy event has been a staple at the Camden Snow Bowl ski area since 1990. Participants don costumes, form two-, three-, and four-person teams, grease up their toboggans, and hit the 400-foot toboggan chute on the side of Ragged Mountain with all they have. With the short walls and wooden trough of a funky old bobsled course, the long, straight chute is covered with ice, sends sledders down at high speeds, and shoots them out across Hosmer Pond to the delight of the gathered spectators. Times are recorded, and the fastest toboggan wins (there are also prizes for best costume, team spirit, etc.). There isn't anything quite like it anywhere else, and everyone is welcome to enter. There is a fee to enter the contest but none to watch.

MARCH

Maine Boatbuilders Show
58 Fore Street, Portland
(207) 774–1067
www.portlandcompany.com/bshow
The age-old art of boatbuilding remains a big deal Down East, and the Maine Boatbuilders Show is a big deal for anyone interested in boats—wooden, fiberglass, sailing, motorized, or otherwise. Every spring, just as armchair sailors have about had it with armchair sailing and are hankering to launch boats and do the real thing, the show fills a vast warehouse with the best watercraft from North America. Maine and New England are well represented, but boatbuilders from as far away as Washington state and parts of Maritime Canada show up for the event. Upwards of 200 exhibitors typically display their wares, everything from the smallest kayak to the largest yacht, and the builders are handy to discuss the making of the vessel and answer questions. Sales are a given. If you are into boats at all, this is for you. There's even food. Admission is $15 at the door.

The Old House Trade Show
Greater Portland Landmarks
165 State Street, Portland
(207) 774–5561
www.portlandlandmarks.org
Portland's resident preservation organization, Greater Portland Landmarks, does a lot of good works in the course of the year, from leading architectural walking tours to educating southern Mainers about the value of their old structures. But its landmark event is the Old House Trade Show every March. (March is truly the month of trade shows in Maine.) A weekendlong immersion in all things *This Old House,* the show features close to 50 exhibitors of historically oriented goods and services, plenty of demonstrations, workshops, and a wealth of advice. If you have a question about your venerable homestead, want to see the latest in reproduction hardware, or need to hire a sensitive builder, this is the place to be.

Maine Maple Sunday
Farms statewide
www.getrealmaine.com
Maine is second only to Vermont when it comes to maple sugar production in the United States, and on the last Sunday of March every year, the state sponsors an open-farm day during the annual harvest. The public is invited to sample the goods and see how the delicious amber delicacy is produced. More than two dozen farms along the coast participate, and some of them have ice cream and pancakes, hay or sleigh rides, sugar bush tours, and other events scheduled to improve on the idea. Kids especially love to explore these agrarian workplaces, and it's a great opportunity for families to see that the treat found at the shopping center actually grows on trees (or in them, rather). Sweet.

APRIL

Fisherman's Festival
Boothbay Harbor Region Chamber of Commerce
State Route 27, Boothbay Harbor
(207) 633–2353
www.boothbayharbor.com
Ever tried to race with a frozen cod in your hands? That's one of the many challenges facing game participants at this Boothbay Harbor fest. Boothbay Harbor may be better known now as a resort than as a fishing town, but it still has one of the largest fleets of any working harbor in the state, and since the early 1970s, the last weekend in April has celebrated them. There's the fish relay race, lobster trap hauling contests, shucking, shelling, and filleting events, and lobster trap racing, during which people run across the tops of a string of floating lobster traps. Food, dancing, a Miss Shrimp Princess Pageant, lighthouse tours, church suppers, and more are all tradition. This is Boothbay at its best—before the huge influx of tourists and summer "complaints" arrive to clutter things up.

MAY

Tour de Cure
Bar Harbor
(888) DIA–BETES
www.tour.diabetes.org
Bicyclists in 70 locations across the country participate in this annual spring "pedalathon" to raise money for diabetes research. But few places present as fine a backdrop for these good works than the one at Acadia National Park. The Tour de Cure is the biggest cycling event of the year in Maine, attracting upwards of 400 bikers. And while these are some fancy pedalers, anyone is welcome to participate and raise money for the cause. You can opt to pedal 25K, 50K, or 100K distances, and you'll get lunch for your efforts. The scenery is good, the cause is great.

Warblers and Wildflowers Festival
Bar Harbor Chamber of Commerce
(207) 288–5103
www.barharborinfo.com
Mainers love the arrival of spring, a season that is about a week long Down East, coming after the months of mud, and they celebrate it any way they can. This one-week event grows more popular with every year, welcoming the return of two great signs of spring: warblers, those small and colorful feathered friends, and wildflowers. (You probably guessed this from the name of the festival.) Activities include bird walks in search of Blackburnian, Canada, and magnolia warblers, garden tours, gallery visits, lectures and discussions, and socials in both Bar Harbor and Acadia National Park. Enjoy the color and the songs.

Down East Spring Birding Festival
Eastport, Lubec, Calais
(207) 733–2201
www.downeastbirdfest.org
More than 400 species of birds visit Maine annually, and about 75 percent of those have had the good sense to visit the "real Maine," the Down East coast. The area sits along the Atlantic Flyway, that superhighway for migrating birds, and every May these summercators

make their way back to the coast in big flocks. It's a sight to see, and folks in the Eastport, Calais, and Lubec areas put together quite a welcoming party in their Down East Birding Festival at the end of May each year. Begun in 2004, the get-together features trips into the field, boat rides, lectures and discussions, and a lot of time behind binoculars looking for feathered friends. Anyone who is into birds won't want to miss it, and anyone who enjoys the outdoors, the Maine coast, and good conversation might think about attending, too.

JUNE

La Kermesse Festival
Downtown Biddeford
(207) 282–1567
www.lakermessefestival.com
Maine isn't exactly overflowing with festivals that celebrate ethnicity, but there are a few, and the biggest is La Kermesse (which in French means "the fair"), the largest French-Canadian party in the country. Maine has a rich Franco-American heritage, and this city of 21,000 is one of the cities where it is most strongly felt, never more so than during La Kermesse, which brings crowds of 50,000 to the city on the last weekend of June. If you're not of French descent, don't worry. You'll be adopted for the length of the event, and organizers have made an effort to broaden its appeal, multiculturally. It's Franco first and foremost, and you'll have an opportunity to try all those dishes you always wanted—from boudin to crepes to our favorite, *poutine*, which is French fries with gravy and cheese. Block parties, French singers and national acts, traditional dancing, and a parade are

> **i** NASCAR's got nothing on Maine. Lobsterboat racing is a huge sport in summertime—rip-roaring contests in souped-up lobsterboats that take place along the length of the coast. Find out the schedule at the Web site www.lobsterboatracing.com and be prepared to get wet.

highlights, and there are the typical festival delights of a midway and fireworks. The 10K La Kermesse Road Race is popular too. Maybe it's all that *poutine*. The bulk of the activities take place at St. Louis Field downtown.

Independence Pops
Portland Symphony Orchestra
477 Congress Street, Portland
(207) 773–6128
www.portlandsymphony.com

Every summer in the week leading up to the Fourth of July, the Portland Symphony Orchestra performs a five-date series of concerts at a handful of places along the coast. Popular, patriotic favorites are the order of the day, and the shows are followed by a fireworks display in the evening. Fans bring lawn chairs, blankets, picnics, and wine, and they enjoy fine summer evenings of Maine's best classical music in beautiful locales. Check the Web site or give a call for this year's dates and locations.

Old Port Festival
Fore and Exchange Streets (a good place to start), Portland
(207) 772–6828
www.portlandmaine.com

Portland's Old Port doesn't really need a festival to attract visitors in June these days. Dozens of shops, restaurants, and bars packed into 6 cobblestoned blocks have a way of reeling people in. The Old Port Festival was set up in 1973, though, back when these venerable Victorian buildings on the waterfront had just been rehabilitated by eager entrepreneurs, and people couldn't be quite so sure what they'd find in this once shady part of town. Today this street party on the first Sunday of June is an eagerly anticipated event and a good time. Things traditionally are kicked off with a parade before noon, after which people mosey around looking at tables set up for the sidewalk sale, enjoy street performances and art displays, and then congregate around ten stages set up at various points where country, jazz, folk, and rock acts play. This being Port-

land, of course, food plays a large role, and there is plenty for kids to do, from face painting to games. The crowds can get huge, and they're usually filled with delighted folks.

Bowdoin Summer Music Festival
Bowdoin College
6300 College Station, Brunswick
(207) 373–1400
www.summermusic.org

Bowdoin College is never quite deserted, the way some schools are in summer. In fact, the liberal arts college is abustle every June through July with the Bowdoin Summer Music Festival. Two hundred music students—high school through college and graduate level—move in for a six-week residency on campus. Renowned teachers and classical artists show up to teach all these kids, see, and everyone gets a chance to play. The school holds performances several times per week, including student concerts, contemporary shows, and, on Friday evenings, faculty and guests the likes of Emanuel Ax, Lucy Shelton, and Eugenia Zukerman performing. Students learn by playing in front of audiences and watching top talents, but fans of chamber, orchestral, and even modern music may benefit the most. Most shows are inexpensive, and the artists can be world class. See the Web site for more details.

Windjammer Days
Boothbay Harbor Chamber of Commerce
Route 27, Boothbay Harbor
(207) 633–7448
www.boothbayharbor.com

Maine has an impressive fleet of windjammers, those classic old, tall-masted ships, and every June they rally in the resort community of Boothbay Harbor for a few days. Nautical nuts will not want to miss this opportunity to tour vessels—which have included navy boats and Coast Guard cutters, too, in the past—and to explore the local Coast Guard base and area boatbuilding facilities. Everyone else will be impressed by all the goings-on that swirl around the boats' visit—there are parades, arts and craft fairs, kids' events, and even fire-works. And it's hard not to appreciate the graceful parade of sail, when the windjammers cruise out into the harbor as a slow and stately armada.

Great Schooner Race
Maine Windjammer Association
P.O. Box 317, Augusta 04332
(800) 807–WIND
www.sailmainecoast.com
People often refer to Penobscot Bay as one of the finest sailing grounds in the world, second only to the Mediterranean for its views and cruising conditions. And if salty panoramas are your thing, there's no better time to pay this Midcoast bay a visit than during the Great Schooner Race, when as many as 28 old wind-jammers vie for top honors in the competition that began in 1976. The sight of these pretty three-masters—most more than 100 feet long—straining in the breeze, huge sails taut, crashing through the chop, crews rushing about—harks back to the great age of sail in Maine and won't soon be forgotten. It's the largest annual gathering of tall ships in North America. The race typically is the last weekend in June, and its course is dependent upon the wind and weather, but there are plenty of good viewing locations in the Penobscot Bay area. The best bet, of course, is to be aboard one of the vessels—most take passengers during the event, and it often doesn't cost any more than any other cruise. If you can't swing that, look to go aboard another passenger boat out of Camden, and if that doesn't work, either, get thee to Camden Harbor and ask around about a mainland point to sit on. At the very least you could watch from atop tall Mount Battie, which stares out over the bay.

Kneisel Hall Chamber Music Festival
P.O. Box 648, Blue Hill 04614
(207) 374–2811
www.kneisel.org
World-class chamber music in Blue Hill, Maine? Sounds unlikely, but it's true, thanks to a trip Austrian violinist Frank Kneisel made to the

area in the late 19th century. Kneisel was the chair of the Department of Strings at what is now called the Juilliard School and in 1902 began bringing his most gifted students to his summer retreat in Blue Hill every year. The tra-dition has continued—the Kneisel Hall Cham-ber Music Festival is now the oldest chamber music fest in the United States—and each summer, a group of talented young chamber musicians ventures north to live and learn on the shores of Blue Hill Bay. On Friday evenings and Sunday afternoons the school offers per-formances to the public, and they are some of the finest classical music concerts anyone's going to see anywhere in Maine.

Festival of the Kayak
Southwest Harbor–Tremont Chamber of Commerce
P.O. Box 1143, Southwest Harbor 04679
(207) 244–9264 or (800) 423–9264
Kayaking has seen explosive growth on the Maine coast since the 1980s, and it's practi-cally impossible to go anywhere on U.S. Route 1 now without seeing the skinny boats stuck to the top of somebody's car. You'll probably never see more in any one Maine place, though, than you do during the Festival of the Kayak in Southwest Harbor. The "quiet side" of Mount Desert Island isn't so quiet when hun-dreds of paddlers arrive to discuss and demonstrate, race and explore for two days in June. Events traditionally kick off with a bit of a competition on Saturday before getting into workshops—compass reading, safety tech-niques, that sort of thing—and the testing of all sorts of display models. (This is a kayak shopper's delight.) An exploratory paddle takes the rest of the afternoon, followed by dinner and discussion. After breakfast Sunday come more paddling and more workshops. Great fun for anyone into "yak smak."

JULY
Fourth of July Celebrations
Used to be the Fourth of July was the official beginning of summer and tourist season in

ℹ️ Some time ago, community organizations discovered garden tours, and now they're one of the principal fundraising methods Down East and a high point of July and August in many communities. You can find out the complete schedule in the April issue of *Down East* magazine or at the Web site of *People, Places, and Plants* magazine— www.ppplants.com.

Maine. That changed long ago, when people started pushing the shoulder seasons as far as possible, but Mainers still enjoy their Independence Day festivities. From Kittery to Calais, there are celebrations up and down the coast. Here are a few high points.

Portland

The best place to watch the fireworks display in the state's largest city is from the Eastern Promenade, a grassy park on the east end of the Portland Peninsula. Portland usually has the largest budget for pyrotechnics and therefore has a great show. A more genteel option to hanging on the Prom and Munjoy Hill might be to go to one of the Portland Symphony Orchestra's performances in the week leading up to the Fourth, because they always have fireworks, too. Contact: Greater Portland Convention and Visitors Bureau, 245 Commercial Street, Portland 04101; (207) 772–5800; www.visitportland.com.

Bath

Known for its midway, its triathlon, its parade, and, of course, the fireworks over the Kennebec River, the five-day Bath Heritage Days has been going strong since 1972. Contact: Southern Midcoast Maine Chamber of Commerce, 59 Pleasant Street, Brunswick; (207) 725–9787; www.midcoastmaine.com.

Thomaston

A one-day extravaganza, Thomaston's Old Fashioned Fourth revolves around a parade and a chicken barbecue, and its fireworks displays are among the best around. Contact:

Prenobscot Bay Regional Chamber of Commerce, P.O. Box 508, Rockland; (207) 596–0376 or (800) 562–2529; www.thereal maine.com.

Bar Harbor

Thanks to some wealthy benefactors, Bar Harbor's fireworks are truly extraordinary, lighting the sky over Frenchman Bay. A parade kicks off the day at 10:00 A.M. Contact: Bar Harbor Chamber of Commerce, 93 Cottage Street, Bar Harbor; (207) 288–5103; www.barharbor maine.com.

Eastport

Eastport has called its Independence Day festivities a "Fourth of July Celebration Unmatched in America," and while that's a hard billing to live up to, the city does go all out. (At the very least it's the most easterly city celebration.) The tiny burgh mixes its Old Home Week in with the Fourth so the streets are jammed with friends, family members, and former residents. The usual Maine suspects— parade, barbecues, fireworks—can be expected but in a bigger and better way. Contact: Eastport Chamber of Commerce, P.O. Box 254, Eastport; (207) 853–4644; www .eastport.net.

Other July Events

Yarmouth Clam Festival
Yarmouth Chamber of Commerce
162 Main Street, Yarmouth
(207) 846–3984
www.clamfestival.com
How many clams does it cost to get into the Yarmouth Clam Festival? Not many. In fact, most of the entertainments at this three-day Greater Portland favorite are free. Not quite as huge as the Maine Lobster Festival, the clam festival has been packing people in since it was founded in the mid-1960s. Kids and teenagers are naturally drawn to the midway set up by Smokey's Greater Shows, with all the arcade games, rides, cotton candy, and questionable carnies you could want. Younger folks like the parade as well. Everyone enjoys the

firefighters' muster, the Maine State Clam Shucking Contest, and the street dancing. Parents are fond of the art show on the library lawn, the "pink elephant" sale across from the First Parish Church, and the live music on stages across the village in the evening. Good times for everyone and loads and loads of clams, sold to benefit various sports teams and community organizations.

North Atlantic Blues Festival
Harbor Park, Rockland
(207) 593–1189 (festival hotline) or
(207) 596–6055
www.northatlanticbluesfestival.com

The coast of Maine is not exactly the first place anyone would go looking for the blues. Perhaps they should. Started in 1994, this July staple has become one of the most prestigious blues fests on the East Coast, even winning a Keeping the Blues Alive award from the Blues Foundation, something that normally goes out to big-city events like the Chicago Blues Festival. Thirteen thousand people can't be wrong, though, and that's the size of the crowd that typically turns out to Harbor Park to listen to the work of some of the top names in the blues—singers and guitar slingers like Susan Tedeschi, Jimmie Vaughan, Eddie Kirkland, James Cotton, Koko Taylor, and Bo Diddley. The stage is set up right on the harbor, there's food, and you don't want to miss the Club Crawl, which fills "Rock City" clubs with area talent during the two days of the festival. Some really good stuff can be found, like local legend Blind Albert and his blues band. Fun, fun, fun. Bring a blanket or a lawn chair, and arrive well before gates open at 10:00 A.M. for optimum viewing. Shows start at 11:00 A.M.

WERU Full Circle Fair
WERU, 1186 Acadia Highway,
East Orland
(207) 469–6600
www.weru.org

WERU 89.9 FM out of Blue Hill has become almost a way of life for a lot of people in Waldo and Hancock Counties since Paul Stookey of Peter, Paul, and Mary fame and a group of volunteers founded the station in 1988. The community radio station plays a kooky mix of music—from jazz to reggae to alternative rock, sometimes in the same show—to the delight of a wide audience in the Midcoast, and every July it sponsors its annual Full Circle Fair somewhere in the Midcoast (used to be in Union, of late it's been in Blue Hill). As might be expected from a musically diverse station, the focus of the fair is music, and several stages are set up and topped with a wide array of performers of local and regional repute—you might see the "altcountry" of Maine's own Delco Ray on one stage and a traveling jam band on another. Many people try to make it to the weekendlong event just to visit its book and CD sale tent, where the station offloads discs that it is no longer playing at very low prices. Others come for the food booths set up by local restaurants—from Indian to Mexican, it's all good—and still others to hear peace activists and other progressives speak on the issues of the moment.

Arcady Music Festival
P.O. Box 780, Bar Harbor 04609
(207) 669–4225
www.arcady.org

Top-shelf chamber music hits stages Down East in late July and August. The Arcady Music Society has been welcoming some truly extraordinary classical talents to Maine since 1980, bringing the likes of the Chamber Orchestra Kremlin, the Essex Quartet, and the T'ang String Quintet to Bar Harbor and various up-country locations for a handful of per-

i Portland's busy boosters, the Portland Downtown District, host free movies shown outdoors in Congress Square on a weekly basis in high summer. These films are family-oriented and sort of a cross between a drive-in and a sit-in, and they're definitely good fun. Check www.portlandmaine.com for this year's coming attractions.

formances each summer. Tickets are usually eminently reasonable, there's often a free, preshow lecture, and the schedule tends to include a bit of whimsy, like adding the New York Ragtime Orchestra to what's usually a classical lineup. Bar Harbor performances typically take place on Thursday evenings in the months of July, August, and September, and are held at various points in town.

Native American Festival
College of the Atlantic
State Route 3, Bar Harbor
(207) 288–3519

It isn't every day that the four Maine Native American tribes—Maliseet, Micmac, Passamaquoddy, and Penobscot—get together. But they do the first Saturday in July on the pretty campus of the College of the Atlantic in Bar Harbor. The school, the Maine Indian Basketmakers Alliance, and the local Abbe Museum, which celebrates Native American culture, all combine to host this day of traditional demonstrations, storytelling, drumming, singing, and dancing. Expert Native American artisans typically demonstrate and sell their work, and the basketry alone is worth the trip. Admission is free.

Open Farm Day
Statewide
(207) 287–3491
www.mainefoodandfarms.com

One of the consequences of all the growth, change, and development Maine has seen since the 1970s is the loss of a lot of family farms. This loss of farms is sad not only for the families involved but for communities, too, which lose good neighbors, access to fresh produce, and open space. The state of Maine has recognized this problem and begun to take steps to help the farms that are left, launching several agricultural campaigns. One of these is Open Farm Day, the last Sunday in July, when agrarian operations all across the state welcome the public in for tours, wagon rides, animal petting, berry picking, and walks around farm meadows. You can see how dairy cows are milked, tickle little lambies, learn about beekeeping, and get your picture taken with a llama. There's usually the opportunity to buy produce and crafts and sample fresh foods. You might not want to leave.

AUGUST

York Days
Short Sands Beach, York
(207) 363–1040
www.gatewaytomaine.org

Not many towns in Maine—or anywhere else in the United States, for that matter—hold 350th anniversary parties. But the southern Maine town of York Beach was settled in 1624 and thus can host such things. The community's York Days festivities take place in late July and early August every year and celebrate the rich heritage of ol' Georganna (that's what York used to be called, throw it around if you want to seem hip). This is all-American Americana, with 10 days of concerts, suppers, beach events, antiques and dog shows, and the ubiquitous parade and fireworks, all set in a white clapboard village that seems ripped out of a history book.

Maine Lobster Festival
Harbor Park, Rockland
(207) 596–0376 or (800) LOB–CLAW
www.mainelobsterfestival.com

Plan far ahead if you want to attend the five-day Maine Lobster Festival in Rockland. It's almost impossible to get a room anywhere nearby due to the extraordinary popularity of this event. Since it was begun in the 1950s, the Lobster Fest has graduated from a fun family fair into a genuine phenomenon with a life of its own (we're talking lines of clothing, shuttle services, and kings and queens here). Tens of thousands of people descend upon the Penobscot Bay city in the last week of July and first week of August to feed at the World's Largest Lobster Cooker. In 2005, for example, more than 12 tons of lobster were devoured, along with untold amounts of clams, mussels, and fried shrimp. Food is the focus, but there's so much more to the festival. Highlights include the lobster crate race, open houses at the Coast Guard base, marine tank tent displays, merchant showcases, King Neptune and his parade, and the unforgettable Sea Goddess pageant. The music tends to be worthy, too, with recent headliners including Willie Nelson, the Dixie Chicks, Ricky Skaggs, and Dwight Yoakam. About the only people who don't like the Maine Lobster Festival are the activists from People for the Ethical Treatment of Animals, who stage protests every year. These protests are usually very clever, though, so even the angry people entertain. Summer in Maine wouldn't be quite the same without it.

Maine Antiques Festival
Union Fairgrounds, Union
(207) 563–1013
www.maineantiquefest.com
There are innumerable antiques shows on the Maine calendar, but none really come close to being the giant antiques and collectibles bazaar that is the Maine Antiques Festival—it's the largest show in northern New England. More than 350 dealers move into the Union Fairgrounds west of Rockland along State Route 17 every August for a couple of days, toting their showcase wares. They set up booths, fill tents, arrange their goods into miniature parlors, and wait for the hordes to arrive. Arrive they do. The roads are jammed for miles in each direction with eager antiquers, some dealers, some just plain folks looking for that special something. There is always plenty of good food available at the fairgrounds, and shoppers will often make a day of it, spending hours and hours visiting every last site. When the festival started back in the early 1980s, it was mostly of interest to people who like country Americana, but now you can find just about anything—including the kitchen sink. Need an armoire? Look no further. Venerable Shaker-style table set? You found it. Veterans of the fair show up on Sunday afternoon, when the real deals can be made, because dealers don't want to have to lug their stuff home. Be prepared to haggle.

Wild Blueberry Festival
Centre Street Church, Machias
(207) 255–4402
www.machiasblueberry.com
Chances are, if you've ever munched on a blueberry, it came from Washington County, Maine. The most Down East county Down East, Washington produces 85 percent of the world's blueberry crop, and every year in mid-August the region salutes that fact with the Maine Wild Blueberry Festival in Machias. A weekendlong immersion in all things berry, the fruity fair is the highlight of summer in the small town of Machias, and most of the events revolve around its stunning Centre Street Congregational Church. The community promises "an old-fashioned country good time," and it delivers, too, with a children's parade, a fish fry, a locally produced musical, an arts and crafts show, a pancake breakfast, a road race, bands and music, and many, many a blueberry. These blue guests of honor show up at the breakfast, at the pie-eating and cooking contests, on a quilt, and even at the post office, in the form of a blueberry letter cancellation. You can eat them by the bucket if you feel like it. The festival is pure, WaCo fun in a really pretty old Maine town, and it will even help prevent cancer (blueberry antioxidants, you see)—where else will you find that?

International Homecoming Festival
St. Croix Valley Chamber of Commerce
P.O. Box 368, Calais 04619
(207) 454–2308 or (888) 422–3112
www.visitcalais.com
So many family and friends would return to the Calais–St. Stephen area every year for the annual International Festival that organizers decided to rename it the International Homecoming Festival. "Two Countries, One Heart" is the fest's motto, and while that may sound a little precious, this celebration of life on the U.S.–Canada border is kind of fun and funky. Taking place over the course of two weeks, the event includes beauty pageants for girls and teens—where else can you win the Miss International crown?—golf tournaments, lots of

Close-up

Common Ground Country Fair

One of the most beloved of all of Maine's summer shindigs, the Common Ground Fair takes place on the third weekend of September every year. People mark that date on their calendars and keep it open at all costs, to be sure they can attend—for many, it's the highlight of the year.

What's there to love? The fair is a celebration of rural life, born in the late 1970s, a time when Waldo County had seen a large influx of countercultural types interested in moving "back to the land." They moved to the country, set up farms, and learned by doing, getting together in September to share ideas and the harvest. That's still what the fair is about today, but it has grown and grown and attracts 60,000 fairgoers every year, most of whom are no longer farmers.

Hosted by the Maine Organic Farmers and Gardeners Association, the fair has many goals but a core few stand out. First, it's organic through and through (all vendors sell organic foods—they don't even allow coffee to be sold on-site), it's all about sustainability, and it places a premium on community and sharing.

Now held at MOFGA's own farm in Unity, the event features new activities every year, but much remains the same. There's always great food, with scores of booths selling everything from Indian curry to the old favorite, turkey dinners from the free-range Turkey Farm in New Sharon. Acres of tents are filled with the wares of Maine country craftsmen and women, many of whom elevate their work to the level of art—there are always remarkable jewelers, canoe builders, and sweater makers—as well as political action booths. There are also stages on which bands play and people dance. Speechifying happens on the Common, usually by progressive activists the likes of Jim Hightower; there's the ever popu-

bands, lumberjack and rock-skipping competitions, a "food fest," a street dance, various suppers, chocolate pudding wrestling, cow patty bingo (yes, real cow patties), a road race, volleyball tournament, and much more. (Did we mention the pudding wrestling?) Events are held at sites on both sides of the border.

SEPTEMBER

Capriccio
Ogunquit Performing Arts
(207) 646–6170
The tiny beach town of Ogunquit has been a haven of the arts since before the turn of the 20th century, and in the early days of September every year they take to the fore, with a

weeklong celebration on the beach and in the village. Events include live theater, musical performances, ballet, poetry readings, a fashion show, and an art show. The largest spectacle just might be the Festival of Kites at the end of the week. This annual event fills the skis over Ogunquit Beach with color and movement—and sometimes awful tangles.

Laudholm Farm Nature Crafts Festival
P.O. Box 1007, Wells 04090
(207) 646–4521
www.laudholm.org
Close to 100 of the area's most talented artisans gather to show their works and wares on the weekend after Labor Day in Wells every year. The show is juried and reportedly com-

lar Parade of Vegetables, which kids love, and there are several days' worth of agricultural workshops and demonstrations. Big crowds gather to see border collies herd sheep, hear talks about small woodlot forestry, pat the animals in the barns, and file through the displays of award-winning fruits and vegetables. Perhaps best of all, people are constantly bumping into friends and family, and it's a beautiful thing.

The Common Ground Country Fair is like your average state fair run by tasteful ex-hippies—and that's definitely a good thing. If you leave the fair without feeling warm and fuzzy and wanting to simplify your life, you have issues. The fair is about a half hour drive from Belfast on Route 137, but it's well worth it, and people commonly drive from out of state to attend. For more information, call (207) 568–4142 or visit www.mofga.org.

Funky art is just one part of the appeal of the Common Ground Fair. JENNIFER SMITH-MAYO

petitive, so you know it won't be all macramé toilet-tissue doilies and pipe cleaner art. Picturesque Laudholm Farm and the Wells National Estuarine Research Reserve will also be busy with music, food, and educational seminars to round out the weekend. Get a jump on your Christmas shopping and spend a day on the beach with food and fun at the same time. How do you beat that?

Windjammer Weekend
Camden-Rockport-Lincolnville Chamber of Commerce, Camden
(207) 236–4404
www.windjammerweekend.com
Enjoy a sea chantey? Attracted to schooner bums? Then get thee to Camden over Labor

Day weekend for Windjammer Weekend, the last of the season's grand parades of sail. The age of tall ships is roasted over the course of three days with songs and music, the telling of tall tales, a schooner bum talent show, nautical workshops, the ever-popular lobster crate races, and fireworks. With Camden's compact harbor abrim with graceful schooners, it's quite a spectacle.

Eastport Salmon Festival
Downtown Eastport
(207) 853–4644
www.eastportme.org
Fish helped build the city of Eastport, one of the most picturesque communities in all of Maine. In the 1880s the sardine canning indus-

try was booming here, with 18 factories providing jobs for a population that was almost three times the 2,000 that it is today. The canneries went bust long ago, but fish—these days salmon in pens in the bay—remain very important to the local economy. And the city on Moose Island gives them a tip of the hat with its Salmon Festival every September on the first Sunday after Labor Day. The day typically includes a road race, boat rides, a walking tour, crafts displays, and barbecued salmon dinner, all before the beautiful edge of Passamaquoddy Bay. If you enjoy salmon, best get yourself Down East.

OCTOBER

PopTech!
P.O. Box 1405, Camden
(207) 230–2425
www.poptech.org

What's Brian Eno doing in Camden, Maine? The eminent recording artist (Roxy Music, solo stuff) and producer (U2, Peter Gabriel, David Bowie, Paul Simon) was speaking at PopTech!, an annual conference that explores science and technology and the future of ideas. Every October this rather remarkable confab attracts some 500 visionaries from the worlds of technology, arts, design, education, business, government, and the sciences to the beautifully restored Camden Opera House. So Eno was in good company. If you're interested in where we're all headed—or just want to ogle celebrities—you'll find PopTech! a fascinating weekend.

York Harvestfest
Greater York Region Chamber of Commerce
1 Stonewall Lane, York Village
(207) 363–4422
www.gatewaytomaine.org

When York claims its celebration is old-fashioned, people should listen, this being one of the oldest towns in the nation. The community's annual Harvestfest is built around all sorts of traditional foods and entertainments—a Native American pow-wow, craft demonstrations, puppet shows,

antique car displays, tours of historic sites, all complemented by an ox roast, chowders, cider, apple crisp, and good old Maine baked beans. Events get under way on the Village Green—just across from Olde York Village (see, it's so old they have to put an *e* on the end) and move to Ellis Park on Short Sands beach for the Hannah Jackson 5K race.

Fall Foliage Fair
Boothbay Chamber of Commerce
Route 27, Boothbay Harbor
(207) 633–2353
www.boothbayharbor.com

Autumn in Maine is as beautiful as it is in Vermont and New Hampshire, perhaps even more so, because the state has the sea off which the colors can reflect. But, perhaps due to marketing, those states are the ones people associate with glowing foliage. Several Maine communities have put together festivals to pay homage to the season (and attract visitors), and one of the better ones is in Boothbay at the Railway Village Museum. More than 100 vendors typically show up to display Maine-made crafts, woodworking, art, and jewelry, and to sell locally canned and baked goods. Local bands play on stages, to the delight of adults, and the trains of the popular little museum chug around their track to entertain the kids. Plenty of chowders and cider are available, too. It's a good excuse to drive down to the Boothbays at a particularly beautiful time of year.

NOVEMBER

Maine Brewers' Festival
Downtown Portland
(207) 771–7571
www.mainebrew.com

Somehow Maine's version of Oktoberfest got bumped into November (which actually makes sense because the second-to-last month of the year, a dark time when the days are short, is now known as "Drink Maine Beer Month" Down East). The Oktoberfest is now called the

Maine Brewers' Festival, a jolly and sudsy gathering of the many brewers that have put the state on the microbrew map since 1993. Anyone who enjoys a pint—or six—wouldn't want to miss it. For the price of entry, attendees are given 12 tickets, each worth a single four-ounce tasting. They also get a souvenir tasting glass to tote around to the more than 20 booths. Of course, you're welcome to buy more. The festivities typically get under way at 3:00 P.M. on a Saturday afternoon and last until after midnight. Besides the beer, there are booths by local restaurants and blues bands to take you into the evening. Don't even think about showing up if you're under 21, because the brewers enlist members of the Portland Rugby Club to do their bouncing. Portland has lots of taxis if you need a post-party lift.

Victorian Holiday
Citywide, Portland
(207) 772–6828
www.portlandmaine.com
There are few better cities in which to celebrate a Victorian holiday than the very Victorian city of Portland, known for its late-19th- and early-20th-century architecture (as well as the Victorian Mansion, an over-the-top museum of all things Victorian). The great monthlong pre-Christmas party actually has a very broad appeal, not limited to history buffs. Things kick off the day after Thanksgiving with the tree lighting in Monument Square and don't let up until New Year's Portland on December 31. Highlights include strolling carolers in Victorian garb, horse-drawn wagon rides downtown, a visit by Father Christmas, window decorating contests, and more. The Old Port is gaily lit; the Portland Symphony Orchestra plays its annual Magic of Christmas concert series, a truly magical batch of shows; and other arts, cultural, and business organizations across town—from the Portland Museum of Art to the Portland Public Market to the Maine Historical Society—host events. Perhaps there will even be an enchanting dusting of snow. It's all very Dickensian.

DECEMBER

Christmas Prelude
Townwide, Kennebunkport
Kennebunkport Business Association, Kennebunkport
(207) 967–0857
www.christmasprelude.com
Often described as "quaint," Kennebunkport makes a particularly fine backdrop for a holiday celebration. And, boy, does this venerable village of historic homes, shops, and restaurants on the Atlantic throw one. Christmas Prelude, it's called, and after hosting it since the 1980s, the community pretty much has it down—the name is even copyrighted now. Dreamed up as a method of drawing tourists to a resort area that was all but boarded up in wintertime, Prelude revolves around shopping but somehow manages to transcend the commercial. The festivities get under way on the first Friday of December and usually begin with shopping, arts and crafts shows, open houses, and walking tours in the afternoon. This activity is followed by a chowder supper and then a tree lighting downtown in Dock Square, and then after that the action shifts to a bonfire for carols. Saturday is all consumed with pancake breakfast, Christmas fairs, free sleigh rides, open houses, lunches and teas, and later dinner and then caroling. One of the more unique elements is the traditional candlelit walk to the local Franciscan monastery for more caroling. Sunday is a quieter day of more craft fairs and the arrival of St. Nick by sea. And there's so much to do, events spill over into the following weekend. This is a rare opportunity to see beyond the resort facade and get a glimpse of Kennebunkport as a small Maine town, with a strong sense of community, and it's particularly welcome at Christmastime.

Sparkle Weekend
Downtown Freeport
Freeport Merchants Association
23 Depot Street, Freeport
(207) 865–1212 or (800) 865–1994
www.freeportusa.com

The town of Freeport doesn't really need any big events to entice shoppers during the holiday season. It already has a couple of the biggest draws any community could want at this time of year—L. L. Bean and several dozen factory outlets. The business organization put together the colorful Sparkle Weekend anyway, and, if you can deal with crowds and parking hassles, it's fun. The village gussies itself up with thousands of lights, sets up a talking Christmas tree, puts together a concert of traditional yuletide favorites—played by 50 tubas—enlists the help of Santa and some strolling carolers, organizes a Wine and Beer Garden, and holds what it claims is New England's only nighttime parade of lights. Whimsy is the word, and it all works. Plus it's free. And while you're in town, you can pick up something for everyone on your shopping list.

Christmas by the Sea
Downtown Camden
(207) 236–4404
www.camdenme.org
Where else in the world does Santa arrive by lobster boat? Well, he actually does so in many Maine towns, but few hold a Christmas candle to the extravaganza enjoyed during the first weekend of December in the picturesque Midcoast communities of Camden and Rockport. We're talking a holiday house tour, carolers strolling through historic neighborhoods, beachside bonfires, craft fairs and yuletide bazaars, carriage rides, free screenings of *It's a Wonderful Life* at a nifty old cinema, old-fashioned baked bean suppers, a concert with the area's famous folksingers, and, yes, plenty of opportunities for shopping at the resort town's stores. The party gets under way on Friday afternoon and doesn't let up until Sunday evening. This is what the holidays should be all about.

DAY TRIPS

One of the great things about living on or visiting the Maine coast is its proximity to the state's famous interior, the woodsy wonderland of moose and mountains and lakes. Baxter State Park, one of the premier wilderness destinations in the East, is within a few hours drive of U.S. Route 1; Moosehead Lake, the largest freshwater body contained in one state east of the Mississippi and a wilderness playground, is about the same distance; and the Rangeley Lakes area, one of the oldest resorts in the state and a picturesque mountain town, is, too. The White Mountains, the tallest peaks in the northeast, are a skip from Portland, visible from various points in the city on a clear day. Of course, if you prefer more cosmopolitan entertainments, a pair of cool cities—Boston, Massachusetts, and Portsmouth, New Hampshire—are just a half hour and an hour away, respectively, from Kennebunk. Or you can head out the state's back door and cross the border into Canada to pay a visit to the Canadian Maritimes and Campobello.

On the Maine coast you can enjoy a day on the beach and head into the city for dinner with relative ease. Maybe shop in Freeport in the afternoon and hit a concert in Boston that night. Or you can spend the morning touring a quiet Atlantic cove in a kayak, and then shove off for a little après-supper canoeing on a remote river up-country later that evening. Many people like to visit the state's two premier parks—Acadia and Baxter—in a week or even a weekend, which is eminently doable (provided you make the necessary reservation at Baxter). The state of Maine has it all going on—really fun cities, picturesque fishing villages, romantic islands, sparkling sea vistas, majestic mountains, miles of spruce forest—and you have access to everything when you set up on the coast.

BAXTER STATE PARK

Baxter State Park
64 Balsam Drive, Millinocket
(207) 523–3140
www.baxterstateparkauthority.com

As wilderness parks go, it's hard to improve on the 200,000 acres of Maine wilderness that Governor Percival Baxter gave to the state back in the 1930s. A hiker's paradise, Baxter State Park was designed to be enjoyed on foot and has some 175 miles of trails. These woodsy walkways climb the state's highest peak, mile-high Mount Katahdin, the northern terminus of the Appalachian Trail, along with a score of other summits, and they wander out to moosey bogs, skirt photogenic lakes and ponds, and follow waterfalls for miles. Truly spectacular stuff.

When Baxter assembled this park two hours north of Bangor, beginning in the 1930s and ending in the 1960s (he left a trust to buy still more land, too), he did so with the provision that it would be managed for wildlife first and foremost, human use a distant second. "Forever wild" is how he put it, and over the years park management has lived up to that decree. No RVs or motorcycles are allowed in, and, unlike Acadia, this isn't a park where you drive around in your car gawking out the window. There is a tote road that traverses its edges, but its famous ribs are rough on cars. In order to see the real goods, you have to park, usually at one of 10 campgrounds, lace up your boots, and strike out into it the woods. And it's an infinitely rewarding place if you do.

Because of its outstanding beauty and wild nature, though, the park is busy these days, especially in the summer months. To camp anywhere you need a reservation, and if you want to find a parking place for a climb of

Katahdin, you might want to consider getting there before 6:00 A.M. The "Mountain of the People of Maine" is the reason why most people make their way here north of Millinocket, and the staging points for all-day hikes up the imposing massif are usually very crowded. People will often arrive in the wee hours of the morning, get in line at the southern gate, and sleep in their cars to be sure they make it in before the parking areas close, which can be as early as 7:00 A.M. If you plan to hike Katahdin, a reservation for at least one night is advisable. Just by being there, campers get first dibs at the trails, the most major of which begin at Roaring Brook, Abol, and Katahdin Stream Campgrounds. People often find that after spending six hours or more hiking straight up, they don't feel much like driving when they get back down. There are oodles of other great climbs here as well, from the challenging ascent of Doubletop to the easygoing route up short but scenic Sentinel Mountain.

The majority of the campgrounds lie along the park's tote road and can be reached by automobile, but a few, like Russell Pond and Chimney Pond, are in the wild backcountry and require a backpack in. The most popular of the roadside areas are Roaring Brook, Katahdin Stream, and the cabin campgrounds of Daicey and Kidney Ponds. The camping is primitive, with just tents and small pop-up trailers allowed, and there are few amenities beyond a fire ring and picnic tables, though some sites do have lean-tos, open-faced Adirondack-style shelters, or even bunkhouses. Regardless of where you stay, you have to use common outhouses, carry out the trash you bring in, and tote your own water. Several lean-to sites are scattered here and there in remote areas for individual stopovers.

Your camping companions might be moose, black bear, deer, American martin, Canada jay, or any number of other beasties. Because the park is so wild, critters are wild about it. Moose are perhaps the biggest attraction for the average visitor, because they're numerous, commonly spotted, and

generally unbothered by respectful people—they willingly pose for pictures. Viewing is great at Sandy Stream Pond, just north of Roaring Brook Campground; at Abol, Tracy, and Stump Ponds near Abol and Katahdin Stream Campgrounds; and anywhere in the backcountry. Bears are a little more skittish.

Reservations for the most popular camping areas can be hard to come by, and Mainers have been known to sleep out in the frigid cold in January to be first in line when the reservation process begins for the year. It's a long drive to the park from the coast—about three and a half hours from the Midcoast and Down East regions—but is it ever worth it. People truly love this place, and it's easy to understand why.

MOOSEHEAD LAKE AREA

Look at a map of Maine, and sprawling Moosehead Lake does indeed resemble the profile of Bullwinkle's noggin. This is the state's largest freshwater body—its blue expanse covers 117 square miles of prime North Woods territory. A vast land of forest and rivers and, yes, moose, surrounds the big lake, whose nose points squarely at the small community of Greenville. The area has been a haven for outdoor lovers of all types since the 1880s, when "sports" from across the Northeast began to flock north in droves, spending a week or more in the woods and on the water hunting and fishing.

Those two pastimes still attract a lot of people to Moosehead, but many more come simply to see a bit of this rugged country, enjoy fresh air and wild views, and look for moose. So many of the awkward brown beasts can be seen wandering near the road and in the woods that the local chamber of commerce has come up with a monthlong celebration of all things moose called Moose-Mainea, and local outfitters have put together moose "safari" tours. MooseMainea features races by canoe, rowboat, and mountain bike, picture contests, and many moose safaris, like the ones offered by Registered Maine Guide

Dan Legere of the **Maine Guide Fly Shop and Guide Service** (207–695–2266). Hiking, kayaking, white-water rafting, and sightseeing trips—out on the lake, aboard the old steamer *Katahdin* (207–695–3390), or above the wilderness, with **Currier's Flying Service** (207–695–2778)—are other popular diversions. When snow flies this place is a snowmobiler's happy zone, with miles and miles of trails through the woods.

A tiny place with an up-country charm, Greenville (pop. 2,000) has enough treats to occupy an afternoon. There are a few cool shops to peruse downtown—**Indian Hill Trading Post** (207–695–3376), a woodsy outfitter with one of everything, and **Moosehead Traders** (207–695–3806), with moose antler furnishings. Some fun dining options await the traveler, too, from **Flatlanders** (207–695–3373), a diner where all the locals show up at one time or another, to the **Blair Hill Inn** (207–695–0224), an upscale place with a fancy chef. Accommodations run the gamut: There's the **Kineo View Motor Lodge** (207–695–4470), a 12-room motel with nice views of Mount Kineo in the middle of the lake; the **Greenville Inn** (207–695–2206 or 800–695–6000), a gracious Victorian hostelry with water views; and the **Birches** (207–534–7305 or 800–825–9453), a "wilderness resort" in nearby Rockwood with lakeside cabins, a great dining room, and a small excursion empire.

The woods around the lake are dotted with intriguing places. To the east is Kokadjo (pop. "not many"), a wee frontier hamlet on the edge of First Roach Pond where you'll find a trading post, some privately owned cabins, and **West Branch Pond Camps** (207–695–2561), a sporting camp of eight rustic cabins on West Branch Pond. To the north is Northeast Carry, an outpost at the spot between the West Branch of the Penobscot and Moosehead where canoes had to be portaged back in the glory days of Maine guides. A little general store is here that'll take you back a few years. And to the west is **Pittston Farm** (207–280–0000), a down-home restaurant on the site of an old logging farm that is legendary in the North Woods for its all-you-can-pile-on buffet.

A huge land owner, Plum Creek, has plans to do a massive development—thousands of homes, golf courses, a ski area, and more, which threatens the future of Moosehead, so see it before it gets spoiled.

For more information on the Moosehead Lake Region, contact the Moosehead Lake Region Chamber of Commerce at (207) 695–2702 or www.mooseheadarea.com.

RANGELEY LAKES REGION

It's hard not to like Rangeley. The town is undeniably appealing, high up in the western mountains of Maine and hard by Rangeley Lake. It's the most elevated community in the state at 2,000 feet and looks out over a landscape of lakes and mountains that trundle to the horizon. Woods cover every inch of ground that isn't water. The mighty Androscoggin River gets its start here, before tumbling south to enter the sea at Brunswick, and the area is famous for its fishing and its large population of moose.

With about 1,200 people, the town of Rangeley—which picturesquely wraps around Rangeley Lake, Mooselookmeguntic Lake, and innumerable small ponds—is the hub of the area, and it's a real cool combination of rugged outdoorsy and up-country gentility. Parks and preserves are everywhere, sportsmen and snowmobilers still flock to the community, and yet it has its own cultural appeal, with a movie theater, a few good restaurants, an offbeat museum, and the shows and concerts put on by Rangeley Friends of the Arts. A lot of affluent city folks have summer homes on the lake, and they don't want to give up their entertainments for the summer.

Downtown Rangeley is a few blocks of shops, eateries, and services on the northeast side of Rangeley Lake. It's the sort of place where you can see a floatplane land while strolling the sidewalk and gas up your snowmobile at a Main Street convenience store in winter. Good meals can be had at the **Range-**

ley Inn (51 Main Street; 207–864–3341 or 800–666–3687), a classic up-country hostelry right downtown, or at **Loon Lodge** (Pickford Road; 207–864–5666), a turn-of-the-20th-century, three-room inn. The Rangeley Inn is also a pleasant place to stay—if you book a room in the inn itself and not in the adjacent motel.

Just up the road from Rangeley to the west is the village of Oquossoc on Mooselook-meguntic Lake. Colonized by wealthy cottagers—there's an interior design firm in this tiny woods community—Oquossoc nonetheless is a pretty wild locale, and there's good hiking to be found on 2,400-foot Bald Mountain. The hairless summit has exceptional ganders at Mooselookmeguntic and Rangeley Lakes and the hundreds of acres of woods that surround. One of the state's better private camping areas, **Stephen Phillips Memorial Preserve** (207–864–2003), is located right on Mooselookmeguntic, with primitive, walk-in sites on the lake and on a couple of undeveloped islands in the middle of it.

To the northeast of Rangeley is Stratton, on the shores of artificially created Flagstaff Lake. This is the spot where the town of Flagstaff was sunk in the 1930s, when the Dead River was dammed. The Bigelow mountain range sprawls behind the lake, and it's one of the state's best hiking areas. And just beyond it on State Route 27 is **Sugarloaf USA** (800–843–5623), the famed ski area, where there is lodging, dining, and adventuring year-round. Golfers are particularly fond of the Sugarloaf links, and the resort has mountain biking, moose safaris, and a host of other offerings during the warm-weather months.

For more information on the Rangeley area, contact the Rangeley Lakes Region Chamber of Commerce at (207) 864–5364 or (800) MT–LAKES.

SCENIC DRIVES IN MAINE

It may seem strange, but only one of the 17 roads in Maine's Designated Scenic Highway program is along the coast. The 16 others wend and wind through the state's gorgeous interior, passing underneath mountains, skirting lakes, and wandering through the North Woods. The one piece of coastal pavement deemed worthy is State Route 182, a stunning alternative to Route 1 Down East, connecting the small towns Franklin and Cherryfield. (Of course, you never see the ocean on this short route either, and the lakes-and-forest landscape it passes looks a lot like the North Woods.) But there are plenty of other picturesque seaside drives the state might consider should it ever decide to designate a few other highways scenic. They make for great detours and are often useful alternate routes.

State Route 103, Kittery Point to York Harbor

This two-lane road at the southern tip of Maine goes through the venerable, all-American village of Kittery Point, a white-clapboard place of fine old homes, before passing along Pepperrell Cove and through sections of the Rachel Carson National Wildlife Refuge, a pretty marshy area frequented by much birdlife.

State Route 24, Orr's and Bailey's Islands

The tip of rock at the end of this photogenic stretch of road in Harpswell is called Lands End, and that's just what it is—the road dead ends at the salty brine of Casco Bay. The views along the rolling road that lead to it are truly fine.

The River Road, Boothbay Harbor to Newcastle

A very pleasant backway between the resort of Boothbay Harbor and the Damariscotta/Newcastle area, the River Road follows the Damariscotta River for several miles. The road plays peekaboo with the salt water, passing sweet old homes all the while.

State Route 131, Thomaston to Port Clyde

This quiet road wanders through fishing village after fishing village, following the St. George River to the sea. It ends in the cool community of Port Clyde, home of the Marshall Point Lighthouse and jumping-off point for trips to Monhegan Island.

Blue Hill Peninsula

Any road down in these parts is a detour worth taking. The East Penobscot Bay villages of Castine, Brooksville, Deer Isle, and Stonington are all truly stunners. And the prospect from Caterpillar Hill in Sedgwick—the whole of Penobscot Bay spread out before you—is priceless.

Mount Desert Island

Home of Acadia National Park, Mount Desert is ringed with photogenic drives. Pick a road.

WHITE MOUNTAINS

It says something that one of the most favored destinations of the Maine Outdoor Adventure Club is the White Mountains of New Hampshire. No knock on Maine here, it's just that the Portland-based outing group is closer to the fabled Whites than they are to the mountains of Maine. Mount Washington is less than a couple of hours from the Forest City, and there is no end of things to do in the woods that surround New England's highest peak.

This is prime hiking country, some of the best woods to walk and mountains to climb in the nation. There are more than 1,200 miles of hiking trails—including the famous Appalachian Trail—and five areas designated as wilderness, the largest more than 45,000 acres. Outdoor enthusiasts will find 23 campgrounds, 14 picnic areas, and unlimited hunting, fishing, swimming, canoeing, and in the winter, skiing. For a taste of the trail offerings, try the 20-minute hike in to the 66-foot Glen Ellis Falls (off State Route 16 in Pinkham Notch, New Hampshire); the four-hour Boulder Loop round-trip, which gives some great views of Mt. Chocorua and the Swift River Valley (off Kancamagus Highway); or the Rob Brook Road trail (off Rob Brook Road), which takes you through some boggy areas where moose and bears have been known to hang out. For the ambitious climber,

In the 20 or so years since it was released, the DeLorme *Maine Atlas and Gazetteer* has become the bible of travel in Maine. The 78 maps it contains within its signature blue covers are more detailed than anything else available—showing old woods roads and overgrown farm byways as well as every piece of blacktop in the state—and you almost can't get lost if you follow them carefully. Most Mainers have a tattered old copy on the backseat of their cars and wouldn't go anywhere without it. You'll find the *Maine Atlas and Gazetteer* at a wide variety of shops and bookstores and you can order one online at www.delorme.com.

there is always Mount Washington. At 6,288 feet, it's the highest peak in the Northeast. Try the Tuckerman Ravine trail, the most direct—and one of the most popular—routes up the mountain. The trail begins at the Appalachian Mountain Club's visitor center on Route 16 in Pinkham Notch. Of course, plenty of the other Presidentials are good fun, too.

People who don't want to or can't hike enjoy the Kancamagus Highway, a 34-mile-long road that cuts right through the heart of the Whites. Those who want to rough it have options aplenty. Try the **Dolly Copp Campground** (Route 16, Pinkham Notch, New Hampshire) in the National Forest, near the base of Mount Washington. There are 176 sites, with a base rate of $18 per night. Or try **Wild River Campground** (Wild River Road, Gilead, Maine), which has 12 wooded sites on the Wild River in the Maine section of the forest. It's $16 a night. At the other end of the spectrum is the **Balsams Grand Resort Hotel** (State Route 26, Dixfield Notch, New Hampshire; 800–255–0600; www.thebalsams.com), a 130-year-old New England castle of sorts surrounded by the Whites. It's fancy enough that you can pretend you're in the Alps. *Ski America Guidebook* called the Balsams "one of the top ten romantic ski resorts in the country." See for yourself.

For more information contact White Mountains Attractions, Route 112, Kancamagus Highway, Woodstock, New Hampshire; (603) 745–8720 or (800) FIND–MTS; www.visit whitemountains.com.

BOSTON

Mainers have always had a proprietary interest in the city of Boston, even if they like to make fun of Massachusetts in general. The city is only an hour and a half from Portland, close enough for an easy day trip. The Red Sox are our baseball team, just as the New England Revolution are our soccer team, and the Celtics our basketball team. (It's not uncommon to see a lot of Maine license plates on cars parked in lots at the big game.) The museums, the aquarium, and the Freedom Trail are where Maine schoolkids go for their field trips, and older kids and adults frequently drive down to the Fleet Center and sundry clubs to see the rock concerts that inevitably skip Maine. Many Pine Tree State residents even drive down to use Logan Airport when they travel, despite the fact that Portland Jetport has connecting flights. One has to look no farther than the Amtrak Downeaster rail service between Portland and Boston for evidence of

i A few secrets when traveling to Boston. Do yourself a favor and take the train—driving in Beantown is always a major hassle, as the city was laid out in horse-and-cart days, and parking is inevitably a huge headache. The Downeaster is fast, relatively inexpensive, and drops you off right downtown, where you can easily connect to the T subway system. If you do drive, gas up before you leave the state, because there are no stations on the highway after Kennebunk. You'll be happier if you take State Route 93 into town, rather than jumping for the first big Boston sign and U.S. Route 1—the old Atlantic Highway is stop-and-go from strip-mall Saugus all the way into the city.

the popularity of the city with Mainers—more than 20,000 riders make the trek every month.

What are they going to do and see? Everyone has different agendas, of course, but it's safe to say that all these travelers are looking for the sort of big-city entertainments that Maine lacks. Museums are particularly popular (a good resource is www.museumsofboston .org), and not just with those schoolkids. When big exhibits come through town, parents pack up the family and walk them through the **Museum of Fine Arts** (617–267–9300), the **Children's Museum** (617–426–8855), and the **Museum of Science** (617–723–2500). (Some people go to the latter simply to see IMAX movies, too, something unavailable in Maine.) The **New England Aquarium** (617–973–5200) is also a large draw, with its penguin pool, shark wall, and auditorium shows.

History is another biggie. Maine was once part of Massachusetts, and Boston is rich with the heritage of those colonial times. From the architecture—places like the Old South Meeting House, Paul Revere House, and Fanueil Hall—to the well-preserved sites along the Freedom Trail to the decks of the *Constitution*, the chronicle of the past is easy to read and surprisingly popular.

And don't forget shopping. Newbury Street is a well-known high-end retail zone, as is Copley Square. People also enjoy the bookstores of Harvard Square in Cambridge, the cut-rate retail of Downtown Crossing, and the tourist-oriented shops of Quincy Market. It's easy enough to shop for CDs and books online, but when it comes to clothes, shoes, and furniture, you often want to see it first, and Boston is the nearest place Mainers can do just that in a big way.

Beantown's Convention and Visitors Bureau is a wealth of information on where to eat, what to see, and where to stay. Call 1–888–SEE BOSTON or visit its Web site—www.bostonusa.com—for ideas.

PORTSMOUTH, NEW HAMPSHIRE

Portsmouth is a truly fine city, with an appeal much like that of Portland, only on a much smaller scale (pop. 23,000). It too has the history, the sea, the progressive vibe, and a restaurant culture similar to the one found in its cousin to the north. In fact, like Portland, the city was recently named one of the 50 best places to live by *Men's Journal* magazine. Many southern Mainers—those from towns like Kittery, the Berwicks, and the Yorks—use the city as their hub, because it's closer than Portland. And many more pour in to buy big-ticket items, thanks to the fact that New Hampshire has no sales tax.

Portsmouth calls itself the nation's third-oldest city and it must be close, having been settled in 1623. The architecture is beautiful. Check out the Strawbery Banke Museum (www.strawberybanke.org), a 10-acre, six-house study of a Portsmouth neighborhood over the course of 300 years. Spread across the city are a variety of other historic homes that scream "Early Americana" and are fascinating to visit. Try the **Jackson House** (76 Northwest Street; 603–436–3205), which was built in 1660 and is the state's oldest home; the **Moffat-Ladd House** (154 Market Street; 603–436–8221), which was built in 1760 and was owned by a signer of the Declaration of Independence; or the **Governor John Langdon House** (143 Pleasant Street; 603–436–3205), a 1784 mansion that features a lot of classic furnishings.

For eats consider the **Blue Mermaid** (409 The Hill; 603–427–2583), an acclaimed local favorite known for its grilled seafood; the **Dolphin Striker** (15 Bow Street; 603–431–5222), one of the oldest but best creative American places in town; **Radici** (142–144 Congress Street; 603–373–6464), an Italian place with an extensive vegetarian menu; or **Lindbergh's Crossing** (29 Ceres Street; 603–431–0887), a Mediterranean bistro in a 200-year-old building on the harbor.

CANADIAN MARITIMES

It doesn't get any more Down East than the coast of New Brunswick. The shore from the U.S. border at Calais and Lubec down into the Canadian Maritimes is very "Mainey." In fact, the small towns and the coastal country feel much like the Pine Tree State did back in, say, the 1950s or 1960s—not overly developed, with unspoiled fishing villages and large stretches of woods. Places like Labrador (admittedly far for a day trip) are seeing an influx of Maine sporting-camp owners, who are expanding their businesses north and east to find country more remote than Maine. Mainers thus feel right at home in the Maritimes, and many vacation here, especially in these days when the American dollar is greatly outpacing the Canadian dollar. Campobello is a fine place to begin an adventure.

Campobello

The New Brunswick island of Campobello, just across the border from Lubec, is the site of the former vacation home of President Franklin D. Roosevelt, which is part of an international park like none other in the world. Stop at the Roosevelt **Campobello International Park Visitor Centre** (506–752–2922; www.fdr.net) to get an overview of the things to do in the park's 2,800 acres. Next door is the focus of the park, the colorful old gambrel-roofed manse to which the Roosevelt family adjourned for fun in the sun. The 34-room "cottage" has been preserved to look much the same as it did when young Franklin and his siblings played on the water here—he spent every summer from 1883 to 1921 on the island, and, unfortunately, it was here that he contracted polio. The cottage is filled with family photos and memorabilia, and its grounds are made for strolling.

There's plenty to do in the park beyond the Roosevelt compound. Perhaps the best way to see the island is by hiking the 8.5 miles of trails, and you can begin right at the visitor center. Less than a mile away is the Friar's Head Picnic Area, which is a nice place to bring a basket for lunch right on the water (people also enjoy eating alfresco at Mullholand Point Picnic Area). Other options include the cliffy trail from Liberty Point and the perimeter walk, which traces the park's border right along the shore. Motorists enjoy drives along Cranberry and Liberty Points, which make fine loops from the visitor center, passing before stunning seascapes.

While on Campobello, don't miss the beach at Herring Cove and the East Quoddy Head Light, another Bay of Fundy sentinel that looks out over prime whale-watching seas. If you need more time, reserve a room at the pleasant **Owen House** (506–752–2977), a nine-room bed-and-breakfast in the village of Welshpool, where you can get a room with a view for less than $100 U.S.

For more information call (506) 752–7043 or visit the Web site www.campobello.com.

RELOCATION

Realtors across Maine know the type: a handsomely dressed and starry-eyed person who arrives in their office at the end of the summer, raving rapturously about a piece of property seen while traveling through Maine. Most definitely from away, this individual would like to change that, having fallen truly, madly, deeply in love while on vacation. This scenario plays out scores of times across the state every year. And for good reason. As so many former visitors, retirees, kids, and just plain old Mainers know—this is a great place to call home.

Houses are affordable, considering the ridiculous prices to which real estate has escalated in other states, and the facts that our health care system is leading the way in several areas and our schools are holding their own. In recent years the state has been seeing waves of retirees who are setting up households here for their golden years and an influx of young families headed by natives who decided they want to come back home to raise their children Down East. And there are plenty of people who hate so much to leave at the end of their vacation that they decide to stay, too. Who can blame them?

REAL ESTATE

We already know Maine is a beautiful place, but its real estate remains relatively affordable compared to points south, especially in coastal sections east of Portland. The median selling price of a Maine home in 2005 was $184,000. Compare that to $400,000 in Seattle, $345,000 in Massachusetts, and $530,000 in places like Sedona, Arizona, and you can see why people get into such a lather about Maine. When it comes to coastal property, the discrepancies are even more dramatic—Down

East in Washington County the median home price in 2005 was $121,000! Contrast that with Cape Cod's average home price of $340,000, factor in the fact that you don't have to wait in lines for hours to get to your place in Eastport, and Maine's looking pretty good. Like everywhere else, the market here cooled a bit in 2006, so it's a good time to be looking.

The prices of coastal homes vary by community, of course, but there are some trends to note. In Kittery Point, which is commuting distance from Boston, homes are going to sell for much more than in the fishing village of Cutler, which is in a fairly remote corner of the state far from any urban area and booming economic sectors. Just about anywhere in York County, which is the fastest-growing section of the state, is going to be more expensive than places up the coast, save for maybe Greater Portland. It's almost accurate to say that prices begin on the high end on the South Coast and fade as you head Down East. That's true for the most part, but there are a few anomalies, which the Portland and York figures show. Likewise, in Hancock County, where Bar Harbor and Acadia are located, the median price was higher than in neighboring Waldo County (home of Belfast) to the south. But as a general rule of thumb, it's true that the farther you go Down East, the lower prices of coastal property will be.

i Real estate ads have long been a specialty of *Down East: The Magazine of Maine.* Each summer there are dozens of pages of full-color advertisements showing homes up for sale across the state. It's a great resource, if only for the pictures alone. Pick up a copy at the newsstand.

Sales of Coastal Maine Homes by County, 2005*

	Total Units Sold	Median Sale Price
York	2,517	$245,000
Cumberland	3,474	$250,000
Sagadahoc	400	$194,688
Lincoln	450	$235,000
Knox	473	$201,000
Waldo	439	$160,000
Hancock	590	$212,500
Washington	49	$121,000

*from Maine Real Estate Information System

The state's largest city and its suburbs are increasingly desirable places to live, and they continue to experience quite rapid development, with homes sprouting up in old fields as quickly as dandelions. Everyone in Maine knows that Cumberland and York Counties have been exploding with growth and sprawl; in fact, there was talk that in the late 1990s Portland, Maine, was one of the fastest-growing areas in the nation. These days the talk is how to control growth and minimize sprawl. But there were other booming pockets along the coast. Waldo County is an example. The advent of credit card giant MBNA in Belfast—and the 7,000 jobs that came with it—helped launch a real estate flurry in the Penobscot Bay city, and it's still suffering from a housing crunch.

The whole of the Midcoast has grown more popular, with places like Damariscotta seeing influxes of retirees as well as summer people who decided to move up full-time. There are a lot of reasons why, beyond cheap real estate. One is simply that people are realizing coastal land is going fast—and "they aren't making any more of it," as the joke goes. Cultural changes have weighed in, as well, with people looking for quiet, crime-free towns to raise their children in. The shock of

9/11 reverberated all the way up to the Maine coast, and Realtors found themselves fielding calls from New Yorkers anxious to get out of the city.

Newcastle Realty's James Cosgrove summed up the real estate climate of 2004 thusly: "Buyers are looking for communities with high quality of life and a place where they can make a connection with their neighbors. In years past the buzzwords were 'privacy' and 'isolation.' Now people talk about being 'in the village' and 'walking distance to town.'"

TAXES

You can't talk real estate in Maine, though, without talking taxes. The Pine Tree State has a reputation for high taxes, and property taxes are part of the reason. Everyone has an opinion on taxes, and so sources vary in reliability and accuracy, due to political slant, but the Maine Municipal Association, a nonprofit, nonpartisan organization representing the interests of Maine's communities, has a wealth of information about the state's tax system on its Web site, www.memun.org/. A highlight for prospective buyers might be the property tax rates section, which lists each community by tax rate. It's a very handy resource.

REAL ESTATE AGENCIES

You can't drive more than a couple of miles on the coast of Maine without coming across a real estate agency. They're everywhere, and they come in all sizes and flavors. Some are housed in a trailer on the side of U.S. Route 1, some tucked away in an old home in a small village, others in fancy downtown offices in Portland. A good Realtor can make a huge difference in your shopping experience, and there are plenty in Maine who will go the extra mile to help you find what you want (and earn their commission). Buyer's brokers—essentially personal Realtors—have become the way to go in Maine, especially for people from away, who can't zip around to anything that appeals and need a lot of help sifting through the options and narrowing down their lists.

It would be impossible to list all of the state's real estate agencies in a single space—try looking on the Web, searching by the town you're interested in, or by contacting the chambers of commerce in the region. Here are some of the more notable ones that can help you search for just the right property on the coast of Maine.

South Coast

Anne Erwin Real Estate
281 York Street
York 03909
(207) 363–6640
www.anneerwin.com

Century 21 Atlantic Realty
433 Route 1, Suite 101
York 03909
(800) 344–5710
www.c21atlantic.com

Re/Max Realty One
439 Route 1
York 03909
(207) 363–2497
www.yorkmaine.com

Perkins Real Estate
19 Beach Street
Ogunquit 03907
(207) 646–5535
www.perkinsre.com

Coldwell Banker Residential Brokerage
183 Port Road, P.O. Box 1143
Kennebunkport 04046
(207) 967–9900
www.newenglandmoves.com

The Downing Agency, Inc. Realtors
10 Storer Street
Kennebunk 04043
(207) 985–3328
www.downingagency.com

Kennebunk Beach Realty
Junction of Routes 9 and 35
Kennebunk 04043
(207) 967–5481
www.kennebunkbeachrealty.com

Pack Maynard and Associates
165 Port Road
Kennebunk 04043
(207) 967–3883
www.pmrealestate.com

Greater Portland

Re/Max Absolute Realty
100 Foden Road
Scarborough 04074
(207) 828–3900
www.realestategreaterportland.com

i A handy source of home-for-sale photos is the digest-size guides put out by Home Handbooks (www.home handbook.com) found in supermarket lobbies the length of the coast. The thumbnail photos are great fun to peruse, and the information is there if you're smitten.

Re/Max Coastal
306 Route 1
South Portland 04106
(800) 883–7362
www.southportlandmehomes.com

Landvest
2 Monument Square
Portland 04101
(207) 774–8518
www.landvest.com

Port Island Realty
73 Federal Street
Portland 04112
(207) 775–7253
www.portisland.com

Re/Max by the Bay
970 Baxter Boulevard
Portland 04103
(207) 773–2345
www.homesinmaine.com

Town and Shore Associates
One Union Wharf
Portland 04101
(207) 773–0262
www.townandshore.com

Re/Max Heritage
765 Route 1
Yarmouth 04096
(207) 846–4300
www.rheritage.com

Midcoast

Legacy Properties
141 Maine Street
Brunswick 04011
(207) 729–2820
www.brunswickmaine.com

Morton Real Estate
240 Maine Street
Brunswick 04011
(207) 729–1863
www.mainere.com

Rob Williams Real Estate
Route 24
Bailey Island 04003
(207) 833–5078
www.baileyisland.com

Homes and Harbors Real Estate
1 Harbor Place
Orrs Island 04079
(207) 833–0500
www.homesandharbors.com

Re/Max Riverside
1 Main Street, Suite 101
Topsham 04086
(207) 725–8505
www.remax-riverside-maine.com

Century 21 Shore and Country
6 Main Street
Topsham 04086
(207) 725–1444
www.century21shoreandcountry.com

CHR Realty
823 Washington Street
Bath 04530
(207) 443–3333
www.chrrealty.com

Court Street Realty
78 Court Street
Bath 04530
(207) 442–7111
www.courtstreetrealty.com

Sharon Drake Real Estate
136 Front Street
Bath 04530
(800) 561–1005
www.sharondrake.com

Roy Farmer Associates
Main Street
Wiscasset 04578
(207) 882–7391

Pottle Realty Group
63 Townsend Avenue
Boothbay Harbor 04538
(207) 633–2222
www.pottlerealtygroup.com

Tindal and Callahan Real Estate
32 Oak Street
Boothbay Harbor 04358
(207) 633–3392
www.tindalandcallahan.com

Antique and Coastal Properties
P.O. Box 312
Southport 04576
(207) 633–0110
www.hywatt.com

Adams and Perley Real Estate
Upper Main Street
Damariscotta 04543
(207) 563–5140

Drum and Drum Real Estate
17 Bristol Road
Damariscotta 04543
(207) 563–1772
www.bestmaineproperties.com

Newcastle Square Realty
87 Main Street
Damariscotta 04543
(207) 563–1003
www.mainecoastproperties.com

L. Dewey Chase Real Estate
2568 Bristol Road
New Harbor 04554
(207) 677–2978
www.ldchase.com

Rubenstein Real Estate
145 Main Street
Thomaston 04861
(207) 354–6654

Cap de Rochemont Realtor
141 Main Street
Rockland 04841
(207) 594–9397
www.derochemont.com

Jordan Real Estate Company
99 Camden Street
Rockland 04841
(207) 594–5503

True Hall Realty
P.O. Box 121
Tenants Harbor 04860
(207) 372–8952
www.truehall.com

Rock Maple Realty
295 Common Road
Union 04862
(207) 785–4305
www.rockmaplerealestate.com

Sterlingtown Realty
Union Common
Union 04862
(207) 785–2000

Camden Real Estate Company
43 Elm Street
Camden 04843
(800) 236–1920
www.camdenre.com

Jaret and Cohn Real Estate
73 Elm Street
Camden 04843
(207) 236–9626
www.jaretcohn.com

Landvest
22 Bayview Street
Camden 04843
(207) 236–3543
www.landvest.com

Trimble Realty Group
39 Main Street
Camden 04843
(207) 236–1003
www.trimblerealty.com

Town and Country Realtors
High Street
Belfast 04915
(207) 338–3500
www.greenkeefe.com

GRF Real Estate Company
230 Searsport Avenue
Belfast 04915
(207) 338–2422
www.grfrealestate.com

United Realty
217 Northport Avenue
Belfast 04915
(207) 338–6000
www.unitedrealtyme.com

Singleton-Rollerson Real Estate
185 West Main Street
Searsport 04974
(207) 548–2280
www.pru-singleton.com

Castine Realty
Main Street, P.O. Box 234
Castine 04421
(207) 326–9392
www.castinerealty.com

Endicott Real Estate and Insurance
Main Street
Castine 04421
(207) 326–8741
www.endicottagency.com

Glenith Gray Real Estate
Reach Road
Sargentville 04673
(207) 359–4448
www.glenithgray.com

Shepard's Select Properties
P.O. Box 115
Stonington 04681
(207) 367–2790
www.shepardselect.com

Compass Point Real Estate
P.O. Box 52
Blue Hill 04614
(207) 374–5300
www.compasspointrealestate.com

DownEast Properties
P.O. Box 402
Blue Hill 04614
(207) 374–2321
www.downeastpropertiesinc.com

Saltmeadow Properties
P.O. Box 1001
Blue Hill 04614
(207) 374–5010
www.saltmeadowproperties.com

Prudential Northeast Properties
105 High Street
Ellsworth 04605
(207) 667–4604
www.prudentialnortheastproperties.com

Sargent Real Estate
P.O. Box 368
Ellsworth 04605
(207) 667–2144
www.sargentre.com

Acadia Area

Lynam Real Estate
P.O. Box C
Bar Harbor 04609
(207) 288–3334
www.lynams.com

Swan Agency Real Estate
P.O. Box 46
Bar Harbor 04609
(207) 288–5818
www.swanagency.com

Landvest
4A Tracy Road
Northeast Harbor 04662
(207) 276–3840
www.landvest.com

Hinckley Real Estate Sales
246 Main Street
Southwest Harbor 04679
(207) 244–7011
www.hinckleyrealestate.com

Down East

Eastland Realty
Route 1
Machias 04654
(207) 255–3912
www.eastlandrealty.com

Drop Anchor Realty
P.O. Box 249
Milbridge 04658
(207) 546–2195
www.dropanchorrealtymaine.com

Bold Coast Realty
460 County Road
Lubec 04652
(207) 733–4344
www.boldcoast.net

Due East Real Estate
183 Country Road
Eastport 04631
(207) 853–2626
www.dueast.com

EDUCATION

In a 2006 study by Morgan Quitno, Maine was ranked the "5th Smartest State" in the nation. Not bad for a state with a small, largely rural population. Rankings were based on 21 factors, including test scores, graduation rates, and education expenditures. From top-level colleges to schools private and parochial, Maine's educational system has begun to come into its own in recent years. According to *Education Week* magazine, Maine's primary school system is in the top 10 in the nation and has one of the best "school climates," which ranks student-to-teacher ratios, parental involvement, and school safety. The magazine also lauded the state for having 97 percent of its schools connected to the Internet.

Students who continue on to college have their choice of some of the nation's best small private schools in Colby, Bates, and Bowdoin; one of the nation's highest-ranking small public liberal arts colleges in the University of Maine at Farmington; and the school with the happiest students (the view is spectacular) in the College of the Atlantic in Bar Harbor. And, of course, there's always the giant University of Maine itself, a school of 10,000 in Orono, that's been the place to go for most Mainers for more than a century. A whole fleet of smaller state universities are spread across the state, and in recent years Maine has been seriously studying the addition of community colleges to the mix, transforming some of the state's technical schools into more traditional two-year colleges. The Pine Tree State is also home to a well-regarded divinity school—Bangor Theological Seminary. Anyone who wants to learn will find some exceptional places to do so Down East.

Public Schools

Maine's 707 public schools traditionally fare pretty well in national surveys. In a study in the late 1990s, the National Educational Goals Panel found Maine to be the state that had most improved its public education system. Proof of this might be that in 1998 the state's eighth-graders were first in the national assessment tests for their writing ability and second for reading ability. Their performance in math and science was respectable as well, in 2000 coming in fifth and eighth, respectively, so their education is well rounded.

What does the state have going for it? Most schools are in rural or suburban areas where class sizes are small and where schools tend to be important parts of community life. There's been a lot of forward-thinking action at the state level as well, with first-in-the-nation moves like former governor Angus King's program to equip every seventh grader with a laptop computer and the establishment of magnet schools for gifted math and science students.

Maine's school system is divided into 70-some School Administrative Units (SADs) and 14 Community School Districts (CSDs) under local control. Many of these districts include two or more towns, which combine resources and expenses, and they're funded by the state and by local property taxes. In a few cases—like Lincoln Academy in Newcastle and George Stevens Academy in Blue Hill—towns pay for students to attend private schools, but these private schools usually accept every student in the area and function like public schools anyway.

The state has a very handy education directory online at www.state.me.us/education/, where you'll find a list of all schools in Maine broken down by community, private and public status, district, and more. There's also a set of useful school links.

Homeschooling

Homeschooling has a pretty long history in the state, and Mainers have long been leaders in the homeschool movement. The Maine Department of Education is a lot more open to the idea than its equivalent in other states, and the hoops parents have to jump through are fewer. The Maine Home Education Association (350 Duck Pond Road, Westbrook 04092), a nonsectarian, nonprofit advocacy group, has a useful Web site—www.geocities .com/mainehomeed/—with links to all sorts of topics related to teaching kids at home.

Private Schools

There are more than 100 private schools in Maine, and they range from Catholic schools like Cheverus in Portland to Montessori to Ashwood Waldorf schools. A majority of these educational institutions are inland, but there are many along the coast. Some areas—

Greater Portland and Camden-Rockport, for example—are particularly rich with alternatives to public schools.

Following is a list of Maine's coastal private schools and the addresses and phone numbers at which to get more information. The number of students given was the number at press time, just to give an idea of school size.

South Coast

Berwick Academy
31 Academy Street
South Berwick 03908
(207) 384–2164
Grades K–12, 600 students, nonsectarian

Cornerstone Kindergarten, Inc.
19 Morse Street
Berwick 03901
(207) 698–5651
Kindergarten, 18 students, nonsectarian

Brixham Montessori Friends School
18 Brickyard Court
York 03909
(207) 351–2700
Grades K–4, 55 students, nonsectarian

Herne Schools of Discovery
117 Woodbridge Road
York 03909
(207) 363–8631
Grades 1–2, 50 students, nonsectarian

School around Us
281 Log Cabin Road
Arundel 04046
(207) 967–3143
Grades K–8, 21 students, nonsectarian

Cocoons LLC
215 Sea Road
Kennebunk 04043
(207) 967–4440
Kindergarten, 14 students, nonsectarian

The New School
38 York Street
Kennebunk 04043
(207) 985–3745
Grades 9–12, 27 students, nonsectarian

Pace Maine
11 Lebanon Street
Sanford 04073
(207) 324–1466
Grades 1–6, 3 students, nonsectarian

Saint Thomas School
69 North Avenue
Sanford 04073
(207) 324–5832
Grades K–6, 268 students, Catholic

Saint James School
25 Graham Street
Biddeford 04005
(207) 282–4084
Grades K–8, 489 students, Catholic

Notre Dame De Lourdes
50 Beach Street
Saco 04072
(207) 283–3111
Grades K–8, 214 students, Catholic

Saco Island School
110 Main Street, Suite 1115
Saco 04072
(207) 283–1435
Grades 9–12, 16 students, nonsectarian

Sweetser Children's Services
50 Moody Street
Saco 04072
(207) 294–4941
Grades K–12, 129 students, nonsectarian

Thornton Academy
438 Main Street
Saco 04072
(207) 282–3361
Grades 9–12, 1,174 students, nonsectarian,
with 60 percent or more publicly funded
students

Greater Portland

Toddle Inn Elementary School
9 Lincoln Drive
Scarborough 04074
(207) 776–5397
Kindergarten, 13 students, nonsectarian

AppleTree School
44 Two Lights Road
Cape Elizabeth 04107
(207) 799–4225
Kindergarten, 22 students, nonsectarian

Ledgemere Country Day School
243 Mitchell Road
Cape Elizabeth 04107
(207) 799–8654
Kindergarten, 60 students, nonsectarian

Aucocisco School
496 Ocean Street
South Portland 04106
(207) 773–7323
Grades 5–12, 38 students, nonsectarian

Casco Bay Montessori School
440 Ocean Street
South Portland 04106
(207) 799–2400
Kindergarten, 25 students, nonsectarian

Greater Portland Christian School
1338 Broadway
South Portland 04106
(207) 767–5123
Grades K–12, 153 students, sectarian

Holy Cross School
436 Broadway
South Portland 04106
(207) 799–6661
Grades K–8, 227 students, Catholic

Levey Day School
400 Deering Avenue
South Portland 04103
(207) 774–7676
Grades K–5, 32 students, sectarian

Lighthouse School
525 Highland Avenue
South Portland 04106
(207) 767–2129
Kindergarten, 120 students, sectarian

Breakwater School
856 Brighton Avenue
Portland 04102
(207) 772–8689
Grades K–5, 166 students, nonsectarian

Cathedral School
14 Locust Street
Portland 04101
(207) 775–1491
Grades K–8, 194 students, Catholic

Catherine McAuley High School
631 Stevens Avenue
Portland 04103
(207) 797–3802
Grades 9–12, 301 students, Catholic

Children's Center
Westbrook College Campus
721 Stevens Avenue
Portland 04103
(207) 797–9366
Kindergarten, 55 students, nonsectarian

Saint Elizabeth School
87 High Street
Portland 04101
(207) 871–7444
Kindergarten, 6 students, Catholic

Saint Joseph Parish School
695 Stevens Avenue
Portland 04103
(207) 797–7073
Grades K–8, 229 students, Catholic

Saint Patrick School
1251 Congress Street
Portland 04102
(207) 775–2521
Grades K–8, 214 students, Catholic

Spurwink School Inc.
899 Riverside Street
Portland 04103
(207) 771–1354
Grades K–12, 231 students, nonsectarian

Waynflete School
360 Spring Street
Portland 04102
(207) 772–6832
Grades K–12, 540 students, nonsectarian

Koala Child Care/Learning Center
969 Spring Street, Box 1068
Westbrook 04092
(207) 775–3337
Kindergarten, 10 students, nonsectarian

The Little Dolphin School
101 County Road
Westbrook 04092
(207) 874–9909
Kindergarten, 36 students, nonsectarian

Children's Odyssey
196 Gray Road
Falmouth 04105
(207) 878–6998
Kindergarten, 31 students, nonsectarian

Pine Grove Child Development Center
32 Foreside Road
Falmouth 04105
(207) 781–3441
Kindergarten, 95 students, nonsectarian

Winfield Children's House
161 Field Road
Falmouth 04105
(207) 797–8101
Kindergarten, 59 students, nonsectarian

North Yarmouth Academy
148 Main Street
Yarmouth 04096
(207) 846–9051
Grades 6–12, 272 students, nonsectarian

Red House Montessori School
392 Walnut Hill Road
North Yarmouth 04097
(207) 829–4379
Kindergarten, 26 students, nonsectarian

Merriconeag Waldorf School
57 Desert Road
Freeport 04032
(207) 865–3900
Grades K–8, 228 students, nonsectarian

Pine Tree Academy
67 Pownal Road
Freeport 04032
(207) 865–4747
Grades K–12, 134 students, sectarian

Midcoast

Children's School of Arts and Science
185 Harding Road
Brunswick 04011
(207) 443–4771
Grades K–8, 27 students, nonsectarian

St. John's Catholic School
39 Pleasant Street
Brunswick 04011
(207) 725–5507
Grades K–8, 224 students, Catholic

Hyde School
616 High Street
Bath 04530
(207) 443–7123
Grades 9–12, 236 students, nonsectarian

Midcoast Montessori School
785 High Street
Bath 04530
(207) 442–9447
Kindergarten, 36 students, nonsectarian

Chop Point School
425 Chop Point Road
Woolwich 04579
(207) 443–3080
Grades K–12, 97 students, sectarian

Sheepscot Valley Children's House
127 Federal Street, P.O. Box 449
Wiscasset 04578
(207) 882–6300
Grades K–3, 68 students, nonsectarian

Center for Teaching and Learning
119 Cross Point Road
Edgecomb 04556
(207) 882–9706
Grades K–8, 75 students, nonsectarian

Deck House School
124 Deck House Road
Edgecomb 04556
(207) 882–7055
Grades 9–12, 12 students, nonsectarian

Lincoln Academy
81 Academy Hill Road
Newcastle 04553
(207) 563–3596
Grades 9–12, 547 students, nonsectarian, with
60 percent or more publicly funded students

Pen Bay Christian School
1 Waldo Avenue
Rockland 04841
(207) 594–6460
Grades K–8, 144 students, sectarian

Ashwood Waldorf School
180 Park Street, P.O. Box 129
Rockport 04856
(207) 236–8621
Grades K–8, 138 students, nonsectarian

Children's House Montessori School
205 West Street, P.O. Box 1106
Rockport 04856
(207) 236–2911
Grades K–8, 98 students, nonsectarian

Riley School Inc.
Warrenton Road, P.O. Box 300
Glen Cove 04846
(207) 596–6405
Grades K–9, 52 students, nonsectarian

Community School
79 Washington Street, P.O. Box 555
Camden 04843
(207) 236–3000
Grades 9–12, 26 students, nonsectarian

Toddy Pond School
561 Oak Hill Road
Swanville 04915
(207) 338–3848
Grades K–8, 7 students, nonsectarian

Bay School
South Street, P.O. Box 269
Blue Hill 04614
(207) 374–2187
Grades K–8, 96 students, nonsectarian

George Stevens Academy
23 Union Street
Blue Hill 04614
(207) 374–2808
Grades 9–12, 384 students, nonsectarian, with
60 percent or more publicly funded students

Liberty School
P.O. Box 857
Blue Hill 04614
(207) 374–2886
Grades 9–12, 58 students, nonsectarian, with
60 percent or more publicly funded students

Kids Peace–New England
Route 180, P.O. Box 787
Ellsworth 04605
(207) 667–0909
Grades 7–12, 49 students, nonsectarian

Acadia Area

Island Montessori School
83 Herrick Road, P.O. Box 418
Southwest Harbor 04679
(207) 244–9968
Kindergarten, 14 students, nonsectarian

Acadia School
55 Kebo Street
Bar Harbor 04609
(207) 288–9980
Grades K–3, 53 students, nonsectarian

DownEast

Machias Valley Christian School
6 Broadway, P.O. Box 219
Machias 04654
(207) 255–3300
Grades K–8, 112 students, sectarian

Washington Academy
High Street, P.O. Box 190
East Machias 04630
(207) 255–8301
Grades 9–12, 298 students, nonsectarian, with
60 percent or more publicly funded students

Higher Education

In Bates, Bowdoin, and Colby Colleges, Maine
has three of the better small, liberal arts institutions of higher education in the nation. The
trio are the best and the brightest as far as
Maine schools go, but there's no shortage of
other choices, from the University of New England in Biddeford to the Maine Maritime Academy in Castine to the College of the Atlantic in
Bar Harbor to the many schools of the University of Maine system (only the coastal representatives are listed here). Students have a lot
of options and can go far with what they take
in at Maine colleges.

Bates College
Lewiston
(207) 786–6255
www.bates.edu
Founded in 1855, Bates is one of the nicest
things about Lewiston, occupying 109 woody
acres in the center of the city. Known for
excellence in the sciences, the school has
small student-to-teacher ratios (as low as 10:1)
and is perennially ranked among the nation's
best in college surveys. The school was number 22 in the *U.S. News and World Report*'s

Maine Photographic Workshops

Who would have guessed when this downtown Rockport school at 2 Central Street was founded in 1973 that it would become a world-renowned institution teaching the best of tomorrow's photographers and filmmakers? Over the years the Maine Photographic Workshops have grown exponentially, and there are now more than 250 one-week workshops and master classes to choose from. (Most of the hipsters you see walking or biking around Camden and Rockport are associated with the school.) Some of the biggest names in the industry teach courses in all aspects of film and photography, from writing the screenplay to doing final edits to darkroom techniques, all right here above Rockport Harbor. Rockport College, a spin-off of "the Workshops," was founded in 1996 and now offers associate's and master's degrees as well. All summer long there are free slide shows open to the public—check the Web site for dates and times—and while they can be hot and stuffy, where else do you get to see legends like Mary Ellen Mark discuss their work? There are also frequent gallery shows. For more information call (207) 236–8581 or (877) 577–7700 or visit www.theworkshops.com.

A "Workshops" workshop. LISA MOSSEL VIETZE

famed "Best American Colleges" issue among the top 217 liberal arts schools. And *Seventeen* magazine called it "cool" to boot. There are 1,700 students here, and they're a bright and active bunch. Most participate in some sort of student-run club or sport, and more than two-thirds go on to graduate school. Founded by abolitionists, the school prides itself on its diverse student body. Tuition and board run about $42,100.

The campus includes the Olin Arts Center (Russell and Bardwell Streets; 207–786–6135), where there are often films and performances open to the public, and the Bates College Museum of Art (Russell Street; 207–786–6158), an excellent small art collection. On Thursdays in the summer there are free concerts that are worth attending. Also a biggie in the summer is the Bates Dance Festival (207–786–6161), which attracts big names from the world of modern dance.

Bowdoin College
Brunswick
(207) 725–3000
www.bowdoin.edu

If you want to be a major political figure in the United States, you could pick a worse college to attend—Bowdoin has turned out scads of high-ranking officials, from presidents to governors (a dozen in Maine) to legislators. Founded in 1794, the liberal arts school has about 1,650 students, evenly divided between men and women, and it accepts about a quarter of its applicants. Its student body represents 48 states and 27 countries, with about 230-some Mainers among them, and class sizes are kept small, with the median being 16. Tuition and board cost is now up to $42,000, and students graduate with Bachelor of Arts degrees in about 40 disciplines.

The 110-acre campus is a pretty place, with more than 80 buildings, the oldest of which date back to 1802. A famous stand of pines provides shade, adding a bit of class to the neighborhood, and there are a lot of fine squares and greens framed by all the brick. Downtown Brunswick is just down the hill, and

Bowdoin's students help keep Main Street vibrant. Free guided tours are available from the admissions office.

Colby College
Mayflower Hill, Waterville
(207) 872–3000
www.colby.edu

The campus of Colby is huge—714 acres—and it's well apart from the rest of Waterville, its own brick kingdom of fine Georgian buildings. Coed since 1871, the school began life as a Baptist institution in 1813, and it is highly regarded for its liberal arts curriculum. There are 54 majors from which to choose—the top four being economics, biology, English, and government—and the school has become nationally recognized for its research- and project-based undergraduate programs. About a third of its applicants are accepted.

The campus of Colby was moved here from downtown Waterville in the 1950s, and it now consists of about 62 structures with an arboretum and bird sanctuary around them. In fact, most of the campus is considered a Maine Wildlife Management Area. There are 1,870 students wandering among all that wildlife going to classes with an average size of 19 students—a third of all classes have less than a dozen. Tuition and board cost about $41,770.

University of New England
11 Hills Beach Road, Biddeford
(800) 477–4UNE
www.une.edu

Another school with twin campuses, UNE has facilities in Biddeford and in downtown Portland (the site of the old Westbrook College). It is Maine's only medical school, and it has about 1,500 undergrads, 500 graduate students, and 500 medical students on its attractive campuses. The Biddeford campus has more than 4,000 feet of ocean frontage. And the school's level of prestige is rising fast— *U.S. News and World Report* has called it one of the best regional universities in the Northeast, has ranked the physician assistant program among the top 25 in the nation, and has recognized UNE's College of Osteopathic Medicine for excellence in primary care, geriatrics, and rural medicine. The marine biology program is growing in repute as well, thanks to the new Marine Science Education Research Center.

Maine Maritime Academy
Castine
(207) 326–4311 or (800) 227–8465
www.mainemaritime.edu
People see the cadets marching around Castine and automatically think of this nautical college as a military institution. It's not. About 60 percent of the school's 861 students are enrolled in the regimental program, which is quasi-military, but they're learning to be sailors in the merchant marine, not the navy. And students study a lot more here than simply commercial sailing. Majors include marine engineering, ocean studies, and marina management, among other things. The school is one of only seven merchant marine colleges in the nation, and it has a fleet of more than 90 vessels, most impressive of which is the *State of Maine,* a 498-foot training vessel that takes up blocks of the town's waterfront when it's not out on a tour. The 50-acre campus is an attractive centerpiece of the downtown of this historic community, all old brick and lawns, and the students here help offset the loss of the tourists and summer people in the fall. The school has a great record of job placement, too.

College of the Atlantic
105 Eden Street, Bar Harbor
(207) 288–5015
www.coa.edu
Students have the choice of exactly one major at this progressive Bar Harbor school: human ecology. But the definition of that discipline is so hazy, they can study whatever they want. Within their degree focus they can concentrate on design, environmental science, landscape and building architecture, marine studies, natural history, museum studies, pub-

For more information on the schools in the University of Maine system, log on to www.maineedu.com.

lic policy, teacher ed, and various humanities. So there is a lot of wiggle room in human ecology, which the school describes as "emphasizing the interrelationships, specifically between humans and our natural, social, and technological environments." It's not for everyone, of course, and the school has a tiny student body—just 300 kids. But in surveys of the nation's colleges they're always recognized as among the happiest in the country, and their campus, right on Frenchman Bay and minutes from Acadia, is often deemed the most beautiful. The school has come a long way since it was founded in 1969, and its list of alumni includes some cool folks.

University of Maine System

There are seven universities in the UMaine system, serving 34,000 students. The University of Maine inland in Orono is the largest, with about 11,000 of those students. UMaine schools on the coast include the University of Southern Maine—which has campuses in Portland and Gorham and actually more students than Orono, but only half or so are full-time—and the University of Machias, with about 1,100 students way Down East. The biggest major at any of these schools is education, with health care and business, respectively, the second and third most popular.

The University of Southern Maine
P.O. Box 9300, Portland 04104
(207) 780–4141 or (800) 800–4USM
www.usm.maine.edu
Divided into two parts—one half in the leafy suburb of Gorham, the other in downtown Portland—USM was founded in 1878, and the two campuses are separated by about 8 miles. Thought of as something of a Maine commuter school, the university has students from 32 states and 15 foreign countries, so it's a lot more diverse than it's given credit for, and

there are about 11,000 of them enrolled in undergraduate and graduate programs. The school confers degrees in 50 majors and has eight colleges: arts and sciences; business; applied science, engineering, and technology; nursing and health; education and human development; law; Lewiston-Auburn College; and the Muskie School of Public Service. Student-to-faculty ratio is kept small (about 13:1) and class sizes are, too, with an average of 22 students. The school was among the "Best Northeastern Colleges" in the 2007 *Princeton Review*.

The University of Maine at Machias
9 O'Brien Avenue, Machias
(207) 255–1200
www.umm.maine.edu
The easternmost college in the nation, UMM is a small school in a small town way Down East. The campus covers about 43 acres in Machias, a beautiful and historic Washington County community hard by the shores of Machias Bay. Of the 1,100 students, 60 percent are women. The school likes to bill the fact that it has a level of attention comparable to the good private schools—the student-to-faculty ratio is 14:1; average class size is 16—but with all the resources of the University of Maine system. It's a nice combination, and the setting is stunning if you can handle remoteness.

Other Educational Opportunities

If you're interested in fine furniture and how it's created, sign up for a one- or two-week course at the respected **Center for Furniture Craftsmanship** (25 Mill Street, Rockport; 207–594–5611; www.woodschool.com). Perhaps boats are more to your liking? Seek out the **Wooden Boat School** (Off Naskeag Point Road, Brooklin; 207–359–4651 or 800–273–7447; www.thewoodenboatschool.com), where traditional boatbuilders learn their craft from the best. Or maybe you fancy yourself an artisan? The **Haystack Mountain School of Crafts** (Deer Isle; 207–348–2306; www.haystack-mtn.org) is famous for its two- and three-week sessions in pottery, glass, fibers, and graphics.

HEALTH CARE

For such a small state in terms of population, Maine comes out at the top of a lot of surveys and polls when it comes to health care. Not too long ago, the cardiac unit at Maine Medical Center in Portland was deemed to be among the best in the nation, and more recently, the OB-GYN department at Miles Memorial Hospital in Damariscotta came out tops in the nation in patient satisfaction. So Maine doctors must be doing something right.

The state has about 40 hospitals spread throughout small communities and has large, state-of-the-art health care centers in Portland and Bangor. Wherever you go, from Kittery to Calais, excellent health care is not far away. Newly arrived Mainers take comfort in the fact that there are good hospitals within a reasonable drive, and Mainers in general have been taking advantage of them, too, turning to the state's hospitals for help close to three million times annually. The state's health care system is fairly hospital-centric, without a lot of the clinics you see in urban areas and with doctors generally being allied with one large center or another.

When they aren't visiting hospitals, Mainers seem to be going to alternative health care providers, of which there are a growing number. In the past Mainers, who tend to be a fairly skeptical lot, have looked askance at health care givers who worked outside the traditional fields of medicine. But today you'll see old-timers going to the acupuncturist and grandmas at the chiropractor. Wellness centers have been popping up along the coast since the 1990s, and certain hospitals even have their own natural or homeopathic offshoots these days. Most of the major alternative disciplines are represented along the coast, with centers in southern Maine, Portland, and more forward-thinking coastal counties like Knox, Waldo, and Hancock.

Hospitals

York Hospital
15 Hospital Drive, York
(207) 363–4321
www.yorkhospital.com
Acute Beds: 79
Long-Term Care Beds: 13

Goodall Hospital
25 June Street, Sanford
(207) 324–4310
www.goodallhosp.org
Acute Beds: 49
Long-Term Care Beds: 74

Southern Maine Medical Center
P.O. Box 626, Biddeford 04005
(207) 283–7000
www.smmc.org
Acute Beds: 150
Long-Term Care Beds: 0

Spring Harbor Hospital
175 Running Hill Road, South Portland
(207) 761–2200
www.springharbor.org
Acute Beds: 111
Long-Term Care Beds: 0

Maine Medical Center
22 Bramhall Street, Portland
(207) 622–0111
www.mmc.org
Acute Beds: 606
Long-Term Care Beds: 0

Mercy Hospital
144 State Street, Portland
(207) 879–3000
www.mercyhospital.com
Acute Beds: 230
Long-Term Care Beds: 0

New England Rehabilitation Hospital
of Portland
335 Brighton Avenue, Portland
(207) 775–4000
www.nerhp.com
Acute Beds: 100
Long-Term Care Beds: 0

Mid Coast Hospital
123 Medical Center Drive, Brunswick
(207) 729–0181
www.midcoasthealth.com
Acute Beds: 104
Long-Term Care Beds: 42

Parkview Adventist Medical Center
329 Maine Street, Brunswick
(207) 373–2000
www.parkviewhospital.com
Acute Beds: 55
Long-Term Care Beds: 0

Miles Memorial Hospital
Bristol Road, Damariscotta
(207) 563–1234
www.mileshealthcare.org
Acute Beds: 38
Long-Term Care Beds: 76

St. Andrews Hospital & Healthcare Center
P.O. Box 417, Boothbay Harbor 04538
(207) 633–2121
www.standrewshealthcare.org
Acute Beds: 25
Long-Term Care Beds: 30

Penobscot Bay Medical Center
6 Glen Cove Drive, Rockport
(207) 596–8000
www.nehealth.org
Acute Beds: 109
Long-Term Care Beds: 123

Waldo County General Hospital
118 Northport Avenue, Belfast
(207) 338–2500
www.wchi.com
Acute Beds: 25
Long-Term Care Beds: 0

Blue Hill Memorial Hospital
57 Water Street, Blue Hill
(207) 374–3400
www.bhmh.org
Acute Beds: 23
Long-Term Care Beds: 0

Maine Coast Memorial Hospital
50 Union Street, Ellsworth
(207) 667–5311
www.mainehospital.org
Acute Beds: 64
Long-Term Care Beds: 8

Mount Desert Island Hospital
P.O. Box 8, Bar Harbor 04609
(207) 288–5081
www.mdihospital.org
Acute Beds: 25
Long-Term Care Beds: 0

Down East Community Hospital
R.R. 1, Box 11, Machias
(207) 255–3356
www.dech.org
Acute Beds: 25
Long-Term Care Beds: 28

Calais Regional Hospital
24 Hospital Lane, Calais
(207) 454–7521
www.calaishospital.com
Acute Beds: 25
Long-Term Care Beds: 0

Acadia Hospital
268 Stillwater Avenue, Bangor
(207) 973–6100
www.acadiahospital.org
Acute Beds: 100
Long-Term Care Beds: 0

Eastern Maine Medical Center
P.O. Box 404, Bangor 04402
(207) 973–7000
www.emh.org
Acute Beds: 411
Long-Term Care Beds: 288

St. Joseph Hospital
360 Broadway, Bangor
(207) 262–1000
www.stjoseph-me.org
Acute Beds: 112
Long-Term Care Beds: 0

Alternative Providers
Acupuncture
Alice Meattey
74 State Road 201, Kittery
(207) 439–5809

Family Acupuncture and Holistic Medicine
170 Cider Hill Road, York
(207) 240–4100

Scott Cormier
P.O. Box 202, Cape Neddick 03902
(207) 233–8808

Heart and Soul
1662 Post Road, Wells
(207) 636–7988

Massagecraft and Acupuncture Clinic
314 Alfred Street, Biddeford
(207) 286–8416
www.massagecraft.com

Family Acupuncture Center
68 Maine Street, Kennebunk
(207) 985–0099

Gate of Hope Center for Acupuncture
554 Main Street, Springvale
(207) 490–4190

Meret C. Liebenstein Bainbridge
884 South Broadway, South Portland
(207) 767–3395

Acupuncture Affiliates
535 Ocean Avenue, Portland
(207) 775–2156

Acupuncture and Chinese Herbal Clinic
4 Sheffield Street, Portland
(207) 772–5368

Acupuncture and Counseling Services
609 Forest Avenue, Portland
(207) 772–6396

Acupuncture and Oriental Medicine
222 St. John Street, Portland
(207) 871–5966

Stephanie A. Baird
222 St. John Street, #125, Portland
(207) 871–5060

Mary Chaney
778 Forest Avenue, Portland
(207) 874–8019

Devereux Hopkins
145 Newbury Street, Portland
(207) 775–0058

Jeffrey Logan
470 Forest Avenue, Suite 209, Portland
(207) 780–8880

Susan Reed
778 Forest Avenue, Portland
(207) 828–1799

Jason Stein
500 Forest Avenue, Portland
(207) 775–2059

Natural Balance Traditional Acupuncture
and Chinese Herbal Medicine
510 Main Street, Gorham
(207) 839–5529

Paul Marks
10 Forest Falls Drive, Suite #1, Yarmouth
(207) 846–6464

John Tsao
6 Bennett Road, Yarmouth
(207) 846–4433

Mary Beth Hassett
210 Main Street, Freeport
(207) 865–1203

Augat Chiropractic
9 Pleasant Street, Brunswick
(207) 725–7177

Marion Brown
98 Maine Street, Brunswick
(207) 725–2268

Winnegance Acupuncture
11 Lakeview Drive, West Bath
(207) 442–0885

HealthPoint Traditional Acupuncture
P.O. Box 184, Damariscotta 04543
(207) 563–6607

Susan Weiser Mason and George Mason
3 Mill Road, Newcastle
(207) 563–1571

Midcoast Acupuncture Clinic
44–46 Park Street, Rockland
(207) 594–1200

Stillpoint
254 Main Street, Rockland
(207) 594–9211

Sally Cook
P.O. Box 447, Rockport 04856
(207) 236–8469

Acupuncture for Adults and Children
39 Mountain Street, Camden
(207) 236–3601
www.acupunctureweb.com

Grove Street Acupuncture
13 Grove Street, Camden
(207) 236–2794

The Wellness Center
69 Elm Street, Camden
(207) 465–4490

Rhonda Feinman, DOM, L.Ac
243 High Street, Belfast
(207) 338–4454

Carol V. Hall
58 East Waldo Road, Belfast
(207) 338–0357

Howard Evans
P.O. Box 838, Blue Hill 04614
(207) 374–9963

Chiropractic

A Lebro Center for Well-Being
135 Rogers Road, Kittery
(207) 439–7246
www.alebrocenter.com

A Seacoast Holistic Center
137 Rogers Road, Kittery
(207) 439–3358

Chiropractic Works
Meadowbrook, York 03909
(207) 363–5966

Gallant Chiropractic Health Clinic
433 Route 1, #114–115, York
(207) 363–7323

Molda Chiropractic
529 Route 1, York
(207) 363–5656

Farrer Chiropractic Center
Route 1, Wells
(207) 646–5400

Life Family Chiropractic Center
913 Post Road, Wells
(207) 641–2225

Merrill Clinic of Chiropractic
2550 Post Road, Wells
(207) 985–2428

Couture Chiropractic Center
36 Main Street, #1, Kennebunk
(207) 985–7133

Family Chiropractic-Kennebunk
R.R. 9, Kennebunk
(207) 985–8877
www.familychiropractors.com

Natural Way Chiropractic
4 Dane Street, Kennebunk
(207) 985–3055

William G. Brink
1047 Main Street, Sanford
(207) 324–5753

Robert W. Schwell
216 Main Street, Sanford
(207) 324–2223

Malon Chiropractic Center
322 Elm Street, Biddeford
(207) 283–0104

Ringuette Chiropractic Center
260 Elm Street, Biddeford
(207) 282–9976

Chasse Chiropractic Office
7 Hutchins Street, Saco
(207) 282–5233

Heidrich Chiropractic Health Center
52 King Street, Saco
(207) 284–2059

Roy Chiropractic Center
626 Route 1, Scarborough
(207) 883–3249
www.roychiropractic.com

Cape Elizabeth Chiropractic
249 Ocean House Road, Cape Elizabeth
(207) 799–1252

Chiropractic Healing Arts Center
85 E Street, One Park Square,
South Portland
(207) 799–0972
www.drdunphy.com

Chiropractic Health Alternatives
558 Main Street, South Portland
(207) 775–2265

South Portland Chiropractic
597 Main Street, South Portland
(207) 774–7242

A Better Way Chiropractic
2001 Congress Street, Portland
(207) 879–5433
www.abetterwaychiropractic.com

Deutsch Chiropractic
94 Auburn Street, #2, Portland
(207) 797–7750
www.deutschwellness.com

Family Chiropractic Center
1020 Forest Avenue, Portland
(207) 797–4815

Goulding Chiropractic
96 India Street, Portland
(207) 775–6782

Margaret J. Hoy
285 Woodford Street, Portland
(207) 772–6400

Wholistic Chiropractor Center
222 Saint John Street, #204, Portland
(207) 329–9742

New England Chiropractic
89 Larrabee Road, Westbrook
(207) 854–2001
www.newenglandchiropractic.net

Westbrook Chiropractic Care
27 Main Street, #B, Westbrook
(207) 854–2626

Gorham Chiropractic Center
17 Donna Street, Gorham
(207) 839–3888

Kerwin Chiropractic Center
164 Main Street, Gorham
(207) 839–8181

Bardwell Chiropractic
40 Forest Falls Drive, Yarmouth
(207) 846–1665

Abby Kramer Chiropractor
202 Route 1, Falmouth
(207) 781–7911

Brown Chiropractic Center
253 Main Street, Yarmouth
(207) 846–5111

Yarmouth Chiropractic
10 Forest Falls Drive, #3, Yarmouth
(207) 846–1481

Freeport Integrated Health Center
174 South Freeport Road, #1F, Freeport
(207) 865–1183

Holistic Chiropractic Center
30 Bow Street, Freeport
(207) 865–3649

Augat Chiropractic Center
9 Pleasant Street, Brunswick
(207) 725–7177

Hagerty Chiropractic Health
16 Lincoln Street, Brunswick
(207) 729–8656

Feldspar Mill Chiropractic Health Center
63C Elm Street, Topsham
(207) 725–6406

Dennis Chiropractic and Rehabilitation
972 Washington Street, Bath
(207) 443–5721

West Family Chiropractic
42 Federal Street, Wiscasset
(207) 882–7800

White Medical Clinic
49 Churchill Street, Wiscasset
(207) 882–7600

Steven Amato
Water Street, Damariscotta
(207) 563–1000

Damariscotta Chiropractic Health
54 Bristol Road, Damariscotta
(207) 563–5500

Waldoboro Chiropractic and Therapeutic
Spa
290 Bremen Road, Waldoboro
(207) 832–6347
www.waldoborochiropracticandspa.com

Bay Chiropractic Center
279 Main Street, Rockland
(207) 596–6700

Kelly Chiropractic
20 Summer Street, Rockland
(207) 594–0000

Penobscot Bay Chiropractic Center
1112 Commercial Street, Rockport
(207) 596–5523

Rockport Family Chiropractic
412 Commercial Street, Rockport
(207) 236–8486

The Wellness Center
69 Elm Street, Camden
(207) 465–4490

Community Chiropractor Clinic
29 Washington Street, Belfast
(207) 338–6463

Horowitz Chiropractic
51 West Main Street, Searsport
(207) 548–6376

Oceanside Chiropractic
316 West Main Street, Searsport
(207) 548–2741

Downeast Chiropractic and Wellness Center
1 Daisy Way, Ellsworth
(207) 664–7575

Nesiba Chiropractic Center
150 Bucksport Road, Ellsworth
(207) 667–4678

Holistic Chiropractic Center
Hadley Point Road, Bar Harbor
(207) 288–3899

Day Spas

O Salon and Spa
58 State Road, Kittery
(207) 439–1100

Lucinda's Day Spa
311 Beech Ridge Road, Scarborough
(207) 839–9000

Akari Hair Care and Day Spa
Fore Street, Portland
(207) 772–9060
www.akarihairspa.com

Radiance Day Spa and Massage
1 City Centre, Portland
(207) 874–2219

Kiowa Day Spa
267 Route 1, Yarmouth
(207) 846–1272
www.kiowadayspa.net

Beau Bella Day Spa and Hair Salon
16 Monument Place, Topsham
(207) 729–2700
www.beaubelladayspa.com

Utopia Day Spa
81 Main Street, Topsham
(207) 725–4845
www.utopiadayspa.biz

Body and Soul Aromatherapy Day Spa
5 Oak Street, Boothbay Harbor
(207) 633–5935
www.bodysouldayspa.com

Sanctuary Day Spa
336 Main Street, Rockland
(207) 594–8403
www.mainesanctuary.com

Cynthia's Day Spa and Salon
24 First South Street, Bar Harbor
(207) 288–3426

Petite Retreat
17 Main Street, Machias
(207) 255–0085

Massage Therapy

A Aha Tactora Relaxation Center
9 Bridge Street, Kittery
(207) 439–0813

Renew and Relax Massage
99 State Road, Kittery
(207) 439–9974

Muscle Matters Therapeutic Massage
226 York Street, York
(207) 363–6683

Norma Bazylinski Massage Therapist
5 Bradgon Lane, Kennebunk
(207) 985–7685

Northern Lights Holistic Health Center
36 Main Street, Kennebunk
(207) 967–9850

Massagecraft and Acupuncture Clinic
314 Alfred Street, Biddeford
(207) 286–8416
www.massagecraft.com

Lucinda's Day Spa
311 Beech Ridge Road, Scarborough
(207) 839–9000

A Healing Touch
222 St. John Street, Portland
(207) 874–9859

Akari Hair Care and Day Spa
Fore Street, Portland
(207) 772–9060
www.akarihairspa.com

Bodyworks Massage Therapy
535 Ocean Avenue, Portland
(207) 761–5889

Marry Craven Massage Therapist
499 Stevens Avenue, Portland
(207) 774–1461

Debbie Elliott Salon and Spa
1 William Street, Portland
(207) 828–0540

Grampa's Garden Herb and Body Shop
87 Market Street, Portland
(207) 774–2225

Natalie Hickey Massage
Old Port, Portland
(207) 775–4010

Kind Hands Strong Hands Massage
142 High Street, Portland
(207) 772–2519

Cynthia McGovern Massage Therapist
449 Forest Avenue, Portland
(207) 775–0940

Pele Rising Bodywork
400 Allen Avenue, Portland
(207) 797–3388

Radiance Day Spa and Massage
1 City Centre, Portland
(207) 874–2219

Shanti Therapeutic Massage Associates
222 Saint John Street, Portland
(207) 772–5051

Von Faulk Trueworthy Silla Massage
Therapists
153 Route 1, Scarborough
(207) 883–1440

Suzanne White Massage Therapist
459 Libby Avenue, Gorham
(207) 839–3667

Kiowa Day Spa
267 Route 1, Yarmouth
(207) 846–1272
www.kiowadayspa.net

Healing Touch Massage Therapy
124 Maine Street, Suite E, Brunswick
(207) 729–4555
www.htouchmassage.com

Sharon Forney Massage
16 Lincoln Street, Brunswick
(207) 725–2310

Jo Ann McAllister Massage
7 Middle Street, Brunswick
(207) 725–1063

Midcoast Well Being Center
310 Bath Road, Brunswick
(207) 729–3100

Wendy Decker Massage Therapy
14 Walker Street, Bath
(207) 443–2572

Harcourt and Rice Massage Therapists
1 Nichols Street, Bath
(207) 443–6005

Body and Soul
Boothbay Harbor
(207) 633–5935
www.bodysouldayspa.com

Boothbay Therapeutic Massage
18 West Street, Boothbay Harbor
(207) 633–5500

Sean Colby
28 Eastern Avenue, Boothbay Harbor
(207) 633–7060

Therapeutic Massage Associates
Elm Street, Damariscotta
(207) 563–1441

Sanctuary Day Spa
336 Main Street, Rockland
(207) 594–8403
www.mainesanctuary.com

Shofestall Ily Neuromuscular Therapist
385 Main Street, Rockland
(207) 594–7919

Helen G. Caddie-Larcenia
3 Liberty Road, Washington
(207) 845–2707

Living Stone Massage Therapy, Hope
(207) 785–2549
www.livingstonemassage.com

The Wellness Center
69 Elm Street, Camden
(207) 465–4490

Evergreen Bodyworks
118 High Street, Belfast
(888) 338–5959

Rose Rapp
72 Rowe Hill Road, Morrill
(207) 342–3955

Spring Tree Therapies
28 Spring Street, Belfast
(207) 338–1117

Unity Massage Therapy
41 School Street, Unity
(207) 948–2948

Sharma Buell
56B Church Street, Ellsworth
(207) 664–0808

Cynthia's Day Spa and Salon
24 First South Street, Bar Harbor
(207) 288–3426

Whole Health Center
Gilbert Farm Road, Bar Harbor
(207) 288–4128
www.thewholehealthcenter.com

Petite Retreat
17 Main Street, Machias
(207) 255–0085

Homeopathic Doctors

Dayton F. Haigney, M.D.
164 York Street, York
(207) 363–0610

Dirk Vandersloot, M.D.
17 Masonic Street, Rockland
(207) 596–0991

Naturopathic Doctors

Maine Naturopathic Health Center
36 Main Street, Suite 1, Kennebunk
(207) 985–3279

Coastal Naturopathic Center
281 Veranda Street, Portland
(207) 772–4447
www.coastalnaturalhealth.com

Maine Whole Health
4 Milk Street, Portland
(207) 773–2517
www.mainewholehealth.com

New England Women's Center
66 Pearl Street, Portland
(207) 772–5227

Sasha Rose
97 India Street, Portland
(207) 347–7132
www.wildwoodmedicine.com

Priscilla Skerry, N.D.
260 Western Avenue, Portland
(207) 772–5227

Michael Russo, N.D.
499 Stevens Avenue, Portland
(207) 774–6688
www.drmrusso.com

True North Health Center
202 Route 1, Falmouth
(207) 781–4488
www.truenorthhealthcenter.org

Rising Tide Natural Medicine
1185 Route 1, Suite 1, Freeport
(207) 865–1222

Julie Taylor, N.D.
171 Park Row, Brunswick
(207) 721–1100

Northern Sun Family Health Care
1 Main Street, Topsham
(207) 798–3993
www.northernsunfamilyhealth.com

Tim Hagney, N.D.
97 Main Street, Belfast
(207) 338–4244

Acadia Naturopathic Clinic
53 Church Street, Ellsworth
(207) 664–0780
www.acadianaturopathic.com

Evergreen Naturopathic Care
142 Hammond Street, Suite 5,
Bangor
(207) 941–0981
www.evergreenclinic.net

Women's Health

Women to Women
3 Marina Road, Yarmouth
(207) 846–6163
www.womentowomen.com

CHURCHES

For a list of Maine's churches by county, click over to the Web site www.mainecouncil ofchurches.org and go to the directory page.

LIBRARIES

The Maine State Library in Augusta maintains a directory of all Maine libraries, with some fascinating stats. Visit its Web site at http://msl1.ursus.maine.edu to see the list.

REGISTERING YOUR CAR

The Maine Bureau of Motor Vehicles has a number of Motor Vehicle Branch Office locations. All are open from 8:00 A.M. to 5:00 P.M. Monday through Friday and closed on all legal holidays. Call (207) 624–9215 and inquire about mobile locations before you head out— there might be one closer than the branch location. Information is also available at www.state.me.us/sos/bmv.

63 Portland Road, Suite 4, Kennebunk
(207) 985–4890

456 Main Street, Springvale
(207) 490–1261

704 Maine Mall Road, South Portland
(207) 822–0730

125 Presumpscot Street, Portland
(207) 822–6400

49 Topsham Fair Mall Road, Topsham
(207) 725–6520

212 New County Road, Rockland
(207) 596–2255

24 Church Street, Ellsworth
(207) 667–9363

376 North Street, Calais
(207) 454–2175

RETIREMENT

Used to be Mainers of retirement age would head south for the winter, enjoying sun and golf while the rest of the state persevered through snow and ice. This pattern is still true for some, but in recent years, the Pine Tree State has seen more and more seniors stay put. Not only that, it has seen an actual influx of people who want to enjoy their golden years on the Maine coast, weather be damned. The state has grown exponentially in the retirement market—villages like Damariscotta and Camden are brimming with the older set—and senior communities have sprouted up all along the coast like mushrooms. They range from assisted-living facilities to simply condo villages where the common theme is age.

Many of these new Mainers have a history with the state, vacationing here for years and years and pining for the day when they could move north permanently. Others are simply drawn by the quality of life enjoyed Down East. The resort communities that cater to tens of thousands of vacationers in summer, with their shops and restaurants, are perfectly suited to serve retirees in winter. Crime is a nonissue, the climate is actually fairly hospitable (global warming?), the pace of life is easy and pleasant, and the state is made up of actual communities where it's not difficult to become involved and feel like you play an important part. Neighbors are still neighbors here, looking out for one another. And the health care system in Maine is now competitive with those found elsewhere. It's a nice place to grow old.

Of course, a lot of people who retire here have no intention of sitting around on their duffs. Many enjoy very active retirements, starting new businesses, exploring the outdoors, joining town boards and volunteering

for worthy causes, and taking advantage of the excellent elder learning opportunities to be found here. Places like Bowdoin College in Brunswick allow seniors to audit courses for free, innumerable communities have great adult ed programs, fitness centers offer eldercize-type workouts, and on and on. The state park system can be enjoyed gratis by people over 65, and Audubon has a wealth of field trips geared toward older folks. A lot of people find themselves busier after leaving the 9-to-5 world behind than they were when they were working. There is no end to the things to do in Maine.

This chapter includes a list of retirement communities, information on elder education, and further resources for retirees.

RETIREMENT COMMUNITIES

Almost 50 retirement communities have been built in Maine, many of them along the coast. These aren't your grandmother's nursing home either, but congregate housing where a meal or two is provided and services are clustered for ease of use. Many do feature an assisted-living option, where doctors and nurses are a more regular presence, but they feel more like elderly villages than anything else.

South Coast

Sentry Hill
2 Victoria Court, York
(207) 363–5116
www.sentryhillatyorkharbor.com
Location, as they say in real estate, is everything, and that certainly applies to Sentry Hill. The sprawling retirement community sits on 12 acres within walking distance of York Harbor Beach, the York Golf and Tennis Club, and

The state of Maine has a wealth of resources available to retirees, including the handy Web site of its Office of Elder Services—www.maine.gov/dhs/beas/. Here you'll find information on everything from Medicaid and prescription drugs to job possibilities and the senior farm-share program, which gets fresh produce to seniors for free.

a nature preserve. The resort community of the Yorks—with all their restaurants and shops—are minutes away by car, and the nearest hospital is a half mile down the road. Sentry Hill offers seniors a whole raft of choices, from two-bedroom condo units to one- and two-bedroom apartments to assisted-living apartments where medical staff is at the ready. There's also a more traditional nursing home and even an option for those suffering from Alzheimer's disease. Housekeeping, transportation, and as many as three meals a day are available, too. Units can be rented or purchased outright, and there are maintenance and entry fees. About 160 seniors have moved in already, and more are sure to follow.

Atria Kennebunk
1 Penny Lane, Kennebunk
(207) 985–5866
www.atriacom.com

Atria is a national chain of retirement communities, and this is its Maine facility. All of the amenities of the Kennebunks—from the sea to the shopping—are right out the doors of these assisted-living apartments (studio, one-bedroom, and two-bedroom). There are 82 units for rent, eight of which are for folks suffering from Alzheimer's. (Rental fees range from $2,600 to $4,000 per month, depending on the unit.) Three meals are served daily, and housekeeping happens on a weekly basis. The facility has a library and a beauty salon on the premises, and the activity calendar is reportedly busy here. Private tours are available.

The Farragut at Kennebunk
71 Farragut Way, Kennebunk
(207) 985–9740 or (877) 985–0300
www.thefarragut.com

"If you're not sixty, you'll wish you were." That's the slogan at the Farragut in Kennebunk, and it's easy to see why someone might have senior envy. Boston, Portland, and Portsmouth are all within an hour and a half of the retirement village's site along the Kennebunk River—and that's if you ever feel the need to leave the Kennebunks, one of Maine's oldest and best resort communities, with neat stores, fine restaurants, beautiful beaches, and superb scenery. Qualified residents here have the option of moving into a single-floor unit or a cottage that looks like a tasteful suburban home, and the amenities are many. On the Farragut's 14 acres are an inn with cafe-style meals, indoor pool and Jacuzzi, computer center, and walking trails, and the facility offers the option of in-home health care and housekeeping. You don't pay for what you don't use, unlike some other places. And an emphasis is placed on being active, so you'll be up and about, and there will always be plenty to do. Units can be purchased—fees are anywhere from $200,000 to $259,000—and then there are monthly maintenance fees. You can even buy right on the saltwater river.

Huntington Common
1 Huntington Common Drive, Kennebunk
(207) 985–2810 or (800) 585–0533
www.huntingtoncommon.com

Both Portland and Portsmouth are handy to the folks living at Huntington Common, one of Maine's larger retirement communities, with more than 200 residents. From condos to Alzheimer's units, the place has a wide array of options for seniors. Most, however, live in independent apartments that are rented for anywhere from $2,000 to $5,600 a month. Three meals a day are served, and amenities include an exercise program, a beauty salon, a library, and an activities room. And then, of course, there's everything to do in the Kennebunks and you're right on the river.

Wardwell Retirement Neighborhood
43 Middle Street, Saco
(207) 284–7061
One of Maine's oldest retirement communities, Wardwell was built in 1890 and now consists of 38 independent apartments and 46 assisted-living units right in downtown Saco. About 100 residents live here, and they enjoy three meals a day, an exercise program, a library, and a hair salon on the premises. Units are rented for $300 to $3,200 a month, and housekeeping and transportation are available.

Greater Portland

Chancellor Gardens
78 Scott Dyer Road, Cape Elizabeth
(207) 799–7332 or (888) 860–6914
www.carematrix.com
Part of the nationwide Carematrix chain, Chancellor Gardens has 58 assisted-living units in the pleasant Portland bedroom community of Cape Elizabeth. They're particularly well outfitted with restaurant-style dining, a library and computer center, a hair salon, a woodshop, an ice-cream shop, a cocktail lounge, and a fitness center all on the campus. Portland is just moments away, and transportation is provided on a regular schedule. The units are rented for $3,200 to $4,900 a month with no additional fees. They take care of everything so you can get down to some serious senior living.

Piper Shores
15 Piper Road, Scarborough
(207) 883–8700 or (888) 760–1042
www.pipershores.org
With 350-some residents, Piper Shores is Maine's largest retirement facility. And, as they say, 350 people can't be wrong—you have to assume the place is doing something right to attract and keep so many retirees. A nonprofit organization, Piper Shores has a continuum of care, with 200 independent apartments and cottages, 20 assisted-living units, and 40 long-term-care beds. And it offers 'most every amenity known to a retirement community— all meals, an exercise program, a pool, library,

activities room, walking trail, beauty salon, movie room, even a wood shop. The shore is a short walk across the road, and Portland, with its symphony, museums, restaurants, and medical-care providers, is just minutes down the road.

The Atrium at Cedars
630 Ocean Avenue, Portland
(207) 772–5456
www.cedarshealthcare.com
The Cedars began its life in 1929 as a home for elderly Jewish folks in Portland. Over the years it changed, adding a nursing component, before opening a nonsectarian retirement community at its present location on Ocean Avenue. The company likes to call the lifestyle it promotes at the Atrium "progressive living," and it certainly seems like the good life, with fine food at the formal dining room and at the cafe, an indoor pool and spa, a fitness center, proximity to all of the great restaurants of Portland, and comfortable apartments. Maintenance and housekeeping can be taken care of, making the hassles few.

The Park at Danforth
777 Stevens Avenue, Portland
(207) 797–7710
www.parkdanforth.com
The Park at Danforth is a big apartment building–style home with 160 units, most of which are set up for independent living, and three dozen of which are assisted-living spaces. The place has a fairly rich history, dating back to 1881 when a few Portland philanthropists opened a house for elderly mariners with no place else to go. Over the years, the mission of the home broadened to include any elderly residents of the Forest City, not just seamen, and today it's a completely modern facility with all the amenities. The rentals range from studio apartments to two-bedroom suites; some are Medicaid eligible, some will set you back about $1,500 a month. The activities calendar is particularly busy here, with something scheduled for every day. You won't want to miss Beano on

Sunday or the trip to the Maine Mall on Friday. Students from the nearby University of Maine visit occasionally to help out and offer instruction in the computer room, and the activity room often hosts art classes or musical entertainment. (It also has a wide-screen TV for watching movies or the big game.) Friends and families are always welcome. Rents range from $1,432 for a one-bedroom studio to $5,000 for an apartment in the assisted-living Clark Terrace.

Seventy Five State Street
75 State Street, Portland
(207) 772–2675
www.75state.org

State Street is hands down the oldest retirement community in Maine, predating the Civil War. It was founded as a home for three elderly Portland women and has grown from there, now housing 170 residents in as many apartments. Unlike many of the other senior housing options in the state—and elsewhere—this is a nonprofit organization, with all resident-derived income being reinvested to enhance the facilities and provide more services. So this building in the West End, one of the nicer residential neighborhoods of Portland, feels a little warmer than some of the operations that are obviously out for money first. The average age here is a little steeper than some other places—the last survey found most occupants to be in their 80s—but the amenities are many. The apartments are all rentals and come in a variety of layouts, from efficiencies to full suites, and they range in price from $1,900 to $4,100 per month. Concierge service is available seven days a week, as is nursing care.

The Woods at Canco
257 Canco Road, Portland
(207) 772–4777
www.thewoodsatcanco.com

Not the woodsiest facility, but, hey, this is the Forest City; these Woods are operated by Holiday Retirement Corporation. There are 128 independent apartments—both one- and two-bedroom—and 13 cottages, and three squares a day. Amenities include a big-screen TV lounge, an activity room, library, and exercise room, and you're 5 miles from golf. All of Portland is available to you, thanks to regularly scheduled trips. Rent is $1,500 to $3,200.

Gorham House
50 New Portland Road, Gorham
(207) 839–5757
www.mainecare.com

Owned by the same people who run Sentry Hill in York, Gorham House is located in the peaceful Portland suburb of Gorham, a leafy college town not far from the city. Established in 1990, the facility offers an array of living choices for a continuum of care (these are rentals): 34 independent apartments, 12 cottage units, 29 assisted-living units, 52 long-term care beds, and 30 Alzheimer's units. The independent-living apartments are well outfitted with full kitchens and come in one- or two-bedroom layouts, and pets are allowed. One meal a day, housekeeping, grocery delivery, and trash removal are all provided free of charge, and there is a full activities calendar. RN care is available on a 24-hour basis. The assisted-living option brings the care right to your apartment, and help is offered with recreational and transportational needs.

OceanView at Falmouth
20 Blueberry Lane, Falmouth
(207) 781–4460
www.oceanviewrc.com

OceanView is one of a trio of retirement villages owned by developer John Wasileski that advertises all over the place, from print to radio. "It's about life, it's about time" is their motto, and in many ways they live up to it. The OceanView campus is located on a side street in Falmouth, Portland's tony easterly neighbor, and includes 71 independent apartments in the Lodge, a large condo building, 107 cottages, and 38 assisted-living apartments. All units are purchased, and they come in pleasant one- or two-bedroom layouts. The complex sits on 45 acres within a few minutes' drive of Portland, so there is the quiet of the country but the convenience of being next to the state's largest city. And, as the name suggests, the water is not far. Activities are aplenty right at OceanView, however, so you needn't travel much. The retirement center offers workouts for the mind—a library and Internet access—as well as for the body—strength training, yoga, and tai chi. It also has an active calendar of social activities, from talks to musical performances to art shows. Best of all, though, are the services provided, from complete maintenance to grocery delivery to a hair salon. It's like living in a small Maine village where everything is taken care of.

Bay Square at Yarmouth
27 Forest Falls Drive, Yarmouth
(207) 846–0044 or (888) 374–6700
www.benchmarkquality.com

Benchmark Quality is a big national corporation with dozens of assisted-living communities in New York and New England. The company's Maine offering is in the Greater Portland community of Yarmouth, 15 or 20 minutes north of the Forest City and just south of Freeport. Bay Square is a 60-unit assisted-living center housed in a big building it describes as a "grand seaside inn," and it has a specialized program for the memory-impaired. Studio, one-bedroom, and two-bedroom apartments are available for rent, and three meals are offered daily. The facilities are right on the Royal River and include a white-linen dining room, walking trails, a beauty salon, a library, a country kitchen, and a sunporch. Exercise programs are there to be enjoyed on a daily basis, and there is a full social calendar. The staff offers 24-hour nursing support as well as all the housekeeping and maintenance services anyone could want. There's a $2,000 entrance fee, and rents range from $3,700 to $4,900.

Midcoast

Sunnybrook Village
340 Bath Road, Brunswick
(207) 443–9100
www.sunnybrookvillage.com

The newest of the retirement villages on the red-hot Brunswick retiree scene, Sunnybrook sounds like a Kate Douglas Wiggin book—you may wonder where Rebecca and the farm are—and it's privately owned rather than part of a soulless chain. There are already 51 people ensconced in its 12 apartments and 39 assisted-living units. Three chef-cooked meals a day, a beauty parlor and a barber shop, rose gardens, a computer center, and a calendar's worth of activities number among the many amenities. Plus, you're in Brunswick, which, among retirees, makes you one of the cool kids.

Thornton Oaks
25 Thornton Way, #100, Brunswick
(207) 729–8033 or (800) 729–8033
www.thorntonoaks.com

The big Thornton Oaks campus went up in 1990 in Brunswick, home of Bowdoin College and Brunswick Naval Air Station, and it now has one of the highest populations of any retirement community in Maine. (The town was voted the best place to retire in New England by *Money* magazine in 2005.) Residential options run the gamut, from completely independent "private" homes to Alzheimer's units. The houses are on 29 acres, with a walking trail, and the owner can choose from a wide variety of floor plans. They all were built in a "New England cottage style" and feature large 14-by-25-foot living/dining areas and two bedrooms and three baths. The fancier models have fireplaces, central air, and whirlpools. While set up like any contemporary suburban development, these homes allow use of all of Thornton Oaks' facilities, including the dining room (catering is available in homes for parties), the arts and crafts room, the library, and the fitness center. Maintenance, of course, is provided. The apartments are in the campus's Matthews Terrace building and come in one-

and two-bedroom arrangements. Large windows, extensive lighting, and lots of closet space keep things comfortable. The activities calendar at Thornton Oaks is something to behold. Foreign affairs, religious, and book discussions are common, there's a lively arts program with classes in flower arranging and that sort of thing, and there are organized bridge and Scrabble competitions. Residents are welcome to audit courses and use the pool at nearby Bowdoin College. Excursions to the Portland Museum of Art, Portland Symphony Orchestra, and Maine State Music Theater are frequent.

The Highlands
26 Elm Street, Topsham
(207) 725–2650 or (888) 760–1042
www.highlandsrc.com
Topsham, just north of Brunswick, has undergone quite a building boom in the past few decades, and the Highlands was part of it, going up in 1989. Part of the Wasileski empire, it is one of the biggest retirement communities in Maine, with more than 300 residents, and the choices are many. There are 106 apartments, more than 125 cottage units, 44 assisted-living units, and 24 Alzheimer's units to provide a continuum of care. Many of these—the single- and duplex-home Estates, for example—can be customized to the owner's specifications. Others, like the six apartments in the 19th-century Benjamin Porter House, are more unique and character laden.

The Highlands campus sprawls across 75 acres, with walking trails wandering about, so there is something of a sense of rural living even though you're five minutes from the restaurants and cultural activities of Brunswick and less than 25 miles from all that Portland has to offer. Not that you need to go anywhere. The facility is very self-sufficient, with fine dining, a fitness center, library and media room, pool, bingo, bridge—even a bank—and regular outings to the Portland Symphony Orchestra, the Maine State Music Theatre, Portland Stage Company, Audubon events,

and more. The Highlands van also whisks residents to Topsham, downtown Brunswick, Cooks Corner, Bath, and the Maine Mall for shopping.

St. Andrews Village
145 Emery Lane, Boothbay Harbor
(207) 633–0920
www.standrewsvillage.com
St. Andrews Village has one of those nifty arrangements that are becoming common among retirement communities—buy into any one of the units on the campus and you can use all the amenities and services even if you live in one of the private cottages. Options here include 25 of these cottages, 30 independent apartments, 12 assisted-living facilities, 8 Alzheimer's units, and 30 long-term care beds. The setting is fine, with 60 acres of Boothbay Harbor out the door. The cottages have two-bedroom layouts, with kitchens, and one-and-a-half or two baths. The Saint Andrews Inn is where the apartments are located, as well as the dining room, library, and services. The calendar of activities is a busy one, with regularly scheduled exercise classes, transportation to town for shopping, eating out, and cultural happenings, and movies, coffees, book clubs, and birthday parties on a monthly basis.

Schooner Cove
35 Schooner Street, Damariscotta
(207) 563–5523
www.standrewshealthcare.org/miles
Situated on the banks of the Damariscotta River, Schooner Cove has a lot going for it. The 59 residents have great views of the tidal river from their two-bedroom apartments, a fine dining room at which to sup, a well-stocked library, and access to medical services should they be needed, with Miles Memorial Hospital a stone's throw away. Chase Point Assisted Living Center and Cove's Edge Nursing Home are right next door, too, ready to serve if needed. There's plenty to do—classes and lectures, afternoon teas, and musical performances occur on a regular basis, and there are fre-

quent trips into town and to points in the area for museum visits, nature walks, and shopping. Housekeeping and other services are taken care of—and the staff is second to none in Maine. This is one of the best.

Bartlett Woods
20 Bartlett Street, Rockland
(207) 594–1159
www.bartlettwoods.com

Newly revitalized Rockland is the home of Bartlett Woods, an active retirement center with 14 cottage units and 34 independent apartments. The cottages are suburban homes clustered together in a woodsy area within walking distance of Rockland's historic downtown. Residents buy into a cooperative equal to the value of their home, which allows them to both create equity and vote on issues that concern all residents. The units are single-floor dwellings with two bedrooms, a full kitchen, a good-size living room, one and one-half baths, and an attached garage. Most have a sunroom. Snow removal, lawn care, and maintenance are all part of the package. Bartlett House is an apartment building with balconies, full kitchens, large living rooms, and one or two bedrooms. All of the services of Bartlett Woods are right here—a library, dining room, computer center, wellness center, and even a hair salon. Pets are welcome.

Camden Gardens
110 Mechanic Street, Camden
(207) 236–0154

Tiny in comparison to the many other retirement communities in Maine, Camden Gardens has just 12 residents living in its eight apartments and two cottages. But they have it good, being close to all of the excellent eateries, shops, outdoor areas, and services of Camden. Built in 1989, the facility has an exercise program, an activities room, and a library, and it provides one meal daily. Housekeeping and transportation are available. The units are rented for $1,950 to $2,500, depending upon the size.

Quarry Hill
30 Community Drive, Camden
(207) 230–6116
www.quarryhill.org

Quarry Hill offers the comforts of living in a resort community but the peace of being on your own 26-acre campus. Its 225 residents make it one of the biggest retiree villages in Maine, and folks live in 37 independent apartments, 45 cottages, 62 assisted-living units, and 24 Alzheimer units. You eat well, have all of the perks of Camden living—good restaurants, boutique shopping, fresh air, ocean, lakes, mountains, great classical concerts in summer, a fine library—and have your own little kingdom to return to. And you know that because it's in tony Camden it's going to be nice. Units range from $239,000 to $369,000 for purchase or $2,000 to $3,000 per month for rent, and there's a $1,000 maintenance fee.

Harbor Hill
2 Footbridge Road, Belfast
(207) 338–5307
www.sandyriverhealth.com

Part of the Sandy River Health empire of Farmington, Harbor Hill is an assisted-living and long-term care center with 85 residents. Those in the assisted-living program can maintain their independence but get help with meals, laundry, and maintenance and enjoy the company of others. Health care is available at a moment's notice. The long-term care is more of a traditional nursing home service. Units are rented for $600 to $6,000 a month.

Penobscot Shores
10 Shoreland Drive, Belfast
(207) 338–2332
www.penobscotshores.com

Clustered onto 20 acres overlooking Penobscot Bay, the 28 apartments and 26 cottages of Penobscot Shores have fine views to go with their shingle-style architecture. This is an independent-living facility with its own cobblestone beach, library, fine dining room, hair salon, activity room, and fitness studio, and access to all that the cool city of Belfast has to offer. Wellness and health-care programs keep you happy and fit, and the maintenance services leave your mind at ease. Transportation is available, too. Penobscot Shores is affiliated with the excellent local Waldo County General Hospital and is only a quarter mile from its beds and services. Units are purchased for $130,000 to $350,000, and then a maintenance fee of $1,200 to $1,400 is paid on a monthly basis. The motto at Penobscot Shores is "the location you want and the lifestyle you deserve," and it certainly makes its case. Local residents have been overheard to say that they couldn't wait to reach retirement age so they can move in.

Parker Ridge Retirement Community
63 Parker Ridge Lane, Blue Hill
(207) 374–2306
www.parkerridge.com

One of the more gracious of Maine's retirement centers, Parker Ridge is a large complex on 90 acres overlooking Blue Hill Bay. The cottages are shingle-sided affairs with gables and pillars, and the Parker Inn is a sprawling, cupola-topped structure that has the feel of an old Maine seaside manse about it. Obviously modern, it has a shingle-style air even though its apartments have blocky balconies tacked onto them. There are 34 independent apartments here, along with 24 freestanding cottages and 13 assisted-living units. The latter enjoy three gourmet meals daily, help with laundry and housekeeping, and transportation into town and to Ellsworth. Residents of the two-bedroom cottages have the options of buying 10 or 20 meals a month in the restaurant-style dining room, and they too get help with repairs and maintenance and access to the on-staff nurse. The facilities and services include a library and wellness program and regular exercise and art classes, movies, and billiards contests. The lawns give way to walking trails, and the bay vistas are beautiful. Purchase prices range from $183,000 for a one-bedroom apartment to $280,000 for a two-bedroom deluxe cottage.

Acadia Area

Birch Bay Village
25 Village Inn Road, Bar Harbor
(207) 288–8014
www.birchbayinfo.com

One of the newest, latest retirement communities in Maine, Birch Bay borders Acadia National Park. The cottage-style homes are terraced on the side of a hill, with outstanding views of the mountains of Mount Desert Island and the waters of Frenchman Bay. Each of the 20 cottages features two bedrooms, a fully applianced kitchen, a screened-in porch, and a terrace. Some have a den and a sunroom. Everyone who buys into the cottages has access to the Birch Bay Village Inn, the main lodge of the community and site of the 37 independent and assisted-living apartments. The inn's dining room and outdoor deck offer dramatic views of the bay and mountains, and inside residents will find a raft of amenities—library, fitness studio, hair salon, and arts and crafts and media rooms. A 1,200-square-foot cottage costs $300,000, with a monthly maintenance fee of about $1,200.

ELDER LEARNING

The sad thing about higher education is that it's generally taught to people when they're too young to truly appreciate it. By the time people hit their golden years, they often find themselves with both the time and the yearning to learn. Maine has a great Senior College program perfect for anyone in this boat, and compared to the fees young students pay, the cost is incredibly small. Sixteen schools and colleges affiliated with the University of Maine host classes for older learners across the state. They're all set up similarly.

Take the Coastal Senior College at the University College of Thomaston, for example. Seniors pay an annual membership fee of $25, which allows them to take classes here or at any other Senior College location. The types of courses vary widely, just as at any other university; recent possibilities included classes in the arts, humanities, social sciences, sciences, technology, health, and finance. These classes might be anything from Irish film to photography to New England writers to alternative healing. They meet for two hours a week for eight weeks, and special events, field trips, lectures, and get-togethers outside of class are common. And you don't ever have to worry about passing in term papers or studying for exams.

Senior College is open to any residents age 55 or older. Spouses, including those under 55, are welcome, too. Quite aside from all the learning going on, the Senior Colleges are a great way to get out and meet like-minded others and add a few dates to the social calendar.

For an overview, click over to www.maine seniorcollege.org.

South Coast

York County Senior College
University College at Saco
University College at Sanford
(207) 324–6012
www.learn.maine.edu/sanford/senior
college.php

Greater Portland

Osher Lifelong Learning Institute
University of Southern Maine
Forest Avenue, Portland
(207) 780–4406
www.usm.maine.edu/eap/seniorcollege

Midcoast

Midcoast Senior College
University College at Bath/Brunswick
9 Park Street, Bath
(207) 442–7349
www.learn.maine.edu/ucbb/msc.php

Coastal Senior College
University College at Thomaston
Route 1, Thomaston
(207) 354–6906
www.coastalseniorcollege.org

Belfast Senior College
University of Maine Hutchinson Center
Route 3, Belfast
(207) 338–8033
www.belfastseniorcollege.org

Acadia Area

Downeast Senior College
University College at Ellsworth
(207) 667–3897
www.learn.maine.edu/ellsworth/dsc.php

Acadia Senior College
College of the Atlantic
105 Eden Street, Bar Harbor
(207) 288–9500
www.acadiaseniorcollege.org

Down East

Sunrise Senior College
University of Maine at Machias
Route 1, Machias
(207) 255–1384
www.maineseniorcollege.org/sunrise_
senior_college.htm

Washington County College for Seniors
Washington County Community College
1 College Drive, Calais
(207) 454–1013
www.wccc.me.edu

i Did you run a company somewhere before retiring to Maine? If so, you could be of great help to the next generation of management by joining the Service Corps of Retired Executives. Offering classes and counseling to young businesspeople, SCORE is a great fit for a small-business friendly state like Maine, and it might be just right for you, too. The state's ambitious entrepreneurs could surely use your help. Contact SCORE's regional hub at (207) 756–8187 or check it out online at www.score53.org/maine chapters.html.

Other Options

While the Senior College system is a fantastic resource, it's not the only way for older students to get back behind the desks at good schools across Maine. Mainers age 65 and older who are interested in a course at a University of Maine campus but can't seem to swing the tuition can apply to have the fee waived. (You'll still have to take care of books and lab fees.) Bowdoin College in Brunswick and Husson College in Bangor likewise allow seniors to audit courses free of charge. For a more hands-on approach, try the state's community colleges (www.mccs.me.edu), where anyone age 65 or older can register for courses free of charge on a space-available basis.

Senior Adult Growth Exchange
Center for Continuing Education
University of Southern Maine
68 High Street, Portland
(207) 780–5900 or (800) 787–0468
Much like Senior College, this USM-based program provides workshops for older area residents at reasonable prices. Students pay $57 ($85 per couple) to participate and then can select a lecture or discussion from the handful offered on the three dates when the SAGE program meets. These are single shots and might be anything from studying family history to genetic engineering in contemporary society.

Elder Arts
Spiral Arts, 156 High Street, Portland
(207) 775–1474
www.spiralarts.org
Run by Spiral Arts, an arts program for people of all ages in Portland, Elder Arts is a series of classes and workshops designed to get Greater Portland seniors interested in the arts and crafts. Classes are very inexpensive or free and are often held at senior centers.

CyberSeniors
One Monument Way, Portland
(888) 676–6622
www.cyberseniors.org
Computers have a way of striking fear and anxiety into many older people, but there's no getting around them in today's society. And they actually are an especially great resource to people who might be a little less mobile than they once were, allowing them to keep in contact with friends and relatives and to explore the world from the comfort of their own living room. Based in Portland and now with chapters in several other northeastern states, CyberSeniors was founded to help seniors get comfortable with computers. Quite aside from the fact that the machines are useful for connecting people, CyberSeniors believes they actually help older folks maintain their independence, their self-worth, and their health. They have set up learning centers across the state—there are a number along the coast—where they teach small groups, with a high teacher-to-student ratio, how to navigate on a PC. The courses are set up on a pay-as-you-can basis, thanks to the generous donations of many individuals and organizations.

SPORTS AND RECREATION

Maine has always been well suited to outdoor recreation, and seniors can find plenty of fun and exercise simply by taking to the hundreds of miles of hiking trails and walking paths across the state. Visiting the state parks, signing up with Maine Audubon, taking a class in boating, doing laps at the Maine Mall in the hours before it opens—the options are endless. Or try a more social outing or fitness program, like those sponsored by many coastal hospitals or community YMCAs. There are many, many possibilities for seniors all along the Maine coast. Here are a few ideas.

Maine State Park System
Statewide
Department of Parks and Lands
286 Water Street, Augusta
(207) 287–3821
www.maine.gov/doc/parks/programs/
parkpasses.html

The Department of Parks and Lands allows people age 65 or older to use the state's park system free, anytime. We're talking day use though, not camping. This privilege is particularly handy for folks who live near a park and would like to use it on a daily basis. Just call and they'll mail you out a free Senior Citizen Pass. Then, as they say, you're golden.

Senior Games
c/o Anita Chandler
P.O. Box 10480, Portland 04104
(207) 396–6500
Maine has had its own Olympics for residents age 50 and older since the mid-1980s. Part of the national network of Senior Games, these contests take place every September and include both team and individual events. Participants can take part in basketball and softball as well as aquatics, canoe and kayak racing, bowling, cycling, field events, football throw, golf, horseshoes, racquetball, softball throw, table tennis, tennis, and track. And there is much opportunity for socializing as well. Gold-winning Mainers have gone on to compete in the nationals.

Lifeline Center for Fitness, Recreation, and Rehabilitation
University of Southern Maine
P.O. Box 9300, Portland 04104
(207) 780–4170
www.usm.maine.edu/lifeline
Based at the University of Southern Maine, Lifeline has been just that for generations of Mainers, helping people recover from physical trauma, quit smoking, improve their health and well-being, and simply find fitness. The center offers a host of programs and classes for seniors in the Greater Portland area, from simple walking and jogging sessions to aerobics, tai chi, and yoga. It also runs more academic health and wellness classes. They're a great resource.

Maine has quite the cadre of volunteers in its Retired and Senior Volunteer Program (RSVP), which encourages folks over 55 to use their life experience and skills to help their neighbors. From teaching kids to read to working in nursing homes and hospitals, it's a nice way to better a community. Find out more at www.maine.gov/dhhs/beas/resource/volun.htm.

City of Portland Parks and Recreation
17 Arbor Street, Portland
(207) 874–8793
www.ci.portland.me.us/rec.htm

Department of Health and Human Services
City Hall
389 Congress Street, Portland
(207) 874–8633
Portland's very active parks and rec department has a full slate of activities designed specifically for people over 60. These might include outings, luncheons, exercise, or educational programs. See the Web site or give a call for the full schedule. The city's Department of Health and Human Services sponsors a groundbreaking program called Eldercize, which incorporates movement from tai chi and dance to get people active.

SERVICES

The American Association of Retired Persons (AARP)
1685 Congress Street, Portland
(207) 775–7774
www.aarp.org/states/me
Joining AARP is a sure sign you've arrived into your golden years. The national retiree advocacy group has an active chapter in Maine, helping seniors in all aspects of life, from lobbying on political issues to setting up volunteer programs to distributing essential information. For the small annual fee of $12.50, anyone over age 50 can get access to a wealth of discounts on travel, lodging, food,

and car rentals, as well as a home-prescription program, and they'll receive a subscription to the AARP newsletter. They get invites to social gatherings and events, they'll learn about issues facing seniors on the Maine coast, and they'll find out about community-service opportunities. It's probably the best $12.50 any retiree will ever spend.

Area Agency on Aging
Southern Maine (serving York County and Greater Portland)
136 Route #1, Scarborough 04074
(207) 396–6500 or (800) 427–7411
www.smaaa.org

Eastern Maine (serving Penobscot, Piscataquis, Hancock, and Washington Counties)
450 Essex Street, Bangor
(207) 941–2685 or (800) 432–7812
www.eaaa.org

The national Agency on Aging program is set up to help older people remain at home and independent, yet retain quality of life, and it has a few chapters in Maine. The agency provides an array of services to people from all walks of life, from health insurance and finance counseling to home repair to Meals on Wheels. Its Community Service Consultants visit homes and provide all sorts of information on helpful programs and benefits available to the elderly. The chapters organize volunteer programs and assist people in finding employment opportunities, too.

INDEX

ABOUT THE AUTHOR

Andrew Vietze is a freelance writer and a registered Maine guide. As managing editor of *Down East: The Magazine of Maine*, he spent years traveling up and down the coast. He's co-authored a digital guide to adventure travel and written for a wide array of regional and national magazines, from *MaineBiz* and *Maine Times* to *Offshore, Hooked on the Outdoors, AMC Outdoors,* and *Time Out New York*. A seasonal ranger at one of the nation's premier wilderness areas, he's currently finishing his first novel, a thriller about the North Woods of Maine during the lumbering era.